VOLUME

6

Eating Disorders

WPA Series
Evidence and Experience in Psychiatry

Other Titles in the *WPA Series* Evidence and Experience in Psychiatry

Volume 1—Depressive Disorders 1999
Mario Maj and Norman Sartorius

Depressive Disorders, Second Edition 2003
Mario Maj and Norman Sartorius

Volume 2—Schizophrenia 1999
Mario Maj and Norman Sartorius

Schizophrenia, Second Edition 2003
Mario Maj and Norman Sartorius

Volume 3—Dementia 1999
Mario Maj and Norman Sartorius

Dementia, Second Edition 2003
Mario Maj and Norman Sartorius

Volume 4—Obsessive–Compulsive Disorder 1999
Mario Maj, Norman Sartorius,
Ahmed Okasha and Joseph Zohar

Obsessive–Compulsive Disorder, Second Edition 2003
Mario Maj, Norman Sartorius,
Ahmed Okasha and Joseph Zohar

Volume 5—Bipolar Disorder
Mario Maj, Hagop S. Akiskal,
Juan José López-Ibor and Norman Sartorius

VOLUME

6

Eating Disorders

Edited by

Mario Maj
University of Naples, Italy

Katherine Halmi
Weill-Cornell Medical College, New York, USA

Juan José López-Ibor
Complutense University of Madrid, Spain

Norman Sartorius
University of Geneva, Switzerland

WPA Series
Evidence and Experience in Psychiatry

WILEY

This publication is designed to provide accurate and authoritative information in regard to the
subject matter covered. It is sold on the understanding that the Publisher is not engaged in
rendering professional services. If professional advice or other expert assistance is required, the
services of a competent professional should be sought.

Other Wiley Editorial Offices

John Wiley & Sons Inc., 111 River Street, Hoboken, NJ 07030, USA

Jossey-Bass, 989 Market Street, San Francisco, CA 94103-1741, USA

Wiley-VCH Verlag GmbH, Boschstr. 12, D-69469 Weinheim, Germany

John Wiley & Sons Australia Ltd, 33 Park Road, Milton, Queensland 4064, Australia

John Wiley & Sons (Asia) Pte Ltd, 2 Clementi Loop #02-01, Jin Xing Distripark, Singapore
129809

John Wiley & Sons Canada Ltd, 22 Worcester Road, Etobicoke, Ontario, Canada M9W 1L1

Wiley also publishes its books in a variety of electronic formats. Some content that appears in
print may not be available in electronic books.

Library of Congress Cataloging-in-Publication Data

Eating disorders / edited by Mario Maj . . . [et al.].
    p. cm. – (WPA series, evidence and experience in psychiatry; 6)
    Includes index.
    ISBN 0-470-84865-0 (alk. paper)
    1. Eating disorders. I. Maj, Mario, 1953– II. Series

    RC552.E18E282112 2003
    616.85'26–dc21

                                                    2002192404

British Library Cataloguing in Publication Data

A catalogue record for this book is available from the British Library

ISBN 0-470-84865-0

Typeset by Dobbie Typesetting Ltd, Tavistock, Devon
Printed and bound in Great Britain by TJ International, Padstow, Cornwall
This book is printed on acid-free paper responsibly manufactured from sustainable forestry in
which at least two trees are planted for each one used for paper production.

Contents

Review Contributors

Francesca Brambilla   Department of Psychiatry, University of Naples SUN, Largo Madonna delle Grazie, 80138 Naples, Italy

Scott J. Crow   Eating Disorders Research Program, Department of Psychiatry, University of Minnesota, 2450 Riverside Avenue, Minneapolis, MN 55454-1495, USA

Martina de Zwaan   Department of General Psychiatry, University Hospital of Vienna, Vienna, Austria

Katherine A. Halmi   Eating Disorder Program, Weill-Cornell Medical College, New York Presbyterian Hospital, Westchester Division, White Plains, NY 10605, USA

Hans Wijbrand Hoek   Parnassia, The Hague Psychiatric Institute, Albardastraat 100, NL-2555 VZ The Hague, The Netherlands

Melanie A. Katzman   New York Presbyterian Hospital, Weill-Cornell Medical College, New York, USA

Palmiero Monteleone   Department of Psychiatry, University of Naples SUN, Largo Madonna delle Grazie, 80138 Naples, Italy

Carol B. Peterson   Eating Disorders Research Program, Department of Psychiatry, University of Minnesota, 2450 Riverside Avenue, Minneapolis, MN 55454-1495, USA

James Roerig   Department of Neuroscience, University of North Dakota School of Medicine and Health Sciences, Fargo, North Dakota, USA

Daphne von Hoeken   Parnassia, The Hague Psychiatric Institute, Albardastraat 100, NL-2555 VZ The Hague, The Netherlands

G. Terence Wilson   Graduate School of Applied & Professional Psychology, State University of New Jersey Rutgers, 152 Frelinghuysen Rd, Piscataway, NJ 08854-8085, USA

Preface

The emergence in the 20th century of the eating disorders anorexia nervosa, bulimia nervosa and variants thereof is documented in a vast literature describing diagnostic refinement, increased incidence and prevalence and a variety of treatment modalities. Anorexia nervosa is now considered a specific syndrome with core clinical features that distinguish it from other psychiatric disorders. Recognition that binge eating and purging behaviors can occur both in patients with anorexia nervosa and in normal weight persons has led to ongoing research attempting to more accurately define and classify the eating disorders. This research includes the study of comorbid psychiatric disorders and specific personality traits or characteristics associated with core eating disorder symptomatology. At the current time investigations are showing a robust association between a perfectionistic personality trait and the restricting type of anorexia nervosa, and between impulsive behaviors, including alcoholism and drug abuse, and binge eating and purging behaviors. A further refinement of the role of anxiety disorders in the development and presentation of eating disorders needs to be clarified.

In the beginning of the 20th century anorexia nervosa was rarely recognized and diagnosed as such. At the end of the century this disorder reached an incidence of 0.1% in the population of industrialized countries. Bulimia nervosa, which was not described as a specific entity until the late 1970s, has a current incidence of about 1% in industrialized countries. Anorexia nervosa has the highest mortality rate of psychiatric disorders. Approximately 0.5% of people with anorexia nervosa die per year. Since this death rate is cumulative, over 20 to 30 years, 10% to 15% of the people with anorexia nervosa will die from this illness. Long-term outcome studies have shown that only one-fourth to one-third of anorexia nervosa patients completely recover. Thus, most of these patients continue to have varying degrees of impairment due to their illness. Bulimia nervosa tends to be a chronic relapsing disorder in which relapses are often associated with stress events. The peak age onset of these eating disorders is during adolescence. Thus, the impairment of function occurs during the most formative years of the patients' life and usually continues through young adulthood, at the time of expected greatest productivity.

Treatment has been more effective for bulimia nervosa than anorexia nervosa. State of the art cognitive-behavioral therapy (CBT) for bulimia nervosa can be expected to eliminate bingeing and purging behavior in about 50% of patients and to significantly reduce this behavior in 80 to 90% of patients. Unfortunately, therapists trained in the specific CBT for bulimia nervosa are rare and thus this form of treatment is not widely available. Treatment of bulimia nervosa is further complicated by the necessity of having to treat other comorbid problems such as alcoholism, drug abuse, impulsive personality disorder problems and depression in the same individual.

There are very few adequate sample size randomly assigned controlled treatment studies for the treatment of anorexia nervosa. There is some indication that early diagnosis and early intensive treatment involving the family with patients under the age of 18 portends a better outcome. Anorexia nervosa patients ill for longer than 6 years tend to defy all treatment intervention. The active resistance to treatment and the reinforcements of the disorder for the anorectic patient are so compelling that treatment remains a significant challenge especially for patients over the legal age of 18. Motivational enhancement techniques have not had considerable impact; however, none of the new enhancement techniques have been studied in a properly controlled design.

Most of the physiological and medical changes in the eating disorders can be attributed to starvation and purging behaviors. Recent investigations of neurotransmitter function and genetics in eating disorder patients may provide some pertinent clues for the development of pharmacological treatment of these disorders. An understanding of the basic physiological aberrations associated with the eating disorders can also provide a foundation for early diagnosis and markers for the progress and effectiveness of a variety of treatment techniques.

This volume of the WPA Series "Evidence and Experience in Psychiatry" aims to review the research developments and controversies concerning the diagnosis and management of eating disorders, and to provide a balanced state of the art update of emerging scientific evidence and accumulated clinical wisdom for psychiatrists from countries all over the world.

Mario Maj
Katherine Halmi
Juan José López-Ibor
Norman Sartorius

1

Classification, Diagnosis and Comorbidities of Eating Disorders: A Review

Katherine A. Halmi

Eating Disorder Program, Weill-Cornell Medical College, New York Presbyterian Hospital, Westchester Division, White Plains, NY 10605, USA

INTRODUCTION

The eating disorders anorexia nervosa, bulimia nervosa and variants thereof are behavioural disorders that have been studied comprehensively with systematic methodologies only in the past 30 years. They are referred to as disorders and not diseases because at present it is unknown if they have a common cause and a common pathology. The eating disorders are classified on the basis of the cluster of symptoms that are present and it is important to keep in mind the purposes of classification. The most useful classification will: a) facilitate meaningful communication among clinicians; b) facilitate research so that investigative findings can be replicated; c) elucidate the phenomena or criteria that one is examining; d) assess treatment efficacy through the use of careful classifying criteria.

Another important matter to consider in naming a disorder is the advantage in communication of common usage and the immediate recognition of a specific disorder. Although the term "anorexia nervosa" has an unsatisfactory aspect (very few patients with this disorder are anorectic or have lost their appetite), the term has been used for more than 100 years and immediately brings to the minds of most clinicians a cluster of signs and symptoms that represents a familiar disorder to them.

In the 20th century the diagnosis of anorexia nervosa went through several phases representing views of the aetiology, such as pituitary disease [1], various psychoanalytical formulations [2,3] or a nervous malnutrition [4]. Finally, the current view evolved that anorexia nervosa is a specific syndrome with core clinical features that distinguish it from other states [5,6].

Eating Disorders. Edited by Mario Maj, Katherine Halmi, Juan José López-Ibor and Norman Sartorius.
©2003 John Wiley & Sons Ltd: ISBN 0-470-84865-0

TABLE 1.1   Anorexia nervosa according to DSM-IV and ICD-10

Key features of DSM-IV anorexia nervosa

A. Weight loss and refusal to maintain weight in a normal range
B. Morbid fear of becoming fat
C. Disturbance in the experience of low weight, including denial and influence on self-evaluation
D. Amenorrhoea

Subtypes
1. Restricting: dieting and exercising only
2. Binge eating/purging, as well as dieting

Key features of ICD-10 anorexia nervosa

A. Weight loss
B. Weight loss is self-induced—avoidance of fattening foods
C. Dread of fatness and perception of being too fat
D. Endocrine disorder involving the hypothalamic–pituitary–gonadal axis (amenorrhoea)
E. No overeating episodes and no sense of compulsion to eat

Comments
Behaviours of self-induced vomiting, purging and use of appetite suppressants and/or diuretics may be present

TABLE 1.2   Bulimia nervosa according to DSM-IV and ICD-10

Key features of DSM-IV bulimia nervosa

A. Recurrent episodes of binge eating
B. Repeated use of self-induced vomiting or laxatives, diuretics, enemas, fasting, exercising excessively or other medications to prevent weight gain
C. Both of the above must occur an average of twice a week for 3 months
D. Body shape and weight unduly influenced self-evaluation
E. Diagnosis of anorexia nervosa is not present

Subtypes
1. Purging: self-induced vomiting, misuse of laxatives, diuretics or enemas
2. Non-purging: only fasting or exercising to counteract calorie intake

Key features of ICD-10 bulimia nervosa

A. Recurrent episodes of overeating (twice a week for 3 months)
B. Persistent preoccupation with eating and sense of compulsion or craving to eat
C. Counteraction of calorie intake by self-induced vomiting or purging, starvation or use of drugs
D. Feeling too fat, with dread of fatness usually leading to underweight

TABLE 1.3   Unspecified eating disorders

DSM-IV eating disorders not otherwise specified

Disorders of eating that do not meet the criteria for anorexia nervosa (AN) or bulimia nervosa (BN)

Examples
1. Meets criteria for AN except amenorrhoea
2. Meets criteria for AN with weight loss but is still in normal weight range
3. Meets criteria for BN except for frequency and chronicity
4. Purging behaviour after small amounts of food
5. Chewing and spitting out food
6. Binge eating disorder: binge eating in the absence of compensatory behaviours for calorie intake

ICD-10 atypical eating disorders

1. Atypical anorexia nervosa: not defined, but recommended researchers make own decisions
2. Atypical bulimia nervosa: involving normal or excessive body weight and researchers make own decision
3. Overeating associated with other psychological disturbances
4. Vomiting associated with other psychological disturbances
5. Other eating disorders
6. Eating disorder, unspecified

TABLE 1.4   Key features of DSM-IV binge eating disorder

A. Recurrent episodes of binge eating
B. Binge eating episodes have three or more of the following:
    1. Eating rapidly
    2. Eating until uncomfortably full
    3. Eating large amounts of food when not physically hungry
    4. Eating alone due to embarrassment of amount of food
    5. Feeling disgusted, depressed or guilty after overeating
C. Marked distress with binge eating
D. Binge eating occurs at least 2 days a week for 6 months on average
E. No use of inappropriate compensatory behaviours (e.g. purging)

In the late 1970s, awareness of the frequency of the symptom of bulimia, both within the anorexia nervosa syndrome and in persons who had many features of anorexia nervosa but without a low body weight, brought about a subtyping of anorexia nervosa and the classification of bulimia nervosa [7–9].

Both the *Diagnostic and Statistical Manual of Mental Disorders* (DSM-IV) [10] and the *10th Revision of the International Classification of Diseases and Related Health Problems* (ICD-10) [11] used descriptive phenomena for the

diagnosis of eating disorders. For anorexia nervosa, both systems acknowledge the weight loss, the fear of becoming fat and the amenorrhoea. The
ICD-10 criterion concerning body image disturbance is limited to the
perception of being too fat, whereas DSM-IV incorporates additional
psychodynamic issues of denial and self-evaluation.

The ICD-10 does not subtype anorexia nervosa, but rather considers those
patients who engage in any type of purging behaviour to be part of the
same diagnosis as those who merely restrict intake and exercise. Patients
who binge eat and weigh very little are diagnosed as having bulimia
nervosa.

The issue of weight status for the diagnosis of bulimia nervosa is unclear
in ICD-10. Criterion D states that patients have an intrusive dread of fatness
"usually leading to underweight". There is a lack of clear distinction
between bulimia nervosa as defined in ICD-10 and another condition in this
classification system labelled hyperorexia nervosa. In the latter condition, as
well as those labelled atypical anorexia nervosa, atypical bulimia nervosa,
overeating and vomiting associated with other psychological disturbances
and other eating disorders, researchers are recommended to design their
own criteria. These categories in ICD-10 are roughly equivalent to the
"eating disorder not otherwise specified" category in DSM-IV. The
ambiguous and overlapping definitions of the various bulimia subtypes
listed in ICD-10 may pose problems for the clinician as well as the
researcher. Although researchers can, of course, make specific criteria for
those patients entering a study, the lack of consistent criteria across studies
makes it difficult, if not impossible, to compare those studies. A summary
of the DSM-IV and ICD-10 systems of diagnoses for eating disorders is
presented in Tables 1.1–1.4.

HISTORICAL ORIGINS

The First Millennium and the Middle Ages

Bulimic behaviours were practiced in the ancient Roman Empire. Wealthy
patricians indulged in orgies of binge eating and vomiting into special
vomitoriums [12]. The Greek physician Galen (AD 130–200) spent a
considerable portion of his life in Rome and defined boulimus (great
hunger) as a digestive dysfunction [12].

There are well documented cases of irreversible self-starvation in the
fasting female saints in the Middle Ages [13]. Of Italian fasting saints, the
most complete biographical account exists for Catherine of Siena [13].
Another example is Princess Margaret of Hungary who lived from 1242 to
1271 [14]. Her history is from a complete copy of depositions by witnesses

who gave evidence in the process of beatification, which began less than 5 years after her death. Princess Margaret was the daughter of a king and raised in a Dominican convent where she excelled in all of her studies and in all of the undesirable chores of the monastery. To an utterly heroic degree, she practised the austerities of fasting, deprivation of sleep, exhausting menial work and other bodily penance. Often, as she sat at the table with the rest of the community, she would let all food pass her untasted. She would often slip out to pray while her sisters ate and was described as being never idle. Margaret intensified her dieting when King Baylor confronted her with suitors and died at the age of 28 years with a mind that was clear and alert and a poor wasted body.

The similarities between the behaviour of Saint Margaret and that of 20th century anorexia nervosa women is obvious. Whether dieting for sainthood or dieting for thinness produces the same determination not to gain weight is still a matter of controversy. Psychiatric diagnostic categories are constrained by history and culture. Dieting seems to be the common risk factor across the centuries. It is most likely that the psychobiological vulnerability factors that induced the development of irreversible starvation in medieval saints were similar to those inciting the emergence of anorexia nervosa in the young women of today. DiNicola [15] has described anorexia nervosa as "anorexia multiforme—a medical chameleon that changes with times".

The 17th and 18th Centuries

Printed pamphlets began to appear in the second half of the 17th century describing cases of self-starvation. In one of these, John Reynolds [16] described an 18-year-old English girl named Martha Taylor who had lost her period and, after a siege of vomiting, stopped taking all solid food. Over the following year she became emaciated. Reynolds wrote "Most of these damsels fall into this abstinence between the age of 14 and 20 years. It's probable that the feminale humours in these virgins may by a long abode in their vessels grow acid. Her age confirms the probability of a ferment in the feminals". Twenty-two years later, Richard Morton [17] described two cases of typical anorexia nervosa symptomatology and distinguished them from consumption. In the 18th century, Robert Whytt described typical anorectic symptomatology in a young man of 14 years and called it a case of "nervous atrophy" [18].

At the end of the 18th century, various encyclopaedias and medical dictionaries included descriptions of bulimia. The *Encyclopaedia Britannica* in 1797 described bulimy as "a disease in which the patient is affected with an insatiable and perpetual desire for eating" [19]. In a medical dictionary,

Motherby [20] describes bulimia in which hunger is terminated by vomiting. Blankaart in 1708, in the *Physical Dictionary* [21], describes bulimia as an extraordinary appetite usually accompanied by a defection of the spirits. A more complete discussion of these early historical references to bulimia can be found in an excellent review article by Stein and Laakso [22].

19th Century—The Victorian Age

Dr Louis-Victor Marcé of Paris described several cases of anorexia nervosa in 1860 [23]. His exact description was "young girls, who at the age of puberty, and after a precocious development, become subject to inappetancy carried to the utmost limits. Whatever the duration of their abstinence, they experience a distaste for food, which the most pressing want is unable to overcome. These patients arrive at a delirious conviction that they can not or ought not to eat. In one word, the gastric nervous disorder becomes cerebro-nervous".

Later in the 19th century the London physician Sir William Gull and the Paris neuropsychiatrist Charles Lasègue published papers on the description and treatment of "hysterical anorexia" [24,25]. The emotional turmoil of the patients was recognized by Lasègue. Gull recommended a treatment that "the patient should be fed at regular intervals, and surrounded by persons who would have moral control over them, relations and friends being generally the worse attendance"[24].

During this period, the USA was still a developing country and most likely had very few cases of fasting women. However, William Chipley, chief medical officer of the Eastern Lunatic Asylum of Kentucky, did publish an article in 1859 on the causes and treatment of sitomania (intense dread of eating or aversion to food) [26].

A New York neurologist, William Alexander Hammond, described in 1879 fasting girls, including the well-publicized Brooklyn girl Molly Fancher [27]. Cases of great self-starvation were also described by the American neurologist Silas Weir Mitchell [28]. In 1895, the Canadian P.R. Inches read a paper on anorexia nervosa before the St John Medical Society in Halifax, Nova Scotia [29]. Thus, by the end of the 19th century, anorexia nervosa had arrived in North America, and by the 20th century the name was commonly used in reference to cases of self-induced starvation.

In the 19th century, recognition of bulimia seemed to be restricted to the European continent. Gull recognized the presence of bulimia in some anorectic patients [24]. In Germany, bulimia is referred to as hyperorexia [30]. In France, Blachez [1869] provides the most complete description of bulimia [31]. He regarded bulimia as a functional problem or a specific form of nervous disorder and recognized that it could alternate with symptoms of anorexia nervosa. For treatment he recommended eating light meals more frequently and careful regulation of the meals. Perhaps the 20th century cognitive–behavioural therapy (CBT) just reinvented the wheel.

CONTEMPORARY CLASSIFICATION APPROACHES

Anorexia Nervosa

In the early 20th century, the confusion between pituitary insufficiency and the disorder of anorexia nervosa was definitively clarified in a book by E.L. Bliss and C.H. Branch, in which endocrine studies, as well as the history and psychological descriptions of anorexia nervosa, were summarized [4]. Later in the 1970s, Hilde Bruch carefully articulated the psychological turmoil of anorexia nervosa patients. She coined the phrase "the relentless pursuit of thinness" and described the "paralyzing sense of ineffectiveness which pervades all thinking and activities" [32].

In a movement to make diagnostic descriptive criteria of psychiatric disorders more precise, Feighner et al. (1972) created a very exacting set of criteria for anorexia nervosa [33]. The first criterion was age of onset prior to 25 years and probably derived from the fact that anorexia nervosa is mainly a disorder of young women. However, in the following ten years, studies by numerous investigators—Halmi et al. [34], Morgan and Russell [35], Theander [36] and Hsu et al. [37]—demonstrated that the occurrence of anorexia nervosa in patients over the age of 25 or even 30 years is not uncommon. In more recent classifications age is no longer an exclusion criterion.

The second Feighner criterion for anorexia nervosa was "anorexia with accompanying weight loss of at least 25% of original body weight". Even though weight loss is an obvious sign in anorexia nervosa, there is no consensus as to how weight loss should be calculated for a diagnostic criterion. Some investigators emphasize a total weight loss and others emphasize weight loss below a normal weight for age and height. The DSM-III [38] required both a weight loss of 25% from original body weight and a refusal to maintain body weight over a minimal normal weight for age and height. No-one has demonstrated that patients with anorexia nervosa can be differentiated on other clinical variables by degree of weight loss. This fact was acknowledged by Russell, who in 1970 published three criteria for anorexia nervosa including the criterion of self-induced loss of weight, which was a comprehensive statement covering weight loss [39]. Feighner's two criteria specifying that no medical illness associated with weight loss or no other psychiatric disorder could be present for the diagnosis of anorexia nervosa have been deleted in subsequent diagnostic criteria. It is now recognized that the diagnosis of anorexia nervosa should be made on positive criteria and that there is always a chance that some physical weight-losing disease would co-exist with anorexia nervosa. Treatment of the specific physical entity does not mean that the eating behaviour and typical anorectic attitudes will change.

The descriptive axial system of classification, which began with DSM-III, allows the possibility of more than one diagnosis on Axis I and an additional diagnosis on the personality disorder Axis II. Subsequent studies described in the comorbidity section have shown that affective disorders, anxiety disorders and substance abuse disorders can exist with anorexia nervosa. Therefore, the "no other psychiatric disorder" exclusion criterion has been deleted from subsequent diagnostic criteria for the diagnosis of anorexia nervosa.

The issue of whether amenorrhoea should be a necessary criterion for the diagnosis of anorexia nervosa remains controversial. Russell [40], in 1969, advocated that amenorrhoea should be a necessary criterion for the diagnosis of anorexia nervosa on the basis of his hypothesis that amenorrhoea is caused by a primary disturbance of hypothalamic function. He stated that the full expression of this disturbance is brought about by psychological stress, and that malnutrition only perpetuates the amenorrhoea of anorexia nervosa. Some investigators agree with Russell that amenorrhoea is a sign of hypothalamic impairment in anorexia nervosa, because it occurs in about one-fifth to one-third of patients with anorexia nervosa before a substantial weight loss occurs [41,42]. Other investigators think that amenorrhoea is merely a reflection of the dieting and physical condition [43]. It is of interest to note that the Feighner criteria did not require amenorrhoea but it was included in a list of six manifestations, of which any two were necessary. The DSM-III criteria did not include amenorrhoea. Russell's hypothesis stimulated much research in the past 25 years and his use of amenorrhoea as a criterion for the diagnosis of anorexia also has emphasized a direction in research.

Several studies have shown that the resumption of menses in anorexia nervosa does not occur merely with restoration to a normal weight, but is associated more significantly with marked psychological improvement [35,41,44]. Weiner [44] pointed out that if 78% of the variance of luteinizing hormone (LH) levels must be accounted for by factors other than weight loss, there can be no simple relationship between weight loss, LH levels and amenorrhoea. His calculations were taken from a study by Brown [45] in which only 22% of the variance in LH levels was accounted for by the degree of weight loss or the percentage below ideal body weight. In this same article, Weiner mentioned that amenorrhoeic runners in the study by Schwartz et al. [46] had increased LH levels when compared with exercising women who maintained their menses. Weiner suggested that this provides evidence against a relationship between weight and gonadotropin levels, because women who lose weight but do not develop anorexia nervosa and have secondary amenorrhoea can have normal LH levels. Some normal weight bulimics have low LH levels and some patients with "psychogenic amenorrhoea" have no weight loss but have low LH levels compared with normal controls. Post-pubertal bulimic women with a normal weight can be amenorrhoeic and have age-inappropriate patterns of gonadotropin secretion. Patients with full recovery of ideal body weight but the persistence of symptoms of anorexia nervosa or bulimia still show age-inappropriate gonadotropin secretion patterns [47].

The entire issue of amenorrhoea is complicated by the fact that it is often difficult to get an accurate history of menstrual patterns. Patients with anorexia nervosa are notoriously disinterested in treatment and do not wish to receive the diagnosis. They often know the diagnostic criteria better than the physicians examining them and will readily say that they are menstruating when they are not, in order to disqualify themselves for the diagnosis of anorexia nervosa. Because of the difficulty in obtaining accurate histories and a few examples of women at a low weight still menstruating, there is current support again for excluding the criterion of amenorrhoea for the diagnosis of anorexia nervosa.

A precise and concise definition of the core psychology of anorexia nervosa is also frought with problems. Bruch [32] defined the relentless pursuit of thinness, denial of cachexia and the general ineffectiveness of these patients as being the core psychological symptoms. Other investigators have focused on the fear of becoming obese [48] or the fear of sexuality and the adult female sexual body [49].

The disturbance of body image is described by patients with anorexia nervosa as "claiming to feel fat even when they are emaciated". This has been fairly well accepted by most investigators. The concept has been broadened from DSM-III to DSM-III-R [50] to a body conceptualization disturbance and then further expanded in DSM-IV to include denial of illness and self-evaluation.

In 1980 seminal papers were published demonstrating that anorectic patients who binge and vomit are distinctly different from anorectic patients who merely starve themselves [7,8]. The bingeing and purging anorectics had a higher association of impulsive behaviours such as suicide attempts, self-mutilation, stealing and substance abuse, including alcohol abuse. They also had a much higher incidence of well-defined personality disorders. In the subsequent decade, 12 adequately designed studies were conducted comparing anorectic restrictors with anorectic bulimics and all showed consistent differences between these subtypes. A summary of these 12 studies demonstrated that impulsive behaviours were more prevalent in anorectic bulimics compared with anorectic restrictors [51]. In addition, it was recognized that the medical problems associated with the bingeing and purging behaviours are distinctly different to those of anorectic restrictors. Both of these facts of impulsive behaviours and medical problems warranted a subclassification of anorexia nervosa into the restricting type and the binge/purge type that occurred in the DSM-IV classification. It should be noted that in DSM-III-R if a patient with anorexia nervosa experienced episodes of binge eating then that patient received a dual diagnosis of anorexia nervosa and bulimia nervosa.

Bulimia Nervosa

The term bulimia merely means binge eating, which is a behaviour that may occur on occasion in otherwise healthy persons. As mentioned above, bulimia is also a behaviour that was recognized to occur in anorexia nervosa as early as the 17th century.

The term bulimia nervosa was coined by Russell in 1979 [9]. At that time Russell conceptualized bulimia nervosa as an "aftermath of the chronic phase of anorexia nervosa". Only 6 of the 30 patients he studied had no history of preceding anorexia nervosa. At that time Russell had only three criteria for the diagnosis of bulimia nervosa. These criteria were: a) a powerful and intractable urge to overeat, resulting in episodes of over-eating; b) avoidance of "fattening" effects of food by inducing vomiting or abusing purgatives or both; c) a morbid fear of becoming fat. These criteria had the problem of being ambiguous, because a person with anorexia nervosa could also meet the criteria for bulimia nervosa. The question became: does such a patient receive both diagnoses or does one take precedence over the other?

The DSM-III did not use Russell's term of bulimia nervosa but rather the term bulimia and included in its diagnostic criteria an exclusion criterion stating that the bulimic episodes are not due to anorexia nervosa. Neither Russell's nor the DSM-III criteria contained a frequency and chronicity criterion. This resulted in the early population prevalence studies producing a rather high prevalence of bulimia, especially in vulnerable groups such as college students. It then became necessary to separate those students who binge occasionally for a lark from those binge eaters who have a distinct impairment of function. Subsequently, rather arbitrary criteria based on clinical experience for frequency and chronicity were placed in the DSM-III-R and DSM-IV criteria for bulimia. Moreover, the DSM changed the name of the disorder from bulimia to bulimia nervosa because the latter implied a psychiatric impairment. A further revision of DSM-IV criteria for bulimia nervosa included emphasis on the sense of lack of control over eating and the undue influence of body shape and weight on self-evaluation. This revision also created a purging subtype and a non-purging subtype of bulimia nervosa. In the latter, inappropriate compensatory behaviours to combat caloric intake included only fasting or excessive exercise. Most patients with the non-purging type of bulimia nervosa were thought to be in the upper part of a normal weight range or actually overweight.

The ICD-10 diagnostic criteria were also revised to contain the same frequency and chronicity criteria that were present in DSM-IV. The criterion emphasizing a sense of compulsion or craving to eat is somewhat similar to the DSM-IV criterion emphasizing the fear of losing control over eating. Likewise, the criterion in ICD-10 of an intrusive dread of fatness is somewhat equivalent to the undue influence of body shape and weight on self-evaluation in the DSM-IV definition of bulimia nervosa. The major difference in these two systems of diagnosis is that DSM-IV has an exclusion criterion for binge eating in the context of anorexia nervosa whereas ICD-10 states that the intrusive dread of fatness in bulimia nervosa usually leads to being underweight. The issue of weight status has created a problem when comparing studies that have used one or the other diagnostic system.

Unspecified Eating Disorders

The current ICD-10 and DSM-IV diagnostic systems have recognized that there are many variants of anorexia and bulimia nervosa that do not meet the specific criteria for these disorders but involve significant impairment of function. In the ICD-10 system they are referred to as atypical anorexia, atypical bulimia nervosa, overeating associated with other psychological disturbances, vomiting associated with other psychological disturbances and eating disorder unspecified. The DSM-IV system simply states that the category of eating disorder not otherwise specified is for disorders of eating that do not meet the criteria for anorexia nervosa or bulimia nervosa. It then gives some examples. The example of binge eating disorder defined as recurrent episodes of binge eating in the absence of the regular use of inappropriate compensatory behaviours characteristic of bulimia nervosa is highlighted and further defined in an appendix. The major problem of binge eating disorder is to distinguish it from the non-purging subtype of bulimia nervosa. It is emphasized in the description of this disorder in DSM-IV [10] that the diagnosis should be considered only when the individual reports a subjective sense of impaired control during episodes of overeating. Many of these individuals are obese and eat throughout the day in addition to their binge eating episodes. Most have a long history of repeated efforts to diet and others have given up all effort to diet. About

30% of individuals in weight-control programmes will have binge eating disorder, and in the non-patient community samples a prevalence rate of 0.7–4% has been reported [10].

CLASSIFICATION RESEARCH STUDIES

Anorexia Nervosa

Both ICD-10 and DSM-IV have a weight criterion for the diagnosis of anorexia nervosa. The ICD-10 specifically states 15% below expected weight for age and height, whereas DSM-IV gives an example of body weight less than 85% of that expected, thus being slightly ambiguous in its definition. Over 20 years ago a study was done to show that there is no specific amount of weight loss associated with other symptoms of anorexia nervosa [52]. Those patients who have had a substantial amount of weight loss but are still in a normal weight range and have many of the core psychological symptoms of anorexia nervosa are, under the present classification system, relegated to the category "eating disorder not otherwise specified".

The criteria "dread of fatness" or "intense fear of gaining weight" are somewhat similar in concept and have remained unchanged throughout the decades.

The third criterion in DSM-IV for anorexia nervosa pertains to body image and has evolved since the late 1970s into a more complex concept. This body image factor is embedded in Criterion C in ICD-10 as "self-perception of being too fat". In an earlier version of Criterion C for anorexia nervosa in DSM-III it was described as a "body image disturbance". This resulted in many studies of a narrow definition of body image related to visual self-perception. Because these studies show that many anorectics do not overestimate their sizes, and that overestimation is not unique to those with anorexia nervosa [53], the criterion was reworded in DSM-III-R to focus on attitudinal and affective dimensions of body image. This newly worded criterion of "overconcern with body size and shape" had a significant overlap between patients with anorexia nervosa and the general female population. Therefore, it was revised in DSM-IV to emphasize the central concern of weight and shape in evaluation of the self, in addition to a reference to denial of the serious consequences of weight loss. The precise wording of "disturbance in the way in which one's body weight or shape is experienced" reflects the person's claiming to feel fat or believing that one area of the body, such as the thighs, is too fat even when obviously underweight. The "undue influence of body weight or shape on self-evaluation" reflects the dominating importance of the latter to the patient. Losing weight and dieting are skills that patients with anorexia nervosa can perform competently and from which they receive strong positive reinforcements. The security of being thin and of dieting compensates for vast insecurities in other areas of life, such as interpersonal relationships and adult role expectations. "Denial of the seriousness of the current low body weight" reflects the person's unwillingness to acknowledge that her emaciated body is not healthy or attractive.

The criterion of amenorrhoea, which is present in both the ICD-10 and DSM-IV systems, continues to be controversial, as mentioned above. A Canadian study [54] between 1989 and 1994 found that 30% of patients who met all other diagnostic criteria for anorexia nervosa did not have amenorrhoea. These authors argued that amenorrhoea adds little to the definition of anorexia nervosa. In ICD-10 amenorrhoea is mentioned as part of a "widespread endocrine disorder". Thus, maintaining this criterion does provide emphasis on the hypothalamic dysfunction that occurs in this syndrome [55] and may help to alert the clinician to potential sequelae, including osteoporosis.

Numerous studies have consistently demonstrated that impulsive behaviours, including stealing, drug abuse, suicide attempts, self-mutilations and mood lability, are more prevalent in anorectic patients who binge and purge compared with anorectic restrictors [7,8]. The anorectic-bulimics also have a higher prevalence of premorbid obesity, familial obesity and debilitating personality traits [56–59]. There are also important physiological differences between bulimic people who lose large amounts of weight and meet the criteria for anorexia nervosa and those who never lose weight [55]. The former patients have all of the physical complications of emaciation. For this reason the DSM-IV criteria have defined an anorexia nervosa restrictor type and an anorexia nervosa binge/purge type. This means that the patients who binge and purge and meet the criteria for anorexia nervosa are diagnosed with anorexia nervosa (binge/purge subtype) rather than bulimia nervosa.

There remains the question of how to classify patients with anorexia nervosa who purge but do not binge. Garner et al. [60] compared anorectic restrictors, anorectic purgers and anorectic binge/purgers and found that the anorectic purging group was significantly similar to the anorectic binge/purge group in a variety of impulsive behaviours as well as the core anorectic and general psychopathology. The authors stated that this evidence, combined with the medical risk associated with purging behaviours and the formidable problems associated with the definition of binge eating, supports a subtyping system for anorexia nervosa based on the presence or absence of purging rather than binge eating.

In a longitudinal prospective study of eating disorders, Herzog et al. [61] had the surprising result at a 4-year follow-up that anorectics who binged and purged had a higher rate of recovery than restricting anorectics. The authors stated that this gave some support to the subtyping of anorexia nervosa.

In a study of 163 Caucasian female twins from a population-based registry, Bulik *et al.* [62] conducted a latent class analysis for nine eating disorder symptoms. In this study a six-class solution provided the best fit, and three of these classes broadly resembled the DSM-IV classification of anorexia nervosa, bulimia nervosa and binge eating disorder. The authors found a convergence between the anorectic class derived from the latent class analysis and the DSM criteria for symptoms of weight loss and fear of fatness, symptoms that were nearly ubiquitously reported. Symptoms of feeling fat, even when thin, and amenorrhoea were less universally endorsed. The authors state that broadening of the body conceptualization criterion in DSM-IV to include undue influence of shape and weight on self-evaluation and the denial of seriousness of the illness may be warranted on the basis of these findings. They also found that amenorrhoea was not a unifying criterion in one of the six classes.

Bulimia Nervosa

One of the major problems in the definition of bulimia nervosa is in defining the size of a binge. The ICD-10 criteria refer to overeating and the DSM-IV criteria to a large amount of food. Fairburn [63] has tried to differentiate between an objective binge and a subjective binge. Many eating episodes that patients consider to be binges contain amounts of food that are well within the range of normal eating behaviour for a meal. Others believe that binges are better characterized by a sense of loss of control over eating than by the consumption of an excessive amount [64]. Thus, the definition of a binge continues to depend heavily on the judgment of the interviewer.

The operational definition of "recurrent binge eating" is also a problem. Both ICD-10 and DSM-IV require binges to occur on average at least twice a week for three months. In DSM-IV this requirement also includes inappropriate compensatory behaviour. These criteria were intended to prevent a diagnostic label from being applied to individuals who had only an occasional problem. The frequency and chronicity criterion was arbitrary, with little information about the frequencies of binge eating in clinical or community samples. Subsequent research studies have used this criterion and thus there is little information gathered on individuals with less frequent problems. A few community studies [65,66] have provided evidence that those who binge on average once a week do not differ from those who binge more often.

The ICD-10 criterion of "self-perception of being too fat with an intrusive dread of fatness" is somewhat equivalent to the DSM-IV "self-evaluation unduly influenced by body shape and weight". There are several studies demonstrating that excessive weight and shape concerns are regularly seen in bulimia nervosa [67,68]. Body weight and shape concerns are highly related to body dissatisfaction. Garfinkel et al. [69] found this to be a significant relationship in a large sample of women with bulimia nervosa, where those with the highest degree of self-loathing displayed the greatest feelings of fatness, dietary restraint and feelings of ineffectiveness. The authors recommended that consideration be given to altering the criterion for overconcern with weight and shape to include the closely linked concept of body dissatisfaction, because it includes the negative affective dimension of body image and reflects deficits in self-esteem regulation that may underlie the concern of being fat. This is an area that needs further study.

The DSM-IV classification subtypes bulimic patients into purging and non-purging types. This subtyping is not present in ICD-10. The subtyping of DSM-IV was based on evidence from a series of studies. Garfinkel et al. [54] found that the purging bulimic group, in comparison with the non-purging bulimics, had earlier ages of onset and higher rates of comorbidity for depression, anxiety disorders and alcohol abuse. They also had higher rates of previous sexual abuse.

In a general population of 250 women with recurrent binge eating, Hay and Fairburn [70] found that the purging type of bulimia nervosa had more severe clinical symptomatology compared with the non-purging type, and came to the conclusion that their data supported retaining a distinction between non-purging bulimia nervosa and purging bulimia nervosa. Another study by Tobin et al. [71] found very few differences between the purging and non-purging bulimic patients on the Eating Disorder Inventory (EDI) and the Hopkins Symptom Checklist.

The criteria for bulimia nervosa will continue to be revised until ongoing studies of the biology of the disorder, including neuroimaging and genetic studies, as well as longitudinal course studies are completed.

In the latent class analysis of eating behaviours in Caucasian female twins [62] mentioned above, the symptom profiles of the bulimic class were compared with the DSM-IV criteria for bulimia nervosa and reasonable convergence for three of the four criteria was found. Nearly all of the women in the bulimic class endorsed binge eating, compensatory behaviours and excessive shape and weight concerns. The most frequent compensatory methods were strict dieting and exercise, followed by fasting, vomiting and laxatives. A lifetime history of anorexia nervosa was reported in 9% of cases. The "out of control" criterion was less defining of this bulimic class. The authors thought that further validation of this criterion is warranted.

Binge Eating Disorder

The potential new diagnostic category of binge eating disorder was proposed by Spitzer *et al.* [72] in 1993. Clinicians and researchers in the field of eating disorders agreed that there was the need for a diagnostic label for individuals who binge eat but do not engage in the inappropriate compensatory behaviour characteristic of bulimia nervosa. Most studies comparing obese individuals with binge eating disorder and obese people without binge eating have found a higher level of psychopathology, including elevated symptoms of depression, in the former [73].

Early field studies have shown binge eating disorder to be common in a non-clinical population (1.5–2.0%) and among the obese seeking treatment (30%) [74]. One of the problems with the binge eating disorder diagnosis is distinguishing it from bulimia nervosa, the non-purging type. In both diagnoses there is a requirement for binge eating and an absence of compensatory purging behaviour. The distinction therefore rests on the presence of the psychopathology related to weight and shape. This may vary over time with the same person and is often difficult to measure. Another study found that attitudes to shape were equally distorted in obese binge eating subjects compared with patients with bulimia nervosa [75]. In a recent review of the binge eating disorder literature, Williamson and Martin [76] came to the conclusion that several important questions must be addressed for considering binge eating disorder as a diagnostic entity. The first is whether healthcare researchers should regard binge eating in this condition as a behavioural feature of obesity rather than a psychiatric syndrome. Because neither dietary restraint nor escape from negative emotional states adequately explains the development of binge eating associated with obesity, the authors ask: what biological and psychological factors play a significant role in the development of binge eating in the absence of compensatory behaviours to control body weight? Finally, does the presence of significant binge eating affect the outcome of traditional behavioural or pharmacological treatments for obesity?

In a study of 250 young women with recurrent binge eating [70], binge eating disorder did not emerge from the cluster analysis. The latent class analysis of Caucasian female twins described above [62] found a large class of individuals, distinct from women with bulimia nervosa, whose primary behavioural manifestation was binge eating without compensatory behaviours. All members in this class endorsed binge eating; however, only half reported feeling out of control. The authors recommended further enquiry into the relationship between the behavioural symptom of binge eating and the cognitive feature of feeling out of control. The women in this class also differed from those in the bulimic class in terms of having a greater propensity towards obesity.

Partial Syndromes of Eating Disorders

Studies of patients with eating disorders who have met some, but not all, of the criteria for anorexia nervosa or bulimia nervosa have produced discrepant results. In one study the severity of eating disorder symptoms in the partial syndrome cases was as great or greater than that of the full symptom cases [77]. In another study, persons with partial syndromes in subclinical eating disorders had lower severity scores than those with full syndrome eating disorders [78]. One study showed that some individuals over time progressed from the less to more severe disturbances in eating behaviour [79]. There is a paucity of research on these partial syndromes, sometimes labelled atypical syndromes. Likewise, there is very little research on a spectrum approach to eating disorders, which would consider them as one syndrome with different degrees of severity and manifestations [80]. The spectrum approach may not be very helpful to the clinicians, who need an immediate communication concerning the specific signs and symptoms of a patient.

COMORBIDITY OF EATING DISORDERS

Affective Disorders

The association between anorexia nervosa and depression has long been recognized by clinicians. One of the first attempts at systematically examining depression was done by Morgan and Russell [35] as part of a follow-up study. The rates of depression remained constant: 42% at presentation and 45% at follow-up. Later, using the Feighner criteria for diagnosis, Cantwell et al. [81] found that 45% of 26 adolescents with anorexia nervosa at a 5-year follow-up had major depression. Three studies used the Diagnostic Interview Schedule (DIS) with DSM-III criteria for the diagnosis of depression. Halmi et al. [82] found a lifetime prevalence of 68% for major depression. This was considerably higher than the 36% and 38% rates of depression present in the other two studies using the DIS [83,84]. In one of the studies the patients were, on average, 8 years younger than in the Halmi study and in the other study only 47 patients out of 149 participated in the DIS interview. Gershon et al. [85] used the Schedule for Affective Disorders and Schizophrenia—Lifetime Interview (SADS-L) to establish the diagnosis of major depressive disorder in 13 of 24 patients with anorexia nervosa (54%). In the Halmi et al. study [82], the lifetime prevalence of depression was not correlated with the outcome of the eating disorder. There was a trend for more major depression to occur in those who binged at some time compared with pure restricting patients. At the time of the

10-year follow-up, there was significantly more *current* major depression in the normal weight bulimics compared with those who had recovered, those with only mild eating disorder symptomatology and those who still had the diagnosis of anorexia nervosa.

Several studies have used the Structured Clinical Interview for DSM-III-R (SCID) for studying comorbidity in patients with eating disorders. Forty-three per cent of female patients with anorexia nervosa or bulimia nervosa met the criteria for major depression in a study done by Kennedy *et al.* [86]. In a study of 105 inpatients with eating disorders, Braun *et al.* [87] found that the lifetime prevalence of any affective disorder was 41.2% in anorectic restrictors, 82% in anorectic bulimics, 64.5% in patients with bulimia nervosa and 78% in patients with bulimia nervosa with a past history of anorexia nervosa. The dual eating disorder diagnosis groups (binge/purge anorexia nervosa and bulimia nervosa with a past history of anorexia nervosa) were more likely to have had a major depression than the single diagnostic groups (anorectic restrictors and bulimia nervosa patients). The anorectic restrictor subgroup was significantly more likely than the other groups to have *no* affective disorder. The majority (64%) of the anorectic restrictors, but only 33% of the patients with bulimia nervosa, developed their eating disorder as their first Axis I disorder. Three other studies found the incidence of lifetime major depression to be higher in the binge/purge anorexia nervosa group than in the anorectic restrictors or in the patients with bulimia nervosa [88–90]. In the study by Herzog *et al.* [90], 66% of the patients with anorexia nervosa, 50% of the patients with bulimia nervosa and 76% of those with both bulimia and anorexia nervosa had an affective disorder. For major depressive disorder, the rates were 37%, 32% and 53%, respectively.

A study in Sweden using structured interviews for DSM-III-R criteria found that 85% of patients with anorexia nervosa had a depressive disorder [91].

In a large-sample twin study in which they derived heritability estimates for anorexia nervosa and examined the comorbid relationship between anorexia nervosa and major depression, Wade *et al.* [92] found a 49.4% incidence rate of major depression in the twins that met the criteria for anorexia nervosa. The authors concluded that genetic factors substantially contributed to the observed comorbidity between anorexia nervosa and major depression.

Several studies have shown a relationship between bulimia nervosa and bipolar disorder. In the study by Herzog *et al.* [90] no patients with anorexia nervosa had bipolar disorder but two patients with bulimia nervosa and three with bulimia and anorexia nervosa had that diagnosis, i.e. about 2% of the bulimia patients. In another study of 31 consecutive eating disorder admissions there were two patients diagnosed as having bipolar disorder, i.e. 6.5% [93]. In another study of the lifetime prevalence of affective disorders in bulimics, 12% of current bulimics and 11% of recovered bulimics had a history of bipolar affective disorder [94].

Because family studies [85] have not found a greater than expected prevalence of eating disorders in probands with affective disorder, it cannot be stated that eating disorders are a *forme fruste* of affective disorders. Affective disorders do seem to put a person at risk for developing an eating disorder and it is most likely that affective disorders and eating disorders have some shared genetic components.

Anxiety Disorders

Two large sample studies using the DIS interview found lifetime prevalences of 65% and 60% for anxiety disorders [82,84]. The two most prevalent anxiety disorders in both studies were social phobia and obsessive–compulsive disorder (OCD). Using the Diagnostic Interview for Genetic Studies with generated DSM-III-R diagnoses, Bulik *et al.* [95] found the prevalence of anxiety disorders to be 60% in anorexia nervosa and 57% in bulimia nervosa. In 90% of the patients with anorexia nervosa and 94% of the patients with bulimia nervosa, anxiety disorder preceded the eating disorder [95]. In another study by Bulik *et al.* [96], using SCID, 65% of patients with bulimia nervosa entering a treatment study had an anxiety disorder diagnosis [96]. In a Spanish 8-year longitudinal study, social phobia was present in 13% of the 46 children who had anorexia nervosa [97]. In another study of bulimia nervosa using DSM-III-R diagnoses, anxiety disorder was present in 36% of patients [98]. Seventy-one per cent of those cases with an anxiety disorder had the onset of that disorder prior to the onset of their bulimia [98].

Schwalberg *et al.* [99] found that 75% of bulimics and 64% of obese binge eaters had one or more anxiety disorders. The anxiety disorders preceded the onset of the eating disorder by at least 1 year in 59% of patients. Among bulimics, 63.6% of the cases of generalized anxiety disorder and 87.5% of those of social phobia preceded the onset of the eating disorder. Among the obese binge eaters the corresponding figures were 87.5% for generalized anxiety disorder and 75% for social phobia [99]. In a French study, 83% of patients with anorexia nervosa and 71% of those with bulimia nervosa had at least one lifetime diagnosis of an anxiety disorder. The most frequent was social phobia: in 55% of the anorectics and in 59% of the bulimics. The comorbid anxiety disorder predated the onset of the eating disorder in 75% of patients with anorexia nervosa and 88% of patients with bulimia nervosa [100].

With so many studies replicating the findings that anxiety disorders preceded the onset of eating disorders in a highly significant number of cases, there may be a reasonable concern that anxiety disorders are a risk factor for the development of eating disorders.

Obsessive–Compulsive Disorder

Because the obsessions and compulsions of OCD are similar to the preoccupations and rituals of patients with eating disorders, it has been proposed that anorexia nervosa is a *forme fruste* of OCD, or part of an OCD spectrum. In structured interview studies of comorbid psychiatric diagnoses in anorexia nervosa, Toner et al. [84] found that 16 of 47 anorectic patients (34%) had a history of OCD and Halmi et al. [82] reported a lifetime rate of 26% (16 of 62 patients) for OCD in an anorectic group. Both studies showed a considerably higher prevalence of OCD in the anorectic patients compared with their control population. The study of Halmi et al. [82] reported that OCD was more frequent in the anorectic patients who had never binged. In two other studies that did not have a control group, Laessle et al. [83] found OCD to be present in 15.4% of anorectics, with no difference between restricting and bulimic subtypes. Hudson et al. [94] found that 69% of anorectic restrictors and 44% of anorectic bulimics met the criteria for OCD. In a study of 105 patients with eating disorders, using SCID, Braun et al. [87] found that 20% of anorectic patients had a lifetime OCD, with no difference between anorectic restrictor and anorectic bulimic subgroups. In a study by Halmi et al. [82], the mothers of anorectic patients had a significantly greater prevalence of OCD (11%) compared with mothers of controls.

In a family study, Cavallini et al. [101] found that obsessive–compulsive spectrum disorders were significantly more prevalent in 458 first-degree relatives of patients with eating disorders: 9.69% vs. 0% in 358 relatives of controls, without differences among the three eating disorder subgroups when compared with the comparison group. Specifically, OCD was more prevalent in relatives with eating disorders: 4.61% vs. 0% in controls, without differences among the three eating disorder subgroups. The authors suggest that genes potentially involved in OCD development may also be candidates for eating disorders.

Cavallini et al. [102] tested the hypothesis that eating disorders and OCD might share the same biological vulnerability by applying a complex segregation analysis to 141 families of probands affected with eating disorders. The authors stated that their analyses could support the hypothesis that a common genetic liability could account for both eating disorders and OCD. In another study, Bellodi et al. [103] examined the occurrence of obsessive–compulsive spectrum disorders among first-degree relatives in 136 nuclear families of probands with eating disorders in Italy. The authors stated that the higher morbidity risk for obsessive compulsive spectrum disorders in the first-degree relatives of the patients with eating disorders (10.34%) lent support to the proposal that OCD and eating disorders are phenotype expressions of the same liability.

In a family study of anorexia nervosa and bulimia nervosa, Lilenfeld [104] found that relatives of anorectic and bulimic probands had an increased risk of clinically subthreshold forms of an eating disorder, major depressive disorder and OCD. The risk of obsessive–compulsive personality disorder was elevated only among relatives of anorectic probands and there was evidence that these two disorders may have shared familial risk factors. The authors concluded that OCD was not likely to share a common cause with eating disorders. However, obsessional personality traits may be a specific familial risk factor for anorexia nervosa.

Two other studies examined the lifetime prevalence of OCD in eating disorder subgroups. Speranza *et al.* [105] found that the current and lifetime prevalences of OCD in patients with eating disorders were significantly higher than in the general population. Anorectic patients had significantly higher current and lifetime comorbidities than bulimic patients (19% and 22.4% vs. 9.7% and 12.9%). Purging anorexia was the diagnostic subtype that presented the higher prevalences (29% and 43%), followed by restricting anorexia and purging bulimia. In the majority of cases (65%) OCD diagnosis preceded the eating disorder diagnosis. In a study from Australia [106], 35 anorectic and 33 bulimic patients were assessed with the Composite International Diagnostic Interview (CIDI). Thirty-seven per cent of the anorectic patients were comorbid for OCD, compared with only 3% of patients with bulimia nervosa. In the majority, OCD preceded the dieting disorder.

Although some authors have argued vehemently that eating disorders, especially anorexia nervosa, are part of an OCD spectrum, all of these family studies have inherent limitations. Eventually the answer will be provided by more sophisticated genome studies.

In a Swedish sample of 51 teenagers with anorexia nervosa, 24 cases had shown behaviour patterns suggestive of autistic-like conditions as children before the onset of anorexia nervosa [107]. One of the three boys in the anorexia nervosa group had Asperger syndrome. Three of the 48 girls had histories suggesting high functioning autism. Eighteen of the girls met the criteria for obsessive–compulsive personality disorder. Because of the problems of social interaction in these patients, the authors suggested that there may be a link with Asperger syndrome and autistic-like conditions. In another study of these same patients, the authors [108] stated that a small subgroup of anorexia nervosa cases showed autism spectrum disorders and had test profiles similar to those observed in autism and Asperger syndrome. At the present time, no other studies have replicated these findings and no family studies of eating disorders have found an increased prevalence of autism spectrum diagnoses.

Substance Abuse

There are many studies suggesting that eating disorders and substance abuse, especially alcoholism, are interrelated. In the study by Halmi *et al.* [82], only 8% of the patients with anorexia nervosa had alcohol abuse and 12% had cannabis abuse; however, there was a significant increase in alcoholism in the families of anorectic patients when all the first-degree relatives were compared with control first-degree relatives. A similar low rate of alcohol or drug dependence in anorectic restrictors was found in the study by Braun *et al.* [87]. Anorectic restrictors were significantly less likely than the whole sample of patients with eating disorders to have any alcohol or drug dependence. Onset of alcohol or substance dependence before the onset of the eating disorder occurred only in the bulimic subjects. Selby and Moreno [109] found that bulimic subjects reported a greater frequency of both personal and family substance abuse problems compared with anorectic patients, obese persons and women with major depression. The bulimic subjects with and without substance abuse problems reported similar frequencies of family substance abuse problems. Striegel-Moore and Hyudic [110] found that adolescent girls diagnosed with an eating disorder were twice as likely to be problem drinkers than girls who did not have an eating disorder. Bushnell *et al.* [111] found that 44% of a clinical sample of bulimic women had a lifetime alcohol or drug disorder. In a review of 51 studies, Holderness *et al.* [112] concluded that the relationship between substance abuse and bulimia nervosa is far stronger than with anorexia nervosa.

In a study comparing bulimia nervosa with and without substance abuse, Lilenfeld *et al.* [113] found that women with bulimia and substance dependence have problems with social anxiety, antisocial behaviour and a variety of personality disturbances, and come from families where there are problems with substance abuse disorders, anxiety, impulsivity and affective instability. The authors raise the possibility that a familial vulnerability for impulsivity and affective instability may contribute to the development of substance dependence in the subgroup of women with bulimia nervosa. Another study compared female patients with comorbid substance-related disorder and eating disorder with female patients who had only substance-related disorder. Essentially there were very few differences between the groups, the major difference being that those with eating disorders were more highly educated and of a higher social economic status [114]. In another study comparing bulimic subjects with and without substance abuse [115], the women with substance abuse had the highest frequency and the most severe history of sexual abuse.

The relationship between substance abuse and bulimia nervosa or anorexia nervosa (binge/purge type) has been replicated many times. Future research studies should elucidate common biological phenomena.

Personality Disorders

Although many of the studies of personality disorders and eating disorders are contradictory, almost all have shown a high preponderance of Cluster B (impulsive) personality disorders associated with the bulimic subtypes compared with the anorectic restrictors. The percentages of DSM-III-R bulimics who have at least one personality disorder are reported to be 77% [116], 62% [117], 61% [118], 43% [119], 33% [120] and 28% [121]. In the Herzog et al. study [121] of 210 patients with eating disorders, the most commonly observed personality disorder was borderline personality disorder (9%). Consistent with previous reports, higher rates of borderline personality disorder were found in the bulimic and anorectic-bulimic groups, whereas avoidant personality disorder was the most prevalent among the anorectic and anorectic-bulimic groups. In the study by Braun et al. [87], 69% of patients had at least one personality disorder. Of the patients who had personality disorders, 93% also had Axis I comorbidity. Thirty-one per cent of the bulimic subgroups and none of the anorectic restrictors had Cluster B disorders. Borderline personality disorder was present in 25% of the bulimic subgroups and was the most common Cluster B condition. Cluster C personality disorders were present in 29.5% of the sample. Avoidant personality disorder was the most common (14.3%), followed by dependent (10.5%), obsessive–compulsive (6.7%) and passive–aggressive (4.8%). The prevalence of Cluster C personality disorders did not vary according to eating disorder subtype.

Steiger et al. [121] found that personality disorder classification did not predict the severity of bulimic symptoms or the responsiveness to treatment of bulimic symptoms.

More recently, a study of 54 patients with eating disorders showed that 26% had at least one personality disorder [122]. Cluster B personality disorders were closely associated with bulimic subtypes. In another study comparing bulimics with and without borderline personality disorder [123], the borderline bulimics showed elevated motor impulsivity, disassociation and rates of sexual abuse.

Many questions need to be answered concerning the relationship of eating disorders with personality disorders. It would be helpful to know if the development of an eating disorder during adolescent years has a formative effect on personality.

SUMMARY

Consistent Evidence

The evidence reviewed over the past decade indicates that eating disorders are more complex and broader in scope than what is precisely defined in DSM-IV and ICD-10. They range from self-imposed severe starvation to uncontrolled binge eating with obesity. Consistent evidence can be summarized as follows.

Anorexia Nervosa

- Dieting behaviour is maintained by self-imposition.
- Presence of a pervasive dissatisfaction with one's body, reflected in feeling too fat.
- An overwhelming fear and reluctance to change behaviour.
- Ability of the restricting type to develop bulimia over the course of time.
- Frequent comorbidity with affective disorders.

Bulimia Nervosa

- Recurrent episodes of overeating in a discrete period of time.
- Recurrent attempts to counteract the caloric intake of the overeating episodes.
- Frequent comorbidity with affective disorders, anxiety disorders, substance use disorders and Cluster B personality disorders.

Unspecified Eating Disorders

- Demonstration in population surveys that partial anorexia nervosa and bulimia nervosa syndromes are more prevalent than the complete defined syndrome.
- Documentation of a binge eating (overeating) condition without the use of compensatory behaviours to counteract caloric intake.
- Identification of the condition in which regular use of self-induced vomiting or laxative abuse occurs by an individual of normal body weight after eating small amounts of food.

Incomplete Evidence

Anorexia Nervosa

The body conceptualization disturbance phenomena in anorexia nervosa are still not well defined. There is considerable variation in the presence and severity of various observed behaviours and psychological states, such as denial of illness, motivation to change behaviour, fear of changing behaviour and sense of adequacy/inadequacy and self-competence.

The specific physiological mechanisms that are related to the psychological set and behaviours of the patient with anorexia nervosa are not well defined. "Hypothalamic disturbance" may well reflect neurotransmitter disturbances and genetic polymorphisms affecting other mechanisms.

Bulimia Nervosa

The definition of a binge is still in question. The exact frequency and chronicity of the binge/purge behaviour that is associated with impairment of function needs to be identified, because there is no evidence for the current arbitrary criterion. There is no consistent evidence that the concern for body shape and weight and the dread of being fat have the same significance to all patients with bulimia nervosa.

Unspecified Eating Disorders

There is incomplete evidence on the course and response to treatment of the numerous variants of eating disorders that are thrown into this category. There is incomplete evidence that partial syndromes actually should be partial or included as part of the complete syndrome of anorexia nervosa or bulimia nervosa.

Areas Still Open to Research

Anorexia Nervosa

The physiological mechanisms underlying the reinforcement and maintenance of the starvation behaviours need to be investigated with the more sophisticated neuroimaging and genetic techniques that are now available. It is very likely that the so-called "hypothalamic impairment" is due to dysfunctioning of neurotransmitters and receptor sites secondary to variations in genetic control.

More systematic and precise psychological investigations need to be devised to elucidate more clearly the overwhelming reluctance and fear of the anorectic patient to change behaviour.

Predictor research is necessary to identify more carefully the restricting type of patient who will remain a restricting type throughout her lifetime, and also to identify those restricting patients who will develop binge eating behaviour.

Bulimia Nervosa

Continued efforts are necessary to define more carefully both binge eating and overeating in order to delineate the parameters of what is actually pathological.

Compelling evidence is needed to separate underweight patients who binge and purge from normal weight persons who engage in these behaviours.

The core psychological set of the patients with bulimia nervosa needs to be investigated more thoroughly. Not all of these patients are overly concerned with their body shape and weight. Some suggestible persons learn binge/purge behaviour as a means of alleviating boredom and handling stress. Binge/purge behaviour also can become an addictive-like phenomenon that can sustain itself without any relationship to body weight and shape concerns. This is an area that needs more careful investigation.

The entire concept of whether eating disorders are part of a spectrum of other Axis I disorders can be determined conclusively only by genetic research. At this time there is not enough evidence to classify bulimia nervosa as part of a spectrum of addictive disorders or affective disorders. It is also not possible to classify anorexia nervosa as part of any spectrum of OCD or affective disorders. Continued careful defining of the phenotypes of bulimia nervosa and anorexia nervosa, along with genetic research, is essential to produce a more accurate classification of these disorders.

Unspecified Eating Disorders

Longitudinal follow-up studies are needed on carefully defined types of eating disorders within this category. This will be helpful in determining a meaningful classification of the specific variants included in this general classification. Continued investigations are needed to delineate more carefully binge eating disorder from the non-purging type of bulimia nervosa.

The Future

Periodic meetings of members of the ICD-10 and DSM-IV eating disorder classification committees should occur, with exchange of research evidence for redefining and more carefully classifying the eating disorders.

REFERENCES

1. Richardson H.B. (1939) Simmonds's disease and anorexia nervosa. *Arch. Intern. Med.*, **63**: 1–5.
2. Waller J.F., Kaufman M., Deutsch F. (1940) Anorexia nervosa: a psychosomatic entity. In *Evolution of Psychosomatic Concepts* (Eds R.M. Kaufman, M. Heilman), pp. 35–46. Hogarth Press, London.
3. Fairbairn W.R.D. (1944) Endopsychic structure considered in terms of object relationships. *Int. J. Psychoanal.*, **25**: 70–93.
4. Bliss E.L., Branch C.H. (1960) *Anorexia Nervosa: Its History, Psychology and Biology*. Hober Medical Division, Harper & Row, New York.
5. Thoma H. (1963) Some psychoanalytic observations on anorexia nervosa. *Br. J. Med. Psychol.*, **36**: 239–245.
6. King A. (1963) Primary and secondary anorexia nervosa syndrome. *Br. J. Psychiatry*, **109**: 470–475.
7. Casper R., Eckert E., Halmi K., Goldberg S., Davis J. (1980) Bulimia: its incidence and clinical importance in patients with anorexia nervosa. *Arch. Gen. Psychiatry*, **37**: 1030–1035.
8. Garfinkel P., Moldofsky H., Garner D. (1980) The heterogeneity of anorexia nervosa; bulimia as a distinct group. *Arch. Gen. Psychiatry*, **37**: 1036–1040.
9. Russell G.F.M. (1979) Bulimia nervosa: an ominous variant of anorexia nervosa. *Psychol. Med.*, **9**: 429–448.
10. American Psychiatric Association (1994) *Diagnostic and Statistical Manual of Mental Disorders*, 4th ed. American Psychiatric Association, Washington.
11. World Health Organization (1992) *International Classification of Diseases and Related Health Problems*, 10th ed. World Health Organization, Geneva.
12. James R. (1743) *A Medical Dictionary*. Osborne, London.
13. Bell R.M. (1985) *Holy Anorexia*. University of Chicago Press, Chicago.
14. SMC (1945) *Margaret, Princess of Hungary*. Blackfriars Publications, London.
15. DiNicola V.F. (1990) Anorexia multiforme: self starvation in historical and cultural context. Part 1: Self starvation as a historical chameleon. *Transcult. Psychiatry Res. Rev.*, **27**: 165–196.
16. Reynolds J. (1669) *A Discourse upon Prodigious Abstinence; Occasioned by the 12 Months Fasting of Martha Taylor, the Famed Derbyshire Damsel*. RW, London.
17. Morton R. (1689) *Phthisiologia. Seu Exercitiationes de Phtisi*. S. Smith, London.
18. Whytt R. (1764) *Observations on the Nature, Causes and Cure of Those Disorders which have been Commonly called Nervous, Hypochondriac or Hysteric*. Becket, DeHondt and Balfour, Edinburgh.

19. Encyclopaedia Britannica (1797) *Bulimy*. Bell and MacFarguhar, Edinburgh.
20. Motherby G. (1785) *A New Medical Dictionary: Or a General Repository of Physic*. Johnson and Robinson, London.
21. Blankaart S. (1708) *The Physical Dictionary*. Crouch and Sprint, London.
22. Stein D., Laakso W. (1988) Bulimia: a historical perspective. *Int. J. Eat. Disord.*, 7: 201–210.
23. Marcé L.V. (1860) On a form of hypochondriac delirium occurring consecutive to dyspepsia and characterized by refusal of food. *J. Psychol. Med. Met. Pathol.*, 13: 264–266.
24. Gull W. (1888) Anorexia nervosa. *Lancet*, i: 516–517.
25. Lasègue C. (1873) On hysterical anorexia. *Med. Times Gaz.* 2: 265–266.
26. Chipley W. (1859) Sitomania: its causes and treatment. *Am. J. Insanity*, 16: 1–42.
27. Hammond W. (1879) *Fasting Girls: Their Physiology and Pathology*. Putnam, New York.
28. Mitchell S.W. (1881) *Lectures on the Diseases of the Nervous System, Especially in Women*. Henry C. Lea's, Philadelphia.
29. Inches P.R. (1895) Anorexia nervosa. *Marit. Med. News (Halifax)*, 7: 73–75.
30. Soltmann D. (1894) Anorexia cerebralis und centrale nutritions neurosin. *Jahrb. Kinderheilkd. Phys. Erzieh.*, 38: 1–13.
31. Blache Z.P. (1869) Boulimie. In *Dictionnaire Encyclopédique des Sciences Médicales*, first series, Vol. 10 (Ed. A. Dechandre), p. 15. Masson, Paris.
32. Bruch H. (1973) *Eating Disorders: Obesity, Anorexia Nervosa, and the Person Within*. Basic Books, New York.
33. Feighner J.P., Robins E., Guze S., Woodruff R., Winokur G., Munoz R. (1972) Diagnostic criteria for use in psychiatric research. *Arch. Gen. Psychiatry*, 26: 57–63.
34. Halmi K.A., Broadland G., Rigas C. (1975) A follow-up study of 79 patients with anorexia nervosa: an evaluation of prognostic factors in diagnostic criteria. *Life Hist. Res. Psychopathol.*, 4: 290–298.
35. Morgan H.G., Russell G.F.M. (1975) Value of family background in clinical features as prediction of long term outcome in anorexia nervosa. *Psychol. Med.*, 5: 355–371.
36. Theander S. (1970) Anorexia nervosa. *Acta Psychiatr. Scand.*, Suppl. 214.
37. Hsu L.K., Crisp A.H., Harding L. (1979) Outcome of anorexia nervosa. *Lancet*, i: 63–73.
38. American Psychiatric Association (1980) *Diagnostic and Statistical Manual of Mental Disorders*, 3rd ed. American Psychiatric Association, Washington.
39. Russell G.F.M., Beardwood C. (1970) Amenorrhea in the feeding disorders: anorexia nervosa and obesity. *Psychother. Psychosom.*, 18: 358–364.
40. Russell G.F.M. (1969) Metabolic, endocrine and psychiatric aspects of anorexia nervosa. *Sci. Basis Med. Annu. Rev.*, 15: 236–255.
41. Falk J.R., Halmi K. (1982) Amenorrhea in anorexia nervosa: examination of the critical body weight hypothesis. *Biol. Psychiatry*, 17: 799–806.
42. Russell G.F.M. (1970) Anorexia nervosa: its identity as an illness and its treatment. In *Modern Trends in Psychological Medicine* (Ed. J.H. Price), pp. 131–164. Butterworths, London.
43. Pirke K.M, Fichter M., Lund R., Doerr P. (1979) Twenty-four hours sleep–wake pattern of plasma LH in patients with anorexia nervosa. *Acta Endocrinol.*, 92: 193–204.
44. Weiner H. (1983) Hypothalamic–pituitary–ovarian axis in anorexia and bulimia nervosa. *Int. J. Eat. Disord.*, 2: 109–116.

45. Brown G.M., Garfinkel P.E., Jeuniewic N., Moldofsky H., Stancer H. (1977). Endocrine profiles in anorexia nervosa. In *Anorexia Nervosa* (Ed. R.A. Vigersky), pp. 123–125. Raven Press, New York.
46. Schwartz B., Cummings D., Riordan E., Selye M., Yen S., Rebar R. (1981) Exercise associated amenorrhea: a distinct entity? *Am. J. Obstet. Gynecol.*, **141**: 662–670.
47. Katz J., Boyar R., Roffwarg H, Hellman L., Weiner H. (1978) Weight and circadian LH secretory pattern in anorexia nervosa. *Psychosom. Med.*, **40**: 549–567.
48. Brady A., Rieger W. (1972) Behavior treatment of anorexia nervosa. In *Proceedings of the International Symposium on Behavior Modification*, pp. 35–42. Appleton-Century-Crofts, New York.
49. Crisp H., Kalucy R. (1982) Aspects of perceptual disorder in anorexia nervosa. *Br. J. Med. Psychol.*, **47**: 349–360.
50. American Psychiatric Association (1987) *Diagnostic and Statistical Manual of Mental Disorders*, 3rd ed., revised. American Psychiatric Association, Washington.
51. DeCosta M., Halmi K.A. (1992) Classifications of anorexia nervosa: question of subtypes. *Int. J. Eat. Disord.*, **11**: 305–313.
52. Halmi K.A. (1974) Comparison of demographic and clinical features in patient groups with differing ages and weights at onset of anorexia nervosa. *J. Nerv. Ment. Dis.*, **150**: 222–225.
53. Lindholm L., Wilson G.T. (1988) Body image assessment in patients with bulimia nervosa and normal controls. *Int. J. Eat. Disord.*, **7**: 527–539.
54. Garfinkel P.E., Kennedy S.H., Kaplan A.S. (1995) Views on classification and diagnosis of eating disorders. *Can. J. Psychiatry*, **40**: 445–456.
55. Halmi K.A. (1999) Eating disorders: anorexia nervosa, bulimia nervosa and obesity. In *American Psychiatric Press Textbook of Psychiatry*, 3rd ed. (Eds K.E. Hales, S.C. Yudofsky, J. Talbott), pp. 983–1002. American Psychiatric Association, Washington.
56. Anderson A.E. (1985) *Practical Comprehensive Treatment of Anorexia Nervosa and Bulimia Nervosa*. Johns Hopkins University Press, Baltimore.
57. Yellowlees A. J. (1985) Anorexia and bulimia in anorexia nervosa: a study of psychosocial functioning and associated psychiatric symptomatology. *Br. J. Psychiatry*, **146**: 648–652.
58. Strober M., Salkin B., Burroughs J., Morrell W. (1982) Validity of the bulimia–restrictor distinctions in anorexia nervosa: parental personality characteristics and familial psychiatric morbidity. *J. Nerv. Ment. Dis.*, **170**: 354–351.
59. Eckert E., Halmi K.A., Marchi P., Cohen J. (1987) Comparison of bulimic and nonbulimic anorexia nervosa patients during treatment. *Psychol. Med.*, **17**: 891–898.
60. Garner D.M., Garner M.V., Rosen L.W. (1993) Anorexia nervosa "restrictors" who purge: implications for subtyping anorexia nervosa. *Int. J. Eat. Disord.*, **13**: 171–185.
61. Herzog D.B., Field A.E., Keller M.B., West J.C., Robbins W.M., Staley J., Colditz G.A. (1996) Subtyping eating disorders, is it justified? *J. Am. Acad. Child Adolesc. Psychiatry*, **35**: 928–936.
62. Bulik C.M., Sullivan P.F., Kendler K.S. (2000) An empirical study of the classification of eating disorders. *Am. J. Psychiatry*, **157**: 886–895.
63. Fairburn C.G. (1987) The definition of bulimia nervosa: guidelines for clinicians and research workers. *Ann. Behav. Med.*, **9**: 3–7.

64. Beglin C. J., Fairburn C.G. (1992) What is meant by the term "binge"? *Am. J. Psychiatry*, **149**: 123–124.

65. Wilson G.T., Eldredge K.L. (1991) Frequency of binge eating in bulimic patients: diagnostic validity. *Int. J. Eat. Disord.*, **10**: 557–561.

66. Fairburn C.G., Cooper P.J. (1984) The clinical features of bulimia nervosa. *Br. J. Psychiatry*, **14**: 238–246.

67. Cooper Z., Cooper P.J., Fairburn C.G. (1989) The validity of the eating disorder examination and its subscales. *Br. J. Psychiatry*, **154**: 807–812.

68. Wilson G.T., Smith D. (1989) Assessment of bulimia nervosa: an evaluation of the Eating Disorders Examination. *Int. J. Eat. Disord.*, **8**: 173–179.

69. Garfinkel P.E., Glodbloom D.S., Olmsted M.P. (1992) Body dissatisfaction in bulimia nervosa: relationship to weight and shape concerns and psychological functioning. *Int. J. Eat. Disord.*, **11**: 151–161.

70. Hay P., Fairburn C. (1998) The validity of the DSM-IV scheme for classifying bulimic eating disorders. *Int. J. Eat. Disord.*, **23**: 7–15.

71. Tobin D.L., Griffing A., Griffing S. (1997) An examination of subtype criteria for bulimia nervosa. *Int. J. Eat. Disord.*, **22**: 179–186.

72. Spitzer R.L., Yanolfski S., Wadden T., Wing R., Marcus M., Stunkard A., Devlin M., Mitchell J., Hasin D., Horne R.L. (1993) Binge eating disorder: its further validation in a multisite study. *Int. J. Eat. Disord.*, **13**: 137–153.

73. Yanovski C.Z., Leet M., Yanovski J.A., Flood M., Gold P.W., Kissileff H.R., Walsh B.T. (1992) Food selection and intake of obese women with binge-eating disorder. *Am. J. Clin. Nutr.*, **56**: 975–980.

74. Marcus M.D., Wing R.R., Hopkins J. (1988) Obese binge eaters: affect, cognitions and response to behavioral weight control. *J. Consult. Clin. Psychol.*, **53**: 433–439.

75. Marcus M.D., Smith D., Santelli R. (1992) Characterization of eating disorder behavior in obese binge eaters. *Int. J. Eat. Disord.*, **12**: 249–255.

76. Williamson D.A., Martin C.K. (1999) Binge eating disorder: a review of the literature after publication of DSM-IV. *Eat. Weight Disord.*, **4**: 103–114.

77. Martin C.K., Williamson D.A., Thaw T.M. (2000) Criterion validity of the multiaxial assessment of eating disorders symptoms. *Int. J. Eat. Disord.*, **28**: 303–310.

78. Cotrufo P., Barretta V., Monteleone P., Maj M. (1998) Full syndrome, partial syndrome and subclinical eating disorders: an epidemiological study of female students in Southern Italy. *Acta Psychiatr. Scand.*, **98**: 112–115.

79. Shisslak C.M., Crago M., Estes L. (1995) The spectrum of eating disorders. *Int. J. Eat. Disord.*, **18**: 209–219.

80. van der Ham T., Meulman J.J., Van Strien C., Van Engeland H. (1997) Empirically based subgrouping of eating disorders in adolescents: a long-itudinal perspective. *Br. J. Psychiatry*, **170**: 363–368.

81. Cantwell D.P., Sturzenberg S., Burroughs J., Salkin B., Green J.K. (1977) Anorexia nervosa: an affective disorder? *Arch. Gen. Psychiatry*, **34**: 1087–1092.

82. Halmi K.A., Eckert E., Marchi P., Apple R., Cohen J. (1991) Comorbidity of psychiatric diagnoses in anorexia nervosa. *Arch. Gen. Psychiatry*, **48**: 712–719.

83. Laessle R.G., Kittl S., Fichter M., Wittchen H.U., Pirke K.M. (1987) Major affective disorder in anorexia nervosa and bulimia: A descriptive diagnostic study. *Br. J. Psychiatry*, **151**: 785–790.

84. Toner B.B., Garfinkel P.E., Garner D.M. (1988) Affective and anxiety disorders in the long-term follow-up of anorexia nervosa. *Int. J. Psychiatry Med.*, **18**: 357–360.

85. Gershon E., Schreiber J., Hamovit J., Dibble E.D., Kaye W., Numberger J.I., Jr., Andersen A.E., Ebert M. (1984) Clinical findings in patients with anorexia nervosa and affected illnesses in their relatives. *Am. J. Psychiatry*, **149**: 1419–1422.

86. Kennedy S.H., Kaplan A.S., Garfinkel P.E., Rockert W., Toner B., Abbey S.E. (1994) Depression in anorexia nervosa and bulimia nervosa: discriminating depressive symptoms and episodes. *J. Psychosom. Res.*, **38**: 773–781.

87. Braun D.L. Sunday S.R., Halmi K.A. (1994) Psychiatric comorbidity in patients with eating disorders. *Psychol. Med.*, **24**: 859–867.

88. Hudson J., Pope H.G., Jr., Jonas J., Yurgelun-Todd D. (1983) Phenomenologic relationship of eating disorders to major affective disorder. *Psychiatry Res.*, **9**: 345–354.

89. Fornari V., Kaplan M., Sandberg D. (1982) Depressive and anxiety disorders in anorexia nervosa and bulimia nervosa. *Int. J. Eat. Disord.*, **12**: 21–29.

90. Herzog D.B., Keller M.B., Lavori P.W., Kenny G.M., Sacks N.R. (1992) The prevalence of personality disorders in 210 women with eating disorders. *J. Clin. Psychiatry*, **53**: 147–152.

91. Ivarsson T., Rastam M., Wentz E., Gillberg I., Gillberg C. (2000) Depressive disorders in teenage-onset anorexia nervosa: a controlled longitudinal, partly community-based study. *Compr. Psychiatry*, **41**: 398–403.

92. Wade T., Bulik C., Neale N., Kendler K. (2000) Anorexia nervosa and major depression: shared genetic and environmental risk factors. *Am. J. Psychiatry*, **157**: 469–471.

93. Grilo C.M., Levy K.N., Becker D.F., Edell W., McGlashan T. (1996) Comorbidity of DSM-III-R Axis I and II disorders among female inpatients with eating disorders. *Psychiatr. Serv.*, **47**: 426–429.

94. Hudson J.I., Pope H.G., Yurgelun-Todd D., Jonas J., Frankenburg F.R. (1987) A controlled study of lifetime prevalence of affective and other psychiatric disorders in bulimic outpatients. *Am. J. Psychiatry*, **144**: 1283–1287.

95. Bulik C.M., Sullivan P.F., Fear J.L., Joyse P.R. (1997) Eating disorders and antecedent anxiety disorders: a controlled study. *Acta Psychiatr. Scand.*, **96**: 101–107.

96. Bulik C.M., Sullivan P.F., Carter F.A., Joyse P.R. (1996) Lifetime anxiety disorders in women with bulimia nervosa. *Compr. Psychiatry*, **37**: 368–374.

97. Pla C., Toro J. (1999) Anorexia nervosa in a Spanish adolescent sample: an 8-year longitudinal study. *Acta. Psychiatr. Scand.*, **100**: 441–446.

98. Brewerton T.D., Lydiard B., Herzog D., Brotman A., O'Neil P., Ballenger J. (1995) Comorbidity of Axis I psychiatric disorders in bulimia nervosa. *J. Clin. Psychiatry*, **56**: 77–80.

99. Schwalberg M.D., Barlow D., Alger S.A., Howard L.J. (1992) Comparison of bulimics, obese binge eaters, social phobics and panic disorder on comorbidity across DSM-III-R anxiety disorders. *J. Abnorm. Psychol.*, **4**: 675–681.

100. Godart N.T., Flament M., Lecrubier Y., Jeammet P. (2000) Anxiety disorders in anorexia nervosa and bulimia nervosa: co-morbidity and chronology of appearance. *Eur. Psychiatry*, **15**: 38–45.

101. Cavallini M.C., Riboldi C., Bellodi L. (1999) Genetic aspects of eating disorders and obsessive–compulsive disorder: genetic models. In *Eating Disorders and Obsessive–Compulsive Disorders: an Etiopathogenetic Link?* (Eds L. Bellodi, F. Brambilla), pp. 27–40. Centro Scientifico Editore, Turin.

102. Cavallini M., Bertelli S., Chiapparino D., Riboldi S., Bellodi L. (2000) Complex segregation analyses of obsessive–compulsive disorder in 141 families of

eating disorder probands, with and without obsessive–compulsive disorder. *Am. J. Med. Genet.*, **96**: 384–391.

103. Bellodi L., Cavallini M., Bertelli D., Chiapparino D., Riboldi C., Smeraldi E. (2001) Morbidity risk for obsessive–compulsive spectrum disorders in first-degree relatives of patients with eating disorders. *Am. J. Psychiatry*, **158**: 563–569.

104. Lilenfeld L.R., Kaye W.H., Greeno G.C., Merikangas K.R., Plotnicov K., Pollice C., Rao R., Strober M., Bulik C.M., Nagy L. (1998) A controlled family study of anorexia nervosa and bulimia nervosa: psychiatric disorders in first-degree relatives and effects of proband comorbidity. *Arch. Gen. Psychiatry*, **55**: 603–610.

105. Speranza M., Corcos M., Godart N., Jeammet P., Flament M. (2001) Obsessive–compulsive disorders in eating disorders. *Eat. Behav.*, **2**: 193–207.

106. Thornton C., Russell J. (1997) Obsessive–compulsive comorbidity in the eating disorders. *Int. J. Eat. Disord.*, **21**: 83–87.

107. Gillberg C., Rastam M. (1992) Do some cases of anorexia nervosa reflect underlying autistic-like conditions. *Behav. Neurol.*, **5**: 27–32.

108. Gillberg I., Gillberg C., Rastam M., Johansson M. (1996) The cognitive profile of anorexia nervosa: a comparative study including a community-based sample. *Compr. Psychiatry*, **37**: 23–30.

109. Selby M.J., Moreno J.K. (1995) Personal and familial substance misuse patterns among eating disorder and depressed subjects. *Int. J. Addict.*, **30**: 1169–1176.

110. Striegel-Moore R.H., Hyudic E.S. (1993) Problem drinking and symptoms of disordered drinking in female high school students. *Int. J. Eat. Disord.*, **14**: 417–425.

111. Bushnell J.A., Wells J.E., McKenzie K., Hornblow A.R., Oakley-Browne M.A., Joyce P.R. (1994) Bulimia comorbidity in the general population and in the clinic. *Psychol. Med.*, **24**: 605–611.

112. Holderness C.E., Brooks-Gunn J., Warren M.P. (1994) Comorbidity of eating disorders and substance abuse: review of the literature. *Int. J. Eat. Disord.*, **16**: 1–34.

113. Lilenfeld L., Kaye W., Greeno C., Merikangas K., Plotnicov K., Pollice C., Rao R., Strober M., Bulik S.M., Nagy L. (1997) Psychiatric disorders in women with bulimia nervosa and their first degree relatives: effects of comorbid substance dependence. *Int. J. Eat. Disord.*, **22**: 253–264.

114. Specher S., Westermeyer J., Thuras P. (2000) Course and severity of substance abuse in women with comorbid eating disorder. *Subst. Abuse*, **21**: 137–147.

115. Deet A., Lilenfeld S.L., Plotnicof K., Pollice C., Kaye W. (1999) Sexual abuse in eating disorder subtypes and control women: the role of comorbid substance abuse in bulimia nervosa. *Int. J. Eat. Disord.*, **25**: 1–10.

116. Powers P.C., Coovert D.L., Brightwell D.R., Stevens B.A. (1988) Other psychiatric disorders among bulimic patients. *Compr. Psychiatry*, **29**: 503–508.

117. Wonderlich S.A., Swift W.J., Slotnick A., Goodman S. (1990) DSM-III-R personality disorders in eating disorder subtypes. *Int. J. Eat. Disord.*, **9**: 607–616.

118. Gartner A.F., Marcus R.N., Halmi K.A., Loranger A.W. (1989) DSM-III-R personality disorders in patients with eating disorders. *Am. J. Psychiatry*, **146**: 1585–1591.

119. Schmidt N.B., Telch M. (1990) Prevalence of personality disorders among bulimics, nonbulimic binge eaters and normal controls. *J. Psychopathol. Behav. Assess.*, **12**: 170–185.

120. Rossiter E.M., Agras W., Telch C., Schneider J.A. (1993) Cluster B personality disorder characteristics predict outcome in the treatment of bulimia nervosa. *Int. J. Eat. Disord.*, **13**: 349–357.
121. Steiger H., Thibaudeau J., Leung F., Houle L., Ghadirian A.M. (1994) Eating and psychiatric symptoms as a function of Axis II comorbidity in bulimic patients. Three-month and six-month response after therapy. *Psychosomatics*, **35**: 41–49.
122. Matsunaga H., Kaye W., McConaha C., Plotnicov K., Pollice C., Rao R. (2000) Personality disorders among subjects recovered from eating disorders. *Int. J. Eat. Disord.*, **27**: 353–357.
123. Steiger H., Leonard S., Kin N., Ladouceur C., Ramdoyal D., Young S. (2000) Childhood abuse and platelet tritiated paroxetine binding in bulimia nervosa: implications of borderline personality disorder. *J. Clin. Psychiatry*, **61**: 428–435.

Commentaries

1.1

Unresolved Issues in the Classification, Diagnosis and Comorbidity of Eating Disorders

Drew Westen[1]

As Katherine Halmi's comprehensive review of the history and current status of diagnosis of eating disorders suggests, the field has made great strides since the 1970s in the delineation of different forms of eating pathology. At the same time, as her review makes clear, numerous issues remain unresolved. I focus here on two issues: the question of dimensional diagnosis and the question of within-diagnosis heterogeneity. Both issues relate to three problems confronting efforts to devise more rigorous, empirically grounded ways of classifying psychiatric disorders: a) the proliferation of diagnoses for eating disorders (now five in DSM-IV, including subtypes) that is an inherent consequence of increasing specificity of categorical diagnoses; b) the importance of attending to patterned heterogeneity within diagnoses that may render generalizations about patients who share a diagnosis (e.g. restricting anorexia) problematic; c) the increasingly cumbersome diagnostic procedures (counting long lists of inclusion and exclusion criteria to make a diagnosis) that often accompany increasing diagnostic specificity, which contributes to a gap between research and practice, unless clinicians find new diagnostic distinctions clinically useful.

A central question in contemporary research on psychiatric classification pertains to the advantages and disadvantages of categorical versus dimensional diagnosis (i.e. diagnosing patients as *having* a specific diagnosis, distinct from other diagnoses, versus diagnosing pathology on a continuum from absent to severe or prototypical) [1,2]. Categorical approaches have clear advantages: we naturally tend to think and speak in categories (e.g. describing a patient to a colleague as "anorexic" rather than "high on fear of fatness, low on weight, high on restricting") and categorical diagnosis *allows* professionals to assume a set of connotations and denotations when they hear or read about a patient or a study, unless

[1] *Center for Anxiety and Related Disorders, Department of Psychology, Boston University, 648 Beacon St., Boston, MA 02215, USA*

expressly stated otherwise (e.g. a patient with anorexia is likely to be substantially underweight and to deny her illness, even though in specific cases she may not). On the other hand, dimensional diagnoses have several advantages: a) they tend to be more reliable (because it is easier for two observers to agree that a patient is relatively high or relatively low on a dimension than to agree when a patient's symptoms hover around the threshold for what is usually an arbitrary cutoff for "caseness"); b) they do not require arbitrary severity or duration criteria (such as bingeing and purging at least twice a week for a specified period of weeks); c) they avoid the problems of "subclinical" diagnoses that fail to meet cutoffs but are nevertheless clinically significant; d) they avoid the problem of "not otherwise specified" (NOS) diagnoses that convey little information but are the primary diagnosis for patients with eating disorders treated in the community in over 30% of cases [3]. Dimensional systems of scaling can be useful even when a disorder is truly taxonic, i.e. when above some empirically determined threshold the individuals are qualitatively different from those below the threshold [4].

A promising approach to clinical diagnosis that has many of the advantages of both categorical and dimensional diagnosis is a prototype-matching approach, in which clinicians simultaneously diagnose patients dimensionally and categorically [5]. For example, instead of counting symptoms and deciding whether a patient is above or below a threshold, the clinician simply makes a 1–5 rating of the extent to which a patient's symptomatology resembles a diagnostic prototype, in which a rating of 4 or 5 (i.e. good or excellent match to the prototype) constitutes, by convention, a categorical diagnosis. For example, a prototype of anorexia taken from current DSM-IV criteria would be as follows:

Patients who match this prototype refuse to maintain their body weight at or above a minimally normal weight for their age and height. They have an intense fear of gaining weight or becoming fat, even though they are, or are in danger of becoming, substantially underweight. They tend to have a disturbance in the way they experience their body weight or shape, and may deny the seriousness of their low body weight. Their body weight or shape exerts undue influence on their views of and feelings about themselves. Patients who match this prototype may also develop amenorrhoea (i.e. cessation of menstruation).

Using a simple prototype matching system of this sort, patients would receive a single rating for anorexia and a single rating for bulimia, with no subtype or NOS diagnoses necessary. To provide more diagnostic information, for patients who receive a rating of 3 or above only, clinicians would rate dimensions such as severity, duration and age of onset, providing more information than currently recorded in either DSM-IV or ICD-10. We are currently testing whether such a system predicts criterion variables that a diagnostic classification should predict (such as adaptive functioning, prognosis, treatment response and aetiology [1,6,7]) as effectively as the current symptom-counting diagnostic algorithms in the DSM and ICD systems, and whether clinicians find it easier to use.

As Halmi's review makes clear, the research literature on eating disorders shows wide divergence of estimates of variables on which one would not expect so much fluctuation across samples, such as estimates of comorbidity for a given disorder (e.g. obsessive–compulsive disorder in anorexics) ranging from the low teens to the upper sixties. Although methodological problems could account for such discordant findings (such as different research centres' thresholds for making an obsessive–compulsive disorder diagnosis using the same structured interview), an equally likely possibility is that patients who share a single diagnosis (e.g. anorexia, restricting type) are highly heterogeneous on variables such as personality that may be crucial both clinically and empirically, and that this heterogeneity may be patterned, not random. For example, using Q-factor analysis (a cluster-analytical technique that does not assume mutually exclusive categories), Westen and Harnden-Fischer [8] identified three personality prototypes that cut across Axis I eating disorder diagnoses: a high-functioning, perfectionist prototype, characterized by generally successful social and occupational adaptation but a tendency towards self-criticism and negative affect; a low-functioning, constricted, overcontrolled prototype, characterized by restriction in virtually all domains of life (emotional, social, sexual, as well as nutritional); and a low-functioning, emotionally dysregulated, impulsive, undercontrolled prototype, characterized by many borderline features. Patients with anorexic symptoms tended to match either the first or second prototype; patients with bulimic symptoms tended to match the first or third. Thus, a given study of patients with bulimia may be including a mixture of high-functioning women with problems of perfectionism and self-esteem, and low-functioning, impulsive women with significant borderline traits. In both the original study and in more recent research from our laboratory [3,9] we have found these prototypes to be far more predictive of criterion variables such as treatment response and aetiology (e.g. history of sexual abuse) than DSM-IV Axis I.

This classification by personality phenotype is just one example, but the data suggest that we should follow up inconsistencies in the empirical literature with careful attention to patterned (rather than random) within- and across-diagnosis heterogeneity. This is particularly true in light of data suggesting that Axis I eating disorder diagnosis (e.g. whether a patient has bulimia, with or without purging) may not be highly predictive of clinically and empirically important variables such as adaptive functioning, prognosis and treatment response [10].

REFERENCES

1. Millon T. (1991) Classification in psychopathology: rationale, alternatives, and standards. *J. Abnorm. Psychol.*, **100**: 245–261.
2. Widiger T. (1992) Categorical versus dimensional classification: implications from and for research. *J. Personal. Disord.*, **6**: 287–300.
3. Morrison C., Westen D. The structure of DSM-IV eating disorder diagnoses: a factor- and cluster-analytic investigation (in preparation).
4. Waller N., Meehl P. (1998) *Multivariate Taxometric Analysis*. Sage, New York.
5. Westen D., Heim A.K., Morrison K., Patterson M., Campbell L. (2003) Classifying and diagnosing psychopathology: a prototype matching approach. In *Rethinking the DSM: Psychological Perspectives* (Eds L. Beutler, M. Malik). American Psychiatric Association, Washington (in press).
6. Skinner H.A. (1986) Construct validation approach to psychiatric classification. In *Contemporary Directions in Psychopathology: Towards the DSM-IV* (Eds T. Millon, G.L. Klerman), pp. 307–329. Guilford, New York.
7. Robins E., Guze S.B. (1970) Establishment of diagnostic validity in psychiatric illness: its application to schizophrenia. *Am. J. Psychiatry*, **126**: 983–986.
8. Westen D., Harnden-Fischer J. (2001) Classifying eating disorders by personality profiles: bridging the chasm between Axis I and Axis II. *Am. J. Psychiatry*, **158**: 547–562.
9. Thompson H., Westen D. Predicting treatment outcome in patients with bulimia using an effectiveness design (in preparation).
10. Eddy K., Keel P., Dorer D., Delinsky S., Franko D., Herzog D. (2003) A longitudinal comparison of anorexia nervosa subtypes. *Int J. Eat. Disord.* (in press).

1.2

The Classification of Eating Disorders: How Many Categorical Distinctions is it Worth Making?

Peter J. Cooper[1]

The history of the classification of eating disorders, authoritatively reviewed by Katherine Halmi, is clearly still in the early stages of being written. As she notes, several issues of nosological importance remain to be resolved, such as the status of binge eating disorder. Despite this, it is of interest that, although the 19th century and early 20th century saw sorties

[1] *Winnicott Research Unit, Department of Psychology, University of Reading, Whiteknights, Reading, UK*

down some dubious avenues, the concept of anorexia nervosa changed remarkably little over the second half of the 20th century. Indeed, the recent refinements to the DSM system have required only its relationship with a newly specified eating disorder (bulimia nervosa) to be clarified, and a distinction to be drawn between those who do and do not engage in a particular set of behaviour (i.e. surrounding bingeing and purging).

There is widespread agreement about the central defining features of anorexia nervosa. Some issues remain controversial, but they are not of real importance in defining what is and is not anorexia nervosa. For example, an issue highlighted by Halmi is the question of whether amenorrhoea should be a necessary diagnostic criterion for anorexia nervosa. This issue is a legacy of Gerald Russell, from the days when he regarded anorexia nervosa as involving a primary hypothalamic disturbance. This is not a view Russell has advanced in recent years. (There is, of course, no empirical barrier to resolving this issue: a comparison, in terms of psychopathological features and clinical outcome, of two groups both satisfying all the other diagnostic criteria, one group with amenorrhoea and one without amenorrhoea, would suffice.)

Where there has been most recent nosological interest and development has been in the specification of forms of eating disorder other than anorexia nervosa. In particular, the emergence of bulimia nervosa as a distinct disorder has entailed considerable argument and debate concerning its necessary criteria. Halmi remains concerned about the defining character-istics and necessary frequency of the central behavioural disturbance, namely a binge. It is, however, questionable whether further thought or research on this question will provide the refinement in classification that Halmi seeks. Although it certainly is true that the DSM-IV specifications on these issues are arbitrary, given that in the case of bulimic episodes, as in so much of psychiatric phenomenology, no sharp boundary between the normal and abnormal exists, the clinically grounded criteria currently specified are probably as good as any set of such criteria that could be produced.

This search for finer and finer distinctions, exemplified by Halmi's specification of areas for research, is laudable and, indeed, is the basis of the revisions contained in successive versions of the DSM. However, in the case of anorexia nervosa and bulimia nervosa, it is questionable whether such endeavour, pursued solely at the phenomenological level, is going to prove either clinically useful or scientifically important. It is salutary that the family history studies consistently reveal that anorexia nervosa, bulimia nervosa and the DSM-IV category of eating disorders not otherwise specified do not breed true, and that there is a shared transmission of vulnerability between these disorders [1,2]. If the presence of one of these disorders raises the risk in family members to this disorder no more than it does to the other disorders, then an understanding of the aetiology of these disorders and an improved ability to treat them is unlikely to come from further fine-grained refinements of the existing classification system. Similarly, although some studies do suggest that severity is a predictor of treatment outcome in bulimia nervosa, there is no suggestion that this is true at the margins, and the debate, therefore, concerning exactly what the defining features of a binge are, and exactly how many of these are necessary for a diagnosis, is most unlikely to prove material to treatment response.

The question must be asked, as indeed it has been [3], whether the fractionation of eating disorders into smaller and smaller subgroups is going to serve either our efforts to understand aetiology or our attempts to improve treatments, because a dimensional approach to these disorders appears to fit the data better than a rigidly categorical one. Of course dimensions are notoriously difficult to deal with and, understandably, given the communication problems associated with them, are avoided by clinicians [4]. However, it is important in pursuing aetiological research to make a distinction between specifying a categorical cutoff on a dimensional variable because it is clinically useful, and specifying a point on a dimension that separates the well from the ill or this kind of illness from that kind of illness.

An area not considered by Halmi, of relevance to a discussion of the classification of eating disorders, is where childhood disturbances in eating fit within the psychiatric nosology of eating disorders. Anorexia nervosa of early onset has now been identified and clearly described, and it is clear that it is phenomenologically indistinguishable from classic anorexia nervosa of adolescent onset [5,6]. However, other childhood disturbances of less certain status have also been described, such as selective eating [5] and food avoidant emotional disorders [7]. These conditions are psychopathologically distinct from anorexia nervosa and bulimia nervosa, and yet they are related to them. Thus, a raised rate of eating disorder psychopathology has been found in the mothers of these children [8,9], and one longitudinal study has found these early disturbances in early feeding to be precursors to adolescent eating disorder [10]. An understanding of the nature of these early disturbances of eating and their relation to the DSM eating disorders would be of help to understanding the pathways to the development of eating disorders.

Halmi concludes her review by providing an extremely useful specification of the classificatory issues that she regards to be in need of further clarificatory research. Central to this specification is the argument that genetic research is essential to producing "a more accurate classification of these disorders". This is an exciting prospect for the future. However, it is clear that the genetic developments will need to be complemented by an equally sophisticated understanding of the family and wider environmental factors that are likely to interact with the genetic substrate to produce the variety of eating disturbances that our current classificatory system attempts to specify.

REFERENCES

1. Lilenfeld L.R., Kaye W.H., Greeno G.C., Merikangas K.R., Plotnicov K., Pollice C., Rao R., Strober M., Bulik C.M., Nagy L. (1998) A controlled family study of anorexia nervosa and bulimia nervosa: psychiatric disorders in first-degree relatives and effects of proband comorbidity. *Arch. Gen. Psychiatry*, **55**: 603–610.
2. Strober M., Freeman R., Lampert C., Diamond J., Kaye W. (2000) Controlled family study of anorexia nervosa and bulimia nervosa: evidence of shared liability and transmission of partial syndromes. *Am. J. Psychiatry*, **157**: 393–401.
3. van der Han T., Jacqueline J., Meulman D., van Strien C., van Engeland H. (1997) Empirical based subgrouping of eating disorders in adolescents: a longitudinal perspective. *Br. J. Psychiatry*, **170**: 363–368.
4. Kendell R.E. (1975) *The Role of Diagnosis in Psychiatry*. Blackwell, Oxford.
5. Bryant-Waugh R. (2000) Overview. In *Anorexia Nervosa and Related Eating Disorders in Children and Adolescents*, 2nd ed. (Eds B. Lask, R. Bryant-Waugh), pp. 27–40. Psychology Press, Hove.
6. Cooper P.J., Watkins E., Bryant-Waugh R., Lask B. (2002) The nosological status of early onset anorexia nervosa. *Psychol. Med.*, **32**: 873–880.
7. Higgs J., Goodyer I., Birch J. (1989) Anorexia nervosa and food avoidance emotional disorder. *Arch. Dis. Childhood*, **64**: 346–351.
8. Stein A., Stein J., Walters E.A., Fairburn C.G. (1995) Eating habits and attitudes among mothers of children with feeding disorders. *Br. Med. J.*, **310**: 228.
9. Whelan E., Cooper P.J. (2000) The association between childhood feeding problems and maternal eating disorder. *Psychol. Med.*, **30**: 69–77.
10. Marchi M., Cohen P. (1990) Early childhood eating behaviors and adolescent eating disorders. *J. Am. Acad. Child Adolesc. Psychiatry*, **29:** 112–117.

1.3

The Problem of Classification and Comorbidity: Relationship to Trauma and Post-traumatic Stress Disorder

Timothy D. Brewerton[1]

Katherine Halmi guides us on a very interesting historical excursion that outlines the development of the recognition and classification of eating disorders. As she points out, the relationship between anorexia nervosa and

[1] *Department of Psychiatry and Behavioral Sciences, Medical University of South Carolina, 67 President St., Charleston, SC 29425, USA*

bulimia nervosa remains problematic to this day in that the DSM-IV and the ICD-10 continue to disagree on the boundaries, particularly on whether bingeing and/or purging occurring at normal weight are fundamentally the same as or different from these symptoms occurring in the context of anorexia nervosa.

Biologically oriented psychiatrists have long wished for a nomenclature that is more aetiologically based, yet a specific, single aetiology underlying eating disorders remains elusive. As the field has developed and grown, it has become apparent that there is probably no one cause of eating disorders but rather there is a complex interaction of factors that span the biopsychosocial spectrum. One of the most extensively studied neuro-transmitters in eating disorders has been serotonin (5-hydroxytryptamine, 5-HT), but it too has failed to elucidate a specific "lesion" that could be useful in terms of classification. A dysregulation hypothesis of the 5-HT system has been proposed that seeks to unify the various eating disorder manifestations and comorbid phenomena [1].

As Halmi has pointed out, a wealth of data link bulimia nervosa and binge/purge behaviours with mood, anxiety, substance use and Cluster B personality disorders. However, one of the anxiety disorders that she did not discuss is post-traumatic stress disorder (PTSD), which has been of increasing interest in the field. Like substance abuse, it appears to occur primarily in association with bulimia nervosa. In the National Women's Study (NWS), a representative sample of over 4000 women from four stratified geographical areas in the USA participated in highly structured telephone interviews by experienced females, who assessed histories of criminal victimization (including behaviourally defined rape, molestation, attempted sexual assault and aggravated assault), PTSD, major depressive disorder (MDD), bulimia nervosa, binge eating disorder (BED) and substance abuse/dependence, using DSM-III-R and DSM-IV criteria [2]. The lifetime prevalence rate for PTSD in the subjects with bulimia nervosa was 37% vs. 12% in the non-bulimia nervosa/BED subjects ($P < 0.001$). Current PTSD prevalence was found to be 22% in the bulimia nervosa group vs. 4% in the non-bulimia nervosa/BED group ($P < 0.001$). The BED subjects also had higher lifetime PTSD rates (22%) (but not current rates) compared with non-bulimia nervosa/BED subjects (4%, $P < 0.01$). These numbers are notable in that they were obtained from a representative group of non-clinical, non-treatment-seeking women, most of whom had never had mental health treatment before, so they are generalizable in the USA. Other recent studies have confirmed an association between eating disorders and PTSD [3–7].

Even before this growing focus on PTSD, there has been the recognition that victimization experiences, particularly those that occur during child-hood, are significantly more likely to be reported in patients with a history of bulimia nervosa compared with those with anorexia nervosa or controls. In a review of studies to date, Wonderlich *et al.* [8] found a robust relationship of child sexual abuse to bulimia nervosa with associated comorbidity but not to the severity of bulimia nervosa *per se*. There was no such link found between child sexual abuse and restricting anorexia nervosa, which was confirmed in the NWS. In the NWS, any form of direct victimization occurred in a majority (54%) of subjects with bulimia nervosa compared with a minority (31%) of non-bulimia nervosa/BED subjects ($P<0.001$). However, PTSD rather than abuse *per se* appears to convey the greatest risk for developing bulimia nervosa. The prevalence rates for bulimia nervosa were significantly higher in women with a history of rape associated with PTSD (10.4%) compared with those with rape without PTSD (2.0%) and those with no rape (2.0%, $P<0.001$).

Interestingly, PTSD is linked to an almost identical spectrum of psychiatric disorders [9]. It then becomes logical that severe victimization and the resultant PTSD may mediate the link between psychiatric comorbidity and bulimia nervosa in many cases. This has been confirmed in unpublished data from the NWS in which a linearly increasing number of comorbid diagnoses were associated with an increasing prevalence of childhood rape and any type of direct victimization. This association between victimization, bulimia nervosa and comorbidity has been reported in other large data sets, including the Virginia Twin Registry, which has the benefit of controlling for genetic factors [10]. Other psychiatric disorders associated with victimization and PTSD include dissociative and somatoform disorders, which also have been related to bulimia nervosa and its symptoms [9]. In the NWS there were links found between severe trauma, PTSD, dissociative symptoms and bulimia nervosa [11]. Subjects with bulimia nervosa endorsed more forgetting of traumatic events (27%) than subjects with BED (12%) or non-eating disorders (11%, $P<0.001$), and dissociative symptoms also predicted comorbidity. Although most studies have been completed in adults, recent findings in children and adolescents are confirming these same relationships [12].

These observations defy the boundaries of our traditional classification schemes. Another way of looking at it is that these findings transcend these same boundaries and lead us to think "outside the box". As a result, some investigators have suggested a group of trauma-related disorders. However, this flies in the face of evidence strongly suggesting that both anorexia nervosa and bulimia nervosa are highly genetic disorders, appearing to share a common genetic vulnerability factor related to perfectionism, obsessive–compulsive personality traits, high harm avoidance and/or behavioural inhibition. However, it appears that traumatic experiences, and especially the presence of PTSD, predispose such genetically loaded individuals towards the bulimic form of the disorder and its associated comorbidity, whereas the absence of overt trauma and PTSD allows the illness to remain in its "purest" form, i.e. restricting anorexia nervosa. From this perspective, we may be dealing with one disorder with different manifestations and permutations.

REFERENCES

1. Brewerton T.D. (1995) Toward a unified theory of serotonin dysregulation in eating and related disorders. *Psychoneuroendocrinology*, **20**: 561–590.
2. Dansky B.S., Brewerton T.D., O'Neil P.M., Kilpatrick D.G. (1997) The National Women's Study: relationship of crime victimization and PTSD to bulimia nervosa. *Int. J. Eat. Disord.*, **21**: 213–228.
3. Rorty M., Yager J. (1996) Histories of childhood trauma and complex post traumatic sequelae in women with eating disorders. *Psychiatr. Clin. North Am.*, **19**: 773–791.
4. Gleaves D.H., Eberenz K.P., May M.C. (1998) Scope and significance of posttraumatic symptomatology among women hospitalized for an eating disorder. *Int. J. Eat. Disord.*, **24**: 147–156.
5. Striegel-Moore R.H., Garvin V., Dohm F.A., Rosenheck R.A. (1999) Eating disorders in a national sample of hospitalized female and male veterans: detection rates and psychiatric comorbidity. *Int. J. Eat. Disord.*, **25**: 405–414.
6. Lipschitz D.S., Winegar R.K., Hartnick E., Foote B., Southwick S.M. (1999) Posttraumatic stress disorder in hospitalized adolescents: psychiatric comorbidity and clinical correlates. *J. Am. Acad. Child Adolesc. Psychiatry*, **38**: 385–392.
7. Matsunaga H., Kaye W.H., McConaha C., Plotnicov K., Pollice C., Rao R., Stein D. (1999) Psychopathological characteristics of recovered bulimics who have a history of physical or sexual abuse. *J. Nerv. Ment. Dis.*, **187**: 472–477.
8. Wonderlich S.A., Brewerton T.D., Jocic Z., Dansky B.S., Abbott D.W. (1997) The relationship of childhood sexual abuse and eating disorders: a review. *J. Am. Acad. Child Adolesc. Psychiatry*, **36**: 1107–1115.
9. Brady K., Killeen T.K., Brewerton T.D., Sylverini S. (2000) Comorbidity of psychiatric disorders and posttraumatic disorder. *J. Clin. Psychiatry*, **61** (Suppl. 7): 22–32.
10. Kendler K.S., Bulik C., Silberg J., Hettema J.M., Myers J., Prescott C.A. (2000) Childhood sexual abuse and adult psychiatric and substance use disorders in women: an epidemiological and cotwin control analysis. *Arch. Gen. Psychiatry*, **57**: 953–959.
11. Brewerton T.D., Dansky B.S., Kilpatrick D.G., O'Neil P.M. (1999) Bulimia nervosa, PTSD and "forgetting": results from the National Women's Study. In *Trauma and Memory* (Eds L.M. Williams, V.L. Banyard), pp. 127–138. Sage Publications, Durham.
12. Brewerton T.D. (2003) Bulimia in children and adolescents. *Child Adolesc. Psychiatr. Clin. North Am.* (in press).

1.4
Getting to the Essence of Eating Disorders
Manfred M. Fichter[1]

Few people—including professionals—know that anorexia nervosa is among the psychiatric disorders with the highest mortality at a relatively young age. Mortality in anorexia nervosa is higher than in schizophrenia or depression [1]. Adequate classification, subclassification and diagnosis make it possible to identify those patients with the highest risk to die early or to have a chronic course. Although much is still to be desired, more effective treatments for patients with eating disorders have been developed that influence the course positively. Thorough classification combined with biological studies, treatment studies and studies on the course of illness eventually will bring us to true nosological entities. Katherine Halmi, who has been a member of the Task Force for the Eating Disorders Work Group for DSM-III, DSM-III-R and DSM-IV, presents a straightforward and clear review of the state of the art in this area.

Eating and food intake can have very different functions. Eating fulfils the biological necessity of keeping us alive, but it can also be a source of pleasure and joy. Food intake plays an important role when we relax or celebrate with other human beings (festivities). For a person who hungers involuntarily, this can be bothersome or painful. On the other hand, an anorexic patient who has achieved the reduction of weight to a pathological level will be proud of the result. Refusal to eat on the level of society can be used as a means of political pressure (hunger strike). Within a family system the refusal to eat of an anorexic girl can—with the lack of other possibilities of expression—be an attempt to find and define herself; it can be a sign of inner resistance and defence against the intrusion of others. The anorexic patient avoids confrontation with the increasing demands of the role of an adult person (sexuality, trust and relationships, profession, achievement) and in a way regresses to an earlier more infantile stage. Eating too much as well as too little can be damaging to mental and physical health.

Katherine Halmi's description makes it clear that William Gull and Charles Lasègue were not the first to describe anorexia nervosa. Numerous other clinicians had described anorexic eating disorders in former centuries. Even bulimic disorders had been described long before 1979, when Russell reported bulimia nervosa as an ominous variant of anorexia nervosa. Halmi briefly mentions the misleading concept of anorexia nervosa as a primary

---

[1] *Roseneck Hospital for Behavioural Medicine, Am Roseneck 6, 83209 Prien, Germany*

pituitary insufficiency. This concept was introduced in Germany by Morris Simmonds [2] and had a profound impact in that country.

In her description of contemporary classification approaches, Katherine Halmi cites Herbert Weiner [3], who expressed the opinion that "78% of the variance of luteinizing hormone (LH) levels must be accounted for by factors other than weight loss and that therefore there can be no simple relationship between weight loss, LH levels and amenorrhea". Starvation experiments with blood probes analysed by radioimmunoassay have shown convincingly that the hypothalamic–pituitary–gonadal axis, the hypothalamic–pituitary–adrenal axis and several other hormonal axes respond very quickly to the reduction of food intake in obese, normal-weight and underweight subjects [4]. Even patients with bulimia nervosa with suboptimal but largely normal body weight and disturbed eating patterns—dieting and fasting on the one hand and bingeing on the other—showed considerable disturbances in their menstrual cycle as well as in the hypothalamic–pituitary–adrenal axis [5,6]. The issue concerning whether amenorrhoea should or should not be a criterion for the diagnosis of anorexia nervosa is of importance. If low body weight is highly correlated with the absence of menses, it would be unnecessary to have amenorrhoea as a criterion for anorexia nervosa, because low body weight definitely is one of the major criteria for the disorder.

The DSM-IV criteria for eating disorders are far more precise than the ICD-10 criteria. For the diagnosis of anorexia nervosa, ICD-10 research criterion D requires a "widespread endocrine disorder involving the hypothalamic–pituitary–gonadal axis in women". According to the results of endocrine starvation research, the "widespread endocrine disorder" observed in anorexia nervosa is a direct consequence of starvation resulting in low body weight. It is therefore not necessary to state it as a distinct criterion. The ICD-10 definitions for atypical anorexia nervosa, atypical bulimia nervosa, overeating associated with other psychological distur-bances, vomiting associated with other psychological disturbances, other eating disorders and unspecified eating disorders are too vaguely defined.

Halmi also points to the weakness of the diagnostic criteria for binge eating disorder, which are briefly described not in the main part but in an appendix of DSM-IV. There is definitely a need for further scientific exploration, because diagnostically the criteria for bulimia nervosa (non-purging type) and for binge eating disorders overlap heavily.

In the comorbidity section of Halmi's review, it is clearly described that mood disorders, anxiety disorders, substance-related disorders and personality disorders are fairly frequent and can be observed more frequently than in the general population in close relatives of patients. Concerning Axis II (personality) disorders, Cluster B disorders (antisocial, borderline, histrionic, narcissistic) tend to be associated with bulimia nervosa whereas Cluster C disorders (avoidant, dependent, obsessive–compulsive) are more closely associated with anorexia nervosa.

Although the last three decades of research in eating disorders have been very productive, many things are still outstanding. Most likely, molecular genetics will revolutionize our current systems of diagnosis and classification. Because eating disorders, as most other psychiatric disorders, are most likely not monogenic, it will be very important for future research how the phenotype is defined. Thus, the classification and diagnosis of eating disorders is a very important field, not only for the present but also for the future.

REFERENCES

1. Harris E.C., Barraclough B. (1998) Excess mortality of mental disorder. *Br. J. Psychiatry*, **173**: 11–53.
2. Simmonds M. (1916) Uber Hypophysenschwund mit tödlichem Ausgang. *Dtsch. Med. Wochenbl.*, **42**: 190–199.
3. Weiner H. (1983) Hypothalamic–pituitary–ovarian axis in anorexia and bulimia nervosa. *Int. J. Eat. Disord.*, **2**: 109–116.
4. Fichter M.M. (1992) Starvation-related endocrine changes. In *Psychology and Treatment of Anorexia Nervosa and Bulimia Nervosa* (Ed. K.H. Halmi), pp. 193–219. American Psychiatric Press, Washington.
5. Pirke K.M., Dogs M., Fichter M.M., Tuschl R.J. (1988) Gonadotropins, estradiol and progesterone during the menstrual cycle in bulimia nervosa. *Clin. Endocrinol.*, **29**: 265–270.
6. Fichter M.M., Pirke K.M., Pöllinger J., Wolfram G., Brunner E. (1990) Disturbances in the hypothalamic–pituitary–adrenal and other neuro-endocrine axes in bulimia. *Biol. Psychiatry*, **27**: 1021–1037.

1.5
Capturing an Elusive Entity: Classification, Diagnosis and Comorbidities in Eating Disorders

Arnold E. Andersen[1]

Katherine Halmi's authoritative review goes beyond its title by providing the most comprehensive comparison of international diagnostic criteria in the context of the fascinating but ever changing history of eating disorders. The two major philosophical contributions of the 20th century were existential philosophy and language philosophy. At issue here is the use of the term eating disorders. The language of diagnosis and classification of

[1] *Department of Psychiatry, University of Iowa, 200 Hawkins Drive, Iowa City, IA 52242, USA*

eating disorders is convoluted, especially in the cross-cultural context. In contrast to schizophrenia, which is relatively constant around the world in its prevalence and in its qualitative abnormalities, the prevalence of eating disorders and their reliance on the imposition of categories upon dimensions make them a slippery entity diagnostically and yet a very real and life-threatening disorder with the highest mortality in psychiatry.

Halmi brings light and comprehensive understanding to the difficulties in the classification and diagnosis of eating disorders but, as with the observation of the electron, one can only observe to a certain degree of closeness without distorting the subject of the observation. Eating disorders are absolutely real to the clinicians, who see them all around the world. Yet, like overlapping Venn circles, it is not clear whether the ICD-10 diagnostic criteria identify the same entities as the DSM IV, and whether either of them currently is adequate. The underlying problems come from several sources. First, eating behaviour is a normal human-motivated behaviour with enormous variation in its natural state. Just when does eating behaviour become abnormal? This is similar to the question of when day becomes night. It is not difficult to tell midnight from noon, but exactly when day changes to night remains uncertain.

Two certain historical assumptions have been called into question in this review. The historical inclusion of amenorrhoea as a crucial criterion for anorexia nervosa remains disproven, inapplicable to males and yet firmly entrenched in the thinking of committees on diagnostic criteria, whether DSM-IV or ICD-10. The momentum of an idea, once useful but out of date now, is as forceful in psychiatry as it is in physics. Secondly, Halmi notes that any disorder that remains at the syndrome stage of understanding is inherently made more ambiguous by reference to a cluster of signs and symptoms rather than to a fundamental aetiology. The syndromic nature of eating disorders is simply a reflection of the current state of understanding. A behaviour is a behaviour is a behaviour. Disorders of behaviour always have multiple entrées into abnormal behaviour. The diagnosis of eating disorders remains a syndromic combination of a self-induced behaviour (self-starvation with or without binge/purge behaviour), a psycho-pathology (a morbid fear of fatness, British emphasis versus a relentless drive for thinness, American emphasis) and finally a functional medical impairment, but a very specific and somewhat archaic one as specified by DSM-IV and ICD-10.

Halmi nuances the shading of the field of eating disorders from clear to obscure by classifying the available evidence into areas of consistent evidence, incomplete evidence, areas open to research and future needs. By agreeing on the essentials and being open to future research on the non-essentials, both clinicians and researchers can be sure that they are studying the same animal. How compelling and how frustrating to not be able to grasp securely an entity that is so real, so dangerous, so widespread as eating disorders and yet elusive in its core and periphery.

Eating disorders are seldom solitary travellers. Other studies have documented that the various subtypes of eating disorders have 2–4 separate comorbid diagnoses by DSM-IV. In many ways the diagnoses of the comorbid conditions are more reliable than the eating disorders themselves, because of the more secure criteria for disorders such as obsessive–compulsive disorder, major depression, etc. Yet the secure identification of comorbid psychiatric diagnoses with the eating disorders begs the question of whether they are primary or secondary, independent or integral, inflationary representations of predisposing vulnerabilities intensified by the eating disorder or intrinsically contributing to the eating disorder. What is clear, as Halmi notes, is that eating disorders are a separate diagnosable recognizable disorder and not a *forme fruste* of any other psychiatric disorder.

Lest the uncertainties and complexities of diagnosis in the international cross-cultural context be seen as discouraging, this treatment of diagnosis classification and comorbidity is the most authoritative and useful to date. Increase in knowledge comes about only with identification of areas of ignorance or conflict. This treatise carries that task forward by lighting candles to the future as well as sighing empathically at the darkness of the present. As more refinement of the subtypes of eating disorders is made, and as more specific delineation of their aetiology is uncovered, eating disorders will follow the natural scientific progression into more fundamentally understood disorders. In the meantime, disorders of normal-motivated behaviours, which are hijacked into problems-solvers for developmental issues, mood disorders and family regulation, such as eating disorders, must be grasped with a secure but a light hold in the hands of knowledge. Held too tightly, they disappear through reductionism, but too loosely held, they blend into the normal range of behaviours. In the meantime, this review on diagnosis, classification, and comorbidity serves as a miner's lamp to illuminate the next several yards of the path to knowledge, with additional segments of the path to be uncovered only as the miner walks further forward through systematic studies in aetiology, mechanism and treatment. These studies will illuminate the true nature of eating disorders.

1.6
How Well Do We Understand Eating Disorders?

Suzanne Abraham[1]

Our understanding and knowledge of eating disorders have escalated over the last 50 years. Katherine Halmi provides a historical account of the recognition of these disorders and discusses the research and diagnostic criteria used by both ICD-10 and DSM-IV. Reading this fine critical review alerts us to how much more information we need to understand. Is it possible that we have not clearly understood the basic elements of eating disorders?

Although accepting that eating disorders range from extreme self-imposed starvation to binge eating obesity, Halmi provides a useful summary of the consistent evidence relating to the diagnoses and comorbidity of anorexia nervosa, bulimia nervosa and unspecified eating disorder. Within this appears the concept of an eating disorder continuum ranging from emaciation to obesity, from rigid controlled eating to totally out of control binge eating and from obsessionality to lack of impulse control.

Consistent evidence presented about anorexia nervosa includes the following aspects:

- *Dieting is maintained by self-imposition.* This control over low body weight is basic and central to the treatment of anorexia nervosa. The reason for the initial weight loss may not have been self-induced (severe viral illness is a common cause of initial weight loss) but the sufferer invariably controls the behaviour supporting the low body weight.
- *Presence of a persuasive dissatisfaction with one's body, reflected in feeling too fat.* Although common, it is possible that feeling fat reflects other features of anorexia nervosa, such as low self-esteem/concept and depressive mood. It may be more important to consider these features in the planning of treatment rather than to concentrate on "feeling too fat". Most young women following the body image and weight challenges of puberty "feel fat" but this does not mean that they have an eating disorder. Women can associate "feeling fat" with negative feelings such as feeling bloated, low in mood, irritable and generally unwell when they are premenstrual.
- *An overwhelming fear and reluctance to change behaviour.* Whether this fear is fear of weight gain, fear of becoming obese (for some women this is a reality because they have already been obese), fear of loss of control over

[1] *Department of Obstetrics and Gynecology, University of Sydney, NSW 2000, Australia*

eating, fear of loss of control over feelings and moods or simply fear of change has not been clarified.

- *Restricting type can become bulimic over time.* This depends on the definition of binge eating. If *bulimic*, as stated above, refers to overeating in response to a negative energy balance of the body, then this is correct; it is a normal physiological reaction to food deprivation. If *bulimic* involves binge eating when the body is not in negative balance then this statement may not be true. It should not be considered a natural progression from anorexia nervosa to bulimia nervosa. Some women experience bulimia nervosa before they achieve serious weight loss leading to a diagnosis of anorexia nervosa, whereas others are bulimic while they have very low body weights and others during weight gain, particularly if treatment does not include learning "normal eating".
- *Frequency of comorbidity with affective disorders.* What is not clearly understood is the timing and interaction of affective disorders and the presence of anorexia nervosa. For some women and men the depressive symptoms appear to be present only at low body weight, whereas others can have depressive episodes after recovery from an eating disorder. Some people suffering from depression may "discover" that weight loss has antidepressant qualities and thus resist weight gain for this reason; in other words, anorexia nervosa is secondary to their primary depressive disorder.

In bulimia nervosa, recurrent episodes of overeating associated with efforts to counteract the energy intake are accepted as a consistent finding. The definition of a binge—what constitutes a subjective binge and what is objective binge eating, the frequency of the behaviour and the energy balance of the sufferer—is not uniformly accepted or understood.

There is agreement that unspecified eating disorders are a group of non-specific eating disorders that show features of both anorexia nervosa and bulimia nervosa and that these occur more often than anorexia and bulimia nervosa. The occurrence of binge eating without compensatory behaviours among women who are obese and the use of compensatory behaviours in normal-weight women are two examples of these partial syndromes. What has not been discussed is the movement of people between the diagnoses, e.g. anorexia nervosa during adolescence to unspecified during recovery, to bulimia nervosa, to unspecified (binge eating disorder) and recovery with obesity in middle age.

Nowadays there is little usefulness in including amenorrhoea in the criteria for anorexia nervosa, because it cannot be ascertained for most sufferers. Measurement of bone density has resulted in women at low weight receiving hormone replacement or oral contraception. When women are taking an oestrogen and progesterone it is not possible to tell if they have secondary amenorrhoea (no spontaneous menstrual periods for 3 months) because they will bleed when the hormones are withdrawn. A "withdrawal bleed" is not indicative of a normal menstrual cycle. A diagnosis of primary amenorrhoea (no periods ever) should not be made until young women are 16 years or older.

Although we use the word "eating" and not "body image" to describe these disorders, the idea exists that there is a body image disturbance/ dissatisfaction with body weight and shape as a central feature for both anorexia nervosa and bulimia nervosa. Halmi alludes to the possibility of other reasons for weight loss and cites examples from history. Currently, young women who are no more concerned and possibly less interested in body shape and weight than other women of their age and socioeconomic class can become preoccupied with nutrition and the content of processed food and lose weight while striving for health and fitness. Once at low body weight, they may fear loss of control of their eating and of their feelings, or fear change itself, but they may not be overly concerned about their body image, at least not until they commence treatment. Experienced chronic patients can also lose interest and stop worrying about their body weight and shape because their life is organized so that they remain at low body weight without any fear of ever losing control. This can, of course, be accepted as an improvement in the severity of the disorder or it could be seen as a measure of continued chronicity of the disorder. It is unfortunate that many clinicians think that refusing to gain body weight when emaciated is indicative of a body image problem.

What eating behaviour constitutes "binge eating" is far from clear. Does the energy balance of a person change the definition?

Halmi shows how far our knowledge about eating disorders has come and highlights how much more we need to understand. Even within "consistent evidence" there are unanswered questions that may affect the management of sufferers with these debilitating disorders. The message appears to be to continue to treat sufferers as individuals until we understand the disorders a little better; in this way, we may stop producing chronic sufferers.

1.7
Validity of Categorical Distinctions for Eating Disorders: From Disorders to Symptoms
Pamela K. Keel[1]

The utility of any diagnostic classification system can be evaluated according to the concepts of aetiological, concurrent and predictive validity [1]. This commentary will utilize these concepts to review briefly the data concerning the validity of differentiating eating disorders from other psychiatric disorders, differentiating anorexia nervosa from bulimia nervosa and then distinguishing among their subtypes.

Although eating disorders have high comorbidity with mood and anxiety disorders and respond to antidepressant medications, research supports the aetiological validity of eating disorders as a category. In a controlled family study, Lilenfeld *et al.* [2] found evidence of independent familial transmission of eating disorders from most other major psychiatric illnesses. Similarly, Kendler *et al.* [3] demonstrated that the genetic risk factors for bulimia nervosa differed from those for major depression and generalized anxiety disorder in multivariate twin analyses; however, bulimia nervosa loaded on the same factor as panic disorder and phobia. Within the category of eating disorders, family studies have failed to support the independent transmission of anorexia and bulimia nervosa [2,4], perhaps explaining the high rate of cross-over between eating disorders [5]. Despite these inconclusive data, several studies support a distinction between anorexia nervosa and bulimia nervosa on the basis of concurrent and predictive validity. Anorexia nervosa is associated with greater impulse control compared with bulimia nervosa [6,7]. In addition, treatment response, course and outcome tend to be worse in patients with anorexia nervosa compared with patients with bulimia nervosa [8–10].

Although reasonably good data support distinctions between eating disorders and other major Axis I disorders and between anorexia and bulimia nervosa, below this level the data become more equivocal. In addition to the differences in impulse control between anorexia nervosa, restricting subtype (ANR) and anorexia nervosa, binge/purge subtype (ANBP) discussed by Katherine Halmi, a recent genome-wide linkage analysis [11] found the strongest evidence for an anorexia nervosa susceptibility locus when restricting analyses to ANR–ANR pairs (versus the more phenotypically heterogeneous AN–AN pairs), supporting the aetiological validity of the subtype categories in anorexia nervosa.

[1] *Department of Psychology, Harvard University, 1320 William James Hall, 33 Kirkland Street, Cambridge, MA 02138, USA*

However, longitudinal studies have found a high rate of cross-over from ANR to ANBP [12,13]. Furthermore, rates of recovery, relapse and mortality do not appear to differentiate between women who present with a diagnosis of ANR or ANBP [9,10].

In the evaluation of eating disorders not otherwise specified, most work has been completed on binge eating disorder and suggests both lower levels of comorbid pathology [14,15] and better course compared with bulimia nervosa [16]. In contrast, comparisons between bulimia nervosa and a disorder characterized by recurrent purging suggest similar levels of comorbid pathology [14,17] and course [18]. In a recent investigation comparing bulimia nervosa (purging subtype) and a purging disorder, we found that objectively large binge episodes were associated with poor impulse control [17].

In summary, the current DSM-IV classification of eating disorders as a distinct category has reasonably good support. There are greater similarities between women with anorexia nervosa and bulimia nervosa than between women with eating disorders and other major psychiatric disorders. Further, the hierarchy in which anorexia nervosa and bulimia nervosa cannot be diagnosed concurrently has empirical support because low weight appears to have a significant impact on course, treatment response and outcome. Data comparing syndromes with binge episodes (bulimia nervosa, ANBP) with those without (ANR, purging disorder) suggest that bingeing may be associated with high levels of impulsiveness, supporting distinctions among both syndromes and subtypes. Although differences can be found, from the level of eating disorder category all the way down to specific eating disorder symptoms, it is unclear whether these latter differences denote distinct categories or whether they represent differences along a continuum of eating pathology.

REFERENCES

1. Kendell R. (1989) Clinical validity. *Psychol. Med.*, **19**: 45–55.
2. Lilenfeld L.R., Kaye W.H., Greeno C.G., Merikangas K.R., Plotnicov K., Pollice C., Rao R., Strober M., Bulik C.M., Nagy L. (1998) A controlled family study of anorexia nervosa and bulimia nervosa: psychiatric disorders in first-degree relatives and effects of proband comorbidity. *Arch. Gen. Psychiatry*, **55**: 603–610.
3. Kendler K., Walters E.E., Neale M.C., Kessler R.C., Heath A.C., Eaves L.J. (1995) The structure of the genetic and environmental risk factors for six major psychiatric disorders in women: phobia, generalized anxiety disorder, panic disorder, bulimia, major depression, and alcoholism. *Arch. Gen. Psychiatry*, **52**: 374–383.
4. Strober M., Freeman R., Lampert C., Diamond J., Kaye W. (2000) Controlled family study of anorexia nervosa and bulimia nervosa: evidence of shared liability and transmission of partial syndromes. *Am. J. Psychiatry*, **157**: 393–401.

5. Keel P., Mitchell J.E., Miller K.B., Davis T.L., Crow S.J. (2000) Predictive validity of bulimia nervosa as a diagnostic category. *Am. J. Psychiatry*, **157**: 136–138.
6. Bulik C.M., Sullivan P.F., Weltzin T.E., Kaye W.H. (1995) Temperament in eating disorders. *Int. J. Eat. Disord.*, **17**: 251–261.
7. Pryor T., Wiederman M.W. (1996) Measurement of nonclinical personality characteristics of women with anorexia nervosa or bulimia nervosa. *J. Person. Assess.*, **67**: 414–421.
8. Peterson C., Mitchell J.E. (1999) Psychosocial and pharmacological treatment of eating disorders: a review of research findings. *J. Clin. Psychol.*, **55**: 685–697.
9. Herzog D., Dorer D.J., Keel P.K., Selwyn S.E., Ekeblad E.R., Flores A.T., Greenwood D.N., Burwell R.A., Keller M.B. (1999) Recovery and relapse in anorexia and bulimia nervosa: a 7.5-year follow-up study. *J. Am. Acad. Child Adolesc. Psychiatry*, **38**: 829–837.
10. Keel P., Dorer D.J., Eddy K.T., Franko D., Charatan D.L., Herzog D.B. (2003) Predictors of mortality in eating disorders. *Arch. Gen. Psychiatry* (in press).
11. Grice D., Halmi K.A., Fichter M.M., Strober M., Woodside D.B., Treasure J.T., Kaplan A.S., Magistretti P.J., Goldman D., Bulik C.M., *et al.* (2002) Evidence for a susceptibility gene for anorexia nervosa on chromosome 1. *Am. J. Hum. Genet.*, **70**: 787–792.
12. Strober M., Freeman R., Morrell W. (1997) The long-term course of severe anorexia nervosa in adolescents: survival analysis of recovery, relapse, and outcome predictors over 10–15 years in a prospective study. *Int. J. Eat. Disord.*, **22**: 339–360.
13. Eddy K., Keel P.K., Dorer D.J., Delinsky S.S., Franko D.L., Herzog D.B. (2002) Longitudinal comparison of anorexia nervosa subtypes. *Int. J. Eat. Disord.*, **31**: 191–201.
14. Tobin D., Griffing A., Griffing S. (1997) An examination of subtype criteria for bulimia nervosa. *Int. J. Eat. Disord.*, **22**: 179–186.
15. Crow S., Zander K.M., Crosby R.D., Mitchell M.E. (1996) Discriminant function analysis of depressive symptoms in binge eating disorder, bulimia nervosa and major depression. *Int. J. Eat. Disord.*, **19**: 399–404.
16. Fairburn C., Cooper Z., Doll H.A., Norman P., O'Connor M. (2000) The natural course of bulimia nervosa and binge eating disorder in young women. *Arch. Gen. Psychiatry*, **57**: 659–665.
17. Keel P., Mayer S.A., Harnden-Fischer J.H. (2001) Importance of size in defining binge eating episodes in bulimia nervosa. *Int. J. Eat. Disord.*, **29**: 294–301.
18. Hay P., Fairburn C.G., Doll H.A. (1996) The classification of bulimic eating disorders: a community-based cluster analysis. *Psychol. Med.*, **26**: 801–812.

1.8
Eating Disorders: From Heterogeneous Disorders to Distinct Diseases?

Laura Bellodi[1]

The problem of classification in psychiatry is a burdensome task and, to date, in the specific case of eating disorders, a clear definition of pathological boundaries does not exist. Deviant eating attitudes and behaviours have been associated with completely different concepts over the centuries: from a concept of holiness and sacrifice in the past, to the myth of beauty and thinness in the present age.

Furthermore, eating disorders have been considered only a problem of medical competence until the last part of the 19th century, when subjects with abnormal eating behaviour started to receive clinical attention also from a psychiatric point of view. This point is crucial, because the different perspective and the attention paid to the cognitive–emotional mechanisms possibly implicated in the development of eating disorders changed substantially the therapeutic approach offered to patients.

In fact, if we consider psychopathological elements as primary events and the behavioural patterns as secondary to these cognitive and emotional aspects, the clinical conditions become more understandable and easier to treat.

The boundary between the pathological condition and an extreme, but still normal, restriction of food intake frequently is not well defined: the latter behaviour may already characterize a population at risk for eating disorders, if cognitive motivation to diet is investigated.

It is of fundamental importance to give attention to the psychopathological core in eating disorders: it is possible to build a solid therapeutic alliance with new patients, before any medical treatment, by showing patients that we are aware of the psychological processes that condition their behaviour. It is important to discuss with them not only their overvalued ideas of beauty and thinness but also the despair and low levels of self-esteem caused by the incapacity to recover an appropriate eating attitude. In available diagnostic systems (DSM-IV, ICD-10), cognitive factors, when compared with "visible" behaviours, still have a limited diagnostic significance, owing to the difficulty in exploring and objectifying the underlying mechanisms.

Furthermore, starting always from a behavioural perspective, the historical clinical separation of anorexia and bulimia is maintained. These

[1] Eating Disorder Unit, Università Vita-Salute, Ospedale San Raffaele, Via Stamina D'Ancona 20, 20127 Milan, Italy

clinical conditions are well recognized to be highly unstable [1]: during a lifetime patients may firstly present anorexia and then bulimia and sometimes *vice versa*. Considering the cognitive core and its key role in the development of the clinical condition, self-evaluation is unduly influenced, both in anorexia and bulimia, by concerns about weight and body image, even though they are characterized by apparently different eating behavioural attitudes. One should wonder whether the diversity between anorexia and bulimia could have only a behavioural origin, while the primary process may not differ substantially between the two conditions. Differences between anorexic and bulimic patients may result from the inability of bulimics to restrict, significantly and continuously, their food intake, starting from identical pathological urges and needs that result in different compensatory behaviours [2]. The main current efforts are oriented to elicit differences between the two disorders, but we believe that it may be useful to look simultaneously for the *apparently* common mechanisms. All clinical and research efforts in psychiatry have to be focused on the attempt to define carefully the core of specific signs and symptoms helpful in identifying reliable and valid entities, which will allow us to move from syndrome dimensions to disease dimensions, as highlighted in Katherine Halmi's review. In spite of these goals, modern systems of classification allow for a modest degree of diagnostic reliability and validity. The lack of knowledge about aetiological processes hampers the possibility to deal with diseases and not with disorders or syndromes. A valid model that organizes the overall information (clinical, biochemical and genetic) about eating disorders is not available: the lack of identification of an unequivocal phenotype slows down the biological and clinical research.

The absence of appropriate classification tools prevents us from estimating the true prevalence of full syndromes (anorexia and bulimia) and of other additional diagnostic categories, i.e. binge eating disorder or eating disorders not otherwise specified, and consequently from estimating the true social impact of these disorders. For this reason, widening the observational field and evaluating the comorbidity and the familial risk for other psychiatric conditions, such as obsessive–compulsive disorder, may help to define better the clinical and aetiopathogenetic boundaries of eating disorders [2] and to solve partially the problem of clinical heterogeneity. In fact, the distinction of genetic and non-genetic forms of eating disorder might be extremely important for the diagnostic definition, treatment and prognosis of patients.

Promising advances in neurobiological studies of feeding and appetite are providing new approaches to the aetiology and pathogenesis of eating disorders; nevertheless, to date, no trait-related markers for eating disorders have been identified: for example, leptin deficiency has been observed in anorexics only during the acute phase of starvation [3]. Focusing attention only on the mechanisms of food intake regulation and therefore facing the eating disorder once again as a primary "medical" condition and not as a complex psychopathological condition is a limiting approach.

Several lines of evidence suggest that patients with eating disorders (anorexia nervosa and bulimia nervosa) may have a trait-related disturbance of serotonin activity [4], indicating a suitable avenue of genetic research for eating disorders: recently, controversial findings suggest the association of genetic polymorphisms related to serotonergic structures [5,6] with eating disorders. The awareness that these studies cover a limited field and that a hurdle divides the understanding of cognitive mechanisms from biological investigations should not discourage the efforts towards a complete and adequate comprehension of eating disorders.

REFERENCES

1. Keel P.K., Mitchell J.E. (1997) Outcome in bulimia nervosa. *Am. J. Psychiatry*, **154**: 313–321.
2. Bellodi L., Brambilla F. (1999) Conclusive remarks. In *Eating Disorders and Obsessive Compulsive Disorder: an Etiopathogenetic Link?* (Eds L. Bellodi, F. Brambilla), pp. 179–183. Centro Scientifico Editore, Milan.
3. Hebebrand J., Blum W.F., Barth N., Coners H., Englaro P., Juul A., Ziegler A., Warnke A., Rascher W., Remschmidt H. (1997) Leptin levels in patients with anorexia nervosa are reduced in the acute stage and elevated upon short-term weight restoration. *Mol. Psychiatry*, **2**: 330–334.
4. Kaye W.H., Lilenfeld L., Berrettini W.H., Strober M., Devlin B., Klump K.L., Goldman D., Bulik C.M., Halmi K.A., Fichter M.M., *et al.* (2000) A search for susceptibility loci for anorexia nervosa: methods and sample description. *Biol. Psychiatry*, **47**: 794–803.
5. Di Bella D., Catalano M., Cavallini M.C., Riboldi C., Bellodi L. (2000) Serotonin transporter linked polymorphic region in anorexia nervosa and bulimia nervosa. *Mol. Psychiatry*, **5**: 233–234.
6. Gorwood P., Ades J., Bellodi L., Cellini E., Collier D.A., Di Bella D., Di Bernardo M., Estivill X., Fernandez-Aranda F., Gratacos M., *et al.* (2002) The 5-HT(2A) - 1438G/A polymorphism in anorexia nervosa: a combined analysis of 316 trios from six European centres. *Mol. Psychiatry*, **7**: 90–94.

1.9
Eating Disorders—A Challenge for Clinicians and Scientists
Bodo Müller[1]

Katherine Halmi's review gives an extensive, detailed and useful overview of the historical background, classification, diagnosis and comorbidity of eating disorders.

Halmi argues for a clear classification of the different eating disorders in order to facilitate meaningful communication among clinicians as well as research. For each eating disorder she describes the empirically based development of the current key symptoms, which is not yet concluded. She emphasizes that there are no clear thresholds for some of the key symptoms of the different eating disorders. The degree of weight loss necessary for the diagnosis of anorexia nervosa is not precisely illustrated either in ICD-10 or in DSM-IV. There is also no indication of how to determine the degree of body image disturbance phenomena in anorexia nervosa. The confusion on some key features of anorexia nervosa and bulimia nervosa and their different subgroups reflects the fact that the empirical examination of these disorders is still ongoing. The lack of consistent criteria across studies makes it difficult, if not impossible, to compare clinical studies.

From previous studies it can be concluded that remission rates in anorexia nervosa increase with time [1]. The results of our prospective 10-year follow-up study in adolescent anorexia nervosa confirm these results and indicate a rather favourable outcome of the eating disorder itself [2]. The recovery rate of 69% found in our study is very similar to the 76% and 74% reported by Strober *et al.* [3] and Theander [4], respectively. Both authors followed up cohorts with juvenile-onset anorexia nervosa for 10–15 years.

The mortality risk in the adolescent type seems to be lower than in the adult-onset disorder. Several studies on adolescent anorexia nervosa report no deaths [3,5], which is in line with our results [2].

Regarding the time course of recovery, we would agree with Strober *et al.* [3] that it is a lengthy process for the majority of anorexic patients. Although eating disorders still show a lengthy and distressing course, there is some evidence from newer studies [2,3] that progress has been made in the treatment of adolescent anorexia nervosa, resulting in a zero mortality and lower rates of chronicity. However, despite recovery from the eating disorder, many patients still suffer from ongoing psychiatric disturbances.

[1] *Department of Child and Adolescent Psychiatry and Psychotherapy, Aachen University, Neuenhofer Weg 21, D-52074 Aachen, Germany*

Further efforts have to be made not only to cope with the eating disorder itself but also with the long-term risk of additional mental disorder.

Comorbidity is an important subject in Halmi's review. Overall Axis I morbidity in our own prospective 10-year follow-up is very similar to the findings described in the study by Halmi et al. [6], also based on a 10-year follow-up interval. Forty-nine per cent of our sample had no current comorbid diagnosis compared with 47% in the sample of Halmi's group [2]. But even recovered patients suffered from a higher psychiatric morbidity than controls. This finding is consistent with the results by Casper and Jabine [7] and by Rastam et al. [8] and supports the view that anorexia nervosa is not a self-contained, age-specific disease, but rather a marker pointing to a high vulnerability to psychiatric disorders.

To our knowledge there are only very few follow-up studies that have assessed the prevalence of personality disorders in anorexia nervosa. More than a quarter of our patients met the full or subthreshold criteria for at least one DSM-III-R personality disorder. Personality disorders grouped in Cluster C of the DSM-III-R categories (avoidant, dependent and obsessive–compulsive) were the most prominent disorders diagnosed in 15% of the probands of our own sample [2,9].

Generally our follow-up study indicates that subjects with a mental disorder (besides the eating disorder) on Axis I or II display a more severe course of illness [2,9]. It is important to note, however, that we do not know in which way the unfavourable relationship works. Although most of the literature suggests that the presence of a comorbid psychiatric disorder complicates the outcome of the eating disorder [7], personality or another mental disorder could also be a "scarring effect" [10] of long-standing anorexia nervosa.

Some authors assume that the high rates of depression, anxiety disorders and obsessive–compulsive disorders in patients with eating disorders are part of an "obsessive–compulsive spectrum disorder", with increased vulnerability in the serotonergic system [9,11]. Elevated concentrations of 5-hydroxyindoleacetic acid in the cerebrospinal fluid after recovery suggest that altered serotonin activity in anorexia and bulimia nervosa may be a trait-related characteristic. Elevated serotonin activity is consistent with behaviours found after recovery from anorexia and bulimia nervosa, such as obsessionality, harm avoidance, perfectionism and behavioural over-control [12]. Recent results in medication with selective serotonin reuptake inhibitors (SSRIs) in eating disorders show different effects. In bulimia nervosa, serotonergic modulating antidepressant medications with SSRIs suppress symptoms independently of their antidepressant effects. But SSRIs are not useful when subjects with anorexia nervosa are malnourished and underweight. However, when given after weight restoration, SSRIs may significantly reduce the high rate of relapse in anorexia nervosa [12].

There is little known about the reasons for hyperactivity in anorexia nervosa patients. Semi-starvation-induced hyperactivity has been viewed as a model for elevated physical activity levels frequently associated with anorexia nervosa. Nevertheless, it is commonly assumed that excessive physical activity is mainly performed by patients to control weight via both increased energy expenditure and appetite suppression. Preliminary results indicate that the hypoleptinaemia that ensues from energy restriction and subsequent weight loss may be one important factor in developing excessive physical activity in humans [13,14].

Halmi argues for a continued careful defining of the phenotypes of bulimia nervosa and anorexia nervosa, along with genetic research. This is essential to produce a more accurate classification of these disorders. Only in this way will it be possible to define precisely the different eating disorders in all their complexity and to develop specific treatment settings by taking comorbidity into account. It will be necessary to learn more about the genetic polymorphism affecting the various mechanisms and how they interact with the numerous environmental risk factors.

REFERENCES

1. Fichter M., Quadflieg N. (1999) Six-year course and outcome of anorexia nervosa. *Int. J. Eat. Disord.*, **26**: 359–385.
2. Herpertz-Dahlmann B., Müller B., Herpertz S., Heussen N., Neudörfl A., Hebebrand H., Remschmidt H. (2001) Prospective ten-year follow-up in adolescent anorexia nervosa—course, outcome and psychiatric comorbidity. *J. Child Psychol. Psychiatry*, **42**: 603–612.
3. Strober M., Freeman R., Morrell W. (1997) The long term course of severe anorexia nervosa in adolescents: survival analysis of recovery, relapse, and outcome predictors over 10–15 years in a prospective study. *Int. J. Eat. Disord.*, **22**: 339–360.
4. Theander S. (1996) Anorexia nervosa with an early onset: selection, gender, outcome, and results of a long-term follow-up study. *J. Youth Adolesc.*, **25**: 419–430.
5. Rastam M., Gillberg I.C., Gillberg C. (1995) Anorexia nervosa 6 years after onset. Part II: Comorbid psychiatric problems. *Compr. Psychiatry*, **36**: 70–76.
6. Halmi K.A., Eckert E., Marchi P., Sampugnaro V., Apple R., Cohen J. (1991) Comorbidity of psychiatric diagnoses in anorexia nervosa. *Arch. Gen. Psychiatry*, **48**: 712–718.
7. Casper R.S., Jabine L.N. (1996) An eight-year follow-up: outcome from adolescent compared to adult onset anorexia nervosa. *J. Youth Adolesc.*, **25**: 499–517.
8. Rastam M., Gillberg G., Gillberg I.C. (1996) A six-year follow-up study of anorexia nervosa subjects with teenage onset. *J. Youth Adolesc.*, **25**: 439–454.
9. Müller B., Herpertz S., Heussen N., Neudörfl A., Wewetzer C., Remschmidt H., Herpertz-Dahlmann B. (2000) Personality disorders and psychiatric morbidity in adolescent anorexia nervosa. Results of a prospective 10 year catamnesis. *Z. Kinderheilkd. Jugend. Psychother.*, **28**: 81–91.

10. Wonderlich S. (1995) Personality and eating disorders. In *Eating Disorders and Obesity* (Eds K.D. Brownell, C.G. Fairburn), pp. 171–176. Guilford, New York.
11. Kaye W.H., Weltzin T.W., Hsu L.K. (1993) Anorexia nervosa. In *Obsessive–compulsive Related Disorders* (Ed. E. Hollander), pp. 49–70. American Psychiatric Press, Washington.
12. Kaye W., Gendall K., Strober M. (1998) Serotonin neuronal function and selective serotonin reuptake inhibitor treatment in anorexia and bulimia nervosa. *Biol. Psychiatry*, **44**: 825–838.
13. Holtkamp K., Herpertz-Dahlmann B., Warnke A., Fichter M., Herpertz S., Hebebrand J. Further evidence for a mediating effect of hypoleptinemia in elevated physical activity levels in patients with anorexia nervosa (submitted for publication).
14. Exner C., Hebebrand J., Remschmidt H., Wewetzer C., Ziegler A., Herpertz S., Schweiger U., Blum W.F., Preibisch G., Heldmaier G., *et al.* (2000) Leptin suppresses semi-starvation induced hyperactivity in rats: implications for anorexia nervosa. *Mol. Psychiatry*, **5**: 476–481.

1.10
Do We Miss the Forest Because of the Trees?

David Clinton[1]

The question of how best to conceptualize eating disorders has long been a matter of debate, as Katherine Halmi's clear and comprehensive review indicates. As she points out, these disorders have been studied systematically only during the past 30 years. The resultant schemes of classification, currently typified by DSM-IV and ICD-10, have increasingly focused on distinguishing subtypes of distinct eating disorders from each other. Although this has increased our knowledge of eating disorders and aided the development of treatment strategies, the complementary question of what characterizes these disorders as a whole has largely been ignored. As a result, we may now be running the risk of failing to notice the forest because of the trees.

A multitude of studies attest to statistically significant differences between specific eating disorder diagnoses in terms of psychiatric symptomatology, comorbidity, psychological profiles and socioeconomic variables. For the most part this means differences between anorexics and bulimics at presentation, because this is where most research has been conducted. Systematic data on the important group of patients with atypical disorders (i.e. eating disorder not otherwise specified) are lacking, despite the fact

[1] *Resource Centre for Eating Disorders, Huddinge University Hospital, Karolinska Institutet, 141 86 Stockholm, Sweden*

that they may represent 30–60% of eating disorder cases [1]. Moreover, differences between specific diagnostic subtypes tend to be small in comparison with the differences between those who have and those who do not have eating disorders, and in terms of the individual differences within the different diagnostic groups.

Recent research has turned attention to the natural clustering of eating-related pathology and the latent structure of eating disorder symptoms [2,3]. These studies support the idea of three basic groups of eating disorders that are broadly similar to anorexia nervosa, bulimia nervosa and binge eating disorder. Williamson et al. [3] also used statistical methods that allowed for the important comparison of categories and dimensions among patients with eating disorders and controls. Not surprisingly, they found that patients with eating disorders were qualitatively (i.e. categorically) different from controls. However, they found only "mixed support" for categorical differences between specific eating disorders when controls were excluded from the analysis.

Other recent studies suggest that differences in eating disorder symptoms between specific eating disorder diagnoses may not be particularly stable over time. In a longitudinal comparison of anorexia nervosa subtypes, Eddy et al. [4] found that only 12% of restricting anorexics never reported regular binge/purge behaviour, and that 8 years after initial assessment 62% of patients who had been diagnosed with restricting anorexia nervosa had crossed over to the binge/purge subtype of the disorder. They argued that the high cross-over rate suggests that the restricting form of anorexia nervosa may represent a phase in the course of the disorder rather than a distinct subtype. In an earlier study, van der Ham et al. [5] examined changes in symptomatology over time. As would be expected, patients could be differentiated on the basis of bulimic or restrictive behaviour at intake. However, over a period of 4 years, the core psychopathology of categories of eating disorder patients tended to become more alike. This was partly due to recovery and improvement and partly due to diminishing differences in bulimic or restrictive behaviour. These findings raise the question of whether our present system of classification is limited in terms of its temporal validity.

Waller [6] has gone as far as to suggest that our attempts to better understand and treat eating disorders may, in fact, have been impeded by classification schemes focusing on distinct criteria for diagnostic subgroups. He maintains that we should focus more attention on what characterizes patients with eating disorders as a whole. This he sees as being "the general concern with control over food, weight and body shape". Similar recommendations have been made by Beumont et al. [7], who contend that problems with the classification of eating disorders can be dealt with no longer by further refining current diagnostic criteria. They also see a need to focus on the defining features of eating disorders as a whole.

Surprisingly few attempts have been made to define eating disorders. Recently, however, Fairburn and Walsh [1] have proposed that eating disorders can be defined as "a persistent disturbance of eating behaviour or behaviour intended to control weight, which significantly impairs physical health or psychosocial functioning. This disturbance should not be secondary to any recognized general medical disorder (e.g. a hypothalamic tumour) or any other psychiatric disorder (e.g. an anxiety disorder)". This move towards defining eating disorders as a whole and focusing on what distinguishes them from other psychiatric disorders and from normal variants of eating behaviour is a promising step. It is also an area clearly in need of more systematic exploration. Using the common characteristics of eating disorders as a point of departure for classification, one can identify other important signs and symptoms and attempt to understand their role in eating disorders and why they are exhibited by certain patients at certain points in time. Focusing on such questions will help us to see the diagnostic forest more clearly, and save us getting lost among the trees.

REFERENCES

1. Fairburn C.G., Walsh B.T. (2002) Atypical eating disorders (Eating disorder not otherwise specified). In *Eating Disorders and Obesity: a Comprehensive Handbook*, 2nd ed. (Eds C.G. Fairburn, K.D. Brownell), pp. 171–177. Guilford Press, New York.
2. Bulik C.M., Sullivan P.F., Kendler K.S. (2000) An empirical study of the classification of eating disorders. *Am. J. Psychiatry*, **157**: 886–895.
3. Williamson D.A., Womble L.G., Smeets M., Netemeyer R., Thaw J., Kutlesic V., Gleaves D. (2002) Latent structure of eating disorder symptoms: a factor analytic and taxometric investigation. *Am. J. Psychiatry*, **159**: 412–418.
4. Eddy K., Keel P., Dorer D., Delinsky S., Franko D., Herzog, D. (2002) Longitudinal comparison of anorexia nervosa subtypes. *Int. J. Eat. Disord.*, **31**: 191–201.
5. van der Ham T., Meulman J., van Strien D., van Engeland H. (1997) Empirically based subgrouping of eating disorders in adolescents: a longitudinal perspective. *Br. J. Psychiatry*, **170**: 363–368.
6. Waller G. (1993) Why do we diagnose different types of eating disorder? Arguments for a change in research and clinical practice. *Eur. Eat. Disord. Rev.*, **1**: 74–89.
7. Beumont P.J.V., Garner D.M., Touyz S.W. (1994) Diagnoses of eating or dieting disorders: what may we learn from past mistakes? *Int. J. Eat. Disord.*, **16**: 349–362.

1.11

Controversies in the Classification of Eating Disorders

David H. Gleaves[1]

Katherine Halmi reviews the current approaches to classification and diagnosis of the eating disorders. She also discusses unresolved issues, problems and areas of controversy. Although there are many such issues worthy of elaboration and/or discussion, below is a brief discussion of the binge/purge type of anorexia and binge eating disorder.

According to the current DSM system, individuals who meet the diagnostic criteria for both anorexia and bulimia nervosa are classified as the binge eating/purging type of anorexia. But should this condition be viewed as a subtype of bulimia nervosa instead? This has been one of the research questions addressed in a recent set of taxometric studies [1–3]. Taxometrics [4] is a group of statistical methods designed to distinguish types from continua, i.e. do phenomena occur on one or more continua with normality and with one another, or are there qualitative discontinuities (taxa)? The results of Gleaves *et al.* [2] suggest that bulimia nervosa and the binge eating/purging type of anorexia may occur on a continuum with one another, whereas both may be qualitatively different from the restricting type of anorexia. Although additional research is needed on the topic, such a reconceptualization is consistent with clinical experience and may help to make sense of additional data reviewed by Halmi. For example, it may not be at all surprising that anorexics who binge and purge have a higher rate of recovery than restricting anorexics. Such a finding is consistent with the fact that the prognosis for bulimia nervosa is generally better than anorexia nervosa.

Halmi describes the current status of binge eating disorder, as well as the history of the diagnoses of bulimia and bulimia nervosa. However, the story is a bit more convoluted. As she notes, the DSM-III category of bulimia was broader than the bulimia nervosa of DSM-III-R and DSM-IV. However, it was not simply because of vague bingeing criteria. Purging also was not a necessary criterion in DSM-III. Because other criteria could be fulfilled, persons who binged but did not purge could have met the DSM-III criteria for bulimia. During this time, however, researchers and clinicians were aware of apparent "subtypes" of persons meeting the diagnostic criteria for bulimia, and the clinical and research literature began to refer to the existence of "binge eaters" (or compulsive overeaters) versus "binge purgers".

[1] *Department of Psychology, Texas A&M University, College Station, TX 77843-4235, USA*

With the publication of DSM-III-R, some sort of compensatory criterion was then required, meaning that persons who binged but did not purge were excluded from the category. Although the distinction between "binge eaters" and "binge purgers" may be a valid one, the change in diagnostic criteria was quite significant because it meant that an entire class of persons who previously had a diagnosable psychiatric disorder after 1980 no longer had one from 1987 onwards. From the practical standpoint, this group of people suddenly found it harder to obtain treatment (or, more specifically, insurance coverage) because they no longer had a diagnosable disorder. Awareness of the existence of this subgroup of individuals with clinically significant eating problems but who did not fulfil the criteria for bulimia nervosa led the push to include binge eating disorder in DSM-IV. However, it was added only as a provisional diagnosis. It allegedly did not make the cut for a variety of reasons, one being the questionable distinction between it and the non-purging subtype of bulimia nervosa.

Although it may have been valid to question this distinction at the time, the more questionable category was arguably the non-purging subtype of bulimia nervosa. Even today, it seems safe to say that we know much less about non-purging bulimia than binge eating disorder. Furthermore, there now appear to be data suggesting that binge eating disorder is meaningfully different from bulimia nervosa. Perhaps most interesting are the data on the relationship between dieting history and onset of bingeing. In one study [5], 55% of participants with binge eating disorder reported bingeing prior to dieting. With bulimia nervosa, dieting almost invariably precedes bingeing. The gender breakdown for binge eating disorder also appears to be markedly different from the other eating disorder; it is the only disorder relatively common among males.

If the goal of science is as Plato wrote "to carve nature at its joints", it seems that we are to continue searching for the meaningful demarcations among the various types of eating disorders. Progress is being made and, although much more research is needed, available data may be pointing to three meaningful diagnoses: a) anorexia nervosa (defined only as the current restricting type); b) bulimia nervosa (including what is currently called the binge eating/purging type of anorexia nervosa); c) binge eating disorder (perhaps including non-purging bulimia, although its status is less resolved).

REFERENCES

1. Gleaves D.H., Lowe M.R., Snow A.C., Green B.A., Murphy-Eberenz K.P. (2000) The continuity and discontinuity models of bulimia nervosa: a taxometric investigation. *J. Abnorm. Psychol.*, **109**: 56–68.

2. Gleaves D.H., Lowe M.R., Green B.A., Cororve M.B., Williams T.L. (2000) Do anorexia and bulimia nervosa occur on a continuum? A taxometric analysis. *Behav. Ther.*, **31**: 195–219.
3. Williamson D.A., Womble L.G., Smeets M.A.M., Netemeyer R.G., Thaw J., Kutlesic V., Gleaves D.H. (2002) The latent structure of eating disorder symptoms: a factor analytic and taxometric investigation. *Am. J. Psychiatry*, **159**: 412–418.
4. Meehl P.E. (1995) Bootstraps taxometrics: solving the classification problem in psychopathology. *Am. Psychol.*, **50**: 266–275.
5. Spurrell E.B., Wilfley D.E., Tanofsky M.B., Brownell K.D. (1997) Age of onset for binge eating: are there different pathways to binge eating? *Int. J. Eat. Disord.*, **21**: 55–65.

1.12
Clinical Experience with the Diagnosis and Treatment of Eating Disorders

Thomas Paul[1]

The main aim of this commentary is to depict, from the perspective of a practising mental health specialist, the classification and diagnosis of eating disorders and the key findings from comorbidity research, and to comment on the relevance of the above for treatment. With regard to the system of classification, the scope of this commentary makes a limitation to DSM-IV necessary. The differences between ICD-10 and DSM-IV, which in some cases are quite substantial, have been delineated by Halmi in her review.

Anorexia nervosa. A condition of being seriously underweight, defined as a weight at or below a minimally normal weight, is the cardinal feature of this diagnosis. Whether this condition must be attributable to a *"refusal* to maintain body weight at or above a minimally normal weight for age and height" (DSM-IV, criterion A) is an issue that warrants discussion. Although either a conscious restriction of food intake to achieve weight loss or a refusal to counteract underweight is generally present at illness onset, in clinical experience anorexic patients often seek treatment with the express desire to increase their weight to normal. The possible earlier refusal seems to yield to increasing discomfort and insight over time. In all other respects these patients fulfil criteria B–D. For this reason it is suggested that "refusal" be eliminated from criterion A.

To achieve simplification of diagnosis with regard to the weight criteria, a guideline of a body mass index (BMI)≤17.5, as suggested in ICD-10, could be instituted. The index is easily calculable and not subject to cultural

[1] *Med.-Psychosomatische Klinik, Birkenweg 10, 24576 Bad Bramstedt, Germany*

influences. In individual cases that seem to justify the diagnosis, exceptions to this guideline would be permitted if all other diagnostic criteria were fulfilled.

Intense fear of gaining weight or becoming fat (DSM-IV, criterion B) can, in general, be established clearly in all anorexic patients, although clear cultural differences have been identified, a fact that can be seen as an indication of Western diagnostic ethnocentricity in DSM-IV.

Criterion C gives rise to more difficulty, because body dissatisfaction and weight concerns have become increasingly normative among women in Westernized countries and thus no longer represent a characteristic specific to anorexic patients. Furthermore, during the course of the illness, tension reduction and possibly even problem avoidance may become the primary factors maintaining the eating disorder. Thus the disorder becomes, as Halmi puts it, an addictive-like phenomenon that can sustain itself without any relationship to body weight and shape concerns. In view of these issues, the question arises of whether this criterion continues to merit inclusion.

The clinical utility of the amenorrhoea criterion (DSM-IV, criterion D) seems questionable at the very least. It is often impossible to determine whether it is fulfilled or not because the majority of patients use oral contraceptives, which artificially induce menstruation. Cases of particularly cachectic patients with anorexia who continued to have regular periods have been reported. On the other hand, Halmi has described several studies that have shown that resumption of the menses does not occur with restoration of normal weight, but is more significantly associated with marked psychological improvement. More recent studies have shown that, in a group comparison, patients suffering from anorexia nervosa with vs. without amenorrhoea did not differ with regard to the seriousness of the eating disorder, body image problems, depression and personality problems [1,2]. With such a lack of clarity in the findings and uncertainty as to the presence of the symptom (due to the use of oral contraceptives or incorrect information given by patients), a lot speaks for Halmi's suggestion that this symptom should no longer be taken into consideration in the diagnosis.

The differentiation between the restricting type and the binge eating/purging type appears to be useful for clinical practice because patients with binge eating/purging type are often characterized by greater impulsiveness and therefore require closer attention during therapy owing to the danger of self-injury or suicide. These patients also suffer more frequently from Axis II disorders, such as emotionally unstable personality disorder, which frequently makes therapy more difficult.

Bulimia nervosa. One of the features essential to this diagnosis is the occurrence of eating *binges* with an accompanying feeling of loss of control.

These features, however, are often not clearly fulfilled and/or can be subject to change and variation over time. The value of differentiating between subjective and objective binges has been pointed out by Fairburn [3]. Because compensatory behaviour is the reaction usually shown following both types of binges, the underlying psychological mechanism seems to be very similar. In the course of bulimia nervosa, the sense of lack of control originally experienced during bingeing is often increasingly replaced by stereotypical behaviour patterns, in that the patients *consciously* integrate binges and compensatory behaviour into their daily schedule and thus attempt to maintain a certain amount of control over their eating behaviour. Many patients purchase food for the express purpose of bingeing and know exactly when, where and with what intensity they will "go on a binge" in the course of the day. These patients only rarely report a sense of loss of control. It therefore seems to merit discussion whether the presence of subjective binges should suffice for criterion A and whether the criterion of loss of control should be extended to include situations in which the patient was *unable to prevent a binge from taking place.*

Determining whether criteria B, C and E are met is usually not a problem, although modification of the criteria to reflect empirical findings and increase precision would be desirable. Fairburn [3], for example, was unable to detect any differences between patients who experienced only one binge per week vs. those who fulfilled the frequency criterion. The same issues apply for criterion D here as for anorexia nervosa (see above).

Binge eating disorder. The inclusion of this disorder into DSM-IV as a criteria set for further study is to be welcomed, because a large number of empirical studies exist that have identified important differences between obese patients who do not binge and obese patients with binge eating disorder. As Halmi pointed out, the differential diagnosis between bulimia nervosa (non-purging type) and binge eating disorder can pose substantial difficulties, because patients with binge eating disorder, when closely questioned, often admit attempting to compensate for their binges in order to avoid weight gain. However, in contrast to patients with bulimia nervosa, these patients are ultimately unsuccessful. Future research needs to address the underlying mechanisms, which may allow differentiation between the two diagnoses. In order to prevent a further surge in the number of patients diagnosed with eating disorders not otherwise specified (EDNOS), the following suggestions may be worth considering: a) limitation of binge eating disorder to obese patients (BMI > 30); b) introduction of two subtypes: compensatory type and non-compensatory type. The compensatory type would consist of patients with binge eating disorder who engage in any type of compensatory behaviour, whereas patients with non-compensatory type employ no form of counter-regulation. Overweight patients with bulimia nervosa and obese patients who fulfil the binge eating disorder criteria A–D and employ compensatory measures then would be diagnosed with binge eating disorder, compensatory type. Through this broadening of the diagnostic criteria it would be possible to differentiate clearly between bulimia nervosa and binge eating disorder. Comparative studies involving the respective subgroups of patients with bulimia nervosa and binge eating disorder would yield information on the utility of such a differentiation.

Comorbidity. The co-occurrence of eating disorders and other psychiatric disorders has been well documented by Halmi. The most frequently reported comorbid disorders are affective and anxiety disorders, obsessive–compulsive disorder, substance abuse and personality disorders. The subtyping of anorexia and bulimia nervosa has proven very useful in this field because in many cases substantial differences have been found between the subgroups. Frequently, comorbid disorders precede the onset of the eating disorder and thus represent a risk for development of the latter. The treatment of patients with eating disorder and comorbid psychiatric disturbances is generally more difficult and the response to therapy is less positive. In this area of research there is a paucity of good psychotherapy studies investigating the implementation of different intervention methods or elements and their sequence. It is now evident that even the best diagnosis is of little use when concrete, differentiated guidelines for appropriate therapy are lacking. Although the first promising endeavours have been made in this field [e.g. 4], further research is necessary.

REFERENCES

1. Garfinkel P.E., Lin E., Goering P., Spegg C., Goldbloom D.S., Kennedy S., Kaplan A.S., Blake Woodsie D. (1996) Should amenorrhoea be necessary for the diagnosis of anorexia nervosa? Evidence from a Canadian community sample. *Br. J. Psychiatry*, **168**: 500–506.
2. Calchelin F.M., Maher B.A. (1998) Is amenorrhoea a critical criterion for anorexia nervosa? *J. Psychosom. Res.*, **44**: 435–440.
3. Fairburn C.G. (1987) The definition of bulimia nervosa: guidelines for clinicians and research workers. *Ann. Behav. Med.*, **9**: 3–7.
4. Safer D.L., Telch C.F., Agras W.S. (2001) Dialectical behavior therapy for bulimia nervosa. *Am. J. Psychiatry*, **158**: 632–634.

1.13
Do Sociocultural Factors Influence the Comorbidity of Eating Disorders?

Hisato Matsunaga and Nobuo Kiriike[1]

Katherine Halmi's authoritative and comprehensive description of classifications of eating disorders clearly illustrates some crucial issues underlying the current operational definition of these disorders. The introduction of systematic diagnostic criteria, such as the DSM criteria, has facilitated an internationally reliable diagnosis of eating disorders. However, it should be noted that psychopathological aspects inherent to eating disorders, such as desire for thinness or distortion of body image, might be influenced by the surrounding culture. In addition, genetic and environmental factors, such as race and culture, may exert significant effects on certain sociocultural contexts and conditions, especially during childhood, and on personality development. These factors are believed to play important roles as determinants of personality disorders also in those with eating disorders [1]. Thus, a comparative examination focusing on psychopathological similarities and differences between people diagnosed as having eating disorders in Japan and those in the Western world should be useful in clarifying the sociocultural effects on psychopathology related to eating disorders. In this regard, comorbid Axis I disorders or personality disorders assessed using internationally reliable instruments can be robust indicators for cross-cultural comparison. Therefore, we tried to compare our data on psychiatric comorbidity in Japanese subjects with eating disorders with the Western findings systematically summarized by Katherine Halmi.

As for comorbid Axis I disorders, assessed using the Structured Clinical Interview for DSM-III-R, patient version (SCID-P) in 171 Japanese subjects with eating disorders (62 with restricting anorexia nervosa, 36 with bulimic anorexia nervosa and 73 with bulimia nervosa), the lifetime prevalence of both mood and anxiety disorders seemed similar to that reported in Western countries [2], being 57% and 43%, respectively. The two most prevalent anxiety disorders were obsessive–compulsive disorder (OCD) and social phobia. Likewise, a closer association with major depression was observed in bulimic subtypes of eating disorder compared with subjects with restricting anorexia nervosa. Compared with Western countries, however, substance abuse was less prevalent in Japanese bulimics, which might be due mainly to sociocultural differences, such as the different availability of drugs. Thus, comorbid Axis I disorders in subjects with eating disorders may be rather culture-free.

---

[1] *Department of Neuropsychiatry, Osaka City University Medical School, Osaka, Japan*

Comorbid personality disorders were evaluated in 108 Japanese patients with eating disorders (36 with restricting anorexia nervosa, 30 with bulimic anorexia nervosa and 42 with bulimia nervosa) using the SCID–Personality Disorders [3]. Fifty-one per cent of these patients met the criteria for at least one personality disorder. In particular, a close relation to Cluster B personality disorders, especially borderline personality disorder, was found in bulimic subtypes of eating disorder. Patients with any personality disorder, especially borderline, had more severe clinical features in terms of bulimic behaviours, concurrent depressive, anxious and obsessive–compulsive symptoms, psychopathology related to eating disorders, and a higher number of suicidal attempts compared with those without personality disorders. Thus, there were few differences between patients with eating disorders in Japan and those in the Western world in terms of the prevalence and type of personality disorders.

Our studies of comorbid disorders appear to support the transcultural similarities of a variety of psychopathological characteristics in patients with eating disorders. Examining the relationship between comorbid Axis I disorders and comorbid personality disorders in subjects with eating disorders may be useful, because the nature and timing of Axis I comorbidity may exert a confounding effect on the assessment of pathology of the personality disorder [4]. For example, 21(40%) of 53 Japanese women with anorexia nervosa concurrently met the DSM-III-R criteria for OCD, manifesting significant impairment due to primary OCD symptoms, with a magnitude of severity similar to that in age-matched OCD women [5]. Compared with OCD women, however, women with anorexia nervosa showed a significantly closer link between OCD and obsessive–compulsive personality disorder.

Overall, concerning the comorbidity of Axis I or personality disorders, Japanese people diagnosed as having eating disorders by DSM criteria are likely to have a substantial commonality in psychopathological characteristics to patients with eating disorders in the Western world. However, the current classification and operational definition of eating disorders still remains controversial, as suggested by Halmi. For further discussion on this issue, it may be useful to examine whether patients categorized as having other types of eating disorder, such as eating disorders not otherwise specified, show the same cultural-free tendency in comorbidity.

REFERENCES

1. Derkesen J. (1995) Sociocultural and economic backgrounds of personality disorders. In *Personality Disorders: Clinical and Social Perspectives* (Ed. J. Derkesen), pp. 279–305. Wiley, Chichester.

2. Iwasaki Y., Matsunaga H., Kiriike N., Tanaka H., Matsui T. (2000) Comorbidity of Axis I disorders among eating disordered subjects in Japan. *Compr. Psychiatry*, **41**: 454–460.
3. Matsunaga H., Kiriike N., Nagata T., Yamagami S. (1998) Personality disorders in patients with eating disorders in Japan. *Int. J. Eat. Disord.*, **23**: 399–408.
4. Halmi K.A. (1997) Co-morbidity of the eating disorders. *Baillière's Clin. Psychiatry*, **3**: 291–302.
5. Matsunaga H., Kiriike N., Iwasaki Y., Miyata A., Yamagami S., Kaye W.H. (1999) Clinical characteristics in patients with anorexia nervosa and obsessive–compulsive disorder. *Psychol. Med.*, **29**: 407–414.

1.14
Eating Disorders: Syndromes with Still Poorly Defined Boundaries

Angélica M. Claudino and Miguel R. Jorge[1]

Eating disorders have been considered, until recently, as culture-bound syndromes, owing to their greater prevalence in wealthy countries of Westernized culture, especially in North America and Europe. Nowadays this hypothesis is being questioned, owing to the growing identification of these problems in the developing countries of Asia, South America and Africa, some of them with very different cultural values from Western ones [1]. The rising number of specialized eating disorder services in university centres in many regions of Brazil in the last decade confirms such an observation.

Possible interpretations of these findings have been based on the concept of "modernization" [2]. In the eating disorders field, this involves not only the influence of Western beauty values spread through the globalization process, but also the whole pressure over social roles faced by subjects living in societies undergoing important economic and political changes.

Watching the gradual dissolution of the conception of eating disorders as culture-bound syndromes, we have to acknowledge that this ongoing process runs parallel to the understanding of what exactly is essential for their diagnosis and classification. For instance, the occurrence of anorexia nervosa "without weight phobia", described in Chinese women [3] and considered in DSM-IV as a possible variation in some cultures, led to the recognition that there are still "huge", basic nosological questions to be solved in the field, e.g. "what should be considered the *core* psychopatho-

[1] *Eating Disorders Program, Department of Psychiatry, Federal University of São Paulo, R. Botucatu 740, São Paulo, CEP 04023-900, Brazil*

logical aspects of anorexia nervosa". Russell [4] suggested an explanation of the changing nature of anorexia nervosa based on the existence of possible invariable pathogenetic factors and variable cultural factors, and DiNicola [5] refers to "anorexia multiforme", but there is still an incomplete basis for a clear definition of the body disturbance phenomena not only in anorexia nervosa but also in bulimia nervosa.

Certainly the main classification systems have been refining the criteria sets since the scientific method has been applied to psychiatric nosology, but, as stated by Katherine Halmi, "eating disorders are more complex and broader in scope than what is precisely defined in DSM-IV and ICD-10". Many gaps of the current diagnostic systems can be identified easily in clinical daily practice: what if a patient purges to control weight but does not binge? How should someone be considered who actively maintains low body weight and eccentric eating habits when it is not possible to identify the dread of fatness with the best of our expertise? Is he/she a patient with a particular form of depression or developing anorexia nervosa? Can someone who deals with affective feelings through frequent binge/purge cycles but does not have a strong concern with weight and shape be considered bulimic? How does one decide between the diagnosis of bulimia nervosa of non-purging type and that of binge eating disorder in a slightly overweight patient?

In clinical settings, we deal with the whole symptomatic picture and with the impairment determined by the disorder, expecting to clarify the diagnosis with follow-up. The problem gets worse when we are doing research and have to define caseness according to the DSM-IV or ICD-10 criteria sets, particularly in community studies. Many of these patients will fall into the "unspecified eating disorders" category and be missed, as we usually "study what we define". It is true that we see our patients walking along the spectrum of eating disorders, but how can we learn more about the diagnosis and classification of eating disorders without broadening the scope of research to the atypical cases?

Psychiatric nosology has to deal with the blurred line between normal and pathological cognitions or behaviours, and this discrimination becomes even more difficult when dealing with beliefs that are highly syntonic with cultural values (such as concerns about weight). The relationship between partial and full syndromes of eating disorders is still unclear: do partial manifestations represent a transitional phase to full presentations? Are there enough qualitative elements to introduce differences within the "continuum of weight concern"? Large longitudinal studies with community samples, such as the Bulik *et al.* [6] investigation of twins looking for eating disorder-related concerns, attitudes and behaviours, are of unmeasurable value. This discrimination will certainly have implications for early intervention and prognosis.

Research in the field is also facing the difficult task of identifying whether eating disorders should be considered as different symptomatological presentations of the same disorder (which might change with time), disorders with subtype classes, different disorders of the same diagnostic group or even disorders that can be variations of other diagnostic groups. Many external validators have been used (demographic data, psychological tests, family history). Multicentre aetiological studies (such as that hosted by the US University of Pittsburgh and the European Genes & Environment Study into Eating Disorders and Obesity) that are currently ongoing might provide us with further elements to improve our knowledge on the diagnosis and classification of eating disorders.

However, as discussed well by Kendler [7], when applying the scientific method to psychiatric nosology, it is necessary to balance its strengths and limitations and recognize what *is* and what *is not* an empirical question. The author suggests that empirical data, systematically and objectively reviewed, be used to *inform* the nosological process, and that decisions that are fundamentally non-empirical be made by considering the empirical implications of the alternatives. Katherine Halmi strengthened this suggestion in the final recommendation of her review.

REFERENCES

1. Nasser M., Katzman M.A., Gordon R.A. (2001) *Eating Disorders in Cultures in Transition.* Taylor and Francis, New York.
2. Katzman M.A., Lee S. (1997) Beyond body image: the integration of feminist and transcultural theories in the understanding of self-starvation. *Int. J. Eat. Disord.,* **22**: 385–394.
3. Lee S., Ho T.P., Hsu L.K.G. (1993) Fat phobic and non-fat phobic anorexia nervosa: a comparative study of 70 Chinese patients in Hong Kong. *Psychosom. Med.,* **23**: 999–1017.
4. Russell G.F.M. (1985) The changing nature of anorexia nervosa. *J. Psychiatr. Res.,* **19**: 101–109.
5. DiNicola V. (1990) Anorexia multiforme: self-starvation in historical and cultural context. Part II: Anorexia nervosa as a culture reactive syndrome. *Transcult. Psychiatr. Res.,* **27**: 245–286.
6. Bulik C.M., Sullivan P.F., Kendler K.S. (2000) An empirical study of the classification of eating disorders. *Am. J. Psychiatry,* **157**: 886–895.
7. Kendler K.S. (1990) Toward a scientific psychiatric nosology. Strengths and limitations. *Arch. Gen. Psychiatry,* **47**: 969–973.

Epidemiology and Cultural Aspects of Eating Disorders: A Review

Hans Wijbrand Hoek

Parnassia, The Hague Psychiatric Institute, The Hague, The Netherlands and Department of Epidemiology, Mailman School of Public Health, Columbia University, New York, USA

Daphne van Hoeken

Parnassia, The Hague Psychiatric Institute, The Hague, The Netherlands

Melanie A. Katzman

New York Presbyterian Hospital, Weill-Cornell Medical College, New York, USA and Institute of Psychiatry, University of London, UK

INTRODUCTION

Several reviews have been written on the epidemiology of eating disorders [1–4] and the impact of culture on weight consciousness [5,6]. The authors themselves have reviewed the epidemiology of eating disorders before [7–10] and discussed the impact of sociocultural factors [6,11–15]. This chapter is a selection of the literature on epidemiology and an update and integration of our previous reviews.

Epidemiological studies of eating disorders have to counter a number of methodological problems in the selection of populations under study and the identification of cases [1,4,7,10]. Problems specific to the eating disorders are their low prevalence in the general population and the tendency of subjects with eating disorders to conceal their illness and avoid professional help. These problems make it necessary to study a very large number of subjects from the general population in order to reach enough differential power for the cases. This is highly time- and cost-intensive.

Eating Disorders. Edited by Mario Maj, Katherine Halmi, Juan José López-Ibor and Norman Sartorius.
©2003 John Wiley & Sons Ltd: ISBN 0-470-84865-0

Several strategies have been used to circumvent this problem, in particular case register and other record-based studies, two-stage studies and studies of special populations.

The limitations of record-based studies are considerable [4]. Register-based frequencies represent cases detected in inpatient and occasionally outpatient care. Treated cases represent only a minority of all cases. Findings from case registers/hospital records are of more value to treatment planning than for generating hypotheses on the aetiology of disease, because there is no direct access to the subjects and the additional information available is usually limited and of demographic nature only.

At present a two-stage screening approach is the most widely accepted procedure for case identification. First a large population is screened for the likelihood of an eating disorder by means of a screening questionnaire, identifying an at-risk population (first stage). Then definite cases are established using a personal interview of subjects from this at-risk population as well as on a randomly selected sample of those not at risk (second stage) [16]. Methodological problems of two-stage studies are poor response rates, sensitivity/specificity of the screening instrument and the often restricted size of the interviewed groups, particularly of those not at risk [2].

Studies of special populations address a particular segment of the general population, selected a priori for being at increased risk, such as female high school/university students, athletes or a particular age cohort. The major methodological problem associated with this type of study is the specificity of the findings to the selected subset of the general population.

Both two-stage studies and studies of special populations have the potential to provide information relevant to the aetiology, because there is direct access to the subjects and the availability of additional information is not restricted by a predetermined registration system. Register-based prevalence studies and prevalence studies of eating disorders using only questionnaires will not be discussed in this review.

In the sections on anorexia nervosa and bulimia nervosa only studies using strict definitions of these eating disorders (meeting Russell, DSM or ICD criteria) are discussed. Another category, the eating disorders not otherwise specified (EDNOS), includes a variety of patients who do not meet all the criteria for anorexia nervosa or bulimia nervosa but who do have symptoms severe enough to qualify as having a clinically significant eating disorder. This heterogeneity makes it a difficult category for the search on possible aetiological factors and as a result there is hardly any reliable epidemiological information available. Therefore, the EDNOS are not included in this review.

In DSM-IV [17], a provision is made for a separate eating disorder category to be researched further: the binge eating disorder (BED). Although there is only limited epidemiological information available, we will briefly review the epidemiology of this disorder.

ANOREXIA NERVOSA

Prevalence

The current standard for assessment of the prevalence of eating disorders are studies employing a two-stage selection of cases. Table 2.1 summarizes the two-stage surveys of anorexia nervosa in young females.

All studies have succeeded in obtaining high response rates of 85% or more, except that of Meadows et al. [21], who reached a response rate of 70%. Those two-stage surveys that identified cases found a prevalence rate of strictly defined anorexia nervosa of between 0.2 and 0.9% of young females, with an average prevalence of 0.3% in Western countries. These rates are possibly minimum estimates. Most studies found much higher prevalence rates for partial syndromes of anorexia nervosa.

Two other studies are discussed here because they are not confined to high-risk populations and give prevalence figures for the entire population. A drawback is that these studies did not use a two-stage procedure for case finding. In a general practice study in The Netherlands, a point-prevalence rate of 18.4 per 100 000 of the total population (95% CI = 12.7–26.8) was found on 1 January 1985 [30]. Lucas et al. [31] used a very extensive case-finding method, which included all medical records of healthcare providers, general practitioners and specialists in the community of Rochester, Minnesota. They also screened records mentioning related diagnostic terms for possible non-detected cases. They found an overall gender- and age-adjusted point prevalence of 149.5 per 100 000 (95% CI = 119.3–179.7) on 1 January 1985.

A main explanation for this difference can be found in the inclusion of probable and possible cases by Lucas et al. Definite cases constituted only 39% (82 out of 208) of all incident cases identified in the period 1935–1989 [32]. Applying this rate to the point prevalence of 149.5 gives an estimated point prevalence of 58.9 per 100 000 for definite cases in Rochester, Minnesota, on 1 January 1985. The remaining difference with the point prevalence reported by Hoek [30] could be explained by the greater variety of medical sources searched by Lucas et al. [31].

TABLE 2.1 Two-stage surveys of prevalence of anorexia nervosa in young females

Study	Subjects			Methods		Prevalence (%)
	Source	Age (years)	n	Screening*	Criteria	
Button and Whitehouse [18]	College students	16–22	446	EAT	Feighner	0.2
Szmukler [19]	Private schools	14–19	1331	EAT	Russell	0.8
	State schools	14–19	1676	EAT	Russell	0.2
King [20]	General practice	16–35	539	EAT	Russell	0
Meadows et al. [21]	General practice	18–22	584	EAT	DSM-III	0.2**
Johnson-Sabine et al. [22]	Schoolgirls	14–16	1010	EAT	Russell	0
Råstam et al. [23]	Schoolgirls	15	2136	Growth chart + questionnaire	DSM-III	0.47
					DSM-III-R	0.23
Whitaker et al. [24]	Highschool girls	13–18	2544	EAT	DSM-III	0.3
Whitehouse et al. [25]	General practice	16–35	540	Questionnaire	DSM-III-R	0.2
Rathner and Messner [26]	Schoolgirls + case register	11–20	517	EAT	DSM-III-R	0.58
Wlodarczyk-Bisaga and Dolan [27]	Schoolgirls	14–16	747	EAT	DSM-III-R	0
Steinhausen et al. [28]	Schoolgirls	14–17	276	EDE-S	DSM-III-R	0.7
Nobakht and Dezhkam [29]	Schoolgirls	15–18	3100	EAT	DSM-IV	0.9

*EAT—Eating Attitudes Test; EDE-S—Eating Disorder Examination, Screening Version.
**Not found by screening (EAT score below threshold).

Incidence

Studies of clinical samples will always show an underestimation of the incidence of eating disorders in the community, because only a minority of people with these disorders come to medical attention. The incidence studies of anorexia nervosa have used psychiatric case registers, medical records of hospitals in a circumscribed area, registrations by general practitioners, or medical records of healthcare providers in a community. All record-based studies will grossly underestimate the true incidence, because not all cases will be referred to mental healthcare or become hospitalized. Therefore, it is unclear whether the increase in cases reported in healthcare facilities reflects an actual increase in the incidence in the community, because it might be due to improved methods of case detection or to the wider availability of services. Table 2.2 summarizes the results of the studies on the incidence of anorexia nervosa that report overall rates for the total population.

The overall rates vary considerably, ranging from 0.10 in a hospital records-based study in Sweden in the 1930s to 12.0 in a medical records-based study in the USA in the 1980s, both per 100 000 population per year.

Incidence rates derived from general practices on average represent more recent onset eating disorders than those based on other medical records. There were two studies of this type [42,44]. In the study in The Netherlands [42], general practitioners using DSM-III-R criteria have recorded the rate of eating disorders in a large ($n = 151\,781$) representative sample (1.1%) of the Dutch population. The incidence rate of anorexia nervosa was 8.1 per 100 000 person-years (95% CI = 6.1–10.2) during the period 1985–1989. During the study period, 63% of the incident cases were referred to mental healthcare, accounting for an incidence rate of anorexia nervosa in mental healthcare of 5.1 per year per 100 000 population. In the period 1995–1996 the incidence of patients with anorexia nervosa referred to mental healthcare did not increase significantly to 5.4 per year per 100 000 population [43]. Turnbull et al. [44] searched the UK General Practice Research Database, covering 550 general practitioners and 4 million patients, for first diagnoses of anorexia in the period 1988–1993. A randomly selected subset of cases was checked with DSM-IV criteria, from which estimates for adjusted incidence rates were made. For anorexia nervosa, they found an age- and gender-adjusted incidence rate of 4.2 (95% CI = 3.4–5.0) per 100 000 population in 1993.

Lucas et al. [31,32] used the most extensive case-finding method (see the section on prevalence). Over the period 1935–1989, they report an overall age- and gender-adjusted incidence rate of anorexia nervosa of 8.3 per 100 000 person-years (95% CI = 7.1–9.4).

TABLE 2.2   Incidence of anorexia nervosa per year per 100 000 population

Study	Region	Source	Period	Incidence
Theander [33]	Southern Sweden	Hospital records	1931–1940	0.10
			1941–1950	0.20
			1951–1960	0.45
			(1931–1960)	(0.24)
Willi et al. [34, 35]	Zurich	Hospital records	1956–1958	0.38
Martz et al. [36]			1963–1965	0.55
			1973–1975	1.12
			1983–1985	1.43
			1993–1995	1.17
Jones et al. [37]	Monroe County	Case register + hospital records	1960–1969	0.37
			1970–1976	0.64
Kendell et al. [38]	North-East Scotland	Case register	1960–1969	1.60
Szmukler et al. [39]	North-East Scotland	Case register	1978–1982	4.06
Kendell et al. [38]	Camberwell	Case register	1965–1971	0.66
Hoek and Brook [40]	Assen	Case register	1974–1982	5.0
Møller-Madsen and Nystrup [41]	Denmark	Case-register	1970	0.42
			1988	1.36
			1989	1.17
Lucas et al. [31,32]	Rochester, MN	Medical records	1935–1949	9.1
			1950–1959	4.3
			1960–1969	7.0
			1970–1979	7.9
			1980–1989	12.0
			(1935–1989)	(8.3)
Hoek et al. [42,43]	The Netherlands	General practitioners	1985–1989	8.1
		Referred to mental healthcare	1985–1989	5.1
		Referred to mental healthcare	1995–1996	5.4
Turnbull et al. [44]	England, Wales	General practitioners	1993	4.2

Time Trends

There has been considerable debate over whether the incidence of eating disorders is, or has been, on the rise. Among the different studies there are diverging incidence rates. Most likely, there is at least partly a methodological explanation for these differences. The main problem lies in the need for long study periods. This results in a sensitivity of these studies to minor changes in absolute incidence numbers and in methods, e.g. variations in

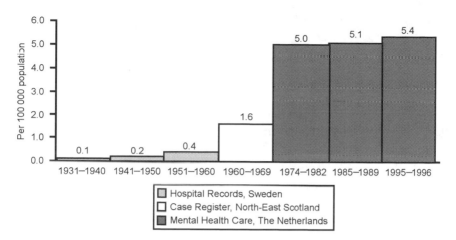

Figure 2.1 Registered yearly incidence of anorexia nervosa

registration policy, demographic differences between the populations, faulty inclusion of readmissions, the particular methods of detection used or the availability of services [3,45].

From the studies that have used long study periods [32,34,35] it may be concluded that there has been an upward trend in the incidence of anorexia nervosa since the 1950s. The increase is most substantial in females aged 15–24 years. Lucas *et al.* [32] found that the age-adjusted incidence rates of anorexia nervosa in females aged 15–24 years showed a highly significant linear increasing trend from 1935 to 1989, with an estimated rate of increase of 1.03 per 100 000 person-years per calendar year. In 10–14-year-old females, a rise in incidence was observed for each decade since the 1950s. The rates for men and for women aged 25 years and over remained relatively low.

Despite the use of different methods, we have made an attempt to combine different studies on the incidence of anorexia nervosa in mental healthcare in Northern Europe (Sweden, North-East Scotland and The Netherlands) to derive a figure over a long period (see Figure 2.1). One might conclude from Figure 2.1 and the studies in Switzerland (see Table 2.2) that prior to 1980 there was an increase over time of the registered incidence of anorexia nervosa in Europe. After 1980, the incidence of anorexia nervosa in Europe seemed to be rather stable [7,8,43].

Although the debate about the extent to which there has been an increase in the true incidence of anorexia nervosa in the 20th century is not yet solved, the increase in incidence rates of registered cases implies that at least there has been an increased demand for healthcare interventions for anorexia nervosa.

Age

Incidence rates of anorexia nervosa are the highest for females aged 15–19 years. These constitute approximately 40% of all identified cases. For example, Lucas *et al.* [32] report an incidence rate of 73.9 per 100 000 person-years for 15–19-year-old women over the period 1935–1989, with a continual rise since the 1930s to a top rate of 135.7 for the period 1980–1989. They report an incidence rate of 9.5 for 30–39-year-old women, 5.9 for 40–49-year-old women, 1.8 for 50–59-year-old women and 0.0 for women aged 60 years and over.

Males

Although anorexia nervosa occurs in men as well as in women, few studies report incidence rates for males. From incidence studies that do report on males, one might conclude that the incidence of anorexia nervosa among males is below 1.0 and probably even below 0.5 per 100 000 population per year [32,42,44]. In those studies where it is reported, the female to male ratio usually is more than 10:1 [10,42].

Mortality

The few follow-up studies of at least 10 years show a mortality of anorexia nervosa of at least 10%. Theander [46] was the first to conduct a very long-term follow-up study. He found a mortality rate of 18% among his group of 94 patients with anorexia nervosa in Sweden.

Sullivan [47] conducted a meta-analysis on crude mortality rates (CMR) for anorexia nervosa in 42 published studies. The CMR found was 5.9% (178 deaths in 3006 patients), translating into 0.56% per year or 5.6% per decade. In the studies specifying cause of death, 54% of the subjects died as a result of complications of the eating disorder, 27% committed suicide and the remaining 19% died of unknown or other causes.

In a meta-analysis on standardized mortality rates (SMR), the overall aggregate SMR of anorexia nervosa in studies with 6–12 years of follow-up is 9.6 (95% CI = 7.8–11.5) and in studies with 20–40 years of follow-up it is 3.7 (95% CI = 2.8–4.7) [48]. Thus, in the long run, subjects with anorexia nervosa have an almost fourfold risk of dying compared with healthy people of the same age and gender.

BULIMIA NERVOSA

Prevalence

In 1990, Fairburn and Beglin [2] provided a review of the prevalence studies on bulimia nervosa. This review yielded the generally accepted prevalence rate of 1% among young females for bulimia nervosa diagnosed according to DSM criteria.

Table 2.3 summarizes two-stage surveys of bulimia nervosa in young females that have been published since the review by Fairburn and Beglin. The aggregated prevalence rate according to DSM-III-R and DSM-IV criteria remains at 1%. In a random, stratified, non-clinical community sample, using a structured interview for the whole sample, the lifetime prevalence for bulimia nervosa was 1.1% in women and 0.1% in men aged 15–65 years using DSM-III-R criteria [52].

The prevalence of subclinical eating disorders is substantially higher than that of full-syndrome bulimia nervosa (e.g. Whitehouse *et al.* [25]: 1.5% for full-syndrome and 5.4% for partial-syndrome bulimia nervosa).

Incidence

There have been only a few incidence studies of bulimia nervosa, most probably because of the lack of criteria for bulimia nervosa in the past. Most case registers use the International Classification of Diseases, currently ICD-10 [53]. The ICD-9 [54] and previous versions did not provide a separate code for bulimia nervosa. Bulimia nervosa was first distinguished as a separate disorder by Russell in 1979 [55] and in DSM-III in 1980 [56]. Before 1980, the term "bulimia" in medical records designated symptoms of heterogeneous conditions manifested by overeating, but not the syndrome as it is known today. Therefore it is difficult to examine trends in the incidence of bulimia nervosa or a possible shift from anorexia nervosa to bulimia nervosa, which might have influenced the previously described incidence rates of anorexia nervosa.

Three studies are reviewed here, those of Soundy *et al.* [57], Hoek *et al.* [42] and Turnbull *et al.* [44]. Soundy *et al.* [57] used a methodology similar to that in the long-term anorexia nervosa study in the same area [31], screening all medical records of healthcare providers, general practitioners and specialists in Rochester, Minnesota, over the period 1980–1990 for a clinical diagnosis of bulimia nervosa as well as for related symptoms. In The Netherlands, the incidence rate of bulimia nervosa using DSM-III-R criteria was examined in a large general practice study representative of the population, covering the period 1985–1989 [42]. Turnbull *et al.* [44] screened

TABLE 2.3 Two-stage surveys of the prevalence of bulimia nervosa in young females (1990–2000)

| Study | Subjects | | | Methods | | Prevalence (%) |
	Source	Age (years)	n	Screening*	Criteria	
Whitaker et al. [24]	Highschool girls	13–18	2544	EAT	DSM-I	4.2
Bushnell et al. [49]	Household census	18–24		DIS	DSM-I	4.5
		25–44				2.0
		(18–44)	(777)			(2.6)
Szabó and Túry [50]	Schoolgirls	14–18	416	EAT, BCDS, ANIS	DSM-II / DSM-III-R	0 / 0
	College girls	19–36	224	EAT, BCDS, ANIS	DSM-III / DSM-III-R	4.0 / 1.3
Whitehouse et al. [25]	General practice	16–35	540	Questionnaire	DSM-III-R	1.5
Rathner and Messner [26]	Schoolgirls + case register	11–20	517	EAT	DSM-III-R	0
Wlodarczyk-Bisaga and Dolan [27]	Schoolgirls	14–16	747	EAT	DSM-III-R	0
Santonastaso et al. [51]	Schoolgirls	16	359	EAT	DSM-IV	0.5
Steinhausen et al. [28]	Schoolgirls	14–17	276	EDE-S	DSM-III-R	0.5
Nobakht and Dezhkam [29]	Schoolgirls	15–18	3100	EAT	DSM-IV	3.2

*EAT—Eating Attitudes Test; DIS—Diagnostic Interview Schedule; BCDS—Bulimia Cognitive Distortions Scale; ANIS—Anorexia Nervosa Inventory Scale; EDE-S—Eating Disorder Examination, Screening Version.

the UK General Practice Research Database, covering a large, representative sample of the English and Welsh population for first diagnoses of anorexia nervosa and bulimia nervosa in 1993. Another general population study on the island of Bornholm, Denmark, is not discussed here because the population under consideration was relatively small (<50 000 inhabitants) [58].

The three studies under consideration all report an annual incidence of bulimia nervosa of around 12 per 100 000 population: 13.5 in Rochester, Minnesota [57], 11.5 for The Netherlands [42] and 12.2 in the UK [44].

Time Trends

The yearly incidence rates in Rochester rose sharply from 7.4 per 100 000 females in 1980 to 49.7 in 1983 and then remained relatively constant at around 30 per 100 000 females until 1990 [57]. This would seem to be related to the publication and subsequent implementation in the field of DSM-III, introducing bulimia nervosa as an official diagnostic category. In The Netherlands, a non-significant trend was found for an increase in the incidence rates of bulimia nervosa: 15% each year in the period 1985–1989 [42]. Turnbull et al. [44] noted a highly significant, threefold increase in bulimia nervosa incidence rates for women aged 10–39 years in the period 1988–1993: from 14.6 in 1988 to 51.7 in 1993.

These incidence rates of bulimia nervosa can only serve as minimum estimates of the true incidence rate, owing to the lack of data, the greater taboo around bulimia nervosa and its lesser perceptibility compared with anorexia nervosa.

Gender

Soundy et al. [57] report an incidence of bulimia nervosa of 26.5 for females and 0.8 for males per 100 000 population, yielding a female to male ratio of 33:1. Hoek et al. [42] report similar rates of 21.9 for females and 0.8 for males per 100 000 population, yielding a female to male ratio of 27:1.

Age

For the highest risk group of 20–24-year-old females, rates of 82 per 100 000 are found: 82.7 according to Soundy et al. [57] and 82.1 according to Hoek et al. [42]. Turnbull et al. [44] report an annual incidence of 1.7 per 100 000 people (men and women) aged 40 years and over.

Mortality

Combination of the results of the meta-analyses by Keel and Mitchell [59] and Nielsen [48] yields a CMR for bulimia nervosa of 0.4% (11 deaths in 2692 patients). No information is available on the distribution of the causes of death.

Nielsen [48] has conducted an update of a previous meta-analysis on SMR. The overall aggregate SMR of bulimia nervosa in studies with 5–11 years of follow-up is 7.4 (95% CI = 2.9–14.9). Longer follow-up periods are not available yet. However, as suggested by Nielsen (personal communication), there may be serious publication bias in this rate. When the mortality information from all 42 bulimia nervosa cohorts is used, not just that of the five cohorts reporting SMR, the SMR changes to 1.56 (95% CI = 0.8–2.7).

Thus, within the first 10 years after detection, subjects with bulimia nervosa run an increased risk of dying compared with healthy people of the same age and gender. But it is still open to debate as to whether this risk is only moderately increased (1.5 times) or, with a sevenfold increase, is close to the risk (more than ninefold increase) of anorexia nervosa.

PATHWAY TO CARE OF ANOREXIA AND BULIMIA NERVOSA

For health policy makers, it is important to know the number of patients in care. Despite their different nature, we have tried to combine the different rates in one model to discuss the morbidity at different levels of care [7,8]. Table 2.4 shows three levels of morbidity in a pathway to care representing the one-year prevalence rates per 100 000 young females at different levels. The one-year period prevalence is given by point prevalence plus annual incidence rate.

Each level in the model of Table 2.4 represents a different population of subjects. In order to move from one level to the next, it is necessary to pass through a filter.

Level 0 represents the community. Our knowledge concerning this level is derived from the two-stage surveys of eating disorders. We have calculated previously that the mean point-prevalence rate for anorexia nervosa is 280 and for bulimia nervosa it is 1000 per 100 000 young females [7,8]. We do not know the incidence rates in the community. Hoek [30] has found that the incidence of anorexia nervosa was about one-third of the point prevalence and that of bulimia nervosa was half the point prevalence in primary care. If we use these primary care figures as estimates for the

TABLE 2.4. One-year period prevalence rates per 100 000 young females at different levels of care

Level of morbidity	Characteristic of filter	Anorexia nervosa	Bulimia nervosa
1. Community		370	1500
→ filter 1:	Detection of disorder		
2. Detected in primary care		160	170
→ filter 2:	Referral to psychiatrist		
3. Total in mental healthcare		127	87

community, the one-year prevalence rates in the community are 370 for anorexia nervosa and 1500 for bulimia nervosa.

Level 1 consists of those patients identified as "psychiatrically ill" by their attending primary care physician. These patients collectively represent psychiatric morbidity as seen from the vantage point of the primary care physician. The rates are derived from the general practice study in The Netherlands [42].

Between eating disorder morbidity in the community and the detection of an eating disorder case by a general practitioner there is a filter. The factors that determine whether or not an individual passes through the first filter are often referred to as the "illness behaviour" of the patient, which is of course affected by and related to the doctor's ability to detect eating disorders and the method and diagnostic system that the doctor uses to label illness behaviour. The biomedical taxonomy of the ICD and DSM systems has been criticized as being very Western and therefore biasing detection, because different methods of classification and help-seeking behaviours may exist in different societies. Even within Western cultures, general practitioners have problems in detecting eating disorders, because they are characterized by taboo and denial. In particular, patients with bulimia nervosa who are of normal weight might be difficult to identify [30].

Patients attending outpatient and inpatient services of mental healthcare represent level 2. In countries like The Netherlands and the UK, the primary care physician is critically placed to determine who will be referred for psychiatric outpatient care, and the general practitioner will therefore be thought of as another filter. Table 2.4 shows that this filter lets through more anorexia than bulimia nervosa patients. The rates for eating disorders have been derived from the number of patients referred by the general practitioner according to the studies in The Netherlands [30,40,42,43].

Being aware of the methodological differences and problems of the studies described, we might conclude from Table 2.4 that roughly one-third of the patients with anorexia nervosa in the community are coming into mental healthcare. In contrast, only a small minority of the community cases with bulimia nervosa appear to be detected in primary care and only 6% of those cases will be seen in mental healthcare.

BINGE EATING DISORDER (BED)

Binge eating disorder (BED) has the status of "diagnostic category in need of further research" in DSM-IV [17]. A general problem with the comparison of studies of BED—and of bulimia nervosa for that matter—lies in the diagnosis of a binge. Studies may differ in the way the boundaries of a binge were set, resulting in subject groups that are not fully comparable.

Just as for anorexia nervosa and bulimia nervosa, we will focus on prevalence studies using a two-stage case identification procedure in the general population. Cotrufo *et al.* [60] were the only ones to use a two-stage procedure. They identified two cases of BED in a group of 919 13–19-year-old females, giving a prevalence rate of 0.2%. The low rate may be due to the relatively young age of the investigated population. Also, the sample size is rather small for a low-frequency disorder.

Hay [61] conducted interviews to determine the prevalence of bulimic-type eating disorders on all subjects in a large general population sample (3001 interviews). The mean age of the cases was 35.2 years. Using DSM-IV criteria, a (point) prevalence for BED of 1% was found. Using a broader definition by Fairburn and Cooper [62], the prevalence was estimated at 2.5%. A weakness of the study was that diagnoses were based on a very limited number of questions (two gating questions and three further probes). No information was given regarding the sensitivity/specificity of the instrument.

In the USA, a rate of 4.5% for recurrent binge eating (two episodes per week during the past 3 months) has been reported among a sample of 1628 18–40-year-old black women, and of 2.6% among 5741 white women of the same age group [63]. Black and white women differed significantly on numerous eating disorder features: black women with BED reported less concern about weight, shape and eating than white women with BED [64].

No reports on crude or standardized mortality rates have been located for BED.

RISK FACTORS

Prospective Studies

The method of choice for assessing risk is a prospective follow-up study. Unfortunately, none of the few available prospective studies employed a two-stage case identification procedure and these studies addressed only a subsample of the general population.

Wlodarczyk-Bisaga and Dolan [27] re-interviewed a high and a low-risk group of 14–16-year-old schoolgirls, defined by their scores on the Eating Attitudes Test (EAT), 10 months after initial assessment. No clinical cases were detected at either measurement point. Patton *et al.* [65] conducted a cohort study over 3 years with 6-month intervals in students initially aged 14–15 years. All new cases of eating disorder that developed during the study had partial/subclinical syndromes of bulimia nervosa. Both dieting and psychiatric morbidity were implicated as risk factors, but from this study it is not clear whether this also holds for full-syndrome eating disorders.

General Population Retrospective Studies

There are many case–control studies on eating disorders, but often they are drawn from selected populations. Fairburn *et al.* [66–68] offer data from a general community sample. They compared subjects with bulimia nervosa [66], BED [67] and anorexia nervosa [68] with each other, with healthy control subjects without an eating disorder (general risk factors) and with subjects with other psychiatric disorders (specific risk factors), recruited from general practices in Oxfordshire, UK. After screening with self-report questionnaires, a retrospective risk-factor interview was carried out that addressed the premorbid period. This interview focused on biological, psychological and social factors thought to place persons at risk for the development of eating disorders. For anorexia nervosa and bulimia nervosa, the great majority of risk factors found were general risk factors, separating eating disorder cases from healthy controls. For BED, only a few general risk factors were identified.

Some specific risk factors separating eating disorder cases from other psychiatric cases were found as well. For anorexia nervosa, they were personal vulnerability factors, particularly childhood characteristics of negative self-evaluation and perfectionism. For bulimia nervosa these were dieting vulnerability factors, such as parental obesity, childhood obesity, and negative comments from family members about eating, appearance and weight.

The results suggest that both bulimia nervosa and BED are most likely to develop in dieters who are at risk of obesity and psychiatric disorder in general [65–67].

Dieting behaviour and disturbed eating attitudes are often used as predictors of the disorder and at the same time are actions and beliefs that comprise part of the syndrome. This touches upon the fundamental issue of a categorical versus a dimensional approach to eating disorders [69].

SPECIFIC RISK TOPICS

Childhood Sexual Abuse

In clinical samples of patients with eating disorders, a relatively large percentage of the women report sexual abuse in childhood. There has been considerable controversy concerning the relationship between childhood sexual abuse and the later development of an eating disorder, but in a recent meta-analysis a small significant positive relationship emerged [70]. Although a causal relation has not been determined, the higher frequencies of eating problems and sexual abuse in women make this finding a concern and lend importance to assessing one when a client presents with the other.

In a review on this subject, childhood sexual abuse was found to be a non-specific risk factor for bulimia nervosa, particularly when there is psychiatric comorbidity [71]. In case–control studies of 10–15-year-old female children receiving treatment for sexual abuse [72] and of women in New Zealand with childhood sexual abuse prior to age 16 years [73], higher levels of disturbed eating behaviours were reported.

Risk Factors in Males

Males with eating disorders do not differ from females with respect to age of onset, dissatisfaction with current body shape and weight control methods [74–76]. Premorbid obesity is a risk factor that is present in about 50% of male cases [77]. Homosexuality appears to be a risk factor in men [78,79]. Russell and Keel [80], in a study of 64 heterosexual and 58 homosexual males, report that homosexual men had more pathological scores on the assessment of body and weight concerns and revealed greater discomfort with sexual orientation. They suggest that future research may benefit from exploring aspects of homosexuality that may contribute specifically to the risk for disordered eating in men.

Social Class

Social class and social rank may be related to the development of eating problems. Although most psychiatric disorders show a higher prevalence in the lower socio-economic classes, it is difficult to determine whether this is the result of the social selection process or a causal factor in the pathology [81].

Anorexia nervosa traditionally was believed to be more prevalent in the upper social classes. Gard and Freeman [82] concluded that the relationship between anorexia nervosa and high socio-economic status is unproven and that studies suggesting such a relation most likely reflect biases in data collection, including sample size, clinical status and referral patterns. However, when reviewing the data from 692 referrals to a UK national specialist centre over 33 years, McClelland and Crisp [83] found referrals for anorexia nervosa from the two highest social classes to be almost twice as high as expected, a finding that they claim is unrelated to differences in clinical features or in access to their service.

Similar to most psychiatric disorders, bulimia nervosa seems to be preponderant in the low socio-economic groups [82].

Level of Urbanization

The incidence of bulimia nervosa is, respectively, three and more than five times higher in urbanized areas and cities than in rural areas in The Netherlands, whereas anorexia nervosa is found with almost equal frequency in areas with different degrees of urbanization [42]. The drift hypothesis, relating urbanization differences to migration for educational reasons, is rejected because the differences remain after adjusting for age. Other social factors involved might include greater availability of high-calorie fast food, an increased pressure to be slender, decreased manual labour and increased "purchased" labour in gyms and workout sessions in urbanized areas. Furthermore, urban life might offer greater challenges to family-based meals which, when coupled with the availability of fast food, lead to unhealthy choices [84].

Occupation

Some occupations appear to run a greater potential risk of being linked to the development of an eating disorder [85]. Typical examples of these are professions within the world of fashion and ballet. We do not know whether this is a result of characteristics of the profession or of the people involved in this area. In other words, are pre-anorexics attracted by the ballet world or are the requirements of the profession conducive to the development of anorexia nervosa? For men, the presentation of eating disorders may be related to the exposure to and expectations of coaches and team members, such as the case of jockeys and wrestlers [86].

SOCIOCULTURAL ASPECTS

Transcultural studies in the 1970s and 1980s showed that anorexia nervosa was rare in non-Western countries [87–92], but studies in the 1990s demonstrated that eating disorders occur in traditional as well as modernizing countries [29,93–100] and in fact suggest that the differentiation based on East and West may be arbitrary.

As our understanding of eating disorders matures, the appreciation of the complexity of cultural causes evolves. The development of cultural understanding indicated that in the 1970s the focus was simplistic and solely on weight and diet pressures, whereas the 1980s saw an awareness of female role stress and the 1990s a recognition of cross-cultural issues [5,6]. At the end of the 20th century the study of cross-cultural cases became more refined, with a goal towards understanding the complex interplay of social and biological risk.

Although eating disorders were once understood to be Western illnesses, data from around the world indicate that culture or national lines do not bind the problem. Methodological problems in epidemiological studies in non-Western countries include not merely the identification of risk but agreeing on the diagnostic terms for the problem itself.

Migration and Transition

Several clinical reports of anorexia nervosa in immigrant families suggest that immigration and acculturation stress are key factors triggering the illness [101–105]. Immigrants are more likely to develop an eating disorder than their peers in their homeland, such as Arab college students in London [106] and Greek and Turkish girls in Germany [107], as well as East European migrants, Asian and black minorities in the USA and the UK and Russian Jews and Vietnamese refugees [5,6,108–114]. The reasons for this increased risk are debatable. Migrating females who are strongly identified with the traditional and patriarchal values of their country of birth may, paradoxically, reveal a greater proclivity to develop eating disorders. This may reflect difficulties experienced in growing up with alternative or noncompatible cultural values [115–117]. Alternatively, contrary findings suggest that eating disorders increase in those migrating women who accept and assimilate the new norms and values, including the standard of thinness [103,109,118,119].

Ethnicity and Cultural Identity

The experience of women from other ethnicities and cultures suggests that altering one's body weight may be a powerful way of accelerating one's acculturation. For example, several case reports of anorexia nervosa in the black communities of the USA and the UK [37,102,120–125] reflect the psychological problems that girls struggle with as they try to achieve a "racial identity" while fitting into a new society. Some thought that integration was possible through rigid dieting and adoption of the prevailing social standards of thinness [102,126]. It has been suggested that thinness became a parameter of black achievement and social mobility within the wider (but thinner) American middle-class society [127].

However, one does not need to leave one's own country to endure the challenges of belonging. A recent study showed that binge eating or vomiting is as likely among black women as in white women [63]. Among the Hispanic, Asian and black population in the USA, a correlation was found between the level of acculturation and morbid concerns over weight, where adherence to the Western culture was speculated to increase the individual's vulnerability to eating pathology [114,126,128–131]. Dieting behaviour was found to be equal among both black and white females in the USA [132]. Dysfunctional eating patterns with a tendency to develop bulimia were found to be more prevalent in the African–Caribbean population in the UK than in their white counterparts [133].

CROSS-CULTURAL VALIDITY OF RESEARCH

Instruments

Because the field of epidemiology is becoming "global", the experience of epidemiological studies in non-Western populations unveils the need for greater cultural sensitivity, the importance of interviews and the complexity of definitions. One factor that hampers community surveys in Asian and other populations is the absence of valid research instruments. As noted by Lee and Katzman [14], surveys in the East typically reveal a low prevalence of anorexia nervosa. One reason may be that the "typical" focus on fat phobia is not reflected in this population. For example, anorexic subjects may not necessarily endorse such items on the EAT scale as "I am terrified of gaining weight" (item 16) and "I am preoccupied with the desire to be thinner" (item 32) when they are manifestly emaciated. As a result, some of them would be screened out as "non-cases".

Lee and Katzman [14] go on to say that "even if Western instruments are accurately translated into the local language, whether they exhibit contextual validity in a non-Western setting remains uncertain". Using the Chinese version of the Eating Disorders Inventory (EDI-1), Lee *et al.* [134] showed that, although the profile of fat phobic patients was similar to that of Canadian patients with restrictive anorexia, that of non-fat phobic patients was anomalous. The latter patients displayed significantly more "general psychopathology" than control subjects, but exhibited even less "specific" or fat phobic psychopathology, as measured on the "drive for thinness" subscale. Likewise, non-fat phobic anorexic patients scored atypically low on the EAT scale.

One possible way to increase the sensitivity of the extant instruments is to include the local language used by starving subjects to explain food refusal. According to Lee and Katzman [14], "Research in mainstream psychiatric epidemiology has already shown that small but culturally relevant changes in the stem questions of research instruments originally based on the DSM system can result in significant changes in the detected rates of non-psychotic disorders. The obvious cultural basis of eating disorders notwithstanding, this approach to epidemiological work is yet to be explored in the field".

Definition of Diagnosis and Concept of Western Culture

Although bulimia nervosa appears to "breed true" in Asian populations, the case of anorexia nervosa is more complex. The DSM-IV requires that food refusal or emaciation in anorexia nervosa be solely attributed to an intense fear of fatness. However, not all Asian anorexic patients exhibit fat concern, especially when they are evidently emaciated. In the context of a retrospective study, Lee *et al.*, in Hong Kong [135], found that 41 (59%) of 70 Chinese anorexic patients, despite the compelling resemblance to their Western counterparts, attributed food refusal to stomach bloating, loss of appetite, no hunger and other rationales not connected with fat concern. A recent study by Nakamura *et al.* [136] showed that atypical patients still commonly occur in Japan.

Three common explanations given for the absence of fat phobia in these patients are "denial" of fat concern, somatized depression and the fact that they were already premorbidly thin and so did not need to shed fat. A further explanation is that they come from subcultures in which fat phobia is not an effective idiom of distress. Rather, rationales such as stomach bloating provide more irrefutable excuses for food refusal in their local worlds of interpersonal experience.

The importance of understanding the local meaning of dieting behaviour and clearly defining what is meant by West or Westernization is illustrated further by research in Curaçao. Initially the incidence rate of anorexia nervosa on the Caribbean island of Curaçao was reported within the lower range of rates published for Western countries [99], but the issue of how one classifies Western versus non-Western society is highly contested. In the Curaçao study, could one really consider an island riddled with fast-food chains, European labels and cruise boat tourists as non-Western?

In an effort to address this question, a new study in Curaçao was conducted that included a case–control comparison and detailing of cultural pressures. The new, not yet published, investigation highlighted the methodological problems of subcultures within cultures and a great deal of immigration and emigration within what initially appear to be culturally intact communities.

Future challenges include the exploration and definition of these key concepts.

SUMMARY

Consistent Evidence

There are many epidemiological studies on eating disorders in Western Europe and the USA that provide consistent prevalence rates. For anorexia nervosa, an average prevalence rate of 0.3% was found for young females. Prevalence rates of bulimia nervosa of 1% in young women and 0.1% in young men seem accurate. Only a minority of these persons with an eating disorder in the community enter into mental healthcare. A tentative conclusion is that the prevalence of binge eating disorder is at least 1%.

Assuming that even the studies with the most complete case-finding methods yield an underestimate of the true incidence, as state of the art we conclude that the overall incidence of anorexia nervosa is at least 8 per 100 000 population per year and the incidence of bulimia nervosa is at least 12 per 100 000 population per year. The incidence rate of anorexia nervosa has increased during the past 50 years, at least until the 1970s, particularly in females 15–24 years old. The registered incidence of bulimia nervosa has increased, but it is hard to examine trends yet, because it was included in the psychiatric classification systems only in 1980 (DSM-III).

Incomplete Evidence

Transcultural studies in the 1970s and 1980s show that anorexia nervosa was very rare in non-Western countries, but studies in the 1990s show that eating disorders do occur also in non-Western countries. The relationship between culture and eating disorders can be interpreted in three ways with varying degrees of "strength" [85,101]: a) strong—culture acts as a causative factor by providing a blueprint for anorexic behaviour; b) moderate—specific cultural factors trigger the eating disorder, which is further determined by many other factors; c) weak—culture is a context for expression of the eating disorder.

The rising rate of eating disorders in non-Western countries will pose a public health challenge to most modernizing countries in Asia, Eastern Europe, Latin America and Africa. In nearly all of these countries, specialized treatment facilities and support groups are barely available. Patients frequently have to detour round various practitioners before they receive some sort of psychological treatment. In non-Western countries many more patients with eating disorders than in Europe are not being treated.

For the purpose of aetiological model building, the mere determination of prevalence and incidence rates is not enough. Risk factor research in eating disorders is still sparse. Although more is becoming known on general and specific risk factors for the onset of an eating disorder, there is still an impressive gap. Furthermore, the developmental mechanisms of these factors are largely unknown.

Some group and individual characteristics, particularly related to dieting, have been identified tentatively as carrying with them an increased risk. One might conclude that dieting behaviour plays a role in the pathogenesis of anorexia nervosa, bulimia nervosa and BED, but only a small proportion of all dieters proceed to develop an eating disorder.

Areas Still Open to Research

Through the late 20th century, the collective fear of fatness in Western cultures was the predominantly accepted sociocultural cause for disordered eating. However, cross-cultural investigations are challenging that view. At the start of the 21st century, the rising identification of eating disorders in diverse countries has pushed the boundaries not only of the imagination but also of the disciplines.

Because only a minority of people who meet strict diagnostic criteria are seen within the mainstream (mental) health system, one area for improvement is the ascertainment of eating disorder cases across all types of healthcare.

The world of epidemiology has become more complex. No longer can we merely count eating disordered thoughts and attitudes. We have to contemplate culture, how it affects the colouring of the illness and how culture in some ways clarifies the meaning of what may be an "individual" diagnosis of a predisposed person. It is an issue whether the definition of eating disorders should be more culture-specific. Although it may seem to do justice to clinical practice, with culture-specific definitions it is almost impossible to make cross cultural comparisons on the incidence and prevalence of eating disorders. On the other hand, changes in diagnostic criteria across revisions of the prevailing classification systems pose difficulties for the comparability of epidemiological results over time.

More refinement is needed in the definition of the essence of "culture", including ethnicity, social grouping, values and attitudes. This is a debate that, in part, lies outside the work field of eating disorder researchers and practitioners. For eating disorder experts, the challenge is to go beyond the comparison of heterogeneous groups such as Blacks and Whites and low- and high-income people. It is important to find out more precisely what the sociocultural stresses are, including the political and economic forces that are involved in the development of an eating disorder and how these interact with biological predisposition and psychological vulnerability.

In the future, we hope to see not only sophisticated epidemiological studies on more specific risk factors but also a parallel examination of the nature of the association between sociocultural aspects and the development of eating disorders.

REFERENCES

1. Szmukler G.I. (1985) The epidemiology of anorexia nervosa and bulimia. *J. Psychiatr. Res.*, **19**: 143–153.
2. Fairburn C.G., Beglin S.J. (1990) Studies of the epidemiology of bulimia nervosa. *Am. J. Psychiatry*, **147**: 401–408.
3. Fombonne E. (1995) Anorexia nervosa. No evidence of an increase. *Br. J. Psychiatry*, **166**: 462–471.
4. Hsu L.K.G. (1996) Epidemiology of the eating disorders. *Psychiatr. Clin. North Am.*, **19**: 681–700.
5. Nasser M. (1997) *Culture and Weight Consciousness*. Routledge, London.
6. Nasser M., Katzman M.A., Gordon R.A. (Eds) (2001) *Eating Disorders and Cultures in Transition*. Routledge, London.
7. Hoek H.W. (1993) Review of the epidemiological studies of eating disorders. *Int. Rev. Psychiatry*, **5**: 61–74.
8. Hoek H.W. (2002) The distribution of eating disorders. In *Eating Disorders and Obesity: A Comprehensive Handbook*, 2nd ed. (Eds C.G. Fairburn, K.D. Brownell), pp. 233–237. Guilford Press, New York.
9. van Hoeken D., Lucas A.R., Hoek H.W. (1998) Epidemiology. In *Neurobiology in the Treatment of Eating Disorders* (Eds H.W. Hoek, J.L. Treasure, M.A. Katzman), pp. 97–126. Wiley, Chichester.
10. van Hoeken D., Seidell J.C., Hoek H.W. (2003) Epidemiology. In *Handbook of Eating Disorders*, 2nd ed. (Eds J.L. Treasure, U. Schmidt, C. Dare, E.F. van Furth), pp. 11–34. Wiley, Chichester.

11. Katzman M.A. (1996) Asia on my mind. Are eating disorders a problem in Hong Kong? *Eating Disorders: The Journal of Treatment and Prevention*, **4**: 378–380.

12. Katzman M.A. (1997) Getting the difference right. It is power not gender that matters. *Eur. Eat. Disord. Rev.*, **5**: 71–74.

13. Katzman M.A., Lee S. (1997) Beyond body image: the integration of feminist and transcultural theories in the understanding of self starvation. *Int. J. Eat. Disord.*, **22**: 385–394.

14. Lee S., Katzman M.A. (2002) Cross-cultural perspectives on eating disorders. In *Eating Disorders and Obesity: a Comprehensive Handbook*, 2nd ed. (Eds C.G. Fairburn, K.D. Brownell), pp. 260–293. Guilford Press, New York.

15. Nasser M., Katzman M.A. (2003) Sociocultural theories of eating disorders: an evolution in thought. In *Handbook of Eating Disorders*, 2nd ed. (Eds J.L. Treasure, U. Schmidt, C. Dare, E.F. van Furth). Wiley, Chichester (in press).

16. Williams P., Tarnopolsky A., Hand D. (1980) Case definition and case identification in psychiatric epidemiology: review and assessment. *Psychol. Med.*, **10**: 101–114.

17. American Psychiatric Association (1994) *Diagnostic and Statistical Manual of Mental Disorders*, 4th ed. American Psychiatric Association, Washington.

18. Button E.J., Whitehouse A. (1981) Subclinical anorexia nervosa. *Psychol. Med.*, **11**: 509–516.

19. Szmukler G.I. (1983) Weight and food preoccupation in a population of English schoolgirls. In *Understanding Anorexia Nervosa and Bulimia. Report of 4th Ross Conference on Medical Research* (Ed. G.I. Bargman), pp. 21–27. Ross, Columbus.

20. King M.B. (1989) Eating disorders in a general practice population. Prevalence, characteristics and follow-up at 12 to 18 months. *Psychol. Med. Monogr. Suppl.*, **14**: 1–34.

21. Meadows G.N., Palmer R.L., Newball E.U.M., Kenrick J.M.T. (1986) Eating attitudes and disorder in young women: a general practice based survey. *Psychol. Med.*, **16**: 351–357.

22. Johnson-Sabine E., Wood K., Patton G., Mann A., Wakeling A. (1988) Abnormal eating attitudes in London schoolgirls—a prospective epidemiological study: factors associated with abnormal response on screening questionnaires. *Psychol. Med.*, **18**: 615–622.

23. Rastam M., Gillberg C., Garton M. (1989) Anorexia nervosa in a Swedish urban region. A population-based study. *Br. J. Psychiatry*, **155**: 642–646.

24. Whitaker A., Johnson J., Shaffer D., Rapoport J.L., Kalikow K., Walsh B.T., Davies M., Braiman S., Dolinsky A. (1990) Uncommon troubles in young people: prevalence estimates of selected psychiatric disorders in a nonreferred adolescent population. *Arch. Gen. Psychiatry*, **47**: 487–496.

25. Whitehouse A.M., Cooper P.J., Vize C.V., Hill C., Vogel L. (1992) Prevalence of eating disorders in three Cambridge general practices: hidden and conspicuous morbidity. *Br. J. Gen. Pract.*, **42**: 57–60.

26. Rathner G., Messner K. (1993) Detection of eating disorders in a small rural town: an epidemiological study. *Psychol. Med.*, **23**: 175–184.

27. Wlodarczyk-Bisaga K., Dolan B. (1996) A two-stage epidemiological study of abnormal eating attitudes and their prospective risk factors in Polish schoolgirls. *Psychol. Med.*, **26**: 1021–1032.

28. Steinhausen H.C., Winkler C., Meier M. (1997) Eating disorders in adolescence in a Swiss epidemiological study. *Int. J. Eat. Disord.*, **22**: 147–151.

29. Nobakht M., Dezhkam M. (2000) An epidemiological study of eating disorders in Iran. *Int. J. Eat. Disord.*, **28**: 265–271.

30. Hoek H.W. (1991) The incidence and prevalence of anorexia nervosa and bulimia nervosa in primary care. *Psychol. Med.*, **21**: 455–460.

31. Lucas A.R., Beard C.M., O'Fallon W.M., Kurland L.T. (1991) 50-year trends in the incidence of anorexia nervosa in Rochester, Minn.: a population-based study. *Am. J. Psychiatry*, **148**: 917–922.

32. Lucas A.R., Crowson C.S., O'Fallon W.M., Melton L.J., III (1999) The ups and downs of anorexia nervosa. *Int. J. Eat. Disord.*, **26**: 397–405.

33. Theander S. (1970) Anorexia nervosa. A psychiatric investigation of 94 female patients. *Acta. Psychiatr. Scand.*, **214** (Suppl.): 1–194.

34. Willi J., Grossmann S. (1983) Epidemiology of anorexia nervosa in a defined region of Switzerland. *Am. J. Psychiatry*, **140**: 564–567.

35. Willi J., Giacometti G., Limacher B. (1990) Update on the epidemiology of anorexia nervosa in a defined region of Switzerland. *Am. J. Psychiatry*, **147**: 1514–1517.

36. Martz J., Milos G., Willi J. (2001) Entwicklung der Inzidenz und andere Aspekte von Anorexia Nervosa im Kanton Zürich, 1956–1995. Doctoral Dissertation, Zürich University.

37. Jones D.J., Fox M.M., Babigian H.M., Hutton H.E. (1980) Epidemiology of anorexia nervosa in Monroe County, New York: 1960–1976. *Psychosom. Med.*, **42**: 551–558.

38. Kendell R.E., Hall D.J., Hailey A., Babigian H.M. (1973) The epidemiology of anorexia nervosa. *Psychol. Med.*, **3**: 200–203.

39. Szmukler G., McCance C., McCrone L., Hunter D. (1986) Anorexia nervosa: a psychiatric case register study from Aberdeen. *Psychol. Med.*, **16**: 49–58.

40. Hoek H.W., Brook F.G. (1985) Patterns of care of anorexia nervosa. *J. Psychiatr. Res.*, **19**: 155–160.

41. Moller-Madsen S., Nystrup J. (1992) Incidence of anorexia nervosa in Denmark. *Acta Psychiatr. Scand.*, **86**: 197–200.

42. Hoek H.W., Bartelds A.I.M., Bosveld J.J.F., van der Graaf Y., Limpens V.E.L., Maiwald M., Spaaij C.J.K. (1995) Impact of urbanization on detection rates of eating disorders. *Am. J. Psychiatry*, **152**: 1272–1278.

43. Hoek H.W., van Hoeken D., Bartelds A.I.M. (2000) No increase in the incidence of anorexia nervosa and bulimia nervosa in the nineties. Presented at the Annual Meeting of the Eating Disorders Research Society, Prien am Chiemsee, 9–12 November.

44. Turnbull S., Ward A., Treasure J., Jick H., Derby L. (1996) The demand for eating disorder care. An epidemiological study using the General Practice Research Database. *Br. J. Psychiatry*, **169**: 705–712.

45. Williams P., King M. (1987) The "epidemic" of anorexia nervosa: another medical myth? *Lancet*, **i**: 205–207.

46. Theander S. (1985) Outcome and prognosis in anorexia nervosa and bulimia: some results of previous investigations, compared with those of a Swedish long-term study. *J. Psychiatr. Res.*, **19**: 493–508.

47. Sullivan P.F. (1995) Mortality in anorexia nervosa. *Am. J. Psychiatry*, **152**: 1073–1074.

48. Nielsen S. (2001) Epidemiology and mortality of eating disorders. *Psychiatr. Clin. North Am.*, **24**: 201–214.

49. Bushnell J.A., Wells J.E., Hornblow A.R., Oakley-Browne M.A., Joyce P. (1990) Prevalence of three bulimia syndromes in the general population. *Psychol. Med.*, **20**: 671–680.

50. Szabo P., Tury F. (1991) The prevalence of bulimia nervosa in a Hungarian college and secondary school population. *Psychother. Psychosom.*, **56**: 43–47.

51. Santonastaso P., Zanetti T., Sala A., Favaretto G., Vidotto G., Favaro A. (1996) Prevalence of eating disorders in Italy: a survey on a sample of 16-year-old female students. *Psychother. Psychosom.*, **65**: 158–162.

52. Garfinkel P.E., Lin E., Goering P., Spegg C., Goldbloom D.S., Kennedy S., Kaplan A.S., Woodside D.B. (1995) Bulimia nervosa in a Canadian community sample: prevalence and comparison of subgroups. *Am. J. Psychiatry*, **152**: 1052–1058.

53. World Health Organization (1992) *The ICD-10 Classification of Mental and Behavioural Disorders: Clinical Descriptions and Diagnostic Guidelines*. World Health Organization, Geneva.

54. World Health Organization (1978) *Mental Disorders: Glossary and Guide to Their Classification in Accordance with the Ninth Revision of the International Classification of Diseases*. World Health Organization, Geneva.

55. Russell G. (1979) Bulimia nervosa: an ominous variant of anorexia nervosa. *Psychol. Med.*, **9**: 429–448.

56. American Psychiatric Association (1980) *Diagnostic and Statistical Manual of Mental Disorders*, 3rd ed. American Psychiatric Association, Washington.

57. Soundy T.J., Lucas A.R., Suman V.J., Melton L.J., III (1995) Bulimia nervosa in Rochester, Minnesota from 1980 to 1990. *Psychol. Med.*, **25**: 1065–1071.

58. Pagsberg A.K., Wang A.R. (1994) Epidemiology of anorexia nervosa and bulimia nervosa in Bornholm County, Denmark, 1970–1989. *Acta Psychiatr. Scand.*, **90**: 259–265.

59. Keel P.K., Mitchell J.E. (1997) Outcome in bulimia nervosa. *Am. J. Psychiatry*, **154**: 313–321.

60. Cotrufo P., Barretta V., Monteleone P., Maj M. (1998) Full-syndrome, partial-syndrome and subclinical eating disorders: an epidemiological study of female students in Southern Italy. *Acta Psychiatr. Scand.*, **98**: 112–115.

61. Hay P. (1998) The epidemiology of eating disorder behaviors: an Australian community-based survey. *Int. J. Eat. Disord.*, **23**: 371–382.

62. Fairburn C.G., Cooper Z. (1993) The eating disorder examination. In *Binge Eating: Nature, Assessment and Treatment*, 12th ed. (Eds C.G. Fairburn, G.T. Wilson), pp. 317–360. Guilford Press, New York.

63. Striegel-Moore R.H., Wilfley D.E., Pike K.M., Dohm F.A., Fairburn C.G. (2000) Recurrent binge eating in black American women. *Arch. Fam. Med.*, **9**: 83–87.

64. Pike K.M., Dohm F.A., Striegel-Moore R.H., Wilfley D.E., Fairburn C.G. (2001) A comparison of black and white women with binge eating disorder. *Am. J. Psychiatry*, **158**: 1455–1460.

65. Patton G.C., Selzer R., Coffey C., Carlin J.B., Wolfe R. (1999) Onset of adolescent eating disorders: population based cohort study over 3 years. *Br. Med J.*, **318**: 765–768.

66. Fairburn C.G., Welch S.L., Doll H.A., Davies B.A., O'Connor M.E. (1997) Risk factors for bulimia nervosa: a community-based case-control study. *Arch. Gen. Psychiatry*, **54**: 509–517.

67. Fairburn C.G., Doll H.A., Welch S.L., Hay P.J., Davies B.A., O'Connor M.E. (1998) Risk factors for binge eating disorder: a community-based case-control study. *Arch. Gen. Psychiatry*, **55**: 425–432.

68. Fairburn C.G., Cooper Z., Doll H.A., Welch S.L. (1999) Risk factors for anorexia nervosa: three integrated case-control comparisons. *Arch. Gen. Psychiatry*, **56**: 468 476.
69. Leung F., Geller J., Katzman M.A. (1996) Issues and concerns associated with different risk models for eating disorders. *Int. J. Eat. Disord.*, **19**: 249–256.
70. Smolak L., Murnen S.K. (2002) A meta-analytic examination of the relationship between child sexual abuse and eating disorders. *Int. J. Eat. Disord.*, **31**: 136–150.
71. Wonderlich S.A., Brewerton T.D., Jocic Z., Dansky B.S., Abbott D.W. (1997) Relationship of childhood sexual abuse and eating disorders. *J. Am. Acad. Child Adolesc. Psychiatry*, **36**: 1107–1115.
72. Wonderlich S., Crosby R., Mitchell J., Thompson K., Redlin J., Demuth G., Smyth J. (2001) Pathways mediating sexual abuse and eating disturbance in children. *Int. J. Eat. Disord.*, **29**: 270–279.
73. Romans S.E., Gendall K.A., Martin J.L., Mullen P.E. (2001) Child sexual abuse and later disordered eating: a New Zealand epidemiological study. *Int. J. Eat. Disord.*, **29**: 380–392.
74. Keel P.K., Klump K.L., Leon G.R., Fulkerson J.A. (1998) Disordered eating in adolescent males from a school-based sample. *Int. J. Eat. Disord.*, **23**: 125–132.
75. Olivardia R., Pope H.G., Jr., Mangweth B., Hudson J.I. (1995) Eating disorders in college men. *Am. J. Psychiatry*, **152**: 1279–1285.
76. Woodside D.B., Garfinkel P.E., Lin E., Goering P., Kaplan A.S., Goldbloom D.S., Kennedy S.H. (2001) Comparisons of men with full or partial eating disorders, men without eating disorders and women with eating disorders in the community. *Am. J. Psychiatry*, **158**: 570–574.
77. Andersen A.E. (2002) Eating disorders in males. In *Eating Disorders and Obesity: a Comprehensive Handbook*, 2nd ed. (Eds C.G. Fairburn, K.D. Brownell), pp. 188–192. Guilford Press, New York.
78. Carlat D.J., Camargo C.A., Jr., Herzog D.B. (1997) Eating disorders in males: a report on 135 patients. *Am. J. Psychiatry*, **154**: 1127–1132.
79. Mangweth B., Pope H.G., Jr., Hudson J.I., Olivardia R., Kinzl J., Biebl W. (1997) Eating disorders in Austrian men: an intracultural and crosscultural comparison study. *Psychother. Psychosom.*, **66**: 214–221.
80. Russell C.J., Keel P.K. (2002) Homosexuality as a specific risk factor for eating disorders in men. *Int. J. Eat. Disord.*, **31**: 300–306.
81. Dohrenwend B.P., Levav I., Shrout P.E., Schwartz S., Naveh G., Link B.G., Skodol A.E., Stueve A. (1992) Socioeconomic status and psychiatric disorders: the causation-selection issue. *Science*, **255**: 946–952.
82. Gard M.C.E., Freeman C.P. (1996) The dismantling of a myth: a review of eating disorders and socioeconomic status. *Int. J. Eat. Disord.*, **20**: 1–12.
83. McClelland L., Crisp A. (2001) Anorexia nervosa and social class. *Int. J. Eat. Disord.*, **29**: 150–156.
84. Nasser M., Katzman M.A. (1999) Transcultural perspectives inform prevention. In *Preventing Eating Disorders: a Handbook of Interventions and Special Challenges* (Eds N. Piran, M. Levine, C. Steiner-Adair), pp. 26–43. Brunner Mazel, New York.
85. Vandereycken W., Hoek H.W. (1993) Are eating disorders culture-bound syndromes? In *Psychobiology and Treatment of Anorexia Nervosa and Bulimia Nervosa* (Ed. K.A. Halmi), pp. 19–36. American Psychopathological Association Series, Washington.
86. Andersen A. (1985) *Practical Comprehensive Treatment of Anorexia Nervosa and Bulimia*. Johns Hopkins Press, Maryland.

87. Buhrich N. (1981) Frequency of presentation of anorexia nervosa in Malaysia. *Aust. N. Zeal. J. Psychiatry*, **15**: 153–155.

88. Ballot N.S., Delaney N.E., Erskine P.J., Langridge P.J., Smit K., van Niekerk M.S., Winters Z.E., Wright N.C. (1981) Anorexia nervosa—a prevalence study. *S. Afr. Med. J.*, **59**: 992–993.

89. Buchan T., Gregory L.D. (1984) Anorexia nervosa in a black Zimbabwean. *Br. J. Psychiatry*, **145**: 326–330.

90. Famuyiwa O.O. (1988) Anorexia nervosa in two Nigerians. *Acta Psychiatr. Scand.*, **78**: 550–554.

91. Lee S., Chiu H.F., Chen C.N. (1989) Anorexia nervosa in Hong Kong. Why not more in Chinese? *Br. J. Psychiatry*, **154**: 683–688.

92. King M.B., Bhugra D. (1989) Eating disorders: lessons from a cross-cultural study. *Psychol. Med.*, **19**: 955–958.

93. Mumford D.B., Whitehouse A.M., Choudry I. (1992) Survey of eating disorders in English-medium schools in Lahore, Pakistan. *Int. J. Eat. Disord.*, **11**: 173–184.

94. Apter A., Abu Shah M., Iancu I., Abramovitch H., Weizman A., Tyano S. (1994) Cultural effects on eating attitudes in Israeli subpopulations and hospitalized anorectics. *Genet. Soc. Gen. Psychol. Monogr.*, **120**: 83–99.

95. Mukai T., Crago M., Shisslak C.M. (1994) Eating attitudes and weight preoccupation among female high school students in Japan. *J. Child Psychol. Psychiatry*, **35**: 677–688.

96. Bello M. (1995) Prevalence of eating disorders in a school population in Buenos Aires, Argentina. Presented at the European Council on Eating Disorders (ECED), Dublin, 21–22 September.

97. Lee A.M., Lee S. (1996) Disordered eating and its psychosocial correlates among Chinese adolescent females in Hong Kong. *Int. J. Eat. Disord.*, **20**: 177–183.

98. Szabo C.P., le Grange D. (2001) Eating disorders and the politics of identity: the South African experience. In *Eating Disorders and Cultures in Transition* (Eds M. Nasser, M. Katzman, R. Gordon), pp. 24–39. Routledge, London.

99. Hoek H.W., van Harten P.N., van Hoeken D., Susser E. (1998) Lack of relation between culture and anorexia nervosa—results of an incidence study on Curaçao. *N. Engl. J. Med.*, **338**: 1231–1232.

100. Ghazal N., Agoub M., Moussaoui D., Battas O. (2001) Prévalence de la boulimie dans une population de lycéens à Casablanca. *Encéphale*, **27**: 338–342.

101. DiNicola V.F. (1990) Anorexia multiforme: self starvation in historical and cultural context. *Transcult. Psychiatry Res. Rev.*, **27**: 165–196.

102. Lacey J.H., Dolan B.M. (1988) Bulimia in British blacks and Asians. A catchment area study. *Br. J. Psychiatry*, **152**: 73–79.

103. Mumford D.B., Whitehouse A.M. (1988) Increased prevalence of bulimia nervosa among Asian schoolgirls. *Br. Med. J.*, **297**: 718.

104. Bhadrinath B.R. (1990) Anorexia nervosa in adolescents of Asian extraction. *Br. J. Psychiatry*, **156**: 565–568.

105. Bryant-Waugh R., Lask B. (1991) Anorexia nervosa in a group of Asian children living in Britain. *Br. J. Psychiatry*, **158**: 229–233.

106. Nasser M. (1986) Comparative study of the prevalence of abnormal eating attitudes among Arab female students of both London and Cairo universities. *Psychol. Med.*, **16**: 621–625.

107. Fichter M.M., Elton M., Sourdi L., Weyerer S., Koptagel-Ilal G. (1988) Anorexia nervosa in Greek and Turkish adolescents. *Eur. Arch. Psychiatry Neurol. Sci.*, 237: 200–208.
108. Bulik C. (1987) Eating disorders in immigrants: two case reports. *Int. J. Eat. Disord.*, 6: 133–141.
109. Furnham A., Alibhai N. (1983) Cross-cultural differences in the perception of female body shapes. *Psychol. Med.*, 13: 829–837.
110. Furnham A., Adam-Saib S. (2001) Abnormal eating attitudes and behaviours and perceived parental control: a study of white British and British-Asian school girls. *Soc. Psychiatry Psychiatr. Epidemiol.*, 36: 462–470.
111. Goldblatt P.B., Moore M.E., Stunkard A.J. (1965) Social factors in obesity. *JAMA*, 192: 97–102.
112. Kope T.M., Sack W.H. (1987) Anorexia nervosa in Southeast Asian refugees: a report on three cases. *J. Am. Acad. Child Adolesc. Psychiatry*, 26: 795–797.
113. Worsley A. (1981) In the eye of the beholder: social and personal characteristics of teenagers and their impressions of themselves and fat and slim people. *Br. J. Med. Psychol.*, 54: 231–242.
114. Davis C., Katzman M.A. (1998) Chinese men and women in the United States and Hong Kong: body and self-esteem ratings as a prelude to dieting and exercise. *Int. J. Eat. Disord.*, 23: 99–102.
115. Ahmad S., Waller G., Verduyn C. (1994) Eating attitudes among Asian schoolgirls: the role of perceived parental control. *Int. J. Eat. Disord.*, 15: 91–97.
116. Lake A.J., Staiger P.K., Glowinski H. (2000) Effect of Western culture on women's attitudes to eating and perceptions of body shape. *Int. J. Eat. Disord.*, 27: 83–89.
117. McCourt J., Waller G. (1995) Developmental role of perceived parental control in the eating psychopathology of Asian and Caucasian schoolgirls. *Int. J. Eat. Disord.*, 17: 277–282.
118. Akan G.E., Grilo C.M. (1995) Sociocultural influences on eating attitudes and behaviors, body image and psychological functioning: a comparison of African-American, Asian-American and Caucasian college women. *Int. J. Eat. Disord.*, 18: 181–187.
119. Furnham A., Baguma P. (1994) Cross-cultural differences in the evaluation of male and female body shapes. *Int. J. Eat. Disord.*, 15: 81–89.
120. Andersen A., Hay A. (1985) Racial and socio economic influences in anorexia nervosa and bulimia. *Int. J. Eat. Disord.*, 4: 479–487.
121. Holden N.L., Robinson P.H. (1988) Anorexia nervosa and bulimia nervosa in British blacks. *Br. J. Psychiatry*, 152: 544–549.
122. Hsu L.K. (1987) Are eating disorders becoming more common in Blacks? *Int. J. Eat. Disord.*, 6: 113–124.
123. Pumariega A.J., Edwards P., Mitchell C.B. (1984) Anorexia nervosa in black adolescents. *J. Am. Acad. Child Adolesc. Psychiatry*, 23: 111–114.
124. Robinson P., Andersen A. (1985) Anorexia nervosa in American blacks. *J. Psychiatr. Res.*, 19: 183–188.
125. Thomas J.P., Szmukler G.I. (1985) Anorexia nervosa in patients of Afro-Caribbean extraction. *Br. J. Psychiatry*, 146: 653–656.
126. Silber T. (1986) Anorexia nervosa in Blacks and Hispanics. *Int. J. Eat. Disord.*, 5: 121–128.
127. Schwartz H. (1986) *Never Satisfied: a Cultural History of Diets, Fantasies and Fat.* Macmillan, New York.

128. Abrams K.K., Allen L.R., Gray J.J. (1993) Disordered eating attitudes and behaviors, psychological adjustment and ethnic identity: a comparison of black and white female college students. *Int. J. Eat. Disord.*, **14**: 49–57.

129. Pumariega A.J. (1986) Acculturation and eating attitudes in adolescent girls: a comparative and correlational study. *J. Am. Acad. Child Adolesc. Psychiatry*, **25**: 276–279.

130. Smith J., Krejcl J. (1991) Minorities join the majority: eating disturbances among Hispanics and native American youth. *Int. J. Eat. Disord.*, **10**: 179–186.

131. Yates A. (1989) Current perspectives on the eating disorders: I. History, psychological and biological aspects. *J. Am. Acad. Child Adolesc. Psychiatry*, **28**: 813–828.

132. Gray J., Ford K., Kelly L. (1987) The prevalence of bulimia in a black college population. *Int. J. Eat. Disord.*, **6**: 733–740.

133. Reiss D. (1996) Abnormal eating attitudes and behaviours in two ethnic groups from a female British urban population. *Psychol. Med.*, **26**: 289–299.

134. Lee S., Lee A.M., Leung T. (1998) Cross-cultural validity of the Eating Disorder Inventory: a study of Chinese patients with eating disorders in Hong Kong. *Int. J. Eat. Disord.*, **23**: 177–188.

135. Lee S., Ho T.P., Hsu L.K. (1993) Fat phobic and non-fat phobic anorexia nervosa: a comparative study of 70 Chinese patients in Hong Kong. *Psychol. Med.*, **23**: 999–1017.

136. Nakamura K., Yamamoto M., Yamazaki O., Kawashima Y., Muto K., Someya T., Sakurai K., Nozoe S. (2000) Prevalence of anorexia nervosa and bulimia nervosa in a geographically defined area in Japan. *Int. J. Eat. Disord.*, **28**: 173–180.

Commentaries

2.1
Epidemiology of Eating Disorders: Issues of Measurement
Stephen Wonderlich[1]

Over the last several decades, the eating disorders anorexia nervosa and bulimia nervosa have generated substantial empirical research and interest in terms of their epidemiology, aetiology and treatment. Sophisticated empirical studies have emerged that examine biological, psychological and cultural causal variables, course, treatment outcome and more recently prevention. However, owing to changes in diagnostic criteria, cross-cultural variability and potential time-related changes in incidence rates, the epidemiology of eating disorders has remained a complex and elusive topic. Hoek and colleagues once again have brought increased clarity to the distribution of the eating disorders in different populations over time. Particularly noteworthy are their attempts to model the time-related trends in eating disorder incidence and also a pathway from estimates of the distribution of eating disordered people in the community to similar estimates in mental health treatment settings. If accurate, the authors' model highlights the great majority of eating disordered individuals who remain out of treatment, particularly those with bulimia nervosa.

Studies of epidemiology will continue to be influenced by the fundamental measurement and classification systems used to make population-based estimates. These classification schemes, based on the *Diagnostic and Statistical Manual* (DSM) of the American Psychiatric Association and the *International Classification of Diseases* (ICD) of the World Health Organization, continue to provide the most frequently used measurement systems for anorexia nervosa and bulimia nervosa. Critical to future studies of the epidemiology of eating disorders will be advances in the measurement of these conditions. Current instruments used to assess eating disorder diagnostic criteria rest on the assumption that these disorders are indeed distinct diagnostic categories that are distinguished qualitatively from more normative behaviours. Such a categorical conceptualization of the eating disorders implies several things: a) anorexia and bulimia nervosa are truly

[1] *University of North Dakota School of Medicine and Health Sciences and Neuropsychiatric Research Institute, Fargo, North Dakota, USA*

separate from normality; b) anorexia nervosa and bulimia nervosa are indeed distinct from each other; c) subtypes of anorexia nervosa and bulimia nervosa also represent qualitatively distinct entities [1].

However, these assumptions, which underlie both DSM and ICD, remain hypotheses in need of empirical testing. In fact, recent taxometric analyses of the dimensionality versus discontinuity (i.e. taxonicity) of the eating disorder diagnoses provide some support for a categorical diagnostic scheme but also raise questions about its limitations [2,3]. These studies imply that anorexia nervosa of restricting type is unique, distinguishing itself from anorexia nervosa of binge/purge type and both subtypes of normal weight bulimia. However, the binge/purge type of anorexia nervosa appears continuous with normal weight bulimia. This interesting finding implies that restricting anorexia may represent a distinct class, but that the binge/purge type of anorexia nervosa may be categorized best as a variation of normal weight bulimia. Furthermore, the evidence to suggest that bulimia nervosa represents a discrete diagnostic entity has been stronger than the evidence suggesting that anorexia nervosa represents such a taxon.

These findings have important implications for the measurement of eating disorders, including assessments in epidemiological studies. For example, if a behavioural problem is clearly taxonic, then diagnostically oriented interviews with threshold-related cut-points and categorical assignment are appropriate. However, if a disorder appears to be non-taxonic or dimensional, measurement schemes that match the structure of the construct will need to be considered. Dimensional measurement systems may need to be incorporated into research protocols that could make allowances for artificially imposed diagnostic thresholds. Obviously, such redefinition of these diagnostic constructs and associated measures could have significant implications for the prevalence and incidence of any disorder under study.

One of the strengths of the epidemiological studies reviewed by Hoek and colleagues is the creative way in which risk factors may be identified for anorexia nervosa and bulimia nervosa. Studying the distributions of eating disorders in different populations of subjects offers clues about risk factors, which may inform the development of conceptual models of aetiology. Once again, however, these data may be limited by issues related to measurement and research designs. Two particularly important issues emerge in cross-sectional efforts to identify risk factors: a) the direction of association between the risk factor and the disease; b) possible biases associated with retrospective recall of life events or life history. Unfortunately, most risk factors for anorexia nervosa and bulimia nervosa have been studied in cross-sectional research designs with adult subjects (who already have the disease) who are asked to remember events, life experiences or history of the disease retrospectively. In such designs, it is often impossible to verify definitively if the risk factor preceded the illness or was a consequence or scar of the illness, a precondition for identifying risk factors [4]. Furthermore, in psychology, there is substantial evidence to suggest that individuals' recollections of their past may be influenced substantially by their present state [5]. Individuals who have a given psychiatric disorder may construct their histories in a manner that helps them to explain the fact that they are ill (often referred to as "effort after meaning" [6]). Also, present mood may colour an individual's recollections of the past in a manner that biases and confounds cross-sectional risk factor studies. Thus, existing research designs often make it impossible for subjects to describe their history in a reliable manner, because the presence of the disease may influence their memory regarding a given risk factor. As Hoek and colleagues point out, prospective longitudinal designs with subjects who do not display the disease at index assessment are critical for the identification of risk factors.

In summary, epidemiological studies are critical both for assessment of the magnitude of an illness in a given population and for the identification of risk factors associated with the variation in distribution of the disease itself. Yet, as in all behavioural science, these studies rest on sound measurement systems that carefully model the constructs of interest. As we continue to refine the nature and measurement of our psychopathological entities, epidemiological studies similarly will be enhanced.

REFERENCES

1. Gleaves D.H., Lowe M.R., Green B.A., Cororve M.B., Williams T.L. (2000) Do anorexia and bulimia nervosa occur on a continuum? *Behav. Ther.*, **31**: 195–219.
2. Williamson D.A., Womble L.G., Smeets M., Netemeyer R.G., Thaw J.M., Kutlesic V., Gleaves D.H. (2002) Latent structure of eating disorder symptoms: a factor analytic and taxometric investigation. *Am. J. Psychiatry*, **159**: 412–418.
3. Gleaves D.H., Lowe M.R., Snow A.C., Green B.A., Murphy-Eberenz K.P. (2000) Continuity and discontinuity models of bulimia nervosa: a taxometric investigation. *J. Abnorm. Psychol.*, **109**: 56–68.
4. Kraemer H.C., Kazdin A.E., Offord D.R., Kessler R.C., Jensen P.S., Kupfer D.J. (1997) Coming to terms with the terms of risk. *Arch. Gen. Psychiatry*, **54**: 337–343.
5. Stone A.A., Shiffman S. (1994) Ecological Momentary Assessment (EMA) in behavioral medicine. *Ann. Behav. Med.*, **16**: 199–202.
6. Pope H.G., Hudson J.I. (1992) Is childhood sexual abuse a risk factor for bulimia nervosa? *Am. J. Psychiatry*, **129**: 455–463.

2.2
Problems in the Identification of Rare Disorders in a Transcultural Frame
Hans-Christoph Steinhausen[1]

Counter to the expectations of the lay public and frequent media reports, the prevalence of eating disorders or, more specifically, anorexia nervosa is relatively low, as shown in the extensive review by Hoek *et al.* Findings from our own epidemiological study of a large sample of adolescents aged 14–17 years in Switzerland provide a hint as to why the lay public might mistake and exaggerate the frequency of eating disorders [1]. From these findings it is clear that it is not the full-blown eating disorders that are frequent in young females, but rather only individual symptoms that form a part of the eating disorder spectrum. Thus, 10% of the sample showed dieting and even 14% displayed fear of fatness. However, when looking at the cumulation of the various symptoms, almost 80% of the girls and 96% of the boys fulfilled only one or two risk criteria. As found in other studies in different parts of the world, dieting is frequent in school populations and a benign practice in the majority of girls [2]. However, extreme dieting is associated with psychiatric morbidity and may be lying on a spectrum with clinical eating disorders [3]. Furthermore, eating disorders at a partial level are more common in adolescent females, and for the most part are brief and self-limiting [4].

Our own epidemiological study followed the most widely accepted procedure for case identification. In a two-stage approach, the population was screened first by use of a questionnaire in order to identify the at-risk population, and then cases were identified with subsequent interviews. Among the various methodological problems, sensitivity and specificity of the screening instrument are of major concern. Various instruments are available and used also for assessment purposes in clinical practice. Internationally, the most widely used questionnaires of this kind are the Eating Attitudes Test (EAT) [5] and the Eating Disorders Inventory (EDI) [6]. Their use in epidemiological research rests on the assumption that one may validly discriminate between cases and controls by the use of sensitive cutoff scores.

Various studies, including our own, however, did not reveal sufficient evidence that these clinically meaningful and informative instruments may also serve epidemiological purposes in terms of discriminant validity. This conclusion had to be delineated from various transcultural applications of the EAT and the EDI. Whereas the EAT total score showed excellent discriminant validity in four Bulgarian clinical and non-clinical samples, this applied only to four out of eight subscales of the EDI [7]. In another

[1] *Department of Child and Adolescent Psychiatry, University of Zürich, CH-8032 Zürich, Switzerland*

series of validation studies, we showed that North American findings are not transferable or descriptive of Middle European findings. When using the EAT and the EDI in East and West Berlin samples at a time when Germany was still a divided country, the scores were lower than in North America and there was evidence of insufficient discriminant validity for both the EAT and the EDI [8–10].

Similar observations have been made in other parts of the world and they not only called into question the validity of various questionnaires based on the dimensional model of psychopathology but also the issue of transcultural applicability. As Hoek *et al.* illustrate, there is an increasing awareness of eating disorders in the recent past in non-Western countries as well, and at the same time the cross-cultural validity of epidemiological research is hampered by insufficient instruments. The authors' conclusion of a lack of contextual validity in a non-Western setting matches our claim that both the denotative and connotative meanings of questionnaire items are to be conveyed, and that the values, anchors and graduations of the items must be adapted to the attitudes and habits of the different cultural groups [7]. With better prerequisites of this kind, instruments may be developed that may serve as culturally sensitive and economic screening devices for epidemiological assessment of eating disorders in various cultures.

REFERENCES

1. Steinhausen H.-C., Winkler C, Meier M. (1997) Eating disorders in adolescence in a Swiss epidemiological study. *Int. J. Eat. Disord.*, 22: 147–151.
2. Patton G.C., Johnson-Sabine E., Wood K., Mann A.H., Wakeling A. (1990) Abnormal eating attitudes in London schoolgirls. A prospective epidemiological study: outcome at twelve months. *Psychol. Med.*, 20: 382–394.
3. Patton G.C., Carlin J.B., Shao Q., Hibbert M.E., Rosier M., Selzer R., Bowes G. (1997) Adolescent dieting: healthy weight control or borderline eating disorder? *J. Child Psychol. Psychiatry*, 38: 299–306.
4. Patton G.C., Coffey C., Sawyer S.M. (2003) The outcome of adolescent eating disorder: findings from the Victorian adolescent health cohort study. *Eur. Child Adolesc. Psychiatry* (in press).
5. Garner D.M., Garfinkel P.E. (1979) The eating attitude test: an index of the symptoms of anorexia nervosa. *Psychol. Med.*, 9: 273–279.
6. Garner D.M., Omsted M.P., Polivy J. (1983) Development and validation of a multidimensional eating disorder inventory for anorexia and bulimia. *Int. J. Eat. Disord.*, 2: 15–34.
7. Boyadjieva S., Steinhausen H.-C. (1996). The Eating Attitudes Test and the Eating Disorders Inventory in four Bulgarian clinical and nonclinical samples. *Int J. Eat. Disord.*, 19: 93–98.
8. Neumärker U., Dudeck U., Vollrath M., Neumärker K.J., Steinhausen H.-C. (1992) Eating attitudes among adolescent patients and normal school girls in

East Berlin and West Berlin. A transcultural comparison. *Int. J. Eat. Disord.*, **12**: 281–289.

9. Steinhausen H.-C., Neumärker K.-J., Vollrath M., Dudeck U., Neumärker U. (1992) A transcultural comparison of the Eating Disorder Inventory in former East and West Berlin. *Int. J. Eat. Disord.*, **12**: 407–416.

10. Steinhausen H.-C. (1984) Transcultural comparison of eating attitudes in young females and anorectic patients. *Eur. Arch. Psychiatry Neurol. Sci.*, **234**: 198–201.

2.3

The Meaning of Numbers

L.K. George Hsu[1]

The comprehensive and timely review of the epidemiology of eating disorders by Hoek *et al.* provides a thorough description of the occurrence of the disorders, admirably fulfilling the first of the purposes of epidemiological studies. They have also made shrewd observations on the risk factors to the extent allowed by the numbers, thereby fulfilling the second purpose of these studies. Can the numbers also inform us of the meaning of these intriguing disorders and allow us to at least speculate on the issue of pathogenesis?

Anorexia nervosa and bulimia nervosa, already among the most common illnesses to affect young women in the West, are evidently becoming more common in many parts of Asia. A sizeable minority of non-Western cases of anorexia nervosa demonstrate non-fat phobic attitudes. On the other hand, almost all non-Western cases of bulimia nervosa demonstrate fat phobia. This difference in the prevalence of fat phobia suggests that although both anorexia and bulimia nervosa have a component of self-starvation, the meaning and purpose of this self-starvation may be different among some members of these two diagnostic categories. It seems safe to observe that many anorexics and most if not all bulimics restrict their dietary intake to control or lose weight, whereas a sizeable minority of patients with anorexia nervosa do so to fulfil other motives, such as a quest for self-control or asceticism. This observation is supported by some of the risk factor studies: bulimics show weight/shape/diet vulnerability factors, whereas anorexics demonstrate self-deficit factors. Ultimately, both anorexia and bulimia nervosa choose self-starvation as the answer to their deficits. As such, binge eating disorder (BED) cannot comfortably be put in the same category as anorexia and bulimia nervosa, because BED is characterized by a desire for overeating and not by a desire for self-starvation.

[1] *Department of Psychiatry, Tufts University School of Medicine, New England Medical Center, 750 Washington Street, Boston, MA 02111, USA*

This observation is challenged by the fact that only a minority of dieters develop anorexia or bulimia nervosa. The risk, however, of developing anorexia or bulimia nervosa is still much higher among dieters than non-dieters. If dieting had not become so popular, one might speculate that anorexia and bulimia nervosa would have remained exceedingly rare. Also, the demarcation between full-syndrome anorexia or bulimia nervosa and their partial-syndrome counterparts is arbitrary and defined by diagnostic working parties. Partial-syndrome bulimia nervosa may carry an ominous prognosis, as indeed may partial-syndrome anorexia nervosa. The fact that benign and almost ubiquitous dieting behaviour merge imperceptibly into subsyndromal disorders should not be disregarded by researchers or clinicians. Points of discontinuity between normal eating behaviour and pathological attitudes and clinical syndromes do not exist unless imposed by diagnostic criteria.

This dimensional perspective may well be supported by the understanding that the pathogenesis of anorexia and bulimia nervosa occurs from an interplay of genes, environmental factors and epigenetic mechanisms. Scientific breakthroughs are rare and we might expect that geneticists will take some time to work out the complex mechanisms involved. In the meantime, epidemiologists may focus on the subsyndromes of the eating disorders and determine their relationship to the full syndromes on the one hand and normal eating behaviour on the other.

What of culture? If a 21st century pre-anorexic (i.e. genetically pre-disposed) young woman is attracted to the world of ballet, is this analogous to a 13th century pre-anorexic attracted to the world of religious asceticism? If so, the challenge to researchers lies not so much in the task of discerning the meaning of dieting in different environments or cultures, but in understanding how the genes or epigenetic mechanisms drive the individual to find fulfilment in self-starvation in that particular culture or environment.

2.4

Eating Pathology—A Continuum of Behaviours?

Adam Drewnowski[1]

Psychiatric epidemiology of eating disorders addresses such key issues as their classification and occurrence, causal risk factors and associated

[1] *School of Public Health and Community Medicine, University of Washington, Seattle, WA 98195, USA*

comorbidities. Limiting their review to anorexia and bulimia nervosa and to record- and interview-based studies, Hoek *et al.* provide a compelling integrative summary of some key work in this area. One question that is asked is whether rising rates of eating disorders among young women are linked to changing societal and cultural attitudes toward body weight.

The estimated prevalence of anorexia nervosa among young women is 0.3%. The generally accepted prevalence rate for bulimia nervosa in this high-risk group is around 1%. Incidence rates refer to new cases per 100 000 population per year. The incidence of bulimia nervosa among 20–24-year-old females, the highest-risk group, is estimated at 82 new cases per 100 000 women per year.

If prevalence rates are to remain stable, new incident cases must be balanced by cases that no longer meet strict diagnostic criteria for bulimia nervosa. From the standpoint of prevention and public health, it is important to know if the new cases have a history of clinical or subclinical eating disorders. A related question is whether former cases that no longer meet DSM diagnostic criteria can be considered as fully recovered, or whether they will re-enter the diagnosis some time later. The authors correctly point out that the heterogeneity of eating disorders not otherwise specified (EDNOS) makes their evaluation difficult. Reliable epidemiological data on partial, subclinical or subthreshold eating disorders are very limited indeed.

One study of 1367 college women combined survey screening and personal interviews in a two-stage design [1]. Participants were assigned to six categories by the severity of eating pathology, established using the Dieting and Bingeing Severity Scale (DBSS). The categories were: non-dieters (9%), casual dieters (26%), moderate dieters (23%), intense dieters (21%), at-risk dieters (19%) and probable bulimia nervosa (2%). Random stratified sampling procedures then were used to select a subset of women ($n = 306$) from each DBSS category for structured clinical interviews. The psychiatric diagnosis was based on DSM-III-R criteria. Women in the three top categories by DBSS were significantly more likely to have bulimia nervosa and subthreshold eating disorders (EDNOS) than those not at risk. Longitudinal studies [2] suggest that incident cases of bulimia nervosa arise largely from the EDNOS population. Conversely, cases that no longer meet stringent diagnostic criteria still engage in bulimic behaviours and may remain at risk for a prolonged period of time [2]. Arguably, eating disorders represent an extreme of a continuum of pathological eating behaviours [1,2].

Patients with eating disorders are known to exhibit other psychopathologies. In particular, links between bulimia nervosa, alcoholism and substance abuse have been established in clinical studies. A survey study of 1796 college women focused on the relationship between subclinical eating disorders and relative rates of alcohol, tobacco and substance use [3]. The women were stratified by the degree of eating pathology, again using the DBSS. Increasing dieting severity was associated with higher prevalence of alcohol and tobacco use, marijuana use and with increasing frequency and intensity of alcohol use. The relationship extended in a continuous and graded manner to subclinical levels of dieting and substance use behaviours [3]. However, no causality could be assigned, because the study was a cross-sectional survey rather than a prospective follow-up investigation.

The authors note that very few prospective follow-up studies on eating disorders are available in the literature. None have followed a two-stage identification procedure or dealt with the population at large. Although the traditional view had linked anorexia nervosa with higher socio-economic status, Hoek et al. note that this may have been a consequence of social selection and physician referral as opposed to causal pathology. The picture that emerges for bulimia nervosa is different altogether. Studies suggest that bulimia nervosa may be associated with urbanization, lower socio-economic group, predisposition to overweight and history of past dieting. In other words, bulimia nervosa appears to follow the same demographic trends as obesity and overweight.

Obesity rates are increasing in Western and non-Western societies alike. Among recognized risk factors for obesity in Western societies are lower socio-economic status, membership in minority groups and the high energy density of the diet. Among postulated risk factors in the developing world are nutrition transition, urbanization and—reportedly—the increasing energy density of the diet. Given that the binge-eating syndrome provides a link between obesity and bulimia nervosa, exploring the epidemiology of binge eating remains a future challenge of population-based research.

REFERENCES

1. Kurth C., Krahn D.D., Nairn K., Drewnowski A. (1995) The severity of dieting and bingeing behaviors in college women: interview validation of survey data. *J. Psychiatr. Res.*, **29**: 211–225.
2. Drewnowski A., Yee D.K., Krahn D.D. (1988) Bulimia in college women: incidence and recovery rates. *Am. J. Psychiatry*, **145**: 753–755.
3. Krahn D., Kurth C., Demitrack M., Drewnowski A. (1992) The relationship of dieting severity and bulimic behaviors to alcohol and other drug use in young women. *J. Subst. Abuse*, **4**: 341–353.

2.5

Culture as a Defining Aspect of the Epidemiology and Aetiology of
Eating Disorders

D. Blake Woodside[1]

A thorough understanding of the epidemiology of anorexia nervosa and
bulimia nervosa is critical for those attempting to understand the aetiology
of the illnesses and plan for treatment. Well-documented secular trends in
the incidence of these disorders [1–3] highlight the importance of the effects
of culture.

Recent advances in our understanding of the genetic basis of both
illnesses [4] will drive us to re-think how we define the very nature of the
conditions. Clearly complex multifactorial conditions, both anorexia
nervosa and bulimia nervosa occur as a result of interactions between
genetic, environmental and individual temperamental influences, some of
which may be heritable themselves. In this respect, the culture in which an
individual is raised and lives constitutes a major part of his or her
environment and, if this is so, it would be important to try to tease apart
those elements of anorexia and bulimia that are actually culture
independent and those that are specific to a given cultural environment.
Such a distinction would permit not only a more targeted approach to
genetic investigation but also would allow for more sophistication in the
development of preventive strategies targeted towards identified environmental and cultural variables. In this regard, recent advances in
understanding the genetic basis of anorexia nervosa make an understanding of culture even more important than previously.

An excellent start to this endeavour has been provided by the work of Lee
et al. in Hong Kong [5,6]. Demonstrating the existence of two subtypes of
anorexia nervosa side by side, Lee et al. argue convincingly that the core
elements of anorexia nervosa include deliberate food avoidance and the
achievement of a low weight. With this way of looking at the illness,
the rationale for food avoidance is an artefact of the culture in which the
individual lives, and is thus relevant only in the context of that specific
culture. His arguments mirror the occasional report in Western society of
individuals with "ascetic" anorexia nervosa: food avoidant, very thin
individuals who lack a body image distortion or a drive for thinness.

Our clinical experience in Toronto supports this view. In addition to Lee's
description of "Chinese" anorexia, we also see individuals from the
subcontinent of India who typically present with somatic concerns as their
rationale for not eating. For example, such an individual may endorse

_____

[1] Inpatient Eating Disorders Program, Toronto General Hospital, Toronto, Canada

abdominal pain or constipation as the reason why he or she is not eating. When placed in a group treatment programme for "Western" anorexia, such individuals often acculturate, i.e. go on to develop a body image distortion and a fear of fatness that replaces their earlier concerns. For individuals who do not acculturate, our clinical team must develop a culture-specific "language" to assist them in understanding their experience. For example, whereas we might re-frame a "feeling" of "fatness" as a response to an upsetting event for a "Western" anorexic, for a woman from India with nausea as the presenting symptom we would need to develop evidence that her level of nausea varied with her apparent level of emotional distress.

Re-defining the culture-independent aspects of anorexia and bulimia nervosa would most likely result in a larger number of individuals being diagnosed with the illnesses, both in Western and non-Western countries. Such a move would not diminish the importance of understanding cultural influences on eating disorders because treatments must be developed in a fashion that is culture sensitive.

Such a change would have very important effects on the study of epidemiology, especially as cultural influences change gradually over time. One might hypothesize that new forms of the illnesses would present themselves, and this would have to be taken into account by those studying the occurrence of the conditions.

Efforts that are currently underway to understand the genetic basis of eating disorders will also assist in identifying cultural variables, because, once genetics can be controlled for, then other influences can be examined more specifically. Elucidating the precise nature of non-genetic factors is especially important given that heritable genetic factors are less likely to be amenable to intervention, and environmental influences may be susceptible to external manipulations.

REFERENCES

1. Lucas A.R., Beard C.M., O'Fallon W.M., Kurland L.T. (1991) 50-year trends in the incidence of anorexia nervosa in Rochester, Minn.: a population-based study. *Am. J. Psychiatry*, **148**: 917–922.
2. Garfinkel P.E., Lin E., Goering P., Spegg C., Goldbloom D., Kennedy S., Kaplan A., Woodside D.B. (1995) Bulimia nervosa in a Canadian community sample. *Am. J. Psychiatry*, **152**: 1052–1058.
3. Garfinkel P.E., Lin E., Goering P., Spegg C., Goldbloom D., Kennedy S., Kaplan A., Woodside D.B. (1996) Is amenorrhoea necessary for the diagnosis of anorexia nervosa? *Br. J. Psychiatry*, **168**: 500–506.
4. Grice D.E., Halmi K.A., Fichter M.M., Strober M., Woodside D.B., Treasure J.T., Kaplan A.S., Magistretti P.J., Goldman D., Kaye W.H., *et al.* (2002) Evidence for a

susceptibility gene for restricting anorexia nervosa on chromosome 1. *Am. J. Hum. Genet.*, **70**: 787–792.

5.   Lee S., Ho T.P., Hsu L.K. (1993) Fat phobic and non-fat phobic anorexia nervosa: a comparative study of 70 Chinese patients in Hong Kong. *Psychol. Med.*, **23**: 999–1017.

6.   Lee S., Katzman M.A. (2002) Cross-cultural perspectives on eating disorders. In *Eating Disorders and Obesity: a Comprehensive Handbook*, 2nd ed. (Eds C.G. Fairburn, K.D. Brownell), pp. 260–293. Guilford Press, New York.

2.6

Unpackaging "Cultures" in Eating Disorders

Sing Lee[1]

Eating disorders are probably the most difficult of all mental disorders to study epidemiologically. This is because of the problems of low base rate, the patients' tendency towards denial or concealment, the variability of core symptoms and the arbitrariness of defining what abnormality is in a given population. The validity of register-based studies is limited by the fact that the help-seeking pattern of subjects with eating disorders is greatly affected by the degree of public awareness of eating disorders, the ego-syntonic nature of these disorders, the emergence of milder forms of eating disorders over time, the professional broadening of diagnostic criteria and the availability of user-friendly services. The latter matters because, in most parts of the world, subjects with eating disorders are being treated in stigmatizing general psychiatric settings that are dominated by acute and chronic psychotic patients. These do not attract eating disordered adolescents and young adults at all. The establishment of specialist treatment centres typically leads to sudden increases in the clinical prevalence of eating disorders.

A less obvious reason why epidemiological work is hampered is the lack of funding for quality studies in many societies. Unlike psychotic or mood disorders, eating disorders are, on the whole, more amenable to psychological interventions than pharmacotherapy. This applies especially to anorexia nervosa. Consequently, commercial sources of support for research and academic meetings are much more difficult to obtain. At major "international" conferences on eating disorders, for example, participants from the developing countries are often hard to find.

Because eating disorders are no longer confined to the developed West, the issue of cultural sensitivity of research instruments requires close

[1] *Department of Psychiatry, Chinese University of Hong Kong, Shatin, Hong Kong*

examination. A logical view is to argue that because cultural values pertaining to eating, body image and social roles of women vary across "Western" and "non-Western" societies, instruments developed in the former lack validity in the latter. Indeed, an accumulating amount of evidence from non-Western communities has demonstrated that the contemporary emphasis on the primacy of "fat phobia" in the aetiological and diagnostic configuration of anorexia nervosa constitutes what Kleinman [1] called a "category fallacy", at least among a portion of subjects with anorexia nervosa [2]. Consequently, to apply standard Western tools of case finding to widely divergent cultural settings may be to realize a self-fulfilling prophecy that the disorder is non-existent or extremely rare there. Moreover, "atypical" cases that may shed light on the aetiology of eating disorders in general will be excluded systematically.

The Western vs. non-Western conceptual frame also oversimplifies the issue of the validity of research instruments in anorexia nervosa. Experienced clinicians have long indicated that even anorexic patients in "Western" communities may not exhibit the intense fear of fatness that forms the basic construct for such commonly used instruments as the Eating Attitudes Test (EAT) [3]. For example, Bruch [4] discussed a distinction between primary and atypical anorexia in the USA. The former group of patients all exhibited the "relentless pursuit of thinness", whereas the latter patients represented a heterogeneous group of food refusers with "various symbolic misinterpretations of the eating function". She rightly suggested that attributions regarding weight and shape among anorexic subjects were not static, but varied with chronicity of illness, age, degree of weight loss and contextual factors. In this connection, a recent study in Hong Kong has shown that the EAT-26 had dubious validity in atypical as well as a proportion of typical anorexia nervosa cases [5]. Although the EAT-26 does measure the collective fear of fatness and the attendant weight control behaviours, using it in the conventional manner would lead to an underestimate of the number of "cases" of anorexia nervosa in community surveys.

Recent efforts to study culture and eating disorders have been hampered by the lack of a suitable instrument to unpackage and measure "culture". This is not surprising, because the latter is a pluralistic, time-dependent and often slippery construct. In addition to epidemiological issues, there are many other connections between "cultures" and eating disorders, as a result of which perhaps no one standard instrument for measuring culture will ever exist. The following are but some of these complex connections:

• Culture may shape the phenomenology (e.g. fat phobia) and course (e.g. emergence of bulimia) of eating disorders.

- Cultural values can influence the decoding of symptoms (e.g. emaciation) that may appear to be superficially similar.
- Historical and sociopolitical factors govern how the same constellation of symptoms is organized into different ethnopsychiatric syndromes (e.g. "apepsia hysterica" vs. DSM-IV anorexia nervosa) in different localities and is responded to dissimilarly in different cultural contexts.
- Inasmuch as the patient and the practitioner exercise considerable agency in the clinical encounter, their cultural and personal background (e.g. gender, ethnicity) may affect diagnosis and treatment in ways that have bearing on outcome.
- Finally, there is the political economy of psychiatric epistemology, i.e. how interests and strategies that are embedded in a confluence of powerful political and economic forces (e.g. the hegemony of the DSM discourse) often unnoticeably shape psychiatric practice, research and the course of an illness itself [2,6].

To get at the deeper relationships between cultures and eating disorders, a cross-disciplinary research approach, including ethnography, will be a useful first step.

REFERENCES

1. Kleinman A. (1988) *Rethinking Psychiatry: From Cultural Category to Personal Experience.* Free Press, New York.
2. Lee S. (2001) Fat phobia in anorexia nervosa: whose obsession is it? In *Eating Disorders and Cultures in Transition* (Eds M. Nasser, M. Katzman, R. Gordon), pp. 40–54. Routledge, London.
3. Garner D.M. Garfinkel P.E. (1979) The Eating Attitudes Test: an index of the symptoms of anorexia nervosa. *Psychol. Med.*, 9: 273–279.
4. Bruch H. (1973) *Eating Disorders: Obesity, Anorexia Nervosa, and the Person Within.* Basic Books, New York.
5. Lee S., Kwok K., Liau C., Leung T. (2002) Screening Chinese patients with eating disorders using the Eating Attitudes Test in Hong Kong. *Int. J. Eat. Disord.*, 32: 91–97.
6. Lee S. (1999) Diagnosis postponed: shenjing shuairuo and the transformation of psychiatry in post-Mao China. *Culture Med. Psychiatry*, 23: 349–380.

2.7
Eating Disorders in Infancy: Epidemiology and Cultural Aspects
Sam Tyano and Miri Keren[1]

Hoek *et al.* provide us with quite an impressive overview of the epidemiological and cultural aspects of eating disorders from adolescence to adulthood. We would like to focus here on the relatively recent topic of eating disorders in infancy, especially from the aspect of continuity versus discontinuity. Feeding disorders, failure to thrive (FTT) and obesity are common problems of infancy. Feeding disorders affect up to 25% of normally developed infants and up to 35% of those with developmental handicaps [1]. Although FTT and feeding disorders may coexist, the frequency of association has not been firmly determined and studies on feeding disorders have been limited by serious methodological problems, such as inconsistent definitions and determination of the presence and severity of feeding problems often based on parental report only.

Relating to the psychopathology of early eating problems, Chatoor *et al.* [2] suggested looking at the clinical entity of non-organic FTT within a developmental perspective. More specifically, they proposed studying at what stage of the first year of development the feeding disorder starts: during the homeostasis stage or physiological regulation (0–3 months), the attachment phase (2–7 months) or during the somatopsychological differentiation phase (6–36 months). As infants progress through these developmental stages, they master phase-appropriate feeding skills required for their progression from reflex sucking to autonomous feeding. This approach puts great emphasis on the quality of the feeding interaction (as opposed to the focus on caloric intake and growth curves as the sole criteria for feeding problems), as reflected in the level of dyadic reciprocity, parental responsiveness and contingency, positive verbal and non-verbal communication, absence of dyadic conflict and "bargaining" interactions and absence of distorted eating behaviours. Chatoor [3] proposed the name "infantile anorexia nervosa" for the feeding disorder of infancy that starts around the phase of somatopsychological differentiation, because the food refusal and the underlying attempt of the infant to achieve autonomy and control with regard to the mother reminds the dynamics of anorexic older children. The infant's temperament and the parent's conflicts over control, autonomy and dependency appear to contribute to this subtype of eating disorder. Diagnosing infantile anorexia has been shown as possible, with high reliability, by child psychiatrists using a Feeding Scale as a diagnostic tool [4].

---

[1] Geha Mental Health Center, Tel-Aviv University Sackler School of Medicine, Israel

Bulimia nervosa in infancy and early childhood is hardly mentioned in the literature, although in our personal clinical experience this entity does exist and is often a significant symptom of a disordered early mother–child relationship. A possible explanation for the scarcity of reports is the fact that overfeeding/overeating is often not considered problematic by the parents or the paediatrician (except when it reaches obesity). The difficulty in identifying bulimia nervosa in adolescence and early adulthood is therefore even more pronounced in early childhood.

Relating to the basic question of continuity versus discontinuity of eating disorders over time, a few but important longitudinal studies have to be mentioned. For instance, a 10-year follow-up of maladaptive eating patterns beginning at ages 1–10 months showed significant stability [5]. A four-year longitudinal study of infants aged 3 to 12 months [6] with early refusal to eat showed a risk of later problems with their eating patterns and behaviour. A recently published 17-year follow-up of some 800 children between the ages of 1 to 10 years and their mothers revealed that risk factors for later development of eating disorders include eating conflicts, struggles with food and unpleasant meals in early childhood. The presence of eating problems in early childhood or an eating disorder in adolescence conferred a strong risk for an eating disorder in young adulthood [7]. The authors recommend making the distinction between eating disorder diagnoses and eating disorder symptoms.

These few but methodologically well-founded longitudinal studies suggest that parent–child conflictual feeding interactions as soon as the first year of life are a risk factor for later eating problems, suggesting at least some continuity in the psychopathology of eating disorders from infancy to late adolescence. Still, we need more longitudinal studies of this kind, with further sophistication of feeding interaction observation tools and diagnostic criteria for eating problems versus eating disorders, in order to generalize these findings.

Finally, to the best of our knowledge, there has not been any published cross-cultural study of eating problems/disorders in infancy and early childhood. In our own clinical experience, in the context of a community-based infant mental health clinic, we do see specific cultural beliefs about ways of feeding very young children; for instance, immigrant families from Russia often have quite a strict pattern of parenting in general and especially around feeding; coerciveness is not viewed as a maladaptive parental behaviour, and forced feeding is very common from one generation to the next.

REFERENCES

1. Lindberg L., Bohlin G., Hagekull B. (1991) Early feeding problems in a normal population. *Int. J. Eat. Disord.*, **10**: 395–405.

2. Chatoor I., Schaefer S., Dickson L., Egan J. (1984) Non-organic failure to thrive: a developmental perspective. *Pediatr. Ann.*, **13**: 829–835, 838, 840–842.
3. Chatoor I. (1989) Infantile anorexia: a developmental disorder of separation and individuation. *J. Am. Acad. Psychoanal.*, **17**: 43–64.
4. Chatoor I., Hirsch R., Ganiban J., Persinger M., Hamburger E. (1998) Diagnosing infantile anorexia: the observation of mother–infant interactions. *J. Am. Acad. Child Adolesc. Psychiatry*, **37**: 959–967.
5. Marchi M., Cohen P. (1990) Early childhood eating behaviors and adolescent eating disorders. *J. Am. Acad. Child Adolesc. Psychiatry*, **29**: 112–117.
6. Dahl M., Sundelin C. (1992) Feeding problems in an affluent society. Follow-up at four years of age in children with early refusal to eat. *Acta Paediatr.*, **81**: 575–579.
7. Kotler L.A., Cohen P., Davies M., Pine D.S., Walsh B.T. (2001) Longitudinal relationships between childhood, adolescent, and adult eating disorders. *J. Am. Acad. Child Adolesc. Psychiatry*, **10**: 1434–1440.

2.8
Treatment Referral and Atypical Eating Disorders: New Directions for Future Research

Paolo Santonastaso[1]

Interest in epidemiological studies has increased along with the growing awareness that clinical samples represent only a minority of all the subjects with eating disorders present in the community. As Hoek *et al.* point out in their review, the pathway to the care of eating disorders is an important issue. Based on data collected in The Netherlands in primary care, they estimated that only about one-third of patients with anorexia nervosa and 6% of patients with bulimia nervosa are seen in mental healthcare facilities.

In a prevalence general population study in Padova (Italy), we gathered more data about this topic [1]. We interviewed 934 female subjects aged 18–24 years, using the Structured Interview for DSM-IV. The lifetime prevalence of anorexia nervosa was 2%, and 53% of subjects with this diagnosis had received some form of treatment, which was of psychological or psychiatric nature in 32% of the cases. The lifetime prevalence of bulimia nervosa was 4.6%, and 30% of subjects with this diagnosis had received some form of treatment, but only six (14%) had been referred for psychological or psychiatric treatment. Thus, our data tend to confirm the estimates of Hoek *et al.* Future epidemiological research should pay particular attention to the factors that influence treatment referral and those that affect the outcome of eating disorders in the absence of a specific treatment.

[1] *Department of Neurology and Psychiatry, University of Padova, Italy*

Few studies to date have examined the prevalence of atypical eating disorders. However, there is a widespread conviction that they represent the majority of eating disorders. Furthermore, little is known about the natural history of these disorders and the rate at which they shift towards full-syndrome eating disorders. In the light of the findings of the study mentioned above [1], I would like to make some considerations on this category of eating disorders.

Generally, those subjects who display all the symptoms of a full eating disorder syndrome but do not reach the required weight threshold in anorexia nervosa or the required frequency of binge eating episodes in bulimia nervosa are defined as having a subthreshold eating disorder [2]. On the other hand, subjects who do not fulfil one of the diagnostic criteria (e.g. subjects with anorexia nervosa without amenorrhoea or subjects with bulimia nervosa without objective binges or compensatory behaviour) are considered to have a partial eating disorder. The general population study by Garfinkel et al. [3] has suggested that partial anorexia nervosa (i.e. anorexia nervosa in subjects who do not fulfil the criterion of amenorrhoea) does not differ from full anorexia nervosa with regard to weight loss, history of sexual abuse, comorbidity rates and family psychiatric history. Similarly, they have demonstrated [4] that subjects who fulfil all the criteria of bulimia nervosa except for a binge eating frequency of once a week do not differ from subjects with full bulimia nervosa. This finding concerning bulimia nervosa was also confirmed from a genetic–epidemiological point of view by Sullivan et al. using a large sample of twins [5].

Our study [1] revealed that, using strict diagnostic criteria that included a minimum duration of the symptoms of at least 3 months, atypical eating disorders do not seem to be significantly more frequent than full eating disorders. The lifetime prevalence of atypical anorexia nervosa was 2.6%, that of atypical bulimia nervosa was 3.1% and that of binge eating disorder was 0.6%. The study revealed that atypical eating disorders, like full eating disorders in the same sample, are significantly associated with physical abuse, a lifetime overweight condition and the use of hypocaloric diets. Atypical anorexia nervosa, rather than full anorexia nervosa, is the most frequent diagnosis that predates the onset of bulimia nervosa: in our sample, two-thirds of subjects with subthreshold anorexia nervosa went on to develop bulimia nervosa. Finally, there are cases of spontaneous remission in both full and atypical eating disorders. This finding is in contrast with the accepted view that eating disorders, especially anorexia nervosa, tend to undergo a chronic course. Although limited by the fact that the observation is cross-sectional, these findings, if confirmed, might lead us to the hypothesis that there are subjects in the general population who develop a more benign form of eating disorder without a chronic course, which sometimes remits without requiring specific treatment. Greater knowledge about remitted cases in the general population would enable us to understand better the mechanisms of chronicity and evaluate the real effectiveness of specific treatments.

REFERENCES

1. Favaro A., Ferrara S., Santonastaso P. The spectrum of eating disorders in young women: a prevalence study in a general population sample (submitted for publication).
2. Fairburn C.G. (1995) Atypical eating disorders. In *Eating Disorders and Obesity. A Comprehensive Handbook* (Eds K.D. Brownell, C.G. Fairburn), pp. 135–140. Guilford Press, New York.
3. Garfinkel P.E., Lin E., Goering P., Spegg C., Goldbloom D.S., Kennedy S., Kaplan A.S., Woodside D.B. (1996) Should amenorrhoea be necessary for the diagnosis of anorexia nervosa? Evidence from a Canadian community sample. *Br. J. Psychiatry*, **168**: 500–506.
4. Garfinkel P.E., Lin E., Goering P., Spegg C., Goldbloom D.S., Kennedy S., Kaplan A.S., Woodside D.B. (1995) Bulimia nervosa in a Canadian community sample: prevalence and comparison of subgroups. *Am. J. Psychiatry*, **152**: 1052–1058.
5. Sullivan P.F., Bulik C.M., Kendler K.S. (1998) The epidemiology and classification of bulimia nervosa. *Psychol. Med.*, **28**: 599–610.

2.9

Understanding the Epidemiology of Eating Disorders

Salvador Cervera[1], Miguel Angel Martínez-González[2] and Francisca Lahortiga[1]

We agree with Hoek *et al.* that a two-stage screening approach is the most appropriate epidemiological design to ascertain the prevalence or the incidence of eating disorders, but it must be emphasized that the sensitivity of the screening tool should be maximized in the first stage and specificity should be increased at the second stage. Thus, investigators may be willing to accept that they will find a large number of positive results in the first stage (usually a questionnaire) and that many of them will be false positives. The second stage (usually a structured interview using DSM-IV criteria) will confirm true positive cases among the large number of positive results found at the first stage. This strategy maximizes the global efficiency of the screening procedure, but it implies that a low cutoff point be set for the screening questionnaire used in the first stage, and this cutoff point

[1] *Department of Psychiatry and Medical Psychology*
[2] *Department of Epidemiology and Public Health, University of Navarre, Pamplona, Spain*

should be lower than in clinical use. The methodological error in an epidemiological study would be to set the cutoff point for the questionnaire at the same level as used in the clinical context.

A case–control approach is useful to estimate relative (but not absolute) risks. The case–control design allows the calculation of odds ratios, which, under the rare disease assumption, validly estimate rate ratios. Therefore, the case–control design is used to identify risk factors. Once bias is excluded, the higher the value of the odds ratio, the higher the likelihood that the risk factor is a truly causal determinant of eating disorders, but it could be very difficult to exclude bias in a case–control design.

The three case–control studies conducted by Fairburn *et al.* [1–3] are examples of a correct epidemiological design with careful prevention and control of biases. They are in fact analytical epidemiological studies and they provide arguments to support the role of perfectionism, low self-esteem and childhood obesity, among others, as causal risk factors for eating disorders.

However, an inherent limitation of the case–control approach is the retrospective evaluation of exposures (the postulated risk factors), which is dependent on the ability of the patient to recall them. It is easy to think that cases (patients) and controls may have a different ability to recall the exposures of interest, leading to a systematic misclassification, i.e. a bias. Moreover, some of the recalled "exposures" by patients may be, in fact, symptoms or consequences of the disorder. Therefore, a recall bias cannot be excluded in any case–control study, and prospective follow-up studies are needed to confirm these findings. Cohort studies with prospective follow-up, adequate control for confounding and validated end-points are usually the best suited designs to find this evidence, but conducting follow-up studies is time-consuming and very demanding. They should include a very large sample ("cohort"), initially free of disease, that is followed up during enough time to observe a sufficient number of new cases of the disease.

In this context, potential threats to the validity of a follow-up study are losses to follow-up and inclusion of subclinical cases in the initial cohort. We have conducted such a cohort study in Spain [4]. A representative sample of the female adolescent population (12–21 years old) of a Spanish Region (Navarre) was invited to participate in our study. Among the 3472 girls invited, 2862 accepted to complete the first stage of the study (participation: 82.4%). After excluding prevalent cases, the cohort at risk of developing new eating disorders during the follow-up was 2743 girls. They were contacted and re-evaluated again by the Eating Attitudes Test (EAT) after 18 months of follow-up using similar procedures as in the initial screening. We successfully followed them up for 18 months (follow-up proportion $= 92\%$). Girls scoring >21 in the EAT and a random sample with score ≤ 21 were invited to a psychiatrist interview. During the follow-up we identified 90 incident cases of eating disorders according to DSM-IV criteria.

Most cases of eating disorder (82%) identified using such a cohort design belonged to the subtype "eating disorders not otherwise specified" (EDNOS). Therefore we suggest that further insights are needed into the aetiology and determinants of the EDNOS subtype of eating disorders to supplement the review by Hoek *et al*. Moreover, we think that a continuum spectrum of disease may be found in eating disorders, ranging from a girl who simply scores high on the EAT (or another screening test) to the full-blown life-threatening clinical picture of anorexia nervosa or bulimia nervosa. In this spectrum, EDNOS would be a first stage of disease and their risk factors are very interesting from a public health and preventive perspective.

Hoek *et al*. affirm that "we do not know the incidence rates in the community". This was true when no cohort study had completed an adequate follow-up period. Now two such studies are available: the first, conducted by Ghadieri and Scott [5] in Sweden, found an incidence of 1.6 for eating disorders during a 2-year follow-up of women aged 20–32 years; the second was designed by us and we found an incidence of 4.8% among women aged 13–22 years.

Regarding risk factors, in our cohort we found that the cumulative incidence of eating disorders progressively decreased with higher levels of self-esteem, whereas the opposite was true for the neuroticism scale [6]. A higher than threefold increase in the cumulative incidence of eating disorders was observed between extreme quartiles for both scales. We previously published [7] similar findings when we assessed prevalent cases (in the baseline population of our cohort). In addition, in a multivariate logistic analysis [8], a higher risk of incident eating disorder was found for several exposures assessed at the beginning of follow-up, such as solitary eating (odds ratio = 2.9; 95% CI = 1.9–4.6) and frequently reading girls' magazines or listening to radio programmes (odds ratio = 2.1; 95% CI = 1.2–3.8 for those most frequently using both media). No independent association was found for television viewing or socio-economic status. A marital status of parents different from "being married" was associated with a significantly higher risk in the multivariate analysis (OR = 2.0; 95% CI = 1.1–3.5).

In conclusion, we have confirmed previous reports from case–control studies supporting that low self-esteem, high levels of neuroticism and solitary eating are powerful predictors of the incidence of eating disorders. In addition, our findings suggest that some familiar factors (divorced, separated, single or widowed parents) and higher levels of exposure to mass media also may be risk factors for the disease. Consistency of findings from different studies is among the important criteria for causal inference in epidemiology. Therefore the findings related to familiar and mass-media exposure require further confirmation.

REFERENCES

1. Fairburn C.G., Welch S.L., Doll H.A., Davies B.A., O'Connor M.E. (1997) Risk factors for bulimia nervosa. A community-based case-control study. *Arch. Gen. Psychiatry*, **54**: 509–517.
2. Fairburn C.G., Doll H.A., Welch S.L., Hay P.J., Davies B.A., O'Connor M.E. (1998) Risk factors for binge eating disorder: a community based, case-control study. *Arch. Gen. Psychiatry*, **55**: 425–432.
3. Fairburn C.G., Cooper Z., Doll H., Welch S.L. (1999) Risk factors for anorexia nervosa: three integrated case-control comparisons. *Arch. Gen. Psychiatry*, **56**: 468–476.
4. Pérez-Gaspar M., Gual P., de Irala-Estévez J., Martínez-González M.A., Lahortiga F., Cervera S. (2000) Prevalencia de trastornos de la conducta alimentaria (TCA) en las adolescentes navarras. *Med. Clín. (Barcelona)*, **114**: 481–486.
5. Ghaderi A., Scott B. (2001) Prevalence, incidence and prospective risk factors for eating disorders. *Acta Psychiatr. Scand.*, **104**: 122–130.
6. Cervera S., Lahortiga F., Martínez-González M.A., Gual P., De Irala-Estévez J., Alonso Y. (2003) Neuroticism and low self-esteem as risk factors for incident eating disorders in a prospective cohort study. *Int. J. Eat. Disord.* (in press).
7. Gual P., Pérez-Gaspar M., Martínez-González M.A., Lahortiga F., De Irala-Estévez J., Cervera S. (2002) Self-esteem, personality, and eating disorders: baseline assessment of a prospective population-based cohort. *Int. J. Eat. Disord.*, **31**: 261–273.
8. Martínez-González M.A., Alonso Y., Gual P., Lahortiga F., De Irala-Estévez J., Cervera S. Parental factors, mass-media influences and the onset of eating disorders in a prospective population-based cohort (submitted for publication).

2.10

The Epidemiology of Eating Disorders: Data from Japan

Yoshikatsu Nakai[1]

Eating disorders are prevalent in Caucasian young females in Western society but comparatively rare in non-Western cultures. However, the prevalence of eating disorders is increasing in several countries in Asia and Africa as well as among ethnic minorities in Western countries.

[1] *College of Medical Technology, Kyoto University, 53 Kawaharacho, Shogoin, Sakyo-ku, Kyoto, Japan*

A nationwide epidemiological survey of eating disorders has been conducted periodically in Japan since 1980, when the number of patients with eating disorders began to increase. Moreover, the results of epidemiological studies, even in limited areas, may be generalized to the Japanese population, because Japan is a country of great uniformity in race, ethnicity and culture.

There had been some descriptions of eating disordered patients before the 19th century in Japan, but detailed descriptions of anorexia nervosa were first reported in 1960, when Japan had become a modern industrial country. The number of patients with anorexia nervosa has been increasing since 1970, when the International Exposition was held in Osaka and the Japanese economy developed remarkably. The model Twiggy visited Japan at that time. In 1980 the Japanese government decided to organize a special research team on eating disorders, because the increase in the number of anorexic patients had become an object of public concern.

This team conducted periodically the nationwide epidemiological survey of eating disorders among Japanese hospitals [1]. The estimated prevalences of anorexia nervosa in 1980, 1985, 1992 and 1998 were 2.5, 3.3, 3.6 and 10.1, respectively, per 100 000 of the total population and 16.2, 22.9, 21.9 and 62.6, respectively, per 100 000 females aged 10–29 years. The proportion of binge/purging subtype of anorexia nervosa increased remarkably in the 1998 survey (47.7%) compared with the 1992 survey (25.6%). The estimated prevalences of bulimia nervosa in 1992 and 1998 were 1.1 and 5.1, respectively, per 100 000 of the total population and 6.6 and 32.7, respectively, per 100 000 females aged 10–29 years.

The author conducted a modified two-stage survey among approximately 9000 students aged 12–24 years in Kyoto prefecture, located in the middle of Japan, in 1985 and 1992 [2]. In Japan, 41.6% of anorexic patients and 29.8% of bulimic patients scored atypically low on the Eating Attitudes Test (EAT). Therefore a large population was screened for anorexia nervosa by means of body mass index ($< 17.5 \, kg/m^2$) and for bulimia nervosa by means of the Bulimic Investigatory Test, Edinburgh (BITE). Then definite cases were established by clinical interview. The prevalence of anorexia nervosa in females was 0.1% in 1985 and 0.15% in 1992. The prevalences of bulimia nervosa in females and males were 0.5% and 0.1%, respectively, in 1992. The prevalences of binge eating disorder (BED) and eating disorders not otherwise specified (EDNOS) in females were 1.0% and 4.6%, respectively, in 1992. Roughly calculated, 60% of patients with anorexia nervosa and 9% of patients with bulimia nervosa in the community are coming to medical facilities.

The author studied the risk factors for anorexia and bulimia nervosa in Japan. Our findings were similar to those of Fairburn et al. [4]: the great majority of risk factors found were general risk factors for psychiatric disorders, but some specific risk factors were found as well. For anorexic patients, they were personal vulnerability factors, particularly perfectionism and negative self-evaluation. For bulimic patients they were dieting vulnerability factors.

A consecutive series of 324 patients with eating disorders were sought 4–9 years after hospitalization [3]. At follow-up, 17 had died. Of the 217 interviewed patients (94 restricting anorexics, 28 bulimic anorexics, 83 bulimics and 12 patients with atypical eating disorders at hospitalization), 130 (60%) had fully recovered, 36 (17%) had partially recovered and 51 (23%) currently had an eating disorder. There was a significant association between psychiatric comorbidity and a worse outcome of the eating disorder and between a worse outcome and a worse psychosocial adaptation. Both mood disorders and anxiety disorders were found to be similar in prevalence and content to those reported in Western countries. However, compared with Western countries, childhood sexual abuse and substance use disorders were less prevalent, which might be due to sociocultural or ethnic differences [3].

The overview of eating disorders in Japan indicated that in the 1970s the focus was on a contribution of the family in classical anorexia nervosa, in the 1980s on weight and diet pressures in bulimia nervosa and in the 1990s on the awareness of female role stress in EDNOS. The overview of eating disorders in Japan as well as in Western society reveals the essential issues for cross-cultural perspectives on eating disorders: not only the standard of thinness but also the role of the family, awareness of female role stress and so on.

REFERENCES

1. Nakai Y. (2000) Epidemiology of eating disorders. *Psychosom. Med.*, **4**: 1–9.
2. Nakai Y., Hamagaki S., Takagi R. (1998) The validity of Bulimic Investigatory Test, Edinburgh (BITE) and the survey of bulimia nervosa. *Clin. Psychiatry (Tokyo)*, **40**: 711–716.
3. Nakai Y., Hamagaki S., Ishizaka Y., Takagi R., Takagi S., Ishikawa T. (2001) Outcome of eating disorders. *Jpn. J. Clin. Psychiatry*, **30**: 1247–1256.
4. Fairburn C.G., Cooper Z., Doll H.A., Welch S.L. (1999) Risk factors for anorexia nervosa: three integrated case control comparisons. *Arch. Gen. Psychiatry*, **56**: 468–476.

2.11
Eating Disorders in the Age of Globalization

Maria Angélica Nunes, Andréa Pinheiro and Ana Luiza Abuchaim[1]

Hoek *et al.* have reviewed, in a straightforward manner, the epidemiological findings on eating disorders and their sociocultural aspects. In Brazil no nationwide study on the prevalence and incidence of anorexia nervosa and bulimia nervosa has been carried out. Nonetheless, some regional studies show a pattern that is similar to that described in developed countries. Only recently, in the 1990s, centres specializing in research on and assistance for eating disorders have been established. Furthermore, there is still no public health network of professionals trained to diagnose such disorders and no governmental programme to address this issue.

In 1996, a population-based epidemiological study of women aged 12–29 years ($n = 513$) living in Porto Alegre, a city in Southern Brazil with a population of over 1.5 million, assessed the prevalence of abnormal eating behaviour and inadequate practices of weight control. Ten per cent of the subjects showed abnormal eating behaviour, with no significant relationship with ethnic background, years of education, occupation or family income. The only factor that showed a statistically significant influence was the overweight/obesity body mass index (BMI). Use of laxatives (8.5%), dieting (7.8%), use of appetite suppressants (5.1%), fasting (3.1%) and vomiting (1.4%) were the most prevalent pathological behaviours [1].

In a second stage of the study, we applied a diagnostic interview for ICD-10. We found ten cases of eating disorders: nine of bulimia nervosa and one of anorexia nervosa.

In 2001, another epidemiological study was carried out in Porto Alegre to assess the prevalence of body dissatisfaction and weight concerns in a representative sample of schoolchildren aged 8–11 years. Preliminary results show that 40% of the children were not satisfied with their body. Among children in the 25–75th percentile, 19% wished that they had a thinner body and 13% wished that they had a bigger body. The following variables showed a significant relationship with the primary outcome: female gender, BMI, and parents' expectations concerning their children's weight. There was no relationship with socio-economic status [2].

The Brazilian version of the Binge Eating Scale was validated recently in a sample of obese individuals seeking weight loss treatment. The instrument had a sensitivity of 98%, a specificity of 50% and a positive predictive value of 65% [3].

---

[1] *Eating Disorders Programme, Fundação Universitária Mário Martins, 221 Dona Laura, 90430-091 Porto Alegre, Brazil*

Transcultural research over the last few years has provided evidence that allows us to understand better the different levels of interaction between biological, psychological and cultural aspects in the aetiology of eating disorders. The idea of culture-bound syndromes is being replaced by the idea of modernization-related factors, such as industrialization, urbanization, cultural misunderstandings, influx of Western culture and media, acculturation and women's role in society. The study that shows that urbanization has no impact on the incidence of anorexia nervosa, as it does for bulimia nervosa, may pave the way to new discoveries on the fundamental differences between the pathogeneses of these two syndromes [4].

Striegel-Moore *et al.* [5] reported that African-American and Caucasian women in the USA show no difference in the frequencies of binge eating and vomiting. Cultural beliefs that were traditionally considered protective of ethnic groups in terms of eating disorders seem to be eroding in the face of acculturation of teenagers towards mainstream American culture: strict diet and adoption of a slender ideal. A similar finding was reported in a study of American schoolchildren, in which weight concerns and body dissatisfaction were highly prevalent, with no relationship to race or socio-economic status [6].

Among the difficulties in carrying out such studies, the most frequently discussed are fitting diagnostic criteria in different cultures and the difficulty of validating research instruments. Studies on Chinese anorexic patients without apparent weight phobia raised questions about whether Western culture diagnostic criteria should be applied in countries where weight phobia is not the rule [7]. As far as the instruments applied are concerned, whether they are questionnaires or structured interviews, the problem resides in the difficulty of validating, translating and adapting the questionnaire to the local language and adapting the semantics of the key questions. The investigator must be familiar with the concept of a heterogeneous cultural setting [8,9].

Important questions arise from these studies: what do we mean by Westernization of a society? Does this refer to industrialization, modernization, urbanization and acculturation, or does it refer to the role of the family or a changing national identity in a global society? What exactly is it about the media's role that is so important? What do we have to learn from the exceptions? Is it true that half of Asian anorexics do not wish to lose weight? If this were the case, why would they develop the clinical picture, and what should we learn from this? Can qualitative methodology contribute to the understanding of cultural representations of the ideal of beauty?

Future investigations may help us to understand better the different levels of cultural influences in the psychopathology of eating disorders and thus may provide us with deeper and more detailed knowledge of the pathogenesis of these syndromes.

REFERENCES

1. Nunes M.A., Barros F., Olinto M.T., Camey S., Mari J.J. (2003) Prevalence of abnormal eating behaviors and inappropriate methods for weight control in young women from Brazil: a population-based study. *Eat. Weight Disord.* (in press).
2. Pinheiro A.P., Giugliani E.R.J., Barros A. Body dissatisfaction, self-esteem and weight concerns in 8–11 year-old schoolchildren of Porto Alegre, Brazil (in preparation).
3. Freitas S., Lopes C.S., Appolinario J.C., Sichieri R. Validation of the Brazilian version of the Binge Eating Scale—a scale to evaluate binge eating in obese patients (submitted for publication).
4. Hoek H.W., Bartelds A.I.M., Bosveld J.J.F., van der Graaf Y., Limpens V.E.L., Maiwald M., Spaaij C.J.K. (1995) Impact of urbanization on detection rates of eating disorders *Am J Psychiatry*, **152**: 1272–1278.
5. Striegel-Moore R.H., Wilfley D.E., Pike K.M., Dohm F.A., Fairburn C.G. (2000) Recurrent binge eating in Black American women. *Arch. Family Med.*, **9**: 63–87.
6. Robinson T.N., Chang J.Y., Haydel K.F., Killen J.D. (2001) Overweight concerns and body dissatisfaction among third-grade children: the impacts of ethnicity and socioeconomic status. *J. Pediatr.*, **138**: 181–187.
7. Hsu L.K.G, Lee S. (1993) Is weight phobia always necessary for a diagnosis of anorexia nervosa? *Am J. Psychiatry*, **10**: 1466–1471.
8. Sen B., Mari J.J. (1986) Psychiatric research in the transcultural setting: experiences in India and Brazil. *Soc. Sci. Med.*, **23**: 277–281.
9. King B.M., Bhugra D. (1989) Eating disorders: lessons from a cross-cultural study. *Psychol. Med.*, **19**: 955–958.

2.12

Eating Disorders in Developing Countries— Do We Need New Criteria?

Ahmed Okasha[1]

For a long time, most people have accepted that sociocultural factors play an important role in the aetiology of eating disorders and, of course, most of us believe that this aetiology is multifactorial. However, the specific sociocultural mechanisms that come into play have been rather poorly understood, and people have been especially interested in the media's role in creating what many people have called the prevailing "pressure to be thin" in American and European societies. Unfortunately, the studies investigating the impact of culture on eating disorders have been rather inconclusive.

Becker [1] reported on Fiji, where women are traditionally expected to have very robust appetites and robust body sizes. The society practically revolves around food and food exchange. While working in Fiji, Becker

[1] *Institute of Psychiatry, Ain Shams University, Cairo, Egypt*

studied the impact of the introduction of television broadcast in a remote village on two separate matched cohorts of adolescent girls in 1995 and 1998. He found a very high prevalence of high Eating Attitudes Test scores, a significant and dramatic increase in indices of disordered eating between those two times and a significant increase in induced vomiting to lose weight (0% in 1995 and 11% in 1998) [2].

DiNicola [3] established the hypothesis that eating disorders are culture-bound syndromes that exist only in the Western world. In his cross-cultural reviews, he also established the acculturation-stress hypothesis or the culture-change syndrome, which meant that if these disorders started to emerge in non-Western cultures it is probably because of their exposure to Western values and ideals through immigration or mass media. The data from the non-Western cultures were, and still are, very limited.

In Egypt (a representative of Arab culture) Okasha et al. [4] found only two cases of anorexia nervosa in their study. A later Egyptian study investigated eating disorders in 371 adolescent girls, age range 13–18 years, using ICD-10 research criteria. Results showed no typical cases of anorexia nervosa or bulimia nervosa, but 32 cases (8.6% of the study sample) fulfilled the diagnostic criteria for atypical bulimia nervosa. It is noteworthy that 6 (1.6% of the sample) out of 32 atypical cases of bulimia nervosa would have fulfilled the criteria for the diagnosis of typical bulimia nervosa if the weight had not been used as a criterion of atypicality [5].

Similar results were obtained by Nasser [6], who carried out a comparative study of abnormal eating attitudes among Arab female students at London and Cairo universities. She did not find any cases of typical anorexia nervosa in either of the samples, but she commented that the test scores of the female college students of her Cairo sample were very high, reflecting a culture change that should be investigated further. The higher prevalence of "atypical" anorexia nervosa syndrome has led some authors to use the term anorexia nervosa, partial syndrome [7]. The rate of clinical bulimia nervosa in Nasser's London sample was 12%. This is the highest rate of bulimia nervosa ever reported for any group of women living in Britain. Mumford et al. [8] reported a 3.4% rate of bulimia nervosa among Asian girls in Bradford.

In 1990, Ford et al. [9] found that body shape dissatisfaction and weight concerns were evident in a sample of Egyptian college students in the American university in Cairo.

It has been suggested that it may be impossible to gain a proper estimate of the prevalence of eating disorders owing to denial and non-participation. Thus, the prevalence of eating disorders may always be an underestimate [10]. Also, the sample size for low prevalence disorders such as eating disorders may constitute an obstacle to their accurate detection [11].

The question that should be posed here is: "should the weight be used as a criterion of atypicality?" Two large-scale investigations have suggested that many bulimics are somewhat overweight for their respective heights [12,13]. Beumont et al. [14] and Killen et al. [15] reported that bulimia nervosa (the binge/purge cycle) might occur in normal-weight and overweight individuals. If the DSM-IV had been used in the Egyptian study, the bulimia nervosa prevalence would have risen to 6.1%, which is in agreement with the results obtained by Rathner et al. [11]. This should draw attention to the fact that the use of different methods of case finding, together with the use of different prevalence measures and the adoption of different definitions of illness, has had considerable impact on prevalence estimates for anorexia nervosa and bulimia nervosa and seems as likely to account for variation between studies as real population differences.

It seems that a convergence between the recent classification systems in order to be able to provide one language for researchers all over the world has become a necessity.

REFERENCES

1. Becker A.E. (1995) Body, Self and Society: the View from Fiji. University of Pennsylvania Press, Philadelphia.
2. Becker A.E., Grinspoon S.K., Klibanski A., Herzog D.B. (1999) Current concepts: eating disorders, N. Engl. J. Med., 340: 1092–1098.
3. DiNicola V.F. (1990) Anorexia multiforme: self starvation in historical and cultural context: II. Anorexia nervosa as a culture reactive syndrome. Transcult. Psychiatry Res. Rev., 27: 245–286.
4. Okasha A., Kamel M., Sadek A., Lotaief F., Bishry Z. (1977) Psychiatric morbidity among university students in Egypt. Br. J. Psychiatry, 131: 149–154.
5. Okasha A., Bishry Z., Khalil A., Ghanem M., Effat S., Elsayed S. (1998) Prevalence and psychodemographic data of eating disorders in a sample of Egyptian adolescent girls. Thesis in Psychiatry, Ain Shams University, Cairo, Egypt.
6. Nasser M. (1986) Comparative study of the prevalence of abnormal eating attitudes among Arab female students of both London and Cairo universities. Psychol. Med., 16: 621–625.
7. Rathner G., Messner K. (1993) Detection of eating disorders in a small rural town: an epidemiological study. Psychol. Med., 23: 175–184.
8. Mumford D.B., Whitehouse A.M., Platts M. (1991) Sociocultural correlates of eating disorders among Asian schoolgirls in Bradford. Br. J. Psychiatry, 158: 222–228.
9. Ford K.A., Dolan B.M., Evans C. (1990) Cultural factors in the eating disorders: a study of body shape preferences of Arab students. J. Psychosom. Res., 34: 501–507.
10. Johnson-Sabine E., Wood K., Patton G., Mann A., Wakeling A. (1988) Abnormal eating attitudes in London schoolgirls. A prospective epidemiological study:

factors associated with abnormal responses on screening questionnaires. *Psychol. Med.*, **18**: 615–622.

11. Rathner G., Tury F., Szabo P., Geyer M., Rumpold G., Forgacs A., Sollner W., Plottner G. (1995) Prevalence of eating disorders and minor psychiatric morbidity in Central Europe before the political changes in 1989: a cross-cultural study. *Psychol. Med.*, **25**: 1027–1035.

12. Halmi K.A., Falk J.R., Schwartz E. (1981) Binge eating and vomiting: a survey of college population. *Psychol. Med.*, **11**: 697–706.

13. Fairburn C.G., Cooper P.J. (1982) Self-induced vomiting and bulimia nervosa: an undetected problem. *Br. Med. J.*, **284**: 1153–1155.

14. Beumont P., Al-Alami M., Touyz S. (1988) Relevance of a standard measurement of under nutrition to the diagnosis of anorexia nervosa: use of Quetelet's Body Mass Index (BMI). *Int. J. Eat. Disord.*, **7**: 399–405.

15. Killen J.D., Taylor C.B., Telch M.J., Saylor K.E., Maron D.J., Robinson T.N. (1986) Self-induced vomiting and laxative and diuretic use among teenagers. Precursors of the binge-purge syndrome? *JAMA*, **255**: 1447–1449.

2.13

The Search for Influences on Eating Disorders

Merry N. Miller[1]

Aetiological factors leading to the development of eating disorders have long been a source of study and speculation. Hoek *et al.* have provided a thorough and useful review of the epidemiology of eating disorders, which can provide clues to aetiology. As they discuss, potential risk factors can be identified through examination of epidemiological and cultural associations, and this has the potential to improve understanding of the development of eating disorders.

Controversy exists about the true occurrence rates of both anorexia nervosa and bulimia nervosa. As Hoek *et al.* mention, true prevalence and incidence rates are obscured by the fact that many individuals with these disorders deny and conceal their pathology. In addition, their overall low prevalence in the general population presents a methodological challenge. The use of two-stage screens and studies of population subsets at higher risk are methods reviewed that provide useful data.

An apparent increase in the incidence of anorexia nervosa over the last half of the 20th century is discussed. Less information is available about changes in rates of bulimia nervosa owing to its relatively recent identification. Nevertheless, evidence is cited suggesting that these rates also have increased since the original description of bulimia nervosa as

[1] *Department of Psychiatry and Behavioral Sciences, East Tennessee State University, Box 70567, Johnson City, TN 37614, USA*

a separate disorder in 1979 [1]. Such a presumable expansion in eating disorder pathology often has been referenced as evidence for a cultural influence on the development of these disorders, particularly in light of the emphasis on thinness in the Western ideals of the late 20th century.

Unfortunately, determination of true prevalence and incidence rates for eating disorders is even more problematic in earlier periods of history. A review of historical evidence suggests the possible existence of eating disorders in previous eras, and raises questions about the true impact of current social pressures on the development of eating disorders [2].

The role of contemporary social factors in the development of eating disorders has been debated. It was believed previously that eating disorders occurred almost exclusively in upper socio-economic groups within Western nations, and primarily among Caucasian females [3]. However, emerging evidence indicates that eating disorders occur in a wide range of ethnic, cultural and socio-economic groups within the USA [4]. In addition, recent reports that reveal the presence of eating disorders in developing Third World nations appears to be increasing [5].

Hoek et al. cite evidence from epidemiological data for a number of potential risk factors for eating disorders. Childhood perfectionism and self-criticism have been linked with anorexia nervosa, and obesity in the parents, childhood obesity, negative comments about weight and dieting behaviour have been linked with bulimia nervosa. Although there has been controversy on the role of sexual abuse, childhood sexual abuse is described as a non-specific risk factor for eating disorders, especially if there is psychiatric comorbidity.

Urbanization is described as a potential risk factor, and is associated with a three- to fivefold increase in the incidence of bulimia nervosa in The Netherlands, whereas anorexia nervosa is found in almost equal frequency in areas of different degrees of urbanization [6]. These data conflict with the findings of Miller et al. [7], in which adolescents in more rural areas were reported to have greater levels of risk for eating disorders. It was hypothesized that cultural factors in rural America may place adolescents at greater risk, including the rapid transition from a traditional agricultural culture to one with more urban influences. Further research into the issue of urban versus rural prevalence of eating disorders is needed.

Acculturation stress is discussed as a potential trigger for the development of eating disorders, reflected in higher eating disorder rates among immigrants. In addition, Hoek et al. comment on the correlation among minority populations within the USA between level of acculturation and morbid concerns over weight, with increased risk associated with adherence to Western culture. It has been reported that US ethnic minority groups are showing a trend towards higher levels of eating disorders [8], and it has been hypothesized that cultural beliefs that previously protected ethnic groups against eating disorders may be eroding as adolescents attempt to acculturate to mainstream American culture [9].

Cross-cultural rates of eating disorders are a topic of much interest at this time. Evidence is accumulating that eating disorders are present across the globe, including in developing Third World countries, with increased rates seen in more Western-oriented cultures [2]. Hoek *et al.* question the true meaning of "Western culture", and point to increasing Western influences even in remote island communities. They also point to some cross-cultural differences in the presentations of eating disorders. The apparent absence of an intense fear of fatness in Asian anorexic patients raises questions about how central this fear is to the disorder.

Both anorexia nervosa and bulimia nervosa are in many ways a challenge to comprehend. The possible role of culture in influencing the development, rate and presentation of these disorders is intriguing and worthy of further study, with implications for understanding the aetiology and for planning the most effective treatment.

REFERENCES

1. Russell G.F.M. (1979) Bulimia nervosa: an ominous variant of anorexia nervosa. *Psychol. Med.*, **9**: 429–448.
2. Miller M.N., Pumariega A.J. (2001) Culture and eating disorders: a historical and cross-cultural review. *Psychiatry*, **64**: 93–110.
3. Bruch H. (1973) *Eating Disorders: Obesity, Anorexia Nervosa and the Person Within*. Basic Books, New York.
4. Dolan B. (1991) Cross-cultural aspects of anorexia nervosa and bulimia: a review. *Int. J. Eat. Disord.*, **10**: 67–78.
5. Ritenbaugh C., Shisslak C., Prince R. (1996) A cross-cultural review in regard to DSM-IV. In *Culture and Psychiatric Diagnosis: A DSM-IV Perspective*. (Eds J.E. Mezzich, II. Fabrega, A. Kleinman, D. Perron), pp. 171–186. American Psychiatric Press, Washington.
6. Hoek H.W., Bartelds A.I.M., Bosveld J.J.F., van der Graaf Y., Limpens V.E.L., Maiwald M., Spaaij C.J.K. (1995) Impact of urbanization on detection rates of eating disorders. *Am. J. Psychiatry*, **152**: 1272–1278.
7. Miller M.N., Verhegge R., Miller B., Pumariega A. (1999) Assessment of risk of eating disorders among adolescents in Appalachia. *J. Am. Acad. Child Adolesc. Psychiatry*, **38**: 437–443.
8. Pate J.E., Pumariega A.J., Hester C., Garner D. (1992) Cross-cultural patterns in eating disorders: a review. *J. Am. Acad. Child Adolesc. Psychiatry*, **31**: 802–809.
9. Pumariega A.J. (1986) Acculturation and eating attitudes in adolescent girls: a comparative and correlational study. *J. Am. Acad. Child Adolesc. Psychiatry*, **25**: 276–279.

2.14
Cross-cultural Psychology and Epidemiology of Eating Disorders

Adrian Furnham[1]

Within psychology there is a profound, and self-serving, disagreement between *universalists* and *cultural specifists*. Thus, some psychologists (i.e. personality theorists and experimental psychologists) rejoice the pan-cultural nature of processes and structures, whereas others (cross-cultural psychologists) revel in finding both cultural and subcultural differences in normal and abnormal behaviour. The issue at the heart of the difference is, of course, the nature–nurture debate, which in psychiatry divides the biological and social psychiatrists. For eating disorders, this means the extent to which one sees sociocultural factors influencing the aetiology, manifestation and prognosis of anorexia and bulimia nervosa.

Hoek *et al.* attempt an epidemiological examination of the data to answer the question of the social origin of eating disorders, their occurrence and their distribution. There are significant advantages but many disadvantages to this approach and the authors spell these out in their review. In addition to those mentioned, it is important to acknowledge that many Third World countries simply do not have the systems and infrastructure to gather salient data on eating disorders over time. All the data come from Europe or North America, which probably have broadly similar attitudes to eating and eating disorders. If we had data from Asia or Africa the results may look very different. The question is whether the "cultures" taking part in the study are sufficiently different to show cultural effects on eating disorders [1].

Hoek *et al.* attempt to examine the time trends to answer the all-important question about whether the incidence of eating disorders is on the increase or decrease. To answer this question one needs longitudinal studies with stability in the diagnostic criteria, which do not exist. The same problem applies to analysis of age, gender and mortality statistics. Analysis of the data on bulimia nervosa is even more problematic: diagnostic criteria are unclear, incidence is low and distinguishability from other disorders is not clear.

The question is whether, given all the methodological problems, an epidemiological approach to the question is of any use *at this stage*. What is also conspicuously missing is any theoretical consideration as to why there may be cultural or temporal changes. There are numerous possibilities that have been considered by theories derived from psychology, sociology and psychiatry. Thus, there is the role-model exposure theory, which suggests

[1] *Department of Psychology, University College London, 26 Bedford Way, London WC1 OAP, UK*

that advertising somehow influences young people's preferences for particular body shapes, which influences their eating behaviour. This is sometimes called the "societal pressure to become thin" hypothesis [2]. Other psychiatric theories suggest that parent–child conflict may be at the source of eating disorders in particular migrant groups [3]. The advantage of a theory is that at least one can see if the available data, at least partly, confirm the hypothesis. At the moment we can only review the admittedly very inadequate existing data, but we need to do so within a number of theoretical frameworks.

In the discussion of the risk factors for eating disorders, I was surprised by the omission of topics such as religion, parenting style and family dynamics. On the other hand, urbanization and occupation seem very minor factors if one reads the literature carefully.

The final two paragraphs of the review pose the central question of the relationship between culture and eating disorders but offer no answers. The question is about the strength and precise nature of cultural predictors of eating disorders. To what extent is the epidemiological approach ever going to be able to answer this question, given all the methodological problems involved? I believe that it will only do so if it is driven theoretically as well as empirically. Once various hypotheses are established, one could examine the evidence from various studies that purport to test them. But perhaps that is conventional meta-analysis rather than epidemiology.

REFERENCES

1. Miller M.N., Pumariega A.J. (2001) Culture and eating disorders: a historical and cross-cultural review. *Psychiatry*, **64**: 93–110.
2. Mautner R.D., Owen S.V., Furnham A.F. (2000) Cross-cultural explanations of body image disturbance in western cultural samples. *Int. J. Eat. Disord.*, **30**: 165-172.
3. Furnham A., Husain K. (1999) The role of conflict with parents in disordered eating among British Asian females. *Soc. Psychiatry Psychiatr. Epidemiol.*, **34**: 498–505.

3

Physical Complications and Physiological Aberrations in Eating Disorders: A Review

Francesca Brambilla and Palmiero Monteleone

Department of Psychiatry, University of Naples SUN, Largo Madonna delle Grazie,
80138 Naples, Italy

INTRODUCTION

Anorexia nervosa and bulimia nervosa are perhaps the most intriguing combinations of psychological and medical impairments, both being pathognomonic and paradigmatic for the nosographic definition of the diseases. Even the eating alterations occurring in the two syndromes, although a definite expression of psychopathological impairments, seem to point out the existence of a physical derangement in the capacity of the patients to perceive and correctly define the internal stimuli of hunger, satiety, food selection and taste sensations [1–11].

The medical complications observed in anorexia and bulimia nervosa have always been considered the consequence of nutritional derangements, on the basis of the similarities with the alterations observed in simple starvation in both experimental animals and humans [12]. In fact, in anorexia nervosa, most of these aberrations start after the beginning of severe food restriction and weight loss and disappear after recovery of normal eating habits and weight, with the possible exception of amenorrhoea, which can start before significant weight loss takes place and does not always disappear with weight normalization [13–17]. Bulimic patients are not starving, but the loss of food obtained with vomiting or the use of laxatives, the biased selection of macro–micronutrients typical of bingeing episodes and the alternation of gorging and severe dieting might lead to malnutrition, resulting in some of the impairments of simple starvation.

What are still not fully defined are the mechanisms by which starvation for anorexia nervosa and malnutrition for bulimia nervosa induce and

Eating Disorders. Edited by Mario Maj, Katherine Halmi, Juan José López-Ibor and Norman Sartorius.
©2003 John Wiley & Sons Ltd: ISBN 0-470-84865-0

maintain the medical complications of the two syndromes. In particular, it is not clear why some patients show the full spectrum of medical complications and others with a very similar clinical picture do not. Moreover, it is not clear what the influence exerted by peripheral medical complications is on the course, response to treatments and prognosis of anorexia and bulimia nervosa.

The same seems to occur for the brain biological alterations that characterize anorexia and bulimia nervosa. The reduced function of serotonin (5-HT) and noradrenaline systems and the increased activity of dopamine systems, frequently observed in anorexia nervosa, have been considered an expression of malnutrition, because they occur in starved experimental animals and sometimes in human simple malnutrition [18–30]. However, it is not clear why these alterations do not occur in all the starving–malnourished anorexics and bulimics and why they do not correlate with the indices of food deficiency. Moreover, it has been observed that long after recovery from anorexia nervosa, when eating habits and weight have normalized, some patients show the persistence of dopamine hyperactivity and noradrenaline hypofunction and the appearance of 5-HT hyperfunction [25,26,31].

Therefore, the significance of peripheral medical alterations and brain biological impairments for the development, course, response to treatment and prognosis of anorexia and bulimia nervosa is still not clear and is worth further study.

SPECIFIC PHYSICAL AND PHYSIOLOGICAL IMPAIRMENTS

Dermatological Alterations

In both restricting type anorexia nervosa (ANR) and bingeing/purging type anorexia nervosa (ANBP), cutaneous changes occur rather precociously, being strictly associated with starvation, self-induced vomiting and abuse of purging drugs (laxatives and diuretics).

Brittle hair, eyelash and nails, loss of hair and eyebrow, and a dystrophic aspect of the skin, which looks dry and scaling, pale or yellowish like old paper or dirty-like brownish because of cornification, are related to nutritional deficiencies, possibly as a consequence of the starvation-linked hypothyroidism, which occurs rather early in the disease. The yellowish colour of the skin seems to be due to hypercarotenaemia, which is frequent in anorexics, because of excessive consumption of carrots and of the general metabolic down-regulation. The skin is often covered by a fine, downy-like hair defined as "lanugo", growing especially on the face, superior lip, back, arms and legs. This aspect is different from that of hypertricosis and is certainly not due to hyperandrogenism, which does not occur in anorexia nervosa, because in anorexics the synthesis of biologically active androgens is reduced, due to a decreased activity of the 5α-reductase enzyme system, possibly linked to the hypothyroidism mentioned above [32–35]. The presence of skin trauma and calluses on the dorsal surfaces of hands, secondary to using the hand as an instrument to induce vomiting, is characteristic and first described in 1979 by Russell (Russell sign) [36]. The lesion may appear anywhere on the dorsum of the hand, but more frequently at the metacarpo-phalangeal joint of each finger; it may be superficial but can progress to hyperpigmentation of the calluses with scarring [37]. It has been reported that these lesions may disappear in a later phase of the disease, because many patients train themselves to vomit reflexly. Poor wound healing is frequent. Facial dermatitis, seborrheic dermatitis and acne are occasionally observed [38].

Peripheral oedema may be present in 20% of anorexics, often during the refeeding phase [39]. A mild form occurs in the presence of normal plasma proteins and albumin levels, its aetiology being unknown. A more severe form follows purgation and chronic laxative abuse, resulting in marked hypoproteinaemia in severely malnourished patients. The subsequent lowering of plasma osmotic pressure allows fluid to pass from vasculature into tissues to produce hypovolaemia. The oedema is rapid in onset, often associated with shock, renal infarction and cardiovascular collapse due to an inability to maintain appropriate fluid volume, and it may be life threatening [40]. Vomiting strain may favour the appearance of petechiae on the face and haemorrhages of the conjunctiva, possibly linked to the fact that platelet number is reduced and capillary vessel permeability is increased [41].

Subcutaneous emphysema of the neck has been described to occur in vomiting patients, even though infrequently, and in some cases it is associated with spontaneous pneumomediastinum. This would be favoured by prolonged starvation, which in experimental animals induces an increase of the superficial tension and a decrease of tissue elasticity in the alveoli [42].

A stable erythema, linked to the abuse of phenolphthalein-containing laxatives or of ipecac, has been reported in anorexics [43]. Cutaneous alterations linked to avitaminoses, such as scurvy or pellagra, have been reported infrequently [43]. More frequent are self-injury signs such as excoriated acne and *ab igne* erythema [43].

In bulimia nervosa, cutaneous impairments are the same as in anorexia nervosa but occur less frequently, with the exception of the Russell sign that is often present in patients with vomiting [36].

Eye Alterations

Cataract formation has been reported very occasionally in anorexia nervosa, possibly being linked to prolonged starvation, anaemia, chronic diarrhoea and hypokalaemia [44]. There are no data regarding bulimia nervosa.

Oral Alterations

Oral complications are common among patients with eating disorders, being mostly related to the chronic regurgitation of gastric acid content in ANBP and bulimia nervosa [45–48].

Angular chelosis is a form of stomatitis characterized by pallor and maceration of the mucosa at the corners of the mouth, often resulting in very painful linear fissures healing in scars. It occurs in ANBP and bulimia nervosa; the lesions are mainly due to the caustic effect of regurgitated gastric acid content, but they may be also the expression of an underlying vitamin deficiency, involving both riboflavin (B2) and pyridoxine (B6), in this case being seen also in ANR [38].

The second most frequent oral alteration occurring in bulimia nervosa and ANBP is enamel erosion (perimolysis). It consists of loss of dentine and tooth enamel at the lingual, palatal and posterior occlusal surfaces of the maxillary teeth, which are generally shortened with irregular incisal edges. The alterations are due to chronic contact with regurgitated gastric acid contents [44].

Caries are frequent in both anorexia and bulimia nervosa, being related to starvation in the former and both vomiting and excessive bingeing of carbohydrate food in the latter [49].

Gingivitis is seen frequently in ANBP and bulimia nervosa, resulting from chronic irritation due to the regurgitated gastric acid content, often associated with a painful pharyngeal erythema [44].

Sialadenosis is a hypertrophy of salivary glands common in ANBP and bulimia nervosa, generally painless and bilateral and more frequent in the parotids, with the glands enlarged two to five times their normal size. The frequency and severity of the disorder are related to the chronicity and frequency of vomiting. The causes seem to be multiple, including chronic regurgitation of the stomach contents leading to cholinergic nerve stimulus, consumption over short periods of high-calorie foods with repetitive stimulation of the glands, chronic metabolic alkalosis and increased autonomic stimulation linked to contact of the oral mucosa with pancreatic proteolytic enzymes acting at the lingual taste receptors. Biopsy of the parotids may reveal increased acinar size and granule secretion, fat infiltration, fibrosis and occasionally areas of inflammation [44,50,51]. The parotid hypertrophy may be more evident in the case of concomitant masseteric hypertrophy, which is especially present in bulimics affected by bruxism [52].

Gastroenteric Alterations

The most commonly reported gastrointestinal symptoms occurring in anorexia and bulimia nervosa are bloating, epigastric pain or lower chest discomfort, flatulence, constipation, decreased or increased appetite, abdominal pain, borborygmi and nausea [53].

Lesions of the oesophagus are frequent in anorexia and bulimia nervosa. They are represented by oesophagitis, erosions and ulcers of the gastro-oesophageal junction, stenosis and breakage of the organ occurring during vomiting episodes [54]. These lesions are mostly due to vomiting, to the frequently spastic motility of the organ and to a neuropathy linked to vitamin deficiencies [55].

In anorexia nervosa, gastric volume is normal or reduced and the smooth muscle of the gastric wall is atrophic and atonic [56], with gastric emptying always being delayed for solid food and hypertonic liquids and normal for hypotonic liquids and physiological solutions [54,57]. These impairments are partly responsible for the belching and the precocious feeling of gastric fullness observed in anorexia nervosa. The inverse correlation between time of gastric emptying and body weight observed in starvation is not present in anorexics, not even after weight recovery [55]. This observation, together with the demonstration that in anorexics the most compromised phase of gastric emptying is that inhibited by the duodenum, has suggested that a congenitally excessive duodenal sensibility might be a predisposing factor for the development of anorexia nervosa. On the other hand, gastroenteric sensitivity to cholinergic and antidopaminergic stimuli is preserved in anorexics [54,55,57].

During refeeding, gastric bloating and other non-specific abdominal discomfort usually occur. Gastric dilatation requiring the immediate evacuation of stomach contents has been reported rarely. Complaints of oesophageal reflux may occur even when self-induced vomiting is not practiced, and is generally due to diminished competence of the gastro-oesophageal sphincter [44].

Studies of gastric acidity have given contrasting results, with most of them providing evidence for normal basal and pentagastrin-stimulated acid secretion. Gastritis and pyloric erosions are occasional, but proximal duodenal and jejunum dilatations are reported frequently [58]. No increased prevalence of *Helicobacter pylori* has been seen in anorexia and bulimia nervosa compared with the general population [59]. Gastric perforation is a rare complication of anorexia nervosa [60].

Constipation, due mostly to drastically reduced calorie intake, invariably accompanies weight loss in anorexia nervosa and is generally worsened by the abuse of laxatives [61]. Abdominal pain is a frequent complaint, being generally diffuse, unaccompanied by tenderness and probably related to gastroparesis or irritable bowel-type syndrome [62]. Rectal sensation, internal anal sphincter relaxation threshold, rectal compliance, sphincter pressure and expulsion pattern, studied by a radiopaque marker technique and anorectal manometry, are normal in anorexia nervosa [61]. Slow colonic transit times and pelvic floor dysfunction occur in undernourished anorexics and normalize after refeeding [63]. Colonic lesions are mostly related to laxative abuse resulting in chronic constipation, with signs of inflammation, atony and dilatation, and the so-called cathartic colon characterized by thinness, atrophy and superficial ulcers of the mucosa, retention cysts and mononuclear infiltration of the submucosa [64,65]. Occasional ischaemic necrosis of the segmental ileum and caecum has been reported in anorexia nervosa, possibly due to poor blood supply linked to severe malnutrition and dehydration [66]. Rectal prolapse has been reported to occur in anorexia and bulimia nervosa, possibly related to constipation, laxative abuse or increased intra-abdominal pressure from forced vomiting [67].

Ultrastructural investigation reveals multiple and diffuse cellular alterations in the intestinal epithelium, Schwann cells and nervous plexuses. Microvilli are reduced; macrophages, including large and increased lysosomes, are augmented [68]. Functional investigations reveal reduced xylose excretion due to enteric atrophy and dismotility, while proteo-wasting enteropathy is more infrequent [39,69].

In bulimia nervosa, most of the impairments of the gastrointestinal tract are similar to those observed in anorexia nervosa [47]. Disordered oesophageal motility, including lower than normal oesophageal sphincter pressure, relaxed sphincter pressure, reduced mean oesophageal body contraction amplitude, altered waveform morphology and reduced progression, is uncommon in bulimia nervosa, the only alterations observed being dysphagia and odynophagia [70]. Gastric capacity is generally larger than normal, being related to the severity of binge eating behaviour and with a highly significant correlation with mean daily food intake [71]. Maximal fullness is reached sooner than maximum tolerated gastric pain, which is generally reduced. Intragastric pressure reached at maximum tolerance is not different from normal. Gastric emptying is slower in bulimics than in normal subjects, probably due to reduced intragastric pressure for a given volume and a lower gradient between stomach and duodenum [71].

Hepatic and Pancreatic Alterations

Abnormalities of hepatic functions are not prominent in eating disorders. In anorexics, starvation may favour hepatic impairments manifested as hepatomegaly, with increase of lactate dehydrogenase, serum glutamic-oxaloacetic transaminase, serum glutamine-pyruvic transaminase, alkaline phosphatase and reduction of cholinesterase and plasma proteins [72]. Histologically, a diffuse steatosis is observed, infrequently evolving in cirrhosis and disappearing with refeeding [73,74].

Pancreatic abnormalities, both morphological and functional, are frequent in anorexia nervosa and tend to persist long after recovery [75]. Morphological changes are mostly represented by atrophy with reduction of acini cells and zymogene granules, increase of fibrous interstitial tissue, cystic dilatation of pancreatic ducts and diffuse calcifications. Functional abnormalities include a reduction of pancreatic enzyme secretion and protein synthesis [54]. Amylase and elastase-1 serum concentrations—a specific index of pancreatic suffering—are increased [76,77], with pancreatitis occurring more frequently during refeeding [78]. Amylase levels correlate with vomiting frequency. The occurrence of pancreatitis may be facilitated by duodenal stasis followed by duodenal-pancreatic reflux.

Cardiovascular Alterations

Cardiovascular abnormalities may occur at some stages of anorexia nervosa in up to 87% of patients and much less frequently in bulimia nervosa. They include sinus bradycardia, less frequently tachycardia, ventricular arrhythmias, lower than normal values of the heart rate coefficients of variations in supine and standing posture, lower than normal ratios of low- and mid-frequency to high-frequency power (which may represent cardiac sympathetic/parasympathetic balance), cardiac failure, reduced left atrial and left ventricular chamber dimension, hypotension and a variety of electrocardiographic changes [79,80]. Bradycardia, ranging from below 60 beats per minute during the day to around 30 beats per minute at night, is probably due to vagal hypertonus [81], whereas the decreased thickness of the ventricular walls, the consequent decreased myocardial contractility, the dehydration with subsequent hypovolaemia and the reduction of cardiac cavities concur to decrease blood pressure [82–84]. The reduced left ventricular chamber dimension and mass, without substantial changes in shape, might be responsible for mitral valve prolapse, which occurs in 28–80% of anorexics [39,83,85]. It has been suggested that mitralic prolapse may be induced also by a central neuroregulatory dysfunction, as supported by its frequent occurrence in other psychiatric disorders (phobias, panic disorder, neuroses) and in patients with neurovegetative disorders [81]. Mitral valve prolapse may be responsible for lipothymic episodes and cardiac rhythm alterations [86]. Arrhythmias may result from electrolytic disturbances, such as hypokalaemia, hypomagnesaemia and altered acid–base balance [87,88], frequently occurring in anorexia nervosa as a result of diuretic and laxative abuse [89]. Heart rate variability is greater in anorexic patients than in controls, correlating inversely with body mass index (BMI) values [80]. During refeeding, anorexics may develop arrhythmias, possibly related to hypophosphataemia occurring during the first weeks of nutritional rehabilitation [90].

Congestive heart failure may occur terminally in anorexics and sometimes has been seen also as a consequence of refeeding. The reason for this is unclear, but rapid glucose-rich hyperalimentation and fluid replacement may potentiate starvation-induced hypophosphataemia and place excessive demands on failing myocardial reserves [40,88]. Sudden death with unexpected cardiovascular collapse may occur as a consequence of arrhythmias linked to electrolytic abnormalities [86]. A lethal cardiomyopathy may be produced by ipecac abuse, because emetin induces a negative inotropic effect and favours the development of defects of conduction due to inhibition of the contracting proteins.

Pericardial effusion has been reported in anorexia nervosa, often without overt symptomatology. The cause of the phenomenon is not clear, but it seems to develop more frequently during refeeding and weight restoration [91].

As seen in simple starvation, electrocardiographic (ECG) alterations occur frequently in anorexics. They include low voltage, prolonged Q time, increased QT dispersion, longer QRS intervals, a shift to the right of the QRS axis, diminished amplitude of the QRS complex and T wave, depression of the ST tract, inversion of T wave, occasional U waves linked to hypokalaemia and hypomagnesaemia, premature atrial and ventricular heart beats and less frequent ventricular tachiarrythmias [86,87,92–96]. The inversion of the T wave and the prolonged Q time, whose occurrence increases the risk of tachiarrythmias, prevail in bulimics and in bingeing/purging anorexics in whom hypokalaemia and hypomagnesaemia are more severe. Sometimes, however, ECG impairments occur also in patients without evident electrolytic alterations, possibly linked to hypertonus of the central autonomic system. Alterations of the repolarization, in fact, occur after sympathetic stimulation of the hypothalamus followed by intramyocardial secretion of catecholamines [81]. Most of the ECG changes are reversible, often improving rapidly with correction of electrolytic disturbances and with return to normal nutrition and hydration [97,98]. Holter monitoring shows normal chronotropic function [99].

Patients with bulimia nervosa show fewer ECG alterations than those with anorexia nervosa. A slightly longer mean QT has been reported [94,100,101].

Hypotension of less than 90/60 mmHg may be present in up to 85% of anorexics and much less frequently in bulimics [102], usually as a result of chronic volume depletion and orthostatic changes, resulting in frequent bouts of dizziness and occasionally frank syncope. Circadian variations of blood pressure (a sharp rise in the morning, another peak in the late afternoon and a nadir during the night) are occasionally present in the starvation phase of anorexia nervosa and revert to normal after refeeding [103].

Pulmonary Alterations

Pulmonary alterations are observed infrequently in anorexia and bulimia nervosa and are usually secondary to vomiting or refeeding. Pneumomediastinum has been observed in anorexia and bulimia nervosa with and without vomiting: patients complain of shortness of breath and pleuritic chest pain aggravated by deep inspiration or coughing, often radiating to the back, neck or shoulders. The process develops when a rapid increase in intra-alveolar pressure leads to alveolar rupture and subsequent tracking of air along perivascular planes to the mediastinum and subcutaneous. The subcutaneous emphysema is detected by a "crunchy" sensation to palpation in the skin overlying the thorax, and is heard also over the pericardium, being synchronous to systole [104].

Pulmonary oedema secondary to congestive heart failure, with dyspnoea, orthopnoea, paroxysmal nocturnal dyspnoea, dullness to percussion of the lung fields and tackles or rales on auscultation may occur in anorexia nervosa during rapid refeeding [104].

Renal Alterations

Impairments of renal function occur in as many as 70% of anorexics and much less frequently in bulimics. They include alterations of glomerular filtration rate and concentration capacity, acute or chronic renal failure, increased blood urea, pitting oedema, hypokalaemic nephropathy, pyuria, haematuria and proteinuria [105–107]. An increased risk of urolithiasis has been noted in anorexia nervosa, perhaps due to a combination of high dietary oxalate intake (from tea, spinach, rhubarb, almond and cashew nuts), chronic dehydration, low urinary excretion and purging [105,108]. Hypokalaemic nephropathy has been seen in anorexia nervosa, as a result of chronic abuse of diuretics or laxatives, and may be followed by chronic renal failure with polyuria, polydipsia and higher than normal creatinine blood concentrations [40,109]. High serum levels of uric acid and creatinine have been seen in anorexia nervosa and are considered predictors of poor outcome of the disease [107].

Muscular System Alterations

The musculature of anorexics is generally atrophic and becomes hypotonic only when starvation is really severe [110]. Bioptic studies have revealed a primary myopathy with prevalent atrophy of type II fibres [111]. This observation is peculiar because the alteration differs from those observed in simple starvation, represented by a mix of type I and II fibre atrophy [112]. Electromyographic studies have revealed increased polyphasic potentials going in parallel with an increase in plasma creatine phosphokinase concentrations [113]. Possible causes of this myopathy are the reduced total body potassium levels and the caloric and protein deficiency, together with an increased physical activity [110].

No muscular alterations have been reported in bulimia nervosa.

Skeletal Alterations

Patients with early onset anorexia nervosa tend to be slightly shorter than their peers [114]. Bony accretion and maturation, characteristic of adolescence, are generally retarded and bony maturation may actually cease during the active phases of the disease [115,116].

Osteoporosis with decreased peak bone mass, decreased mineral density, decreased total body mineral content and pathological fractures have been reported to occur frequently in anorexia nervosa, being significantly correlated with the duration of the illness and with BMI, with severe spinal osteopenia being present in at least 50% of patients [117–125]. Overt osteopenia is uncommon in anorexia nervosa [125]. It is not clear whether or not strenuously exercising anorexics have greater bone density [118].

The primary cause of the alterations is still not fully clarified. A combination of malnutrition, oestrogen deficiency, excessive cortisol secretion and insulin-like growth factor I (IGF-I) deficiency is possibly involved in their pathogenesis. Starvation does not seem to play a major role in bone alterations of anorexics, because no correlations have been observed between bone density and serum albumin (a marker of protein calorie nutrition), daily calcium intake, serum calcium, phosphorus, alkaline phosphatase, 25-hydroxyvitamin D, 1,25-dihydroxyvitamin D or parathyroid hormone levels [118,123,126]. Bone biopsies of anorexics show no evidence of hyperparathyroidism or osteomalacia [127]. However, it has been demonstrated that refeeding is associated with an increase of bone mineral density and total body mineral content [125]. The oestrogen deficiency probably results in disordered calcium regulation, loss of bone collagen [128] and an increase in the rate of bone remodelling and bone resorption relative to formation, leading to a net loss of bone mass [129]. However, reports so far have shown no association between bone loss and oestradiol concentrations and no benefit from oestrogen substitution therapy [118,130,131]. Hypercortisolism is present in anorexia nervosa, and may be an important aetiological factor in the development of osteopenia by inhibiting bone formation [123]. An inadequate skeletal consolidation occurring at puberty may be at the basis of osteoporosis, more so than a premature skeletal involution.

Osteoporosis and osteopenia have been reported to occur also in anorexic men, with the same characteristics but with a greater severity than in anorexic women [132]. This alteration might be due to the markedly reduced secretion of testosterone typical of anorexic men, as suggested by the positive correlation existing between plasma testosterone concentrations and the bone mineral density in women [35,132]. However, decreased mineral density is reported also for bulimic men whose testosterone secretion is not decreased [132].

Bilateral osteonecrosis of the talus has been reported in anorexia nervosa [133].

Haematological Alterations

Multiple haematological alterations are reported in anorexia nervosa and much less frequently in bulimia nervosa.

Leuconeutropenia, with white blood cell number much inferior to $5000/mm^3$, relative lymphocytosis and multilobed polymorphonuclear leucocytes, has been reported in two-thirds of anorexics [51,110,134,135]. This alteration could be due to hypoplasia of the bone marrow with reduction of fat, a gelatinous transformation and increased mucopolysaccharide ground substance, with markedly reduced cell production, atrophic intramedullar adipose tissue and accumulation of amorphous eosinophil extracellular material. Areas of necrosis of medullar cells, circumscribed to the gelatinous zones, have also been reported [136–139]. Gelatinous transformation and cellular necrosis represent different ends of an insufficient medullar nutrition, the former occurring when the caloric deficiency develops gradually and the latter when the starvation is acute and extremely rapid or when other threatening events, e.g. a severe infection, occur concomitantly. Other possible causes of leucopenia are an altered neutrophil distribution between central and marginal pools or a diminished neutrophil life span [140]. Both anorexics and bulimics may have bone marrow suppression secondary to excessive consumption of phenolphthalein-containing laxatives. The alteration disappears with normal nutrition and weight recovery [141]. No similar alterations have been reported in bulimia nervosa.

Anaemia has been reported to occur in at least one-third of anorexics [135,142], usually normochromic and normocytic. The bone marrow alterations reported above for leucopenia may be the cause of anaemia. Occasionally, macrocytic anaemia with elevated mean cell volume due to vitamin B_{12} deficiency may be observed. Frequently, together with anaemia there is acanthocytosis, a disorder of the red blood cell membrane. Acanthocytosis cells tend to sediment slowly and therefore reduce the erythrocyte sedimentation rate [143]. The cause of the disorder in anorexia nervosa is unknown, but it seems to be secondary to abnormalities in cholesterol metabolism [140]. Iron deficiency anaemia may occur in anorexia nervosa, being normochromic when the haemoglobin level is above 11 g/dl or microcytic, hypochromic and with anisocytosis when the haemoglobin level is below 11 g/dl [44]. Bulimic patients do not seem to have red blood cell impairments.

Thrombocytopenia has been described in nearly one-third of anorexics [142]. Purpura and petechiae are infrequent in anorexia nervosa [39,113,135,136]. Generally, no platelet alterations are observed in bulimia nervosa.

Immune System Alterations

There is a vast literature showing signs of immunosuppression in anorexia and bulimia nervosa. They include decreased total lymphocyte, CD4+ and CD51 lymphocyte subset counts and significantly lower percentage and number of CD8+ lymphocytes, with normal CD19 cell subset counts, in anorexia nervosa [144–149]. Higher than normal acute-phase response proteins [150] and decreased complement factors [151] are reported in anorexia nervosa. Transforming growth factor β concentrations are significantly increased in patients with untreated anorexia nervosa and return to normal values with weight gain [152].

Cytokine secretion has been investigated substantially in eating disorders, because some of them are known to induce anorexia and weight loss [153]. Data on proinflammatory monocytic cytokines are contradictory. Blood and cerebrospinal fluid (CSF) concentrations of interleukin 1β (IL-1β), tumor necrosis factor α (TNF-α), interleukin 6 (IL-6) and interferon γ (IFN-γ) have been reported to be normal in anorexia nervosa [151,152,154–162]. However, peripheral blood mononuclear cells (PBMC) harvested from anorexics show an increased spontaneous release of TNF-α, a normal production of this cytokine after stimulation with endotoxin, phytohaemagglutinin or tumor cells [151,154,163–165] and a decreased secretion after lipopolysaccharide stimulation [151]. Soluble TNF-α receptor I and II and soluble IL-1 receptor antagonist are normal, whereas soluble IL-6 receptor concentrations are increased in symptomatic anorexics [166]. Plasma levels of the cytokine receptor protein gp-130 and the leukaemia inhibitory factor receptor are increased in anorexia nervosa, whereas the anti-inflammatory Clara cell 16K protein is increased in bulimia nervosa [162]. Interleukin-3-like activity production by PBMC is lower in anorexics than in controls [158]. Interleukin 2 (IL-2) blood concentrations are lower than normal in anorexics [162]. *In vitro* production of IL-2 by phytohaemagglutinin-stimulated PBMC is also decreased [151,154,158,165]. The production of IFN-γ is reduced and tends to normalize after successful refeeding and nutritional rehabilitation [151,167].

The cause for these alterations is not clear, possibly being related to nutritional deficiencies or increased hypothalamic–pituitary–adrenal (HPA) axis function [153].

Metabolic Alterations

Glucose metabolism is altered in anorexia nervosa, with low–normal glycaemic levels but a diabetic-like or a flat glucose response on the glucose tolerance test [39,72,168,169]. These impairments may be due partly to decreased intestinal motility or to reduced glucose absorption, as demonstrated by the D-xylose absorption test [102]. The glucose production is guaranteed by the metabolization of glycogen from the liver, which is accompanied by ketosis and ketonuria. Insulin and glucagon concentrations may be normal or reduced, and correlate inversely with the degree of weight loss [76,170,171]. The insulin peaks after glucose stimulation are prolonged. However, insulin sensitivity is increased due to an increased number of its specific receptors [170], in contrast to the old theory of insulin resistance in anorexia nervosa [172]. All these alterations revert to normal after refeeding and weight gain [169]. In bulimia nervosa, no signs of altered glucose metabolism have been observed [173].

Lipid alterations are present in at least 50% of anorexics and are mainly represented by hypercholesterolaemia, due to an increase in LDL cholesterol because of its reduced excretion [174–176]. Plasma levels of HDL, VLDL and triglycerides are generally normal [177]. The lipid alteration has been found not to correlate with thyroid dysfunction, severity of weight loss, type of food consumption, presence of vomiting or laxative abuse. It may be caused by diminished activity of the 5α-reductase enzyme system involved in androgen metabolism, because 5α-compounds have cholesterol-lowering properties [32,33]. Metabolization of adipose tissue also has been considered responsible for the hypercholesterolaemia [174]. The alteration reverts after refeeding and weight gain [169].

In bulimia nervosa, hypercholesterolaemia unrelated to thyroid dysfunction and low free fatty acid levels have been reported [173,178]. The cause of these alterations is unknown.

In anorexia nervosa, total protein concentration in blood is reduced, with the globulin more than the albumin levels being lower than normal [72,107]. Protein catabolism involves destruction of the muscular mass. Together with dehydration, hypovolaemia, diminished plasmatic renal flow and diminished glomerular filtration, this induces an increase of blood urea. Strangely enough, an unexplained reduced urinary excretion of methylhistidine—a specific index of muscular catabolism—is observed in anorexia nervosa [179]. Very low albumin levels seem to be highly predictive of death [107]. Analysis of amino acid concentrations in plasma and red blood cells reveals a minimal reduction of the essential amino acids threonine, valine, isoleucine and leucine, normal or reduced tryptophan levels and normal or reduced tryptophan/neutral amino acid ratio. The tryptophan/neutral amino acid ratio seems to be higher in actively exercising anorexics [180–184].

Electrolyte and Vitamin Alterations

Electrolytic alterations are frequent in anorexia and bulimia nervosa, partly due to starvation-malnutrition, partly to vomiting and partly to laxative and diuretic abuse with ensuing fluid depletion and hypovolaemia. The most frequent impairments are hypokalaemia, hyponatraemia, hypochloraemia and hypochloraemic metabolic alkalosis with increased pCO_2. Hypokalaemia is mostly due to vomiting, whereas the abuse of diuretics and laxatives worsens the hypochloraemia; hyponatraemia, instead, seems to be linked to prolonged starvation [40,185,186].

Phosphoraemia and calcaemia are generally normal in anorexia and bulimia nervosa [118]. Hyperphosphataemia may be present in anorexics with severe vomiting [186], but in restricting anorexics the body stores of phosphate are depleted, usually with only a modest reduction of plasma levels [31]. Severe hypophosphataemia is due to vomiting, diarrhoea and abuse of diuretics. It may be seen, however, also during refeeding as a result of transfer of phosphate into cells for phosphorylation of glucose and for protein synthesis. This may result in myocardial dysfunction and neurological complications such as convulsions [187,188].

Hypomagnesaemia is found in up to 25% of anorexics and is associated with refractory hypocalcaemia (linked also to increased excretion of urinary calcium with renal calculi production) and hypokalaemia, which revert only after magnesium replacement [40,105,108,189,190]. All these electrolytic impairments may induce severe alterations of cardiac rhythm. Iron deficiency with depressed total iron binding capacity may be present in anorexia and bulimia nervosa, generally secondary to poor consumption of iron-rich foods [44,191,192].

Copper concentrations of hair are normal in anorexia nervosa [192]. Zinc deficiency has been reported in plasma, urine and tissues of undernourished anorexics. This alteration correlates positively with duration and severity of the disease and negatively with depressive symptomatology [192–194]. The zinc deficiency is likely to be due to starvation, impaired intestinal absorption of the metal or increased excretion through sweat. It is worth mentioning that zinc deficiency induces anorexia, weight loss, delayed growth and sexual development, depressed mood, ageusia, hair loss and skin alterations resembling those of anorexia nervosa.

All the metal alterations regress in anorexia nervosa after nutritional rehabilitation [192].

Hypercarotenaemia with normal plasma vitamin-A-binding protein and retinol-binding protein is frequently present in anorexia nervosa, especially the ANR type, and correlates with the severity of starvation [192,195,196]. The pathogenesis of this alteration has not been clarified fully. The impaired metabolism of vitamin A could be due to lipid dysmetabolism, hypothyroidism and excessive consumption of vegetables rich in carotene. The zinc deficiency could contribute to the increase in circulating levels of carotene, because it diminishes the synthesis of retinol-binding protein [196,197]. No carotene alterations have been observed in bulimia nervosa [196].

Riboflavin and pyridoxine deficiencies have been reported in anorexia nervosa. Vitamin B_{12} and folate concentrations in blood are reported to be generally low in anorexics [44,192]. Vitamin B_{12}- and vitamin C-related pellagra and scurvy have been reported infrequently in anorexia nervosa [43]. Blood 25-dihydroxyvitamin D, 1,25-dihydroxyvitamin D and 24,25-dihydroxyvitamin D concentrations are significantly lower than normal in anorexia nervosa, whereas vitamin-D-binding protein values are normal [198].

Neurophysiological Alterations

Impaired temperature regulation has been noted in anorexics [199], particularly concerning autonomic modifications required to respond to changes in environmental temperature. Anorexics exposed to cold do not increase or stabilize their core temperature and do not shiver, and when exposed to heat they exhibit minimal or absent vasodilatation and an abnormal elevation in core temperature [51]. Temperature impairments have been observed very infrequently in bulimia nervosa [106].

Sleep studies in anorexia nervosa have yielded conflicting results. Most investigations report that sleep is less deep than in controls, is frequently disrupted, the total sleep time is reduced and there is early morning wakening [200–202]. Rapid eye movement (REM) sleep latency has been reported to be shortened [203,204] or normal [202,205]. Abnormalities of sleep appear to correlate with low body weight and resolve with recovery. In bulimia nervosa no sleep alterations have been reported [201,205,206].

Endocrine Alterations

Hypothalamic–Pituitary–Adrenal (HPA) Axis

Bliss and Migeon [207] first reported increased plasma levels of cortisol in underweight anorexic patients. This finding has been replicated by several authors, who have also reported normal blood concentrations of adreno-corticotropic hormone (ACTH) and increased urinary cortisol levels in the symptomatic phase of anorexia nervosa [208–213]. The cortisol and ACTH circadian rhythms are often normal, but plasma cortisol concentrations are generally increased throughout the day. The number and amplitude of cortisol secretory bursts are usually increased in underweight anorexics [214–215]. These data support hyperactivity of the HPA axis in the symptomatic phase of anorexia nervosa. The hypercortisolaemia has been explained by both an enhanced synthesis of cortisol [210] and a reduced peripheral clearance of the hormone, with a prolongation of its half-life [209]. Because hypercortisolaemia seems to revert with the recovery of body weight [216], it has been assumed to be secondary to malnutrition. In support of this idea, it has been reported that increased plasma levels of cortisol, with a reduced metabolic clearance, and normal concentrations of ACTH also occur in subjects with protein-calorie malnutrition [217]. These subjects, however, in contrast to underweight anorexics, do not display an enhanced production of the steroid hormone. Therefore, in anorexia nervosa, hypercortisolaemia cannot be explained by sole chronic malnutrition.

Dynamic assessments of HPA axis activity suggest that hypothalamic and/or suprahypothalamic alterations may be responsible for the increased cortisol production in anorexia nervosa. Most anorexic patients have an abnormal cortisol suppression during the dexamethasone suppression test (DST) [218,219]. Although in the symptomatic phase of the illness the DST has no clinical significance, its positivity in weight-recovered patients has been associated with a poor prognosis [220], possibly reflecting a continuous stress condition negatively affecting outcome. Moreover, normal or increased cortisol responses to stimulation with ACTH, and a decreased ACTH response to corticotropin-releasing factor (CRF), are reported in underweight anorexics [214,221]. The ACTH response to CRF seems to normalize in long-term weight-restored patients [214,222]. These results are consistent with the finding of enhanced levels of CRF in the CSF of both underweight and weight-recovered anorexic subjects [222,223]. Therefore, although peripheral changes in cortisol metabolism cannot be excluded, it is likely that a central hypersecretion of CRF is responsible for the HPA axis hyperactivity in anorexia nervosa. The origin of this CRF hypersecretion is still debated [224]. Even so, the demonstration that CRF is able to promote anorexia, increase physical activity and reduce sexual behaviour in animals [225] may support a role for this peptide also in the determinism and/or maintenance of some anorexic symptoms.

From a clinical point of view, anorexics, despite their pronounced hypercortisolaemia, never display cushingoid features. Two major explanations can be provided for this phenomenon: a) anorexic patients have a reduced sensitivity to glucocorticoids because of a defect of glucocorticoid receptors; b) their malnutrition leads to a reduced availability of substrates necessary to develop the effects of glucocorticoids. The demonstration that, in underweight anorexics, the number of glucocorticoid receptors on mononuclear leucocytes does not differ from normal subjects or patients with Cushing's disease [226,227], whereas their affinity is decreased as in patients with Cushing's disease [227], suggests that anorexics lack the metabolic substrate for both the cushingoid fat distribution and the neoglucogenesis secondary to hypercortisolism.

Adrenal glands are also the main sources of the circulating androgen dehydroepiandrosterone (DHEA) and its sulphated form (DHEAS). The secretion of these steroids is driven by the CRF–ACTH system. Therefore, because of the above alterations of the HPA axis in anorexia nervosa, changes in circulating DHEA and DHEAS are expected in anorexic patients. Initial work on small patient samples provided evidence for a decreased production of both DHEA and DHEAS in underweight anorexics [228,229]. This reduction, together with the increase in cortisol levels, leads to decreased DHEA/cortisol and DHEAS/cortisol ratios, reflecting a dissociation in the adrenal secretion similar to that occurring in the pubertal stage of sexual maturation. Therefore, it was hypothesized that, in acutely ill postpubertal anorexics, there is a regression to a prepubertal status of functioning, affecting not only the reproductive axis (see below) but also the HPA axis. However, this hypothesis has not been confirmed by a recent larger study [213], which has found increased plasma levels of DHEA,

DHEAS and cortisol with a preservation of their ratios in underweight anorexic women.

The most widely reported alteration of the HPA axis in bulimia nervosa is the non-suppression on the DST in a percentage of patients ranging from 20% to 60%, without significant correlations with severity and chronicity of the illness, concomitant depressive symptoms or previous history of anorexia nervosa [230–233]. This alteration disappears after successful treatment of bulimia nervosa, and is not predictive of treatment outcome [234]. However, in spite of DST non-suppression, the circadian rhythm of cortisol is reported to be unaltered in patients with bulimia nervosa [221]. This discrepancy has been explained partially by the finding of reduced dexamethasone plasma levels in non-suppressor compared with suppressor bulimics [230]. Therefore, changes in the absorption and/or metabolism of dexamethasone may explain non-suppression on the DST in some bulimic patients. Morning baseline plasma concentrations of cortisol are reported to be either normal or increased [212,213], whereas urinary excretion of free cortisol and 17-hydroxycorticosteroids, as well as cortisol responses to CRF or ACTH, are reported to be normal [186,214,230]. Thus, in contrast to anorexic patients, HPA axis activity is only slightly altered in normal-weight bulimic subjects.

Hypothalamic–Pituitary–Gonadal (HPG) Axis

Amenorrhoea is a key diagnostic feature of anorexia nervosa. It is related to a status of hypogonadotropic hypogonadism with low plasma concentrations of luteinizing hormone (LH), follicle-stimulating hormone (FSH) and oestrogens. In the symptomatic phase of the illness, the circadian pattern of gonadotropin secretion resembles that in the prepubertal stage, with secretory pulses almost completely absent during the day and occasionally present at night [235–237]. This regression to a prepubertal stage of functioning of the hypothalamic–pituitary–gonadal (HPG) axis is confirmed by dynamic assessments. Indeed, the HPG axis response to exogenous gonadotropin-releasing hormone (GnRH) administration is characterized by low or absent secretion of LH and FSH (with a prevalence for FSH response over LH), like before pubertal maturation [238,239]. Moreover, emaciated anorexics exhibit a normal negative feedback of oestrogens on the HPG axis, but lack the oestrogen positive feedback [240], which is a functional capacity that is acquired in the late stages of pubertal maturation. Indeed, the LH response to clomiphene administration is blunted in these subjects [241].

All the abnormalities of the HPG axis are reverted by low-dose pulsatile administration of GnRH [242], which supports the idea that, in emaciated anorexics, HPG dysfunctions are related to deficient or dysrhythmic hypothalamic GnRH release. The origin of this GnRH dysregulation is not completely clear. It is known that a critical minimum body weight is necessary for normal HPG axis functioning, because oestrogens are synthesized from androgens in the fat tissue [243]. Therefore, it has been hypothesized that the low body fat mass of underweight anorexics may be responsible for a deficient aromatization of androgens to oestrogens, with a consequent hypoestrogenaemia and a failing of the positive oestrogen feedback on hypothalamic GnRH secretion. Baseline LH concentrations and LH response to GnRH are reported to correlate with the degree of body weight loss and body fat percentage [244]. However, this relationship is not confirmed by all the authors [245] and oestradiol substitution fails to correct the abnormal LH secretion in anorexics [15]. Furthermore, the critical body weight hypothesis is not consistent with the observation that, in some patients, amenorrhoea precedes body weight loss [245] or persists after the recovery of normal weight [14]. Therefore, factors other than body weight changes may be involved in the determinism of HPG axis dysfunctions in anorexia nervosa. One of these factors could be the increased physical activity of anorexics, because in athletic women with amenorrhoea the menstrual dysfunction was found to correlate with the intensity of physical exercise rather than body fat mass. Moreover, Falk and Halmi [13] found that in patients with eating disorders menstrual irregularities are related to the anorectic behaviour as well as the body weight. It has been proposed that an increased endogenous opioid tonus could be responsible for the HPG axis dysfunctions in anorexia nervosa, because opioid peptides have been shown to be involved in the pathogenesis of amenorrhoea in lean non-anorexic women [246] and in exercise-associated amenorrhoea [247]. However, in amenorrhoeic anorexics, treatment with the opioid antagonist naltrexone is not able to restore menstrual cyclicity [248].

Clinically, besides being involved in amenorrhoea, oestrogen deficiency is likely to be implicated in the pathogenesis of osteopenia. The decrease in bone density of anorexic patients correlates with the duration of amenorrhoea [123]; oestrogen administration, however, does not result in the amelioration of osteopenia in undernourished patients, suggesting that other factors are likely to be involved in the determinism of bone changes in anorexia nervosa [118,130,131].

Menstrual irregularities, such as oligomenorrhoea or amenorrhoea, occur in almost half of the women with bulimia nervosa, especially in those with concomitant anxious or depressive symptoms and a more chronic course of bulimic attacks [249]. With regard to the HPG axis activity, normal or decreased levels of 17β-oestradiol, decreased levels of progesterone and either normal or decreased values of plasma gonadotropins with a reduced circadian pulsatility are reported in bulimia nervosa [250–253]. These alterations are more evident in bulimics with a reduced calorie intake [233] or with a weight loss greater than 15% of the usual body weight [254]. In contrast to anorexia nervosa, however, it has been shown that in bulimia nervosa the LH secretion is deranged more in the amplitude than in the frequency of secretory pulses, and the LH response to GnRH is normal or even enhanced [255]. These HPG axis irregularities are ascribed to food restriction and protein malnutrition of bulimic patients. In addition, Kaye *et al.* [256] have shown that, in bulimics, binge episodes induce a dramatic increase in plasma prolactin (PRL) levels; hence, repeated hyperprolactin-aemia could impair HPG axis activity, because of the inhibitory action of this hormone on GnRH release [257].

Hypothalamic–Growth Hormone–Somatomedin Axis

In emaciated anorexics, increased plasma levels of growth hormone (GH) and reduced plasma concentrations of IGF-I or somatomedin C are commonly present [30,241,258–260]. Increased GH levels seem to be negatively correlated to the caloric ingestion, because they decrease with the amelioration of nutritional intake before a significant recovery of body weight has taken place [261]. Besides the reduced IGF-I levels, decreased plasma concentrations of GH binding protein (GHBP), resembling those of prepubertal children, are present in undernourished anorexics [262,263]. Because GHBP represents the extracellular domain of GH receptors, its decrease in the blood reflects a reduced sensitivity to GH in anorexia nervosa. Therefore, the decrease of both IGF-I and GHBP in emaciated anorexics points to a state of GH resistance, which is probably why hypersecretion of GH in these patients does not result in acromegalic manifestations. It has been shown that also the concentrations of IGF-I binding proteins (IGFBP), especially IGFBP-3, are reduced in emaciated anorexics [264]. This result has not been replicated by other authors, who report increased levels of circulating IGFBP, which would result in a decrease of free IGF-I. Because free IGF-I is the biologically active form [265], its reduction would be consistent with the decreased sensitivity of symptomatic anorexics to GH. However, free IGF-I levels are reported to be normal in anorexia nervosa [266].

The GH response to GH-releasing hormone (GHRH) is increased in anorexic patients [30,267,268] and the decrease in peripheral IGF-I may play a role in this phenomenon, because this somatomedin exerts a negative feedback on GH secretion. It has been demonstrated recently that the administration of recombinant human IGF-I in anorexic patients signifi-cantly reduces basal GH levels and decreases, but does not restore, the GH response to exogenous GHRH [269]. This finding suggests that, besides the reduced negative feedback of peripheral IGF-I, a central dysregulation of GH secretion also occurs in anorexia nervosa. In particular, the hyperresponsiveness of GH to GHRH is not inhibited by the cholinergic antagonist pirenzepine [270], nor is it increased by the cholinergic agonist pyridostigmine [271,272]. Because acetylcholine has a stimulatory action on hypothalamic somatostatin, these findings support the idea that GH hypersecretion in anorexia nervosa is partially linked to a reduced somatostatin tone because of an increased hypothalamic cholinergic activity [273]. However, assessment of somatostatin secretion has provided conflicting results, because either low or normal levels of this hormone have been found in symptomatic anorexic patients [274,275]. Paradoxical responses of GH to both GnRH and thyrotrophin-releasing hormone (TRH) [276–278] and a lack of suppression of the GH response to GHRH by CRF administration [279] occur in anorexia nervosa. Finally, GH responses to insulin, clonidine, L-dopa and apomorphine are lower than normal in underweight anorexics [30,280], suggesting a dysfunction in both the noradrenergic and dopaminergic modulation of GH secretion.

It seems evident that in underweight anorexics peripheral mechanisms, such as the decreased IGF-I production, resulting from both the reduced calorie intake and concomitant receptor alterations, increase GH secretion because of impairment of the negative regulatory feedback. Concomitantly, primary or secondary hypothalamic or supra-hypothalamic changes may further affect GH production.

From a clinical point of view, the dysregulation of the hypothalamic–GH–IGF-I axis may be involved in the pathogenesis of osteopenia, because IGF-I has a trophic effect on the bone. Moreover, in prepubertal subjects, the "resistance" to GH may be responsible for a delay or a stop in the growth, with the possibility that when these alterations resolve the final height be lower than that determined genetically [281]. The recently available recombinant human IGF-I or GH could have therapeutic applications in anorexic patients in order to prevent bone loss or bone fractures and to facilitate a more rapid metabolic recovery. In this regard, Grinspoon et al. [265,282] have reported recently that the administration of recombinant human IGF-I in severely osteopenic anorexic women increases the markers of bone turnover in the short term and ameliorates bone density in the medium term (9 months); the latter effect is potentiated by concomitant oral contraceptive administration. Moreover, Hill et al. [283] have shown that anorexic patients treated with recombinant human GH achieve medical/cardiovascular stability more rapidly.

Both increased and normal baseline GH levels with a normal circadian rhythm are reported in individuals with bulimia nervosa [30,276,284,285]. Circulating IGF-I, instead, is reduced [286,287]. Growth hormone responses to clonidine or apomorphine are blunted or normal [30,284,288] and, as with anorexia nervosa, the administration of TRH induces an abnormal increase in GH secretion that persists after the normalization of eating behaviour [255,276,284].

Hypothalamic–Pituitary–Thyroid Axis

Decreased circulating levels of triiodothyronine (T_3) with increased concentrations of reversed T_3 (rT_3), which is biologically inactive, and normal thyroxine (T_4) and thyroxine-stimulating hormone (TSH) levels are common in symptomatic anorexic patients [289,290]. The decrease in circulating T_3 has been attributed classically to a reduced peripheral deionization of T_4 with a simultaneous increased formation of rT_3, which delineates a "low T_3 syndrome". This condition is adaptive to the chronic reduction in caloric intake and the decreased resting energy expenditure of the organism. With normal refeeding and recovery of body weight, the low T_3 syndrome resolves. According to some authors, the normalization of circulating T_3 in recovering anorexics is related more to the speed than to the entity of weight recovery [291]. However, in emaciated anorexics the low T_3 level has been found not always associated with increased rT_3, which suggests that factors other than changes in the peripheral metabolism of T_3 may contribute to this state. It has been argued that low IGF-I as well as hypercortisolaemia may be implicated [292,293]. In spite of the reduction of circulating T_3, TSH is not increased in symptomatic anorexics. This phenomenon can be explained by the fact that, in a condition of low energy expenditure, a decrease in endogenous metabolic processes occurs in all the cells of the organism, including pituitary thyrotropes, which interpret the low T_3 levels as sufficient for the metabolic needs of the organism; in such a condition, TSH secretion does not increase.

Even if baseline production of TSH is not altered in anorexia nervosa, its central modulation seems to be deranged. Indeed, in underweight anorexic patients, the TSH response to exogenous TRH is time-delayed [294,295] and, in some cases, lower than normal [296]. The delayed TSH response to TRH has been related to nutritional status, because a similar phenomenon occurs in non-anorexic women after significant weight loss [297] and disappears in anorexics who recover their body weight [276,295]. However, a persisting delayed TSH response to TRH has been also described in weight-recovered anorexics [298]. It has been suggested that an impaired hypothalamic TRH secretion could be responsible for the deranged TSH response to exogenous TRH. In support of this idea, decreased concentrations of endogenous TRH have been detected in the CSF of both emaciated and weight-restored anorexics [299]. Finally, atrophy of the thyroid gland may occur in underweight anorexics [300]; this alteration has been related to the low IGF-I levels, because thyroid size is clearly influenced by this peptide [301].

Baseline concentrations of T_4 and T_3 are generally unaltered in subjects with bulimia nervosa [186,295,302]. Occasionally, low circulating T_3 can also be detected [303]. Baseline concentrations of TSH are mostly normal in bulimia nervosa [186,276,304], whereas the TSH response to TRH is normal [186,276,295], blunted [233] or delayed [284,305].

Hypothalamic–Prolactin Axis

The majority of studies report normal baseline concentrations of PRL in underweight anorexics [239,276,296,306,307]. However, slightly reduced or even increased plasma PRL concentrations can also occur [211–213,308,309]. Hafner *et al.* [310] reported normal diurnal but increased nocturnal concentrations of PRL in anorexic patients, and argued that this alteration could be related to nutritional factors, because a vegetarian diet selectively decreases nocturnal secretion of the lactotrope hormone. The PRL response to TRH is reported to be normal by most of the authors [239,276,296,306,307] and paradoxical responses to both GnRH and GHRH can be detected in the symptomatic phase of anorexia nervosa [311,312].

Investigation of the central neurotransmitter modulation of PRL secretion in anorexia nervosa has provided evidence for altered dopaminergic and serotonergic regulation. Indeed, PRL responses to dopamine antagonists (metoclopramide) and to indirect (*d*-fenfluramine) and direct (*m*-chlorophenylpiperazine) 5-HT agonists are blunted in emaciated anorexics [29,211,212,313,314]. The serotonergic dysregulation seems to be related to the nutritional status, because PRL responses to both *d*-fenfluramine and *m*-chlorophenylpiperazine normalize in weight-restored patients [314–316].

Normal, decreased or increased baseline PRL levels can be observed in bulimic patients [186,212,251,252,276,317–320], whereas the PRL response to TRH is generally normal [276,317].

The hypothalamic serotonergic control of PRL secretion has been investigated comprehensively in bulimia nervosa. Initial work suggested an impaired PRL response to L-tryptophan in bulimics with concomitant depressive disorders [320]. Subsequent studies reported decreased PRL responses to both *d*-fenfluramine and *m*-chlorophenylpiperazine that are not related to psychopathology [212,252,318–320]. In particular, because the PRL response to *d*-fenfluramine correlates with the frequency of binge/vomit episodes, it is speculated that the blunted PRL response to serotonergic stimulation represents a specific neuroendocrine correlate of bingeing behaviour [212,252]. However, in patients with binge eating disorder, who binge without vomiting or purging and do not incur malnutrition, the PRL response to d-fenfluramine is normal, suggesting that the impaired serotonergic modulation of PRL secretion in severely ill bulimic patients is related to nutritional factors and not to the bingeing behaviour [212,252].

Melatonin

Melatonin is the main secretory product of the pineal gland. In humans, as well as in other species, melatonin shows a characteristic circadian rhythm with low plasma concentrations during the day and high plasma levels at night [321]. This secretion pattern is driven by the light/dark cycle. However, other factors such as stress, nutritional patterns and body weight changes have a role in the modulation of the melatonin circadian rhythm. It has been shown in animals that food deprivation increases the nocturnal secretion of the pineal hormone [322], whereas in humans a positive correlation between body weight and nocturnal melatonin is reported [323]. Furthermore, in obese subjects, body weight reduction profoundly affects the circadian profile of the hormone, with a flattening of its nocturnal secretion and the occurrence of diurnal secretory peaks [324].

Given this background and the well-known role of melatonin in the regulation of reproductive activity [321], studies have been performed to assess melatonin secretion in eating disorders. Initial works showed either a reduction or no change in the 24-h melatonin secretion in severely underweight anorexics [325,326], with the decreased nocturnal production of the hormone significantly related to concomitant depression [327]. Subsequent studies, instead, reported a profound derangement of the melatonin circadian rhythm in severely undernourished anorexics, with higher than normal plasma hormone levels throughout the 24-h cycle, secretory peaks during the day and phase changes in the nocturnal peak [215,328,329]. Kennedy et al. [330,331] did not confirm a derangement of circadian rhythm of melatonin in either emaciated or weight-restored anorexics, but reported an increased diurnal urinary excretion of 6-sulphatoxymelatonin (the main metabolite of the pineal hormone) in emaciated patients who binge and purge. Thus, it seems that in anorexia nervosa the circadian melatonin secretion is disrupted because of an enhanced diurnal production of the hormone, and this alteration is more evident in anorexic patients with binge/purge behaviour. The increased diurnal secretion of melatonin could be involved in the pathophysiology of amenorrhoea, because of the inhibitory role of the pineal hormone on reproductive activity.

No changes in the melatonin circadian rhythm occur in bulimia nervosa [332,333].

Central and Peripheral Appetite-regulating Peptides

A large number of central and peripheral peptides are known to be involved in the regulation of eating behaviour and body weight. In recent years, several studies have investigated the possible role of these substances in the pathophysiology of eating disorders. Interest has focused especially on neuropeptide Y (NPY), opioid peptides, galanin, cholecystokinin and leptin.

Hypothalamic NPY is among the most potent stimulators of hunger and preferential carbohydrate intake. Underweight anorexics have significantly elevated CSF concentrations of NPY that do not normalize after short-term weight restoration [334]. In long-term weight-restored patients the CSF concentration of NPY is found to be normal but those weight-recovered subjects who continue to have amenorrhoea still have significantly elevated concentrations of NPY [334]. Because NPY is involved in the modulation of the HPG axis [335], the persistent elevation of NPY in the CSF after weight gain could contribute to persistent amenorrhoea in those patients.

Although the elevation of NPY may represent a homeostatic mechanism to stimulate feeding and decrease energy expenditure, it is also likely that increased NPY activity could contribute to the obsessive and paradoxical interest in calorie intake and food preparation of anorexic patients. Alternatively, as suggested by Kaye [334], the chronic elevation of NPY could induce a down-regulation of NPY receptors, leading to the food refusal and avoidance of sweet foods typically found in symptomatic anorexics.

The CSF and plasma concentrations of NPY are normal during the symptomatic phases of bulimia nervosa and after clinical recovery [336,337].

Similarly to NPY, endogenous opioids stimulate hunger and promote a preferential carbohydrate intake. An initial study reported an increased overall opioid tonus in the CSF of underweight anorexics, without differentiating among the various opioid peptides [338]. Subsequent work by the same group [339] showed decreased CSF levels of β-endorphin in emaciated anorexics; these reduced levels persist in short-term weight-restored patients and normalize in long-term weight-recovered subjects. The CSF dynorphin levels are normal in both emaciated and weight-restored anorexics [340,341].

Peripheral concentrations of β-endorphin are reported to be either reduced or increased in underweight anorexics [342–344]. Moreover, Brambilla et al. [345] report a loss of the β-endorphin circadian rhythm in symptomatic anorexics, with an increased nocturnal secretion of the opioid peptide and blunted responses to clonidine, 5-hydroxytryptophan and domperidone stimulations. Because endogenous opioids have an inhibitory action on hypothalamic LH-releasing hormone release, it is possible that the increased overall opioid tonus of underweight anorexics could contribute to their HPG axis dysfunctions. However, underweight anorexics do not show an increase of LH secretion after administration of the opiate antagonists naloxone and naltrexone [248,346], which suggests that some other endogenous factors are responsible for the deranged LH secretion in anorexia nervosa.

The CSF concentrations of β-endorphin are decreased, while dynorphin levels are normal in subjects with bulimia nervosa [347]. Moreover, normal, decreased or increased levels of β-endorphin have been detected in the blood of bulimic individuals [348–350]. Finally, normal levels of this opioid peptide are reported in PBMC of bulimic patients [351].

Hypothalamic galanin is an orexigenic peptide that stimulates a preferential fat intake. Plasma levels of this peptide are normal in anorexic patients [344,352,353]. The CSF levels of galanin, instead, are normal in anorexics who have been weight-restored for more than 6 months [354], but decreased in those who have been weight-restored for more than 1 year [355]. The possibility that a decreased CSF concentration of galanin could be a trait marker of anorexia nervosa deserves further investigation.

No change of galanin secretion is reported in bulimia nervosa [356].

Cholecystokinin (CCK), produced both centrally and peripherally, is thought to be a satiety-inducing hormone. In anorexia nervosa, inconsistent results have been reported concerning the baseline plasma levels of CCK [274,344,357]. However, decreased levels of CCK8 have been found in PBMC, a peripheral compartment that mimics the secretion and regulation of neurohormones in central neurons [358]. Moreover, a more rapid and stronger post-prandial rise of serum CCK occurs in undernourished patients [357,359]. It can be argued that a too rapid and strong CCK-induced satiety signal might contribute to food refusal in anorexia nervosa, even when meals are quantitatively very reduced. In contrast to this hypothesis, some authors have reported a normal post-prandial rise of circulating CCK in underweight anorexics [360,361] as well as a normalization of this response in weight-restored patients [357].

In subjects with bulimia nervosa, concentrations of CCK in the CSF [362] and in PBMC [351] are reported to be decreased. A normal or blunted CCK rise after meal has been observed [359,360]. The decreased values of CCK do not correlate to either BMI or the frequency of binge/vomit episodes, but are significantly related to anxiety, hostility, aggression and impairment of interpersonal sensitivity [362]. Moreover, intravenous CCK is able to suppress a single binge in a few bulimics [363]. This finding, together with the reported decreased basal values and blunted post-prandial rise of CCK, may support the idea that impaired CCK secretion may be responsible for the bingeing behaviour in bulimic patients.

The recently discovered peripheral hormone leptin, which is secreted by white adipocytes and is responsible for genetic obesity in the mouse, has gained widespread interest in eating disorder pathophysiology, because it is a potent satiety factor and is involved in the fasting-induced inhibition of the gonadal axis [364]. In particular, leptin behaves as a peripheral sensor of the body fat mass: when adipose stores of the organism increase, leptin is produced in larger amounts, which signals to the brain the need to reduce food ingestion and to increase energy expenditure. However, factors other than adipocyte size and fat content, especially energy availability and the macro–micronutrient composition of the diet, influence leptin production [364].

Given this background, it is not surprising that in underweight people with anorexia nervosa the plasma leptin levels are consistently reduced and correlate with patients' BMI and body fat mass [365–368]. During the recovery of body weight, a progressive increase in leptin concentrations is observed in anorexic individuals [366]. Furthermore, it has been shown that, in anorexics undergoing nutritional treatment, a too rapid weight gain, which implies a substantial increase in circulating leptin, is associated with a poor prognosis [369]. Because leptin is a satiety factor, this finding would suggest that a too rapid increase of leptin production during nutritional rehabilitation would result in a possible excessive suppression of appetite and an enhanced energy expenditure that contrast with the therapeutic process. Finally, given the stimulatory role of leptin on the HPG axis, its reduced production in anorexia nervosa could be involved in the determinism of menstrual alterations. In this regard, evidence has been provided that a critical leptin level is needed to maintain menstrual cyclicity in underweight women [370].

In normal-weight subjects with bulimia nervosa, circulating leptin is reported to be either decreased or normal [253,367,368,371,372]. Studies showing reduced leptin levels in bulimics indicate that this alteration was not related to changes in patients' BMI or body fat mass [368,371,372]. Moreover, leptin response to acute fasting is completely blocked in symptomatic bulimics [253]. These results suggest that the deranged leptin physiology in bulimia nervosa reflects changes in subjects' nutritional parameters and/or eating patterns rather than modifications of body fat mass.

Because leptin behaves as a satiety factor, it is possible that its reduced production contributes to the binge eating behaviour of bulimics. Indeed, human laboratory studies suggest that bulimic patients have diminished satiety responses [6], that could be mediated by either a decreased tonic production of leptin or a lack of its adequate response to acute changes in the energy intake.

SUMMARY

Consistent Evidence

It is clear that in patients with eating disorders medical complications are very common and usually occur as consequences of nutritional derangements secondary to the aberrant eating and abnormal compensatory behaviours. In the most severe cases, impairments of peripheral organs and apparata represent a significant threat to the patient's life. In emaciated anorexics, immediate risks come from starvation-induced cardiovascular and renal alterations, which may lead to the development of severe arrhythmias and sudden death. Cardiovascular risks are increased in those subjects who vomit and/or abuse diuretics and laxatives, because of the severe electrolytic perturbations that can follow these aberrant behaviours. In the longer term, underweight anorexics are exposed to consequences of the progressive impairment in bone density that increases the likelihood of pathological fractures. There is consistent evidence in the literature that bone alterations are linked to the hypoactivity of HPG and hypothalamic–GH–somatomedin axes and, in some individuals, to the increased production of cortisol. Moreover, it is evident that in emaciated anorexics the impaired function of the reproductive axis and the reduced activity of the thyroid gland aim to preserve residual energy stores for vital functions and reduce the basal metabolic needs of the organism. It is also evident that, with a few exceptions, medical complications resolve with the recovery of body weight and the discontinuation of aberrant behaviours.

In bulimia nervosa, medical complications are less severe and occur less frequently than in anorexia nervosa. Therefore, they rarely represent a serious threat to the patient's life. The most harmful complications are represented by oesophageal and/or gastric ruptures, secondary to the massive ingestion of food in the course of binge episodes, and cardiac arrhythmias induced by severe electrolytic imbalance following vomit and diuretic or laxative abuse.

It is important to remember that in patients with eating disorders those medical complications not representing life-threatening conditions increase the patients' burden of suffering and therefore need clinical consideration and appropriate treatment.

Incomplete Evidence

There is considerable variation in the literature regarding the nature and severity of alterations in secretion of some endogenous hormones and central and peripheral appetite-regulating substances in patients with eating disorders. These changes are summarized in Tables 3.1 and 3.2. It has

TABLE 3.1 Summary of neuroendocrine changes in the acute phases of anorexia nervosa and bulimia nervosa

	Anorexia nervosa	Bulimia nervosa
Hypothalamic–pituitary–adrenal axis		
Plasma cortisol	↑	→↑
Urinary cortisol	↑	→
Plasma ACTH	→↓	
Dexamethasone Suppression Test	↑	↑
Cortisol response to ACTH	→	↗
ACTH response to CRF	↓	→
CSF CRF	↑	
Plasma DHEA, DHEA-S	↑↓	↑
Hypothalamic–pituitary–gonadal axis		
Plasma oestradiol	↓	→↓
Plasma LH	↓	→↓
Plasma FSH	↓	→↓
LH response to GnRH	↓	→
Hypothalamic–growth hormone axis		
Plasma GH	↑	→↓
Plasma IGF-I	↓	↓
Plasma GHBP	↓	
GH response to GHRH	↑	
GH response to clonidine	↓	→↓
GH response to apomorphine	↓	→↓
Hypothalamic–thyroid axis		
Plasma T$_3$	↓	→↓
Plasma rT$_3$	↑	
Plasma T$_4$	→	→
Plasma TSH	→	→
TSH response to TRH	↓ or delayed	→↓ or delayed
CSF TRH	↓	
Hypothalamic–prolactin axis		
Plasma PRL	↑→↓	↑→↓
PRL response to TRH	→	→
PRL response to 5-HT agonists	↓	↓
Melatonin		
Circadian rhythm	↑*	→

↑, increased; →, unchanged; ↓, decreased; *, increased plasma levels with secretory peaks during the day; ACTH, adrenocorticotropin hormone; CRF, corticotropin-releasing factor; DHEA, dehydroepiandrosterone; DHEA-S, sulphated dehydroepiandrosterone; LH, luteinizing hormone; FSH, follicle-stimulating hormone; GnRH, gonadotropin-releasing hormone; GH, growth hormone; IGF-I, insulin-like growth factor I; GHBP, growth hormone binding protein; TSH, thyroxine-stimulating hormone; TRH, thyrotropin-releasing hormone; PRL, prolactin; CSF, cerebrospinal fluid; 5-HT, serotonin.

TABLE 3.2 Summary of the changes in central and peripheral appetite-regulating peptides in the acute phases of anorexia nervosa and bulimia nervosa

	Anorexia nervosa	Bulimia nervosa
Neuropeptide Y		
CSF neuropeptide Y	↑	→
Opioid peptides		
CSF overall opioid tonus	↑	
CSF β-endorphin	↓	↓
CSF dynorphin	→	→
Plasma β-endorphin	↓↑	↑→↓
Galanin		
Plasma galanin	→	→
CSF galanin	→*↑**	
Cholecystokinin (CCK)		
Plasma CCK	→↓	↓
CCK response to meal	→↑	→↓
Leptin		
Plasma leptin	↓	→↓
Leptin response to acute fasting		↓

↑, increased; →, unchanged; ↓, decreased; *, in anorexics weight-restored for more than 6 months; **, in anorexics weight-restored for more than 1 year; CSF, cerebrospinal fluid; CCK, cholecystokinin.

been proposed that some of these aberrations are not merely the consequence of malnutrition, but they may be implicated in the pathophysiology of anorexia and bulimia nervosa. In particular, aberrant post-prandial rises in CCK have been suggested to be involved in both the food refusal of anorexic patients and the bingeing behaviour of bulimic individuals. Similarly, it has been suggested that reduced peripheral leptin may be involved in the pathogenesis of amenorrhoea in underweight anorexics and in the altered modulation of satiety in bulimia nervosa. However, the roles of these peptides in the pathophysiology of eating disorders are still not well defined. Finally, it has been proposed recently that the administration of recombinant human IGF-I together with oral contraceptives may be useful in the treatment of bone alterations in anorexia nervosa. This evidence, however, is still preliminary.

Areas Still Open to Research

The reports in the literature on the medical complications and physiological aberrations of eating disorders leave some questions open.

- First of all, the pathogenesis of medical alterations and physiological aberrations has not been clarified definitely. In fact, if for most of them a cause–effect link with global starvation-malnutrition or with a lack of specific micro–macronutrients has been demonstrated soundly, for others this is not so clear. In fact, even though each alteration develops after substantial eating restriction and weight loss have started and disappears after restoration of normal eating habits and weight, the correlations between some impairments and nutritional indices (BMI, body fat mass, etc.) are not always significant. It may be suggested that certain alterations are not linked to starvation-malnutrition in general, but rather to the lack of specific micro–macronutrients, whose deficiency does not necessarily lead to reduction of body weight or fat mass, but just to specific dysmetabolism. Only after correction of the micro–macronutrient deficiencies do the impairments subside, independently of BMI or fat mass restoration. Thus, investigation of the possible cause–effect links between medical alterations and total or partial food deficiency is today mandatory. Alternatively, some impairments may be due indirectly to starvation-malnutrition, being secondary to the occurrence of other nutritionally linked alterations. This possibility must be investigated before dismissing the hypothesis of nutritional deficiencies as being the cause of medical impairments in eating disorders. Anyway, it must be pointed out that secondary physiological aberrations also may contribute to the pathophysiology of eating disorders, favouring the maintenance of aberrant behaviours. This is especially true for alterations of hormones and appetite-regulating substances. Indeed, although most of these have been interpreted to represent secondary changes, most likely reflecting adaptive mechanisms to chronic malnutrition and prolonged starvation, it is possible that they may sustain certain symptoms. For example, in anorexia nervosa, an increased secretion of CRF seems to occur as a consequence of starvation; CRF has been shown to induce anorexia, decrease sexual behaviour and promote excessive physical activity in the experimental animal [225]. Therefore, the possibility exists that, in anorexia nervosa, CRF changes, although secondary to starvation, play a role in the maintenance of certain symptoms and aberrant behaviours. This is an area certainly worthy of further investigations.
- The second point worth mentioning is the fact that some alterations persist after restoration of normal eating habits and weight. Typical is the amenorrhoea occurring in anorexia nervosa, which is certainly linked to starvation-malnutrition and to weight and fat mass loss, but may persist long after normalization of these parameters. The cause of this phenomenon is not clear, but it has been demonstrated that it correlates with the persistence of some psychopathological aspects of the disorder

and seems to disappear only with their correction. This may suggest that the cause of the alteration is complex, depending on both nutritional deficiencies and psychopathological impairments. However, we cannot exclude the fact that the psychopathological alterations are due to nutritional deficiencies, and that they just need a longer eating pattern rehabilitation than that required for medical complications in general.

- The third point that stems from the data reported above is the lack of investigation on the feedback effects that the medical alterations typical of anorexia and bulimia nervosa may exert on the course and prognosis of these disorders. It has been suggested generically that severe starvation and extremely low BMI for anorexia nervosa or very high frequency of bingeing/purging for bulimia nervosa are negative prognostic factors, and that a nutritional rehabilitation is indispensable to obtain a complete psychological recovery. But what is the mechanism of action of the nutritional alterations in worsening the prognosis of eating disorders? It may be that specific metabolic alterations, such as low lipid or protein blood and tissue concentrations, induce modifications of neuronal membrane composition (lipids) or neurotransmitter secretion and function (proteins), thus resulting in impaired central nervous system (CNS) efficiency with ensuing specific psychopathological aspects. In turn, the CNS alterations may have their own time of recovery that is not always coincident with the peripheral nutritional rehabilitation. Unfortunately, we have only experimental animal data in this regard, human data still being sparse and not always consistent.
- The fourth point that has never been taken soundly into consideration is the influence that medical alterations may exert on the capacity of anorexics and bulimics to respond to therapies. Again, it has been suggested generically that excessive food restriction and weight loss are negative prognostic factors for the response of anorexics to therapies, and that excessive purging does the same in bulimics. This led to the suggestion that nutritional rehabilitation for both disorders, obtained during a prolonged hospitalization, should always precede any therapeutic intervention. However, it has never been explained why excessively severe eating impairments in anorexia and bulimia nervosa prevent a significant therapeutic response and what is the mechanism of action for it. It could be suggested that the medical alterations may prevent or alter a correct absorption of psychotropic drugs used in anorexia and bulimia nervosa, acting through the above reported impairments of gastrointestinal function in general and intestinal absorption in particular. Or, in anorexia nervosa, a reduced drug absorption could be linked to the relative hypothyroidism observed during severe starvation. But what about psychotherapeutic treatments? It could be that the starvation-induced metabolic alterations can prevent

normal neurotransmitter secretion and function, with no ensuing response to treatments. Again, these hypotheses have never resulted in sufficiently sound investigations.

- Finally, no long-lasting follow-up has ever been done on the possible persistence of medical complications or on their reappearance after apparent recovery from anorexia and bulimia nervosa. Have these alterations really and definitely disappeared, or may they reappear in relation to rather modest fluctuations of eating habits? In other words, do the functions of peripheral organs and apparata completely normalize and stabilize after recovery from anorexia and bulimia nervosa or have they become sensitized to modest fluctuations of quantity and quality of food consumption, becoming more easily impaired? And what can be the prognostic influence of these subthreshold dysfunctions?

In conclusion, the major challenge for future investigations of physiological aberrations in eating disorders is to delineate carefully the interactive effects of these aberrations and discern how they may perpetuate the disturbed behaviours, cognitions and motivations present in patients with eating disorders.

REFERENCES

1. Owen W.P., Halmi K.A., Gibbs J., Smith G.P. (1985) Satiety responses in eating disorders. *J. Psychiatr. Res.*, **19**: 279–284.
2. Nakai Y., Kinoshita F., Koh T., Tsujii S., Tsukada T. (1987) Perception of hunger and satiety induced by 2-deoxy-*d*-glucose in anorexia nervosa and bulimia nervosa. *Int. J. Eat. Disord.*, **6**: 49–57.
3. Drewnowski A., Halmi K., Pierce N., Gibbs J., Smith J.P. (1987) Taste and eating disorders. *Am. J. Clin. Nutr.*, **46**: 442–450.
4. Drewnowski A., Pierce B., Halmi K.A. (1988) Fat aversion in eating disorders. *Appetite*, **10**: 119–131.
5. van Binsbergen C.J.M., Odink J., van der Berg H., Koppeschaar H., Coeling-Bennink H.J.T. (1988) Nutritional status in anorexia nervosa: clinical chemistry, vitamins, iron and zinc. *Eur. J. Clin. Nutr.*, **42**: 929–937.
6. Walsh T.B., Kissileff H.R., Cassidy S.M., Dantzic S. (1989) Eating behavior of women with bulimia. *Arch. Gen. Psychiatry*, **46**: 54–58.
7. Rodin J., Bartoshuk L., Peterson C., Schank D. (1990) Bulimia and taste: possible interactions. *J. Abnorm. Psychol.*, **99**: 32–39.
8. Halmi K.A. (1992) Psychobiology of eating behavior. In *Psychobiology and Treatment of Anorexia Nervosa and Bulimia Nervosa* (Ed. K.A. Halmi), pp. 79–92. American Psychiatric Press, Washington.
9. Halmi K.A. (1996) The psychobiology of eating behavior in anorexia nervosa. *Psychiatry Res.*, **62**: 23–29.
10. Sunday S.R., Einthorn A., Halmi K.A. (1992) Relationship of perceived macronutrients and caloric content to affective cognitions about food in

eating-disordered, restrained and unrestrained subjects. *Am. J. Clin. Nutr.*, **55**: 362–371.

11. Rolls B.J., Andersen A.E., Moran T.H., McNelis A.L., Baier H.C., Fedoroff I.C. (1992) Food intake, hunger, and satiety after preloads in women with eating disorders. *Am. J. Clin. Nutr.*, **55**: 1093–1103.

12. Fichter M.M., Pirke K.M. (1982) Hypothalamic–pituitary function in starving healthy subjects. In *The Psychobiology of Anorexia Nervosa* (Eds K.M. Pirke, D. Ploog), pp. 124–135. Springer, Berlin.

13. Falk J.R., Halmi K.A. (1982) Amenorrhea in anorexia nervosa: examination of the critical body weight hypothesis. *Biol. Psychiatry*, **17**: 799–806.

14. Lecomte P., Kabir-Gros N., Lansac J. (1984) Gonadal function in anorexia nervosa patients in the postcritical phase. *Ann. Endocrinol. (Paris)*, **45**: 397–401.

15. Buvat J., Buvat-Herbaut M., Lemaire A., Racadot A., Fourlinnie J.C. (1984) Comparison of estrogen priming effects with body weight restoration effects on the gonadotropin pattern of patients with anorexia nervosa. *Horm. Res.*, **20**: 224–230.

16. Kohmura H., Miyake A., Aono T., Tanizawa O. (1986) Recovery of reproductive functions in patients with anorexia nervosa: a 10-year follow-up study. *Eur. J. Obstet. Gynecol. Reprod. Biol.*, **22**: 293–296.

17. Treasure J.L., Wheeler M., King E.A., Gordon P.A., Russell G.F. (1988) Weight gain and reproductive function: ultrasonographic and endocrine features in anorexia nervosa. *Clin. Endocrinol.*, **29**: 607–616.

18. Halmi K.A., Dekirmenjian H., Davis J.M., Casper R., Goldberg S. (1978) Catecholamine metabolism in anorexia nervosa. *Arch. Gen. Psychiatry*, **35**: 458–460.

19. Johnston J.L., Leiter L.A., Burrow J.N., Garfinkel P.E., Anderson G.H. (1984) Excretion of urinary catecholamine metabolites in anorexia nervosa: effect of body composition and energy intake. *Am. J. Clin. Nutr.*, **40**: 1001–1006.

20. Owen W.P., Halmi K.A., Lasley E., Stokes P. (1983) Dopamine regulation in anorexia nervosa. *Psychopharmacol. Bull.*, **19**: 578–581.

21. Ebert M.H., Kaye W.K., Gold P.W. (1984) Neurotransmitter metabolism in anorexia nervosa. In *The Psychobiology of Anorexia Nervosa* (Eds K.M. Pirke, D. Ploog), pp. 58–72. Springer, Berlin.

22. Gerner R.H., Cohen D.J., Fairbanks L., Anderson G.M., Young J.G., Scheini M., Linnoila M., Shaywitz B.A., Hare T.A. (1984) CSF neurochemistry of women with anorexia nervosa and normal women. *Am. J. Psychiatry*, **141**: 1441–1444.

23. Kaye W.H., Ebert M.H., Raleigh M., Lake C.R. (1984) Abnormalities in CNS monoamine metabolism in anorexia nervosa. *Arch. Gen. Psychiatry*, **41**: 350–355.

24. Kaye W.H., Gwirtsman H.E. (1985) Mood changes and patterns of food consumption during bingeing and purging: are there underlying neurobiologic relationships? In *A Comprehensive Approach to the Treatment of Normal Weight Bulimia* (Eds W.H. Kaye, H.E. Gwirtsman), pp. 19–36. American Psychiatric Press, Washington.

25. Kaye W., Frank G., Klump K. (1999) Psychophysiology of obsessional behaviors in anorexia and bulimia nervosa. In *Eating Disorders and Obsessive-Compulsive Disorder: an Etiopathogenetic Link?* (Eds L. Bellodi, F. Brambilla), pp. 57–76. Centro Scientifico Editore, Turin.

26. Jimerson D.C., Lesem M.D., Kaye W.H., Brewerton T.D. (1988) Symptom severity and neurotransmitter studies in bulimia. *Psychopharmacology*, **96** (Suppl.): 124.

27. van Binsbergen C.J., Odink J., van der Beek E.J., Westenberg H.M.G., Coeling Bennink H.J.T. (1991) Biogenic amines in anorexia nervosa: circadian rhythm in urinary excretion and influence of posture and physical task load on plasma catecholamines. *Psychosom. Med.*, **53**: 440–452.

28. Bowers M.B., Jr., Mazure C.M., Greenfeld D.G. (1994) Elevated plasma monoamine metabolites in eating disorders. *Psychiatry Res.*, **52**: 11–15.

29. Brewerton T.D., Jimerson D.C. (1996) Studies of serotonin function in anorexia nervosa. *Psychiatry Res.*, **62**: 31–42.

30. Brambilla F., Bellodi L., Arancio C., Ronchi P., Limonta D. (2001) Central dopaminergic function in anorexia and bulimia nervosa: a psychoneuroendocrine approach. *Psychoneuroendocrinology*, **26**: 393–409.

31. Pirke K.M., Eckert M., Ofers B., Goebl G., Spyra B., Schweiger U., Tuschl R.J., Fichter M.M. (1989) Plasma norepinephrine response to exercise in bulimia, anorexia nervosa and controls. *Biol. Psychiatry*, **25**: 799–802.

32. Boyar R.M., Bradlow H.L. (1977) Studies of testosterone metabolism in anorexia nervosa. In *Anorexia Nervosa* (Ed. R.A.Vigersky), pp. 263–270. Raven Press, New York.

33. Schwabe A.D., Lippe B.M., Chang R.J., Pops M.A., Yager J. (1981) Anorexia nervosa. *Ann. Intern. Med.*, **94**: 371–381.

34. Lacey J.H. (1982) Anorexia nervosa and a bearded female saint. *Br. Med. J.*, **285**: 1816–1817.

35. Brambilla F., Bellodi L., Arancio C., Limonta D. Ferrari E., Solerte B. (2001) Neurotransmitter and hormonal background of hostility in anorexia nervosa. *Neuropsychobiology*, **43**: 225–232.

36. Russell G. (1979) Bulimia nervosa: an ominous variant of anorexia nervosa. *Psychol. Med.*, **9**: 429–448.

37. Williams J.F., Friedman I.M., Steiner H. (1986) Hand lesions characteristic of bulimia. *Am. J. Dis. Child.*, **140**: 28–29.

38. Strumia R., Varotti E., Manzato E., Gualandi M. (2001) Skin signs in anorexia nervosa. *Dermatology*, **203**: 314–317.

39. Silverman J.A. (1983) Clinical and metabolic aspects of anorexia nervosa. *Int. J. Eat. Disord.*, **2**: 159–166.

40. Hall R.C., Beresford T.P. (1989) Medical complications of anorexia and bulimia. *Psychiatr. Med.*, **7**: 165–192.

41. Alcalay J., Ingber A., Sandbank M. (1986) Mask phenomenon: postemesis facial purpura. *Cutis*, **38**: 28.

42. Donley A.J., Kemple T.J. (1978) Spontaneous pseudomediastinum complicating anorexia nervosa. *Br. Med. J.*, **2**: 1604–1605.

43. Gupta M.A., Gupta A.K., Haberman H.F. (1987) Dermatologic signs in anorexia nervosa and bulimia nervosa. *Arch. Dermatol.*, **123**: 1386–1390.

44. Carney C.P., Andersen A.E. (1996) Eating disorders. Guide to medical evaluation and complications. *Psychiatr. Clin. North Am.*, **19**: 657–679.

45. Clark D. C. (1985) Oral complications of anorexia nervosa and/or bulimia: with a review of the literature. *J. Oral Med.*, **40**: 134–138.

46. Scheutzel P. (1996) Etiology of dental erosion intrinsic factors. *Eur. J. Oral Sci.*, **104**: 178–190.

47. Anderson L., Shaw J.M., McCargar L. (1997) Physiological effects of bulimia nervosa on the gastrointestinal tract. *Can. J. Gastroenterol.*, **11**: 451–459.

48. Milosevic A. (1999) Eating disorders and the dentist. *Br. Dent. J.*, **186**: 109–113.

49. House R.C., Grisius R., Bliziotes M.M. (1981) Perymolisis: unveiling the surreptitious vomiter. *Oral Surg. Med. Pathol.*, **51**: 152–155.

50. Walsh B.T., Croft C.B., Katz J.L. (1981) Anorexia nervosa and salivary gland enlargement. *Int. J. Psychiatr. Med.*, **11**: 255–261.
51. Scharp C.W., Freeman C.P. (1993) The medical complications of anorexia nervosa. *Br. J. Psychiatry*, **162**: 452–462.
52. Taylor V.E., Sneddon J. (1987) Bilateral facial swelling in bulimia. *Br. Dent. J.*, **163**: 115–117.
53. Chami T.N., Andersen A.E., Crowell M.D., Schuster M.M., Whitehead W.E. (1995) Gastrointestinal symptoms in bulimia nervosa: effects of treatment. *Am. J. Gastroenterol.*, **90**: 88–92.
54. Cuellar R.E., Van Thiel D.H. (1986) Gastrointestinal consequences of the eating disorders: anorexia nervosa and bulimia. *Am. J. Gastroenterol.*, **81**: 1113–1124.
55. Stacher G., Kiss A., Wiesnagrotzki S., Bergman H., Hobart J., Schneider C. (1986) Oesophageal and gastric motility disorders in patients categorized as having primary anorexia nervosa. *Gut*, **27**: 1120–1126.
56. Evans D.S. (1968) Acute dilatation and spontaneous rupture of the stomach. *Br. J. Surg.*, **55**: 940–942.
57. Robinson P.H., Clarke M., Barrett J. (1988) Determinants of delayed gastric emptying in anorexia nervosa and bulimia nervosa. *Gut*, **29**: 458–464.
58. Scobie B.A. (1973) Acute gastric dilatation and duodenal ileus in anorexia nervosa. *Med. J. Aust.*, **2**: 932–934.
59. Hill K.K., Hill D.B., Humphries L.L., Maloney M.J., McClain C.J. (1999) A role for *Helicobacter pylori* in the gastrointestinal complaints of eating disorder patients? *Int. J. Eat. Disord.*, **25**: 109–112.
60. Nakao A., Isozaki H., Iwagaki H., Kanagawa T. ,Takakura N., Tanaka N. (2000) Gastric perforation caused by a bulimic attack in an anorexia nervosa patient: report of a case. *Surg. Today*, **30**: 435–437.
61. Chun A.B., Sokol M.S., Kaye W.H., Hutson W.R., Wald A. (1997) Colonic and anorectal function in constipated patients with anorexia nervosa. *Am. J. Gastroenterol.*, **92**: 1879–1883.
62. Waldholtz B., Andersen A.E. (1990) Gastrointestinal symptoms in anorexia nervosa: a prospective study. *Gastroenterology*, **98**: 1415–1419.
63. Chiarioni G., Bassotti G., Monsignori A., Menegotti M., Saladini C., Di Matteo G., Vantini I., Whitehead W.E. (2000) Anorectal dysfunction in constipated women with anorexia nervosa. *Mayo Clin. Proc.*, **75**: 1015–1019.
64. Wittoesch J.H., Jackman R.J., McDonald J.R. (1958) *Melanosis coli*: general review and a study of 887 cases. *Dis. Colon Rectum*, **1**: 172–180.
65. Oster J.R., Materson B.J., Rogers A.I. (1980) Laxative abuse syndrome. *Am. J. Gastroenterol.*, **74**: 451–458.
66. Yamada Y., Nishimura S., Inoue T., Tsujimura T., Fushimi H. (2001) Anorexia nervosa with ischemic necrosis of the segmental ileum and cecum. *Intern. Med.*, **40**: 304–307.
67. Malik M., Stratton J., Sweeney W.B. (1997) Rectal prolapse associated with bulimia nervosa: report of seven cases. *Dis. Colon Rectum*, **40**: 1382–1385.
68. Rienemann J.F., Schenk J., Ehler R. (1978) Ultrastructural changes of colonic mucosa in patients with chronic laxative abuse. *Acta Hepatogastroenterol.*, **25**: 213–218.
69. Heizer W.D., Warshaw A.L., Waldman T.A. (1969) Protein-losing gastroenteropathy and malabsorption associated with factitious diarrhea. *Ann. Intern. Med.*, **68**: 839–852.
70. Nickl N.J., Brazer S.R., Rockwell K., Smith J.W. (1996) Patterns of esophageal motility in patients with stable bulimia. *Am. J. Gastroenterol.*, **91**: 2544–2547.

71. Geliebter A., Hashim S.A. (2001) Gastric capacity in normal, obese, and bulimic women. *Physiol. Behav.*, **74**: 743–746.

72. Umeki S. (1988) Biochemical abnormalities of the serum in anorexia nervosa. *J. Nerv. Ment. Dis.*, **176**: 503–506.

73. Halmi K., Falk J.R., Schwartz E. (1981) Binge-eating and vomiting: a survey of college population. *Psychol. Med.*, **11**: 697–706.

74. Herzog D.B., Keller M.B., Lavori P.W. (1988) Outcome in anorexia nervosa and bulimia nervosa. A review of the literature. *J. Nerv. Ment. Dis.*, **176**: 131–143.

75. Brown N.W., Treasure J.L., Campbell I.C. (2001) Evidence for a long-term pancratic damage caused by laxative abuse in subjects recovered from anorexia nervosa. *Int. J. Eat. Disord.*, **29**: 236–238.

76. Kobayashi N., Tamai H., Uehata S., Komaki G., Mori K., Matsubayashi S., Nakagawa T. (1988) Pancreatic abnormalities in patients with eating disorders. *Psychosom. Med.*, **50**: 607–614.

77. Gwirtsman H.E., Kaye W.H., George D.T., Carosella N.W., Greene R.C., Jimerson D.C. (1989) Hyperamylasemia and its relationship to binge-purge episodes: development of a clinically relevant laboratory test. *J. Clin. Psychiatry*, **50**: 196–204.

78. Keane F.B., Fennell J.S., Tomkin G.H. (1978) Acute pancreatitis, acute gastric dilatation, duodenal ileus following refeeding in anorexia nervosa. *Irish J. Med. Sci.*, **147**: 191–192.

79. Fohlin L. (1977) Body composition, cardiovascular and renal function in adolescent patients with anorexia nervosa. *Acta Paediatr. Scand.*, **268** (Suppl.): 1–20.

80. Rechlin T., Weis M., Ott C., Bleichner F., Joraschky P. (1998) Alterations of autonomic cardiac control in anorexia nervosa. *Biol. Psychiatry*, **43**: 358–363.

81. Johnson G.L., Humphries L.L., Shirley P.B., Mazzoleni A., Noonan J.A. (1986) Mitral valve prolapse in patients with anorexia nervosa and bulimia. *Arch. Intern. Med.*, **146**: 1525–1529.

82. Gottdiener J.S., Gross H.A., Henry W.L., Borer J.S., Ebert M.H. (1978) Effects of self-induced starvation on cardiac size and function in anorexia nervosa. *Circulation*, **58**: 425–433.

83. de Simone G., Scalfi L., Galderisi M., Celentano A., Di Biase G., Tammaro P., Garofalo M., Mureddu G.F., de Divitiis O., Contaldo F. (1994) Cardiac abnormalities in young women with anorexia nervosa. *Br. Heart J.*, **71**: 287–292.

84. Eidem B.W., Cetta F., Webb J.L., Graham L.C., Jay M.S. (2001) Early detection of cardiac dysfunction: use of myocardial performance index in patients with anorexia nervosa. *J. Adolesc. Health*, **29**: 267–270.

85. Oka Y., Matsumoto S., Seumatsu H., Ogata E. (1987) Mitral valve prolapse in patients with anorexia nervosa: a two dimensional echocardiographic study. *Jpn. Heart J.*, **28**: 873–882.

86. Isner J.M., Roberts W.C., Heymsfield S.B., Yager J. (1985) Anorexia nervosa and sudden death. *Ann. Intern. Med.*, **102**: 49–52.

87. Arik T.H., Dresser K.B., Benchimol A. (1985) Cardiac complications of intensive dieting and eating disorders. *Arizona Med.*, **42**: 72–74.

88. Schocken D.D., Holloway J.D., Powers P.S. (1989) Weight loss and the heart. Effects of anorexia nervosa and starvation. *Arch. Intern. Med.*, **149**: 877–881.

89. Warren S.E., Steinberg S.M. (1979) Acid-base and electrolyte disturbances in anorexia nervosa. *Am. J. Psychiatry*, **136**: 415–418.

90. Kohn M.R., Golden N.H., Shenker I.R. (1998) Cardiac arrest and delirium: presentation of a refeeding syndrome in severely malnourished adolescents with anorexia nervosa. *J. Adolesc. Health*, **22**: 239–243.

91. Frolich J., von Gontard A., Lehmkuhl G., Pfeiffer E., Lehmkuhl U. (2001) Pericardial effusion in anorexia nervosa. *Eur. Child Adolesc. Psychiatry*, **10**: 54–57.

92. Gould L., Reddy C.V., Singh B.K., Zen B. (1980) Evaluation of cardiac conduction in anorexia nervosa. *Pace*, **3**: 660–665.

93. Webb J.G., Birmingham C.L., MacDonald I.L. (1988) Electrocardiographic abnormalities in anorexia nervosa. *Int. J. Eat. Disord.*, **7**: 785–790.

94. Cooke R.A., Chambers J.B., Singh R., Todd G.J., Smeeton N.C., Treasure J., Treasure T. (1994) QT interval in anorexia nervosa. *Br. Heart J.*, **72**: 69–73.

95. Swenne I., Larsson P.T. (1999) Heart risk associated with weight loss in anorexia nervosa and eating disorders: risk factors for QTC interval prolongation and dispersion. *Acta Paediatr.*, **88**: 304–309.

96. Galetta F., Franzoni F., Cupisti A., Belliti D., Prattichizzo F., Rolla M. (2002) QT interval dispersion in young women with anorexia nervosa. *J. Pediatr.*, **140**: 456–460.

97. Hoffman R.S., Hall R.C. (1989) Reversible E.K.G. changes in anorexia nervosa. *Psychiatr. Med.*, **7**: 211–216.

98. Swenne I. (2000) Heart risk associated with weight loss in anorexia nervosa and eating disorders: electrocardiographic changes during the early phase of refeeding. *Acta Paediatr.*, **89**: 447–452

99. Lupoglazoff J.M., Berkane N., Denjoy I., Maillard G., Leheuzey M.F., Mouren-Simeoni M.C., Casasoprana A. (2001) Cardiac consequence of adolescent anorexia nervosa. *Arch. Mal. Coeur Vaiss.*, **94**: 494–498.

100. Contaldo F., Di Paolo M.R., Mazzacano C., Di Biase G., Giumetti D. (1990) Hypopotassiemia and prolongation of the Q-T interval in a patient with severe malnutrition caused by bulimia and post-prandial vomiting. *Rec. Progr. Med.*, **81**: 266–268.

101. Panagiotopoulos C., McCrindle B.W., Hick K., Katzman D.K. (2000) Electro-cardiographic findings in adolescents with eating disorders. *Pediatrics*, **105**: 1100–1105.

102. Warren M.P., van de Wiele R.L. (1973) Clinical and metabolic features of anorexia nervosa. *Am. J. Obstet. Gynecol.*, **117**: 435–449.

103. Awazu M., Matsuoka S., Kamimaki T., Watanabe H., Matsuo N. (2000) Absent circadian variation of blood pressure in patients with anorexia nervosa. *J. Pediatr.*, **136**: 524–527.

104. Overby K.J., Litt I.F. (1988) Mediastinal emphysema in an adolescent with anorexia nervosa and self-induced emesis. *Pediatrics*, **81**: 134–136.

105. Brotman A.W., Stern T.A., Brotman D.L. (1986) Renal disease and dysfunction in two patients with anorexia nervosa. *J. Clin. Psychiatry*, **47**: 433–434.

106. Palla B., Litt I.F. (1988) Medical complications of eating disorders in adolescents. *Pediatrics*, **81**: 613–623.

107. Herzog W., Deter H.C., Fiehn W., Petzold E. (1997) Medical findings and predictors of long-term physical outcome in anorexia nervosa: a prospective 12-year follow-up study. *Psychol. Med.*, **27**: 269–279.

108. Silber T.J., Kass E.J. (1984) Anorexia nervosa and nephrolithiasis. *J. Adolesc. Health Care*, **5**: 50–52.

109. Fleming B.J., Genuth S.M., Gould A.B., Kamionkowski M.D. (1975) Laxative-induced hypokalemia, sodium depletion and hyperreninemia. Effects of

potassium and sodium replacement on the renin-angiotensin-aldosterone system. *Ann. Intern. Med.*, **83**: 60–62.

110. Alloway R., Shur E., Obrecht R., Russell G.F. (1988) Physical complications in anorexia nervosa. Haematological and neuromuscular changes in 12 patients. *Br. J. Psychiatry*, **153**: 72–75.

111. Slettebo M., Lindboe C.F., Askevold F. (1984) The neuromuscular system in patients with anorexia nervosa. *Clin. Neuropathol.*, **3**: 217–224.

112. Dastur D.K., Daver S.M., Manghani D.K. (1979) Changes in muscle in human malnutrition with an emphasis on the structure in protein-calorie malnutrition. In *Progress on Neuropathology* (Ed. H.H. Zimmermann), pp. 125–138. Raven Press, New York.

113. Alloway R., Reynolds E.H., Spargo E., Russell G.F.M. (1985) Neuropathy and myopathy in two patients with anorexia and bulimia nervosa. *J. Neurol. Neurosurg. Psychiatry*, **48**: 1015–1020.

114. Crisp A.H. (1969) Some skeletal measurements in patients with primary anorexia nervosa. *J. Psychosom. Res.*, **13**: 125–142.

115. Lacey J.H., Crisp A.H., Hart G., Kirkwood B.A. (1979) Weight and skeletal maturation: a study of radiological and chronological age in an anorexia nervosa population. *Postgrad. Med. J.*, **55**: 381–385.

116. Ayers J.W., Gidwani G.P., Schmidt I.M.V., Gross M. (1984) Osteopenia in hypoestrogenic young women with anorexia nervosa. *Fertil. Steril.*, **41**: 224–228.

117. Brincat M., Parsons V., Studd J. (1983) Anorexia nervosa. *Br. Med. J.*, **287**: 1306.

118. Rigotti N.A., Nussbaum S.R., Hertzog D.B., Neer R.M. (1984) Osteoporosis in women with anorexia nervosa. *N. Engl. J. Med.*, **311**: 1601–1606.

119. Rigotti N.A., Neer R.M., Jameson L. (1986) Osteopenia and bone fracture in a man with anorexia nervosa and hypogonadism. *JAMA*, **256**: 385–388.

120. Brotman A.W., Stern T.A. (1985) Osteoporosis and pathologic fractures in anorexia nervosa. *Am. J. Psychiatry*, **142**: 495–496.

121. Warren M.P., Shane E., Lee M.J., Lindsay R., Dempster D.W., Warren L.F., Hamilton W.G. (1990) Femoral head collapse associated with anorexia nervosa in a 20-year-old ballet dancer. *Clin. Orthopaed.*, **251**: 171–176.

122. Bachrach L.K., Guido D., Katzman D., Litt I.F., Marcus R. (1990) Decreased bone density in adolescent girls with anorexia nervosa. *Pediatrics*, **86**: 440–447.

123. Biller B.M., Saxe V., Herzog D.B., Rosenthal D.J., Holtzman S., Klibanski A. (1989) Mechanism of osteoporosis in adult and adolescent women with anorexia nervosa. *J. Clin. Endocrinol. Metab.*, **68**: 548–554.

124. Nishizawa K., Iijima M., Tokita A., Yamashiro Y. (2001) Bone mineral density of eating disorder. *Nippon Rinsho*, **59**: 554–560.

125. Jagielska G., Wolanczyk T., Komender J., Tomaszewicz-Libudzic C., Przedlacki J., Ostrowski K., (2001) Bone mineral content and bone mineral density in adolescent girls with anorexia nervosa: a longitudinal study. *Acta Psychiatr. Scand.*, **104**: 131–137.

126. Carmichael K.A., Carmichael D.H. (1995) Bone metabolism and osteopenia in eating disorders. *Medicine (Baltimore)*, **74**: 254–267.

127. Szmukler G.I., Brown S.W., Parsons S.W., Darby A. (1985) Premature loss of bone in chronic anorexia nervosa. *Br. Med. J.*, **290**: 26–27.

128. Savvas M., Treasure J., Studd J., Fogelman I., Moniz C., Brincat M. (1989) The effect of anorexia nervosa on skin thickness, skin collagen and bone density. *Br. J. Obstet. Gynaecol.*, **96**: 1392–1394.

129. Dalsky G.P. (1990) Effect of exercise on bone: permissive influence of estrogen and calcium. *Med. Sci. Sport Exerc.*, **22**: 281–285.

130. Hay P.J., Hall A., Delahunt J.W., Harper G., Mitchell A.W., Salmond C. (1989) Investigation of osteopaenia in anorexia nervosa. *Aust. N. Zeal. J. Psychiatry*, **23**: 261–268.

131. Klibanski A., Biller B.M., Schoenfeld D.A., Herzog D.B., Saxe V.C. (1995) The effects of estrogen administration on trabecular bone loss in young women with anorexia nervosa. *J. Clin. Endocrinol. Metab.*, **80**: 898–904.

132. Andersen A.E., Watson T., Schlechte J. (2000) Osteoporosis and osteopenia in men with eating disorders. *Lancet*, **355**: 1967–1968.

133. Milos G., Willi J., Hauselmann H. (2001) Bilateral osteonecrosis of the talus and "standing obsession" in a patients with anorexia nervosa. *Int. J. Eat. Disord.*, **29**: 363–369.

134. Bowers T.K., Eckert E. (1978) Leukopenia in anorexia nervosa. Lack of increased risk of infection. *Arch. Intern. Med.*, **138**: 1520–1523.

135. Lambert M., Hubert C., Depresseux G., van de Berg B., Thissen J.P., Nagant de Deuxchaisnes C., Devogelaer J.P. (1997) Hematological changes in anorexia nervosa are correlated with total body fat mass depletion. *Int. J. Eat. Disord.*, **21**: 329–334.

136. Mant M.J., Faragher B.S. (1972) The haematology of anorexia nervosa. *Br. J. Haematol.*, **23**: 737–749.

137. Amrein P.C., Friedman R., Kosinski K., Ellman L. (1979) Hematologic changes in anorexia nervosa. *JAMA*, **241**: 2190–2191.

138. Smith R.R., Spivak J.L. (1985) Marrow cell necrosis in anorexia nervosa and involuntary starvation. *Br. J. Haematol.*, **60**: 527–530.

139. van de Berg B.C., Malghem J., Devuyst O., Maldague B.E., Lambert M.J. (1994) Anorexia nervosa: correlation between MR appearance of bone marrow and severity of disease. *Radiology*, **193**: 859–864.

140. Kay J., Stricker R.B. (1983) Haematologic and immunologic abnormalities in anorexia nervosa. *South. Med. J.*, **76**: 1008–1010.

141. Steinberg S.E., Nasraway S., Peterson L. (1987) Reversal of severe serous atrophy of the bone marrow in anorexia nervosa. *J. Parent. Enter. Nutr.*, **11**: 422–423.

142. Rieger W., Brady J.P., Weisberg E. (1978) Hematologic changes in anorexia nervosa. *Am. J. Psychiatry*, **135**: 984–985.

143. Anyan W.R., Jr. (1974) Changes in the erythrocyte sedimentation rate and fibrinogen during anorexia nervosa. *J. Pediatr.*, **85**: 525–527.

144. Pirke K.M., Nerl C., Jurgen-Kristian K., Fichter M.M. (1992) Immunological findings in anorexia and bulimia nervosa. *Int. J. Eat. Disord.*, **11**: 185–189.

145. Fink S., Eckert E., Mitchell J., Crosby R., Pomeroy C. (1996) T-lymphocyte subsets in patients with abnormal body weight: longitudinal studies in anorexia nervosa and obesity. *Int. J. Eat. Disord.*, **20**: 295–305.

146. Marcos A., Varela P., Toro O., Nova E., Lopez-Vidriero I., Morande G. (1997) Evaluation of nutritional status by immunological assessment in bulimia nervosa: influence of body mass index and vomiting episodes. *Am. J. Clin. Nutr.*, **66**: 491S–497S.

147. do Carmo I., Palma-Carlos M.L., Melo A., Jorge Z., Macedo A., Nunes S., Galvao-Teles A., Palma-Carlos A.G. (1997) Characterization of leukocytes, lymphocytes and lymphocyte subsets in eating disorders. *Allerg. Immunol.*, **29**: 261–268.

148. Mustafa A., Ward A., Treasure J., Peakman M. (1997) T-lymphocyte subpopulations in anorexia nervosa and refeeding. *Clin. Immunol. Immunopathol.*, **82**: 282–289.

149. Allende L.M., Corell A., Manzanares J., Madruga D., Marcos A., Madrono A., Lopez-Goyanes A., Garcia-Perez M.A., Moreno J.M., Rodrigo M., Sanz F., Amaiz-Villena A. (1998) Immunodeficiency associated with anorexia nervosa is secondary and improves after refeeding. *Immunology*, **94**: 543–551.

150. Tracey K.J., Lowry S.F., Cerami A. (1987) Physiological responses to cachectin. In *Tumor Necrosis Factor and Related Cytokines*. Ciba Foundation Symposium, pp. 88–108. Wiley, Chichester.

151. Schattner A., Steinbock M., Tepper R., Schonfeld A., Vaisman N., Hahn T. (1990) Tumor necrosis factor production and cell-mediated immunity in anorexia nervosa. *Clin. Exp. Immunol.*, **79**: 62–66.

152. Pomeroy C., Eckert B., Hu S., Eiken B., Mentink M., Crosby R.D., Chao C.C. (1994) Role of interleukin-6 and transforming growth factor-β in anorexia nervosa. *Biol. Psychiatry*, **36**: 836–839.

153. Maes M., Van West D. (1999) Cytokine production in anorexia nervosa and obsessive-compulsive disorder: a review. In *Eating Disorders and Obsessive-Compulsive Disorder: an Etiopathogenetic Link?* (Eds L. Bellodi, F. Brambilla), pp. 111–124. Centro Scientifico Editore, Turin.

154. Emeric Sauval E., Polack E., Bello M., Guitelman A., Finkielman S., Nahmod V., Arzt E. (1989) Anorexia nervosa and bulimia: a model for the study of immune-neuroendocrine interactions in response to human CRH. *Neuroendocrinol. Lett.*, **11**: 270–273.

155. Licinio J., Listvak S., Altemus M.E., Wong M.L., Demitrack M., Tamarkin L., Kling M. Gold P.W. (1990) Serum and CSF interleukin-1 in bulimia nervosa. *Biol. Psychiatry*, **27**: 147A.

156. Licinio J., Altemus M.E., Wong M., Gold P.W. (1991) Circulating levels of interleukin-2 in patients with anorexia nervosa. *Biol. Psychiatry*, **29**: 56A.

157. Licinio J., Altemus M.E, Heterington M.M., Bernat A., Gold P.W. (1992) 24-hour rhythms of circulating interleukin-1-alpha in actively binging and purging patients with bulimia nervosa. Presented at the 5th International Conference on Eating Disorders, New York, 24–26 April.

158. Bessler H., Karp L., Notti I.., Apter A., Tyano S., Djaldetti M., Weizman R. (1993) Cytokine production in anorexia nervosa. *Clin. Neuropharmacol.*, **16**: 237–243.

159. Mitchell J.E., Eckert E., Pomeroy C. (1994) The role of cytokines in anorexia nervosa. *Neuropsychopharmacology*, **10**: 2065.

160. Vaisman N., Barak Y., Hahn T., Karov Y., Malach L., Barak V. (1996) Defective *in vitro* granulopoiesis in patients with anorexia nervosa. *Pediatr. Res.*, **40**: 108–111.

161. Brambilla F., Bellodi L., Brunetta M., Perna G. (1998) Plasma concentrations of interleukin-1β, interleukin-6 and tumor necrosis factor-α in anorexia and bulimia nervosa. *Psychoneuroendocrinology*, **23**: 439–447.

162. Monteleone P., Maes M., Fabrazzo M., Tortorella A., Bosmans E., Kenis G., Maj M. (1999) Immunoendocrine findings in patients with eating disorders. *Neuropsychobiology*, **40**: 57–62.

163. Vaisman N., Schaltner A., Hahn T. (1989) Tumor necrosis factor production during starvation. *Am. J. Med.*, **87**: 115.

164. Schattner A., Tepper R., Steinbock M., Hahn T., Schoenfeld A. (1990) TNF, interferon-γ and cell-mediated cytotoxicity in anorexia nervosa; effect of refeeding. _J. Clin. Lab. Immunol._, **32**: 183–184.
165. Holden R.J., Pakula I.S. (1996) The role of tumor necrosis factor-alpha in the pathogenesis of anorexia and bulimia nervosa, cancer cachexia and obesity. _Med. Hypoth._, **47**: 423–438.
166. Brambilla F., Monti D., Franceschi C. (2001) Plasma concentrations of interleukin-1-beta, interleukin-6 and tumor necrosis factor-alpha, and of their soluble receptors and receptor antagonist in anorexia nervosa. _Psychiatry Res._, **103**: 107–114.
167. Polack E., Nahmod V.E., Emeric Sauval E., Bello M., Costas M., Finkielman S., Arzt E. (1993) Low lymphocyte interferon-gamma production and variable proliferative response in anorexia nervosa patients. _J. Clin. Immunol._, **13**: 445–451.
168. Crisp A.H. (1965) Some aspects of evolution, presentation and follow-up of anorexia nervosa. _Proc. R. Soc. Med._, **58**: 814–820.
169. Beumont P.J.V., Russell J. (1982) Anorexia nervosa. In _Handbook of Psychiatry and Endocrinology_ (Eds P.J.V. Beumont, G.D. Burrows), pp. 63–79. Elsevier, Amsterdam.
170. Wachschlicht-Rodbard H., Gross H.A., Rodbard D., Ebert M.H., Roth J. (1979) Increased insulin binding to erythrocytes in anorexia nervosa: restoration to normal with refeeding. _N. Engl. J. Med._, **300**: 882–887.
171. Alderdice J.T., Dinsmore W.W., Buchanan K.D., Adams C. (1985) Gastrointestinal hormones in anorexia nervosa. _J. Psychiatr. Res._, **19**: 207–213.
172. Kalucy R.S., Crisp A.H., Chard T., McNeilly A., Chen C.N., Lacey J.H. (1976) Nocturnal hormonal profiles in massive obesity, anorexia nervosa and normal females. _J. Psychosom. Res_, **20**: 595–604.
173. Weingarten H.P., Hendler R., Rodin J. (1988) Metabolism and endocrine secretion in response to a test meal in normal-weight bulimic women. _Psychosom. Med._, **50**: 273–285.
174. Klinefelter H.F. (1965) Hypercholesterolemia in anorexia nervosa. _J. Clin. Endocrinol. Metab._, **25**: 1520–1521.
175. Crisp A.H., Blendis L.M., Pawan G.L. (1968) Aspects of fat metabolism in anorexia nervosa. _Metabolism_, **17**: 1109–1118.
176. Nestel P.J (1974) Cholesterol metabolism in anorexia nervosa and hypercholesterolemia. _J. Clin. Endocrinol. Metab._, **38**: 325–328.
177. Mordasini R., Klose G., Greten H. (1978) Secondary type II hyperlipoproteinemia in patients with anorexia nervosa. _Metabolism_, **27**: 71–79.
178. Pauporte J., Walsh B.T. (2001) Serum cholesterol in bulimia nervosa. _Int. J. Eat. Disord._, **30**: 294–298.
179. Richard J.L., Rodier M., Bringer J., Bellett M.H., Mirouze J. (1982) L'adaptation métabolique à la dénutrition chronique chez l'anorectique mentale. Effet de la réalimentation. _Nouv. Press Med._, **11**: 3327–3330.
180. Schweiger U., Warnhoff M., Pahl J., Pirke K.M. (1986) Effects of carbohydrate and protein meals on plasma large neutral amino acids, glucose, and insulin plasma levels of anorectic patients. _Metabolism_, **35**: 938–943.
181. Halmi K., Struss A.L., Owen W.P., Stegink L.D. (1987) Plasma and erythrocyte amino acid concentrations in anorexia nervosa. _J. Parent. Enteral Nutr._, **11**: 458–464.
182. Schreiber W., Schweiger U., Werner D., Brunner G., Tuschl R.J., Laessle R.G., Krieg J. C., Fichter M.M., Pirke K. M. (1991) Circadian pattern of large neutral

aminoacids, glucose, insulin and food intake in anorexia nervosa and bulimia nervosa. *Metabolism*, **40**: 503–507.

183. Askenazy F., Candito M., Caci H., Myquel M., Chambon P., Darcourt G., Puech A.J. (1998) Whole blood serotonin content, tryptophan concentrations, and impulsivity in anorexia nervosa. *Biol. Psychiatry*, **43**: 188–195.

184. Favaro A., Caregaro L., Burlina A.B., Santonastaso P. (2000) Tryptophan levels, excessive exercise, and nutritional status in anorexia nervosa. *Psychosom. Med.*, **62**: 535–538.

185. Mars D.R., Anderson N.H., Riggall F.C. (1982) Anorexia nervosa: a disorder with severe acid–base derangement. *South. Med. J.*, **75**: 1038–1042.

186. Mitchell J.E., Bantle J.P. (1983) Metabolic and endocrine investigations in women of normal weight with the bulimia syndrome. *Biol. Psychiatry*, **18**: 355–365.

187. Silvis S.E., Paragas P.D., Jr. (1972) Paresthesias, weakness, seizures and hypophosphatemia in patients receiving hyperalimentation. *Gastroenterology*, **62**: 513–520.

188. Cumming A.D., Farquhar J.R., Bouchier I.A. (1987) Refeeding hypophosphataemia in anorexia nervosa and alcoholism. *Br. Med. J.*, **295**: 490–491.

189. Mitchell J.E., Pyle R.L., Eckert E.D., Hatsukami D., Lentz R. (1983) Electrolyte and other physiological abnormalities in patients with bulimia. *Psychol. Med.*, **13**: 273–278.

190. Fonseca V., Havard C.W. (1985) Electrolyte disturbances and cardiac failure with hypomagnesaemia in anorexia nervosa. *Br. Med. J.*, **291**: 1680–1682.

191. Takkunen H., Seppanen R. (1975) Iron deficiency and dietary factors in Finland. *Am. J. Clin. Nutr.*, **28**: 1141–1147.

192. Casper R.C., Kirschner B., Sandstead H.H., Jacob R.A., Davis J.M. (1980) An evaluation of trace metals, vitamins, and taste function in anorexia nervosa. *Am. J. Clin. Nutr.*, **33**: 1801–1808.

193. Ainley C.C., Cason J., Carlsson L., Thompson R.P., Slavin B.M., Norton K.R. (1986) Zinc state in anorexia nervosa. *Br. Med. J.*, **293**: 992–993.

194. Katz R.L., Keen C.L., Litt I.F., Hurley L.S., Kellams-Harrison K.M., Glader L.J. (1987) Zinc deficiency in anorexia nervosa. *J. Adolesc. Health Care*, **8**: 400–406.

195. Bhanji S., Mattingly D. (1981) Anorexia nervosa: some observations on "dieters" and "vomiters", cholesterol, and carotene. *Br. J. Psychiatry*, **139**: 238–241.

196. Jaffe A.C., McAiley L.G., Singer L. (1987) Carotenemia in normal-weight bulimia: a finding unrelated to other physical manifestations of the syndrome. *Int. J. Eat. Disord.*, **6**: 749–755.

197. Pops M.A., Schwabe A.D. (1968) Hypercarotenemia in anorexia nervosa. *JAMA*, **205**: 533–534.

198. Aarskog D., Aksnes L., Markestad T., Trygstad O. (1986) Plasma concentrations of vitamine D metabolites in pubertal girls with anorexia nervosa. *Acta Endocrinol.*, **279** (Suppl.): 458–467.

199. Mecklenburg R.S., Loriaux D.L., Thompson R.H., Andersen A.E., Lipsett M.B. (1974) Hypothalamic dysfunction in patients with anorexia nervosa. *Medicine*, **53**: 147–159.

200. Lacey J.H., Crisp A.H., Kalucy R.S., Hartmann M.K., Chien C.N. (1975) Weight gain and the sleeping electroencephalogram: study of 10 patients with anorexia nervosa. *Br. Med. J.*, **4**: 556–558.

201. Walsh B.T., Goetz R., Roose S.P., Fingeroth S., Glassman A.H. (1985) EEG-monitored sleep in anorexia nervosa and bulimia. *Biol. Psychiatry*, **20**: 947–956.

202. Levy A.B., Dixon K.N., Schmidt H. (1988) Sleep architecture in anorexia nervosa and bulimia. *Biol. Psychiatry*, **23**: 99–101.

203. Neil J.F., Merikangas J.R., Foster F.G., Merikangas K.R., Spiker D.G., Kupfer D.J. (1980) Waking and all-night sleep EEGs in anorexia nervosa. *Clin. Electroenceph.*, **11**: 9–15.

204. Katz J.L., Kuperberg A., Pollack C.P., Walsh B.T., Zumoff B., Weiner H. (1984) Is there a relationship between eating disorders and affective disorder? New evidence from sleep recordings. *Am. J. Psychiatry*, **141**: 753–759.

205. Levy A.B., Dixon K.N., Schmidt H. (1987) REM and delta sleep in anorexia nervosa and bulimia. *Psychiatry Res.*, **20**: 189–197.

206. Hudson J.I., Pope H.G., Jr., Jonas J.M., Stakes J.W., Grochocinski V., Lipinski J.F., Kupfer D.J. (1987) Sleep EEG in bulimia. *Biol. Psychiatry*, **22**: 820–828.

207. Bliss E., Migeon C.J. (1957) Endocrinology of anorexia nervosa. *J. Clin. Endocrinol. Metab.*, **17**: 766–776.

208. Garfinkel P.E., Brown G.M., Stancer H.C., Moldofsky H. (1975) Hypothalamic-pituitary function in anorexia nervosa. *Arch. Gen. Psychiatry*, **32**: 739–744.

209. Boyar R.M., Hellman L.D., Roffwarg H., Katz J., Zumoff B., O'Connor J., Bradlow H.L., Fukushima D.K. (1977) Cortisol secretion and metabolism in anorexia nervosa. *N. Engl. J. Med.*, **296**: 190–193.

210. Walsh B.T., Katz J.L., Levin J., Kream J., Fukushima D.K., Hellman L.D., Weiner H., Zumoff B. (1978) Adrenal activity in anorexia nervosa. *Psychosom. Med.*, **40**: 499–506.

211. Monteleone P., Brambilla F., Bortolotti F., La Rocca A., Maj M. (1998) Prolactin response to d-fenfluramine is blunted in people with anorexia nervosa. *Br. J. Psychiatry*, **172**: 438–442.

212. Monteleone P., Brambilla F., Bortolotti F., Maj M. (2000). Serotoninergic dysfunction across the eating disorders: relationship to eating behaviour, purging behaviour, nutritional status and general psychopathology. *Psychol. Med.*, **30**: 1099–1110.

213. Monteleone P., Luisi M., Colurcio B., Casarosa E., Monteleone P., Ioime R., Genazzani A.R., Maj M. (2001) Plasma levels of neuroactive steroids are increased in untreated women with anorexia nervosa or bulimia nervosa. *Psychosom. Med.*, **63**: 62–68.

214. Gold P.W., Gwirtsman H.E., Avgerinos P.C., Nieman L.K., Gallucci W.T., Kaye W.H., Jimerson D., Ebert M., Rittmaster R., Loriaux D.L., *et al.* (1986) Abnormal hypothalamic–pituitary–adrenal function in anorexia nervosa: pathophysiologic mechanism in underweight and weight-corrected patients. *N. Engl. J. Med.*, **314**: 1335–1342.

215. Ferrari E., Fraschini F., Brambilla F. (1990) Hormonal circadian rhythms in eating disorders. *Biol. Psychiatry*, **27**: 1007–1020.

216. Walsh B.T., Katz J.L. Levin J., Kream J., Fukushima D.K., Weiner H., Zumoff B. (1981) The production rate of cortisol declines during recovery from anorexia nervosa. *J. Clin. Endocrinol. Metab.*, **53**: 203–205.

217. Smith S.R., Bledsoe T., Chetri M.K. (1975) Cortisol metabolism and the pituitary–adrenal axis in adults with protein-calorie malnutrition. *J. Clin. Endocrinol. Metab.*, **40**: 43–52.

218. Schweitzer I., Szmukler G.I., Maguire K.P., Harrison L.C., Tuckwell V., Davies B.M. (1990) The dexamethasone suppression test in anorexia nervosa. The influence of weight, depression, adrenocorticotropic hormone and dexa-methasone. *Br. J. Psychiatry*, **157**: 713–717.

219. Muller E., Cavagnini F., Panerai A.E., Massironi R., Ferrari E., Brambilla F. (1987) Neuroendocrine measures in anorexia nervosa: comparisons with primary affective disorders. *Adv. Biochem. Psychopharmacol.*, **43**: 261–271.
220. Herpetz Dahlmann B., Remschmidt H. (1990) The prognostic value of the dexamethasone suppression test for the course of anorexia nervosa in comparison with depressive diseases. *Z. Kind. Jugenpsych.*, **18**: 5–11.
221. Walsh B.T., Roose S.R., Katz J.L., Dyrenfurt I., Wright L., Wiele R.V., Glassman A.H.. (1987) Hypothalamic–pituitary-adrenal-cortical activity in anorexia nervosa and bulimia. *Psychoneuroendocrinology*, **12**: 131–136.
222. Hotta M., Shibash T., Masuda A., Imaki T., Demura H., Ling N., Shizume K. (1986) The response of plasma adrenocorticotropin and cortisol to cortico-tropin-releasing hormone (CRH) and cerebrospinal fluid immuno-reactive CRH in anorexia nervosa patients. *J. Clin. Endocrinol. Metab.*, **62**: 319–324.
223. Kaye W.H., Gwirtsman H.E., George T.D., Ebert M.H., Simerson D.C., Tomai T.P., Chrousos G.P., Gold P.W. (1987) Elevated cerebrospinal fluid levels of immuno-reactive corticotropin-releasing hormone in anorexia nervosa: relation to state of nutrition, adrenal function and intensity of depression. *J. Clin. Endocrinol. Metab.*, **64**: 203–208.
224. Licinio J., Wong M.L., Gold P.W. (1996) The hypothalamic–pituitary–adrenal axis in anorexia nervosa. *Psychiatry Res.*, **62**: 75–83.
225. Wiersma A., Baauw A.D., Bohus B., Koolhaas J.M. (1995) Behavioural activation produced by CRH but not α helical CRH CRH-receptor antagonist when microinfused into the central nucleus of the amygdala under stress-free conditions. *Psychoneuroendocrinology*, **20**: 423–432.
226. Girardin E., Garoscio-Cholet M., Dechaud H., Lejeone H., Carrier E., Tourniaire J. (1991) Glucocorticoid receptors in lymphocytes in anorexia nervosa. *Clin. Endocrinol.*, **35**: 79–84.
227. Invitti C., Redaelli G., Balgi G., Cavagnini F. (1999) Glucocorticoid receptors in anorexia nervosa and Cushing's disease. *Biol. Psychiatry*, **45**. 1467–1471.
228. Zumoff B., Walsh B.T., Katz J.L., Levin J., Rosenfeld R.J., Kream J., Weiner H. (1983) Subnormal plasma dehydroisoandrosterone to cortisol ratio in anorexia nervosa: a second hormonal parameter of ontogenic regression. *J. Clin. Endocrinol. Metab.*, **56**: 668–672.
229. Winterer J., Gwirtsman H.E., George D.T., Kaye W.H., Loriaux D.L., Cutler G.B. (1985) Adrenocorticotropin stimulated adrenal androgen secretion in anorexia nervosa: impaired secretion at low weight with normalization after long term weight recovery. *J. Clin. Endocrinol. Metab.*, **61**: 693–697.
230. Walsh B.T., Roose S.R., Lindy D.C., Gladis M., Glassman A.H. (1987) Hypothalamic–pituitary–adrenal axis in bulimia. In *The Psychobiology of Bulimia* (Eds J.I. Hudson, H.G. Pope), pp. 3–11. American Psychiatric Press, Washington.
231. Gwirtsman H.E., Roy P., Yager R.H. (1983) Neuroendocrine abnormalities in bulimia. *Am. J. Psychiatry*, **140**: 559–563.
232. Mitchell J.E., Pyle R.L., Hatsukami D., Bouttkottl I. (1984) The dexamethasone suppression test in patients with bulimia. *J. Clin. Psychiatry*, **45**: 508–511.
233. Fichter M.M., Pirke K.M., Pollinger J., Wolfram G., Brunner E. (1990) Disturbances in the hypothalamo-pituitary-adrenal and neuroendocrine axes in bulimia. *Biol. Psychiatry*, **27**: 1021–1037.
234. Hughes P.L., Wells L.A., Cunningham C.J. (1986) The dexamethasone suppression test in bulimia before and after successful treatment with desipramine. *J. Clin. Psychiatry*, **47**: 515–521.

235. Allouche J., Bennet A., Barbe P., Plantavid M., Caron P., Louvet J.P. (1991) LH pulsatility and *in vitro* bioactivity in women with anorexia nervosa-related hypothalamic amenorrhea. *Acta Endocrinol.*, **125**: 614–620.

236. Boyar R.M., Katz K.J. (1977) Twenty-four hour gonadotropin secretory pattern in anorexia nervosa. In *Anorexia Nervosa* (Ed. R. Vigersky), pp.177–187. Raven Press, New York.

237. Pirke K.M., Fichter M.M., Lund R., Doerr P. (1979) Twenty-four hour sleep pattern of plasma LH in patients with anorexia nervosa. *Acta Endocrinol.*, **92**: 193–204.

238. Nillius S.J., Fries H., Wide L. (1985) Successful induction of follicular maturation and ovulation by prolonged treatment with LH-releasing hormone in women with anorexia nervosa. *Am. J. Obstet. Gynecol.*, **122**: 921–928.

239. Beumont P.J.V., George G.C.W., Pimstone B.L., Vinik A.I. (1976) Body weight and the pituitary response to hypothalamic releasing hormones in patients with anorexia nervosa. *J. Clin. Endocrinol. Metab.*, **43**: 487–496.

240. Wakeling A., De Souza V.F.A., Bearwood C.J. (1977) Assessment of the negative and positive feed-back effects of administered oestrogen on gonadotropin release in patients with anorexia nervosa. *Psychol. Med.*, **7**: 397.

241. Brown G.M., Garfinkel P.E., Jeuniewic N., Moldofsky H., Stancer H.C. (1977) Endocrine profiles in anorexia nervosa. In *Anorexia Nervosa* (Ed. R.A. Vigersky), pp. 123–136. Raven Press, New York.

242. Marshall J.C., Kelch R.P. (1979) Low dose pulsatile gonadotropin-releasing hormone in anorexia nervosa: a model of human pubertal development. *J. Clin. Endocrinol. Metab.*, **49**: 712–718.

243. Frisch R.E., McArthur J.W. (1974) Menstrual cycles: fatness as a determinant of minimum weight for height necessary for their maintenance or onset. *Science*, **185**: 949–951.

244. Jeuniewic N., Brown G.M., Garfinkel P.E., Moldofsky H. (1978) Hypothalamic function as related to body weight and body fat in anorexia nervosa. *Psychosom. Med.*, **40**: 187–198.

245. Hurd H.P., Palumbo P.J., Charib H. (1977) Hypothalamic–endocrine dysfunction in anorexia nervosa. *Mayo Clin. Proc.*, **52**: 711–716.

246. Genazzani A.D., Petraglia F., Gastaldi M., Volpogni C., Gamba O., Genazzani A.R. (1995) Naltrexone treatment restores menstrual cycles in patients with weight loss-related amenorrhea. *Fertil. Steril.*, **64**: 951–956.

247. McArthur J.W., Turnbull B.A., Pehrson J., Bauman M., Henley K., Turner A., Evans W.J., Bullen B.A., Skrinar G.S. (1993) Nalmefene enhances LH secretion in a proportion of oligo-amenorrheic athletes. *Acta Endocrinol.*, **128**: 325–333.

248. Armeanu M.C., Berkhout G.M., Schoemaker J. (1992) Pulsatile luteinizing hormone secretion in hypothalamic amenorrhea, anorexia nervosa, and polycystic ovarian disease during naltrexone treatment. *Fertil. Steril.*, **57**: 762–770.

249. Copeland P.M., Natalie R., Sacks M.S., Herzog D.B. (1995) Longitudinal follow-up of amenorrhea in eating disorders. *Psychosom. Med.*, **57**: 121–126.

250. Pirke K.M., Fichter M.M., Chlond C., Schweiger U., Fruth C., Streitmatter A., Wolfram G. (1987) Gonadotropin secretion pattern in bulimia nervosa. *Int. J. Eat. Disord.*, **6**: 655–661.

251. Muhlbauer H.D., Ziolko H.U. (1986) Abnormalities of anterior pituitary responsiveness to hypothalamic hormones in bulimia. *Pharmacopsychiatry*, **19**: 241–242.

252. Monteleone P., Brambilla F., Bortolotti F., Ferraro C., Maj M. (1998) Plasma prolactin response to d-fenfluramine is blunted in bulimic patients with frequent binge episodes. *Psychol. Med.*, **28**: 975–983.
253. Monteleone P., Bortolotti F., Fabrazzo M., La Rocca A., Fuschino A., Maj M. (2000) Plasma leptin response to acute fasting and refeeding in untreated women with bulimia nervosa. *J. Clin. Endocrinol. Metab.*, **85**: 2499–2503.
254. Weltzin T.E., Cameron J., Berga S., Kaye W.H. (1994) Prediction of reproductive status in women with bulimia nervosa by past high weight. *Am. J. Psychiatry*, **151**: 136–138.
255. Levy B.A. (1989) Neuroendocrine profile in bulimia nervosa. *Biol. Psychiatry*, **25**: 98–119.
256. Kaye W.H., Gwirtsman H.E., George T.D. (1989) The effect of bingeing and vomiting on hormonal secretion. *Biol. Psychiatry*, **25**: 768–780.
257. Selmanoff M. (1985) Rapid effects of hyperprolactinemia on basal prolactin secretion and dopamine turnover in the medial and lateral median eminence. *Endocrinology*, **116**: 1943–1952.
258. de la Fuente J., Welles L. (1981) Human growth hormone in psychiatric disorders. *J. Clin. Psychiatry*, **42**: 270–274.
259. Masuda A., Shibasaki T., Hotta M., Suematsu H., Shizume K. (1988) Study on the mechanism of abnormal growth hormone secretion (GH) in anorexia nervosa: no evidence of involvement of a low somatomedin-C level in the abnormal GH secretion. *J. Endocrinol. Invest.*, **11**: 297–302.
260. Rappaport R., Prevot C., Czernichow P. (1980) Somatomedin activity and growth hormone secretion. Changes related to body weight in anorexia nervosa. *Acta Paediatr. Scand.*, **69**: 37–41.
261. Pirke K.M., Fichter M.M., Pahl J. (1985) Noradrenaline, triiodothyronine, growth hormone and prolactin during weight gain in anorexia nervosa. *Int. J. Eat. Disord.*, **4**: 499–503.
262. Murata A., Yasuda T., Niimi H. (1992) Growth hormone-binding protein in patients with anorexia nervosa determined in two assay system. *Horm. Metab. Res.*, **24**: 279–299.
263. Katelslegers J.M., Maiter D., Maes M., Underwood L.E., Thissen J.P. (1996) Nutritional regulation of the growth hormone and insulin-like growth factor binding proteins. *Horm. Res.*, **45**: 252–257.
264. Counts D.R., Gwirtsman H., Carlsson L.M.S., Lesem M., Cuttler G.B., Jr. (1992) The effect of anorexia nervosa and refeeding on growth hormone-binding protein, the insulin-like growth factors (IGFs) and IGF-binding proteins. *J. Clin. Endocrinol. Metab.*, **75**: 762–767.
265. Grinspoon S., Baum H., Lee K., Anderson E., Herzog D., Klibanski A. (1996) Effects of short-term recombinant human insulin-like growth factor I administration on bone turnover in osteopenic women with anorexia nervosa. *J. Clin. Endocrinol. Metab.*, **81**: 3864–3870.
266. Argente J., Caballo N., Barrios V., Munoz M.T., Pozo J., Chowen J.A., Morande G., Hernandez M. (1997) Multiple endocrine abnormalities of the growth hormone and insulin-like growth factor axis in patients with anorexia nervosa: effects of short- and long-term weight recuperation. *J. Clin. Endocrinol. Metab.*, **82**: 2084–2092.
267. Rolla M., Ferdeghini M., Androni A., Bellitti D., Ceragioli M., Paolicchi R. (1986) Evaluation of growth hormone response to growth hormone releasing factor in patients with anorexia nervosa. *Psychiatry Res.*, **16**: 92.

268. Brambilla F., Ferrari E., Cavagnini F., Invitti C., Zanoboni A., Massironi R., Catalano M., Cocchi D., Muller E.E. (1989) α_2-adrenoreceptor sensitivity in anorexia nervosa: GH response to clonidine or GHRH stimulation. Biol. Psychiatry, 25: 256–264.

269. Gianotti L., Pincelli A.I., Scacchi M., Rolla M., Bellitti D., Akvat E., Lanfranco F., Torsello A., Ghigo E., Cavagnini F., et al. (2000) Effect of recombinant human insulin-like growth factor I administration on spontaneous and growth hormone (GH)-releasing hormone-stimulated secretion in anorexia nervosa. J. Clin. Endocrinol. Metab., 85: 2805–2809.

270. Rolla M., Andreoni A., Bellitti D., Cristofani R., Ferdeghini M., Muller E.E. (1991) Blockade of cholinergic muscarinic receptors by pirenzepine and GHRH-induced GH secretion in the acute and recovery phase of anorexia nervosa and atypical eating disorders. Biol. Psychiatry, 29: 1079–1091.

271. Ghigo E., Arvat E., Gianotti L., Nicolosi M., Valetto M.R., Avagnina S., Bellitti D., Rolla M., Muller E.E., Capanni F. (1994) Arginine but not pyridostigmine, a cholinesterase inhibitor, enhances the GHRH-induced GH rise in patients with anorexia nervosa. Biol. Psychiatry, 36: 689–695.

272. Stoving R.K., Andersen M., Flybjers A., Frystik J., Hangaard J., Vinten J., Koldkjaer O.G., Hagen C. (2002) Indirect evidence for decreased hypothalamic somatostatinergic tone in anorexia nervosa. Clin. Endocrinol., 56: 391–396.

273. Muller E.E., Rolla M. (1996) Aspects of the neuroendocrine control of somatotropic function in calorically restricted dogs and patients with eating disorders: studies with cholinergic drugs. Psychiatry Res., 62: 51–63.

274. Gerner R.H., Yamada T. (1982) Altered neuropeptide concentrations in cerebrospinal fluid of psychiatric patients. Brain Res., 238: 298–302.

275. Kaye W.H., Rubinow D., Gwirtsman H.E., George D.T., Jimerson D.C., Gold P.W. (1988) CSF somatostatin in anorexia nervosa and bulimia: relationship to the hypothalamic–pituitary–adrenal cortical axis. Psychoneuroendocrinology, 13: 265–272.

276. Kiriike N., Nishiwaki S., Izuniya Y., Maeda Y., Kawakitia Y. (1987) Thyrotropin, prolactin and growth hormone responses to thyrotropin-releasing hormone in anorexia nervosa and bulimia. Biol. Psychiatry, 22: 167–176.

277. Maeda K., Tanimoto K., Chiara K. (1987) Abnormal growth hormone release following luteinizing hormone releasing hormone in anorexia nervosa. Jpn. J. Psychiatry Neurol., 41: 41–45.

278. Brambilla F., Cocchi D., Nobile P., Muller E.E. (1981) Anterior pituitary responsiveness to hypothalamic hormones in anorexia nervosa. Neuropsychobiology, 7: 225–237.

279. Barbarino A., Corsello S.M., Della Casa S., Tofani A., Sciuto R., Rota C.A., Bollanti L., Barini A. (1990) Corticotropin-releasing hormone inhibition of growth hormone-releasing hormone-induced growth hormone release in man. J. Clin. Endocrinol. Metab., 71: 1368–1374.

280. Blickle J.F., Reville P., Stephan F., Meyer P., Demangeat C., Sapin R. (1984) The role of insulin, glucagon and growth hormone in the regulation of plasma glucose and free fatty acid levels in anorexia nervosa. Horm. Metab. Res., 16: 336–340.

281. Nussbaum M., Baird D., Sonnenblick M., Cowan K., Shenker R. (1985) Short stature in anorexia nervosa patients. J. Adolesc. Health Care, 6: 453–455.

282. Grinspoon S., Thomas L., Miller K., Herzog D., Klibanski A. (2002) Effects of recombinant human IGF-I and oral contraceptive administration on bone density in anorexia nervosa. J. Clin. Endocrinol. Metab., 87: 2883–2891.

283. Hill K., Bucuvalas J., McCline C., Kryscio R., Martini R.T., Alfaro M.P., Maloney M. (2000) Pilot study of growth hormone administration during the refeeding of malnourished anorexia nervosa patients. *J. Child Adolesc. Psychopharmacol.*, **10**: 3–8.

284. Coiro V., Capretti L., Volpi R., D'Amato L., Marchesi C., De Ferri A., Rossi G., Bianconi L., Marcato A., Chiodera P. (1990) Growth hormone responses to growth hormone-releasing hormone, clonidine and insulin-induced hypoglycemia in normal weight bulimic women. *Neuropsychobiology*, **23**: 8–14.

285. Coiro V., Volpi R., Marchesi C., Capretti L., Speroni G., Rossi G., Caffarri G., De Ferri A., Marcato A., Chiodera P. (1992) Abnormal growth hormone and cortisol, but not thyroid-stimulating hormone responses to intravenous glucose tolerance test in normal-weight, bulimic women. *Psychoneuroendocrinology*, **17**: 639–646.

286. Berelowitz M., Szabo M., Frohman L., Firestone S., Chu L., Hintz R.L. (1981) Somatomedin-C mediates growth hormone negative feedback by effects on both hypothalamus and the pituitary. *Science*, **212**: 1279–1281.

287. Levy A.B., Malarkey W.B. (1988) Growth hormone and somatomedin-C in bulimia. *Psychoneuroendocrinology*, **13**: 359–362.

288. Kaplan A.S., Garfinkel P.E., Warsh J.J., Brown G.M. (1986) Neuroendocrine responses in bulimia. In *Disorders of Eating Behaviour: A Psychoneuroendocrine Approach* (Eds E. Ferrari, F. Brambilla), pp. 241–245. Pergamon Press, Oxford.

289. Burman K.D., Virgesky R.A., Loriaux D.L., Strum D., Djuh Y.Y., Wright F.D., Wartofsky L. (1977) Investigations concerning deiodinative pathways in patients with anorexia nervosa. In *Anorexia Nervosa* (Ed. R.A. Vigersky), pp. 255–262. Raven Press, New York.

290. Casper R.C., Frohman L. (1982) Delayed TSH release in anorexia nervosa following injection of thyrotropin-releasing hormone (TRH). *Psychoneuroendocrinology*, **7**: 59–68.

291. Moore R., Mills I.H. (1979) Serum T3 and T4 levels in patients with anorexia nervosa showing transient hyperthyroidism during weight gain. *Clin. Endocrinol.*, **10**: 443–448.

292. Jorgensen J.O., Moller J., Laursen T., Orskof H., Christiansen J.S., Weeke J. (1994) Growth hormone administration stimulates energy expenditure and extrathyroidal conversion of thyroxine to triiodothyronine in a dose-dependent manner and suppresses circadian thyrotropin levels: studies in GH deficient adults. *Clin. Endocrinol.*, **41**: 609–614.

293. Hangaard J., Ancersen M., Grodum E., Koldkjaer O., Hagen C. (1996) Pulsatile thyrotropin secretion in patients with Addison's disease during variable glucocorticoid therapy. *J. Clin. Endocrinol. Metab.*, **81**: 2502–2507.

294. Moshang T., Utiger R.D. (1977) Low triiodothyronine euthyroidism in anorexia nervosa. In *Anorexia Nervosa* (Ed. R.A. Vigersky), pp. 263–270. Raven Press, New York.

295. Norris P.D., O'Malley B.P., Palmer R.L. (1985) The TRH test in bulimia and anorexia nervosa: a controlled study. *J. Psychiatr. Res.*, **19**: 215–219.

296. Wakeling A., De Souza V.F.A., Gore M.B.R., Sabur M., Kingstone D., Boss A.M.B. (1979) Amenorrhea, body weight and serum hormone concentrations, with particular reference to prolactin and thyroid hormones in anorexia nervosa. *Psychol. Med.*, **9**: 265–272.

297. Vigersky R.A., Anderson A.E., Thompson R.H., Loriaux D.L. (1977) Hypothalamic dysfunction in secondary amenorrhea associated with simple weight loss. *N. Engl. J. Med.*, **297**: 1141–1147.

298. Kiyoara K., Tamai H., Karibe C., Kobayashi N., Fuji S., Fukino O., Nakagawa T., Kumagay L.F., Nagataki S. (1987) Serum thyrotropin (TSH) response to thyrotropin-releasing hormone (TRH) in patients with anorexia nervosa and bulimia: influence of changes in body weight and eating disorders. *Psychoneuroendocrinology*, **12**: 21–28.

299. Lesem M.D., Kaye W.H., Bissette G., Jimerson D.C., Nemeroff C.F. (1994) Cerebrospinal fluid TRH immunoreactivity in anorexia nervosa. *Biol. Psychiatry*, **35**: 48–53.

300. Stoving R.K., Bennedbaek F.N., Hegedus L., Hagen C. (2001) Evidence of diffuse atrophy of the thyroid gland in patients with anorexia nervosa. *Int. J. Eat. Disord.*, **29**: 230–235.

301. Cheung N.W., Boyages S.C. (1997) The thyroid gland in acromegaly. An ultrasonographic study. *Clin. Endocrinol.*, **46**: 545–549.

302. Devlin M.J., Walsh B., Kral J.G., Heymsfield S.B., Pi-Sunyer F.X., Dantzic S. (1990) Metabolic abnormalities in bulimia nervosa. *Arch. Gen. Psychiatry*, **47**: 144–148.

303. Pirke K.M., Pahl J., Schweiger U., Warnhof M. (1985) Metabolic and endocrine indices of starvation in bulimia: a comparison with anorexia nervosa. *Psychiatry Res.*, **15**: 33–39.

304. Spalter A.R., Gwirtsman H.E., Demitrack M.A., Gold P.V. (1993) Thyroid function in bulimia nervosa. *Biol. Psychiatry*, **137**: 937–940.

305. Levy B.A., Dixon K.N., Malarkey W.B. (1988) Pituitary response to TRH in bulimia. *Biol. Psychiatry*, **24**: 98–109.

306. Macaron C., Wilber J.F., Green O., Freinkel N. (1978) Studies of growth hormone (GH), thyrotropin (TSH) and prolactin (PRL) secretion in anorexia. *Psychoneuroendocrinology*, **3**: 181–185.

307. Isaacs A.J., Leslie R.D.G., Gomez J., Baylis R. (1980) The effect of weight gain on gonadotropins and prolactin in anorexia nervosa. *Acta Endocrinol.*, **94**: 145–150.

308. Mecklenburg R.S., Loriaux D.L., Thompson R.H., Andersen A.E., Lipsett M.B. (1974) Hypothalamic dysfunction in patients with anorexia nervosa. *Medicine (Baltimore)*, **53**: 147–152.

309. Rolla M., Andreoni A., Bellitti D., De Vescovi S., Mariani G. (1985) Effects of dopamine antagonists (domperidone, metoclopramide) on the release of the adenohypophyseal hormones in patients at different stages of anorexia nervosa. In *Adolescence in Females* (Eds C. Flamigni, S. Venturosi, R. Givens), pp. 475–479. Year Book Medical Publishers, Chicago.

310. Hafner R.J., Crisp A.H., McNeilly A.S. (1976) Prolactin and gonadotropin activity in females treated for anorexia nervosa. *Postgrad. Med. J.*, **52**: 76–79.

311. Beumont P.J.V., Abraham S.F., Turtle J. (1980) Paradoxical prolactin response to gonadotropin-releasing hormone during weight gain in patients with anorexia nervosa. *J. Clin. Endocrinol. Metab.*, **51**: 1283–1285.

312. De Marinis L., Mancini A., D'Amico C., Zuppi P., Tofani A., Della Casa S., Saporosi A., Sambo P., Fiumara C., Calabro F., *et al.* (1991) Influence of naloxone infusion on prolactin and growth hormone response to growth hormone-releasing hormone in anorexia nervosa. *Psychoneuroendocrinology*, **16**: 499–504.

313. Halmi K.A., Owen W.P., Lasley E., Stokes P. (1983) Dopaminergic regulation in anorexia nervosa. *Int. J. Eat. Dis.*, **2**: 129–133.

314. Hadigan C.M., Walsh B.T., Buttinger C., Hollander E. (1995) Behavioral and neuroendocrine responses to meta-CPP in anorexia nervosa. *Biol. Psychiatry*, 37: 504–511.
315. O'Dwyer A.M., Lucey J.V., Russell G.F.M. (1996) Serotonin activity in anorexia nervosa after long-term weight restoration: response to D-fenfluramine challenge. *Psychol. Med.*, 26: 353–359.
316. Ward A., Brown N., Lightman S., Campbell I.C., Treasure J. (1998) Neuroendocrine, appetitive and behavioural responses to D-fenfluramine in women recovered from anorexia nervosa. *Br. J. Psychiatry*, 172: 351–358.
317. Copeland P.M., Herzog D.P., Carr D.B., Klibanski A., McMolaughlin R.A., Martin J.B. (1988) Effect of dexamethasone on cortisol and prolactin responses to meals in bulimic and normal women. *Psychoneuroendocrinology*, 13: 273–278.
318. Jimerson D.C., Wolfe B.E., Metzger E.D., Finkelstein D.M., Cooper T.B., Levine J.M. (1997) Decreased serotonin function in bulimia nervosa. *Arch. Gen. Psychiatry*, 54: 529–534.
319. Levitan R.D., Kaplan A.S., Joffe R.T., Levitt A.J., Brown G.M. (1997) Hormonal and subjective responses to intravenous meta-chlorophenylpiperazine in bulimia nervosa. *Arch. Gen. Psychiatry*, 54: 521–557.
320. Brewerton T.D., Mueller E.A., Lesem M.D., Brandt H.A., Quearry B., George D.T., Murphy D.L., Jimerson D.C. (1992) Neuroendocrine responses to m-chlorophenylpiperazine and L-tryptophan in bulimia. *Arch. Gen. Psychiatry*, 49: 852–861.
321. Reiter R.J. (1991) Pineal melatonin: cell biology of its synthesis and of its physiological interactions. *Endocrinol. Rev.*, 12: 151–180.
322. Chick C.L., Johansson G.E.K., Ho A.K., Brown G.M. (1985) Effects of food restriction on serum melatonin levels in male rats. *Neuroendocrinol. Lett.*, 7: 147–153.
323. Arendt J., Hampton S., English J., Kwasowski P., Marks V. (1982) Twenty-four hour profiles of melatonin, cortisol, insulin, C-peptide and GIP following a meal and subsequent fasting. *Clin. Endocrinol.*, 16: 89–95.
324. Tamarkin L., Abastillas P., Chen H.C., McNemar A., Sidbury J.B. (1982) The daily profile of plasma melatonin in obese and Prader-Willi syndrome children. *J. Clin. Endocrinol. Metab.*, 55: 491–496.
325. Birau N., Alexander D., Bertholdt S., Meyer C. (1984) Low nocturnal melatonin serum concentration in anorexia nervosa. Further evidence for body weight influence. *IRCS Med. Sci.*, 12: 477–482.
326. Dalery J., Claustrat B., Brun J., De Villard R. (1985) Plasma melatonin and cortisol levels in eight patients with anorexia nervosa. *Neuroendocrinol. Lett.*, 7: 159–164.
327. Kennedy S., Garfinkel P.E., Parienti V., Costa D., Brown G.M. (1989) Changes in melatonin levels but not cortisol levels are associated with depression in patients with eating disorders. *Arch. Gen. Psychiatry*, 46: 73–78.
328. Brambilla F., Fraschini F., Esposti G., Bossolo P.A., Marelli G., Ferrari E. (1988) Melatonin circadian rhythm in anorexia nervosa and obesity. *Psychiatry Res.*, 23: 267–276.
329. Arendt J., Bhanji S., Franey C., Mattingly D. (1992) Plasma melatonin levels in anorexia nervosa. *Br. J. Psychiatry*, 161: 361–364.
330. Kennedy S., Brown G.M., McVey G., Garfinkel P.E. (1991) Pineal and adrenal function before and after refeeding in anorexia nervosa. *Biol. Psychiatry*, 30: 216–234.

331. Kennedy S.H., Brown G.M., Ford C.G., Ralevski E (1993) The acute effects of starvation on 6-sulphatoxy-melatonin output in subgroups of patients with anorexia nervosa. *Psychoneuroendocrinology*, **18**: 131–140.

332. Kennedy S., Costa D., Parienti V., Brown G.M. (1987) Melatonin regulation in bulimia. In *The Psychobiology of Bulimia* (Eds J.I. Hudson, H.G. Pope), pp. 74–97. American Psychiatric Press, Washington.

333. Ferrari E., Magri F., Pontiggia B., Rondanelli M., Fioravanti M., Solerte S.B., Sevegnini S. (1997) Circadian neuroendocrine functions in disorders of eating behaviour. *Eat. Weight Disord.*, **2**: 196–202.

334. Kaye W.H. (1996) Neuropeptide abnormalities in anorexia nervosa. *Psychiatry Res.*, **62**: 65–74.

335. Crowley W.R., Kalra S.P. (1987) Neuropeptide Y stimulates the release of luteinizing hormone-releasing hormone from medial basal hypothalamus *in vitro*: modulation by ovarian hormones. *Neuroendocrinology*, **46**: 97–103.

336. Kaye W.H., Berrettini W.H., Gwirtsman H.E., George D. (1990) Altered cerebrospinal fluid neuropeptide Y and peptide YY immunoreactivity in anorexia and bulimia nervosa. *Arch. Gen. Psychiatry*, **47**: 548–556.

337. Gendall K.A., Kaye W.H., Altemus M., McConaha C.W., La Via M.C. (1999) Leptin, neuropeptide Y, and peptide YY in long term recovered eating disorder patients. *Biol. Psychiatry*, **46**: 292–299.

338. Kaye W.H., Pickar D., Naber D., Ebert M.H. (1982) Cerebrospinal fluid opioid activity in anorexia nervosa. *Am. J. Psychiatry*, **139**: 643–645.

339. Kaye W.H., Berrettini W.H., Gwirtsman H.E., Chretien M., Gold P.W., George D.T., Jimerson D.C., Ebert M.H. (1987) Reduced cerebrospinal fluid levels of immunoreactive pro-opiomelanocortin related peptides (including β endorphin) in anorexia nervosa. *Life Sci.*, **41**: 2147–2155.

340. Gerner R.H., Sharpe B. (1982) CSF β-endorphin immunoreactivity in normal schizophrenic, depressed and anorexic subjects. *Brain Res.*, **237**: 244–247.

341. Lesem M.D., Berrettini W.H., Kaye W.H., Jimerson D.C. (1991) Measurement of CSF dynorphin A 1-8 immunoreactivity in anorexia nervosa and normal weight bulimia. *Biol. Psychiatry*, **29**: 244–252.

342. Brambilla F., Cavagnini F., Invitti C., Poterzio F., Lampertico M., Sali L., Maggioni M., Candolfi D., Panerai E., Muller E.E. (1985) Neuroendocrine and psychopathological measures in anorexia nervosa: resemblances to primary affective disorders. *Psychiatry Res.*, **16**: 165–176.

343. Baranowska B. (1990) Are disturbances in opioid and adrenergic system involved in the hormonal dysfunction of anorexia nervosa? *Psychoneuroendocrinology*, **15**: 371–379.

344. Baranowska B., Radzikowska M., Wasilewska-Dziubinska E., Roguski K., Borowiec M. (2000) Disturbed release of gastrointestinal peptides in anorexia nervosa and in obesity. *Diabetes Obes. Metab.*, **2**: 99–103.

345. Brambilla F., Ferrari E., Petraglia F., Facchinetti F., Catalano M., Genazzani A.R. (1991) Peripheral opioid secretory pattern in anorexia nervosa. *Psychiatry Res.*, **39**: 115–127.

346. Garcia-Rubi E., Vasquez-Aleman D., Mendez J.P., Salinas J.L., Garza-Flores J., Ponce-de-Leon S., Perez-Palacios G., Ulloa-Aguirre A. (1992) The effects of opioid blockade and GnRH administration upon luteinizing hormone secretion in patients with anorexia nervosa during the stages of weight loss and weight recovery. *Clin. Endocrinol.*, **37**: 520–528.

347. Brewerton T.D., Lydiard R.B., Ballenger J.C. (1992) CSF β-endorphin and dynorphin in bulimia nervosa. *Am. J. Psychiatry*, **149**: 1086–1090.

348. Waller D.A., Kiser R.S., Hardy B.W., Fuchs I., Feigenbaum L.P., Vavy R. (1986) Eating behaviour and plasma β-endorphin in bulimia. *Am. J. Clin. Nutr.*, **44**: 20–23.
349. Fullerton D.T., Swift W.J., Getto J.C., Carlson I.H. (1986) Plasma immunoreactive β-endorphins in bulimics. *Psychol. Med.*, **16**: 59–63.
350. Fullerton D.T., Swift W.J., Getto J.C., Carlson I.H., Gutzman Z.D. (1988) Differences in plasma β-endorphin levels of bulimics. *Int. J. Eat. Disord.*, **7**: 191–200.
351. Brambilla F., Brunetta M., Draisci A., Peirone A., Perna G., Sacerdote P., Manfredi B., Panerai A.E. (1995) T-lymphocyte cholecystokinin-8 and β-endorphin concentrations in eating disorders: II. Bulimia nervosa. *Psychiatry Res.*, **59**: 51–56.
352. Baranowska B., Radzikowska M., Wasilewska-Dziubinska E., Plonowski A., Roguski K. (1997) Neuropeptide Y, galanin, and leptin release in obese women and in women with anorexia nervosa. *Metabolism*, **46**: 1384–1389.
353. Invitti C., Brunani A., Pasqualinotto L., Dubini A., Bendinelli P., Maroni P., Cavagnini F. (1995) Plasma galanin concentrations in obese, normal weight and anorectic women. *Int. J. Obesity*, **19**: 347–349.
354. Berrettini W.H., Kaye W.H., Sunderland T., May C., Gwirtsman H.E., Mellow A., Albright A. (1988) Galanin immunoreactivity in human CSF: studies in eating disorders and Alzheimer's disease. *Neuropsychobiology*, **19**: 64–68.
355. Frank G.K., Kaye W.H., Sahu A., Fernstrom J., McConaha C. (2001) Could reduced cerebrospinal fluid (CSF) galanin contribute to restricted eating in anorexia nervosa? *Neuropsychopharmacology*, **24**: 706–709.
356. Pirke K.M., Philipp E., Friess E., Kellner B., Wilknes T., Krieg J.C., Fichter M.M. (1993) The role of gastrointestinal hormone secretion in eating disorders. *Adv. Biosci.*, **90**: 75–79.
357. Harty R.F., Pearson P.H., Solomon T.E., McGuigan J.E. (1991) Cholecystokinin, vasoactive intestinal peptide and peptide histidine methionine responses to feeding in anorexia nervosa. *Regul. Peptides*, **36**: 141–150.
358. Brambilla F., Brunetta M., Peirone A., Perna G., Sacerdote P., Manfredi B. (1995) T-lymphocyte cholecystokinin-8 and β-endorphin concentrations in eating disorders: I. Anorexia nervosa. *Psychiatry Res.*, **29**: 43–50.
359. Phillipp E., Pirke K.M., Kellner M.B., Krieg J.C. (1991) Disturbed cholecystokinin secretion in patients with eating disorders. *Life Sci.*, **48**: 2443–2450.
360. Pirke K.M., Kellner M.B., Fries E., Krieg J.C., Fichter M.M. (1994) Satiety and colecystokinin. *Int. J. Eat. Disord.*, **15**: 63–69.
361. Geracioti T.D., Jr., Liddle R.A., Altemus M., Demitrack M.A., Gold P.W. (1992) Regulation of appetite and cholecystokinin secretion in anorexia nervosa. *Am. J. Psychiatry*, **149**: 958–961.
362. Lydiard B.R., Brewerton T.D., Fossey M.D., Laraia M.T., Stuart G., Beinfeld M.L., Ballenger J.C. (1993) CSF cholecystokinin octapeptide in patients with bulimia nervosa and in normal comparison subjects. *Am. J. Psychiatry*, **150**: 1099–1101.
363. Mitchell J.E., Pyle R.L., Eckert E.D. (1985) Bulimia. In *American Psychiatric Association Annual Review* (Eds R.E. Hales, A. Frances), pp. 464–480. American Psychiatric Press, Washington.
364. Wauters M., Considine R.V., Van Gaal L.F. (2000) Human leptin: from an adipocyte hormone to an endocrine mediator. *Eur. J. Endocrinol.*, **143**: 293–311.
365. Herpertz S., Albers N., Wagner R., Pelz B., Kopp W., Mann K., Blum W.F., Senf W., Hebebrand J. (2000) Longitudinal changes of circadian leptin, insulin

and cortisol plasma levels and their correlation during refeeding in patients with anorexia nervosa. *Eur. J. Endocrinol.*, **142**: 373–379.

366. Hebebrand J., Blum W.F., Barth N., Coners H., Englaro P., Juul A., Ziegler A., Warnke A., Racher W., Remschmidt H. (1997) Leptin levels in patients with anorexia nervosa are reduced in the acute stage and elevated upon short-term weight restoration. *Mol. Psychiatry*, **2**: 330–334.

367. Ferron F., Considine R.V., Peino R., Lado I.G., Dieguez C., Casanueva F.F. (1997) Serum leptin concentrations in patients with anorexia nervosa, bulimia nervosa and non-specific eating disorders correlate with the body mass index but are independent of the respective disease. *Clin. Endocrinol.*, **46**: 289–293.

368. Monteleone P., Di Lieto A., Tortorella A., Longobardi N., Maj M. (2000) Circulating leptin in patients with anorexia nervosa, bulimia nervosa or binge-eating disorder: relationship to body weight, eating patterns, psycho-pathology and endocrine changes. *Psychiatry Res.*, **94**: 121–129.

369. Remschmidt H., Schmidt M.H., Gutenbrunner C. (1990) Prediction of long term outcome in anorectic patients from longitudinal weight measurements during inpatient treatment: a cross validation study. In *Child and Youth Psychiatry: European Perspectives. Vol. 1. Anorexia Nervosa* (Eds H. Remschmidt, M.H. Schmidt), pp. 150–167. Hogrefe & Huber, Toronto.

370. Kopp W., Blum W.F., Von Prittwitz S., Ziegler A., Lubbert H., Emons G., Herzog W., Herpertz S., Deter H.C., Remschmidt A., *et al.* (1997) Low leptin levels predict amenorrhea in underweight and eating disordered females. *Mol. Psychiatry*, **2**: 335–340.

371. Jimerson D.C., Mantzoros C., Wolfe B.E., Metzger B.D. (2000) Decreased serum leptin in bulimia nervosa. *J. Clin. Endocrinol. Metab.*, **85**: 4511–4514.

372. Brewerton T.D., Lesem M.D., Kennedy A., Garvey W.T. (2000) Reduced plasma leptin concentrations in bulimia nervosa. *Psychoneuroendocrinology*, **25**: 649–658.

Commentaries

3.1
Bringing the Soma into Psychosomatic Aspects of Eating Disorders

Janet Treasure[1]

Anorexia nervosa is a pervasive illness that reaches parts of the body that other illnesses do not, because the starvation and malnourishment that are integral to eating disorders compromise all organs. The review by Brambilla and Monteleone is a *tour de force* covering every system of the body. Most physical and physiological changes appear to be reversible after weight gain, and so there has been a tendency to dismiss their importance in favour of psychological processes. However, new technologies promise to make our understanding of this aspect of eating disorders more sophisticated. Much of the knowledge base underpinning this chapter is new. The hormone leptin was discovered less than a decade ago and now we know that a cornucopia of new neurotransmitters and hormones are involved in the regulation of appetite and body composition.

The thoughtful questions raised at the end of the review herald the new avenues that need to be explored. I have therefore repeated these questions and added some thoughts of my own to add heat to the debate.

- *The pathogenesis of medical alterations and physiological aberrations has not been definitely clarified.* A key question, as yet unanswered, is: how many of these changes are primary rather than secondary? If we want to look at primary, causal mechanisms, then those systems that are intimately connected to the brain, such as the neuroendocrine and the appetite control systems, are obvious candidates. The current state of progress in defining the pathophysiology within these systems is clearly depicted in the tables within the review. It is an area in which it is to be hoped that there will be an exponential increase in knowledge. New technologies such as knock out, knock in, switch on and off, animal models and other aspects of functional genomics and proteomics are rapidly increasing our knowledge base.

[1] *Department of Psychiatry, Guy's Hospital, London SE1 9RT, UK*

Functional brain scanning provides a new window into aspects of neural function that have eluded us so far. For example, there is an atypical response to food in that the frontal lobe and limbic system become activated in people with eating disorders [1,2]; furthermore, people with bulimic features have less dorsolateral frontal activation [3].

• *Some alterations persist after restoration of normal eating habits and weight.* Data about this important aspect are sparce, perhaps because longitudinal studies are so hungry for resources. It is possible that malnutrition during this critical adolescent phase of physical and brain development may interrupt or derail normal maturation. Furthermore, some sequelae of the illness may leave permanent scars. Bone and brain spring immediately to mind.

Adolescence is the time when peak bone mass develops. There is a little evidence that if anorexia nervosa develops before growth has finished, i.e. in the prepubertal period, there is stunting in height [4]. It remains unclear whether optimal bone mass can be achieved if the illness develops during this phase.

The human brain also has a prolonged period of maturation. This allows for a long period in which the environment interacts with the hardware of the brain. The cortex develops in stages and there is considerable plasticity. Adolescence is accompanied by dramatic reductions in cortico-cortical connectivity in frontal regions [5] and this synaptic pruning is thought to be the central neurodevelopmental event that leads to full adult functioning [6]. It is possible that malnutrition during this phase of brain development may lead to long-lasting changes in brain functioning. Although this is somewhat speculative, it is possible that the rigidity and deficits in set shifting found in anorexia nervosa [7–9] may be caused by an interruption in this process of pruning within the frontal lobe. In turn, this may prevent maturation of the frontal lobe, and functions such as flexibility may be compromised. The reduction in brain mass and other structural changes seen in anorexia nervosa persist over time, despite weight recovery [10]. It is important that we understand more about these long-term risks, so that patients and their carers are fully informed. This links well into the next point.

• *There are no/few investigations about how feedback effects of the medical alterations typical of anorexia and bulimia nervosa influence the course and prognosis of these disorders.* This is a very important point. There is interest in using the technique of motivational interviewing in the management of eating disorders [11–13]. One of the key components in this technique is the use of feedback. For example, the drinkers' check-up is the cornerstone of motivational enhancement therapy for people with alcoholism [14,15]. This includes feedback of a complex assessment package, including general medical health, neuropsychological functioning, etc. There perhaps needs to be an equivalent eater/non-eater check-up in which there is structured feedback about medical, psychological and social risk. At the Maudsley Hospital we have developed a medical risk assessment tool that is shared between professionals, carers and people with anorexia nervosa and is the first step in providing such feedback.

- *How do these medical alterations affect the capacity of people with eating disorders to respond to treatment?* Once again, this is an area in which there is very little evidence. At one time it was thought that it was not possible to do any form of psychotherapy if people were underweight and the standard treatment was admission to an inpatient unit for refeeding, followed by psychotherapy aimed to reduce relapse. However, effective treatment can take place without a preliminary phase of weight gain. In adolescents, outpatient treatment involving the family is effective [16–18]. Furthermore, in adults who are not at high medical risk, outpatient approaches can be as effective as inpatient treatment [19–21]. Finally, adults with moderate-risk anorexia nervosa can respond differentially to individual specific therapies rather than treatment as usual [22] or dietary advice [23].

Nevertheless, the capacity of some people with anorexia nervosa is impaired to such a degree that they need structured inpatient treatment. Also, people with a more severe form of anorexia nervosa in which there has been a long duration of illness may respond only to a prolonged course of inpatient treatment [24]. In extreme cases, this needs to be implemented under the aegis of mental health law [25].

However, these views about the balance between control vs. freedom in the management of anorexia nervosa are culturally grounded. The analysis written above is from the perspective of Great Britain. The guidelines outlined by the American Psychiatric Association advocate a more conservative approach: "Generally patients who weigh less than approximately 85% of their individually estimated healthy weights have considerable difficulty gaining weight in the absence of a structured programme. Those weighing less than about 75% of their individually estimated healthy weights are likely to require a 24-hour hospital programme". "Once weight loss is severe enough to cause the indications for immediate medical hospitalization treatment may be less effective, refeeding may entail greater risks and prognosis may be more problematic than when intervention is provided earlier."

Until further research is undertaken, it is impossible to argue which of these approaches represents best practice. In conclusion, all we can say is watch this space.

REFERENCES

1. Naruo T., Nakabeppu Y., Sagiyama K., Munemoto T., Homan N., Deguchi D., Nakajo M., Nozoe S. (2000) Characteristic regional cerebral blood flow patterns in anorexia nervosa patients with binge/purge behavior. *Am. J. Psychiatry*, **157**: 1520–1522.
2. Naruo T., Nakabeppu Y., Deguchi D., Nagai N., Tsutsui J., Nakajo M., Nozoe S.S. (2001) Decreases in blood perfusion of the anterior cingulate gyri in anorexia nervosa restricters assessed by SPECT image analysis. *BMC Psychiatry*, **1**: 2.
3. Uher R., Murphy T., Brammer M., Dalgleish T., Phillips M., Ng V., Andrew C., Williams S., Campbell I., Treasure J. Functional neural correlates of eating disorders. Personal communication, 2002.
4. Russell G.F. (1985) Premenarchal anorexia nervosa and its sequelae. *J. Psychiatr. Res.*, **19**: 363–369.
5. Huttenlocher P.R. (1979) Synaptic density in human frontal cortex: developmental changes and the effects of aging. *Brain Res.*, **163**: 195–205.
6. Woo T.U., Pucak M.L., Kye C.H., Matus C.V., Lewis D.A. (1997) Peripubertal refinement of the intrinsic and associational circuitry in monkey prefrontal cortex. *Neuroscience*, **80**: 1149–1158.
7. Brecelj M., Tchanturia K., Rabe-Hesketh S., Treasure J. (2003) Childhood obsessive–compulsive personality traits in eating disorders: an approach to the broader phenotypic definition. *Am. J. Psychiatry* (in press).
8. Tchanturia K., Serpell L., Troop N., Treasure J. (2001) Perceptual illusions in eating disorders: rigid and fluctuating styles. *J. Behav. Ther. Exp. Psychiatry*, **32**: 107–115.
9. Tchanturia K., Morris R., Surguladze S., Treasure J. (2003) Perceptual and cognitive set shifting tasks in acute anorexia nervosa and following recovery. *Eat. Weight Disord.* (in press).
10. Katzman D.K., Christensen B., Young A.R., Zipursky R.B. (2001) Starving the brain: structural abnormalities and cognitive impairment in adolescents with anorexia nervosa. *Semin. Clin. Neuropsychiatry*, **6**: 146–152.
11. Schmidt U., Treasure J. (1997) *A Clinicians Guide to Management of Bulimia Nervosa (Motivational Enhancement Therapy for Bulimia Nervosa)*. Psychology Press, Hove.
12. Treasure J.L., Ward A. (1997) A practical guide to the use of motivational interviewing in anorexia nervosa. *Eur. Eat. Disord. Rev.*, **5**: 102–114.
13. Kaplan A.S. (2002) Psychological treatments for anorexia nervosa: a review of published studies and promising new directions. *Can. J. Psychiatry*, **47**: 235–242.
14. Agostinelli G., Brown J.M., Miller W.R. (1995) Effects of normative feedback on consumption among heavy drinking college students. *J. Drug Educ.*, **25**: 31–40.
15. Miller W.R., Benefield R.G., Tonigan J.S. (1993) Enhancing motivation for change in problem drinking: a controlled comparison of two therapist styles. *J. Consult. Clin. Psychol.*, **61**: 455–461.
16. Eisler I., Dare C., Hodes M., Russell G., Dodge E., Le Grange D. (2000) Family therapy for adolescent anorexia nervosa: the results of a controlled comparison of two family interventions. *J. Child Psychol. Psychiatry*, **41**: 727–736.
17. Robin A.L., Siegel P.T., Moye A. (1995) Family versus individual therapy for anorexia: impact on family conflict. *Int. J. Eat. Disord.*, **17**: 313–322.
18. Robin A.L., Gilroy M., Dennis A.B. (1998) Treatment of eating disorders in children and adolescents. *Clin. Psychol. Rev.*, **18**: 421–446.

19. Crisp A.H., Norton K., Gowers S., Halek C., Bowyer C., Yeldham D., Levett G., Bhat A. (1991) A controlled study of the effect of therapies aimed at adolescent and family psychopathology in anorexia nervosa. *Br. J. Psychiatry*, **159**: 325–333.
20. Gowers S., Norton K., Halek C., Crisp A.H. (1994) Outcome of outpatient psychotherapy in a random allocation treatment study of anorexia nervosa. *Int. J. Eat. Disord.*, **15**: 165–177.
21. Meads C., Gold L., Burls A. (2001) How effective is outpatient care compared to inpatient care for the treatment of anorexia nervosa? A systematic review. *Eur. Eat. Disord. Rev.*, **9**: 229–241.
22. Dare C., Eisler I., Russell G., Treasure J., Dodge L. (2001) Psychological therapies for adults with anorexia nervosa: randomised controlled trial of outpatient treatments. *Br. J. Psychiatry*, **178**: 216–221.
23. Serfaty M.A. (1999) Cognitive therapy versus dietary counselling in the outpatient treatment of anorexia nervosa: effects of the treatment phase. *Eur. Eat. Disord. Rev.* **7**: 334–350.
24. Kaechele H., Kordy H., Richard M. and Research Group TR-EAT (2001) Therapy amount and outcome of inpatient psychodynamic treatment of eating disorders in Germany. Data from a multicentre study. *Psychother. Res.*, **11**: 239.
25. Treasure J.L. (2002) Compulsory treatment in the management of eating disorders. In *Eating Disorders and Obesity: A Comprehensive Handbook*, 2nd ed. (Eds C.G. Fairburn, J.D. Brownell), pp. 340–344. Guilford Press: New York.

3.2
Medical Findings in Eating Disorders:
Clinical Perspectives on Cause and Consequence

David C. Jimerson[1]

Among the major psychiatric syndromes, eating disorders have a notably high association with physiological alterations, including serious medical comorbidities. The review by Brambilla and Monteleone provides a systematic overview and extensive reference list detailing the impact of eating disorders on the body's physiological systems, from the gastrointestinal tract through the immune and neuroendocrine pathways. Anorexia nervosa is often associated with potentially life-threatening medical consequences that play a major role in influencing treatment considerations in the low weight state, and call for collaborative efforts across mental health, nutrition and medical disciplines [1]. Although the medical problems associated with bulimia nervosa are generally less severe, the clinician needs to remain alert to the effects of dieting, binge eating and purging, including the possibility of potentially life-threatening alterations in electrolytes [2].

[1] *Beth Israel Deaconess Medical Center and Harvard Medical School, 330 Brookline Avenue, Boston, MA 02215, USA*

One prominent theme that surfaces repeatedly throughout the review is our current uncertainty regarding the precise relationship between physiological symptoms and dysregulated eating patterns. For example, although amenorrhoea in women with anorexia nervosa is commonly assumed to be a result of weight loss with an associated decrease in body fat, it is unclear why some women develop amenorrhoea prior to the onset of the low weight episode. Additionally, a few studies have evaluated the role of decreased calorie intake and weight loss *per se*, in comparison to alterations in dietary macronutrient and micronutrient content, in the medical sequelae of anorexia nervosa. Changes in meal size and frequency are likely to affect gastrointestinal physiology. Additionally, some medical problems have been linked to patients' use of diet pills or purgatives (e.g. the cardiomyopathy associated with the use of syrup of ipecac).

On a related matter, the authors call attention to the fact that medical symptoms and laboratory findings may be quite variable among anorexic patients at a similar body mass index. Little is known regarding the extent to which these variations reflect the influence of age of onset, rate of weight loss, duration of the low weight state, exercise patterns and familial/genetic influences. Similarly, it is unknown why some systems seem to return towards normal quite rapidly with weight restoration (e.g. the restoration of serum leptin concentrations) [3], whereas other abnormalities (e.g. amenorrhoea) are more persistent.

It is also generally unknown whether the nutritional and physiological changes associated with eating disorders may affect the course of illness, either through peripheral consequences or effects on central nervous system (CNS) neurotransmitters and neuromodulators. As the authors note, although the decrease in circulating leptin is not likely to contribute to the reduced food intake characteristic of anorexia nervosa, it may contribute to amenorrhoea and other neuroendocrine symptoms. In another example, dieting has been shown to lower blood tryptophan levels in healthy women, potentially resulting in decreased synthesis of the CNS neurotransmitter serotonin [4]. This decrease in central serotonin function could contribute to the impaired satiety response and high-calorie binge episodes associated with bulimia. A marked decrease in CNS serotonin function may play a role in the lack of response to antidepressant medications in low-weight patients with anorexia nervosa [5], in comparison with preliminary evidence for therapeutic benefit following weight restoration and symptom remission [6].

A challenge facing clinical investigators is the fact that physiological studies during the acute phase of anorexia nervosa or bulimia nervosa are likely to be influenced by patients' nutritional abnormalities. Thus, for both disorders it is difficult to quantify the actual caloric, macronutrient and micronutrient pattern of the diet. As one approach to the identification of persistent trait-related neurobiological alterations, a number of investigators have begun to study patients following dietary stabilization and remission from acute illness. However, abnormal attitudes toward body shape and weight tend to persist, and it is difficult to assess whether dietary and exercise patterns have returned to normal [7]. Nonetheless, future long-itudinal studies following illness remission will be important in helping to clarify which biological alterations represent a predisposition for initial onset or recurrence of illness.

REFERENCES

1. American Psychiatric Association Workgroup on Eating Disorders (2000) Practice guideline for the treatment of patients with eating disorders (revision). *Am. J. Psychiatry*, **157**: 1–39.
2. Wolfe B.E., Metzger E.D., Levine J.M., Jimerson D.C. (2001) Laboratory screening for electrolyte abnormalities and anemia in bulimia nervosa: a controlled study. *Int. J. Eat. Disord.*, **30**: 288–293.
3. Mantzoros C., Flier J.S., Lesem M.D., Brewerton T.D., Jimerson D.C. (1997) Cerebrospinal fluid leptin in anorexia nervosa: correlation with nutritional status and potential role in resistance to weight gain. *J. Clin. Endocrinol. Metab.*, **82**: 1845–1851.
4. Cowen P.J., Clifford E.M., Walsh A.E., Williams C., Fairburn C.G. (1996) Moderate dieting causes 5-HT2C receptor supersensitivity. *Psychol. Med.*, **26**: 1155–1159.
5. Attia E., Haiman C., Walsh B.T., Flater S.R. (1998) Does fluoxetine augment the inpatient treatment of anorexia nervosa? *Am. J. Psychiatry*, **155**: 548–551.
6. Kaye W.H., Nagata T., Weltzin T.E., Hsu L.K., Sokol M.S., McConaha C., Plotnicov K.H., Weise J., Deep D. (2001) Double-blind placebo-controlled administration of fluoxetine in restricting- and restricting-purging-type anorexia nervosa. *Biol. Psychiatry*, **49**: 644–652.
7. Wolfe B.E., Metzger E.D., Levine J.M., Finkelstein D.M., Cooper T.B., Jimerson D.C. (2000) Serotonin function following remission from bulimia nervosa. *Neuropsychopharmacology*, **22**: 257–263.

3.3
Eating Disorders: Minimizing Medical Complications and Preventing Deaths
Walter Kaye[1]

Brambilla and Monteleone's scholarly and comprehensive review covers an important area that does not get the attention it deserves, particularly for

[1] *Department of Psychiatry, Western Psychiatric Institute and Clinics, University of Pittsburgh Medical Center, 3600 Forbes Ave., Pittsburgh, PA 15260, USA*

anorexia nervosa, which has the highest death rate of any psychiatric illness. Approximately 0.5% of people with anorexia nervosa die per year [1]. This death rate is cumulative, so, over 20–30 years 10–15% of the people with anorexia nervosa will die from this illness. The greater majority of those deaths are caused by complications of malnutrition and emaciation. Thus, recognizing and understanding these medical symptoms and the physiological abnormalities underlying these complications is essential for diagnosis and adequate treatment.

Because anorexia is a relatively rare disorder, it is likely that many medical specialists are unfamiliar with this illness. In my experience, medical specialists are often overly aggressive in terms of refeeding anorexia or treating many of the medical complications. As Brambilla and Monteleone point out, it is likely that most of these medical problems and physiological abnormalities are secondary to starvation and malnutrition, or perhaps the lack of specific micro–macronutrients. Starvation is an unusual problem in Western cultures. Medical doctors are experienced in treating illnesses caused by some injury, infection or underlying molecular abnormality, and they tend to attempt aggressively to reverse the pathophysiology with medications and other somatic interventions. However, in anorexia nervosa, these physiological disturbances are compensations or consequences of diminished energy supplies. Aggressive treatments—even too much food—may overwhelm physiological systems and cause problems in themselves. Thus, judiciously adding nutrition and weight gain is the first line of treatment for many of these medical complications and, with sufficient time and treatment, many of them are reversible or at least reduced in severity.

In this era of managed care, third-party providers tend to focus on brief hospitalizations that seek to reverse the most flagrant medical complications, such as abnormal electrolytes or bradycardia. Brief hospitalization, however, will not reverse the entrenched medical problems that occur in anorexia nervosa. Although extended care may not "cure" the illness, it is likely that prolonged treatment minimizes morbidity and mortality. Recent studies [2] suggest that perhaps 50–70% of people with anorexia nervosa have a good outcome, but recovery may take 5–10 years. Thus, minimizing medical complications and preventing deaths is important, because some people who appear to have a chronic illness will recover if given adequate support. No managed care company would argue that they need to withhold care for the complications of diabetes because this is a chronic illness with high morbidity and mortality. Third-party providers need to extend similar benefits to the treatment of people with eating disorders, which probably have better long-term outcome than most chronic medical illnesses.

Brambilla and Monteleone's review makes the important point, not often mentioned in literature, that it may not be absolute malnutrition that is responsible for medical complications. Rather, there may be disturbances of specific micro–macronutrients. People with anorexia nervosa often eat in a ritualized and stereotypical fashion, consuming exactly the same foods for months or even years. Consequently, they may become depleted of essential nutrients, which may be idiosyncratic to each person's diet.

Physiological abnormalities also may drive the vicious circle that people with anorexia enter, i.e. malnutrition seems to exaggerate obsessional behaviours, and cognitive distortions may impair insight so that patients spiral out of control and consequently die from this illness. Alterations caused by starvation also may impede therapies, e.g. by changing drug absorption or response. This is an important area of further investigation.

REFERENCES

1. Sullivan P.F. (1995) Mortality in anorexia nervosa. *Am. J. Psychiatry*, **152**: 1073–1074.
2. Strober M., Freeman R., Morrell W. (1977) The long-term course of severe anorexia nervosa in adolescents: survival analysis of recovery, relapse, and outcome predictors over 10–15 years in a prospective study. *Int. J. Eat. Disord.*, **22**: 339–360.

3.4
Clinical Impact of the Endocrine Alterations in Patients with Eating Disorders: Adaptation or Inappropriate Response?

René K. Støving, Kim Brixen and Claus Hagen[1]

Anorexia nervosa is associated with multiple endocrine and metabolic alterations. Numerous studies on refeeding have failed to demonstrate consistently any alterations independent of starvation or malnutrition [1]. Brambilla and Monteleone summarize important data in their comprehensive review on the physical complications in eating disorders. They also draw attention to the fact that endocrine alterations, although secondary, are implicated in physical complications and affect the clinical course and survival. A number of questions related to the growth hormone (GH)–insulin-like growth factor (IGF) axis, the endocrine function of adipose tissue and insulin seem especially pertinent.

[1] *Department of Endocrinology (M) and Centre for Eating Disorders, Odense University Hospital, DK-5000 Odense C, Denmark*

Growth hormone resistance is related to growth retardation, osteopenia and thyroid atrophy. Furthermore, in anorexia nervosa there is evidence that low serum IGF-I is implicated in amenorrhoea [2]. Normal serum levels of free and biologically active IGF-I have been reported in anorexia nervosa [3], which challenges the GH resistance hypothesis. However, measurement of free IGF-I still involves methodological problems. The above study [3] used a non-equilibrium, direct immunoradiometric method. In contrast, we used a validated equilibrium assay followed by ultrafiltration and found that serum free IGF-I levels as well as free/total IGF-I ratios were decreased profoundly in anorexics [4,5], supporting the GH resistance hypothesis. As discussed by Brambilla and Monteleone, the altered GH–IGF axis function may be due to a central dysregulation. We used deconvolution analysis, designed to remove mathematically the impact of hormone kinetics and uncover pituitary GH secretory events. Also, we applied entropic analysis, which quantifies serial irregularity of hormone concentration patterns not reflected in pulsatility measurements. Our data strongly support that enhanced GH secretion in anorexia nervosa is due to markedly altered neuroendocrine regulation of the GH–IGF axis [6]. Anabolic stimulation using recombinant IGF-I or GH may, in theory, have beneficial effects in anorexia nervosa when combined with nutritional support, behavioural regimes and psychotherapy. It is strongly advisable, however, to consider the lesson from critical illness. In the 1990s, numerous trials demonstrated beneficial effects of treatment with recombinant GH or IGF-I on surrogate outcomes in patients suffering from critical illness. Nevertheless, two well-designed, randomized, placebo-controlled multicentre trials disclosed that GH increased mortality in these patients [7].

An endocrine role for adipose tissue in the regulation of energy balance has been established through the identification of leptin. Leptin is a satiety factor; however, as pointed out by Brambilla and Monteleone, it also seems to be an adipocyte-mediated signal that relates nutritional status to hypothalamic regulators of reproductive function. Thus, a critical leptin level seems to be necessary for the maintenance of menstruation. In healthy subjects, leptin exhibits diurnal variations with a nocturnal peak, but this is strikingly absent in normal-weight athletes [8] as well as in patients with anorexia nervosa [9]. This suggests that absence of leptin oscillations could be of particular significance to hypothalamic amenorrhoea in eating disorders.

Brambilla and Monteleone state that insulin sensitivity is increased in anorexia nervosa. This contrasts with the old theory of insulin resistance in anorexia nervosa. In line with this, we recently observed increased serum levels of adiponectin in patients with anorexia nervosa. Adiponectin is a newly identified adipocyte-specific hormone of considerable interest with regard to the regulation of energy balance and insulin action. Circulating adiponectin levels in humans are positively correlated with insulin sensitivity, as assessed by glucose disposals during euglycaemic hyper-insulinaemic clamps [10].

The outcome of anorexia nervosa has hardly improved since this condition was described for the first time in 1873 [11]. Brambilla and Monteleone's review addresses several critical questions that should be answered before substantial advantages in the treatment of eating disorders can be expected.

REFERENCES

1. Stoving R.K., Hangaard J., Hagen C. (2001) Update on endocrine disturbances in anorexia nervosa. *J. Pediatr. Endocrinol. Metab.*, **14**: 459–480.
2. Richards J.S., Russell D.L., Ochsner S., Hsieh M., Doyle K.H., Falender A.E., Lo Y.K., Sharma S.C. (2002) Novel signaling pathways that control ovarian follicular development, ovulation, and luteinization. *Rec. Prog. Horm. Res.*, **57**: 195–220.
3. Argente J., Caballo N., Barrios V., Munoz M.T., Pozo J., Chowen J.A., Morande G., Hernandez M. (1997) Multiple endocrine abnormalities of the growth hormone and insulin-like growth factor axis in patients with anorexia nervosa: effects of short- and long-term weight recuperation. *J. Clin. Endocrinol. Metab.*, **82**: 2084–2092.
4. Stoving R.K., Flyvbjerg A., Frystyk J., Fisker S., Hangaard J., Hansen-Nord M., Hagen C. (1999) Low serum levels of free and total insulin-like growth factor I (IGF-I) in patients with anorexia nervosa are not associated with increased IGF-binding protein-3 proteolysis. *J. Clin. Endocrinol. Metab.*, **84**: 1346–1350.
5. Frystyk J., Ivarsen P., Stoving R.K., Dall R., Bek T., Hagen C., Orskov H. (2001) Determination of free insulin-like growth factor-I in human serum: comparison of ultrafiltration and direct immunoradiometric assay. *Growth Horm. IGF Res.*, **11**: 117–127.
6. Stoving R.K., Veldhuis J.D., Flyvbjerg A., Vinten J., Hangaard J., Koldkjaer O.G., Kristiansen J., Hagen C. (1999) Jointly amplified basal and pulsatile growth hormone (GH) secretion and increased process irregularity in women with anorexia nervosa: indirect evidence for disruption of feedback regulation within the GH–insulin-like growth factor I axis. *J. Clin. Endocrinol. Metab.*, **84**: 2056–2063.
7. Takala J., Ruokonen E., Webster N.R., Nielsen M.S., Zandstra D.F., Vunde-linckx G., Hinds C.J. (1999) Increased mortality associated with growth hormone treatment in critically ill adults. *N. Engl. J. Med.*, **341**: 785–792.
8. Laughlin G.A., Yen S.S. (1997) Hypoleptinemia in women athletes: absence of a diurnal rhythm with amenorrhea. *J. Clin. Endocrinol. Metab.*, **82**: 318–321.
9. Stoving R.K., Vinten J., Handberg A., Ebbesen E.N., Hangaard J., Hansen-Nord M., Kristiansen J., Hagen C. (1998) Diurnal variation of the serum leptin concentration in patients with anorexia nervosa. *Clin. Endocrinol.* **48**: 761–768.
10. Weyer C., Funahashi T., Tanaka S., Hotta K., Matsuzawa Y., Pratley R.E., Tataranni P.A. (2001) Hypoadiponectinemia in obesity and type 2 diabetes:

close association with insulin resistance and hyperinsulinemia. *J. Clin. Endocrinol. Metab.*, **86**: 1930 1935.
11. Bergh C., Sodersten P. (1998) Anorexia nervosa: rediscovery of a disorder. *Lancet*, **351**: 1427–1429.

3.5
So Much to Learn and So Little Time
Janice Russell[1]

In the conclusion of Brambilla and Monteleone's masterly exposition of the complex neuroendocrine situation in anorexia nervosa and bulimia nervosa, a number of intriguing issues are addressed. These include the effect of emaciation *per se* versus that of nutritional deprivation or deprivation of specific nutritional elements, the time course and non-homogeneity of recovery in various axes, the effect of the psychopathological state on treatment efficacy and the need for a prolonged period of nutritional rehabilitation. The latter is relevant to current health funding policies, which are proving to be problematic in clinical management and research in eating disorders. The authors also raise the question of how secondary the medical complications and neuroendocrine perturbations really are and whether these can resurface in response to minor changes in nutritional intake or eating habits. They point out that little systematic research has been performed to address these issues. Our questions and models have been too linear and far too simple.

All this is very timely in view of Steinhausen's [1] recent assertion that outcome in anorexia nervosa has not improved in the 20th century. The illness remains prevalent with a disturbing mortality rate and a substantial likelihood of chronicity. Perhaps the situation with bulimia nervosa is more optimistic, if less clear. It was, after all, only officially described little more than two decades ago, but its incidence has been rising. Palmer and Treasure [2] discussed the need for specialized services in managing anorexia nervosa and their optimal direction. Constrained health finances in both public and private sectors have dictated otherwise and we are pushed to find quicker and cheaper ways to treat all our eating disordered patients, with little time for evaluation and proper research. Time again seems to be the missing ingredient in the therapeutic mix, even where other resources would appear to be adequate. The same applies to the evidence base of many of our treatment modalities, be these physical or psychological. This of course does not detract from the need to

[1] *Eating Disorders Program, Northside Clinic, Greenwich 2065 NSW, Australia*

improve the efficacy of nutritional rehabilitation and its consequence of appropriately prompt resolution of physical complications and physiological aberrations in anorexia nervosa, bulimia nervosa and even some cases of eating disorders not otherwise specified. This mandates a thorough understanding of the viciously reverberating cycles of nutritional deprivation, adaptation and perverse reward [3] that underpin all these conditions.

Here, an examination of energy metabolism is pertinent. Emaciated patients with anorexia nervosa appear to waste energy in that their diet-induced thermogenesis represents a higher proportion of resting energy expenditure than in controls or in themselves following modest weight restoration [4]. This phenomenon is seen after high carbohydrate and not after high fat loads, furthermore, it is more prominent in high exercisers and is associated with a respiratory quotient in excess of unity, indicative of net lipogenesis. Twenty-four hour energy expenditure is significantly higher in high exercisers [5]. The avidity for lipogenesis could be related to a biological imperative to repair fat-containing tissues metabolized for energy requirements. Using proton magnetic resonance spectrometry, Schlemmer et al. [6] demonstrated degradation of myelin sheaths in acutely ill patients with anorexia nervosa. The therapeutic implication is that a higher fat intake is beneficial in refeeding and, not surprisingly, high exercisers do require significantly more dietary energy [5]. Higher fat supplements such as those used for patients following pulmonary surgery would be recommended for patients so emaciated as to require enteral feeding.

In bulimia nervosa nutritional deprivation is pervasive despite normal body weight, as evidenced by ketone bodies even during short-term abstinence from purging. In conjunction with hypoglycaemia and hyperinsulinaemia, this is likely to be an important perpetuating factor in binge eating [7] and can be addressed only by reinstitution of a regular balanced eating pattern, hence the need for prolonged and expert nutritional counselling and not infrequently initial behavioural containment.

Promising areas for exploration and manipulation include corticotropin-releasing factor (CRF), as discussed by Brambilla and Monteleone, with its anorexogenic effect and its relevance to depression, stress and starvation, the orexogenic peptides galanin, ghrelin [8] and neuropeptide Y (NPY) and the satiety-inducing peptide cholecystokinin (CCK). Leptin, however, which generated so much excitement at its discovery, has not really lived up to its promise therapeutically, despite its not inconsiderable contribution to the understanding of the neuroendocrinology of weight and eating disorders. Weight and energy homeostasis in humans seems to have a floor and no ceiling. Efficient though the former might be under ordinary conditions, and excessively so in affluent societies, as the rising prevalence of obesity would indicate, in the eating disorders it serves to exacerbate the disturbance of behaviour and psyche that constitutes the other half of the therapeutic challenge.

The average eating disordered patient who is ill enough to require specialized inpatient or other high-intensity care will need at least several weeks of this in a multidisciplinary medical psychiatry setting followed by a prolonged period of outpatient management often extending over several years. Even when the illness is less severe in terms of physical and psychological complications, treatment is rarely expedient or inexpensive—a fact that funding authorities remain reluctant to grasp. Yet surely the long-term investment in the health of numerous young people would seem to be worthwhile, in view of reduction of risk with respect to sudden death, osteoporosis, growth retardation, infertility, pubertal and developmental delay, irreversible brain changes, major organ failure, psychiatric comorbidity, general dysfunction and ill health [1,9–12]. Current advances in the management of infertility all too often result in pregnancy without resolution of the eating disorder, to the ongoing detriment of all concerned. Adequate resources for managing and researching eating disorders might afford the best form of prevention for these pernicious conditions and we might look forward to improved health in succeeding generations. We who work with eating disordered patients and their families can only hope that the clinical recommendations and future directions for research specified by Brambilla and Monteleone can be realized before it is too late for too many.

REFERENCES

1. Steinhausen H.-C. (2002) The outcome of anorexia nervosa in the 20th century. *Am. J. Psychiatry*, **159**: 1284–1293.
2. Palmer R.L., Treasure J. (1999) Providing specialised services for anorexia nervosa. *Br. J. Psychiatry*, **175**: 306–309.
3. Russell J.D., Hunt G.E. (1996) Anorexia nervosa—more than an eating disorder. *Nature Med.*, **2**: 366–367.
4. Russell J., Baur L.A., Beumont P.J.V., Byrnes S., Gross G., Touyz S. Abraham S., Zipfel S. (2001) Altered energy metabolism in anorexia nervosa. *Psychoneuroendocrinology* **26**: 51–63.
5. Russell J., Zipfel S., Baur L.A., Hebebrand J., Davies P., Abraham S., Herzog W., Beumont P. (2001) Influence of exercise on energy metabolism in anorexia nervosa. Presented at the Eating Disorders Research Society Meeting, Bernalillo, 28 November–1 December.
6. Schlemmer H.-P., Moeckel R., Marcus A., Hentschel F., Goepel C., Becker G., Koepke J., Gueckel F., Schmidt M.H., Georgi M. (1998) Proton magnetic resonance spectroscopy in acute, juvenile anorexia nervosa. *Psychiatry Res.*, **82**: 171–179.

7. Russell J., Hooper M., Hunt G. (1996) Insulin response in bulimia nervosa as a marker of nutritional depletion. *Int. J. Eat. Disord.*, **20**: 307–313.
8. Cuntz U., Otto B., Fruehauf R., Wawarta R., Folwaczny C., Riepl R., Heiman P., Lehnert P., Fichter M.D., Tschop M. (2001) Ghrelin—a novel weight-regulating hormone—and its role in anorexia nervosa. Presented at the Eating Disorders Research Society Meeting, Bernalillo, 28 November–1 December.
9. Halmi K.A. (1999) Eating disorders: defining the phenotype and reinventing the treatment. *Am. J. Psychiatry*, **156**: 1673–1675.
10. Hendren R.L., De Becker I., Pandina G.J. (2000) Review of neuroimaging studies of child and adolescent psychiatric disorders from the past 10 years. *J. Am. Acad. Child Adolesc. Psychiatry*, **39**: 815–828.
11. Russell J., Gross G. (2000) Anorexia nervosa and body mass index. *Am. J. Psychiatry*, **157**: 12.
12. Zipfel S., Lowe B., Reas D., Deter H.-C., Herzog W. (2000) Long-term prognosis in anorexia nervosa: lessons from a 21-year follow-up study. *Lancet*, **355**: 721–722.

3.6

Medical Abnormalities in Eating Disorders

Yoshikatsu Nakai[1]

Frequently, a person with an eating disorder such as anorexia nervosa or bulimia nervosa does not disclose symptoms or may even conceal them because of ignorance and/or denial of available treatment. Therefore, physicians must be able to recognize and manage the medical abnormalities of eating disorders, because physicians are usually involved in the initial diagnosis. However, the reliability of the physical signs of eating disorders is poor even among specialists [1]. Many medical abnormalities develop after the onset of eating disorders. On the other hand, a past history of physical illness is a significant risk factor for early-onset eating disorders. Furthermore, an increased number of diabetes mellitus cases followed by the development of eating disorders have been reported. The coexistence of diabetes and eating disorders leads to poor glycaemic control and an increased risk of long-term complications.

One of the serious and not uncommon complications of eating disorders is coma. Coma may occur as a consequence of cardiovascular collapse. However, a hypoglycaemic attack should be considered first as a cause of coma in patients with the binge/purge type of anorexia nervosa. Coma usually occurs in these patients suddenly after binge/purging without any early signs of hypoglycaemia, such as cold sweats. The normotensive,

[1] *College of Medical Technology, Kyoto University, 53 Kawaharacho, Shogoin, Sakyo-ku, Kyoto, Japan*

hypokalaemic, hypochloraemic metabolic alkalosis seen in many eating disordered patients with purging is known as pseudo-Bartter's syndrome and has significant therapeutic implications. Despite potassium repletion, potassium levels remain low, unless the hypovolaemic state is judiciously normalized to restore the functionality of the renin–angiotensin–aldosterone axis. There is an increase of vasopressin in plasma and cerebrospinal fluid during abstinence from bingeing and purging. The disturbance in osmo-regulation may aggravate the maintenance of adequate fluid volume in these patients, whereas the increase in centrally directed vasopressin may have relevance to their obsessional preoccupation with aversive consequences of eating.

In the early days, medical abnormalities of eating disorders usually were assessed by the detailed description of signs and symptoms. Afterwards, laboratory tests have been used for the assessment of these abnormalities. Recently, the abnormalities of endocrine and immune systems and of the central nervous system (CNS) have been disclosed. In particular, the abnormalities of appetite-related substances have received great attention. Among them, interest has focused on serotonin, corticotropin-releasing hormone (CRH) and tumor necrosis factor alpha (TNF-α) in the pathogenesis of eating disorders. Interestingly, these are stress-related as well as appetite-related substances and are also involved in the pathogenesis of some other psychiatric disorders. Chronic hypersecretion of CRH may play a role in the aetiology of anorexia nervosa as well as depression. To date, four CRH-like peptides and two CRH receptors have been identified in vertebrates. There are few reports about the function of receptors for serotonin and CRH in eating disorders and other psychiatric disorders even after the molecular cloning of these receptors.

The cytokine TNF-α has immunological and metabolic activities. In addition, TNF-α can stimulate a variety of neuroendocrine and behavioural responses that have been observed also in eating disorders. The action of TNF-α is reflected by soluble forms of the two TNF-α receptors (sTNF-RI and -RII). There are no reliable data on plasma TNF-α concentrations in eating disordered patients. Plasma concentrations of TNF-α and sTNF-RII were significantly increased in anorexic and bulimic patients compared with controls [2,3] when measured using a sensitive radioimmunoassay. The TNF-α in the CNS can be released into peripheral blood, suggesting that the elevated plasma levels of TNF-α in eating disordered patients may be due to altered brain production [3]. If the receptor function for these substances in eating disorders and other psychiatric disorders were clarified, the development of specific antagonists would open up new avenues for treatment.

It has been hypothesized that some signals from the peripheral tissues to the CNS may be responsible for the pathogenesis of eating disorders. From this point of view, two attractive peptides have been identified recently: leptin from adipose tissues [4] and ghrelin from the stomach [5]. In both anorexic and bulimic patients, plasma leptin levels were significantly low and plasma ghrelin levels were significantly high compared with normal controls. Abnormalities of these peptides in anorexic patients may be an adaptation to starvation. On the other hand, these abnormalities in bulimic patients may play an important role in the pathogenesis of bulimia nervosa. As an alternative, they may simply reflect the changes of eating patterns [6]. The function of the receptors for these peptides in eating disordered patients should be clarified in order to draw conclusions.

REFERENCES

1. Tyler I., Birmingham C.L. (2001) The interrater reliability of physical signs in patients with eating disorders. *Int. J. Eat. Disord.*, **30**: 343–345.
2. Nakai Y., Hamagaki S., Takagi R., Taniguchi A., Kurimoto F. (1999) Plasma concentrations of tumor necrosis factor-α (TNF-α) and soluble TNF receptors in patients with anorexia nervosa. *J. Clin. Endocrinol. Metab.*, **84**: 1226–1228.
3. Nakai Y., Hamagaki S., Takagi R., Taniguchi A., Kurimoto F. (2000) Plasma concentrations of tumor necrosis factor-α (TNF-α) and soluble TNF receptors in patients with bulimia nervosa. *J. Clin. Endocrinol.*, **53**: 383–388.
4. Friedman J.M., Halaas J.L. (1998) Leptin and the regulation of body weight in mammals. *Nature*, **385**: 763–770.
5. Kojima M., Hosoda H., Matsuo H., Kangawa K. (2001) Ghrelin: discovery of the natural endogenous ligand for the growth hormone secretagogue receptor. *Trends Endocrinol Metab.*, **12**: 118–123.
6. Nakai Y., Hamagaki S., Kato S., Seino Y., Takagi R., Kurimoto F. (1999) Leptin in women with eating disorders. *Metabolism*, **48**: 217–220.

3.7
Physiological Aberrations: Cause and Consequence?

Kelly L. Klump[1]

As Brambilla and Monteleone articulately describe, anorexia nervosa and bulimia nervosa are disorders that are unique in their ominous combination of psychological and medical impairments. The direct physical complications of these disorders surpass those of any other psychiatric condition and contribute to the significant morbidity and mortality of their sufferers. A central question that is being posed

[1] *Department of Psychology, Michigan State University, 129 Psychology Research Building, East Lansing, MI 48824, USA*

increasingly about these biological dysfunctions concerns the nature of the physiological disturbance—are they merely consequences of starvation and aberrant eating patterns, or do they contribute to the aetiology of the disorder itself?

Brambilla and Monteleone note that many of these disturbances, such as dermatological, gastroenteric and cardiovascular alterations, do appear to be consequences of abnormal eating patterns. However, recent research has begun to identify biological alterations that may represent aetiological mechanisms by which the disorder becomes manifested. Brambilla and Monteleone highlight some of these data in their review, noting that there is a persistence of serotonin, noradrenaline and dopamine system disturbances after recovery from eating disorders. These findings suggest that a dysregulation in one or more of these systems may contribute to the development of eating pathology.

Recent evidence also suggests that neuroendocrine disturbances may represent aetiological as well as concomitant effects. Amenorrhoea and oligomenorrhoea are invariably present in anorexia nervosa, and are frequently present in bulimia nervosa. These menstrual disturbances are clearly the result of starvation and aberrant eating patterns. However, recent twin data indicate that there may be other neuroendocrine disturbances that contribute to, rather than correlate with, eating pathology. These studies have found dramatic increases in the heritability of disordered eating symptoms in girls around puberty [1]. Indeed, findings suggest that there are no genetic influences on eating pathology before puberty, but that genes account for roughly 50% of the variance in disordered eating during and after this developmental period. Possible explanations for this finding include the activation of aetiological genes associated with pubertal biochemical changes, including increases in oestrogen and progesterone (in girls). Could it be that some of the genes contributing to eating pathology are related to these ovarian hormones, and that changes in neuroendocrine systems represent aetiological as well as concomitant effects?

Several lines of evidence from both animal and human studies indirectly support this hypothesis. The preponderance of female sufferers, pubertal age of onset and virtual absence of sufferers after menopause all highlight a potential role for ovarian hormones in eating disorder development. In addition, human [2] and animal [3–6] studies have both shown oestrogen and progesterone to have direct effects on food intake.

Finally, studies of depression—a disorder frequently comorbid with eating pathology—have found ovarian and stress hormones to contribute significantly to the increased prevalence of the disorder in girls after puberty [7]. These studies examined whether hormone concentrations or physical changes (e.g. weight gain, development of pubic hair, etc.)

significantly predicted depressive symptoms during puberty. Findings revealed significant predictive relationships between hormones and depression that were not present for the physical appearance variables. These results are highly significant in suggesting that hormones are associated with increased psychiatric symptoms in girls after puberty—could the same be true for eating disorder symptomatology?

The exact nature of such an aetiological hormonal disturbance in eating disorders remains unclear. At the very least, twin findings suggest that the disturbance may have genetic underpinnings. One possibility is that the genes that code for these hormones contribute to a dysregulation in the neuroendocrine system, which then contributes to disordered eating. However, it is also possible that ovarian hormones contribute indirectly to eating pathology through their effects on gene transcription. Unlike protein or amine hormones, steroid sex hormones exert their effects in the brain by diffusing through cell membranes and binding to nuclear receptors, which function as activators or repressors of gene transcription and subsequent protein synthesis. This mechanism suggests that either the genes involved in ovarian hormone production or the genes that these hormones affect may be aetiologically related to eating pathology.

All of these conjectures are highly speculative and additional genetic and phenotypic research is needed. Genetic research should focus on twin and molecular genetic designs that can examine possible shared transmission between genes involved in hormones and those influencing eating pathology. Phenotypic researchers should focus their efforts on studying relationships between hormones and disordered eating in menstruating women who may or may not have eating disorders. Focusing on menstruating women will allow researchers to examine possible aetiological effects rather than just sequelae of the illness.

REFERENCES

1. Klump K.L., McGue M., Iacono W.G. (2003) Differential heritability of eating attitudes and behaviors in pre-pubertal versus pubertal twins. *Int. J. Eat. Disord.* (in press).
2. Gladis M.M., Walsh B.T. (1987) Premenstural exacerbation of binge eating in bulimia nervosa. *Am. J. Psychiatry*, **144**: 1592–1595.
3. Blaustein J.D., Wade G.N. (1977) Ovarian influences and meal pattern in rats: effects of progesterone and role of gastrointestinal transit. *Physiol. Behav.*, **19**: 23–27.
4. Varma M., Chai J.K., Meguid M.M., Laviano A., Gleason J.R., Yang Z.J., Blaha V. (1999) Effect of estradiol and progesterone on daily rhythm in food intake and feeding patterns in Fischer rats. *Physiol. Behav.*, **68**: 99–107.

5. Kemnitz J.W., Gibber J.R., Lindsay K.A., Eisele S.G. (1989) Effects of ovarian hormones on eating behavior, body weight, and glucoregulation in rhesus monkeys. *Horm. Behav.*, **23**: 235–250.
6. Ganesan R. (1994) The aversive hypophagic effects of estradiol. *Physiol. Behav.* **55**: 279–285.
7. Angold A., Costello E.J., Erkanli A., Worthman C.M. (1999) Pubertal changes in hormone levels and depression in girls. *Psychol. Med.*, **29**: 1043–1053.

3.8
Anorexia Nervosa and Bulimia Nervosa — Neuroendocrine Disturbances

Boguslawa Baranowska[1]

The endocrine disturbances in anorexia nervosa are a consequence of: a) hypothalamic–pituitary dysfunction; b) disturbances in peripheral hormonal metabolism as a result of starvation. The hypothalamic–pituitary disorder includes a disturbed central control of appetite, thermo-regulation and behaviour, as well as a dysfunction of neurohormone secretion. It is obvious that the disturbed secretion of neurohormones leads to a dysfunction of the hypothalamic–pituitary–gonadal, hypothalamic–pituitary–adrenal, hypothalamic–pituitary–thyroid and hypothalamic–growth hormone–somatomedin axes.

The functional deficiency of gonadotropin-releasing hormone (GnRH) is due to the increased opioid, dopaminergic and melatonin activity and to the decreased leptin and adrenergic activity.

Indirect evidence of GnRH deficiency can be seen in the reduced luteinizing hormone (LH) pulsatility, the disturbed diurnal rhythm of LH, the blunted response of LH to clomiphene, the blunted response of LH to GnRH injection (25 μg) and normalization of this response while increasing the dose of GnRH (100 μg). The clinical result of GnRH deficiency is hypothalamic amenorrhoea.

The increased serum cortisol concentration is a result of the raised synthesis of cortisol, the increased corticotropin-reducing factor (CRF) activity and the lowered clearance of cortisol. Normal or low thyroxine-stimulating hormone (TSH) concentrations and the delayed response of TSH to thyrotropin-releasing hormone (TRH) were observed. Also, low serum triiodothyronine (T_3) levels and high reversed T_3 are a result of the

[1] *Neuroendocrinology Department, Medical Centre of Postgraduate Education, Fieldorfa 40, 04-158 Warsaw, Poland*

changes in the peripheral metabolism. An increased serum growth hormone (GH) concentration and exaggerated GH response to GH-releasing hormone GHRH and TRH can be observed and may be connected with the increase of ghrelin activity, the increased sensitivity of somatotrophs to GHRH and the decreased somatostatin activity, as well as the lower leptin activity.

The disturbed peripheral hormonal metabolism is associated with starvation. Examples are: a) the decreased peripheral conversion of thyroxine (T_4) to T_3 and an increase of reversed T_3; b) the changes in metabolism of cortisol (the decrease of cortisol clearance leads to discrepancy between serum cortisol concentrations and metabolites of cortisol); c) the changes in androgen metabolism (the increase of testosterone and the decrease of dehydroepiandrosterone in the dramatic period of weight loss).

Some neuropeptides play an important role in the control of appetite and in the mechanism of hormone secretion. In anorexia nervosa the abnormal control of appetite and many hormonal disturbances may be a consequence of abnormal neuropeptide activity. Plasma neuropetide Y (NPY) concentrations are low, whereas cerebrospinal fluid (CSF) levels are increased. This discrepancy may be due to the changed permeability of the brain–blood barrier as a result of starvation. Plasma leptin levels in anorexic patients are very low and the feedback mechanism of leptin–NPY is strongly disturbed. The low production of leptin does not cause an increase of NPY [1,2].

The opioid activity is changed too [3]. The nocturnal secretion of β-endorphin is increased, but we can observe a loss of β-endorphin circadian rhythm and a blunted response of β-endorphin to clonidine and domperidone. It has been reported that plasma vasoactive intestinal peptide (VIP), ghrelin and melatonin are augmented, whereas plasma cholecystokinin levels are lowered.

Multiple endocrine dysfunctions have been observed in bulimia nervosa. Our results indicate that the plasma leptin concentration in bulimia nervosa is significantly higher than in anorexia nervosa but lower than in controls [4]. Monteleone et al. [5] observed lower leptin concentrations in normal-weight untreated bulimic patients compared with controls. They demonstrated that after acute refeeding the plasma leptin level increased in bulimic patients but did not reach the values observed in normal controls. We found that the plasma NPY level in bulimia nervosa was significantly higher than in anorexic or healthy women [4]. The observed increase of NPY in bulimia nervosa was independent of body mass index (BMI), because the BMI in bulimia nervosa was normal. It may be speculated that factors other than changes in body weight may be involved in the increased production of NPY in bulimia nervosa.

REFERENCES

1. Baranowska B., Radzikowska M., Wasilewska-Dziubinska E., Roguski K., Borowiec M. (2000) Disturbed release of gastrointestinal peptides in anorexia nervosa and in obesity. *Diabetes Obes. Metab.*, **2**: 99–103.
2. Baranowska B., Wasilewska-Dziubinska E., Radzikowska M., Plonowski A., Roguski K. (1997) Neuropeptide Y, galanin and leptin release in obese women and in women with anorexia nervosa. *Metabolism*, **46**: 1384–1389.
3. Baranowska B. (1990) Are disturbances in opioid and adrenergic systems involved in the hormonal dysfunction of anorexia nervosa? *Psychoneuroendocrinology*, **5**: 371–379.
4. Baranowska B., Wolinska-Witort E., Wasilewska-Dziubinska E., Roguski K., Chmielowska M. (2001) Plasma leptin, neuropeptide Y (NPY) and galanin concentrations in bulimia nervosa and in anorexia nervosa. *Neuroendocrinol. Lett.*, **22**: 356–358.
5. Monteleone P., Bortolotti R., Fabrazzo M., La Rocca A., Fuschino A., Maj M. (2000) Plasma leptin response to acute fasting and refeeding in untreated women with bulimia nervosa. *J. Clin. Endocrinol. Metab.*, **85**: 2499–2503.

3.9
The Consequences of Starvation
Reinhold G. Laessle[1]

Anorexia and bulimia nervosa are psychosomatic syndromes characterized by an extremely disordered eating behaviour. The psychologically triggered malnutrition is related to numerous physiological aberrations and physical complications, described in Brambilla and Monteleone's authoritative and comprehensive review. I will reflect on the consequences of starvation caused by either continuous or intermittent dieting, as can be observed in anorexia and bulimia nervosa.

- *Metabolic adaptation to starvation.* The metabolic adaptation to starvation can be subdivided into three phases. During the first phase (following an overnight fast), glycogen reserves are utilized, and glucose and free fatty acids from lipolysis contribute equal parts to the body's energy needs. This is indicated by high levels of ketone bodies, such as β-hydroxybutyric acid. In the second phase (following a short-term, 3-day, fast), when glycogen stores have been depleted, the calorie requirement is met by amino acids, which are oxidized directly or used in gluconeogenesis. This process is indicated by high levels of cortisol. In the third phase (following a prolonged fast of 3 weeks or longer),

[1] *University of Trier, 54286 Trier, Germany*

adaptation processes occur that reduce the basal energy consumption of the body. The body temperature is lowered and the blood pressure and heart rate are reduced. These changes are brought about by a decrease in triiodothyronine levels and by a reduction of catecholamine production, both of which can be seen in patients.

- *Endocrine adaptation to starvation.* Growth hormone levels are elevated in starvation. Total fasting also causes several alterations in the hypothalamus–pituitary–adrenal system. Cortisol stimulates gluconeogenesis and thus plays a role in maintaining an adequate blood glucose concentration necessary for survival. Therefore, it is not surprising that all abnormalities of cortisol secretion and the prolonged half-life in plasma are normalized rapidly when starving subjects or anorexic patients start eating again.
- *Somatic effects of starvation.* Changes in body composition occur as a consequence of starvation. Muscular mass is decreased by about 40% and fat tissue by 70%. Victims of starvation and semi-starvation excrete large amounts of urine of low specific gravity. The ability of the kidneys to concentrate is reduced. An atrophy of the heart, accompanied by a marked reduction of cardiac function, has been observed [1].
- *Physiological effects of starvation.* Gastric motility is reduced and body temperature is lower during semi-starvation. The sympathetic nervous system is dysregulated, as indicated by a reduction in resting plasma noradrenaline and a blunted response to stimulation [2]. Severe reduction of gonadal hormone secretion can be induced by dieting in normal healthy subjects.

All the consequences of starvation depend on the type of food restriction, the duration of food deprivation and the original body composition of the patient. The observations during starvation in normal subjects emphasize how necessary it is to gain knowledge of the individual eating behaviour and preferences in patients with eating disorders. Future research on the psychobiological interactions will enable us to improve the still unsatisfactory long-term treatment outcome for eating disorders.

REFERENCES

1. Keys A., Brozek J., Henschel A., Micholson O., Taylor H.L. (1950) *The Biology of Human Starvation.* University of Minnesota Press, Minneapolis.
2. Pirke K.M., Kellner M., Philipp E., Laessle R.G., Krieg J., Fichter M. (1992) Plasma norepinephrine after a standardized test meal in acute and remitted patients with anorexia nervosa and healthy controls. *Biol. Psychiatry*, **31**: 1074–1077.

3.10
Biological Abnormalities in Eating Disorders

Josefina Castro[1]

Anorexia and bulimia nervosa are two psychiatric disorders in which psychological symptoms lead to physical consequences, which, in turn, contribute to maintaining the disorder. Once the disorder is established, it is a vicious circle from which it is very difficult to escape without intensive and usually prolonged treatment. For clinicians treating eating disorders, knowledge of these physical alterations is very important and Brambilla and Monteleone present a broad-ranging and thorough exposition of all of them.

Mortality in eating disorders is usually related to cardiac or electrolyte alterations. Non-fatal physical sequelae are also common in anorexia and bulimia nervosa, especially if they are not resolved during adolescence. Because these disorders usually begin during puberty and adolescence, they can affect growth, peak bone mass or sexual development. If the disorder lasts for several years, e.g. into the third decade of life, lasting physical sequelae are almost inevitable. Nevertheless, many alterations can be reversed if a good outcome is achieved during the first few years: for instance, cardiac abnormalities, such as bradycardia or reduced atrial and ventricular dimensions, seem to reverse completely after weight recovery in adolescents with a short duration of disorder [1]. Osteopenia in young patients also can improve and a catch-up effect has been described in bone mass if normal weight is attained during adolescence in both female [2] and male [3] anorexic patients. Patients with abnormal bone mineral density but good outcome have a higher increase in bone mass than adolescents from the general population.

In the last decade, the repercussions of eating disorders on the structure and function of the brain have been examined. Neuroimaging studies have shown a reduction in total grey and white matter volumes in anorexic patients compared with controls [4]. Other studies have shown that the loss of grey matter persists after weight recovery in some patients [5,6]. Lower weight in anorexic patients is also associated with poorer performance on cognitive tasks [7]. Functional neuroimaging also shows a reduction of brain activity, both global and regional [8]; it is not clear whether these abnormalities are reversible or if some are already present before the onset of the disorder. It has been suggested that they may contribute to the predisposition of the patient to developing an eating disorder.

_____

[1] *Child and Adolescent Psychiatry and Psychology Department, University Hospital, 1 Sabino de Arana, Barcelona 08028, Spain*

Some biological abnormalities in eating disorders are clearly a consequence of malnutrition and purging behaviour. Nevertheless, other alterations may represent a biological substrate in some adolescents at risk of presenting anorexia or bulimia nervosa. This biological substrate may lead to an eating disorder by itself or, more probably, may require the initial loss of weight to develop into the complete syndrome of an eating disorder. Brain abnormalities and serotonin, noradrenaline or dopamine alterations in eating disorders may persist long after recovery. More research in these areas should broaden our understanding of eating disorders.

REFERENCES

1. Mont L.L., Castro J., Herreros B., Paré C., Azqueta M., Magriña J., Puuig J., Toro J., Brugada J. Reversibility of cardiac abnormalities in adolescents with anorexia nervosa after weight recovery. Unpublished manuscript.
2. Castro J., Lázaro L., Pons F., Halperin I., Toro J. (2001) Adolescent anorexia nervosa: the catch-up effect in bone mineral density after recovery. *J. Am. Acad. Child Adolesc. Psychiatry*, **40**: 1215–1221.
3. Castro J., Toro J., Lázaro L., Pons F., Halperin I. (2002) Bone mineral density in male adolescents with anorexia nervosa. *J. Am. Acad. Child Adolesc. Psychiatry*, **41**: 613–618.
4. Katzman D.K., Lambe E.K., Mikulis D.J., Ridgley J.N., Goldbloom D.S., Zipursky R.B. (1996) Crebral gray matter and white matter volume deficits in adolescent girls with anorexia nervosa. *J. Pediatr.*, **129**: 794–803.
5. Katzman D.K., Zipursky R.B., Lambe E.K., Mikulis D.J. (1997) A longitudinal magnetic resonance imaging study of brain changes in adolescent with anorexia nervosa. *Arch. Pediatr. Adolesc. Med.*, **51**: 793–797.
6. Lambe E.K., Katzman D.K., Mikulis D.J., Kennedy S.H., Zipursky R.B. (1997) Cerebral gray matter volume deficits after weight recovery from anorexia nervosa. *Arch. Gen. Psychiatry*, **54**: 537–542.
7. Kingston K., Szmukler G., Andrewes D., Tress B., Desmond P. (1996) Neuropsychological and structural brain changes in anorexia nervosa before and after refeeding. *Psychol. Med.*, **26**: 15–28.
8. Delvenne V., Goldman S., De Maertelaer V., Wikler D., Damhaut P., Lotstra F. (1997) Brain glucose metabolism in anorexia nervosa and affective disorders: influence of weight loss or depressive syptomatology. *Psychiatry Res.*, **16**: 83–92.
9. Gordon I., Lask B., Bryant-Waught R., Christie D., Timimi S. (1997) Childhood-onset anorexia nervosa: towards identifying a biological substrate. *Int. J. Eat. Disord.*, **22**: 159–165.

3.11
Towards an Understanding of the Biological Causes
and Consequences of Eating Disorders

Gabriella F. Milos[1]

Eating disorders are common among adolescent girls and young women and are associated with potentially serious medical complications, which often go undetected and untreated. All patients with eating disorders should be evaluated and treated for medical complications of the disease at the same time that psychotherapy and nutritional counselling are undertaken [1]. Anorexia nervosa is a complex illness with a high risk of morbidity and mortality [2]. The somatic complications of bulimia nervosa can be dangerous, although little is known about the long-term prognosis of patients with untreated bulimia nervosa.

Eating disorders cause changes and abnormalities in many organs and organ systems. In their review, Brambilla and Monteleone provide a clear presentation of the numerous changes to organs as well as the complex metabolic and endocrinological aberrations, and consider eating disorders to be "the most intriguing combination of psychological and medical impairments".

Brambilla and Monteleone pose the fundamental question: to what extent can the changes in anorexia nervosa be attributed to simple starvation and malnutrition and therefore be interpreted as secondary phenomena, or to what extent may endocrine disorders be considered the primary cause of the illness? At present this question must remain unanswered, but it may stimulate further interesting research.

Dysfunctions in the hypothalamus play an important role in regulating the appetite and are therefore of great significance where the pathogenesis of eating disorders is concerned.

The part played by cortisol and adrenocorticotropic hormone (ACTH) in the chain of pathological alterations in eating disorders is a central one. In anorexia and bulimia nervosa, cortisol and ACTH show a normal circadian rhythm. In anorexia nervosa a raised level of plasma cortisol concentration occurs during the whole day; it reaches its highest levels in the evening. The raised level of cortisol is explained by the increased secretion and the simultaneously reduced clearance. Hypercortisolaemia readjusts only after normal weight has been regained.

---

[1] Eating Disorders Unit, Psychiatric Out-Patients Department, University Hospital, Culmannstrasse 8, 8091 Zürich, Switzerland

Hypercortisolaemia is interpreted as being not simply the result of starvation and malnutrition but also an intrinsic alteration. Several studies prove that weight gain in anorexic patients leads to fat distribution concentrated on the torso, with little subcutaneous fat on the extremities [3–6]. The hypercortisolaemia mentioned by Brambilla and Monteleone could provide the endocrinological explanation for this fat distribution during weight gain in anorexia nervosa.

The pathognomonic amenorrhoea used for the diagnosis of anorexia nervosa is explained by a hypogonadotropic hypogonadism that is accompanied by a low concentration of luteinizing hormone (LH), follicle-stimulating hormone (FSH) and oestrogens. The theory is presented that the low fat mass leads to hypoestrogenaemia. However, in current research the question why certain anorexic patients have amenorrhoea even after achieving their normal weight is not yet answered. In analogy to athletic women, the explanation for irregularities in menstruation possibly lies in their intense physical activity rather than in their being under-weight.

The rarely reversible loss of bone mass in anorexia nervosa is also discussed. In normal physiological conditions the bone mass increases significantly until growth has been completed. From that point until 30 years of age (peak bone mass) the bone mass increases very little. Because peak bone mass is considered to be the key to osteoporosis [7] and anorexia nervosa often starts in this phase of bone building, sufferers of anorexia are frequently confronted with a life-long insufficient bone structure and its consequences. The effect of amenorrhoea in the pathogenesis of osteopenia/osteoporosis is controversial. Studies show [8,9] that oestrogen replacement brings no decisive gain in bone mass. The authors assume, therefore, that other factors must play an important role in respect of the loss of bone mass.

Neuropeptide Y is the strongest stimulator of feelings of hunger and the intake of carbohydrates. It is presumed that this peptide is associated with the not infrequently persisting amenorrhoea after normalization of weight. Cholecystokinin is a hormone that is produced centrally and peripherally and signals satiety. In bulimia nervosa the cholecystokinin levels correlate with anxiety, aggressive behaviour and difficulties in interpersonal relations. However, they do not seem to correlate with the body mass index (BMI) or the frequency of binge/purge episodes.

Although there are numerous research studies on the endocrinological alterations in eating disorders, many pathophysiological and neuroendo-crinological mechanisms remain unclear. There is a considerable discrepancy between biological knowledge and its poor application in the treatment of eating disorders in clinical practice.

REFERENCES

1. Becker A.E., Grinspoon S.K., Klibanski A., Herzog D.B. (1999) Eating disorders. *N. Engl. J. Med.*, **340**: 1092–1098.
2. Zipfel S., Lowe B., Reas D.L., Deter H.C., Herzog W. (2000) Long-term prognosis in anorexia nervosa: lessons from a 21-year follow-up study. *Lancet*, **355**: 721–722.
3. Iketani T., Kiriike N., Nagata T., Yamagami S. (1999) Altered body fat distribution after recovery of weight in patients with anorexia nervosa. *Int. J. Eat. Disord.*, **26**: 275–282.
4. Orphanidou C.I., McCargar L.J., Birmingham C.L., Belzberg A.S. (1997) Changes in body composition and fat distribution after short-term weight gain in patients with anorexia nervosa. *Am. J. Clin. Nutr.*, **65**: 1034–1041.
5. Zamboni M., Armellini F., Turcato E., Todisco P., Gallagher D., Dalle Grave R., Heymsfield S., Bosello O. (1997) Body fat distribution before and after weight gain in anorexia nervosa. *Int. J. Obes. Relat. Metab. Disord.*, **21**: 33–36.
6. Mayo-Smith W., Hayes C.W., Biller B.M., Klibanski A., Rosenthal H., Rosenthal D.I. (1989) Body fat distribution measured with CT: correlations in healthy subjects, patients with anorexia nervosa, and patients with Cushing syndrome. *Radiology*, **170**: 515–518.
7. Valla A., Groenning I.L., Syversen U., Hoeiseth A. (2000) Anorexia nervosa: slow regain of bone mass. *Osteoporos. Int.*, **11**: 141–145.
8. Rigotti N.A., Nussbaum S.R., Herzog D.B., Neer R.M. (1984) Osteoporosis in women with anorexia nervosa. *N. Engl. J. Med.*, **311**: 1601–1606.
9. Klibanski A., Biller B.M., Schoenfeld D.A., Herzog D.B., Saxe V.C. (1995) The effects of estrogen administration on trabecular bone loss in young women with anorexia nervosa. *J. Clin. Endocrinol. Metab.*, **80**: 898–904.

3.12
A Special Situation of Malnutrition Triggering Organism Adaptive Changes

Ascensión Marcos[1]

Patients with eating disorders are suffering not only from malnutrition but also from a great variety of symptoms, resulting in a series of adaptive mechanisms, whereby nervous, endocrine and immune systems are involved and interrelated with each other. This is the reason why patients with malnutrition (marasmus or kwashiorkor) from developing countries, where there is a lack of food, do not show the same medical complications as patients with eating disorders. Obviously, not eating for not having anything to eat is not the same as not eating to avoid eating.

---

[1] *Group of Immunonutrition, Department of Metabolism and Nutrition, Instituto del Frío, Consejo Superior de Investigaciones Científicas, C/José Antonio Novais, 10, Madrid 28040, Spain*

In the case of anorexia nervosa or bulimia nervosa, even though some of the immune impairments are similar to those observed in simple malnutrition, they are less frequent and less severe and the immune function seems to be better preserved than would be expected. In fact, these patients, even those severely malnourished, seem to be relatively free from infectious diseases.

In view of this unexpected outcome, different theories have appeared that try to explain the possible causes and mechanisms involved. We are going to analyse the latest findings as follows.

It is well known that cytokine participation is essential in triggering certain mechanisms involved in infection processes. In fact, infection-induced malnutrition, the most common form of cytokine-induced malnutrition, results from the actions of proinflammatory cytokines such as tumor necrosis factor alpha (TNF-α) and interleukins 1 and 6 (IL-1 and IL-6). These cytokines are able to initiate an acute-phase reaction that is quite stereotyped, including fever, loss of appetite, a decreased food intake, cellular hypermetabolism and multiple endocrine and enzyme responses. However, in the specific case of eating disorders, patients do not show this stereotyped reaction, especially fever [1]. In our research group we consider the presence of fever to be a symptom of improvement, even during hospitalization, and it is commonly a motive to congratulate the patients, because at least their immune system seems to be alert.

Proinflammatory cytokines are able to activate the hypothalamic–pituitary–adrenal axis and also have a direct stimulatory effect on adrenal *in vitro* corticosterone secretion. In turn, glucocorticoids alter the production of these cytokines as a feedback mechanism in order to get a balanced homeostasis. Although all these cytokines are impaired in protein-energy malnutrition, they do not seem to be depleted in eating disorders. On the contrary, a spontaneous and elevated production has been reported, contributing to weight loss, cachexia and osteoporosis in patients with anorexia nervosa [2].

Hypothetical implications during infection processes have been reported recently. Among the central and peripheral appetite-regulating peptides, leptin seems to play a pivotal role in the adaptive mechanisms triggered in these syndromes. Patients with eating disorders typically show a decreased plasma leptin concentration and an increased cortisol concentration. Proinflammatory cytokines seem to be maintained at high levels in patients with anorexia nervosa, which might indicate that the negative feedback mechanism mediated by cortisol is not working. However, when an infection occurs, high plasma cortisol levels could regulate IL-1β production through a cortisol receptor in monocytes, i.e. preventing the normal increased IL-1β secretion in response to an infection. Also during infection episodes, leptin levels are normally increased in plasma, which in turn seem to activate proinflammatory cytokine production by macrophages. However, it could be hypothesized that an incapacity to increase leptin due to neuroendocrine alterations and body mass index fluctuations in these patients would result in a suppression of the expected increase of these cytokines, and consequently lead to the surprising lack of infection symptoms described in these syndromes [3]. However, it still remains unclear if there is a lack of infection or simply a lack of typical symptoms related to infectious processes.

Most of the results found in this field in the literature are controversial. Looking for a reason why these differences exist, we observed that several studies have started from groups of patients in different initial situations. This fact could justify the controversial results observed. Therefore, we consider it important that research in this field be focused on groups of patients that are as homogeneous as possible. The following factors should be strictly taken into account: a) the age of the patients at time of the study; b) the age of the patients at the onset of the disorder; c) the time when the diagnosis takes place; d) the existence of an appropriate treatment; e) the duration of the illness up until the time of the study; f) the type of anorexia nervosa or bulimia nervosa; g) the use of laxatives and/or diuretics; h) the appearance of vomiting.

REFERENCES

1. Nova E., Samartín S., Gómez S., Morandé G., Marcos A. (2002) The adaptive response of the immune system to the particular malnutrition of eating disorders. *Eur. J. Clin. Nutr.*, **56**(Suppl. 3): 534–537.
2. Marcos A., Montero A., López-Varela S., Morandé G. (2001) Eating disorders (obesity, anorexia and bulimia), immunity and infection. In *Nutrition, Immunity and Infection Disease in Infants and Children* (Eds K. Tontisirin, R. Suskind), pp. 243–279. Nestlé Nutrition Services, Vevey.
3. Nova E., Gómez-Martínez S., Morandé G., Marcos, A. (2002) Cytokine production capacity by blood mononuclear cells from in-patients with anorexia nervosa. *Br. J. Nutr.*, **88**: 183–188.

4

Pharmacological Treatment of Eating Disorders: A Review

Martina de Zwaan

Department of General Psychiatry, University Hospital of Vienna,
Austria, and Department of Neuroscience,
University of North Dakota School of Medicine and Health Sciences,
Fargo, North Dakota, USA

James Roerig

Department of Neuroscience,
University of North Dakota School of Medicine and Health Sciences,
Fargo, North Dakota, USA

INTRODUCTION

This review explores the literature concerning the pharmacological treatment of anorexia nervosa, bulimia nervosa and binge eating disorder (BED), emphasizing controlled investigations that utilize a wait-list control condition or other comparison sample. Each type of eating disorder will be reviewed separately. Controlled treatment studies have, for the most part, been conducted on bulimia nervosa. Recently, more attention has been devoted to evaluating the drug treatment of BED. Because relatively less treatment outcome research has been conducted on anorexia nervosa, we will also discuss some of the uncontrolled psychopharmacological studies. These data will aid the clinician in choosing treatments that have clear support for their use and, in addition, enable the clinician to identify when the standard treatments have been exhausted and when a wider exploration of possible solutions to refractory patients is required.

Eating Disorders. Edited by Mario Maj, Katherine Halmi, Juan José López-Ibor and Norman Sartorius.
©2003 John Wiley & Sons Ltd: ISBN 0-470-84865-0

ANOREXIA NERVOSA

The use of pharmacotherapy in anorexia nervosa remains controversial today. Research in this area is difficult owing to a variety of factors, including the relatively low prevalence (0.1%) of anorexia nervosa, and the fact that acutely ill anorexic patients have a potentially life-threatening illness that often makes research unadvisable. In addition, patients with anorexia nervosa show a marked resistance and ambiguity about treatment. In light of the seriousness of the illness, the majority of studies are inpatient in nature and virtually all the pharmacotherapy data involve the addition of the experimental treatment modality to "usual care", which in some circumstances may include intensive weight restoration programmes. Thus the risk of a ceiling effect masking any drug effect is possible. As for most disease states, a relatively large number of case reports, case series and open label studies raise hopes for significant efficacy of a variety of treatments. However, attempts to confirm these reports with placebo-controlled, double-blind randomized trials tempers the enthusiasm considerably.

In choosing outcome criteria, the most relevant results in anorexia nervosa are improved eating, weight gain and, later, maintenance of weight gain. Additional outcomes may be instructive, including changes of body image attitudes, fears and beliefs, as well as alterations in comorbid conditions such as depression, anxiety and obsessive–compulsive symptoms.

Antidepressants

The use of antidepressant pharmacotherapy in anorexia nervosa has been explored since the 1980s with varying results. Trials with antidepressants were prompted by the observation that many patients with anorexia nervosa have depressive symptoms and there is an increased risk for major depression in first-degree relatives of eating disorder patients. Table 4.1 lists the uncontrolled reports of antidepressant use. Because there are only a few controlled studies available, we have to turn to open trials for clues to rational pharmacological management of anorexia nervosa. Interestingly, all the uncontrolled trials focus on selective serotonin reuptake inhibitors (SSRIs), specifically fluoxetine, citalopram and sertraline, with two studies comparing fluoxetine to nortriptyline and amineptine and one study comparing fluoxetine to venlafaxine. As with tricyclic antidepressants (TCAs), treatment with SSRIs is based on the findings that patients with anorexia nervosa frequently exhibit depressive symptoms. However, SSRIs may also act by affecting obsessive–compulsive symptomatology. In addition, dysfunction of the serotonergic system has been postulated as a

TABLE 4.1 Uncontrolled studies using antidepressants in patients with anorexia nervosa (AN)

Authors	No. of patients	Age (years)	Drop-outs (%)	Treatment duration	Agent (dose/day)	Outcome	Comments
Ferguson [1]	1 (outpatient)	42	–	12 months	FLX (80 mg)	15% underweight, weight gain 6 lb	History of compulsive overeating, AN, BN and obesity
Lyles et al. [2]	1–B/P (outpatient)	16	–	6 months	FLX (20 mg)	Weight gain, remission of bulimic symptoms, improvement of depression and distortion of body image	
Gwirtsman et al. [3]	5–R 1–B/P	Range 19–38	–	2–13 months	FLX (20–60 mg)	Weight gain 41.1 to 49.9 kg, improvement of depression and obsessional thoughts	Chronic refractory AN, comorbid MDD and OCD
Kaye et al. [4]	15–R 19–B/P (outpatients)	Mean 20 (SD = 7)	8.8	11±6 months Relapse prevention	FLX (20–60 mg)	29/31 maintained weight at 85% of average body weight. Eating behaviour, mood and obsessive symptoms improved. Response: good, 10; partial, 17; poor, 4. E responded better than B/P	Fluoxetine started after inpatient weight restoration. Psychotherapy variable over the study population
Brambilla et al. [5]	22–R (outpatients)	Mean 21 (SD = 5)	–	4 months	FLX (60 mg) NOR (75 mg)	No difference between drug groups. Both exhibited significant weight gain and reduced EDI, depression and anxiety scores	Both groups received CBT and dietary counselling

(continued)

TABLE 4.1 (*Continued*)

Authors	No. of patients	Age (years)	Drop-outs (%)	Treatment duration	Agent (dose/day)	Outcome	Comments
Brambilla et al. [6]	13—B/P (outpatients)	Mean 23.1 (SD = 6.8)	–	4 months	AMIN (300 mg) FLX (60 mg)	No difference between drug groups. Both exhibited significant weight gain and reduced EDI, depression and anxiety scores. Very little influence on bulimic symptoms	Both groups received CBT and dietary counselling
Bergh et al. [7]	CIT—8 Controls—19	CIT Mean 20.5 Range 10–34 Controls Mean 16.5 Range 10–29	–	–	CIT	Weight loss: CIT 5.4 kg (0.7–11) Non-drug group 0.2 kg	Both groups received psychotherapy. No dose, duration of treatment or type of psychotherapy given
Pallanti et al. [8]	32—R (outpatients)	Mean 22.3 (SD = 4) Range 17–33	8.7	6 months	CIT (20–60 mg)	Significant weight gain: from 77.7% (SD = 3.7) to 81.3% (SD = 5.7) of ideal body weight; 46.9% met criteria for satisfactory response	Drug started during refeeding. Patients not depressed. Non-responders had significantly lower initial body weight
Strober et al. [9]	33—R (outpatients)	Mean 17.6 Range 14–24	12	24 months Relapse prevention	FLX (mean 33.9 mg, SD = 18.3)	No difference in probability of maintaining weight post-discharge compared with matched historic case–control sample	Patients discharged from hospital at 93.3% of ideal body weight
Strober et al. [10]	33—R (inpatients)	Mean 17.6 Range 14–24	12	6 weeks	FLX (mean 33.9 mg, SD = 18.3)	No difference on global clinical severity ratings of eating behaviour or weight phobia compared with matched historic case–control sample	All patients received usual care. FLX started after weight regain

Study	Sample	Mean BMI		Duration	SSRIs and doses	Results	Notes
Ferguson et al. [11]	SSRIs—24 No SSRIs—16 (inpatients)	SSRIs Mean 23 (SD = 10); No SSRIs Mean 21 (SD = 8)	—	—	Various SSRIs and doses	No differences between groups	Retrospective chart review of 40 admissions to inpatient unit
Ricca et al. [12]	24—EDNOS (outpatients)	FLX Mean 19.1 (SD = 3.6); VEN Mean 18.9 (SD = 3.8)	FLX 8.3 VEN 8.3	6 weeks	FLX (40 mg) VEN (75 mg)	Weight gain: FLX: 15.8 ± 0.5 to 18.7 ± 1.1lb; VEN: 15.7 ± 0.6 to 18.3 ± 1.3lb. State Trait Anxiety scale significantly improved in VEN vs. FLX group	CBT in both groups
Calandra et al. [13]	4—R 2—B/P	Mean 22.1 (SD = 4.2)	—	8 weeks	CIT (20 mg)	No effect on weight; improvement in body dissatisfaction	At least four concurrent individual psychotherapy sessions
Santonastaso et al. [14]	22—R (outpatients) SER+ CBT—11; CBT alone—11	SER + CBT Mean 19 (SD = 3.2) CBT alone Mean 19.6 (SD = 6)	SER + CBT 9 CBT 9	14 weeks Follow-up = 64 weeks	SER (50–100 mg)	14 weeks: BMI: SER + CBT = CBT; 64 weeks: SER + CBT > CBT in improving depression, ineffectiveness, lack of interoceptive awareness and perfectionism	
Frank et al. [15]	5 EDNOS	Range 14–19	—	3–10 months	SER (75–150 mg)	Weight gain, improvement in comorbid depression and obsessive-compulsive symptoms	Partial hospital programme
Fassino et al. [16]	CIT—26 Control—26	CIT Mean 24.3 (SD = 5.3) Controls Mean 25.2 (SD = 8.6)	CIT 29.6 Controls 30	3 months	CIT 20 mg	Both groups had significant weight gain, no difference between groups. CIT group had significant improvements vs. baseline in depressive and obsessive-compulsive symptoms, impulsiveness, and trait anger.	Baseline BMI: CIT 16.19 (SD = 0.8) Controls 15.6 (SD = 1.4)

AMI = amitriptyline; AMIN = amineptine; BMI = body mass index; BN = bulimia nervosa; B/P = binge/purge subtype; CBT = cognitive–behavioural therapy; CIT = citalopram; CLO = clomipramine; EDI = Eating Disorder Inventory; EDNOS = eating disorders not otherwise specified (anorexic-like); FLX = fluoxetine; MDD = major depressive disorder; NOR = nortriptyline; OCD = obsessive–compulsive disorder; R = restricting subtype; SER = sertraline; SSRIs = selective serotonin reuptake inhibitors; VEN = venlafaxine.

pathogenetic factor in anorexia nervosa. There is considerable evidence for a reduced serotonergic activity in underweight patients with anorexia nervosa. In long-term weight-restored patients there is some indication of increased serotonergic activity, which may explain some of the pathology that frequently persists after weight recovery in some patients, such as perfectionism, harm avoidance and behavioural overcontrol [17].

Two open trials investigated maintenance therapy with fluoxetine after inpatient weight restoration [4,9], whereas the remainder deal with treatment during the refeeding period. Overall, considering the trials that include clearly diagnosed subjects with anorexia nervosa, four of nine uncontrolled trials [3,5,6,8] and one maintenance trial [4] suggest a positive effect of the drug on weight gain and relapse prevention. However, one trial [7] reported actual weight loss with citalopram treatment in 8 of 30 patients. The authors argue that SSRIs inhibit food intake, thus explaining the efficacy of SSRIs in treating obese patients and patients with bulimia nervosa. Even though this is the only report on a putative weight loss with SSRIs in patients with anorexia nervosa, clinicians should monitor patients' weight closely when using these antidepressants. Two trials appeared to involve patients with subsyndromal anorexia nervosa (eating disorders not otherwise specified, EDNOS) rather than patients meeting the full criteria for anorexia nervosa [12,15]; both of the studies were interpreted positively. The remainder of the uncontrolled trials are single case reports.

Gwirtsman et al. [3] presented a heterogeneous group of cases that included one patient who purged, whereas the others appear to be of the restricting subtype. Pallanti et al. [8] included a more homogeneous group, all restrictors with low to absent depression and obsessive–compulsive symptoms. However, the non-responders had a significantly lower baseline weight. This study also employed citalopram doses of greater than 30 mg/day, whereas the negative studies used 20 mg/day. Brambilla et al. [5,6] reported on two randomized trials that focused on the restricting and binge/purge subtypes of anorexia nervosa. Both trials were of the same design, treating patients with cognitive–behavioural therapy (CBT), dietary counselling and either nortriptyline vs. fluoxetine or amineptine vs. fluoxetine. The premise of these trials was to investigate the efficacy of a norepinephrine reuptake inhibitor (nortriptyline) and a dopaminergic drug (amineptine) vs. a serotonin reuptake inhibitor (fluoxetine) in the two subtypes of anorexia nervosa. Study results demonstrated a significant increase in body mass index (BMI) and reductions in eating-related and general psychopathology over the 4-month trials. No difference between the drugs was observed, even though they act on different central neurotransmitter systems with very minor cross-reactivity. The authors felt that, despite the open design of the trials, the efficacy was probably related to the pharmacotherapies, because the patients had received past psychotherapy without improvements.

Recently Fassino et al. [16] reported an open label comparison between citalopram 20 mg/day and wait list. Both groups had significant weight gain from baseline to 3 months with no difference between the two groups. The subjects were not severely underweight (citalopram group, BMI = 16.19±0.81; wait list controls, BMI = 15.62±1.42). The citalopram group had significant improvements compared to baseline in depressive and obsessive-compulsive symptoms, impulsiveness, and trait anger.

In summary, a few uncontrolled studies appear to suggest that there is at least some evidence that pharmacotherapy can be helpful in some patients. Weight gain was reported in several trials and maintenance of weight also was observed. However, the confounding factor is the use of other therapies with the pharmacotherapy and the lack of parallel control groups. Thus, it is difficult to determine the amount of response to be attributed to the antidepressant.

The controlled trials provide a somewhat clearer view of the contribution of antidepressant treatment. Overall, two of the five placebo-controlled trials listed in Table 4.2 suggest a therapeutic effect of the antidepressant being studied, usually after patients have re-established their normal weight. Two of the three negative studies initiated the antidepressant at the time of refeeding [18,19] or started fluoxetine when the patients had achieved only 65% of their goal weight [13]. In addition, in two studies [11,12] the antidepressant doses used were below those used to treat depression (e.g. 50 mg/day of clomipramine).

Halmi et al. [20] compared amitriptyline and cyproheptadine (a serotonin antagonist) to placebo. The use of TCAs seems appropriate for patients with anorexia nervosa because, in depressed patients, tricyclics not only alleviate mood but also lead to an increase in appetite with at times considerable weight gain. However, weight gain might also be more a side effect and may not be permanent in patients with anorexia nervosa. The drug therapies were initiated when the population completed a pretreatment period of 7 days. Thus, the patients in the amitriptyline group had increased their weight to 82.4±7.8% of their target weight prior to the start of drug treatment. The cyproheptadine group achieved 80.5±6.6% of their target weight. The results of the study suggest a mild but significant drug effect for amitriptyline and cyproheptadine. Patients on both drugs attained their target weights an average of 10.5 days earlier than patients taking placebo. Cyproheptadine demonstrated greater treatment efficiency in the non-bulimic group and impaired treatment efficiency in the bulimic patients. In addition, cyproheptadine exhibited a significant antidepressant effect compared to placebo on day 14 of the trial. The authors suggest that cyproheptadine may be useful in non-bulimic

TABLE 4.2 Controlled studies using antidepressants in patients with anorexia nervosa

Authors	No. of patients	Age (years)	Drop-outs (%)	Treatment duration	Agent (dose/day)	Outcome	Comments
Lacey and Crisp [18]	CLO—8 Plc—8 14—R 2—B/P (inpatients)	—	—	Variable	CLO (50 mg)	No difference between CLO and Plc	All patients received behaviour therapy. Dose of CLO was low
Biederman et al. [19]	AMI—11 Plc—14 (inpatients and outpatients)	AMI Mean 18.4 (SD = 4.9) Plc Mean 13.2 (SD = 4.3)	—	5 weeks	AMI (mean 115 mg, SD = 31)	No difference between AMI and Plc. High refusal rate to enter study (n = 18). Side effects with AMI	All patients received psychotherapy. Dose of AMI was low
Halmi et al. [20]	AMI—23 CYP—24 Plc—25 33—B/P (inpatients)	Mean 20.6 (SD = 5.1) Range 13–36	AMI 26 CYP 17 Plc 36	4 weeks	AMI (maximum 160 mg) CYP (32 mg)	CYP and AMI > Plc ir reducing time to target weight. CYP only effective in restricting group. CYP had antidepressant effect. Side effects with AMI	All patients received psychotherapy and refeeding programme
Attia et al. [21]	FLX—15 Plc—16 12—R 19—B/P (inpatients)	Mean 26.2 (SD = 7.4)	FLX 27 Plc 25	7 weeks	FLX (mean 56 mg)	No difference between FLX and Plc	All patients received psychotherapy
Kaye et al. [22]	FLX—16 Plc—19 all patients–R (outpatients)	FLX Mean 23 (SD = 9) Plc Mean 22 (SD = 6)	FLX 37.5 Plc 84.2	12 months Relapse prevention	FLX (20 mg)	FLX > Plc in preventing relapse (63% vs. 16% completed 1 year without relapse)	All patients received psychotherapy

AMI = amitriptyline; B/P = binge/purge subtype; CLO = clomipramine; CYP = cyproheptadine; FLX = fluoxetine; Plc = placebo; R = restricting subtype.

anorexic patients to increase the rate of weight gain. They advise against using it in the bulimic anorexic subgroup.

Recently, research has focused on the use of SSRIs as relapse prevention agents in weight-restored patients. Kaye et al. [22] reported on the use of fluoxetine as a maintenance therapy in patients with anorexia nervosa who had re-established their normal weight. Thirty-five patients were randomized after inpatient weight gain to fluoxetine or placebo and followed for 1 year. The primary outcome variable was retention in the trial. In the event of relapse or emergence of substantial symptoms, the patient, the patient's family or the study physician could remove the subject from the trial. Results of the study demonstrated that 10 of the 16 (63%) fluoxetine patients remained in treatment for 1 year vs. only 3 of the 19 (16%) placebo patients ($P = 0.006$). In the fluoxetine group, the mean dose was 38 (SD = 21) mg/day for the completers and 43 (SD = 15) mg/day for the drop-outs. Only the fluoxetine completers had an increase in weight and a reduction of core eating disorder symptoms, obsessive thoughts and depressed and anxious mood. Thus, the authors suggest that fluoxetine may be effective in weight-restored anorexic patients in preventing relapse. They attribute the ineffectiveness of the SSRIs in low-weight anorexic patients to the inability to influence effectively the serotonin system in the presence of malnutrition. This is felt to be related to the poor dietary intake of tryptophan, which is a precursor to serotonin (5-HT), but also of other nutrients such as essential fatty acids, zinc and pyridoxine [17]. In addition, food restriction reduces 5-HT synthesis and down-regulates its receptor density in the brain. Consequently, it has been argued that treatment with SSRIs should be initiated after nutritional improvement.

In contrast to the results in bulimia nervosa, controlled trials in anorexia nervosa appear to bear out the suggestions of the open studies in that the antidepressants, usually used as an add-on to multidisciplinary treatment regimens, are modestly if at all effective in severely weight-reduced anorexic patients. However, with the establishment of weight that approaches the normal target weight, it appears to be easier to demonstrate effectiveness. The role of fluoxetine as maintenance therapy initially observed in the open trial by Kaye et al. [4] appears to be confirmed in the double-blind, placebo-controlled trial [22].

Cyproheptadine

Cyproheptadine is a 5-HT_{2a} receptor antagonist. In addition to this effect, it is also a mild anticholinergic and antihistaminergic drug and tends to be quite sedating. Three controlled trials have been published utilizing cyproheptadine [20,23,24]. Of the three, only the study by Halmi et al.

[20] was positive. This trial compared cyproheptadine with amitriptyline and placebo over a 4-week treatment period and is described in detail above. Cyproheptadine, when compared with placebo, significantly decreased the number of days necessary to achieve normal weight (see Table 4.2).

Antipsychotics

Antipsychotic agents are currently designated as "typical" or "atypical". Typical agents are generally prominent dopamine (D_2) receptor antagonists. In addition, they have variable effects on histamine, acetylcholine and α-adrenergic receptors. They present a side effect profile that includes acute extrapyramidal side effects (EPS), tardive dyskinesia, sedation, orthostatic hypotension and constipation, dry mouth and blurred vision. Atypical agents entered the market in the USA with the marketing of clozapine in 1990 and now include risperidone, olanzapine, quetiapine and ziprasidone. These agents differ from the typical antipsychotics in that they have prominent $5-HT_{2a}$ blocking effects compared with their D_2 effects, which is thought to provide a more tolerable side effect profile and potentially increase their efficacy spectrum [25]. In general these agents have little or no EPS and are felt to have a much reduced risk of tardive dyskinesia. In schizophrenia they appear to be effective in refractory patients and to have efficacy in the area of negative symptoms and cognition [26–31]. Improvements have been demonstrated also for depressive and obsessional symptoms [32–36]. Atypical antipsychotics are associated with mild to prominent weight gain, with clozapine and olanzapine demonstrating the greatest effect, risperidone and quetiapine associated with somewhat less gain and ziprasidone reported to be weight-neutral [37,38].

Interest in the application of antipsychotic therapy in anorexia nervosa is associated not only with the weight gain side effect but also with the speculation that the antipsychotic effect would be helpful in ameliorating the distorted body image and unrealistic interpretation of weight that resemble delusions. Typical agents that have been explored include chlorpromazine [39], pimozide [40,41] and sulpiride [42]. In general no effects on weight or eating behaviour were discernable in the three controlled trials listed in Table 4.3. In addition, side effects of typical agents have been reported in patients with anorexia nervosa, including tardive dyskinesia, seizure activity and an increase in purging behaviour [39,43]. Also, pimozide has the potential for dose-related QT prolongation, flattening, notching and inversion of the T wave and U wave appearance in the electrocardiogram (ECG), which makes it a difficult agent to study and/or use [44].

TABLE 4.3 Controlled studies using neuroleptics in patients with anorexia nervosa

Authors	No. of patients	Age (years)	Drop-outs (%)	Treatment duration	Agent (dose/day)	Outcome	Comments
Vandereycken and Pierloot [40]	18 (inpatients)	Median 21.5 Range 15–36	16.7	3 weeks Cross-over	Pimozide (4 or 6 mg)	No difference between drug and placebo phases	All patients treated with a uniform contingency management programme. Patients not classified as R or B/P
Weizman et al. [41]	10 (inpatients)	Mean 6.0 (SD = 1.1) Range 15–18	–	20 weeks	Pimozide (3 mg)	No difference vs. behavioural therapy	
Vandereycken [42]	18 (inpatients)	Mean 23.5 (SD = 8.1)	–	3 weeks Cross-over	Sulpiride (300 or 400 mg)	No difference between drug and placebo phases	All patients treated with a uniform contingency management programme. Patients not classified as R or B/P

B/P = binge/purge subtype; R = restricting subtype.

TABLE 4.4 Uncontrolled studies using "atypical" antipsychotics in patients with anorexia nervosa (AN)

Authors	No. of patients	Age (years)	Drop-outs (%)	Treatment duration	Agent (dose/day)	Outcome	Comments
Fisman et al. [45]	1	13	–	12 months	RIS (1 mg)	2.3 kg increase, maintained for 1 year	Comorbidity: autism, laxative use
Hansen [46]	1	49	–	7 months	OLA (5 mg)	BMI: 12 to 19.9. Insight changed markedly, preoccupation with food and body image became less prominent, increased self-esteem	Comorbidity: OC symptoms, MDD
Jensen and Mejlhede [47]	3	50	–	2 months	OLA (5 mg)	BMI: 13.8 to 21.5	AN
		30	–	9 months	OLA (5 mg)	BMI: 15.8 to 19	AN, BN
		34	–	2 months	OLA (5 mg)	BMI: 18.5 to not available	AN, BPD
La Via et al. [48]	2—B/P	15	–	3.5 months	OLA (10 mg)	ABW: 46 to 92%. Substantial reduction in core eating disorder behaviours and agitation	
		27	–	22 days	OLA (10 mg)	ABW: 80 to 89%	AN-B/P
Newman-Toker [49]	2	19	–	5 months	RIS (1.5 mg)	BMI: 14.6 to 19.8. Delusional thinking improved	AN-R QTc increased 400 to 421 ms
		12	–	9 months	RIS (1.5 mg)	BMI: 15.9 to 19.7	AN-R

Study	N	Mean		Duration	Drug	Results	Comments
Mehler et al. [50]	5	Range 12–17	—	7.25 weeks	OLA (5–12.5 mg)	BMI: 13.6 to 17. Reduction of delusional thinking, fear of weight gain, losing control, body image disturbances, compulsive activity	Rapid onset of effect (several days). One patient developed binge eating. Several patients stopped drug when normal weight was achieved and continued to do well
Ruggiero et al. [51]	AMIS—12 CLO—13 FLX—10 35—R (inpatients)	Mean 24.2	—	3 months	AMIS (50 mg) CLO (57.7 mg) FLX (28 mg)	Weight increase not significantly different between groups: AMIS 1?%, CLO 3.3%, FLX 4.5%. No difference in weight phobia, body image, amenorrhoea	Refeeding programme
Gaskill et al. [52]	OLA—23 Controls—23 (inpatients)	—	—	—	OLA Mean 5.5 mg Range 1.25–15	No difference in weight gain	OLA patients had more chronic and symptomatic disease. Calorie intake was maximized for both groups
Carver et al. [53]	RIS—15 Controls—15	—	—	44.7 days	RIS (0.5–1.5 mg)	No difference, trend for shorter hospital stay with RIS	"Refractory" AN
Powers et al. [54]	18	Mean 26.8 SD = 12.3	2%	10 weeks	OLA (10 mg)	10 of 14 completers gained an average of 8.75 lb, 4 completers lost an average of 2.25 lb, 4 dropouts gained an average of 3.25 lb	3 of 4 completers who lost weight had low OLA plasma levels. Subjects who gained weight had significant improvements on rating scales between baseline and week 10

ABW = average body weight; AMIS = amisulpiride; BMI = body mass index; BN = bulimia nervosa; B/P = binge/purge subtype; BPD = borderline personality disorder; CLO = clomipramine; FLX = fluoxetine; MDD = major depressive disorder; OC = obsessive–compulsive; OLA = olanzapine; R = restricting subtype; RIS = risperidone.

Atypical antipsychotics have been explored in a large number of case reports and case series (see Table 4.4). All of the case reports for risperidone and olanzapine show a positive outcome on weight gain. However, if weight gain is not paralleled by an attitudinal change and improvement in eating behaviour, it is usually not permanent. A number of these patients had a psychiatric comorbidity, including obsessive–compulsive symptoms, borderline personality disorder and agitation. In addition, core eating disorder behaviours were improved, as well as delusional thinking (fear of gaining weight and losing control, body image disturbances), compulsive activity and loss of realistic perceptions. Several patients stopped the atypical agent after weight regain and continued to do well.

Two case series, one involving olanzapine [52] and the other risperidone [53], did not show differences between active drug and control patients. The olanzapine report was an open, non-randomized series with comparison to controls that did not receive the pharmacotherapy. Both groups had their calorie intake maximized and thus a ceiling effect may have been operative. Also, the olanzapine group had a greater number of previous hospitalizations, longer lengths of stay for the current hospitalization and more eating-related psychopathology. The risperidone study was a retrospective, observational chart review that, at this time, is presented in abstract form. Details of the trial are not available. However, the authors report trends towards positive results on weight gain, average calorie intake over the course of hospitalization and length of stay.

Ruggiero et al. [51] reported an open label comparison of clomipramine, fluoxetine and the atypical agent amisulpride. Amisulpride is thought to be an "atypical" atypical antipsychotic because it does not have effects at the 5-HT_{2a} receptor [55]. However, it has a comparable clinical profile to the other atypical agents. The pharmacotherapy was initiated at the beginning of the weight restoration phase of treatment for 35 patients with the restricting subtype of anorexia nervosa. The patients were evaluated at baseline and after 3 months. The mean weight increase for the clomipramine group was not significant. The amisulpride and fluoxetine groups both showed significant increases in mean weight from baseline to the end of the trial: $38.4\pm8.3\,\text{kg}$ to $42.6\pm10.1\,\text{kg}$ ($P = 0.016$), and $40.9\pm6.9\,\text{kg}$ to $42.7\pm7.5\,\text{kg}$ ($P = 0.045$), respectively. There was no significant difference between the two drug groups for weight gain, weight phobia, body image, amenorrhoea or bulimic behaviour.

More recently a 10 week open label study evaluating olanzapine was reported by Powers et al. [54]. Twenty patients with AN (either restricting or binge purge subtype) were enrolled and treated with olanzapine 10 mg/day. Rating scales included the Positive and Negative Syndrome Scale

(PANSS), rated at baseline and at weeks 5 and 10, the EDI-2, the Hamilton Depression Scale (HAMD) and the Clinical Global Impression (CGI). Non-drug treatments included weekly medication monitoring sessions and group medication adherence sessions. Those who were involved in psychotherapy for one month prior to the study could continue the therapy; however, no CBT was allowed and no new therapy could be initiated while in the study. Eighteen patients received drug therapy, 4 patients dropped out. Ten of 14 patients who completed the study gained an average of 8.75 pounds. Three patients reached ideal body weight and four lost a mean of 2.25 pounds. The rating scale scores all improved significantly for those who completed the study and gained weight. For those completers that lost weight the rating scale scores were not significantly different from baseline. Between baseline and termination from the study, four drop-out patients gained a mean of 3.25 pounds. Compliance appeared to play a role in the outcome of the subjects. Olanzapine mean plasma levels, obtained at week 5 and 10, were 20.6 and 13.26 ng/ml respectively. Two patients who completed the study but lost weight had plasma levels < 0.5 ng/ml at both assessment points. Another completer who had gained weight at week 5 but lost weight by week 10 was found to have a week 5 plasma level of 38.18 ng/ml and a week 10 level reported as unobtainable. Olanzapine was well tolerated and adverse reactions were minimal. Sedation was the most common side effect and diminished over two weeks. No problems with movement disorders were found.

Obviously, case reports and open trials are often positive in nature. However, the effects in these reports appear to be similar for the atypical agents. In light of the improved side effect profile of these agents and the potential broader spectrum of efficacy, the case reports and series would support future evaluation. Randomized, double-blind, placebo-controlled trials in the weight restoration phase of treatment with varying lengths of follow-up periods would help to evaluate the place of these agents in the treatment of anorexia nervosa. Controlled trials are in process to evaluate fully the potential of these agents.

Zinc

A variety of case reports concerning the beneficial effects of zinc supplementation have appeared in the literature. It has been suggested that zinc deficiency is a sustaining factor for abnormal eating in selected patients [56]. Zinc deficiency has several symptoms in common with anorexia nervosa, including weight loss, altered taste, amenorrhoea, gastric distention, mood changes and cutaneous findings [57–61]. Increases in weight and improvement in behaviour were reported in case studies. Unfortunately, it is difficult to determine individuals' zinc status [62,63]. It seems probable that during the restricted intake associated with weight loss in the anorexic patient a zinc deficiency could occur.

Case reports led to three controlled trials. Katz et al. [60] reported a trend towards greater weight gain in the supplemented group, but this trend did not reach significance. Significantly lower depression and anxiety scores were found in the supplemented group compared with the placebo group. The second trial [64] was marred by a high drop-out rate in the supplemented group. However, the authors reported that the control group readily normalized their zinc serum levels with the institution of a normal diet. Birmingham et al. [65] reported that the rate of increase in BMI was twofold greater in the supplemented group compared with the control group, which was statistically significant ($P = 0.03$). Thus, there appears to be some benefit to assuring that anorexic patients are supplemented with zinc in doses between 15 and 45 mg of elemental zinc/day. At this dose the cost is minimal and the adverse reaction/toxicity risk is low.

Miscellaneous Agents

A variety of agents have been reported to have some beneficial effects in anorexic patients, including narcotic antagonists (naloxone, naltrexone) [66,67], lithium [68–70] and valproic acid combined with clonazepam [71]. In light of the above, it is interesting to consider the case report by Mendelson [72] concerning tramadol, a μ-opioid receptor agonist that also acts as a norepinephrine and 5-HT reuptake inhibitor [73]. A reduction of ritualistic eating behaviour and a corresponding weight gain were observed. The patient had failed a prior course of 60 mg/day fluoxetine treatment over 6 months.

Single controlled studies of a variety of agents are listed in Table 4.5. Minimal therapeutic effect was found with lithium [74], tetrahydrocannabinol (THC) [75] or clonidine [76]. THC led to dysphoric mood in several of the patients. The trials in low-weight patients were prompted by the observation that these substances can stimulate eating behaviour and appetite.

A controlled trial of growth hormone (GH) administration was reported by Hill et al. [77]. Patients with anorexia nervosa have been reported to have elevated GH levels when malnourished, with low levels of insulin-like growth factor I (IGF-I) [79,80]—a polypeptide that mediates the anabolic effects of GH [77]. Data in malnourished patients indicate that recombinant human growth hormone (rhGH) administration can promote nitrogen retention and increase IGF-I levels [81]. This study included 15 anorexic patients admitted for inpatient treatment. The subjects were randomized to

TABLE 4.5 Controlled treatment studies with other medications in anorexia nervosa

Authors	No. of patients	Age (years)	Drop-outs (%)	Treatment duration	Agent (dose/day)	Outcome	Comments
Gross et al. [74]	Li—8 Plc—8	Li Mean 20.6 (SD = 1.8) Plc Mean 18.8 (SD = 2.6)	—	4 weeks	Li (variable)	At the end of treatment, more weight gain in Li group	Behaviour treatment programme, refeeding, individual and group psychotherapy
Gross et al. [75]	11 (inpatients)	Mean 23.6 (SD = 1.8)	3	2 weeks Cross-over	THC (7.5–30 mg) Diazepam (3–15 mg)	No difference in weight gain. Several patients had dysphoric response	Refeeding, behaviour modification and psychotherapy
Casper et al. [76]	4 (inpatients)	Range 19–28	—	4 weeks Cross-over	Clonidine (0.5–0.7 mg)	No difference in weight gain. Side effects: blood pressure, pulse	Additional psychotherapy
Hill et al. [77]	15	Range 12–18	—	4 weeks	GH (0.05 mg/ kg s.c.)	Cardiovascular stability: GH > Plc, but no difference in weight gain or duration of hospitalization	Refeeding programme, usual care. Cardiovascular stability = two consecutive mornings without orthostasis determined by pulse
Marrazzi et al. [78]	6—B/P (outpatients)	Range 20–36	—	6 weeks Cross-over	Naltrexone (200 mg)	Binge/purge frequency significantly reduced vs. Plc	Weekly psychotherapy

B/P = binge/purge subtype; GH = growth hormone; Li = lithium; Plc = placebo; R = restricting type; THC = tetrahydrocannabinol.

receive rhGH or placebo for 28 days. The dose of rhGH was 0.05 mg/kg subcutaneously each day. The rhGH group achieved cardiovascular stability (two consecutive mornings that the patient was no longer orthostatic by pulse) significantly faster than those on placebo (17 vs. 37 days, $P = 0.02$). Non-significant improvements were seen in weight gain and duration of hospitalization. This pilot study requires replication and extension. The trial was conducted in the anorexic patients without any incident.

Lastly, Marrazzi et al. [78] reports on the use of 200 mg/day naltrexone in divided doses in the treatment of patients with bulimia and patients with anorexia. All six anorexic patients were of the binge/purge subtype. A superiority of naltrexone over placebo was found in the reduction of binge eating and purging, as well as the urge to binge. Despite the relatively high dose, there were no elevations of liver enzymes in the trial.

Patients with anorexia nervosa commonly complain of early satiety and bloating, symptoms that may contribute to food avoidance. Consequently, prokinetic agents have been examined in the treatment of anorexia nervosa. Metoclopramide [82], domperidone [83] and cisapride [84] have been shown to improve gastric emptying in the short-term treatment of anorexia nervosa. However, controlled studies did not show differences in weight gain between metoclopramide [85], domperidone [86] or cisapride and placebo [87,88]. Cisapride has been removed from the market due to potential risks of QTc widening in the ECG.

Conclusions

The state of research on pharmacotherapy for patients with anorexia nervosa is somewhat disappointing and exciting at the same time. In acute treatment, weight gain is the primary outcome to ensure the safety of the patient. Few drugs have proven helpful in promoting or accelerating weight gain. Amitriptyline and cyproheptadine at higher doses appear to be helpful in improving weight gain in some hospitalized patients with anorexia nervosa. The SSRIs are noticeable by their apparent lack of efficacy at this stage of the illness. However, in weight-restored anorexic patients fluoxetine appears to offer benefit as a maintenance treatment for reducing relapse, in conjunction with psychological interventions. Relapse is known to be very common within the first year after successful inpatient weight restoration. A therapeutic agent that assists anorexic patients in maintaining weight outside the hospital is therefore an important addition to the therapeutic armamentarium of patients with anorexia nervosa.

Despite the propensity of SSRIs for causing weight loss in volunteers and depressed patients, only one open study reported weight loss with citalopram [7]. Fluoxetine does not appear to be contraindicated in underweight patients. Medication can be considered as an adjunct to a combined treatment approach, especially in the presence of a comorbid mood, obsessive–compulsive or anxiety disorder. However, because depressive symptoms in severely underweight patients may not respond to antidepressant medication, it is often preferred to wait to initiate a medication trial until some weight gain has occurred and the depressive, obsessive or compulsive symptoms persist [89].

There are no published controlled studies employing a combination of psychotherapy and medication. Investigations are underway, including a multicentered trial, to compare CBT, fluoxetine and CBT combined with fluoxetine. Results are not yet available.

Considerations of potential side effects and medical complications are likely to play an important role in guiding the choice of medication in this group of patients. The potential for side effects in low-weight patients argues in favour of beginning at a relatively low dose and titrating the dosage slowly.

There is evidence that, despite low weight and frequent medical comorbidity, patients with anorexia nervosa tolerate SSRIs well, even in dosages greater than those used for depression [1,3].

Loss of medication through self-induced vomiting may be a potential problem in patients with the bulimic subtype of anorexia nervosa. There are few data on optimal dosages or optimal drug levels in anorexic patients; guidelines might be based on studies in depressed patients or patients with bulimia nervosa. It may be necessary to initiate multiple trials of medication before achieving a successful therapeutic outcome.

Traditional (typical) antipsychotics have not proven helpful, despite the weight gain side effect and the presence of ideas and beliefs that often are of almost delusional intensity and severity. Although no controlled data are available at this time, small case series and single case reports appear to suggest that the atypical agents, such as risperidone and olanzapine, should be investigated in randomized, placebo-controlled designs. With the reduction or absence of EPS, the atypicals are substantially more tolerable than the older neuroleptics and may prove to have benefit.

Zinc supplementation and naltrexone have shown some promise in small controlled trials. Larger studies are needed to replicate and extend these preliminary findings. There have been many dead ends in the search for a helpful agent in the treatment of anorexia nervosa. With luck, several of the potential trails that are now being followed will result in useful additions to the treatment of these individuals.

Changes in body protein and fat composition can significantly affect pharmacokinetics. Depletion of body protein due to inadequate nutrition has the potential to increase the percentage of free or unbound drug in blood. In the case of medication with a relatively narrow therapeutic index, side effects and toxicity may become apparent at a relatively low dose. Assessment of serum albumin concentrations, therefore, is a useful part of the initial screening and medical follow-up of patients with anorexia nervosa. Decrease in total body fat can decrease the volume distribution of fat-soluble drugs, resulting in an increase in their plasma levels. Thus, considerations should be given to measure blood levels of antidepressants in low-weight patients.

It must be noted that the majority of the medication trials have been conducted with adults, even though anorexia nervosa frequently has its onset in adolescence and even childhood. The literature on the pharmacological treatment of children and adolescents is very limited, but some of the open studies include very young patients [9,10].

BULIMIA NERVOSA

Treatment studies of bulimia nervosa are more easily conducted, because of its higher prevalence and ability to be managed in an outpatient setting. In addition, compared with anorexia, the patients show a greater willingness to be treated.

Medication vs. Placebo

Over the course of the past 20 years, a sizable treatment literature on the use of pharmacotherapy in the treatment of bulimia nervosa has developed. Various classes of drugs have been used experimentally. Much of the available literature has focused on the use of antidepressant drugs, first TCAs and monoamine oxidase inhibitors (MAOIs) and, more recently, SSRIs. Antidepressant drugs were used first because of the observed frequent association of bulimia nervosa with depressive illness, although the nature of this association is unclear. The drug that has been studied in the most patients is fluoxetine, which remains the only US Food and Drug Administration (FDA) approved drug for bulimia nervosa. To date, more than 20 controlled studies have been completed. Several comprehensive review articles and meta-analyses are available [90–96]. The placebo-controlled studies are summarized in Table 4.6. There are, however, numerous methodological shortcomings with most of the studies published to date: small sample sizes, substantial drop-out rates, inclusion only of normal-weight women over the age of 18 years who display some form of purging behaviour, additional psychotherapy, differences in placebo run-in periods, great variations in placebo response rates (from deterioration to 50% reduction in binge eating frequency) and differences in statistical analyses. In order to avoid misleading conclusions, all tables report the results of intent-to-treat analyses. If only completer analyses are available, they are specifically marked. Despite the fact that bulimia nervosa frequently has its onset during adolescence and early adulthood, the majority of the medication trials have been conducted with adults and thus their results may not be applicable to children and adolescents.

Taken together, the trials show a definite effect of antidepressant drugs in bulimia nervosa. Although the percentage reductions of binge eating and purging behaviour are impressive in these studies, the percentage of subjects free of symptoms at the end of treatment is usually low. Abstinence rates at the end of treatment have ranged from 0% to 68%, with a mean of 24% [92]. Placebo responses are similarly variable, but are generally less than half the size of the response for active drug treatment [96]. In addition, some trials [101,107,114–116] have failed to support the superiority of antidepressants over placebo in the treatment of bulimia nervosa. No differential effect regarding efficacy among the various classes of antidepressants could be demonstrated. However, there are no studies directly comparing two different classes of antidepressant medication. The recommended doses and blood levels are usually the same as those stated for the treatment of depression, with a tendency for higher dosages to be more effective, especially for fluoxetine, which was effective in a dose of 60 mg/day but not of 20 mg/day [116].

The therapeutic effect of antidepressants may be mediated by the antidepressant or anxiolytic effect or the improvement in impulse control. Antidepressants might have a direct effect on ingestive behaviour (appetite and satiety), by increasing synaptic concentrations of monoaminergic transmitters, particularly 5-HT. The role of 5-HT as a pathogenetic factor in the development and/or maintenance of bulimia nervosa has been discussed extensively [17]. However desipramine, which has been shown to be effective in reducing binge eating and is still the drug of second choice in the USA, has negligible serotonergic properties.

In summary, the use of a single antidepressant agent is clinically more effective for the treatment of bulimia nervosa when compared with placebo. However, the results are far from optimal and there is evidence that medication is less effective than CBT and less acceptable to many patients than psychological treatments [119].

Attrition and Side Effects

Because there is little evidence for superiority of response to a single class of antidepressants, differences in side effects may be a significant factor in the clinical choice of the antidepressant.

Patients treated with antidepressants are more likely to drop out due to adverse events (measure of tolerability). Bacaltchuk *et al.* [91], in their meta-analysis, reported a drop-out rate due to side effects of 10.5% for

TABLE 4.6 Controlled studies using antidepressants in patients with bulimia nervosa (BN)

Authors	Diagnosis	No. of completers/ no. randomized to study	Drop-outs (%)	Agent (dose/day)	Duration of treatment (weeks)/ duration of follow-up (months)	Outcome		Descriptive outcome
						% reduction in binge eating	% abstinent at termination	
Pope et al. [97]	DSM-III	9/11	18.2	IMI (maximum 200 mg)	6/1–5	70*	0	HAMD reduction: IMI > Plc. Follow-up: all patients received one or more trials of medication; remission 26% (of 22)
		10/11	9.1	Plc		2.2	0	
Agras et al. [98]	DSM-III	10/10	0	IMI (maximum 300, mean 167 mg)	16/–	72.5*	30 (V)	Changes on BDI and EAT not significantly different
		10/12	16.7	Plc		43.1	10 (V)	
Mitchell et al. [99]	DSM-III	31/54	42.6	IMI (maximum 300 mg)	10/–	49.3* (D)	16 (D)	HAMD and HAMA reduction: IMI > Plc
		26/31	16.1	Plc		2.5 (D)	–	
Alger et al. [100]	DSM-III-R	22/28 (total)	21.4 (total)	IMI (200 mg)	8/–	22 (C)	–	
				NAL (150 mg)		30 (C)	–	
				Plc		30 (C)	–	
Mitchell and Groat [101]	DSM-III	16/21	23.8	AMI (150 mg), some BT	8/–	72.1 (C)	–	HAMD reduction: AMI > Plc. Depressed BN improved less. Minimal BT seems effective
		16/17	5.9	Plc, some BT		51.8 (C)	–	

Study	Criteria			Drug (dose)				Comments
Hughes et al. [102]	DSM-III	7/10	30	DESI (200 mg)	6/1	91* (D)	–	Follow-up: all patients got medication; 68% (of 22) in remission
		9/12	25	Plc		+19	–	
Barlow et al. [103]	DSM-III	24/47	48.9	DESI (150 mg, cross-over) Plc	6/–	62* (C)	4.2 (C)	Data for first phase not given separately. Effect as early as in week 1
Blouin et al. [104]	DSM-III	–		DESI (150 mg)	6/–	2.4 (C)	–	FEN, DESI > Plc. FEN > DESI. Data for first phase not given separately
		10/17	41.2			–	–	
		12/19	36.8	FEN (60 mg) Both drugs cross-over with Plc		–	–	
Walsh et al. [105]	DSM-III-R	31/40	22.5	DESI (maximum 300 mg)	6/4	47*	12.5	No reduction in HAMD. Follow-up: open continuation trial; high relapse rate
		32/38	15.8	Plc		+7	7.9	
Agras et al. [106]	DSM-III-R	–/12	17 (total)	DESI 16 weeks	32/–	12.7	–	No placebo control group
		–/12		DESI 24 weeks		44.1	42	
Sabine et al. [107]	Features of BN	14/20	30	MIA (30–60 mg)	8/–	0 (C)	0 (C)	No difference in HAMD reduction. Lack of effect probably due to low dose
		22/30	26.7	Plc		0 (C)	0 (C)	
Horne et al. [108]	DSM-III	37/55	12.3 (total)	BUP (maximum 450 mg)	8/–	65.6*	30 (C)	No difference in HAMD reduction; 3.8% (n = 4) of subjects had generalized tonic–clonic seizures; early termination (n = 22); effect after 1 week
		12/26		Plc		23.2	0 (C)	

(continued)

TABLE 4.6 (Continued)

Authors	Diagnosis	No. of completers/ no. randomized to study	Drop-outs (%)	Agent (dose/day)	Duration of treatment (weeks)/ duration of follow-up (months)	Outcome % reduction in binge eating	Outcome % abstinent at termination	Descriptive outcome
Pope et al. [109]	DSM-III-R	17/23	26.1	TRA (mean 355, maximum 400 mg)	6/–	31* (D)	10 (D)ⁱ	No difference in HAMD reduction
		20/23	13	Plc		+21 (D)	0 (D)	
Walsh et al. [110]	DSM-III	10/20	50	PHEN (maximum 90 mg)	8/–	65.7* (D)	42.9 (D)	Problems with side effects
		13/18	27.8	Plc		6.2 (D)	0 (D)	
Walsh et al. [111]	DSM-III	18/31	41.9	PHEN (maximum 90 mg)	8/–	64.2* (D)	34.8 (D)	HAMD reduction: PHE > Plc. Effective in depressed and non-depressed patients; problems with side effects
		21/31	32.3	Plc		5.5 (D)	3.7 (D)	
Rothschild et al. [112]	DSM-III + atypical depression	5/8	–	PHEN (minimum 45 mg)	6/–	–	–	PHE > IMI and trend towards superiority over placebo in improving bingeing and purging
		3/6	–	IMI (minimum 150 mg)		–	–	
		6/10	–	Plc		–	–	

Study	Diagnosis	n	%	Treatment	Weeks			Results
Kennedy et al. [113]	DSM-III Five also current AN	18/29	37.9	ISO (60 mg), cross-over Plc	6/–	–	33 (C)	HAMD, HAMA reduction: ISO > Plc
Kennedy et al. [114]	DSM-III-R	15/19	21.1	BRO (mean 175, maximum 200 mg)	8/–	61.5 (C)	19 (C)	Significant difference in reduction of vomiting. HAMD, HAMA, EAT, EDI: no significant change
		13/17	23.5	Plc		50 (C)	13 (C)	
Carruba et al. [115]	DSM-IV	28/38	26.3	MOC (600 mg)	6/–	22.4 (C)	–	
		24/39	38.5	Plc		44.1 (C)	–	
Fluoxetine Collaborative Group [116]	DSM-III-R	89/129	31	FLX (60 mg)	8/–	67* (median)	23	HAMD reduction: FLX > Plc (only with 60 mg)
		98/129	24	FLX (20 mg)		45 (median)	11	
		79/129	38.8	Plc		33 (median)	11	
Goldstein et al. [117]	DSM-III-R	170/296	42.6	FLX (60 mg)	16/–	50* (median)	18.3	
		49/102	52	Plc		18 (median)	12	
Romano et al. [118]	DSM-IV (responders to 8-week drug treatment)	30/76	60.5	FLX (60 mg)	52/–	–	–	Relapse: FLX 22.4% Plc 29.7%. First 3 months more relapse with Plc. Drop-outs (other than relapse) 61.3%
		28/74	62.2	Plc		–	–	

* = active treatment significantly superior to placebo.

AMI = amitriptyline; BRO = brofaromine; BT = behaviour therapy; BUP = bupropion; BDI = Beck Depression Inventory; C = completers; DESI = desipramine; EAT = Eating Attitudes Test; EDI = Eating Disorder Inventory; D = Some drop-outs included; FLX = fluoxetine; FEN = fenfluramine; HAMA = Hamilton Anxiety Rating Scale; HAMD = Hamilton Depression Rating Scale; IMI = imipramine; ISO = isocarboxazid; MIA = mianserin; Plc = placebo; PHEN = phenelzine; MOC = moclobemide; NAL = naltrexone; TRA = trazodone; V = vomiting.

antidepressants compared with 5.1% for placebo. Compared with placebo, MAOIs presented the lowest tolerability. The analysis of drop-outs due to any cause (measure of acceptability) showed no statistically significant difference between antidepressants and placebo. The overall drop-out rates were high, with 34.6% for drug and 31.4% for placebo. With regard to acceptability, the results were in opposite directions for TCAs and SSRIs. In TCA studies, drop-outs were more likely in the drug group, whereas in SSRI trials they were more likely for placebo.

A particular problem of treatment with TCAs is that of weight gain, whereas fluoxetine tends to produce a modest weight loss [120–122] and even an increase in dietary restraint [123]. However, decreased appetite and weight loss may ultimately exert a detrimental effect, because they may allow patients to continue to restrict eating during treatment with fluoxetine or another appetite-reducing drug, which may prove counter-therapeutic. It is generally agreed that patients with bulimia nervosa should learn to overcome their fear that normal eating will result in significant weight gain. Giving up restraint will also help to interrupt the cycle of fasting and binge eating. Discontinuation of fluoxetine may lead to increased appetite, subsequent weight regain and the return of bulimic behaviour [121]. Other side effects of SSRI treatment, such as headache, nausea, insomnia and effects on sexual function, are likely to be similar to those experienced by patients with major depression.

Other side effects of TCAs include dry mouth, constipation and orthostatic hypotension, all of which may be particularly problematic in patients with bulimia nervosa. Decrease in protective saliva may increase the risk of enamel destruction due to vomiting. If fasting is among the patient's compensatory behaviours, constipation and hypotension will be aggravated further by TCAs. The TCA effects on cardiac rhythm may exacerbate arrhythmias due to hypokalaemia or cardiomyopathy caused by severe ipecac abuse.

Bupropion is contraindicated in patients with bulimia nervosa, because of the high risk of generalized seizures [108]. Irreversible MAOIs, even though effective in patients with bulimia nervosa, are relatively rarely used in this patient population, because of the necessity of dietary limitations to avoid tyramine reactions ("cheese effect"). Reversible MAO-B inhibitors, such as brofaromine and moclobemide [114,115], have not been shown to be superior to placebo.

Inadequate Response to Antidepressant Medication

For the bulimic patient whose response to a medication is unsatisfactory, initial considerations include poor compliance with medication, loss of medication through self-induced vomiting or rapid metabolism resulting in low serum levels. Measurement of plasma levels may prove helpful in evaluating these possibilities. There is evidence that response to treatment, but not adverse events, is related to plasma drug levels [124]. In the case of low plasma levels, a dosage increase may be the first consideration.

Switching to an alternative antidepressant also might be useful. One open-label study suggests that about half of the patients who demonstrate an inadequate response to an initial trial of an antidepressant achieve remission of symptoms during a second trial with a different drug [125]. This supports the contention that the usual clinical practice of sequential antidepressant trials for affective disorder also may be useful for bulimia nervosa treatment.

The option of trying a second antidepressant agent to reduce side effects or increase efficacy has been evaluated in only one controlled study. Walsh *et al.* [126] utilized desipramine for 8 weeks, followed by fluoxetine for non-responders. Notably, the rate of abstinence and reduction in binge eating (29% and 69%, respectively) tended to be higher than those seen in single drug trials, suggesting that sequential use may be a useful strategy. In addition, the use of sequential antidepressants was as effective as CBT (plus placebo). It is worth noting that two-thirds of the patients were switched to fluoxetine during the course of the study.

There are no studies on the use of medication combinations or augmentation rather than sequencing of medication.

Outcome Criteria and Dimensions of Response

It is important to reach a consensus about how successful treatment outcome should be defined. Treatment response to pharmacological interventions has focused primarily on the change in frequency of self-reported binge eating and/or vomiting episodes and on the number of patients who achieve complete remission at the end of treatment.

Improvement in the frequency of self-induced vomiting generally parallels the decrease in bingeing. Few studies have reported on other compensatory behaviours, such as laxative abuse, excessive exercise and fasting, probably because of difficulties in reliable quantification of these behaviours [127]. There is little information on the extent to which dieting and fasting behaviours are replaced by normal meal patterns. Characteristics of the binge episodes (e.g. duration, amount, sense of lack of control) are generally unavailable.

Other measures of outcome, such as secondary eating pathology (e.g. dietary restraint, dysfunctional cognitions, body image), general psychopathology (depression, anxiety, self-esteem, interpersonal problems) and weight change were used inconsistently and yield inconclusive results.

Drug treatment is often accused of not addressing "the underlying problem". However, there is evidence that behavioural improvement is associated also with clinically significant attitudinal change [128].

Depression was assessed more frequently and, interestingly, most trials have not shown a correlation between improvement in mood and reduction in bulimia nervosa symptoms. Many, but not all, studies found a significantly higher reduction of depression ratings in patients receiving active drug than in those receiving placebo [97,99,101,111,113,128]. The lack of significant findings regarding differential changes in depression ratings in active and placebo groups in other studies may, in part, reflect mild to moderate depressive symptomatology among patients who met study selection criteria.

In general, measures of global improvement (e.g. CGI) show significant improvement in the drug-treated groups compared with the placebo groups. Only one study has compared social adjustment and did not observe significant changes following treatment [105].

Other relevant dimensions of response, e.g. modulation of the cognitive aspects of bulimia nervosa, social functioning and quality of life, should be assessed in future trials. Further research is needed to answer specifically the question of whether antidepressant treatment can alter attitudes and cognitions in the long term.

Alternative Medications

In addition to antidepressants, a wide variety of other medications have been investigated in placebo-controlled trials in patients with bulimia nervosa, including opiate antagonists [100,125,129–131], lithium [132], d-fenfluramine [104,133,134], L-tryptophan [135], anticonvulsants [136–138] and, most recently, ondansetron [139].

In a controlled trial of topiramate [138], with 69 patients receiving a median dose of 100 mg (25 to 400 mg), the mean weekly binge eating frequency decreased by 50% in the topiramate group and by 29% in the placebo group. The use of topiramate in eating disorders is problematic because of disturbing side effects such as paresthesias and hypoaesthesias, as well as cognitive impairments such as decreased concentration, attention, word fluency and even confusion. When used, the drug has to be titrated very slowly, increasing the dosage by only 25 to 50 mg per week.

In general, none of the above drugs can be recommended for routine use without additional controlled studies. The fenfluramides have been withdrawn from the market worldwide, owing to a high incidence of valvular disease, and the use of tryptophan is limited by the reported association with eosinophilia–myalgia syndrome. Lithium did not demonstrate effectiveness and, furthermore, there are obvious hazards in treating patients who may experience abnormalities in fluid and electrolyte regulation.

Treatment of "compulsive eating" with anticonvulsants was based on the theory that bulimia, given its episodic, uncontrollable nature, might be a variant of psychomotor epilepsy. However, there is insufficient evidence as to the efficacy of anticonvulsants in bulimia nervosa and the rationale for their use now would seem to be outdated.

There is convincing evidence that endogenous opioid peptides are involved in the regulation of food intake. The controlled studies using naltrexone show contradictory results, with three studies finding no significant difference between naltrexone and placebo [100,125,132]. Higher dosages than used for detoxification or relapse prevention in alcohol and drug abuse seem to be more effective (e.g. 200 mg/day); however, higher dosages can be associated with potentially severe adverse effects, including nausea, vomiting and the elevation of liver enzymes. Experienced clinicians occasionally add naltrexone to existing antidepressant treatment. There are case reports describing treatment success with this augmentation strategy [140].

There is a large body of literature on open studies and case reports using newer antidepressants and other drugs in patients with bulimia nervosa that have not been followed by controlled clinical trials: reboxetine [141], milnacipran [142], methylphenidate [143], flutamide [144], ipsapirone [145], sertraline [146], paroxetine [147], pimozide [148], sodium valproate [149], nomifensine [150], and methylamphetamine [151]. However, the value of open studies is very limited.

Finally, bright light therapy has been investigated in several open and three controlled brief-duration studies of bulimia nervosa [152–154]. Two of the three controlled studies found a significant reduction in binge eating episodes after bright light therapy [153,154] compared with dim light. It has been suggested that bright light therapy might be a potential strategy for augmenting the effects of pharmacotherapy; however, more studies are warranted.

Length of Antidepressant Treatment

The time course of action of the medications appears to be similar to that found in major depression, with a tendency for improvement to occur more quickly for bulimia nervosa than for depression, often as early as in the first week of treatment [101,103,108]. In the large multicentre trial with fluoxetine, most of those subjects who eventually would benefit from the drug had done so within the first two weeks of treatment [116]. However, it is generally recommended that treatment failure should be considered only if adequate doses have been administered for 8–12 weeks.

For the most part, placebo-controlled trials have incorporated a relatively brief duration of treatment (e.g. 6–8 weeks). Given the chronic, frequently relapsing course of treated patients, short-term results are of limited clinical value. Evidence for superiority of drug to placebo over more extended 16–24-week trials have been demonstrated for imipramine and desipramine as well as for fluoxetine [98,106,117]. Usually, there is rapid relapse when the medication is withdrawn [106,121,155,156]. In one controlled study [106,157], patients who received desipramine for a 16-week period rapidly relapsed after withdrawal of the drug, whereas patients who had received desipramine for a 24-week period demonstrated maintenance over a subsequent 1-year follow-up period without further treatment. This result would suggest that initial successful antidepressant treatment should be at least 6 months in duration for bulimia nervosa. In practice, successful antidepressant treatment is often maintained for longer periods of time [156].

Long-term Efficacy of Antidepressants

Few data are available regarding the long-term efficacy of pharma-cotherapy. Pope et al. [156] continued medication over the course of a 2-year period after initial treatment with imipramine or placebo. Fifty per cent of patients achieved and maintained remission over that time and also showed reductions in depressive symptoms. However, the authors note that "in many patients considerable experimentation was necessary to achieve optimal results". Only 25% of subjects received a single medication during the follow-up period. Several patients relapsed when the medication was discontinued (for whatever reason) and others relapsed while continuing on the same medication. Other uncontrolled follow-up studies showed similar results [158].

Two controlled studies reported a significant relapse rate (30–45%) while on maintenance medication in improved patients followed for 4–6 months [105,155]. The most recent placebo-controlled, double-blind study was conducted with fluoxetine over a 1-year period after response to acute fluoxetine treatment [118] (Table 4.6). A total of 232 patients received single-blind acute therapy. Of those, 41 had complete remission of vomiting (17.7%) and 150 met the response criteria (at least 50% reduction of vomiting episodes) and were randomly assigned to fluoxetine 60 mg/day or placebo for a 1-year period. Fluoxetine treatment prolonged the time to relapse, whereas among placebo-treated patients most of the relapses occurred during the first 3 months after randomization. However, the total number of relapsers did not differ between groups (22.4% vs. 29.7%) and, in addition, the attrition rate not attributable to relapse was high (60.5% vs. 62.2%). Relapse was defined as returning to the baseline frequency of vomiting for two consecutive weeks. Of the 150 patients who entered the maintenance phase and were randomized, only 19 remained in the study until the 1-year follow-up. Whether relapse while on continuous drug treatment is due to poor compliance with the medication regimen, to alterations in receptor sensitivity or to other changes is not known.

In summary, there is unfortunately little evidence that continued treatment over an extended period of time with a single antidepressant is more effective than the use of a placebo. Initial improvement and even remission is frequently followed by relapse while on the same medication. The therapeutic effect may be lost even when medication is maintained. These findings raise the question of whether raising the dose, substituting a second antidepressant when relapse has occurred with the first medication or adding a second drug would improve outcome. Open-label studies suggest that the use of different antidepressants after relapse might be a useful approach [155,156].

Predictors of Outcome

Treatment planning would benefit greatly if we could identify potential predictors of favourable outcome to different treatment approaches. For CBT, putative variables have been proposed; however, the results are inconsistent. These include a prior history of anorexia nervosa, low body weight, low self-esteem, comorbid personality disorders and severity of core eating disorder symptoms [159]. Recent research has concentrated on the early identification of non-responders among patients receiving CBT. An early significant reduction in binge eating or purging appeared to be the best predictor for a good outcome [160].

Although there is agreement with regard to the high comorbidity between bulimia nervosa and depression, it is not clear whether depression antedates, coexists with or is a consequence of the eating disorder. Depression at baseline does not seem to be a predictor of response to antidepressant medication. In two studies, samples of non-depressed patients were recruited specifically and seemed to do about equally well on medication as did depressed subjects [161,162]. Therefore, such drugs may have an antibulimic effect separate from their antidepressant effect. However, it is not entirely possible to determine if the effects of antidepressants on bulimic symptoms are completely independent of their effect of depressive symptoms. In some cases the depression will respond but the bulimia nervosa will not [163].

TABLE 4.7 Controlled studies using combination treatment in patients with bulimia nervcsa (involving cognitive–behavioural therapy)

Authors	No. of completers/ no. randomized to study	Drop-outs (%)	Treatment approach	Duration of treatment (weeks)/ duration of follow-up (months)	Outcome		Descriptive outcome
					% reduction in binge eating	% abstinent at termination	
Mitchell et al. [99]	29/34	14.7	G-CBT + Plc	10/–	89.1 (D)	45 (D)	Combined treatment superior only in reducing depression and anxiety. High drop-out rate with IMI alone
	39/52	25	G-CBT + IMI		91.7 (D)	51 (D)	
	31/54	42.6	IMI (maximum 300 mg)		49.3 (D)	16 (D)	
	26/31	16.1	Plc		2.5 (D)	–	
Agras et al. [106]	–/12	17 (total)	I-CBT + DESI 16 weeks	32/–	57.3 (IT)	–	Advantage of 24-week combined treatment. Relapse after 16 weeks of DESI. CBT prevents relapse after DESI
	–/12		I-CBT + DESI 24 weeks		89.2 (IT)	70 (IT)	
	–/12		DESI 16 weeks		+ 12.7 (IT)	–	
	–/12		DESI 24 weeks (maximum 350 mg, mean 168 mg)		44.1 (IT)	42 (IT)	
	–/23		I-CBT 24 weeks		71.3 (IT)	55 (IT)	

Study			Treatment				Comments
Leitenberg et al. [164]	6/7	14.3	I-CBT	20/6	—	71.4 (IT,V)	Terminated early, high drop-out rate with DESI. No advantage of combined treatment over CBT alone. Follow-up: abstinence rates 57% vs. 0 vs. 28.6% (IT,V)
	3/7	57.1	DESI		—	0 (IT,V)	
	5/7	28.6	I-CBT+DESI (serum level 150–275 ng/ml)		—	57 (IT,V)	
Goldbloom et al. [165]	14/24	41.7	I-CBT	16/–	80 (C)	43 (C)	High drop-out rate or lost for final assessment, which was 4 weeks after last group session. No advantage for combined treatment over CBT alone
	12/23	47.8	FLX (60 mg)		70 (C)	17 (C)	
	12/29	58.6	I-CBT+FLX		87 (C)	25 (C)	
Walsh et al. [126]	–/25	34 (total)	I-CBT+Plc	16/–	64.5 (IT)	24 (IT)	No difference in drop-out rates. CBT > SUP; Med > Plc; Med improves outcome of CBT
	–/23		I-CBT+Med DESI (maximum 300 mg), followed by FLX (maximum 60 mg)		87 (IT)	52 (IT)	
	–/28				68.8 (IT)	29 (IT)	
	–/22		SUP+Plc		46.3 (IT)	18 (IT)	
	–/22		SUP+Med		55 (IT)	18 (IT)	
Jacobi et al. [166]	11/19	42.1	G-CBT	16/12	42 (IT)	26.3 (IT)	No advantage for combined treatment over CBT alone. Follow-up: abstinence rates 21.1% ($n = 10$) vs. 6.3% ($n = 8$) vs. 5.6% ($n = 9$) (IT)
	12/16	25	FLX (60 mg)		46 (IT)	12.5 (IT)	
	12*/18	33.3	G-CBT+FLX		50 (IT)	16.7 (IT)	

*Only 7 patients took the medication until the end of treatment

C = completer analysis; CBT = cognitive-behavioural therapy; D = some drop-outs included; DESI = desipramine; FLX = fluoxetine; G = group; I = individual; IMI = imipramine; IT = intent-to-treat analysis; Med = desipramine followed by fluoxetine; Plc = placebo; SUP = supportive therapy; V = vomiting.

In conclusion, to date, matching specific treatments to particular patients is not possible because reliable predictors of drug treatment outcome have not been identified yet.

Combination Treatments

Six studies have evaluated systematically various combination treatments in outpatients with bulimia nervosa. Although differing in many respects, these studies suggest that CBT is superior to drug therapy alone. The studies are summarized in Table 4.7.

Three studies compared CBT alone, medication alone and their combination. They must be interpreted with caution because they are all hampered by high drop-out rates. Leitenberg *et al*. [164] found that CBT alone was more effective than desipramine alone, and combining these two forms of treatment did not improve the results of CBT. The study was terminated early because of the high drop-out rate in the desipramine-only condition (4 of 7 patients), mostly due to unsatisfactory results and side-effects. Goldbloom *et al*. [165] also reported a high drop-out rate; however, this was true for all three groups. In their study there was evidence that the combination of fluoxetine and CBT was superior to fluoxetine alone but not to psychotherapy alone. Also, in the study by Jacobi *et al*. [166] the drop-out rate was unexpectedly high. Abstinence rates for completers were highest for CBT alone at post-treatment and at the 1-year follow-up. Taken together, these three studies did not show an advantage of a combined treatment over CBT alone.

Of the three remaining studies, one used imipramine [99] and one used desipramine [106], agents that have been largely supplanted by the SSRIs in recent years. Again, neither study found that adding antidepressants to CBT improved the outcome of CBT significantly, as measured by binge eating and purging, nor did it increase the speed of the therapeutic response. Mitchell *et al*. [99] found that adding medication to CBT reduced depression significantly more than CBT alone, whereas Agras *et al*. [106] found that adding CBT to desipramine given for 16 weeks appeared to prevent the relapse of binge eating when the medication was withdrawn.

Walsh *et al*. [122] applied a two-stage medication intervention in which a second antidepressant (fluoxetine) was employed if the first (desipramine) was either ineffective or poorly tolerated. It is worth noting that 74% of the patients were switched to fluoxetine during the course of the study. Somewhat surprisingly, the use of sequential antidepressants was as effective as CBT (plus placebo). In addition, this is the only study clearly showing that medication added to CBT proved superior to CBT plus placebo with regard to the reduction of binge eating and purging. However, when antidepressants were combined with CBT, the acceptability of the psychological approach was significantly reduced, as indicated by a higher drop out rate [90]. On the other hand, a combined approach may make antidepressants more acceptable.

Even though clinical recommendations at this point must be viewed as preliminary, augmentation of CBT with antidepressants can be recommended. However, the modest gain of adding medication to psychotherapy must be weighed against the risk of side effects: potentially higher drop-out rates and the costs of medication and monitoring.

There are three more studies using combined treatment, but they did not involve outpatient CBT (Table 4.8). One study added fluoxetine to a comprehensive inpatient programme [120]. Fluoxetine did not add to the effect of intensive inpatient treatment, which most likely demonstrates a ceiling effect. In another study [121], medication was added to 8 weeks of nutritional counselling. No differences were found between nutritional counselling with fluoxetine and nutritional counselling with placebo. However, after discontinuation of the drug, patients on fluoxetine were more likely to have a recurrence of symptoms. The percentage of binge-free patients fell from almost 70% after 8 weeks of treatment to 35.7% 3 months after fluoxetine was withdrawn. In addition, patients on fluoxetine lost weight during treatment and regained weight to 2.4 kg higher than baseline during the 3-month follow-up.

Finally, fluoxetine was added to a self-help condition [92]. Fluoxetine alone was superior to placebo in reducing vomiting episodes and a self-help manual was superior to no manual at all. The combination of the medication and the manual was superior to the use of the drug alone, suggesting a possible utility for such manuals in the treatment of women with bulimia nervosa who receive pharmacotherapy. Reduction of binge eating episodes and abstinence rates did not differ between groups.

Sequential Treatment

Sequential treatment studies examine whether a second level of treatment would be effective for those who fail the first treatment (Table 4.9). Mitchell *et al.* [168] randomized bulimic patients who remained symptomatic after 16 weeks of CBT to 16 weeks of either interpersonal psychotherapy (IPT) or medication therapy (fluoxetine) initiated at a dose of 60 mg/day. For those who had not achieved abstinence at this dosage within a period of 8 weeks, fluoxetine was discontinued and desipramine was initiated, beginning at a dose of 50 mg/day with subsequent increases to a maximum of 300 mg/ day. Eligibility for randomization was based on self-reported purging during the last 2 weeks of CBT treatment. Initial CBT led to a remission rate

TABLE 4.8 Controlled studies using combination treatments in patients with bulimia nervosa (*not* involving cognitive–behavioural therapy)

Authors	No. of completers/ no. randomized to study	Drop-outs (%)	Treatment approach	Duration of treatment (weeks)/ duration of follow-up (months)	Outcome		Descriptive outcome
					% reduction in binge eating	% abstinent at termination	
Fichter et al. [120]	20/20	0	Inpatient treatment + Plc	5/–	25.4	–	No advantage of addition of FLX; ceiling effect?
	19/19	0	Inpatient treatment + FLX (60 mg)		46.7	–	
Beumont et al. [121]	23/34	32.4	NC + FLX (60 mg)	8/3	84.2 (IT)	69.6	EDE: R, WC, SC lower after FLX. More weight loss, more regain with FLX. Follow-up: relapse after FLX stopped; abstinence rates 35.7% (n = 17) vs. 60.9% (n = 23)
	26/33	21.2	NC + Plc		80.3 (IT)	61.5	
Mitchell et al. [92]	21/22		pSH + Plc	16/–	59.7 (D)	24 (D)	Reducing vomiting: FLX > Plc and SH > no SH; pSH added to FLX improves results of FLX
	19/21		pSH + FLX (60 mg)		66.8 (D)	26 (D)	
	25/26		FLX (60 mg)		50.3 (D)	16 (D)	
	18/22		Plc		32.4 (D)	9 (D)	

D = some drop-outs included; EDE = Eating Disorder Examination; FLX = fluoxetine; IT = intent-to-treat analysis; NC = nutritional counselling; Plc = placebo; pSH = pure self-help; R = restraint; SC = shape concerns; WC = weight concerns.

TABLE 4.9 Controlled studies using antidepressants as second treatments in patients with bulimia nervosa

Authors	Diagnosis	No. of completers/ no. randomized to study	Drop-outs (%)	Agent (dose/day)	Duration of treatment (weeks)/ duration of follow-up (months)	Outcome % reduction in binge eating	Outcome % abstinent at termination	Descriptive outcome
Walsh et al. [167]	DSM-IV PT non-responders	12/13 8/9	7.7 11.1	FLX (60 mg) Plc	8/-	81.8* (IT) +20 (IT)	38 (IT) 0 (IT)	FLX effective for some patients who do not respond to CBT or IPT
Mitchell et al. [168]	DSM-IV CBT non-responders	16/31 21/31	48.4 32.3	FLX (maximum 60 mg), followed by DESI (maximum 300 mg) IPT	16/6	– –	10 (IT) 16 (IT)	
Fichter et al. [169]	DSM-III-R after inpatient treatment	18/37 30/35	51.4 14.3	FLV (maximum 300 mg) Plc	15/1	+11 (IT) +170 (IT)	65* (IT) 35 (IT)	Less deterioration of symptoms with FLV. Follow-up: no relapse off medication

*Active treatment significantly superior to placebo.
CBT = cognitive-behavioural therapy; FLV = fluvoxamine; FLX = fluoxetine; IPT = interpersonal psychotherapy; IT = intent-to-treat analysis; Plc = placebo; PT = psychotherapy.

of 39.2%, 27.8% dropped out and 32.9% ($n = 64$) remained symptomatic. Sixty-two patients subsequently were randomized to either IPT or medication. Sequencing the treatment led to a high attrition rate, with 32% during IPT and 48% during medication treatment. The rates of abstinence achieved during secondary treatment were low, with 16% for the subjects assigned to treatment with IPT and 10% for those assigned to medication. The authors conclude that sequencing treatment cannot be recommended, because it appears to be of little clinical utility. They stress the importance of early identification of non-responders to CBT, so that strategies can be implemented to add additional therapies early in the course of the primary treatment or shift them to alternative therapies. It has been suggested that patients who do not achieve a significant reduction in bulimic behaviour early during CBT treatment might profit from the addition of antidepressants [160].

More promising findings on the use of fluoxetine as a second-line treatment were reported in a small study by Walsh *et al.* [167]. They randomly assigned 22 patients with bulimia nervosa who had not responded to or had relapsed following CBT or IPT to receive 60 mg/day placebo or fluoxetine for 8 weeks. Five (38%) of the 13 patients receiving fluoxetine were abstinent during the last 28 days of the study, compared with none of the patients receiving placebo. The frequency of binge eating and purging decreased in patients receiving fluoxetine but increased in placebo-treated patients. The authors conclude that pharmacotherapy may benefit some patients who do not satisfactorily respond to psychotherapy.

Antidepressants for Relapse Prevention after Inpatient Psychotherapy

One study examined the efficacy of fluvoxamine in patients with bulimia nervosa after intensive inpatient treatment [169] (Table 4.9). Seventy-two patients were randomized to fluvoxamine or placebo for 3 weeks in the hospital, followed by 12 more weeks after discharge. At the end of inpatient treatment, roughly 60% of all patients were binge-free. Drop-out rates were high in the fluvoxamine-treated group (51%), with side effects (nausea, dizziness and drowsiness) accounting for 22% of the drop-outs. Twelve weeks after discharge, most patients showed some deterioration of symptoms; however, this was less pronounced in patients receiving fluvoxamine. About 65% of the patients receiving fluvoxamine were binge-free, compared with about 34% of the patients receiving placebo. Interestingly, there was no rebound of symptoms 4 weeks after withdrawal of fluvoxamine. Inpatient treatment is more commonly available in Europe compared to the USA. Discharge from intensive inpatient treatment is a difficult step, frequently associated with some worsening of symptoms. In addition, subsequent outpatient care often is not readily available after discharge and antidepressants might bridge the interval until further treatment can begin.

Stepped-care Programmes

The stepped-care approach allows for the provision of therapies that are or could be widely available (self-help and medication). The use of highly specialized CBT treatment could be reserved for the group of patients who fail to respond to the less expensive and/or more available treatments. Relatively few therapists are trained in manual-based CBT. This strategy is only beginning to be evaluated formally. Stepped care raises important clinical issues. It is unclear when the therapist should switch from one level of treatment to another. In addition, there is still the possibility that failure to respond to an initial, low-intensity level of care might discourage patients from pursuing subsequent treatment. The role of medication within a stepped-care framework remains to be established [159].

An ongoing study (Mitchell et al., personal communication) employs a sequential stepped-care approach. CBT, which is currently the state-of-the-art treatment, with the addition of fluoxetine at week 4 in those predicted to be non-responders, is compared with assisted self-help delivered first, followed by the use of fluoxetine, and—if needed—followed by CBT. Effectiveness and cost-effectiveness will be compared. Results are not yet available.

With regard to cost-effectiveness, there is only one study trying to calculate the costs involved [123]. The authors found that medication given alone for 24 weeks appeared to be associated with lower costs per recovered patient at a 1-year follow-up than 24 weeks of CBT.

Conclusions

Antidepressants are one of the alternatives in the therapeutic armamentarium for the treatment of patients with bulimia nervosa. In contrast to the lack of availability of therapists trained to conduct CBT for bulimia nervosa, drug therapy is readily available and easily administered. However, its use as sole therapy does not seem sufficient for effective treatment of most of these patients. Fluoxetine is the most systematically studied antidepressant agent. Even if it is not superior to other drugs in terms of efficacy, its better acceptability may justify its use as a first-line antidepressant in bulimia nervosa. A daily dose of 60 mg is more effective than the antidepressant dose of 20 mg. Eight weeks seems to be an appropriate period to obtain a relevant improvement. If no or only partial response is noted, an alternative therapeutic approach is indicated. Most studies were conducted in young adult bulimic patients without severe comorbidity, many of whom were volunteers responding to advertisements. Bulimic patients with current or prior use of psychotropic medication, comorbid depression, personality disorders, substance abuse and other relevant clinical conditions are usually excluded [170]. Thus, some of the patients who are most difficult to treat may be excluded from controlled treatment trials. Treatment trials may select more resilient patients who have a better prognosis. This patient selection seriously impairs the generalizability of results.

It is of note that the number of pharmacological studies is declining with time. The effects of SSRIs other than fluoxetine, as well as newer antidepressants, still need to be studied in controlled trials. As in other areas, there appears to be a publication bias in the medication treatment of bulimia nervosa. There are at least two unpublished reports of negative multicentre, multinational studies comparing fluvoxamine with placebo that show a lack of greater efficacy of fluvoxamine compared with placebo [171,172].

The question remains as to which patients with bulimia nervosa should receive drug treatment. Owing to the lack of evidence from controlled studies, most of the following guidelines derive from clinical observations and should be viewed as tentative. Drug treatment should be provided to: a) patients who are significantly depressed when entering treatment, for the antidepressant effect of the drug rather than specifically for the antibulimic effect; b) patients with very severe symptoms, the rationale being that it can be difficult to engage and keep them in psychotherapy; c) patients who decline psychotherapy; d) patients who do not respond to psychotherapy, even though the results of controlled studies on drug treatment of psychotherapy non-responders are equivocal. Although there are no studies supporting it, the addition of antidepressants might be helpful in patients who do not achieve an early significant reduction in bulimic episodes.

Clinicians involved in the medication management of bulimic patients should adhere to the following guidelines: a) there is more evidence on the beneficial effect of fluoxetine at a dosage of 60 mg/day than any other drug, and this, combined with its relatively favourable side effect profile, makes it the drug of first choice; b) there is reasonable evidence to support the use of more than one trial of antidepressants if the first trial proves unsuccessful; c) it would seem reasonable that the minimum duration of successful treatment should be 6 months. As for other psychiatric disorders, initiation of psychotropic medication for bulimia nervosa should be preceded by a comprehensive psychiatric assessment and review of medical history [89]. Baseline laboratory tests should include a complete blood count, serum electrolytes, liver function tests, blood urea nitrogen, creatinine, thyroid function tests and an ECG [173].

BINGE EATING DISORDER (BED)

Much of what we know about the treatment of obese patients with BED is based on extrapolation from two related groups: normal-weight patients with bulimia nervosa and obese patients not selected for binge eating. Some studies were designed primarily to promote binge cessation and others to promote weight loss. The more recent studies have embraced both of these goals.

Because BED has been incorporated only recently in the DSM, treatment research on BED is at a different developmental stage compared to bulimia nervosa. There is little doubt that non-purging bulimia nervosa and BED overlap considerably. As in bulimia nervosa, studies of comorbidity have suggested that BED is associated with major depressive disorder.

Pharmacotherapy Targeting Weight

Studies focusing on weight reduction are confronted with the well-known problem of obesity being associated with poor long-term maintenance of weight reduction. The majority of individuals who attempt to lose weight are ultimately unsuccessful.

Several studies of SSRIs for obesity suggest that this medication results in short-term weight loss, but most patients regain most or all of their lost weight even while still taking the medication [174]. Two controlled studies assessed putative differential effects of SSRI treatment on weight loss in obese binge eaters and non-binge eaters (Table 4.10). Marcus et al. [175] found that 60 mg/day fluoxetine added to behaviour therapy enhanced weight loss in both obese binge eaters and non-binge eaters. Once fluoxetine treatment was terminated, all patients rapidly regained weight. Fluvoxamine at a dose of 100 mg/day did not have an additional weight loss benefit when added to dietary management or behaviour therapy for weight loss either in binge eaters or in non-binge eaters [178]. The combination of phentermine and dl-fenfluramine ("Phen-Fen") has achieved promising results in the treatment of obese patients not selected for the presence or absence of binge eating [179]. This combination of appetite suppressants

TABLE 4.10 Treatment studies comparing obese binge eaters and non-binge eaters in weight loss programmes involving medication

Authors	Diagnosis	No. of completers/no. randomized to study	Drop-outs (%)	Agent (dose/day)	Setting	Duration of treatment (weeks)/ duration of follow-up (months)	Outcome (weight)
Marcus et al. [175]	BES > 29 (B) BES < 17 (NB)	11/22 10/23	50 56.5	FLX (60 mg) + BT vs. Plc + BT	Double-blind randomized	52/3–6	Weight loss: B = NB and FLX + BT > Plc + BT (−13.9 vs. +0.6 kg) (C) Follow-up: rapid weight regain after FLX stopped (5.4 vs. 0.3 kg) (C)
de Zwaan B et al. [176]	NB	15/22 31/42	31.8 26.2	FLV (100 mg) + G-CBT Plc + G-CBT FLV (100 mg) + G-NC Plc + G-NC	Double-blind randomized	18/12	Weight loss: B = NB (6.1 vs. 5.6 kg), CBT = NC and FLV = Plc (C) Follow-up: weight regain, B not significantly different from NB (4.6 vs. 1.6 kg) (C)
Alger et al. [177]	BES≥27 (sB) BES 18–20 (mB) BES≤17 (NB)	16/22 11/17 12/16	27.3 35.3 25	PHEN (15 mg) + FEN (60 mg)	Open	24/30 extended treatment	Weight loss: sB = mB = NB (35 vs. 26 vs. 26 lbs) (IT) Early termination of study: valvular insufficiency in 7 patients (20% of 35 patients investigated)

B = binge eaters; BES = Binge Eating Scale; BT = behaviour therapy; C = completer analysis; CBT = cognitive–behaviour therapy; FEN = dl-fenfluramine; FLV = fluvoxamine; FLX = fluoxetine; G = group; IT = intent-to-treat analysis; mB = moderate binge eaters; NB = non-binge eaters; NC = nutritional counselling; PHEN = phentermine; Plc = placebo.

was also tested openly in the binge eating subgroup of the obese and has proved effective with regard to weight loss [177]. Again, the presence or severity of binge eating at baseline did not predict the amount of weight loss after 6 months of drug treatment. However, the study was terminated early because of the occurrence of valvular damage in seven patients. Eventually, the fenfluramides were withdrawn from the market worldwide owing to the development of valvular heart disease and primary pulmonary hypertension.

All three studies found similar drop-out rates for binge eaters and non-binge eaters.

Pharmacotherapy Targeting Binge Eating

A sizeable literature supports the effect of antidepressants in the short-term treatment of bulimia nervosa. Most placebo-controlled trials have found medication to be superior to placebo also in reducing binge eating and weight in obese patients with BED (Table 4.11). This includes desipramine [180], d-fenfluramine [181], fluvoxamine [182], imipramine [100,185], sertraline [183] and, most recently topiramate [184]. Small or open studies are also available for paroxetine [186], inositol [187] and sibutramine [188].

As in bulimia nervosa, desipramine appears to be very effective in reducing binge eating frequency in obese subjects with BED and this effect seems to be independent of its antidepressant properties. Dietary restraint increases and hunger decreases, which consequently has been suggested to be the mechanism of action of desipramine in the treatment of binge eating. However, these effects are not necessarily of therapeutic advantage and also might explain the rapid relapse after withdrawal from desipramine.

Topiramate is a novel antiepileptic agent that has been shown to produce considerable weight loss in patients with epilepsy. Like other antiepileptic drugs, it also may have mood-stabilizing properties and open studies have reported positive effects on binge eating episodes [189,190]. A double-blind study reported promising results, with reductions of binge eating frequency and binge eating days of 94% [184]. However, topiramate has several central nervous system side effects, the most disturbing being cognitive impairment, seriously questioning this drug's indication in patients with BED.

Sibutramine, a novel 5-HT and norepinephrine reuptake inhibitor, represents a new class of US FDA approved agents for the treatment of obesity [191]. An open study reported remission of binge eating and purging in 7 out of 10 patients treated with a dose of 15 mg/day [188]. The results of an ongoing multicentre study are not available yet.

TABLE 4.11 Controlled treatment studies focusing on eating behavior (and weight) in obese binge eaters

Authors	Diagnosis	No. of completers/ no. randomized to study	Drop-outs (%)	Agent (dose/day)	Duration of treatment (weeks)/ duration of follow-up (months)	Outcome % reduction in binge eating	% abstinent at termination	Descriptive outcome
McCann and Agras [180]	DSM-III-R BN (non-purging) Mean BMI = 31	10/15	33.3	DESI (100–300 mg)	12/1	63.2* (C)	60 (C)	Weight loss: DESI = Plc (3.5 vs. 1.2 kg) DESI reduced dietary restraint and hunger Follow-up: rapid relapse of binge eating after DESI stopped
		13/15	13.3	Plc		+5.7 (C)	15 (C)	
Alger et al. [100]	BES ≥25 2 episodes/ week overweight	33/41 (total)	19.5 (total)	IMI (150–200 mg)	8/–	73 (C)	–	IMI reduced binge duration. Weight loss not significant. Change in depression: IMI = NAL = Plc
				NAL (100–150 mg)		48 (C)	–	
				Plc		50 (C)	–	
Stunkard et al. [181]	DSM-IV BED	12/14	14.3	FEN (30 mg)	8/4	–	80* (S)	No weight loss in either group Follow-up: rapid relapse after FEN stopped
		12/14	14.3	Plc		–	33 (C)	

Study	Classification	N	BMI	Drug (dose)	Duration	%	% (C)	Results
Hudson et al. [182]	DSM-IV BED	29/42	30.9	FLV (50–300 mg, mean = 260 mg)	9/–	–	45* (C)	Weight loss: FLV > Plc. Changes in depression: FLV = Plc. Remission: intent-to-treat, 38% vs. 26%
		38/43	11.6	Plc		–	24 (C)	
McElroy et al. [183]	DSM-IV BED	13/18	27.8	SER (50–200 mg, mean = 187 mg)	6/–	85.1* (C)	53.8* (C)	Weight loss: SER > Plc (12.3 vs. 5.3 lb). Changes in depression: SER = Plc. Remission: intent-to-treat, 38.9% vs. 12.5%
		13/16	18.8	Plc		46.5 (C)	15.4* (C)	
Hudson et al. [184]	DSM-IV BED	52/61 (total)	14.8 (total)	TOP (50–600 mg, mean = 213 mg)	14/–	94*	–	Weight loss: TCP (5.9 kg) > Plc. Reduction in binge days: 93% vs. 46%
				Plc		46	–	

*Active treatment significantly superior to placebo.
BED = binge eating disorder; BES = Binge Eating Scale; BMI = body mass index; BN = bulimia nervosa; C = completer analysis; DESI = desipramine; FEN = fenfluramine; FLV = fluvoxamine; IMI = imipramine; NAL = naltrexone; Plc = placebo; S = analysis in patients with adequate serum levels; SER = sertraline; TOP = topiramate.

It is important to note that the reduction of binge eating does not necessarily result in significant weight loss [100,180,181] or a consistent reduction in depressive symptoms [182,183].

In general, medication trials have either no or only a short follow-up period after termination of drug treatment, and there is not enough knowledge about the benefits of long-term treatment on binge eating behaviour. As in bulimia nervosa, attrition rates are generally higher for medication trials than for psychotherapy trials of BED [192], and in some studies there was an extremely strong placebo effect, with reductions of binge eating frequency of 50% [100,182,184]. Stunkard et al. [181] recruited 50 patients for their d-fenfluramine trial. All received single-blind placebo for a period of 4 weeks. The average number of binges fell from 6 to 1.8 per week and 22 patients no longer met the frequency criterion for BED. These results suggest that BED often may improve even with placebo. Therefore, caution should be exercised in interpreting the results of open-label pharmacological studies of BED. Also, these results argue for a conservative approach in offering treatment to such patients, because many will tend to improve with only placebo treatment.

Pharmacotherapy Combined with CBT for BED

Medication does not appear to add much to the effectiveness of CBT in reducing binge eating [123,193,194]. Only one study found that imipramine increased the reduction of binge eating episodes when added to psychological treatment during acute treatment, and the result persisted even 6 months after withdrawal of the drug [185].

However, antidepressant medication may enhance weight loss beyond the effects of CBT [123,141,185,193]. In a study in which patients who had completed 3 months of group CBT received either open-label desipramine plus weight loss treatment or weight loss treatment alone [157], the desipramine-treated patients lost significantly more weight during treatment and also during follow-up. There were, however, no clear indications that the addition of desipramine led to a greater reduction in binge eating during treatment and at a 3-month follow-up. In this study patients who entirely stopped binge eating during the CBT phase lost significantly more weight than those who were not abstinent. Hence, early abstinence appears to facilitate weight loss. This suggests that treating the eating disorder first and then treating the weight problem might be a useful approach to the management of the overweight binge eater. Because only half of the patients stop binge eating after treatment with CBT, a second level of treatment that would benefit poor responders to CBT might be useful. Laederach-Hofmann et al. [185] accordingly showed that adding low-dose imipramine to diet counselling and psychological support may help patients to lose weight after at least 6 months off medication. In an open study, Devlin et al. [195] added fluoxetine and phentermine to individual CBT. They reported an abstinence rate of binge eating of 86% and a weight reduction of 19 lb. However, as opposed to the two studies mentioned above, there was a significant weight regain, particularly following medication discontinuation. In a randomized but open five-group design study, Ricca et al. [193] found a significant reduction in monthly binge eating frequency only in patients receiving individual CBT alone or combined with fluoxetine or fluvoxamine. Patients who received either of the drugs alone did not demonstrate a significant reduction of binge eating episodes. The same pattern of results was found for changes in BMI. However, there was again a trend towards a greater reduction of BMI in patients treated with CBT plus fluoxetine or fluvoxamine. At a 1-year follow-up, patients in the CBT, CBT/fluoxetine and CBT/fluvoxamine groups maintained most of the weight lost, and the eating behaviour was not significantly different when compared with that at the end of treatment. Fluoxetine and fluvoxamine did not appear to improve the medium-term outcome in a relevant manner. The authors suggest that the benefits of adding fluoxetine or fluvoxamine to CBT are only marginal in the treatment of BED.

Two recently presented controlled combination studies used a 4 cell design: individual CBT plus fluoxetine (60 mg) or placebo, fluoxetine alone, and placebo alone. Grilo et al. [194] found significantly higher remission rates for CBT compared to either fluoxetine or placebo alone. Fluoxetine did not differ from placebo. Fluoxetine did not add to the effects of CBT. Patients who were abstinent of binge eating lost 7.7 lbs, whereas patients who were not abstinent lost only 2.6 lbs (p = 0.02). The results of the 2 year follow-up are not available yet. Devlin [195] reported the results of an ongoing study using an almost identical design. In addition to CBT and fluoxetine, all patients received a 16-session group behavioral eating and weight management treatment (LEARN-BED). Again, fluoxetine did not add to the effects of individual CBT and did not differ from placebo.

Conclusions

As in bulimia nervosa, antidepressants should be considered as an option in patients with BED. Usually, the initial choice of medication is an SSRI. Even though the reduction of binge eating with antidepressants can be substantial, it must be kept in mind that many patients also improve without treatment. It must be emphasized that reduction of binge eating does not necessarily lead to weight loss; however, complete abstinence from binge eating is positively related to weight reduction. Consequently, there is some evidence that treating the eating disorder first and then dealing with weight might be the best sequence.

Antidepressants can increase the amount of weight lost when combined with psychological treatment; however, rebound weight gain after termination of the drug is likely. Medication doses and duration of treatment might be similar to those employed in the treatment of bulimia nervosa. Four weeks of treatment at an adequate dose should be considered an adequate trial [196] and sequential trials of antidepressants may be necessary to achieve optimal response.

SUMMARY

In the area of eating disorders, the role of drug treatment has considerably less support compared with other psychiatric disorders, such as schizophrenia, bipolar disorder and major depressive disorder. Many studies have been conducted, but unfortunately there have been many unproductive directions taken in the search for helpful agents for eating disorders. Although several pharmacotherapies have demonstrated improvement in symptoms, it is important to note that only a minority of bulimic patients actually achieve full abstinence at the end of treatment. In addition, rigorous entry criteria used in the trials may seriously impair the generalizability of results. Lastly, the publication of negative studies should be encouraged in order to avoid publication bias and consequently overoptimistic conclusions.

Anorexia Nervosa

Consistent Evidence

A wide variety of agents have been explored in the acute treatment of anorexia nervosa, including antidepressants (five randomized controlled trials, RCTs), antipsychotics (three RCTs), cyproheptadine (three RCTs), prokinetic drugs (four RCTs), zinc (three RCTs), lithium (one RCT), THC (one RCT), clonidine (one RCT) and GH (one RCT). The results of these trials have been disappointing with regard to weight gain. No medication has been shown to be clearly more effective than placebo if one considers clinical significance. This may be related to the "usual care" the subjects receive, which often includes intensive weight restoration programmes and psychotherapy that obscure the effect of the drug. If so, the drug effects were certainly not large and it could be argued that drug therapy is not indicated at this point in the illness.

Incomplete Evidence

Somewhat better results have been found in the maintenance treatment of weight-restored anorexia nervosa patients. The SSRI fluoxetine has demonstrated significant efficacy as a relapse prevention agent over 1 year. However, this is the only RCT available to date. Considering the high risk of relapse after weight restoration, a therapeutic agent that may help patients to maintain weight would be an important addition to the therapeutic armamentarium for anorexia nervosa; therefore, this result needs further confirmation.

Areas Still Open to Research

The positive results of small case series and single case reports suggest that atypical antipsychotics such as olanzapine and risperidone should be investigated in randomized, placebo-controlled trials. Not only have the weights improved for these patients, but also the eating-related psychopathology and general psychopathology such as anxiety, agitation and obsessive thoughts.

Given the chronic course of anorexia nervosa, short-term studies are of limited clinical value and long-term studies are warranted. Because of the difficulties in recruiting patients with anorexia nervosa, multisite studies should be strongly encouraged. Also, the majority of medication trials have been conducted with adults, even though anorexia nervosa usually begins during adolescence. Pharmacological treatment studies in children and adolescents are warranted.

Bulimia Nervosa

Consistent Evidence

The literature has progressed to the point where fairly firm recommendations can be made on the use of drugs in the treatment of patients with bulimia nervosa. Even though various classes of drugs have been used, antidepressants have emerged as the drugs of choice in the treatment of bulimia nervosa. There are more than 20 double-blind, placebo-controlled trials available using all classes of antidepressant drugs, with fluoxetine accounting for the largest number of patients. These studies demonstrate effectiveness in reducing the frequency of core bulimic symptoms and comorbid psychopathology, including depression and anxiety. Side effect profiles remain a significant factor in the clinical choice of the antidepressant. At the time of writing, fluoxetine is the only US FDA approved drug for the treatment of bulimia nervosa in adults.

Incomplete Evidence

Several other medications have been studied in bulimia nervosa (e.g. opiate antagonists, ondansetron, other SSRIs, 5-HT and noradrenaline reuptake inhibitors), although the results are still inconclusive and additional controlled studies are needed.

More recently the literature has evolved to include alternative treatment models, such as the use of drugs in psychotherapy non-responders (two RCTs), use of drugs as relapse prevention agents after successful in- or outpatient treatment (two RCTs), and studies comparing the relative efficacy of psychotherapies, self-help and pharmacotherapies and their combination (nine RCTs). In general, one can conclude that studies employing CBT have found this therapy to have a more powerful effect than is achieved with drug therapy alone. The combination of CBT with medication appears to be superior to medication alone. Whether the combination of CBT and medication is superior to CBT alone is less clear. Some additional benefit was achieved by the addition of medication in some but not all studies; however, the cost–benefit ratio of additional pharmacotherapy is questionable.

The effect of antidepressants on relapse prevention is inconclusive, although one large multicentre trial suggested some effect. The therapeutic effect may be lost even when medication is maintained. These findings raise the question of appropriate dosing, substituting a second antidepressant when relapse has occurred with the first medication or adding a second drug. Open-label studies suggest that the use of different antidepressants after relapse might be a useful approach.

Areas Still Open to Research

Apart from fluoxetine, other SSRIs and newer antidepressants need to be studied in the treatment of bulimia nervosa. The issue of sequential medication trials has not been studied adequately. There are no studies directly comparing two classes of antidepressants regarding their efficacy, tolerability and cost-effectiveness. The possible utility of drug augmentation strategies for patients with bulimia nervosa receiving antidepressant treatment has not been addressed adequately. In addition, emphasis should be placed on identifying non-responders early during the course of a psychotherapy and evaluating the pharmacotherapy at that point in treatment.

The applicability of pharmacotherapy to the non purging subtype, to males or to individuals with subthreshold forms of the disorder is open to study, as is the exploration of potential predictors of favourable outcome that might allow us to match patients to certain forms of pharmacotherapy. Finally, the development of new treatments for those who are currently regarded as treatment resistant, particularly those with marked problems of impulsivity and high rates of comorbidity for personality disorders, is required.

Binge Eating Disorder (BED)

Consistent Evidence

Because early studies have incorporated the experiences already gathered from the bulimia nervosa and obesity literature and because the methodologies applied in BED trials were more stringent, the results are less diverse. As in bulimia nervosa, antidepressants should be considered as an option in patients with BED (five RCTs). However, even though the reduction in binge eating frequency with antidepressants can be substantial, many patients improve without treatment and there is a risk of relapse after withdrawal of the drug. Also, the reduction in binge eating frequency does not necessarily lead to weight loss; however, complete abstinence from binge eating is related positively to weight reduction. Medication seems to be inferior to psychotherapy (e.g. CBT) and in the short term does not add to the efficacy of psychological treatments on binge eating frequency. Antidepressants can increase the amount of weight lost when combined with psychological treatment; however, rebound weight gain after termination of the drug is common.

Incomplete Evidence

Because BED has been incorporated only recently in the DSM, treatment research on BED is at an early stage. Even so, many of the open questions in bulimia nervosa, such as maintenance treatment, prognostic factors and treatment of those with comorbid illnesses and treatment resistance, also pertain to BED.

Areas Still Open to Research

Most patients with BED are overweight and there are no reliable weight loss strategies available. Studies with drugs that have been shown to reduce weight, such as sibutramine, are ongoing or recently completed and not available yet in patients with BED.

More research should be devoted to the development of new drugs for obesity. There is still a lack of long-term treatment studies. Because there is some evidence that BED is an unstable diagnosis with a tendency to remit over time, long-term studies need to be conducted comparing the natural course with long-term treatment.

REFERENCES

1. Ferguson J. (1987) Treatment of an anorexia nervosa patient with fluoxetine. *Am. J. Psychiatry*, **144**: 1239.
2. Lyles B., Sarkis E., Kemph J.P. (1990) Fluoxetine and anorexia. *J. Am. Acad. Child Adolesc. Psychiatry*, **29**: 984–985.
3. Gwirtsman H.E., Guze B.H., Yager J., Gainsley B. (1990) Fluoxetine treatment of anorexia nervosa: an open clinical trial. *J. Clin. Psychiatry*, **51**: 378–382.
4. Kaye W.H., Weltzin T.E., Hsu L.K.G., Bulik C.M. (1991) An open trial of fluoxetine in patients with anorexia nervosa. *J. Clin. Psychiatry*, **52**: 464–471.
5. Brambilla F., Draisci A., Peirone A., Brunetta M. (1995) Combined cognitive-behavioral, psychopharmacological and nutritional therapy in eating disorders. *Neuropsychobiology*, **32**: 68–71.
6. Brambilla F., Draisci A., Peirone A., Brunetta M. (1995) Combined cognitive-behavioral, psychopharmacological and nutritional therapy in eating disorders. II. Anorexia, binge-purging type. *Neuropsychobiology*, **32**: 64–67.
7. Bergh C., Eriksson M., Lindberg G., Södersten P. (1996) Selective serotonin reuptake inhibitors in anorexia. *Lancet*, **348**: 1459–1460.
8. Pallanti S., Quercioli L., Ramacciotti A. (1997) Citalopram in anorexia nervosa. *Eat. Weight Disord.*, **2**: 216–221.
9. Strober M., Freeman R., DeAntonio M., Lampert C., Diamond J. (1997) Does adjunctive fluoxetine influence post-hospital course of anorexia nervosa? A 24-month perspective, longitudinal follow-up and comparison with historical controls. *Psychopharmacol. Bull.*, **33**: 425–431.
10. Strober M., Pataki C., Freeman R., DeAntonio M. (1999) No effect of adjunctive fluoxetine on eating behavior or weight phobia during the inpatient treatment of anorexia nervosa: a historical case-control study. *J. Child Adolesc. Psychopharmacol.*, **9**: 195–201.
11. Ferguson C.P., La Via M.C., Crossan P.J., Kaye W.H. (1999) Are selective serotonin reuptake inhibitors effective in underweight anorexia nervosa? *Int. J. Eat. Disord.*, **25**: 11–27.
12. Ricca V., Mannucci E., Paionni A., DiBernardo M., Cellini M., Cabras P.L., Rotella C.M. (1999) Venlafaxine vs. fluoxetine in the treatment of atypical anorectic outpatients: a preliminary study. *Eat. Weight Disord.*, **4**: 10–14.

13. Calandra C., Gulino V., Inserra L., Giuffrida A. (1999) The use of citalopram in an integrated approach to the treatment of eating disorders: an open trial. *Eat. Weight Disord.*, **4**: 207–210.
14. Santonastaso P., Friederici S., Favaro A. (2001) Sertraline in the treatment of restricting anorexia nervosa: an open controlled trial. *J. Child Adolesc. Psychopharmacol.*, **11**: 143–150.
15. Frank G.K., Kaye W.H., Marcus M.D. (2001) Sertraline in underweight binge eating/purging-type eating disorders: five case reports. *Int. J. Eat. Disord.*, **29**: 495–498.
16. Fassino S., Leombruni P., Daga G.A., Brustolin A., Migliaretti G., Cavallo F., Rovera G.G. (2002) Efficacy of citalopram in anorexia nervosa: a pilot study. *Eur. Neuropsychopharmacol.*, **12**: 453–459.
17. Kaye W., Gendall K., Strober M. (1998) Serotonin neuronal function and selective serotonin reuptake inhibitor treatment in anorexia and bulimia nervosa. *Biol. Psychiatry*, **44**: 835–838.
18. Lacey J.H., Crisp A.H. (1980) Hunger, food intake and weight: the impact of clomipramine on a refeeding anorexia nervosa population. *Postgrad. Med. J.*, **56** (Suppl. 1): 79–85.
19. Biederman J., Herzog D.B., Rivinus T.M., Harper G.P., Ferber R.A., Rosenbaum J.F., Harmatz J.S., Tondorf R., Orsulak P.J., Schildkraut J.J. (1985) Amitriptyline in the treatment of anorexia nervosa: a double-blind, placebo-controlled study. *J. Clin. Psychopharmacol.*, **5**: 10–16.
20. Halmi K.A., Eckert E., LaDu T.J., Cohen J. (1986) Anorexia nervosa: treatment efficacy of cyproheptadine and amitriptyline *Arch. Gen. Psychiatry*, **43**: 177–181.
21. Attia E., Haiman C., Walsh B.T., Flater S.R. (1998) Does fluoxetine augment the inpatient treatment of anorexia nervosa? *Am. J. Psychiatry*, **155**: 548–551.
22. Kaye W.H., Nagata T., Weltzin T.E., Hsu L.K., Sokol M.S., McConaha C., Plotnicov K.H., Weise J., Deep D. (2001) Double-blind placebo-controlled administration of fluoxetine in restricting- and purging-type anorexia nervosa. *Biol. Psychiatry*, **49**: 644–652.
23. Vigersky R.A., Loriaux D.L. (1977) The effect of cyproheptadine in anorexia nervosa: a double-blind trial. In *Anorexia Nervosa* (Ed. R.A. Vigersky), pp. 349–356. Raven Press, New York.
24. Goldberg S.C., Halmi K.A., Eckert E.D., Casper R.C., Davis J.M. (1979) Cyproheptadine in anorexia nervosa. *Br. J. Psychiatry*, **134**: 67–70.
25. Owens M.J., Risch S.C. (2001) Atypical antipsychotics. In *Essentials of Clinical Psychopharmacology* (Eds A.F. Schatzberg, C.B. Nemeroff), pp. 125–154. American Psychiatric Press, Washington.
26. Beasley C.M., Jr., Tollefson G., Tran P. Satterlee W., Sanger T., Hamilton S. (1996) Olanzapine versus placebo and haloperidol: acute phase results of the North American double-blind olanzapine trial. *Neuropsychopharmacology*, **14**: 111–123.
27. Tollefson G.D., Sanger T.M. (1997) Negative symptoms: a path analytic approach to a double-blind, placebo- and haloperidol-controlled clinical trial with olanzapine. *Am. J. Psychiatry*, **154**: 466–474.
28. Chouinard G., Jones B., Remington G., Bloom D., Addington D., MacEwan G.W., Labelle A., Beauclair L., Arnott W. (1993) A Canadian multicenter placebo-controlled study of fixed doses of risperidone and haloperidol in the treatment of chronic schizophrenic patients. *J. Clin. Psychopharmacol.*, **13**: 25–40.
29. Marder S.R., Meibach R.C. (1994) Risperidone in the treatment of schizophrenia. *Am. J. Psychiatry*, **151**: 825–835.

30. Meltzer H.Y., McGurk S.R. (1999) The effects of fluoxetine, risperidone, and olanzapine on cognitive function and schizophrenia. *Schizophr. Bull.*, **25**: 233–255.

31. Purdon S.E., Jones B.D., Stip E., Labelle A., Addington D., David S.R., Breier A., Tollefson G.D. (2000) Neuropsychological change in early phase schizophrenia during twelve months of treatment with olanzapine, risperidone, or haloperidol. *Arch. Gen. Psychiatry*, **57**: 249–258.

32. Mendelowitz A.J., Liberman S.A. (1995) New findings in the use of atypical antipsychotics: focus on risperidone. *J. Clin. Psychiatry*, **2**: 1–12.

33. Ramasubbu R., Ravindran A., Lapierre Y. (2000) Serotonin and dopamine antagonism in obsessive–compulsive disorder: effective atypical antipsychotic drugs. *Pharmacopsychiatry*, **33**: 236–238.

34. Konig F., von Hippel C., Petersdorff T., Neuhoffer-Weiss M., Wolfersdorf M., Kaschka W.P. (2001) First experiences in combination therapy using olanzapine with SSRIs (citalopram, paroxetine) in delusional depression. *Neuropsychobiology*, **43**: 170–174.

35. Ghaemi S.N., Cherry E.L., Katzow J.A., Goodwin F.K. (2000) Does olanzapine have antidepressant properties? A retrospective preliminary study. *Bipolar Disord.*, **2**: 196–199.

36. Stoll A.L., Haura G. (2000) Tranylcypromine plus risperidone for treatment-refractory major depression. *J. Clin. Psychopharmacol.*, **20**: 495–496.

37. Wirshing D.A., Wirshing W.C., Kysar L., Berisford M.A., Goldstein D., Pashdag J., Mintz J., Marder S.R. (1999) Novel antipsychotics: comparison of weight gain liabilities. *J. Clin. Psychiatry*, **60**: 358–363.

38. Allison D.B., Mentore J.L., Heo M., Chandler L.P., Cappelleri J.C., Infante M.C., Weiden P.J. (1999) Antipsychotic-induced weight gain: a comprehensive research synthesis. *Am. J. Psychiatry*, **156**: 1686–1696.

39. Dally P., Sargant W. (1966) Treatment and outcome of anorexia nervosa. *Br. Med. J.*, **2**: 793–795.

40. Vandereycken W., Pierloot R. (1982) Pimozide combined with behavior therapy in the short-term treatment of anorexia nervosa. *Acta Psychiatr. Scand.*, **66**: 445–450.

41. Weizman A., Tyano S., Wijsenbeek H., Ben David M. (1985) Behavior therapy, pimozide treatment and prolactin secretion in anorexia nervosa. *Psychother. Psychosom.*, **43**: 136–140.

42. Vandereycken W. (1984) Neuroleptics in the short-term treatment of anorexia nervosa: a double-blind placebo-controlled study with sulpiride. *Br. J. Psychiatry*, **144**: 288–292.

43. Condon J.T. (1986) Long-term neuroleptic therapy and chronic anorexia nervosa complicated by tardive dyskinesia. A case report. *Acta Psychiatr. Scand.*, **73**: 203–206.

44. Dulcan M.K., Bregman J., Weller E.B., Weller R. (2001) Treatment of childhood and adolescent disorders. In *Essentials of Clinical Psychopharmacology* (Eds A.F. Schatzberg, C.B. Nemeroff), pp. 459–517. American Psychiatric Press, Washington.

45. Fisman S., Steele M., Short J., Byrne T. Lavallee C. (1996) Case study: anorexia nervosa and autistic disorder in an adolescent girl. *J. Am. Acad. Child Adolesc. Psychiatry*, **35**: 937–940.

46. Hansen L. (1999) Olanzapine in the treatment of anorexia nervosa. *Br. J. Psychiatry*, **175**: 592.

47. Jensen V.S., Mejlhede A. (2000) Anorexia nervosa: treatment with olanzapine. *Br. J. Psychiatry*, **177**: 187.
48. La Via M.C., Gray L., Kaye W.H. (2000) Case reports of olanzapine treatment of anorexia nervosa. *Int. J. Eat. Disord.*, **27**: 363–366.
49. Newman-Toker J. (2000) Risperidone in anorexia nervosa. *J. Am. Acad. Child Adolesc. Psychiatry*, **39**: 941–942.
50. Mehler C., Wewetzer C., Schulze U., Warnke A., Theisen F., Dittmann R.W. (2001) Olanzapine in children and adolescents with chronic anorexia nervosa. A study of five cases. *Eur. Child Adolesc. Psychiatry*, **10**: 151–157.
51. Ruggiero G.M., Laini V., Mauri M.C., Ferrari V., Clemente A., Lugo F., Mantero M., Redaelli G., Zappulli D., Cavagnini F. (2001) A single blind comparison of amisulpride, fluoxetine and clomipramine in the treatment of restricting anorectics. *Prog. Neuro-Psychopharmacol. Biol. Psychiatry*, **25**: 1049–1059.
52. Gaskill J.A., Treat T.A., McCabe E.B., Marcus M.D. (2001) Does olanzapine affect the rate of weight gain among inpatients with eating disorders? *Eat. Disord. Rev.*, **12**: 1–2.
53. Carver A.E., Miller S., Hagman J., Sigel E. (2002) The use of risperidone for the treatment of anorexia nervosa. Presented at the Academy of Eating Disorders Annual Meeting, Boston, 25–28 April.
54. Powers P.S., Santana C.A., Bannon Y.S. (2002) Olanzapine in the treatment of anorexia nervosa: an open label trial. *Int. J. Eat. Disord.*, **32**: 146–154.
55. Leucht S., Pitschel-Walz G., Engel R.R., Kissling W. (2002) Amisulpride, an unusual "atypical" antipsychotic: a meta-analysis of randomized controlled trials. *Am. J. Psychiatry*, **159**: 180–190.
56. McClain C.J., Stuart M.A., Vivian B., McClain M., Talwalker R., Snelling L., Humphries L. (1992) Zn status before and after zinc supplementation of eating disorder patients. *J. Am. Coll. Nutr.*, **11**: 694–700.
57. McClain C.J., Kasarskis E.J., Allen J.J. (1985) Functional consequences of zinc deficiency. *Prog. Food Nutr. Sci.*, **9**: 185–226.
58. Bakan R. (1979) The role of zinc in anorexia nervosa: etiology and treatment. *Med. Hypoth.*, **5**: 731–736.
59. Moynahan E.J. (1976) Zinc deficiency and disturbances of mood and visual behavior. *Lancet*, **i**: 91.
60. Katz R.L., Keen C.L., Litt I.F., Hurley L.S., Kellams-Harrison K.M., Glader L.J. (1987) Zinc deficiency in anorexia nervosa. *J. Adolesc. Health Care*, **8**: 400–406.
61. Esca S.A., Brenner W., Mach K. Gschnait F. (1979) Kwashiorkor-like zinc deficiency syndrome in anorexia nervosa. *Acta Dermatol. Venereol.*, **59**: 361–364.
62. Hambridge K.M. (1988) Assessing the trace element status of man. *Proc. Nutr. Soc.*, **47**: 37–44.
63. Sandstead H. (1991) Assessment of zinc nutriture. *J. Lab. Clin. Med.*, **118**: 299–300.
64. Lask B., Bryant-Waugh R. (1993) Zinc deficiency and childhood-onset anorexia nervosa. *J. Clin. Psychiatry*, **54**: 63–66.
65. Birmingham C.L., Goldner E.M., Bakan R. (1994) Control trial of zinc supplementation and anorexia nervosa. *Int. J. Eat. Disord.*, **15**: 251–255.
66. Luby E.D., Marrazzi M.A., Kinzie J. (1987) Treatment of chronic anorexia nervosa with opiate blockade. *J. Clin. Psychopharmacol.*, **7**: 52–53.
67. Moore R., Mills I.H., Forster A. (1981) Naloxone in the treatment of anorexia nervosa: Effect on weight gain and lipolysis. *J. R. Soc. Med.*, **74**: 129–131.
68. Barcai (1997) Lithium in adult anorexia nervosa. A pilot report on two patents. *Acta Psychiatr. Scand.*, **55**: 97–101.

69. Reilly P.P. (1977) Anorexia nervosa. *Rhode Island Med. J.*, **60**: 419–422, 455–456.
70. Stein G.S., Hartshorn S., Jones J., Steinberg D. (1982) Lithium in a case of severe anorexia nervosa. *Br. J. Psychiatry*, **140**: 526–528.
71. Tachibana N., Sugita Y., Teshima Y., Hishikawa Y. (1989) A case of anorexia nervosa with epileptic seizures showing favorable responses to sodium valproate and clonazepam. *Jpn. J. Psychiatry Neurol.*, **43**: 77–84.
72. Mendelson S.D. (2001) Treatment of anorexia nervosa with tramadol. *Am. J. Psychiatry*, **158**: 963–964.
73. Raffa R.B., Friderichs E., Reiman W., Shank R.P., Codd E.E., Vaught J.L. (1992) Opioid and nonopioid components independently contribute to the mechanism of action of tramadol, an "atypical" opioid analgesic. *J. Pharmacol. Exp. Ther.*, **260**: 275–285.
74. Gross H.A., Ebert M.H., Faden V.B., Goldberg S.C., Kaye W.H., Caine E.D., Hawks R., Zinberg N. (1981) A double-blind control trial of lithium carbonate primary anorexia nervosa. *J. Clin. Psychopharmacol.*, **6**: 376–381.
75. Gross H., Evert M.H., Faden V.B., Goldberg S.C., Kaye W.H., Caine E.D., Hawks R., Zinberg N. (1983) A double-blind trial of Δ^9-tetrahydrocannabinol in primary anorexia nervosa. *J. Clin. Psychopharmacol.*, **3**: 165–171.
76. Casper R.C., Schlemmer R.F., Javaid J.I. (1987) A placebo-controlled crossover study of oral clonidine in acute anorexia nervosa. *Psychiatry Res.*, **20**: 249–260.
77. Hill K., Bucuvalas J., McClain C. (2000) Pilot study of growth hormone administration during the refeeding to malnourished anorexia nervosa patients. *J. Child Adolesc. Psychopharmacol.*, **10**: 3–8.
78. Marrazzi M.A., Bacon J.P., Kinzie J., Luby E.D. (1995) A detailed longitudinal analysis on the use of naltrexone in the treatment of bulimia. *Int. Clin. Psychopharmacol.*, **10**: 173–176.
79. Counts D.R., Gwirstman H., Carlsson L.M., Lesem M., Cutler G.B. (1992) The effects of anorexia nervosa and refeeding on growth hormone-binding protein, the insulin-like growth factors (IGFs) and the IGF-binding proteins. *J. Clin. Endocrinol. Metab.*, **75**: 72–767.
80. Hill K.K., Hill D.B., McClain M., Humphries L.L., McClain D. (1993) Serum insulin-like growth factor I concentration in the recovery of patients with anorexia nervosa. *J. Am. Coll. Nutr.*, **12**: 475–478.
81. Clemmons D.R., Underwood L.E. (1992) Role of insulin-like growth factor I and growth hormone in reversing catabolic state. *Horm. Res.*, **38**: 37–40.
82. Domstad P.A., Shih W.J., Humphries L., DeLand F.H., Digenis G.A. (1987) Radionuclide gastric emptying studies in patients with anorexia nervosa. *J. Nucl. Med.*, **28**: 816–819.
83. Stacher G., Kiss A., Wiesnagrotzki S., Bergmann H., Hobart J., Schneider C. (1986) Oesophageal and gastric motility disorders in patients categorized as having primary anorexia nervosa. *Gut*, **27**: 1120–1126.
84. Stacher G, Bergmann H., Wiesnagrotzki S., Kiss A., Schneider C., Mittelbach G., Gaupmann G., Hobart J. (1987) Intravenous cisapride accelerated delayed gastric emptying and increases antral contraction amplitude with primary anorexia nervosa. *Gastroenterology*, **92**: 1000–1006.
85. Moldofsky H., Jeuniewic N., Garfinkel P.J. (1977) Primary report of meto-clopramide in anorexia nervosa. In *Anorexia Nervosa* (Ed. R.A. Vigersky), pp. 373–376. Raven Press, New York.
86. Craigen D., Kennedy S.H., Garfinkel P.E., Jeejeebhoy K. (1987) Drugs that facilitate gastric emptying. In *The Role of Drug Treatments for Eating Disorders* (Eds P.E. Garfinkel, D.M. Garner), pp. 161–176. Brunnel/Mazel, New York.

87. Stacher G., Abatzi-Wenzel T.A., Wiesnagrotzki S., Bergmann H., Schneider C., Gaupmann G. (1993) Gastric emptying, body weight and symptoms in primary anorexia nervosa. Long-term effects of cisapride. Br. J. Psychiatry, 162: 398–402.

88. Szmukler G.I., Young G.P., Miller G., Lichtenstein M., Binns D.S. (1995) A controlled trial of cisapride in anorexia nervosa. Int. J. Eat. Disord., 17: 347–357.

89. American Psychiatric Association (2000) Practice guideline for the treatment of patients with eating disorders (revision). Am. J. Psychiatry, 157 (Suppl. 1): 1–39.

90. Bacaltchuk J., Hay P. (2002) Antidepressants versus placebo for people with bulimia nervosa (Cochrane Review). In The Cochrane Library. Update Software, Oxford.

91. Bacaltchuk J., Hay P., Mari J.J. (2000) Antidepressants versus placebo for the treatment of bulimia nervosa: a systematic review. Aust. N. Zeal. J. Psychiatry, 34: 310–317.

92. Mitchell J.E., Peterson C.B., Myers T., Wonderlich S. (2001) Combining pharmacotherapy and psychotherapy in the treatment of patients with eating disorders. Psychiatr. Clin. North Am., 24: 315–323.

93. Krüger S., Kennedy S.H. (2000) Psychopharmacotherapy of anorexia nervosa, bulimia nervosa and binge eating disorder. J. Psychiatry Neurosci., 25: 497–508.

94. Peterson C.B., Mitchell J.E. (1999) Psychosocial and pharmacological treatment of eating disorders: a review of research findings. J. Clin. Psychol., 55: 687–697.

95. Lennkh C., de Zwaan M., Kasper S. (1997) New aspects of diagnosis and pharmacotherapy of eating disorders. Int. J. Psychiatry Clin. Pract., 1: 21–35.

96. Jimerson D.C., Wolfe B.E., Brotman A.W., Metzger E.D. (1996) Medications in the treatment of eating disorders. Psychiatr. Clin. North Am., 19: 739–744.

97. Pope H.G., Jr., Hudson J.I., Jonas J.M., Yurgelun-Todd D. (1983) Bulimia treated with imipramine: a placebo-controlled, double-blind study. Am. J. Psychiatry, 140: 554–558.

98. Agras W.S., Dorian B., Kirlkey B.G., Arnow B., Bachman J. (1987) Imipramine in the treatment of bulimia: a double blind controlled study. Int. J. Eat. Disord., 6: 29–38.

99. Mitchell J.E., Pyle R.L., Eckert E.D., Hatsukami D., Pomeroy C., Zimmerman R. (1990) A comparison study of antidepressants and structured group therapy in the treatment of bulimia nervosa. Arch. Gen. Psychiatry, 47: 149–157.

100. Alger S.A., Schwalberg M.D., Bigaouette J.M., Michalek A.V., Howard L.J (1991) Effect of a tricyclic antidepressant and opiate antagonist on binge-eating behavior in normoweight bulimic and obese, binge-eating subjects. Am. J. Clin. Nutr., 53: 865–871.

101. Mitchell J.E., Groat R. (1984) A placebo-controlled double-blind trial of amitriptyline in bulimia. J. Clin. Psychopharmacol., 4: 186–193.

102. Hughes P.L., Wells L.A., Cunningham C.J., Ilstrup D.M. (1986) Treating bulimia with desipramine. Arch. Gen. Psychiatry, 43: 182–186.

103. Barlow J., Blouin J., Blouin A., Perez E. (1998) Treatment of bulimia with desipramine: a double-blind crossover study. Can. J. Psychiatry, 33: 129–133.

104. Blouin A.G., Blouin J.H., Perez E.L., Bushnik T., Zuro C., Mulder E. (1988) Treatment of bulimia with fenfluramine and desipramine. J. Clin. Psychopharmacol., 8: 261–269.

105. Walsh T., Hadigan C., Devlin M., Gladis M., Roose S. (1991) Long-term outcome of antidepressant treatment for bulimia nervosa. *Am. J. Psychiatry*, **148**: 1206–1212.

106. Agras W., Rossiter E., Arnow B., Schneider J., Telch C., Raeburn S., Bruce B., Perl M., Koran L. (1992) Pharmacologic and cognitive-behavioral treatment for bulimia nervosa: a controlled comparison. *Am. J. Psychiatry*, **149**: 82–87.

107. Sabine E.J., Yonace A., Farrington A.J., Barratt K.H., Wakeling A. (1983) Bulimia nervosa: a placebo-controlled, double-blind therapeutic trial of mianserin. *Br. J. Clin. Pharmacol.*, **15**: 195S–202S.

108. Horne R.L., Ferguson J.M., Pope H.G., Hudson J.I., Lineberry C.G., Ascher J., Cato A. (1988) Treatment of bulimia with bupropion: a multicenter controlled trial. *J. Clin. Psychiatry*, **49**: 262–266.

109. Pope H.G., Jr., Keck P.E., Jr., McElroy S.L., Hudson J.I. (1989) A placebo-controlled study of trazodone in bulimia nervosa. *J. Clin. Psychopharmacol.*, **9**: 254–259.

110. Walsh B.T., Stewart J.W., Roose S.P., Gladis M., Glassman A. (1985) A double-blind trial of phenelzine in bulimia. *J. Psychiatr. Res.*, **19**: 485–489.

111. Walsh B.T., Gladis M., Roose S.P., Stewart J.W., Stetner F., Glassman A.H. (1988) Phenelzine vs placebo in 50 patients with bulimia. *Arch. Gen. Psychiatry*, **45**: 471–475.

112. Rothschild R., Quitkin H.M., Quitkin F.M., Stewart J.W., Ocepek-Welikson K., McGrath P.J., Tricamo E. (1994) A double-blind placebo-controlled comparison of phenelzine and imipramine in the treatment of bulimia in atypical depressives. *Int. J. Eat. Disord.*, **15**: 1–9.

113. Kennedy S.H., Piran N., Warsh J.J., Prendergast P., Mainprize E., Whynot C., Garfinkel P.E. (1988) A trial of isocarboxazid in the treatment of bulimia nervosa. *J. Clin. Psychopharmacol.*, **8**: 391–396.

114. Kennedy S.H., Goldbloom D.S., Ralevski E., Davis C., D'Souza J.D., Lofchy J. (1993) Is there a role for selective MAO-inhibitor therapy in bulimia nervosa? A placebo-controlled trial of brofaromine. *J. Clin. Psychopharmacol.*, **13**: 415–422.

115. Carruba M.D., Cuzzolaro M., Riva L., Bosello O., Liberty S., Castra R., Delle Grave R.D., Santononastaso P., Garosi V., Nisoli E. (2001) Efficacy and tolerability of moclobemide in bulimia nervosa: a placebo-controlled trial. *Int. Clin. Psychopharmacol.*, **16**: 27–32.

116. Fluoxetine Bulimia Nervosa Collaborative Study Group (1992) Fluoxetine in the treatment of bulimia nervosa: a multicenter placebo-controlled double-blind trial. *Arch. Gen. Psychiatry*, **49**: 139–147.

117. Goldstein D.J., Wilson M.G., Thompson V.L., Potvin J.H., Rampey A.H., The Fluoxetine Bulimia Nervosa Research Group (1995) Long-term fluoxetine treatment of bulimia nervosa. *Br. J. Psychiatry*, **166**: 660–666.

118. Romano S.J., Halmi K.A., Koke S.C., Lee J.S. (2002) A placebo-controlled study of fluoxetine in continued treatment of bulimia nervosa after successful acute fluoxetine treatment. *Am. J. Psychiatry*, **159**: 96–102.

119. Wilson G.T., Fairburn C.G. (1993) Cognitive treatments for eating disorders. *J. Consult. Clin. Psychol.*, **61**: 261–269.

120. Fichter M.M., Leibl K., Rief W., Brunner E., Schmidt-Auberger S., Engel R.R. (1991) Fluoxetine vs placebo: a double-blind study with bulimic inpatients undergoing intensive psychotherapy. *Pharmacopsychiatry*, **24**: 1–7.

121. Beumont P.J.V., Russell J.D., Touyz S.W., Buckley C., Lowinger K., Talbot P., Johnson G.F.S. (1997) Intensive nutritional counseling in bulimia nervosa: a

role for supplementation with fluoxetine? *Aust. N. Zeal. J. Psychiatry*, **31**: 514–524.

122. Walsh B., Wilson T., Loeb K., Devlin M., Pike K., Roose S., Fleiss J., Waternaux C. (1997) Medication and psychotherapy in the treatment of bulimia nervosa. *Am. J. Psychiatry*, **154**: 523–531.

123. Agras W.S., Rossiter E.M., Arnow B., Telch C.F., Raeburn S.D., Bruce B., Koran L.M. (1994) One-year follow-up of psychosocial and pharmacologic treatment for bulimia nervosa. *J. Clin. Psychiatry*, **55**: 179–183.

124. Ceccherini-Nelli A., Guidi L. (1993) Fluoxetine: the relationship between response, adverse events, and plasma concentration in the treatment of bulimia nervosa. *Int. Clin. Psychopharmacol.*, **8**: 311–313.

125. Mitchell J.E., Pyle R.L., Eckert E.D., Hatsukami D., Pomeroy C., Zimmerman R. (1989) Response to alternative antidepressants in imipramine nonresponders with bulimia nervosa. *J. Clin. Psychopharmacol.*, **9**: 291–293.

126. Walsh B.T., Wilson G.T., Loeb K.L., Devlin M.J., Pike K.M., Roose S.P., Fleiss J., Waternaux C. (1997) Medication and psychotherapy in the treatment of bulimia nervosa. *Am. J. Psychiatry*, **154**: 523–531.

127. Wolf B.E. (1995) Dimensions of response to antidepressant agents in bulimia nervosa: a review. *Arch. Psychiatr. Nurs.*, **9**: 111–121.

128. Goldbloom D.S., Olmsted M.P. (1993) Pharmacotherapy of bulimia nervosa with fluoxetine: assessment of clinical significant attitudinal change. *Am. J. Psychiatry*, **150**: 770–774.

129. Jonas J.M., Gold M.S. (1988) The use of opiate antagonists in treating bulimia: a study of low-dose versus high-dose naltrexone. *Psychiatry Res.*, **24**: 195–199.

130. Marrazzi M.A., Markham K.M., Kinzie J., Luby E.D. (1995) Binge-eating disorder: response to naltrexone. *Int. J. Obesity*, **19**: 143–145.

131. Igoin-Apfelbaum L., Apfelbaum M. (1987) Naltrexone and bulimic symptoms. *Lancet*, **7**: 1087–1088.

132. Hsu L.K.G., Clement L., Santhouse R., Ju E.S.Y. (1991) Treatment of bulimia nervosa with lithium carbonate. A controlled study. *J. Nerv. Ment. Dis.*, **179**: 351–355.

133. Russell G.F.M., Checkley S.A., Feldman J., Eisler I. (1988) A controlled trial of d-fenfluramine in bulimia nervosa. *Clin. Neuropharmacol.*, **11** (Suppl. 1): S146–S159.

134. Fahy T.A., Eisler I., Russell G.F. (1993) A placebo-controlled trial of d-fenfluramine in bulimia nervosa. *Br. J. Psychiatry*, **162**: 597–603.

135. Krahn D., Mitchell J. (1985) Use of L-tryptophan in treating bulimia. *Am. J. Psychiatry*, **142**: 1130.

136. Wermuth B.M., Davis K.L., Hollister L.E., Stunkard A.J. (1977) Phenytoin treatment of the binge-eating syndrome. *Am. J. Psychiatry*, **134**: 1249–1253.

137. Kaplan A.S., Garfinkel P.E., Darby P.L., Garner D.M. (1983) Carbamazepine in treatment of bulimia. *Am. J. Psychiatry*, **140**: 1225–1226.

138. Hoopes S.P., Reimherr F.W., Karvois D., Karim R., Kamin M., Rosenthal N.E. (2002) A randomized controlled trial of topiramate for the treatment of bulimia nervosa. Presented at the Eating Disorders Research Society Annual Meeting, 20–23 November.

139. Faris P.K., Kim S.W., Meller W.H., Goodale R.L., Oakman S.A., Hofbauer R.D., Marshall A.M., Daughters R.S., Banerjee-Stevens D., Eckert E.D., *et al.* (2000) 5-HT$_3$ antagonist therapy of bulimia nervosa: a peripherally active agent for a central nervous system eating disorder? *Gastroenterology*, **119**: 272–273.

140. Neumeister A., Winkler A., Wober-Bingoel C. (1999) Addition of naltrexone to fluoxetine in the treatment of binge-eating disorder. *Am. J. Psychiatry*, **156**: 797.

141. El-Giamal N., de Zwaan M., Bailer U., Lennkh C., Schüssler P., Strnad A., Kasper S. (2000) Reboxetine in the treatment of bulimia nervosa: a report of seven cases. *Int. Clin. Psychopharmacol.*, **15**: 351–356.

142. El-Giamal N., de Zwaan M., Bailer U., Strnad A., Schüssler P., Kasper S. Milnacipran in the treatment of bulimia nervosa: a report of 16 cases. *Eur. Neuropsychopharmacol.* (in press).

143. Sokol M.S., Gray N.S., Goldstein A., Kaye W.H. (1999) Methylphenidate treatment for bulimia nervosa associated with a cluster B personality disorder. *Int. J. Eat. Disord.*, **25**: 233–237.

144. Bergman L., Eriksson E. (1996) Marked symptom reduction in two women with bulimia nervosa treated with the testosterone receptor antagonist Flutamide. *Acta Psychiatr. Scand.*, **94**: 137–139.

145. Geretsegger C., Greimel K.V., Roed I.S., Keppel Hesselink J.M. (1995) Ipsapirone in the treatment of bulimia nervosa: an open pilot study. *Int. J. Eat. Disord.*, **17**: 359–363.

146. Roberts J.M., Lydiard R.B. (1993) Sertraline in the treatment of bulimia nervosa. *Am. J. Psychiatry*, **150**: 1753.

147. Pigott T.A., Sunderland B.A., Horn L. (1986) A pilot study of paroxetine in the treatment of bulimia nervosa Presented at the 149th Annual Meeting of the American Psychiatric Association, Washington, 10–16 May.

148. Faltus F. (1993) Pimozide in the therapy of eating disorders. *Cesk. Psychiatr.*, **1**: 24–26.

149. Herridge P.L., Pope H.G. (1985) Treatment of bulimia and rapid-cycling bipolar disorder with sodium valproate: a case report. *J. Clin. Psychopharmacol.*, **5**: 229–230.

150. Nassr D.G. (1986) Successful treatment of bulimia with nomifensine. *Am. J. Psychiatry*, **143**: 373–374.

151. Ong Y.L., Checkley S.A., Russell G.F.M. (1983) Suppression of bulimic symptoms with methylamphetamine. *Br. J. Psychiatry*, **143**: 288–293.

152. Blouin A.G., Blouin J.H., Iverson J., Carter J., Goldstein C., Goldfield G., Perez E. (1996) Light therapy in bulimia nervosa: a double-blind, placebo-controlled study. *Psychiatry Res.*, **60**: 1–9.

153. Lam R.W., Lee S.K., Tam E.M., Grewal A., Yatham L.N. (2001) An open trial of light therapy for women with season affective disorder and comorbid bulimia nervosa. *J. Clin. Psychiatry*, **62**: 3.

154. Halmi K.A., Braun D.L., Sunday S.R., Fornari V.M. (1999) Bright light therapy decreases winter binge frequency in women with bulimia nervosa: a double-blind, placebo-controlled study. *Compr. Psychiatry*, **40**: 442–448.

155. Pyle R.L., Mitchell J.E., Eckert E.D., Hatsukami D., Pomeroy C., Zimmerman R. (1990) Maintenance treatment and 6-month outcome for bulimia patients who respond to initial treatment. *Am. J. Psychiatry*, **147**: 871–875.

156. Pope H.G., Hudson J.I., Jonas J.M., Yurgelin-Todd D. (1985) Antidepressant treatment of bulimia: a two-year follow-up study. *J. Clin. Psychopharmacol.*, **5**: 320–327.

157. Agras W.S., Telch C.F., Arnow B., Eldredge K., Wilfley D.E., Reaburn S.D., Henderson J., Marnell M. (1994) Weight loss, cognitive-behavioral, and desipramine treatments in binge-eating disorder. An additive design. *Behav. Ther.*, **25**: 225–238.

158. Hudson J.I., Pope H.G., Keck P.E., McElroy S.L. (1989) Treatment of bulimia nervosa with trazodone: short-term response and long-term follow-up. *Clin. Neuropharmacol.*, **12**: S38–S46.
159. Wilson G.T., Vitousek K.M., Loeb K.L. (2000) Stepped care treatment for eating disorders. *J. Consult. Clin. Psychol.*, **68**: 564–572.
160. Agras W.S., Crow S.J., Halmi K.A., Mitchell J.E., Wilson G.T., Kraemer H.C. (2000) Outcome predictors for the cognitive behavior treatment for bulimia nervosa: data from a multisite study. *Am. J. Psychiatry*, **157**: 1302–1308.
161. Blouin J., Blouin A., Perez E., Barlow J. (1989) Bulimia: independence of antibulimic and antidepressant properties of desipramine. *Can. J. Psychiatry*, **34**: 24–29.
162. Goldstein D.J., Wilson M.G., Ascroft R.C., Al-Banna M. (1999) Effectiveness of fluoxetine therapy in bulimia nervosa regardless of comorbid depression. *Int. J. Eat. Disord.*, **25**: 19–27.
163. Brotman A.W., Herzog D.B., Woods S.W. (1984) Antidepressant treatment of bulimia: the relationship between bingeing and depressive symptomatology. *J. Clin. Psychiatry*, **45**: 7–9.
164. Leitenberg H., Rosen J., Vara L., Detzer M., Srebnik D. (1994) Comparison of cognitive-behavior therapy and desipramine in the treatment of bulimia nervosa. *Behav. Res. Ther.*, **32**: 37–45.
165. Goldbloom D.S., Olmsted M., Davis R., Clewes J., Heinmaa M., Rockert W., Shaw B. (1997) A randomized controlled trial of fluoxetine and cognitive behavioral therapy for bulimia nervosa: short-term outcome. *Behav. Res. Ther.*, **35**: 803–811.
166. Jacobi C., Dahme B, Dittmann R.W. (2002) Cognitive-behavioral, fluoxetine and combined treatment for bulimia nervosa: short-term and long-term results. *Eur. Eat. Disord. Rev.*, **10**: 179–198.
167. Walsh B.T., Agras W.S., Devlin M.J., Fairburn C.G., Wilson G.T., Kahn C., Chally M.K. (2000) Fluoxetine for bulimia nervosa following poor response to psychotherapy. *Am. J. Psychiatry*, **157**: 1332–1334.
168. Mitchell J.E., Halmi K., Wilson G.T., Agras W.S., Kraemer H., Crow S. (2002) A randomized secondary treatment study of women with bulimia nervosa who fail to respond to CBT. *Int. J. Eat. Disord.*, **32**:271–281.
169. Fichter M.M., Kruger R., Rief W., Holland R., Doehne J. (1996) Fluvoxamine in prevention of relapse in bulimia nervosa: effects on eating-specific psychopathology. *J. Clin. Psychopharmacol.*, **16**: 9–18.
170. Mitchell J.E., Fletcher L., Hanson K., Pederson-Mussell M., Seim H., Crosby R., Al-Banna M. (1997) The relative efficacy of fluoxetine and manual-based self-help in the treatment of outpatients with bulimia nervosa. *J. Clin. Psychopharmacol.*, **21**: 298–304.
171. Freeman C. (1998) Drug treatment for bulimia nervosa. *Biol. Psychiatry*, **37**: 72–79.
172. Corcos M., Flament M., Atger F., Jeammet P. (1996) Pharmacological treatment of bulimia nervosa. *Encéphale*, **12**: 133–142.
173. Mitchell J.E., Tareen B., Sheehan W., Agras S., Brewerton T.D., Crow S., Devlin M., Eckert E., Halmi K., Herzog D., *et al.* (2000) Establishing guidelines for pharmacotherapy trials in bulimia nervosa and anorexia nervosa. *Int. J. Eat. Disord.*, **28**: 1–7.
174. Goldstein D.J., Rampey A.H., Jr., Enas G.G., Potvin J.H., Fludzinski L.A., Levine L.R. (1994) Fluoxetine: a randomized clinical trial in the treatment of obesity. *Int. J. Obesity*, **18**: 129–135.

175. Marcus M.D., Wing R.R., Ewing L., Kern E., McDermott M., Gooding W. (1990) A double-blind, placebo-controlled trial of fluoxetine plus behavior modification in the treatment of obese binge-eaters and non-binge-eaters. Am. J. Psychiatry, 147: 876–881.

176. de Zwaan M., Nutzinger D.O., Schönbeck G. (1992) Binge eating in overweight females. Compr. Psychiatry, 33: 256–261.

177. Alger S.A., Malone M., Cerulli J., Fein S., Howard L. (1999) Beneficial effects of pharmacotherapy on weight loss, depressive symptoms, and eating patterns in obese binge eaters and non-binge eaters. Obesity Res., 7: 469–476.

178. de Zwaan M., Mitchell J.E. (1992) Opiate antagonists and eating behavior in humans: a review. J. Clin. Pharmacol., 32: 1060–1072.

179. Weintraub M. (1992) Long-term weight control study: conclusions. Clin. Pharmacol. Ther., 51: 642–646.

180. McCann U.D., Agras W.S. (1990) Successful treatment of nonpurging bulimia nervosa with desipramine: a double-blind, placebo controlled study. Am. J. Psychiatry, 147: 1509–1513.

181. Stunkard A., Berkowitz R., Tanrikut C., Reiss E., Young L. (1996) d-Fenfluramine treatment of binge-eating disorder. Am. J. Psychiatry, 153: 1455–1459.

182. Hudson J.I., McElroy S.L., Raymond N.C., Crow S., Keck P.E., Carter W.P., Mitchell J.E., Strakowski S.M., Pope H.G., Coleman B., et al. (1998) Fluvoxamine in the treatment of binge-eating disorder. Am. J. Psychiatry, 155: 1756–1762.

183. McElroy S.L., Casuto L.S., Nelson E.B., Lake K.A., Soutullo C.A., Keck P.E., Jr., Hudson, J.I. (2000) Placebo-controlled trial of sertraline in the treatment of binge eating disorder. Am. J. Psychiatry, 157: 1004–1006.

184. Hudson J., McElroy S.L., Arnold L.M., Shapira N.A., Keck P.E., Rosenthal N. (2001) Topiramate in the treatment of binge eating disorder: a placebo-controlled trial. Presented at the Eating Disorders Research Society Annual Meeting, Bernalillo, 28 November–1 December.

185. Laederach-Hofman K., Graf C., Horber F., Lippuner K., Lederer S., Michel R., Schneider M. (1999) Imipramine and diet counseling with psychological support in the treatment of obese binge eaters: a randomized, placebo-controlled double-blind study. Int. J. Eat. Disord., 26: 231–244.

186. Prats M., Diez-Quevedo C., Avila C., Planell L.S. (1994) Paroxetine treatment for bulimia nervosa and binge-eating disorder. Presented at the Sixth International Conference on Eating Disorders, New York, 29 April–1 May.

187. Gelber D., Levine J., Belmaker R.H. (2001) Effect of inositol on bulimia nervosa and binge eating. Int. J. Eat. Disord., 29: 345–348.

188. Appolinario J.C., Godoy-Matos A., Fontenelle L.F., Carraro L., Cabral M., Vieira A., Coutinho W. (2002) An open-label trial of sibutramine in obese patients with binge-eating disorder. J. Clin. Psychiatry, 63: 28–30.

189. Shapira N.A., Goldsmith T.D., McElroy S.L. (2000) Treatment of binge-eating disorder with topiramate: a clinical case series. J. Clin. Psychiatry, 61: 368–372.

190. Appolinario J.D., Coutinho W., Fontenelle L. (2001) Topiramate for binge-eating disorder. Am. J. Psychiatry, 158: 967–968.

191. Ryan D.H., Kaiser P., Bray G.A. (1995) Sibutramine: a novel new agent for obesity treatment. Obesity Res, 4: 553S–559S.

192. Wilfley D.E., Cohen L.R. (1997) Psychological treatments of bulimia nervosa and binge eating disorder. Psychopharmacol. Bull., 33: 437–454.

193. Ricca V., Mannucci E., Mezzani B., Moretti S., Di Bernardo M., Bertelli M., Rotella C.M., Faravelli C. (2001) Fluoxetine and fluvoxamine combined with

individual cognitive-behaviour therapy in binge eating disorder: a one-year follow-up study. *Psychother. Psychosom.*, **70**: 298–306.

194. Grilo C.M., Masheb R.M., Heninger G., Wilson G.T. (2002) Controlled comparison of cognitive behavioral therapy and fluoxetine for binge eating disorder. Presented at the Academy of Eating Disorders Annual Meeting, Boston, 25–28 April.

195. Devlin M. (2002) Psychotherapy and medication for binge eating disorder. Presented at the Academy of Eating Disorders Annual Meeting, Boston, 25–28 April.

196. Hudson J., Carter W., Pope H. (1996) Antidepressant treatment of binge-eating disorder: research findings and clinical guidelines. *J. Clin. Psychiatry*, **57** (Suppl. 8): 73–79.

Commentaries

4.1
Pharmacotherapy of Eating Disorders: Only a Few Conclusions Can be Drawn

James E. Mitchell[1]

As de Zwaan and Roerig's review indicates, the literature on the pharmacotherapy of eating disorders has grown exponentially over the last 20 years and has reached a point where certain conclusions can be drawn with a fair amount of conviction.

Probably the most important conclusion concerns the limitations of pharmacotherapy for patients with eating disorders. Although many of our colleagues in other areas of psychiatry can raise convincing arguments that pharmacotherapy is a necessary (but not necessarily sufficient) treatment for many mental disorders (schizophrenia and manic–depressive illness obviously come to mind), the role of pharmacotherapy is clearly ancillary in the treatment of patients with anorexia nervosa and bulimia nervosa, although to be cautious one must conclude that the data on binge eating disorder (BED) are still too scarce to make any firm conclusions.

The second issue that will strike even the casual observer is the relative lack of data concerning anorexia nervosa compared with bulimia nervosa, despite the fact that the former has been the object of study for a much longer period of time. The reasons for this include: a) the relative rarity of the condition; b) the fact that patients with anorexia nervosa require a multiplicity of interventions, making it difficult to design treatment trials to control for all the necessary treatment variables; c) the patients' resistance to treatment; d) the fact that many anorexic patients are adolescents, which complicates the issues of informed consent and randomized treatment trials.

Therefore, one must conclude that, if significant headway is to be made in pharmacotherapy studies of anorexia nervosa, multisite designs will be necessary and a consortium to undertake such studies should be established. Such a group, given the proper resources, probably could

[1] *Neuropsychiatric Research Institute, 700 1st Ave. So., PO Box 1415, Fargo, ND 58103, USA*

negotiate effectively with pharmaceutical firms for the use of new agents as they became available and this might have a significant impact on the field.

Given the current state of knowledge, and in particular the most recent research findings, what are the most important outcomes to consider regarding the pharmacotherapy of anorexia nervosa? I would suggest that there are three observations, all of which require further work, which at least tentatively would suggest important findings: a) selective serotonin reuptake inhibitors (SSRIs) appear not to work in patients with anorexia nervosa when they are at low weight, an observation that is of both clinical and theoretical importance; b) SSRIs may help to prevent relapse in weight-restored patients with anorexia nervosa (given the high risk for relapse and the high morbidity/mortality, this result suggests that all patients should be considered for maintenance SSRI therapy following the weight restoration); c) atypical antipsychotics may benefit many of these patients (the results admittedly are preliminary, but this group of agents appears most promising; in a sense it is unfortunate that they are labelled antipsychotics, given the fact that they probably have a number of effects other than those in psychotic illness).

What have been the areas of most neglect? The observation of the possible benefit of zinc therapy clearly deserves to be followed up, because this is an intervention with very modest risks. Also, the whole field of the prevention of bone loss in patients with anorexia nervosa requires a renewed research focus.

In terms of possible research directions regarding anorexia nervosa, the molecular genetics of this illness is beginning to unravel and the results of these studies may suggest new possible targets for drugs. Also, for adolescent patients, the family-based interventions—which in the studies published to date appear to have a great deal of efficacy for younger onset shorter duration patients—should be coupled with pharmacological interventions such as relapse prevention agents to see if this could be beneficial.

Relative to bulimia nervosa, the data seem quite clear at this point that structured forms of psychotherapy, particularly cognitive–behavioural therapy (CBT), are more powerful than drug therapy and that pharmacotherapy alone is probably an adequate treatment. The use of drug therapy in those patients whose rate of improvement suggests that they are not likely to be complete responders to CBT, in combination with self-help approaches (both supervised and unsupervised) and as part of "stepped-care" strategies, appears to be an interesting possibility.

The results in the relapse prevention trials thus far have been disappointing, with high rates of relapse and, in particular, high rates of drop-out. However, the design of these trials may have been problematic in some way. One wonders how effective these agents would be in preventing relapse in individuals who have actually achieved abstinence, because, at least in the psychotherapy literature, abstinence appears to be a very important predictor of continued treatment response. In the relapse prevention studies conducted to date, most patients on medication were symptomatic but improved. Also, we have not adequately addressed the possible utility of augmentation strategies for patients receiving antidepressant treatments. The literature in this area is quite rich for a number of other conditions. Why this option has not been pursued more aggressively in subjects with bulimia nervosa is unclear.

The data on BED are insufficient. What we can conclude thus far is that interventions designed for bulimia nervosa seem to have a positive impact on many patients with BED, in terms of both improvement in binge eating symptoms and reduction in weight, although weight reductions to date have been modest and of short duration. The main problem here is that many patients with BED are quite overweight and at medical risk for the complications of obesity. Also, their main reason for seeking treatment is their desire for weight loss. Therefore, the main problem currently in the BED literature remains the lack of safe and effective agents that are capable of inducing substantial weight loss. Both orlistat and sibutramine clearly have some impact on weight, but the effect is usually modest and agents with greater effectiveness are highly desirable. Results of the trial of sibutramine in BED should prove of considerable interest, given the pharmacological profile of the drug and its effects both on weight and theoretically on binge eating.

4.2

Pharmacotherapy for the Eating Disorders: A Clinical Perspective

Pierre Beumont[1]

For an active clinician, reviews of various treatment approaches to dieting and patients with eating disorders often appear rather monocular. These are complex illnesses that pose multiple problems, both psychiatric and medical. To consider their treatment exclusively in terms of their assumed characteristic features is inadequate. Anorexia nervosa is not merely the syndrome of food refusal and weight loss, with or without purging behaviours; bulimia nervosa is not simply the syndrome of episodic bulimia (gorging) combined with compensatory behaviours to limit weight gain; binge eating disorder (BED) is not simply bulimic episodes in obese persons

_____

[1] Department of Psychological Medicine, University of Sydney, Australia

without compensatory behaviours. De Zwaan and Roerig's excellent review reports the literature relating to the effects of pharmacotherapy on the key features of these illnesses. I would not wish to add to it. Rather, the purpose of my commentary is to look at the broader picture as it confronts the clinician, without the limitation of assuming that eating disorders are only about eating and not eating [1].

The physical manifestations of anorexia nervosa are as important as its psychiatric and behavioural features—perhaps more important. Although it is an illness of low prevalence (0.2–0.5% lifetime risk for women in our society), it has major psychiatric and medical morbidity, and its mortality rate is higher than that of any other psychiatric illness. For this reason, a medical practitioner always must be part of the team treating an anorexic patient and pharmacological treatment of some sort or other is often necessary.

Most patients who present in a state of severe emaciation are medically compromised: however, there is no single medication that is immediately indicated. The priority is to identify physical morbidity and treat it appropriately, and to institute a programme of nutritional rehabilitation. Dehydration may require fluid replacement. On the other hand, the patient may present with hyponatraemia. Despite the frequent presence of severe hypoglycaemia, it is important to be extremely cautious about giving intravenous glucose. To do so is likely to restart a dormant metabolism that will impose demands particularly for phosphates and for other electrolytes such as magnesium that the body, owing to its chronic state of starvation, is unable to meet. For this reason initial refeeding must be slow, and administration of prophylactic phosphates and thiamine is indicated to avoid the potentially fatal refeeding syndrome. Potassium levels are also likely to be dangerously low, posing the risk of cardiac arrhythmias. Again, extreme caution is necessary with replacement, because hyperkalaemia is as dangerous as hypokalaemia. Although patients with anorexia nervosa often do not present with a concurrent infection, if they do it is likely to be masked by their illness. Fever—the usual indicator of infection—is obscured by the patient's general hypothermia [2]. An apparent normal temperature may indicate a pyrexial response in an anorexic patient. If an infective process is present, then it needs to be treated appropriately, if necessary with antibiotics.

The next priority is restoration of nutrition. Fortunately, there are no specific nutritional abnormalities to consider. What is needed is ordinary food, in sufficient quantities to reverse starvation and then gradually restore a normal body composition. The problem is how best to give the nutrition in view of the patient's fear of and inability to eat normally. Usually a high-energy diet, prescribed by a dietitian, is encouraged by supportive nurses who are consistent in insisting on the patient's compliance. Behavioural therapy strategies to bring about weight gain are described elsewhere in this volume. There is a temptation to prescribe heavy sedation, e.g. with chlorpromazine, to counter the patient's opposition to eating, but to do so raises major ethical problems and also imposes risks of its own. If the situation is critical, nasogastric feeding would be safer. In order to provide a balanced diet with sufficient energy it is often useful to use a dietary replacement product, either as a supplement or in substitution for ordinary food.

Because the cause of food avoidance in anorexia nervosa is not really anorexia (loss of appetite), appetite stimulants such as cyproheptadine to promote eating are not likely to be effective, and indeed this has been demonstrated adequately in the literature. Arising from a rather unlikely and complex theory about the aetiology of illness [3], naloxone was suggested as a means of bringing about weight gain, but it too was not effective. The only pharmacological intervention that has been shown to be effective is zinc (zinc, like phosphates, magnesium, calcium and potassium, is often depleted). Supplementation with zinc has been shown to improve the rate of weight gain in a controlled trial [4]. Drugs whose side-effects include weight gain (chlorpromazine, fluoxetine) may contribute to refeeding as well, but the evidence is not convincing. However, there is one good trial that indicates that fluoxetine helps in the prevention of relapse.

The refeeding process is often uncomfortable because the patient's bowel function has adapted to small amounts of food. Delayed gastric emptying and a reduced bowel motility contribute to the patient's discomfort. Drugs such as metoclopramide may be helpful in this situation. Cisapride, which was recommended previously, is to be avoided because of its potential cardiac effects. Severe constipation often complicates refeeding, particularly in persons who had previously abused laxatives in order to lose weight. It should be treated conservatively, with a high-fibre diet, plenty of fluids and a stool softener. However, if extreme, a cathartic or suppository enema should be used: there is a real risk of faecal impaction. Dependent oedema is also a common complication of refeeding, not only in those who have abused laxatives or diuretics. Again, conservative treatment is recommended, e.g. lying down with the legs raised.

The next consideration is that of psychopharmacology. There is no evidence that any psychotropic drug reverses the characteristic psychopathology or behaviour of patients with anorexia nervosa. Antidepressant drugs are those that have been tried most frequently, but with little benefit. Over the last 3 years there have been a number of anecdotal reports that atypical antipsychotics, particularly olanzapine, do exert a beneficial effect, although the mechanism for this is not yet understood. Current research is investigating this issue, to discern whether the benefit is consistent between patients and whether the effect is really via a psychotropic action, perhaps lowering the intensity of the patient's obsessive ideas about food and body.

Depression, obsessive–compulsive symptoms (sometimes restricted to eating), anxiety and even psychotic symptoms are common comorbidities. The first priority is to ensure that these are not signs of an impending delirium, e.g. in a patient developing a refeeding syndrome. Tricyclic antidepressants are potentially dangerous for anorexic patients because of their potential to prolong the QT interval on the electrocardiogram. The selective serotonin reuptake inhibitors (SSRIs) appear safe. A large proportion of anorexic patients today receive an SSRI, either because of depressive or obsessive–compulsive symptoms, but there have been no studies showing that medication adds benefit to the routine treatment of refeeding and psychotherapy.

Osteopenia leading to osteoporosis is a serious long-term complication and only full restoration of body weight appears to prevent it [5]. Hormone replacement with oestrogens is still commonly prescribed, but there is little evidence that it is effective. Recently, the use of bisphosphonates has been explored, but no clear guidelines are yet available.

In total contrast to anorexia nervosa, bulimia nervosa is an illness whose characteristic features respond to psychopharmacology. There have been a great number of studies showing beneficial effects of antidepressant drugs, particularly SSRIs and especially fluoxetine, and there is no reasonable doubt about effectiveness. Interestingly, the action appears independent of the drug's antidepressant effect: changes to bulimic behaviour are not mirrored by changes of depressive symptomatology. To exert an optimal anti-bulimic effect, the dosage of drug must be higher than that indicated for depression, e.g. fluoxetine is prescribed at a dose of 60 mg/day.

Drugs for bulimia nervosa are not the optimal treatment. These patients have been shown to respond very well to a number of psychotherapies, including cognitive–behavioural therapy, educational behavioural therapy (intensive nutritional counselling) and interpersonal psychotherapy. Generally, patients prefer a psychotherapeutic approach to drug treatment, and there are fewer drop-outs in the psychotherapy groups in controlled studies. It would seem that treatment with a drug such as fluoxetine is indicated when the patient has difficulty in accessing psychological treatments, and also during the initial period while awaiting therapy. There is little evidence that the addition of medication to psychotherapy conveys any additional benefit. Unlike the response to psychotherapeutic strategies, the response to medication appears to dissipate as soon as the drug is discontinued [6].

Because eating disorders not otherwise specified (EDNOS) are so heterogeneous, it is difficult to discern any guidelines for the use of drugs in their treatment, and there have been very few studies of the issue.

However, many studies of anorexic and bulimic patients have been less than scrupulous in ensuring that the patients fulfilled all their diagnostic criteria, and many of the subjects would be diagnosed more correctly with EDNOS [6]. In any case, those patients with EDNOS whose illness represents a *forme fruste* of anorexia nervosa or bulimia nervosa (sub-clinical or at least subsyndromal) should be treated similarly to those with the full illness. Other patients with EDNOS present different psycho-pathology, e.g. the severely depressed patient whose food refusal is intrinsic to her depression. In such cases energetic treatment of the underlying illness is indicated. A large minority of patients with EDNOS may be grouped under the rubric of BED. Essentially, these are patients who regularly overeat or even have true bulimia (gorging) episodes, but without the compensatory behaviours that characterize bulimia nervosa. Reversing this behaviour by means of psychopharmacology does not seem to work, and the current view is that these patients are best treated by psychological techniques that encourage dietary restraint (which is certainly not the case for either anorexia nervosa or bulimia nervosa). Because many patients with BED are clinically obese, they should be treated like other obese subjects, with the use of cholesterol-lowering drugs and antihypertensives when indicated.

Pharmacotherapy is not particularly helpful in reversing the core psychopathologies of eating disorders. Pressing questions about pharma-cotherapy to which this clinician would like to see researchers address themselves are:

- Are antidepressants useful in treating the depressed mood of patients with anorexia and bulimia nervosa, irrespective of their effect on eating?
- Tricyclics prolong the QT interval and predispose to cardiac arrhythmias. Should they be avoided in these patients, who are already vulnerable?
- What pharmacological interventions are indicated for the obsessional symptoms that are often prominent? Clomipramine can cause severe constipation.
- What is the optimal regime for a patient whose treatment is hampered by severe constipation or oedema?
- Given that psychotherapeutic approaches appear to be more effective than pharmacology in treating bulimia nervosa, but nevertheless that some antidepressants such as fluoxetine do exert anti-bulimic effects, what are the indications for drugs in this condition?
- What to do about osteoporosis?
- The patient with chronic anorexia nervosa faces years of ill-health and disability. Which medications are useful in its management? Antide-pressants? Nutritional supplements?

REFERENCES

1. Beumont P.J.V. (2003) Withershins from Woop-Woop: what kinds of illnesses are eating disorders? *Eur. Child Adolesc. Psychiatry* (in press).
2. Birmingham C.L., Hodgson D.M., Fung J., Brown R., Wakefield A., Bartrop R., Beumont P. (2003) Reduced febrile response to bacterial infections in anorexia nervosa. *Int. J. Eat. Disord.* (in press).
3. Mills I.H., Medlicott L. (1984) The basis of naloxone treatment in anorexia and the metabolic response to it. In *The Psychobiology of Anorexia Nervosa* (Eds K.M. Pirke, D. Ploog), pp. 161–171. Springer, Berlin.
4. Birmingham C.L., Goldner E.M., Bakan R. (1994) Control trial of zinc supplementation and anorexia nervosa. *Int. J. Eat. Disord.*, **15**: 251–255.
5. Zipfel S., Seibel M.J., Lowe B., Beumont P.J., Kasperk C., Herzog W. (2001) Osteoporosis in eating disorders: a follow-up study of patients with anorexia and bulimia nervosa. *J. Clin. Endocrinol. Metab.*, **86**: 5227–5233.
6. Wilson G.T., Fairburn C.G. (1998) Treatments for eating disorders. In *A Guide to Treatments that Work* (Eds P.E. Nathan, J.M. Gorman), pp. 501–529. Oxford University Press, New York.

4.3

Psychopharmacological Therapy of Disorders of Eating Behaviour: Past and Future

Francesca Brambilla[1]

Psychopharmacological therapies are still not well defined approaches to the treatment of disorders of eating behaviour, mostly because of methodological problems that are seen also in therapies of other psychopathological conditions. In fact, treatments of mental disorders are still centred either on broad-ranging nosological definitions or on single specific symptoms in the context of psychopathological conditions, being only seldom directed towards the correction of the possibly primary causes of the disorders. This is a step that was taken long ago in general medicine, and is one reason for the positive results obtained with the treatment of most pathologies. In psychiatry, instead, there is still a fluctuation between psychopharmacological treatments not specifically centred on the mostly unknown biological causes of the mental disorders and the psychological therapies that ignore the basic biochemical alterations underlying psychopathological conditions.

For anorexia nervosa and bulimia nervosa, it has been demonstrated repeatedly that psychological treatments, when chosen appropriately and done correctly, are successful, at best, in no more than half of the patients

[1] *Department of Psychiatry, University of Naples SUN, Largo Madonna delle Grazie, Naples, Italy*

treated and it is not known why recovery takes place in one group of patients and not in others, what to do in the latter, why in both groups the two pathologies may relapse and what to do to prevent this, and whether or not the treatments act on the aetiopathogenesis of the diseases or only on their symptomatology, course and prognosis. Ignoring the importance of these aspects may be responsible for the too frequent unsuccessful results.

On reviewing the literature on the psychopharmacological therapies of eating disorders, there is no doubt that the results are very disappointing because the efficacy of treatments is no better than that of psychotherapies, the number of drop-outs is too high and the relapses are too frequent. Moreover, in most cases only eating-related symptoms (eating habits, weight loss and recovery, etc.) have been reported or taken into consideration as parameters to define recovery, whereas it is well known that in most patients some psychopathological aspects persist after remission of the eating problems and are often responsible for their relapses.

The poor success of pharmacological treatments may result from the fact that we treat disorders when we do not know exactly what they are, why they develop, why some remit spontaneously and others do not and why they do or do not relapse. This is not acceptable, and totally new approaches should be considered in the future.

The first methodological point to be considered in the search for future fully successful pharmacological treatments of eating disorders involves the determination of the aetiopathogenesis of anorexia nervosa, bulimia nervosa and binge eating disorder (BED), because the correction of the biological background causing the three disorders is obviously the primary core of any therapeutic approach. Brain imaging and neurochemical and genetic studies are moving ahead slowly, providing only hints about the pathologies that may precede the three disorders and be their causes. This means that the necessary aetiopathogenetically linked therapeutic approach is still far from being available, although it is well known that it is the indispensable basic step for successful treatment.

A second important methodological problem is that it has not been decided clearly what must be treated first in patients with eating disorders. Are we trying to confront the causes of the disease or are we only trying to improve the brain pathologies present during their course and responsible for their active symptomatology? This is an extremely important point because the brain pathologies that precede eating disorders may be different from those observed during their course, owing to starvation or even malnutrition and the resulting metabolic impairments that characterize eating disorders being able to alter brain biochemical functions. What should be corrected first: the aetiopathogenetic causes of the diseases or the brain pathologies that develop during their course? This looks like a theoretical question but it is not, because it has been reported that without correction of starvation-linked brain impairments there is no full and stable response to psychopharmacological or psychological treatments. In fact, the starvation-induced deficiency of brain serotonin and the starvation-linked neuropeptide and hormonal impairments that characterize eating disorders may block the capacity of brain neuronal and synaptic complexes to respond to the administration of psychotropic drugs [1]. The importance of the sequence of treatments must be defined and validated, taking into consideration also the need for post-recovery psychiatric assistance. In fact, when the patients have recovered symptomatologically, it might be necessary to look for brain alterations that may be remnants of the acute disorders or be their cause, or in any case be responsible for relapses.

The third important point to be taken into consideration is the fact that psychopharmacological therapies, as mentioned before, have not been used to correct the possible biological impairments present in the diseases. Mostly, tricyclic antidepressants or selective serotonin reuptake inhibitors (SSRIs) have been chosen without specifying why, apart from the possible correction of a depressive symptomatology, which certainly does not represent the core of the diseases. Antidepressants have been given to anorexics or bulimics without having a specific motivation for doing so and without taking into consideration their biochemical effects, which should end up in different brain biochemical manipulations and in different clinical results. The choice for one or another specific pharmacotherapy must be motivated either aetiopathogenetically or symptomatologically. The effects obtained by drugs mainly acting on noradrenergic, dopaminergic or serotoninergic systems, or on all of them, are obviously not the same. A correct pharmacological treatment should be preceded by the study of the biological background of the diseases and their symptoms, by the choice of the parameters that we want to improve and by selection of the type of manipulation needed to correct the biochemical and related clinical impairments.

The fourth point regards the fact that no studies of the dose–response curves and the pharmacodynamics of psychopharmacological drugs have ever been done during treatments of eating disorders. Because there is very little knowledge about the capacity of anorexic and bulimic patients to absorb, metabolize and excrete substances, food or drugs, and because impairments of the gastric and colonic mucosa have been reported in both anorexia and bulimia nervosa [2, 3], it is not known whether or not pharmacological administrations result in therapeutically sufficient blood levels and consequently brain levels of the drugs used in each specific patient. This, obviously, may result in inappropriate protocols of treatments and negative results possibly linked to insufficient blood levels of the drugs in patients. It must be pointed out also that most pharmacological trials have been too short (2–6 weeks) and therefore may have missed any possible positive results that occur after longer observations.

The fifth point is that of the goals to be reached. Eating disorders are complex multifactorial diseases, possibly related to multiple biochemical impairments. However, each of them may be either responsible for the entire disease or for some specific aspects of it. It is well known that there is an array of biological impairments more or less constantly present during the course of an eating disorder, but it is not definitely clear what the pathogenetic responsibilities of each of them are. In the meantime, it is not known how psychopharmacological manipulations change the patterns of one or other biochemical alteration and the link between the various impairments. Thus, studies should be made of the specific effects of each psychotropic drug, in order to motivate its use in patients.

It must be recognized that all the points reported above, and many more deriving from them, are the indispensable premises for the correct pharmacological treatment of any disorder, including eating disorder. Up to now, none of these have been taken into consideration, and it is not surprising that poor results have been obtained by pharmacotherapies. There is probably no reason to restudy most of the old drugs used by totally new protocols designed to include the above-reported considerations, because the few brain biological data that we do have now tend to exclude their use. We must probably use drugs, doses and protocols different from those used up to now. What is clear at the moment is that negating the utility of psychopharmacological therapies on the basis of the failures or of the poor results of the trials conducted up to now is incorrect or even absurd, in view of their scientific imprecision.

The history of the pharmacotherapy of eating disorders must be rewritten, starting from tomorrow.

REFERENCES

1. Kaye W.H., Nagata T., Weltzin T.E., Hsu L.K., Sokol M.S., McConaha C., Plotnicov K.H., Weise J., Deep D. (2001) Double blind placebo controlled administration of fluoxetine in restricting- and purging-type anorexia nervosa. *Biol. Psychiatry*, **49**: 644–652.
2. Anderson L., Shaw J.M., McCargar L. (1997) Physiological effects of bulimia nervosa on the gastrointestinal tract. *Can. J. Gastroenterol.*, **11**: 451–459.
3. Chun A.B., Sokol M.S., Kaye W.H., Hutson W.R., Wald A. (1997) Colonic and anorectal function in constipated patients with anorexia nervosa. *Am. J. Gastroenterol.*, **92**: 1879–1883.

4.4
Pharmacological Treatment of Eating Disorders: Much Progress, Many Problems

B. Timothy Walsh[1]

From several perspectives, the eating disorders appear to be especially promising targets for pharmacological interventions. Individuals with eating disorders frequently describe psychological symptoms of other psychiatric disorders, such as major depression and anxiety, which are known to respond to medication. More is known about the neurobiological controls of eating behaviour than about those that govern the regulation of mood and cognition, providing a foundation on which pharmacological treatments can be based [1]. Furthermore, the prominent symptoms of eating disorders, such as binge eating, purging and disturbances of weight, are arguably easier to assess than the more subjective phenomena that are the hallmarks of many other psychiatric disorders, thereby making it easier for investigators to measure the efficacy of pharmacological interventions. The comprehensive and discerning review of de Zwaan and Roerig documents that in several instances these theoretical advantages have led to substantial advances, whereas in others the evidence for the utility of pharmacological intervention remains impressively thin.

A major success has been the demonstration of the utility of antidepressant medication in the treatment of bulimia nervosa. One of the tables of de Zwaan and Roerig's review lists over 20 controlled trials of this class of agent, and the accumulated data leave no doubt that antidepressant medication is a useful intervention that has a place in the treatment of this syndrome. Furthermore, the relative ease of use and low frequency of side-effects of the selective serotonin reuptake inhibitors (SSRIs) make this intervention widely available, even in non-specialist settings. But, as de Zwaan and Roerig appropriately note, the results of a single course of antidepressant treatment are often disappointing: only a minority of patients achieve remission with such treatment. Furthermore, the information base concerning what pharmacological interventions are clearly useful as second-line treatments is disappointingly small. Having extensively examined antidepressants, the field has begun only tentatively to explore novel interventions, such as sibutramine, ondansetron and topiramate, and such innovation is overdue.

More recent studies of binge eating disorder have attempted to extend the model of bulimia nervosa to this newly defined entity. There are good

[1] New York State Psychiatric Institute and Columbia University, 1051 Riverside Drive (Unit 98), New York, NY 10032, USA

indications that pharmacotherapy has a role to play in the treatment of binge eating disorder, but this area of study is still in a relatively early stage of development. The non-specific psychological difficulties associated with binge eating disorder, such as depression, are generally less extreme than those associated with bulimia nervosa, and, by definition, individuals with binge eating disorder do not regularly engage in inappropriate compensatory behaviour, such as vomiting. Nonetheless, studies of pharmacological treatment have encountered some challenges not characteristic of the trials in bulimia nervosa. First, as de Zwaan and Roerig point out, most patients with binge eating disorder hope not only to eliminate their binge eating and to improve their sense of psychological well-being, but also to lose weight. The pharmacological treatments examined to date have had difficulty in addressing all three aims. In addition, the magnitude of the response of individuals with binge eating disorder to non-specific interventions, including the use of placebo, may be substantial, complicating the detection of the effects of medication. More work is needed, and fortunately already is underway.

Most investigators will concur wholeheartedly with the description of the state of pharmacotherapy for anorexia nervosa as "disappointing". The number of trials remains small, and the work to date has not yielded impressively effective interventions. The oldest of eating disorders remains the most challenging to treat. New efforts have begun recently, some using medications to prevent relapse after patients have gained weight and others examining the utility of atypical antipsychotic agents, which can be associated with substantial weight increases. Hopefully, these and other new ideas will be fruitful, because progress in the pharmacotherapy of anorexia nervosa is long overdue.

REFERENCE

1. Smith G.P. (2000) The controls of eating: a shift from nutritional homeostasis to behavioral neuroscience. *Nutrition*, **16**: 814–820.

4.5
Medicating Disordered Eating: Moving Toward the Next Generation of Studies

Michael J. Devlin[1]

The goal of developing pharmacological interventions for patients suffering from the complex clusters of nutritional, psychological and behavioural symptoms known as the eating disorders is, in many ways, a humbling one. When we consider what an ideal drug for an eating disorder should do—eliminate long-standing aberrations of eating behaviour, correct nutritional imbalances, enhance self-esteem and loosen its connection to body image and eliminate anxiety about weight gain, all with a minimum of unwanted effects—it is difficult to imagine how a drug could be sufficiently focused and versatile to accomplish all these changes. What is striking is that the drugs that have been used, often based on models that subsequently have proved to be limited in their explanatory power, have actually yielded some of these outcomes to some degree in some individuals. The review by de Zwaan and Roerig of pharmacological treatment for eating disorders summarizes what I see as the first two generations of studies in this field, and points the way towards the third generation of studies. This generation of studies may begin to close the gap between our knowledge of efficacy, which is substantial and growing, and our understanding of therapeutic mechanism, which remains quite limited.

The initial generation of studies of anorexia nervosa included, for the most part, inpatient studies in which antipsychotic or antidepressant drugs were given in the context of behaviourally based inpatient treatment, in an attempt to speed or ease the process of weight gain. For bulimia nervosa, the initial studies used antidepressants in the context of outpatient clinical management, usually with binge/purge frequency as the major outcome variable. Studies in obese patients with binge eating disorder (BED) were based on and resembled those of bulimia nervosa except that, in some cases, appetite suppressants were used instead of, or in addition to, antidepressants. These early studies yielded a number of important lessons. Firstly, we learned that flawed models sometimes can yield effective treatments. Although the concept of eating disorders as a variant form of depression [1] soon gave way to more sophisticated understandings, antidepressant medication was found to have short-term efficacy in the treatment of bulimia nervosa whether or not the patient had a comorbid depressive disorder. Secondly, we learned that, despite

[1] *Eating Disorders Research Unit, New York State Psychiatric Institute, 1051 Riverside Drive, New York, NY 10032, USA*

their similarities, anorexia nervosa and bulimia nervosa have distinct medication response patterns. Serotonin reuptake inhibitors, although helpful for patients with bulimia nervosa, have marginal or no utility in treating anorexia nervosa, at least in the acute phase [2]. Thirdly, we learned the difference between short-term superiority to placebo vs. long-term clinical utility. Antidepressants of a variety of classes were shown to bring about greater binge/purge suppression than placebo, but only a minority of patients with bulimia nervosa achieved a sustained remission with drug treatment alone. Finally, we learned that, with regard to binge eating, short-term placebo response rates can be considerable and can vary widely from centre to centre.

The second generation of studies attempted to move beyond these early studies in a number of ways. Importantly, we became more sophisticated about targeting our interventions to a specific phase of illness. Thus, for example, fluoxetine, although not beneficial in the treatment of acute anorexia nervosa, was reported by some to yield better outcomes in the post-hospital relapse prevention phase [3]. We began to investigate combined psychotherapeutic and psychopharmacological approaches, finding, for example, that medication adds little to cognitive–behavioural therapy in treating bulimia nervosa, although the use of a sequence of medications rather than a single medication may tell a different tale [4]. For obese patients with BED, investigators explored how best to sequence [5] or combine [6] treatments that would address the various goals of binge suppression, weight loss and self-acceptance.

These many important studies have brought us to the point where we can begin to ask some particularly exciting third-generation questions. For instance, what are the factors that predict better or worse response to a given pharmacological intervention? A detailed knowledge of these moderator variables is, of course, the key in tailoring treatment to the individual. We are also beginning to undertake the ambitious enterprise of asking what it is that mediates change. Although treatments may work for unanticipated reasons, an understanding of the mechanism of action will clearly allow for the most efficient and effective usage of our resources. A fuller knowledge of how treatment works, and for whom, may guide us in developing novel interventions for those individuals for whom existing treatments do not work. Psychotherapy studies have begun to identify systematically the outcome predictors [7] and mechanisms of change [8], paving the way for similar studies of medication treatment. The current generation of studies also, it is hoped, will allow us to determine the effective ingredients of pharmacological treatment and perhaps provide a theoretical basis for the development of new drugs to help our patients with a minimum of adverse effects. Ideally, we will have an empirical basis to guide us in determining when a particular medication will be helpful or even necessary, when it is superfluous and when it is unlikely to help a patient who is failing.

Is there a fourth generation? I believe that there will be and that it may begin sooner than we think. Advances in neuroimaging, genetics and neurobiology are increasing our understanding of aetiology and pathophysiology to a level that has been unimaginable until recently. Two brief examples pertaining to other psychiatric disorders will illustrate the point. A recent study of patients with social phobia detected associations between changes in regional cerebral blood flow response to a social stressor and treatment success, regardless of whether the treatment intervention was pharmacological or psychological. Moreover, these changes in blood flow response were related to 1-year outcome [9]. A study using positron emission tomography imaging in patients with obsessive–compulsive disorder found that left orbitofrontal cortex metabolism was positively correlated with subsequent response to behavioural therapy but negatively correlated with response to fluoxetine treatment [10]. Studies such as these (which soon will begin to appear in the eating disorders literature), by providing a biological basis for treatment selection and by pointing more clearly to what is fundamentally disordered in our patients, will guide us to novel and more effective ways of restoring patients to health. It is my hope and expectation that, rather than being *surprisingly* effective, the pharmacological approaches of the future will be *understandably* effective, because we appreciate more fully why and how they are working.

REFERENCES

1. Cantwell D.P., Sturzenberger S., Burroughs J., Salkin B., Green J.K. (1977) Anorexia nervosa. An affective disorder? *Arch. Gen. Psychiatry*, **34**: 1087–1093.
2. Attia E., Haiman C., Walsh B.T., Flater S.R. (1998) Does fluoxetine augment the inpatient treatment of anorexia nervosa? *Am. J. Psychiatry*, **155**: 548–551.
3. Kaye W.H., Nagata T., Weltzin T.E., Hsu L.K., Sokol M.S., McConaha C., Plotnicov K.H., Weise J., Deep D. (2001) Double-blind placebo-controlled administration of fluoxetine in restricting- and purging-type anorexia nervosa. *Biol. Psychiatry*, **49**: 644–652.
4. Walsh B.T., Wilson G.T., Loeb K.L., Devlin M.J., Pike K.M., Roose S.P., Fleiss J., Waternaux C. (1997) Medication and psychotherapy in the treatment of bulimia nervosa. *Am. J. Psychiatry*, **154**: 523–531.
5. Agras W.S., Telch C.F., Arnow B., Eldredge K., Wilfley D.E., Raeburn S.D., Henderson J., Marnell M. (1994) Weight loss, cognitive-behavioral, and desipramine treatments in binge eating disorder: an additive design. *Behav. Ther.*, **25**: 235–238.
6. Devlin M.J. (2001) Binge eating disorder and obesity—a combined treatment approach. *Psychiatr. Clin. North Am.*, **24**: 325–335.

7. Agras W.S., Crow S.J., Halmi K.A., Mitchell J.E., Wilson G.T., Kraemer H.C. (2000) Outcome predictors for the cognitive behavioral treatment of bulimia nervosa: data from a multisite study. *Am. J. Psychiatry*, **157**: 1302–1308.
8. Wilson G.T., Fairburn C.G., Agras W.S., Walsh B.T., Kraemer H.C. (2002) Cognitive-behavioral therapy for bulimia nervosa: time course and mechanisms of change. *J. Consult. Clin. Psychol.*, **70**: 267–274.
9. Furmark T., Tillfors M., Marteinsdottir I., Fischer H., Pissiota A., Langstrom B., Fredrikson M. (2002) Common changes in cerebral blood flow with patients with social phobias treated with citalopram or cognitive-behavioral therapy. *Arch. Gen. Psychiatry*, **59**: 425–433.
10. Brody A.L., Saxena S., Schwartz J.M., Stoessel P.W., Maidment K., Phelps M.E., Baxter L.E., Jr. (1998) FDG-PET predictors of response to behavioral therapy and pharmaco-therapy in obsessive compulsive disorder. *Psychiatry Res.: Neuroimag.*, **84**: 1–6.

4.6

Clinical Decision-making From a Spotty Evidence Base: Connecting the Dots in Eating Disorders Treatment

Joel Yager[1]

de Zwaan and Roerig provide an extremely thorough, thoughtful, balanced and realistic appraisal of existing evidence regarding the current state of the art of pharmacological treatment for eating disorders. Their interpretive tasks have been made particularly difficult by the fact that the available data are spotty, often contradictory and generally based on limited clinical designs and small sample sizes. Still, this database is all that is available to join with the often contradictory clinical experience and practice biases in determining the treatment approaches for our patients.

Although evidence-based medicine suggests that the myths and internalized treatment algorithms by which we practise should be highly informed by the results of controlled clinical trials, pitifully few controlled trials have been conducted in eating disorders, particularly for anorexia nervosa. As de Zwaan and Roerig emphasize, in this area evidence is murky and few uncontestable bottom-line findings can be championed. Multiple putative mechanisms of medication actions with potentially different routes in different individuals have been posited. Consequently, proponents of different clinical persuasions can all point to something in these data tables to support their personal views—the glass, simultaneously half-full and half-empty, is dirty. Should medications be used in treating anorexia nervosa? Most studies seem to point to ceiling effects regarding

[1] *Department of Psychiatry, University of New Mexico School of Medicine, 2400 Tucker N.E., Albuquerque, NM 87131-5326, USA*

the rate and amount of weight gain for inpatients treated for anorexia nervosa. Adding selective serotonin reuptake inhibitors (SSRIs) and perhaps atypical antipsychotics to high-quality nursing-care-facilitated nutritional rehabilitation does not seem to do much for most inpatients in good treatment settings.

But, what about patients with premorbid affective, anxiety or obsessive–compulsive disorders? What about treatment-resistant or more chronic inpatients with anorexia nervosa? What about patients being treated in less ideal inpatient or outpatient treatment settings? Is zinc underused? Will atypical antipsychotics or opioid-related medications play a role? The fact is, we just do not know, as a result of which desperate clinicians and patients often venture into uncharted territories and bravely try new medications, leading to the large number of tantalizingly positive case reports and small case series meriting follow-up cited in this review. (Of course, we are unfortunately not privy to the large number of cases and small case series that fail various treatment innovations. Perhaps we need a journal that specializes in publishing negative case reports and case series.) Basic prudent clinical judgment should prevail: what are the relative risks and benefits of adding what sorts of medications for what patients at what points in time? Can they or can they not hurt? How do patients and families in conjunction with their caregivers view these approaches?

Although controlled studies concerning bulimia nervosa and binge eating disorder are more numerous, they still leave much to be desired. Given the high rates of complex comorbidities so often seen in patients with bulimia nervosa, vast fields of ignorance still confront the data-seeking clinician. My personal way of connecting the data dots suggests that combinations of cognitive–behavioural (at least) psychotherapies and medications offer individual patients the highest odds of fullest remission, at least in the short term. A recent randomized controlled trial showing that the antiepileptic agent topiramate is more effective than placebo in reducing binge eating and purging, resulting in overall clinical improvement, potentially opens up new areas of theory and treatment [1]. However, owing to potential cognitive side effects, this medication has to be assessed more thoroughly before its place in treatment can be assessed fully—there is no free lunch. And, as de Zwaan and Roerig point out, the entire area of systematically augmenting and combining medications for these disorders is virginal.

With regard to research designs, what is striking is that many of the more carefully constructed clinical trials for bulimia nervosa have such high drop-out rates. Placebo-controlled studies have higher drop-out rates than open-labelled studies. To my mind, these high drop-out rates are due at least partly to the fact that controlled studies often are set up in ways that experienced clinicians do not usually practise. Randomized trial treatment sequences often are artificial and miserly in what they offer regarding total available care. This suggests that novel clinical designs, based on more careful assessment of what actually transpires both psychotherapeutically as well as psychopharmacologically in successful office-based treatments of complex patients, may lead to the conduction of better studies, at least studies in which more effective patient retention occurs. I conjecture that treatment algorithms in successful clinical practice are highly nuanced and complex, but they are usually not whimsical. When obvious first strategies do not work, clinicians often combine elements of cognitive–behavioural therapy, interpersonal psychotherapy, psychodynamic techniques, family interventions and other psychotherapeutic strategies with sometimes creative medication sequencing and combinations based on their appraisal of the patient's individual situation and local conditions. We trust that sufficiently rigorous study designs ultimately will be capable of testing these assumptions.

REFERENCE

1. Hoopes S.P., Reimherr F.W., Kamin M., Karvois M.S., Rosenthal N.E., Karim R. (2002) Topiramate treatment of bulimia nervosa. Presented at the Annual Meeting of the American Psychiatric Association, Philadelphia, 18–23 May.

4.7
New Treatments for People with Eating Disorders: Hope Renewed
Josue Bacaltchuk[1] and Phillipa Hay[2]

Recent advances in the research of pharmacological treatments for anorexia nervosa and bulimia nervosa support the existence of more effective medications for these conditions. The inclusion of binge eating disorder (BED)—a more prevalent eating disorder—in Appendix B of DSM-IV and the availability of psychotropic agents with weight reduction and/or impulse control properties, such as sibutramine and topiramate, have renewed the interest and investment of pharmacological research in eating disorders.

The comprehensive overview by de Zwaan and Roerig highlights the lack of evidence for beneficial effects of the use of antidepressants, typical neuroleptics, zinc or cyproheptadine for anorexia nervosa. Promising results with fluoxetine in preventing relapse among weight-restored patients must be replicated further. In addition, recent case reports of weight gain induced by olanzapine justify the need for more careful

[1] Department of Psychiatry, Federal University of São Paulo, Brazil
[2] Department of Psychiatry, University of Adelaide, Australia

evaluation of the potential benefits and risks of atypical antipsychotics in the treatment of anorexia nervosa.

Antidepressants have been studied extensively for the treatment of bulimia nervosa and BED, mostly in randomized controlled trials (RCTs). Three systematic reviews conducted by our group [1] found that antidepressants reduce bulimic episodes and improve depressive symptoms compared with placebo in the short-term treatment of bulimia nervosa. However, the role of different classes of antidepressants in maintenance treatment warrants further investigation. Although a clinically relevant improvement in bulimic symptoms was seen in patients treated with cognitive–behavioural therapy compared with psychotropic agents, the differences were not significant. Cognitive–behavioural therapy was more acceptable to patients than antidepressants. Remission rates with the use of antidepressants were low (20%). In addition, combined treatment (antidepressants plus psychotherapy) increased the rate of short-term remission (42–49%) but was associated with higher drop-out rates than psychotherapy alone. The efficacy of these single or combined approaches for BED seems to be comparable.

Recently we have seen an emerging interest in two new agents for the treatment of bulimia nervosa and BED: topiramate and sibutramine. The risk of addiction has not encouraged the use of sibutramine—a serotonin and norepinephrine reuptake inhibitor and anti-obesity agent—in bulimia nervosa. However, data from a 12-week RCT conducted by our group in Brazil [2] in 60 obese patients with BED demonstrate a 47% remission rate at endpoint with 15 mg of sibutramine daily compared to 27% with placebo. Sibutramine induced weight loss and was well tolerated.

Topiramate is a novel neuropsychiatric agent that may represent a potential therapeutic advance in multiple episodic or impulse control conditions, including migraine, bipolar disorder, post-traumatic stress disorder, borderline personality disorder, substance abuse and eating disorders—the latter particularly when characterized by binge eating behaviour. This broad spectrum is possibly due to its activity on multiple neurotransmitter systems, including GABA-enhancing and anti-glutamate effects, inhibition of sodium and calcium channels and carbonic anhydrase inhibition. In patients with bulimia nervosa and BED, topiramate may reduce carbohydrate craving and ameliorate impaired satiety, affective instability and impulsive behavioural patterns. Its weight loss properties could be useful for some subgroups of patients who do not want to gain weight or need to lose weight.

A 10-week RCT compared topiramate with placebo in 68 outpatients with bulimia nervosa. Twenty-five per cent of patients were binge-free at endpoint vs. 12% for placebo. Both binge and purge frequency decreased by 50% with topiramate, compared to 29% and 22% with placebo. Treatment with topiramate was well tolerated and only one subject withdrew from the study due to adverse events. The median dose of topiramate was 100 mg/day [3].

In a 14-week RCT assessing the use of topiramate or placebo for 61 patients with BED associated with obesity, a greater than 90% reduction in both binge frequency and binge days was observed with topiramate. This was associated with a 6 kg weight loss and good tolerability. Six patients on topiramate discontinued the study due to adverse events: three due to headache and two due to paraesthesias. The median dose at the last visit was 213 mg/day [4].

These results, along with the burden of disease and the high rates of comorbid psychiatric illness and personality disorders found among patients with eating disorders, indicate that a multidimensional approach, including psychotherapy, psychotropics, nutritional counselling, treatment of medical complications and family therapy, should always be considered when initiating treatment.

Antidepressants, and particularly topiramate, may have a binge/purge controlling effect in patients presenting bulimia nervosa, BED, the binge/purge type of anorexia nervosa or an eating disorder not otherwise specified. However, a favourable effect on the cognitive and affective dimensions of eating disorders still needs to be shown.

Future studies should try to overcome the methodological limitations of the existing literature and examine a more representative cohort of individuals with eating disorders commonly seen in clinical settings. In order to increase sample sizes and reduce bias, collaborative multicentre, transnational RCTs are warranted.

REFERENCES

1. Bacaltchuk J., Hay P., Trefíglio R.P. (2001) Antidepressants versus psychological treatments and their combination for bulimia nervosa. *Cochrane Database Syst. Rev.*, 2001; CD 003385.
2. Appolinario J.C., Bacaltchuk J., Claudino A., Morgan C., Zanella M.T., Sichieri R., Godoy-Matos A., Coutinho W. A two-center double blind randomized placebo-controlled study of sibutramine for obese patients with binge eating disorder (submitted for publication).
3. Reimherr F.W., Hoopes S.P., Karvois D., Rosenthal N.R., Karim R., Kamin M. (2002) Topiramate in the treatment of bulimia nervosa: additional efficacy. Presented at the Annual American Psychiatric Association Meeting, Philadelphia, 18–23 May.
4. McElroy S.L., Arnold L.M., Shapira N.A., Keck P.E., Rosenthal N.R., Karim R., Kamin M., Hudson J.I. (2002) Topiramate in the treatment of binge eating disorder associated with obesity: a randomized placebo-controlled trial. Presented at the Annual American Psychiatric Association Meeting, Philadelphia, 18–23 May.

4.8
Is Psychopharmacological Treatment of Patients with Eating Disorders Necessary?

Cecilia Bergh[1]

Patients with eating disorders, particularly those with anorexia nervosa, are considered difficult to treat. Few, if any, interventions have proved effective in randomized controlled trials (RCT) [1]. By contrast, many RCTs have shown that cognitive–behavioural therapy (CBT) is effective in bulimia nervosa. However, only 50% of the patients respond to CBT. Addition of psychoactive drugs may be helpful but, as is made clear in de Zwaan and Roerig's in-depth review, in comparison with CBT, their effects are minor. The most thoroughly studied drugs are the selective serotonin reuptake inhibitors (SSRIs), but their effects are also small. In anorexia, there is in fact no demonstration that an SSRI is helpful. This is not surprising, because SSRIs are indirect serotonergic agonists, and serotonin suppresses food intake, which is why serotonin agonists are used to treat obesity. Also, many anorexic patients are peripubertal and, because serotonin is inhibitory both to pituitary gonadotropin secretion and sexual behaviour, SSRIs might delay sexual maturation. Furthermore, as Figure 4.8.1 shows, symptoms of depression, anxiety and obsession among anorexic patients admitted to our clinic do not differ between those who are treated with SSRIs and those who are not.

Many clinicians think of anorexia nervosa as a chronic disorder with frequent periods of relapse after weight restoration. Relapse prevention is therefore a main issue. In an often cited RCT, SSRIs were found to reduce the rate of relapse in anorexics in remission [2]. However, in that study the high and rapid rate of relapse among placebo-treated controls—16/19 (84%) relapsed in 4 months—was more conspicuous than the reduction in relapse among the SSRI-treated patients: 6/16 (37%) relapsed in 8 months, which is in fact also a high rate. This dramatic rate of relapse raises the issue of how the body weight of the patients was restored. Most weight-restored anorexic patients described in the literature display a variety of psychiatric symptoms. They may not fulfil the diagnostic criteria of an eating disorder, but they can only be considered to be in remission if these psychopathological symptoms are thought of as independent of their eating disorder. The presence of an altered neurochemical parameter in such patients, as well as bulimics in remission, is often considered a risk factor for the eating disorder (e.g. [3]) but, obviously, is more likely concomitant to their psychiatric comorbidity.

---

[1] Karolinska Institutet, Center for Eating Disorders, Novum, S-141 57 Huddinge, Sweden

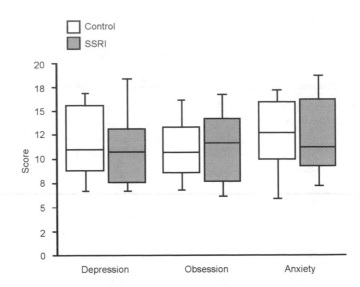

Figure 4.8.1 Score (medians, box plots and outliers) on the Comprehensive Psychopathological Rating Scale in 22 anorexic patients treated with 20–60 mg/day fluoxetine (SSRI) and in 28 anorexic patients not given fluoxetine (Control) at the time of admission

The evidence for the usefulness of SSRIs and most other psychoactive drugs in patients with eating disorders is therefore weak. However, knowledge in the neurobiology of eating behaviour and body weight control is rapidly expanding, and pharmacological manipulation of signalling molecules from peripheral fat stores (e.g. leptin) soon might offer new treatment strategies [4]. While we await the outcome of this research, we withdraw all psychoactive drugs when treating our patients. Instead, we implement non-invasive methods targeting what we believe are the main symptoms in anorexia and bulimia. Thus, patients are trained to eat using computer support, their physical activity is restricted, they rest in warm rooms after eating and they participate in a programme of social restoration. Supply of external heat has a rapid anti-anxiolytic effect and most psychiatric problems yield as the eating behaviour is normalized and the body weight is restored in anorexics, and as the eating behaviour is normalized and bingeing and purging are eliminated in bulimics. A recent RCT testifies to the effectiveness of this strategy, not only in bringing the patients into remission but also in minimizing relapse [5]. The development of new tools, including psychopharmacological tools, that may further improve this treatment is awaited with great interest.

REFERENCES

1. Ben-Tovim D.I., Walker K., Gilchrist P., Freeman R., Kalucy R., Esterman A. (2001) Outcome in patients with eating disorders: a 5-year study. *Lancet*, **357**: 1254–1257.
2. Kaye W.H., Nagata T., Weltzin T.E., Hsu L.K., Sokol M.S., McConaha C., Plotnicov K.H., Weise J., Deep D. (2001) Double-blind placebo-controlled administration of fluoxetine in restricting- and restricting-purging-type anorexia nervosa. *Biol. Psychiatry*, **49**: 644–652.
3. Kaye W.H., Frank G.K., Meltzer C.C., Price J.C., McConaha C.W., Crossan P.J., Klump K.L., Rhodes L. (2001) Altered serotonin 2A receptor activity in women who have recovered from bulimia nervosa. *Am. J. Psychiatry*, **158**: 1152–1155.
4. Adan R.A., Vink T. (2001) Drug target discovery by pharmacogenetics: mutations in the melanocortin system and eating disorders. *Eur. Neuropsychopharmacol.*, **11**: 483–490.
5. Bergh C., Brodin U., Lindberg G., Södersten P. (2003) Randomized controlled trial of a new treatment for anorexia and bulimia nervosa. *Proc. Natl. Acad. Sci. USA* (in press).

4.9
Evidence vs. Experience in Eating Disorders
Robert H. Belmaker[1]

The title of this series is "Evidence and Experience in Psychiatry" and indeed medicine is an empirical field that some have said is an art. Psychiatry in recent years has increasingly emphasized, and rightly so, its scientific aspects, and evidence-based medicine is clearly a philosophy that is more and more important and applicable in psychiatry. However, in all areas of medicine we know that individual clinical patients generate the ideas that later form the hypotheses for controlled trials. Without clinical experience, without chance observations and without an individual making a guess (perhaps basic science based, but a guess nonetheless) there would be no development of clinical science and evidence-based medicine. Moreover, we know that controlled clinical trials give us the results in the mean, i.e. we may decide that selective serotonin reuptake inhibitors (SSRIs) are significantly better than placebo for bulimia nervosa. However, the variance within the clinical population is clearly tremendous. Some patients have a nearly miraculous full therapeutic response and some patients show no benefits whatsoever. Would an evidence-based clinician continue the SSRI treatment of a patient who did not seem to respond? When would he/she be justified in stopping the "best evidence-based treatment"?

[1] *Department of Psychiatry, Ben Gurion University of the Negev, PO Box 4600, Beersheva, Israel*

Controlled clinical trials can give us some information about predictors of good response, but these predictors are often confounded by the placebo response that is included within the drug response, i.e. a predictor of good response might not necessarily be a differential predictor of response to drug only. In the field of anorexia nervosa, bulimia nervosa and binge eating disorder, the role of experience is perhaps more important than in almost any other area of psychiatry. These illnesses are so variable and so polymorphic over time that clinical intuition is critical to optimal use in the practice of the available treatments. The clinician is often dealing with young people, even teenagers, whose eating disorders have become an important battleground in their struggle for independence and identity. A physician who achieves a therapeutic alliance is in a much better position to achieve compliance than the physician who finds him/herself in despair with these admittedly very frustrating patients.

The efficacy of SSRIs in bulimia nervosa compared with their lack of efficacy in anorexia nervosa is one of the most puzzling aspects in this field, given the overlap in symptomatology and patient groups. One wonders what the data are telling us and whether we are missing a key combination that could unlock the pharmacology of this field. Although leptin and its derivative treatments have been disappointing so far, they have clearly not been studied adequately and small negative studies run a great risk of type 2 error. The study of cannabinoids in eating disorders has been greatly held back by the stigma of abuse surrounding these drugs. The danger to life and health involved in eating disorders, especially anorexia nervosa, certainly justifies strong pressure from the psychiatric profession to continue and expand the study of cannabinoids as treatments.

4.10
Pharmacotherapy for Eating Disorders: Beyond Serotonin?
Christopher Paul Szabo[1]

Eating disorders are among the most prevalent and lethal of all psychiatric conditions. Although interventions are predominantly of a psychosocial nature, the outcomes following such treatments are less than optimal. It is thus understandable that the search for effective pharmacological interventions has been ongoing for decades. The extensive review of the literature on pharmacological interventions in the treatment of eating disorders by de Zwaan and Roerig attests to this.

[1] Department of Psychiatry, University of the Witwatersrand, Johannesburg, South Africa

In spite of some 20 years of endeavour, data are somewhat inconsistent and, on the whole, quite disappointing. If one conceptualizes intervention strategies hierarchically, pharmacological interventions are generally second line. In fact the use of medication is more likely aimed at physical morbidity than psychopathology, or at associated dimensions of psycho-pathology (e.g. mood, anxiety or behaviour) rather than core features of the eating disorder. In recent times, however, there has been a shift in this regard with respect to anorexia nervosa, bulimia nervosa and the more recently described binge eating disorder (BED). Specifically, it has been found that the serotonin reuptake inhibitor class of drugs may be helpful in maintaining improvement in weight-restored anorexics [1], in reducing the frequency of bingeing and purging in bulimia nervosa [2], as well as in reducing the frequency of binge episodes among BED sufferers [3].

With regard to sufferers of anorexia nervosa, the finding by Kaye et al. [1] is challenged to some degree by those of Strober et al. [4] that fluoxetine add-on therapy to weight-restored anorexics did not confer a superior outcome with respect to a comparison group not receiving fluoxetine over a 24-month period. It has been suggested that serotonergic agents are not effective in underweight anorexics, potentially as a consequence of the starvation state resulting in decreased availability of substrate for the production of serotonin, thus neutralizing the primary action of the drug [5].

Concerning bulimia nervosa, it is interesting to note that desipramine, a noradrenergic agent, appears to be an effective anti-bulimic agent [6,7]. More recently, Walsh et al. [8] found that the addition of either fluoxetine or desipramine to a cognitive–behavioural therapeutic approach conferred improved outcome vs. placebo or medication alone. Hence, despite understandable pessimism regarding the role for pharmacological inter-ventions in the treatment of eating disorders, it appears that methodological refinement is highlighting the patient groups most likely to benefit from such intervention (in anorexia nervosa) and the treatment approaches (i.e. combination) most likely to yield improved outcome (in bulimia nervosa). At this stage, research into the role of pharmacotherapy in the treatment of BED is limited, but early indications are that such approaches, using specific agents, are worthwhile.

Most of the treatment studies have utilized "antidepressant" medica-tions. It appears that the role of alternative agents, e.g. "antipsychotics" or "antiepileptics", has not been researched rigorously, and the data at hand are of questionable utility in terms of informing clinical practice. A concern raised by the research and treatment studies is the apparent preoccupation with serotonin as the target neurotransmitter, which, although not without some merit, renders efforts somewhat unidimensional. Recent research has challenged the notion that serotonergic dysregulation is linked to core features of eating disorders [9]. This contention is supported by earlier work [10,11]. It seems that what we know, at this level, speaks more about the biology of disordered eating than the biology of eating disorders, and that aberrations are a function of state rather than trait changes. The implications are significant insofar as these research findings are suggesting the need for a critical review of current knowledge and a search for new directions concerning the biology of eating disorders. This may yield an improved understanding and further optimize the pharmacological interventions.

REFERENCES

1. Kaye W.H., Nagata T., Weltzin T.E., Hsu L.K., Sokol M.S., McConaha C., Plotnicov K.H., Weise J., Deep D. (2001) Double-blind placebo-controlled administration of fluoxetine in restricting- and purging-type anorexia nervosa. *Biol. Psychiatry*, **49**: 644–652

2. Goldstein D.J., Wilson M.G., Thompson V.L., Potvin J.H., Rampey A.H., The Fluoxetine Bulimia Nervosa Research Group (1995) Long-term fluoxetine treatment of bulimia nervosa. *Br. J. Psychiatry*, **166**: 660–666.

3. Hudson J.I., McElroy S.L., Raymond N.C., Crow S., Keck P.E., Carter W.P., Mitchell J.E., Strakowski S.M., Pope H.G., Coleman B., *et al.* (1998) Fluvoxamine in the treatment of binge-eating disorder. *Am. J. Psychiatry*, **155**: 1756–1762.

4. Strober M., Freeman R., DeAntonio M., Lampert C., Diamond J. (1997) Does adjunctive fluoxetine influence the post-hospital course of restrictor-type anorexia nervosa? A 24-month prospective, longitudinal followup and comparison with historical controls. *Psychopharmacol. Bull.*, **33**: 425–431.

5. Ferguson C.P., La Via M.C., Crossan P.J., Kaye W.H. (1999) Are selective serotonin reuptake inhibitors effective in underweight anorexia nervosa? *Int. J. Eat. Disord.*, **25**: 11–17.

6. Hughes P.L., Wells L.A., Cunningham C.J., Ilstrup D.M. (1986) Treating bulimia with desipramine: a double-blind placebo-controlled study. *Arch. Gen. Psychiatry*, **43**: 182–186.

7. Barlow J., Blouin J., Blouin A., Perez E. (1988) Treatment of bulimia with desipramine: a double-blind, crossover study. *Can. J. Psychiatry*, **33**: 129–133.

8. Walsh T.B., Wilson T.G., Loeb K.L., Devlin M.J., Pike K.M., Roose S.P., Fleiss J., Waternaux C. (1997) Medication and psychotherapy in the treatment of bulimia nervosa. *Am. J. Psychiatry*, **154**: 523–531.

9. Monteleone P., Brambilla F., Bortolotti F., La Rocca A., Maj M. (2000) Serotonergic dysfunction across the eating disorders: relationship to eating behaviour, nutritional status and general psychopathology. *Psychol. Med.*, **30**: 1099–1110.

10. O'Dwyer A.-M., Lucey J.V., Russel G.F.M. (1996) Serotonin activity in anorexia nervosa after long-term weight restoration: response to D-fenfluramine challenge. *Psychol. Med.*, **26**: 353–359.

11. Monteleone P., Brambilla F., Bortolotti F., La Rocca A., Maj M. (1998) Prolactin response to d-fenfluramine is blunted in people with anorexia nervosa. *Br. J. Psychiatry*, **172**: 438–442.

4.11
New Trends in the Pharmacotherapy of Binge Eating Disorder

José Carlos Appolinario[1]

The pharmacological treatment of eating disorders has changed in the last decades. There has been substantial research on the pharmacotherapy of anorexia nervosa, bulimia nervosa and the newly emerging category of binge eating disorder (BED). I would like to comment on recent reports and some unpublished data about the use of an anti-obesity agent (sibutramine) and an anticonvulsant (topiramate) in BED.

The rationales for the use of anti-obesity agents in BED are: a) binge eating may be characterized by increased appetite and reduced satiety; b) BED is associated with overweight and obesity; c) binge eating behaviour is associated with depression; d) some anti-obesity agents reduce appetite, increase satiety, induce weight loss and may reduce depressive symptoms. The first report of the use of anti-obesity agents to treat BED was a positive placebo-controlled trial of d-fenfluramine (now withdrawn from the market) [1]. The results of an open study [2] suggested that sibutramine may be an effective and safe treatment for obese binge eaters. In this study 10 obese patients with BED were evaluated. Treatment with 15 mg/day sibutramine was administered for 12 weeks. Seven patients completed the trial. They showed a complete remission of BED at the end of the study. The mean number of days with binge episodes per week changed significantly from 5.2 at baseline to 0.8 at the end of the study ($P < 0.01$). The Beck Depression Inventory mean score showed a reduction from 25.7 to 14.9. There was a reduction in body weight (mean = 4.0 kg or 8.9 lb) from baseline to the final visit. The most common adverse reactions reported during the study (dry mouth, nausea and constipation) were benign in nature and lasted for only a few weeks. Several possible mechanisms of binge eating reduction related to sibutramine can be proposed. It may be a direct central effect on eating behaviour or the result of an antidepressant action. Because patients experienced body weight reduction without any nutritional counselling, direct or indirect effects of the drug on energy expenditure could not be excluded. Based on this preliminary evidence, our group has just concluded a double-blind randomized controlled trial of sibutramine in obese patients with BED, which is currently under statistical analysis to be published in the near future.

In a recently published open-label trial with topiramate [3], 8 female obese binge eaters with no neuropsychiatric comorbidity were studied. To

[1] *Obesity and Eating Disorders Group, Institute of Psychiatry, Federal University, and State Institute of Diabetes and Endocrinology, Rio de Janeiro, Brazil*

reduce the central nervous system side effects, the dosage of topiramate was gradually increased: 25 mg b.i.d. for 2 weeks followed by an increase of 25 mg every week up to the target dose of 150 mg/day (75 mg b.i.d). Six patients concluded the trial. Four out of six patients displayed a total remission of the binge eating episodes and the remaining two presented a marked reduction in binge frequency. The most common adverse events (paraesthesias, fatigue and somnolence) were transient and disappeared after the final dose was achieved. More recently, in a double-blind placebo-controlled trial, McElroy et al. [4] confirmed such preliminary findings. In this study, 61 obese patients with BED were treated for 16 weeks. Topiramate was associated with a significantly greater reduction, in relation to placebo, of the number of binge days per week, of eating-related psychopathological symptoms and of weight. The mean topiramate dose was 213 mg/day. The agent was well tolerated. Although topiramate's mechanism of action in BED remains unknown, we can speculate that the observed binge eating reduction could be related to: a) a direct effect on the eating-disturbed psychopathology; b) an antidepressant action; c) a mood stabilizer effect controlling impulsiveness, thereby reducing the urges to eat; d) the influence of topiramate on weight control.

Pharmacological therapy may be an important part of BED treatment. Selective serotonin reuptake inhibitors have been shown to be effective in patients with BED. Sibutramine and topiramate may represent novel pharmacological options in such patients. These agents may address both the disturbed eating behaviour and associated obesity.

REFERENCES

1. Stunkard A., Berkowitz R., Tanrikut C., Reiss E., Young L. (1996) d-Fenfluramine treatment of binge-eating disorder. Am. J. Psychiatry, 153: 1455–1459.
2. Appolinario J.C., Godoy-Mattos A., Fontenelle L.F., Carraro L., Cabral M., Vieira A., Coutinho W. (2002) An open trial of sibutramine in obese patients with binge eating disorder. J. Clin. Psychiatry, 63: 28–30.
3. Appolinario J.C., Fontenelle L.F., Papelbaum M., Bueno J.R., Coutinho W. (2002) Topiramate use in obese patients with binge eating disorder: an open study. Can. J. Psychiatry, 47: 271–273.
4. McElroy S.L., Arnold L.M., Shapira N.A. (2001) Topiramate in the treatment of binge eating disorder associated with obesity. Presented at the Annual Meeting of the American Psychiatric Association Institute in Psychiatric Services, Orlando, 10–14 October.

Psychological Interventions for Eating Disorders: A Review

G. Terence Wilson

Graduate School of Applied and Professional Psychology, Rutgers University, 152 Frelinghuysen Road, Piscataway, NJ 08854-8085, USA

INTRODUCTION

The two best known eating disorders are anorexia nervosa and bulimia nervosa. In addition, many patients present with atypical eating disorders, classified in DSM-IV [1] as "eating disorder not otherwise specified" (EDNOS). The most prominent of the latter is binge eating disorder (BED). This review summarizes the effects of psychological treatments in these three disorders. The focus is on those treatments that have been evaluated in controlled clinical trials.

BULIMIA NERVOSA

Bulimia nervosa is characterized by the presence of binge eating, namely the uncontrolled consumption of unusually large amounts of food, extreme compensatory attempts to control weight, and dysfunctional concern with the importance of body weight and shape. Individuals with bulimia nervosa diet in a rigid and dysfunctional manner, a pattern that leads to binge eating. Body weight is typically normal or low to normal. Psychiatric comorbidity is common, especially depression, substance abuse and personality disorder.

Cognitive–Behavioural Therapy (CBT)

First formulated by Fairburn [2] in Oxford, manual-based CBT consists of cognitive and behavioural procedures for developing a regular pattern of

Eating Disorders. Edited by Mario Maj, Katherine Halmi, Juan José López-Ibor and Norman Sartorius.
©2003 John Wiley & Sons Ltd: ISBN 0-470-84865-0

eating that includes previously avoided foods, for acquiring more constructive skills to cope with high-risk situations for binge eating and purging, for modifying abnormal attitudes and for preventing relapse at the conclusion of acute treatment [3]. Treatment is time-limited, directive and problem-oriented.

CBT for bulimia nervosa has been evaluated intensively in numerous randomized controlled trials in North America and Europe. The treatment has been shown to be superior consistently to waiting-list control groups, which show no improvement across a range of measures. On average, CBT eliminates binge eating and purging in roughly 50% of all patients. The percentage reduction in binge eating and purging across all patients treated with CBT is typically 80% or more, and CBT has broad effects on both the specific psychopathology of bulimia nervosa and associated psychiatric problems. Dysfunctional dieting is decreased and patients' attitudes about their body shape and weight are improved. In addition, there is usually a reduction in the level of general psychiatric symptoms and an improvement in self-esteem and social functioning. Therapeutic improvement is typically well maintained at 1 year following treatment.

Cognitive–Behavioural Therapy versus Pharmacological Treatment

Beyond CBT, the most intensively researched treatment for bulimia nervosa has been antidepressant medication. Both tricyclics and fluoxetine have been shown to be significantly more effective than pill placebo in the short term [4]. Consequently, antidepressant medication provides a stringent standard of comparison for the effects of CBT.

Studies comparing the relative and combined efficacy of CBT and antidepressant medication have been the subject of meta-analyses and other reviews [4–6]. The results can be summarized as follows: a) CBT is more effective than treatment with a single antidepressant drug and is especially superior to medication in producing complete remission of binge eating and purging; b) CBT appears to be more acceptable to patients and the drop-out rate is typically lower than in pharmacological treatment; c) the combination of CBT with antidepressant medication is significantly more effective than medication alone; d) the combination has not been shown yet to improve reliably on the outcome of CBT alone—a possible problem here is that the statistical power in some of the studies might have been insufficient to demonstrate a combined effect, e.g. although Walsh et al. [7] found no statistically significant effect of the combined CBT plus medication condition, this combination was associated with a higher remission rate for binge eating and vomiting (50%) than placebo plus CBT (24%); e) the combination of CBT and antidepressant medication may be more effective than CBT alone in reducing anxiety and depressive symptoms; f) CBT results in superior long-term maintenance, e.g. Mitchell *et al.* [8] showed poor maintenance of improvement in patients who had received medication, in contrast to those who had received psychological treatment [9]. Fluoxetine has been shown to be significantly more effective than pill placebo in the treatment of non-responders to CBT and interpersonal psychotherapy (IPT) [10].

The relative durability of the effect of CBT must be underscored. The dearth of evidence of the long-term effects is a major limitation of treatment with antidepressant medication. In the only controlled study of its kind to date, Romano *et al.* [11] conducted a 52-week double-blind relapse prevention trial of fluoxetine versus pill placebo after acute response to the drug. Although fluoxetine was superior to pill placebo in delaying time to relapse, patients in both conditions deteriorated over the course of follow-up. Moreover, of the 76 patients assigned to the fluoxetine condition, 63 (83%) dropped out. The corresponding figure for placebo was 92%.

Cognitive–Behavioural Therapy versus Alternative Psychotherapies

CBT has proved superior to other psychological treatments with which it has been compared [5,6]. The exception to this finding is the outcome of two studies comparing CBT with IPT, which was originally developed by Klerman *et al.* as a short-term treatment for depression. The primary focus of IPT is to help patients to identify and modify current interpersonal problems; IPT is non-interpretive and non-directive. As adapted for bulimia nervosa [13], IPT focuses exclusively on interpersonal issues, with little or no attention directed to the modification of binge eating, purging, disturbed eating or overconcern with body shape and weight. Specific eating problems are viewed as a means of understanding the interpersonal context that is assumed to be their cause.

Fairburn *et al.* [14] compared CBT with both IPT and a narrow behavioural treatment that was essentially a stripped down version of CBT. At post-treatment, IPT was as effective as CBT at reducing the frequency of binge eating, but it was clearly inferior with respect to vomiting, dietary restraint and attitudes toward body shape and weight. During the 1-year follow-up, however, patients who received IPT showed continuing improvement to the point where their outcome was comparable to that of those who received CBT. Forty-four per cent of IPT patients were no longer binge eating or purging and IPT was as effective as CBT on all measures by the 8- and 12-month follow-ups. Both CBT and IPT fared significantly better than the comparison behaviour therapy condition over the course of follow-up, resulting in a 95% reduction in binge eating and a 91% reduction in vomiting [15]. The patients were followed up once more after an average of almost 6 years. Those patients who had received CBT or IPT were doing equally well, with 63% and 72%, respectively, having no DSM-IV eating disorder compared with 14% among those who had received behaviour therapy [16].

The results of this study by Fairburn *et al.* in Oxford suggested that there is an alternative evidence-based psychological treatment to CBT. Agras *et al.* [17] conducted a multisite study comparing exactly the same CBT with IPT with a large sample size of 110 patients in each treatment. The findings largely replicated the previous Oxford study by Fairburn *et al.* At post-treatment, CBT was significantly superior to IPT in the number of patients who had ceased all binge eating and purging over the preceding 4 weeks. The proportions were 29% vs. 6% in the intent-to-treat analysis and 45% vs. 8% in the analysis of only those patients who completed treatment. Cognitive–behavioural therapy was also significantly superior in reducing dietary restraint, but not in modifying another core clinical feature of bulimia nervosa, namely dysfunctional concerns with body shape and weight. Nor were there any differences between the two treatments on measures of associated psychopathology, such as depression, self-esteem or interpersonal functioning.

The follow-up findings showed a different picture. At 4- and 8–12-month follow-ups there were no statistically significant differences between the two therapies in terms of remission from binge eating and purging over the preceding 4 weeks using intent-to-treat analyses. Fairburn [18] reported that a completer analysis of the follow-up data revealed a trend ($P = 0.55$) for CBT to be more effective than IPT. The post-treatment course of patients in the two treatments was not dissimilar. For example, 66% of those who had recovered with CBT at the end of treatment remained recovered at follow-up, compared with 57% (4/7) of those treated with IPT. For those remitted at the end of CBT, 29% (6/21) recovered, compared with 33% (8/24) for the IPT group. Of the remaining participants, 7% (4/57) had recovered at follow-up in the CBT group, compared with 9% (7/79) in the IPT group. The percentages in each category at the end of treatment were similar for both treatments. These findings suggest that the absence of a statistically significant difference between CBT and IPT over follow-up may be more a function of their differential post-treatment status (a regression towards the mean effect) than any delayed "catch-up" property of IPT.

Two additional findings of this study should be emphasized. First, CBT was quick-acting, achieving much of its ultimate therapeutic effect within the first 6 weeks of treatment. The same finding has been reported in other studies of CBT for bulimia nervosa [19,20]. Second, consistent with the underlying theoretical model, the effects of CBT were partially mediated by treatment-induced changes in dietary restraint [21].

The Agras *et al.* study [17] is the largest comparative outcome study of bulimia nervosa to date. Administration of the two therapies was monitored carefully on a weekly basis throughout the study by two experienced supervisors at each of the two sites in the USA. Moreover, each treatment was monitored independently and continually by the investigator (Fairburn) who had originally developed each protocol and conducted the earlier study at Oxford. However, a limitation of the study was the absence of a third comparison treatment to control for factors such as the passage of time and non-specific therapeutic influences. Given the absence of statistically significant differences at follow-up, conclusions about specific long-term effects cannot be drawn. Lacking this control for non-specific therapeutic influences, it is impossible to conclude definitively that IPT has any specific therapeutic effects. However, the results of the previous controlled study indicate that both IPT and CBT were significantly superior to an exclusively behavioural form of CBT that was equivalent in therapist contact and ratings of suitability and expectancy, suggesting that IPT may have a specific mode of action in the treatment of bulimia nervosa.

Guided Self-help

The principles and techniques of CBT can be implemented in the form of guided self-help (GSH), which is a briefer, less costly and more disseminable form of treatment than the specialized and professionally administered CBT summarized above [22]. In Australia, Banasiak *et al.* [23] compared GSH with a delayed treatment control group in the treatment of patients with bulimia nervosa in a primary care setting. Guided self-help was significantly more effective than the delayed treatment, producing clinically significant improvement that was maintained at a 6-month follow-up. Earlier studies, using a more eclectic self-help manual, also suggested that GSH is effective at least for a subset of bulimia nervosa patients [24,25].

Predictors of Change

Reliable predictors of response to CBT—or alternative pharmacological and psychological treatments—have not been identified. A range of pretreatment patient characteristics have been proposed as predictor variables, including past history of anorexia nervosa or previous low body weight, low self-esteem, comorbid personality disorders and severity of core eating disorder symptoms. Possibly the most consistent finding has been that borderline personality disorder predicts a poorer outcome [26] but in general the results across studies have been inconsistent and of little practical clinical value [19]. Another promising finding has been reported by Stice and Agras [27]: using cluster analysis, they were able to subtype patients with bulimia nervosa along the dimensions of dietary restraint and negative affect. The high restraint/high negative affect group responded significantly less well to CBT than did the high restraint/low negative affect subgroup. Grilo et al. [28] also have identified the same subgroups of bulimia nervosa patients.

Instead of concentrating the search for predictors on pretreatment patient characteristics, the pragmatic approach of identifying rapid responders to treatment might prove more useful. Recent research has shown that much of the overall improvement achieved with CBT is evident after the first few weeks of treatment [20,21]. Using a signal detection analysis, Agras et al. [19] showed that reduction in purging at session 6 provided a better prediction of outcome than any pretreatment variable. Adopting this criterion, 70% of patients were triaged and treated correctly. Only 6% of patients who would have recovered with CBT would have been triaged incorrectly to a second treatment.

Few studies have examined post-treatment predictors of longer term outcome. Fairburn et al. [3] found that among patients who had recovered in terms of behavioural change, 9% of those with the least dysfunctional concern with body shape and weight disturbance relapsed, compared with 29% and 75% among those with moderate and severe degrees of concern about body shape and weight. In a study of 143 patients with bulimia nervosa who had received group CBT treatment, Mussell et al. [29] found that symptom remission (total absence of binge eating and purging) during the final 2 weeks of treatment was the best predictor of outcome at a 6-month follow-up. Most recently, Halmi et al. [30] found that, among patients treated with CBT who were in remission at post-treatment, those who relapsed reported a higher level of preoccupation with eating, a lower motivation for change and had maintained remission from binge eating and purging for a shorter period of time during treatment. The latter finding may be especially important. The goal of acute treatment should be to achieve full remission from symptoms; partial responders are at greater risk for relapse. A similar pattern of findings emerges in the treatment of major depression with CBT [31].

Conclusions

Manual-based CBT is well-tolerated and reliably produces broad, clinically significant change in both the specific and associated psychopathology of bulimia nervosa. Therapy-induced improvement has been well maintained at follow-up in most (e.g. [16]) but not all (e.g. [30]) studies.

A distinctive feature of CBT is that it has a rapid onset of action, resulting in significant improvement within the first 2 months of treatment. The success of CBT is, at least in part, attributable to the reduction of dysfunctional dieting.

Despite its strong evidence-based foundation, CBT is used relatively infrequently by clinical practitioners [32]. More effective dissemination of CBT among mental health providers is a priority. Preliminary evidence indicates that GSH, based on cognitive–behavioural principles, can be effective in treating bulimia nervosa in a primary care setting [23].

CBT currently results in only partial improvement or no therapeutic effect at all for a significant minority of patients. Innovative treatment strategies are needed to help these treatment-resistant patients. Clinical research is currently focused on developing an expanded and enhanced CBT approach for bulimia nervosa and related problems (e.g. [33]).

Clinical Recommendations

Manual-based CBT is the treatment of choice for bulimia nervosa. Combining CBT with a selective serotonin reuptake inhibitor is indicated in cases of severe comorbid depression.

IPT should be considered as an alternative approach if available resources do not include practitioners trained in manual-based CBT. At present there is no evidence from clinical trials that psychodynamic therapy is effective.

Therapists should closely monitor patients' early response to CBT. If there is no indication of response (significant reduction in frequency of binge eating or purging) to properly administered CBT by 10 sessions, then alternative approaches should be considered. When CBT fails, the use of fluoxetine is indicated.

ANOREXIA NERVOSA

Anorexia nervosa is characterized by severe restriction of food intake and refusal to maintain body weight at a normal level. Patients with anorexia nervosa are preoccupied with thoughts about food, eating, shape and weight; they engage in ritualistic eating habits, and have an intense fear of becoming fat despite being seriously underweight. A subset of patients with anorexia nervosa engage in periodic binge eating and self-induced vomiting. Common associated psychopathology includes depressive and anxiety symptoms, obsessional features, perfectionism and social withdrawal. A salient clinical characteristic of anorexia nervosa is that the disorder is ego-syntonic.

In marked contrast to bulimia nervosa, few controlled treatment trials exist despite the seriousness of the disorder. Moreover, the studies that have been completed are limited by small sample sizes and less rigorous methodology than is the case with bulimia nervosa. Reasons for the dearth of treatment outcome research include: the low incidence of the disorder, which makes complicated multisite studies a necessity; difficulties in recruiting patients who do not view themselves as having a significant problem; the severity of the disorder and high drop-out rate from outpatient therapy; and hence the length of treatment that is required.

Cognitive–Behavioural Therapy

Originally, behaviour therapy for anorexia nervosa consisted of application of the principles of operant conditioning to restore weight during inpatient treatment [34]. These limited interventions were effective in increasing weight during inpatient stays, but subsequent research showed that patients lost weight and relapsed when they were discharged.

In the 1980s, Garner and Bemis [35] described the use of cognitive therapy for anorexia nervosa, a treatment derived from Beck et al.'s [36] cognitive therapy for depression. The primary target of this treatment is the modification of patients' negative thinking and dysfunctional assumptions regarding eating and body shape and weight. Current applications of CBT in the treatment of anorexia nervosa have been strongly influenced by this cognitive approach [37].

Two studies have compared CBT with nutritional counselling. In the first, Serfaty et al. [38] randomly assigned patients with anorexia nervosa either to 20 sessions of individual CBT ($n = 25$) or dietary counselling, a treatment consisting of nutritional advice and supportive therapy ($n = 10$). Two patients dropped out of CBT compared with all 10 of those allocated to dietary counselling. Based on an intent-to-treat analysis, 70% of patients treated with CBT no longer met the diagnostic criteria for anorexia nervosa at 6 months, although they remained significantly underweight on average.

Pike et al. [39] completed a study of relapse prevention in patients with anorexia nervosa who had been treated in an inpatient setting. All had achieved at least 90% of expected body weight for a minimum of 2 weeks and their calories were derived mainly from food rather than liquid supplements prior to discharge. The 33 patients were assigned randomly to 50 sessions of either individual CBT or nutritional counselling over a 12-month period. The relapse rate among individuals receiving CBT was lower than for those receiving nutritional counselling (22% vs. 53%) and a Kaplan Meier survival analysis revealed a significant difference in the time to relapse. The nutritional counselling group relapsed earlier in treatment than the CBT group ($P < 0.005$). The overall treatment failure rate (relapse and drop-out combined) was significantly greater for nutritional counselling (73%) compared with CBT (22%). A significantly greater percentage of individuals in the CBT condition met the Morgan–Russell criteria for "good outcome" compared with the nutritional counselling group (44.4% vs. 6.7%; $P < 0.02$).

Treasure *et al.* [40] compared a very basic behavioural outpatient treatment (in which patients monitored their daily food intake, set progressive eating and weight goals and discussed weight and shape issues) with a "cognitive analytical therapy" that "integrates psychodynamic factors with behavioural ones and focuses on interpersonal and transference issues" in adult patients with anorexia nervosa. Both treatments were administered over 20 weekly sessions. Of the 30 patients assigned to treatment, 10 from each condition completed the trial (i.e. a 33% drop-out rate). Both groups of treatment completers gained weight, with 40% and 50%, respectively, reaching 85% average body weight. Given that these results were obtained with a simple form of behaviour therapy, the added value of more elaborate CBT needs to be determined [4].

Family Therapy

Dysfunctional family processes have been implicated in the development and maintenance of anorexia nervosa, and family therapy has been the most studied of psychological treatments for anorexia nervosa [41].

A series of studies from the Maudsley hospital in London have shown that a particular brand of family therapy seems to be effective. Russell *et al.* [42] compared family therapy with individual supportive psychotherapy in 57 patients who had received inpatient therapy. Treatment lasted for 1 year. For those patients with a young age of onset (under 19 years) and short duration of disorder (less than 3 years), family therapy was significantly more effective than individual psychotherapy both at post-treatment and a 5-year follow-up. For patients with an older age of onset or longer duration, the two treatments were comparable. Outcome for these patients was poor.

Subsequent research by the Maudsley group focused on different methods of implementing family therapy. For example, le Grange *et al.* [43] compared what they called conjoint family therapy, in which the whole family was treated together, with family counselling, in which parents were treated separately from their daughter. Both treatments were brief, with an average of nine sessions over a 6-month period. The patients were 18 adolescents whose ages ranged from 12 to 17 years. At a 32-week reassessment, the two groups did not differ in their weight, which was in the normal range. A subsequent study of 40 patients replicated these results [41]. Taken together, these findings suggest that brief therapy separately involving parents and their daughters can be effective, and they challenge long-standing assumptions about the practice of family therapy for anorexia nervosa [41].

The specific nature of this Maudsley model of family therapy is very different from other forms of family therapy that have been described in the clinical literature. Instead of distancing parents from involvement in their daughter's eating problems, this approach requires parents to take full control of refeeding. The therapy provides support for the parents in this task, as well as for the patient in gradually reasserting control over her life [41].

Robin *et al.* [44] compared behavioural family systems therapy (BFST) with ego-oriented individual therapy (EOIT) in recent-onset adolescent girls. Both treatments resulted in significant increases in BMI, but BFST was significantly superior to EOIT both at post-treatment and 1-year follow-up. At post-treatment, 55% of the BFST patients and 46% of the EOIT patients had achieved the target weights set by their paediatricians and had resumed menstruating. At follow-up, the figures were 82% and 50%, respectively, although this difference did not reach statistical significance. Both therapies produced significant reductions in negative communication and parent–daughter conflict within the families. Whether the greater efficacy of the BFST treatment was due to its cognitive–behavioural approach or more generally to an advantage of family therapy over individual treatment cannot be determined from this study.

Two findings from this study have specific relevance for family therapy. One is that the BFST was similar to the Maudsley model, with its focus on helping parents to assume direct responsibility for modifying their daughters' eating. The other is that individual therapy produced significant change in family functioning, thus supporting le Grange *et al.*'s [43] results in demonstrating that conjoint family therapy is not needed to modify interactions between the adolescent anorexic patient and her family.

Inpatient versus Outpatient Treatment

Wide differences exist across services and even countries in the extent to which inpatient treatment is required for treating anorexic patients. Available research offers little guidance in this respect.

A widely cited study by Crisp *et al.* [45] provides one of the few comparisons. Patients were assigned randomly to the following treatments: a) inpatient treatment until normal weight was restored, followed by 12 sessions of individual outpatient therapy, with the average length of hospitalization being 20 weeks; b) 12 sessions of outpatient individual and family psychotherapy; c) 10 sessions of outpatient group psychotherapy for patients and parents; d) no treatment. Patients assigned to the "no treatment" condition were referred back to their local physician. Only six received no treatment of any kind. The others received either outpatient or inpatient treatment elsewhere during the course of the study.

Drop-outs occurred in all treatments, but the rate was greatest in the outpatient group treatment, in which the mean number of sessions attended was only five compared with 8.25 in the individual and family treatment. Among those who completed treatment, the mean weight gains at follow-up 1 year after initial assessment were significantly greater than for the control condition.

As Wilson and Fairburn [4] note, two findings from this study stand out. First, brief outpatient treatment was as effective as much longer, intensive inpatient treatment. Second, all three treatments were associated with a clinically significant amount of weight gain at 1-year follow-up. However, several methodological limitations make it difficult to interpret the results of this study. One is that the two outpatient treatments were administered by different sets of therapists, which confounds therapist with therapy. A second limitation was that assessment of outcome was conducted by a member of the research staff who was not blind to the treatment the patients had received. A 2-year follow-up showed that patients who had received outpatient individual and family therapy had gained significantly more weight and showed greater improvement in social and psychosexual functioning than those in the control condition [46]. The failure to report the status of the other two treatment conditions is unfortunate and clouds the interpretation of the study.

Conclusions

It appears that adolescent patients with an early onset and short duration have the best prognosis. Family therapy enjoys the most empirical support at present in treating adolescent patients.

Compelling issues of cost-effectiveness and dissemination of treatment call for evaluation of the relative merits of inpatient, day patient and outpatient treatment.

Increased research on promising psychological treatments is a priority, especially as there is no evidence of the efficacy of pharmacological therapy [47].

Clinical Recommendations

The lack of necessary research makes it impossible at this time to offer evidence-based recommendations for the treatment of anorexia nervosa. Clinical experience and preliminary research evidence suggest that family therapy can be recommended as the most promising treatment of adolescents with anorexia nervosa. The specific method with the most support involves the parents taking direct responsibility for refeeding their teenage daughter. This approach can be implemented successfully with the entire family or with the parents and patient being treated separately. The recent publication of a manual-based version of this form of family therapy should prove helpful to practitioners [48].

There is some evidence that individual CBT is helpful in preventing relapse in weight-restored patients. Furthermore, specific CBT techniques for modifying dysfunctional overconcern with body shape and weight might be effective as part of a more comprehensive programme [49]. These findings, taken in conjunction with the efficacy of CBT in treating bulimia nervosa, which has many overlapping features with anorexia nervosa, makes CBT a preferred option.

BINGE EATING DISORDER

BED is characterized by recurrent episodes of binge eating in the absence of the extreme methods of weight control seen in bulimia nervosa. There are marked differences between patients with BED vs. those with bulimia nervosa. Individuals with BED neither purge regularly nor engage in excessive exercise. Furthermore, they report significantly less dietary restraint than patients with bulimia nervosa [50,51]. It is now well-established that the binge eating occurs within the context of a general tendency to overeat. Not surprisingly, patients seeking treatment for BED are typically overweight (BMI > 25) or obese (BMI > 30) [52,53]. However, an important similarity between BED and bulimia nervosa is their comparable level of overconcern and preoccupation with body shape and weight [50].

Patients with BED often have significant levels of comorbid Axis I and Axis II disorders, although their severity is often less than in patients with bulimia nervosa [51,54]. The presence of psychiatric comorbidity represents a very reliable difference between obese individuals with BED and obese individuals without BED [55]. The former also have more chaotic eating habits, consume larger amounts of food in and between binge episodes and exhibit higher levels of eating disinhibition (i.e. eating in response to emotional states) [53,54].

Ideally, comprehensive treatment of BED should address not only binge eating and associated eating disorder psychopathology but also comorbid psychiatric disorders (e.g. depression) and obesity.

Specialized psychological treatments for BED directly target binge eating and associated eating disorder psychopathology. Weight loss has typically not been a goal of these treatments.

Cognitive–Behavioural Therapy

This treatment is adapted from manual-based CBT for bulimia nervosa [15]. The emphasis is on developing regular patterns of moderate eating, decreasing rigid (and typically unsuccessful) dietary restriction, developing more adaptive cognitive and behavioural skills for coping with high-risk situations for binge eating, and modifying dysfunctional overconcern with body weight and shape. CBT remains the most extensively researched treatment for BED, and has been shown to be effective in numerous controlled studies.

Cognitive–Behavioural Therapy versus Waiting-list Control

Several studies have shown that CBT is significantly more effective than a waiting-list control condition in reducing binge eating as well as associated eating disorder psychopathology [56]. For example, Agras et al. [57] found that CBT resulted in an 84% reduction in mean frequency of binge eating, with a 55% remission rate. The corresponding figures for a waiting-list control were only 8% and 9%, respectively.

Cognitive–Behavioural Therapy versus Antidepressant Medication

Grilo et al. [58] randomly assigned 108 BED patients to one of four treatment conditions for 16 weeks of individual treatments: a) fluoxetine (60 mg/day); b) placebo; c) fluoxetine (60 mg/day) combined with CBT; d) pill placebo combined with CBT. Administration of the medication was double-blind. Eighty per cent of the patients completed the treatments. At the end of acute treatment, remission rates among completers (defined as zero binges for 28 days) were as follows: 29% (fluoxetine), 30% (placebo), 55% (CBT plus fluoxetine) and 73% (CBT plus placebo). Completer analyses and intent-to-treat analyses of these remission rates, as well as of dimensional measures of binge eating, cognitive (attitudinal) features of eating disorders and associated psychological distress (depression), produced consistent findings. Fluoxetine was not superior to placebo, CBT plus fluoxetine and CBT plus placebo did not differ, and both CBT conditions were superior to fluoxetine and to placebo. As in other studies of CBT, weight loss was minimal overall, but greater among those who had ceased binge eating at post-treatment.

These findings are important on several counts. First, they indicate that CBT does have specific treatment effects. Both the medication and pill placebo conditions control for non-specific influences, including therapist contact and active involvement in the treatment process. Second, CBT proved to be superior to the antidepressant medication that has been shown to be effective in some studies [59].

In a preliminary report of another comparative study, Devlin et al. [60] found that adding CBT, but not fluoxetine, to group behavioural weight loss treatment significantly improved outcome.

Cognitive–Behavioural Therapy versus Alternative Psychological Treatments

In contrast to the Grilo et al. [58] findings with medication, CBT has not been shown to be superior to alternative psychological treatments.

Two well-controlled studies have shown that, although CBT is effective, it is equivalent in efficacy to IPT. In the first, Wilfley et al. [61] compared group CBT with a group adaptation of the IPT treatment originally applied to bulimia nervosa by Fairburn et al. [14] and a waiting-list control condition. At post-treatment, IPT and CBT were significantly more effective than the waiting-list condition, but they did not differ from each other. Nor did the two therapies differ at 1-year follow-up. Patients showed a significant increase in binge eating during follow-up, although the rates remained below pretreatment levels. In the second study, which is the largest controlled study to date, Wilfley et al. [62] compared 20 sessions of group CBT with IPT for overweight and obese BED patients. Using intent-to-treat analyses, post-treatment abstinence rates were 79% for CBT and 73% for IPT. At 12-month follow-up, the abstinence rates were 59% and 62%. Both therapies produced significant reductions in concerns about shape, weight and eating as measured by the Eating Disorder Inventory (EDI), as well as psychiatric symptoms. Both treatments were associated also with a statistically significant but clinically small reduction in BMI. However, patients who ceased binge eating showed significantly more weight loss than those who remained symptomatic. Similarly, Agras et al. [63] reported that patients who had ceased binge eating after 12 weeks of

CBT lost significantly more weight at 1-year follow-up than did non-abstainers.

IPT has also been investigated as a secondary treatment for BED patients who failed to respond to an initial trial of CBT [54], but no incremental improvement was found.

Cognitive–Behavioural Therapy versus Behavioural Weight Loss Treatment

Marcus *et al.* [64] compared CBT with behavioural weight loss (BWL) treatment and a waiting-list control condition in a study in which all treatments were administered individually. The publication of the results of this well-designed study has been limited to a brief abstract, suggesting that at post-treatment both CBT and BWL produced significantly greater reductions in days on which binge eating occurred during the previous month than the waiting-list control. Unlike CBT, BWL also resulted in substantial weight loss. Nauta *et al.* [65] compared a form of cognitive therapy with behavioural treatment in 37 overweight or obese BED patients. The cognitive therapy, administered in 15 weekly group sessions, was a derivative of Beck's [66] treatment in which the primary focus was on identifying and challenging "dysfunctional cognitions about shape, weight, eating, dieting or negative self-schemas". The two treatments produced roughly equivalent improvements in binge eating at post-treatment. A 6-month follow-up, however, revealed that the remission rate in the cognitive therapy group (86%) was significantly higher than in the behavioural treatment group (44%). Cognitive therapy also resulted in greater improvement in dysfunctional concerns about shape, weight, eating and self-esteem than behavioural treatment.

Behavioural Weight Loss Treatment

Behavioural weight control programmes, entailing both moderate and severe calorie reduction, have proved successful in treating binge eating in overweight BED patients [56,67].

As summarized above, both Marcus *et al.* [64] and Nauta *et al.* [65] found that CBT and BWL were comparable in reducing binge eating and associated eating disorder psychopathology. Using an additive experimental design, Agras *et al.* [68] compared a 9-month BWL programme with two alternative treatments: an initial 3-month CBT treatment aimed at reducing binge eating, followed by the BWL programme (CBT/BWL); and a combined CBT and BWL programme, supplemented by the addition of desipramine over the last 6 months of treatment (CBT/BWL/D). There were no significant differences among the three treatments at the end of 9 months on either binge eating frequency or weight loss.

Other studies of BWL aimed primarily at the treatment of obesity have found significant reductions in binge eating (e.g. [69,70]). However, unlike studies of CBT and IPT for BED, assessment of eating disorder psychopathology in these studies of BWL has had limitations. For example, most studies have relied on the Binge Eating Scale [71], which does not assess binge eating frequency and has low convergence with the interview-based EDI [72].

BWL has also resulted in improvements in the measures of depression [69,73]. Finally, BWL produces significant weight loss in obese BED patients, at least in the short term [64,65,68].

Behavioural Weight Loss and Dietary Restraint

It is commonly believed that dietary restriction is contraindicated in the treatment of BED patients, just as it would be unwise in bulimia nervosa [74]. However, there is no evidence that BWL and the moderate dietary restriction that it involves either triggers or exacerbates binge eating in obese patients with BED [75,76]. Even more telling is the finding that severe dietary restriction (a very low calorie diet) reduces binge eating rather than worsening the problem [53,77]. The likely explanation is that BED patients differ from those with bulimia nervosa. In bulimia nervosa, binge eating represents periodic breakdowns in otherwise excessive dietary control. Patients with BED, however, show little dietary restriction between binge eating episodes [53].

Self-help Strategies

As noted above, GSH, based on a cognitive–behavioural approach, is a less costly option than specialized psychotherapy that appears to be effective for at least a subset of patients. Carter and Fairburn [78] compared a pure self-help treatment (PSH), in which BED subjects were mailed a self-help book [79] and advised to follow its recommendations, with one in which they also received up to eight 25-min supportive sessions (GSH). The GSH was conducted by non-specialist therapists with no formal clinical qualifications. Treatment lasted for 12 weeks. Both treatments were compared with a waiting-list control condition. The two interventions produced significant and lasting improvements in binge eating. The remission rates for PSH and GSH were 43% and 50%, respectively, in intent-to-treat analyses. Both were superior to the waiting-list control, but similar to one another in reducing binge eating frequency and general psychopathology over the 12 weeks.

Binge eating results for the full sample across the 9 months of the study, however, were better in GSH.

Locb et al. [80] compared guided and unguided use of the Fairburn [79] self-help manual in a randomized trial with 40 binge eaters, 83% of whom met the diagnostic criteria for BED. Unlike the Carter and Fairburn [78] study, these experimental conditions were designed to mimic the two least intensive interventions in a stepped-care-based speciality treatment setting. The GSH therapists were well-experienced in the treatment of eating disorders. In addition, patients in the unguided self-help (USH) condition maintained regular contact with the clinic by mailing weekly self-monitoring forms. If records revealed major problems or if no records were received, participants were telephoned. Over the 3 months, both the USH and GSH groups experienced significant reductions in binge eating frequency, shape and weight concerns, other symptoms of eating-related psychopathology and general psychopathology. In intent-to-treat analyses, binge eating remission rates were 30% for USH and 50% for GSH. Similar to the results obtained by Carter and Fairburn [78], the GSH condition was superior to USH in reducing binge eating and its associated symptomatology.

Conclusions

Research on the treatment of BED is at an early stage.

Methodological limitations include small sample sizes, failure to use the most comprehensive and valid assessment measures and the absence of long-term follow-up. Nevertheless, the evidence indicates that psychological treatments are effective in reducing binge eating and associated psychopathology in patients with BED but they have not been shown to provide clinically significant weight loss.

BWL has had similar results in producing weight loss in both obese and non-obese patients with BED. As in the treatment of obesity as a whole, the challenge is to develop methods for maintaining weight loss during treatment.

Reliable predictors of treatment outcome have yet to be identified. However, as in bulimia nervosa, Cluster B personality disorders appear to be a negative prognostic factor [51].

Treatment outcome of BED differs from that of bulimia nervosa in at least two important respects. First, remission rates appear to be significantly better. Second, in contrast to bulimia nervosa, CBT and IPT produce equivalent effects in BED. The latter appears to be part of a more general lack of specificity among treatments [81], including fewer differences between antidepressant medications and placebo [58] and a high placebo response rate [67].

Clinical Recommendations

Given current research, the first choice for treatment in BED would be BWL, for the following reasons: a) it seems to be as effective as specialized psychotherapies in reducing binge eating and other eating disorder psychopathology; b) it results in weight loss, at least in the short term; c) it does not require the professional expertise demanded by specialized psychotherapies and hence can be administered by a wider range of different healthcare professionals.

GSH, using a cognitive–behavioural self-help programme, is a less costly and more efficient treatment than CBT or IPT that can be recommended for initial treatment within a stepped-care framework. Patients who fail to respond to BWL or GSH should be considered for more intensive treatment with either CBT or IPT. There is little basis for choosing between CBT and IPT. The latter might make more sense for patients who are unwilling to monitor their eating or for whom interpersonal difficulties play a significant role in the maintenance of their disorder.

SUMMARY

Consistent Evidence

- Bulimia nervosa: Manual-based CBT for bulimia nervosa has been shown consistently to be effective in well-controlled studies by different groups of investigators in different countries. Stunkard [82] cited this reliable finding as one of the major accomplishments in the field of eating disorders over the preceding 25 years. IPT has received far less intensive evaluation than CBT but has shown positive effects.
- BED: CBT has been shown to be consistently effective in treating BED. Unlike the treatment of bulimia nervosa, however, CBT does not appear to be superior to alternative treatments. IPT has received far less intensive evaluation than CBT but has shown positive effects.
- Anorexia nervosa: Consistent evidence for the efficacy of any treatment for anorexia nervosa is lacking.

Incomplete Evidence

- Bulimia nervosa: Preliminary findings on the efficacy of GSH require replication and extension. Identifying patients for whom this briefer, less intensive treatment is effective is a priority.

- BED: An immediate need is research on the long-term effects of the different psychological therapies that have proved effective in the short term. This is especially relevant to BWL, which appears to be as effective as specialized CBT in the short term. The potential effects of the predictable regain in body weight over the long term on eating disorder psychopathology and associated psychiatric problems are of theoretical as well as practical importance. More systematic evaluation of treatment effects, comparable to the methodological rigour of studies on bulimia nervosa, is also necessary.
- Anorexia nervosa: Family therapy (the "Maudsley model") has shown promising results in the treatment of anorexia nervosa in adolescent patients. It remains to compare this form of family therapy with alternative treatments that control for non-specific treatment influences.

Areas Still Open To Research

- Bulimia nervosa: Manual-based CBT is effective but not effective enough. A significant number of patients are not helped by this approach. Innovative and more powerful treatment strategies, based on a broader understanding of cognitive–behavioural principles of psychological change, are needed.
- BED: Psychological treatments have produced consistent short-term improvements in binge eating, associated eating disorder psycho-pathology and general psychiatric comorbidity. The challenge is to develop methods for producing sustained weight loss in obese patients with BED.
- Anorexia nervosa: The most glaring gap in treatment research on eating disorders is the absence of controlled studies on anorexia nervosa. The reasons for this unsatisfactory situation are identified earlier in this review. On the more positive side, several controlled studies are ongoing and the results can be expected within the near future. Some of the research in progress is designed to evaluate different forms of manual-based CBT. The focus on CBT makes sense. The similarities between bulimia nervosa and anorexia nervosa have been well-documented. The psychopathological mechanisms that maintain anorexia nervosa are likely to be similar to those that fuel bulimia nervosa [33]. CBT is effective in treating bulimia nervosa and hence, on both theoretical and clinical grounds, it can be argued that it might be well-suited to the treatment of anorexia nervosa [83].

REFERENCES

1. American Psychiatric Association (1994) *Diagnostic and Statistical Manual of Mental Disorders*. American Psychiatric Association, Washington.
2. Fairburn C.G. (1981) A cognitive behavioral approach to the management of bulimia. *Psychol. Med.*, **11**: 707–711.
3. Fairburn C.G., Peveler R.C., Jones R., Hope R.A., Doll H.A. (1993) Predictors of twelve-month outcome in bulimia nervosa and the influence of attitudes to shape and weight. *J. Consult. Clin. Psychol.*, **61**: 696–698.
4. Wilson G.T., Fairburn C.G. (2002) Eating disorders. In *Treatments that Work*, 2nd ed. (Eds P.E. Nathan, J.M. Gorman), pp. 559–592. Oxford University Press, New York.
5. Hay P.J., Bacaltchuk J. (2000) Psychotherapy for bulimia nervosa and binging (Cochrane Review). In *The Cochrane Library*, Issue 4. Update Software, Oxford.
6. Whittal M.L., Agras W.S., Gould R.A. (1999) Bulimia nervosa: a meta-analysis of psychosocial and pharmacological treatments. *Behav. Ther.*, **30**: 117–135.
7. Walsh B.T., Wilson G.T., Loeb K.L., Devlin M.J., Pike K.M., Roose S.P., Fleiss J., Waternaux C. (1997) Medication and psychotherapy in the treatment of bulimia nervosa. *Am. J. Psychiatry*, **154**: 523–531.
8. Mitchell J.E., Pyle R.L., Eckert E.D., Hatsukami D., Pomeroy C., Zimmerman R. (1990) A comparison study of antidepressants and structured intensive group psychotherapy in the treatment of bulimia nervosa. *Arch. Gen. Psychiatry*, **47**: 149–157.
9. Pyle R.L., Mitchell J.E., Eckert E.D., Hatsukami D.K., Pomeroy C., Zimmerman R. (1990) Maintenance treatment and 6-month outcome for bulimic patients who respond to initial treatment. *Am. J. Psychiatry*, **147**: 871–875.
10. Walsh B.T., Agras W.S., Devlin M.J., Fairburn C.G., Wilson G.T., Kahn C., Chally M.K. (2000) Fluoxetine in bulimia nervosa following poor response to psychotherapy. *Am. J. Psychiatry*, **157**: 1332–1333.
11. Romano S.J., Halmi K.A., Sarkar N.P., Koke S.C., Lee J.S. (2002) A placebo-controlled study of fluoxetine in continued treatment of bulimia nervosa after successful acute fluoxetine treatment. *Am. J. Psychiatry*, **159**: 96–102.
12. Klerman G.L., Weissman M.M., Rounsaville B.J., Chevron E.S. (1984) *Interpersonal Psychotherapy of Depression*. Basic Books, New York.
13. Fairburn C.G. (1997) Interpersonal psychotherapy for bulimia nervosa. In *Handbook of Treatment for Eating Disorders* (Eds D.M. Garner, P.E. Garfinkel), pp. 278–294. Guilford Press, New York.
14. Fairburn C.G., Jones R., Peveler R.C., Carr S.J., Solomon R.A., O'Connor M.E., Burton J., Hope R.A. (1991) Three psychological treatments for bulimia nervosa. *Arch. Gen. Psychiatry*, **48**: 463–469.
15. Fairburn C.G., Marcus M.D., Wilson G.T. (1993) Cognitive behaviour therapy for binge eating and bulimia nervosa: a comprehensive treatment manual. In *Binge Eating: Nature, Assessment and Treatment* (Eds C.G. Fairburn, G.T. Wilson), pp. 361–404. Guilford Press, New York.
16. Fairburn C.G., Norman P.A., Welch S.L., O'Connor M.E., Doll H.A., Peveler R.C. (1995) A prospective study of outcome in bulimia nervosa and the long-term effects of three psychological treatments. *Arch. Gen. Psychiatry*, **52**: 304–312.
17. Agras W.S., Walsh B.T., Fairburn C.G., Wilson G.T., Kraemer H.C. (2000) A multicenter comparison of cognitive–behavioural therapy and interpersonal psychotherapy for bulimia nervosa. *Arch. Gen. Psychiatry*, **157**: 1302–1308.

18. Fairburn C.G. (2001) Designing treatment trials: can we do better? Presented at the Eating Disorders Research Society Annual Meeting, Bernalillo, 1 December.

19. Agras W.S., Crow S.J., Halmi K.A., Mitchell J.E., Wilson G.T., Kraemer H.C. (2000) Outcome predictors for the cognitive–behavioural treatment of bulimia nervosa: data from a multisite study. Am. J. Psychiatry, 57: 459–466.

20. Wilson G.T., Loeb K.L., Walsh B.T., Labouvie E., Petkova E., Liu X., Waternaux C. (1999) Psychological v. pharmacological treatments of bulimia nervosa: Predictors and processes of change. J. Consult. Clin. Psychol., 67: 451–459.

21. Wilson G.T., Fairburn C.G., Agras W.S., Walsh B.T., Kraemer H.D. (2002) Cognitive behaviour therapy for bulimia nervosa: time course and mechanisms of change. J. Consult. Clin. Psychol., 70: 267–274.

22. Wilson G.T., Vitousek K., Loeb K.L. (2000) Stepped-care treatment for eating disorders. J. Consult. Clin. Psychol., 68: 564–572.

23. Banasiak S.J., Paxton S.J., Hay P.J. (2002) Cognitive–behavioural guided self-help for bulimia nervosa in primary care. Paper presented at the International Conference on Eating Disorders, Boston, 26 April.

24. Thiels C., Schmidt U., Treasure J., Garthe R., Troop N. (1998) Guided self-change for bulimia nervosa incorporating use of a self-care manual. Am. J. Psychiatry, 155: 947–953.

25. Treasure J., Schmidt U., Troop N., Tiller J., Todd G., Turnbull S. (1996) Sequential treatment for bulimia nervosa incorporating a self-care manual. Br. J. Psychiatry, 168: 94–98.

26. Rossiter E.M., Agras W.S., Telch C.F., Schneider J.A. (1993) Cluster B personality disorder characteristics predict outcome in the treatment of bulimia nervosa. Int. J. Eat. Disord., 13: 349–358.

27. Stice E., Agras W.S. (1999) Subtyping bulimic women along dietary restraint and negative affect dimensions. J. Consult. Clin. Pscyhol., 67: 460–469.

28. Grilo C.M., Masheb R.M., Berman R.M. (2001) Subtyping women with bulimia nervosa along dietary and negative effect dimensions: a replication in a treatment-seeking sample. Eat. Weight Disord., 6: 53–58.

29. Mussell M.P., Mitchell J.E., Crosby R.D., Fulkerson J.A., Hoberman H.M., Romano J.L. (2000) Commitment to treatment goals in prediction of group cognitive-behavioral therapy treatment outcome for women with bulimia nervosa. J. Consult. Clin. Psychol., 68: 4342–437.

30. Halmi K.A., Agras W.S., Mitchell J., Wilson G.T., Crow S., Bryson S.W., Kraemer H. (2002) Relapse predictors of patients with bulimia nervosa who achieved abstinence through cognitive behavioral therapy. Arch. Gen. Psychiatry 59: 1105–1107.

31. Jarrett R.B., Kraft D., Doyle J., Foster B.M., Eaves G.G., Silver P.C. (2001) Preventing recurrent depression using cognitive therapy with and without a continuation phase. Arch. Gen. Psychiatry, 58: 381–388.

32. Wilson G.T., Agras W.S. (2001) Practice guidelines for treatment of eating disorders. Behav. Ther., 32: 219–234.

33. Fairburn C.G., Cooper Z., Shafran R. (2003) Cognitive behaviour therapy for eating disorders: a "transdiagnostic" theory and treatment. Behav. Res. Ther. (in press).

34. Agras W.S., Kraemer H. (1984) The treatment of anorexia nervosa: do different treatments have different outcomes. In Eating and its Disorders (Eds A.J. Stunkard, E. Stellar), pp. 193–208. Raven Press, New York.

35. Garner D.M., Bemis K.M. (1985) A cognitive-behavioral approach to anorexia nervosa. In Handbook of Psychotherapy for Anorexia Nervosa and Bulimia (Eds D.M. Garner, P.E. Garfinkel), pp. 107–146. Guilford Press, New York.

36. Beck A.T., Rush A.J., Shaw B.F., Emery G. (1979) *Cognitive Therapy of Depression.* Guilford Press, New York.
37. Garner D.M., Vitousek K.M., Pike K.M. (1997) Cognitive-behavioral therapy for anorexia nervosa. In *Handbook of Treatment for Eating Disorders* (Eds D.M. Garner, P.E. Garfinkel), pp. 94–144. Guilford Press, New York.
38. Serfaty M.A., Turkington D., Heap M., Ledsham L., Jolley E. (1999) Cognitive therapy v. dietary counselling in the outpatient treatment of anorexia nervosa: effects of the treatment phase. *Eur. Eat. Disord. Rev.*, 7: 334–350.
39. Pike K.M., Walsh B.T., Vitousek K., Wilson G.T., Bauer J. (2002) Cognitive behavioral therapy in the relapse prevention of anorexia nervosa. Unpublished manuscript, Columbia University.
40. Treasure J., Todd G., Brolly J., Nehmed A., Denman F. (1995) A pilot study of a randomized trial of cognitive analytical therapy vs. educational behavioral therapy for adult anorexia nervosa. *Behav. Res. Ther.*, 33: 363–367.
41. Dare C., Eisler I. (2002) Family therapy and eating disorders. In *Eating Disorders and Obesity* (Eds C.G. Fairburn, K.D. Brownell), pp. 314–319. Guilford Press, New York.
42. Russell G.F.M., Szmukler G.I., Dare C., Eisler I. (1987) An evaluation of family therapy in anorexia nervosa and bulimia nervosa. *Arch. Gen. Psychiatry*, 44: 1047–1056.
43. le Grange D., Eisler I., Dare C., Russell G.F.M. (1992) Evaluation of family treatments in adolescent anorexia nervosa: a pilot study. *Int. J. Eat. Disord.*, 12: 347–358.
44. Robin A.L., Siegel P.T., Moye A. (1995) Family v. individual therapy for anorexia: impact on family conflict. *Int. J. Eat. Disord.*, 17: 313–322.
45. Crisp A.H., Norton K., Gowers S., Halek C., Bowyer C., Yeldham D., Levett G., Bhat A. (1991) A controlled study of the effect of therapies aimed at adolescent and family psychopathology in anorexia nervosa. *Br. J. Psychiatry*, 159: 325–333.
46. Gowers S., Norton K., Halek C., Crisp A.H. (1994) Outcome of outpatient psychotherapy in a random allocation treatment study of anorexia nervosa. *Int. J. Eat. Disord.*, 15: 165–178.
47. Walsh B.T. (2002) Pharmacological treatment of anorexia nervosa and bulimia nervosa. In *Eating Disorders and Obesity* (Eds C.G. Fairburn, K.D. Brownell), pp. 325–329. Guilford Press, New York.
48. Lock J., le Grange D., Agras W.S., Dare C. (2001) *Treatment Manual for Anorexia Nervosa: a Family-based Approach.* Guilford Press, New York.
49. Key A., George C.L., Beattie D., Stammers K., Lacey H., Waller G. (2002) Body image treatment within an inpatient programme for anorexia nervosa: the role of mirror exposure in the desensitization process. *Int. J. Eat. Disord.*, 31: 185–190.
50. Striegel-Moore R.H., Cachelin F.M., Dohm F.A., Pike K.M., Wilfley D.E., Fairburn C.G. (2001) Comparison of binge eating disorder and bulimia nervosa in a community sample. *Int. J. Eat. Disord.*, 29: 157–165.
51. Wilfley D.E., Schwartz M.B., Spurrell E.B., Fairburn C.G. (2000) Using the Eating Disorder Examination to identify the specific psychopathology of binge eating disorder. *Int. J. Eat. Disord.*, 27: 259–269.
52. Striegel-Moore R.H., Wilfley D.E., Pike K.M., Dohm F.A., Fairburn C.G. (2000) Recurrent binge eating in Black American women. *Arch. Fam. Med.*, 9: 83–87.
53. Yanovski S.Z., Sebring N.G. (1994) Recorded food intake of obese women with binge eating disorders before and after weight loss. *Int. J. Eat. Disord.*, 15: 135–150.

54. Marcus M.D. (1993) Binge eating in obesity. In *Binge Eating: Nature, Assessment and Treatment* (Eds C.G. Fairburn, G.T. Wilson), pp. 77–96. Guilford Press, New York.
55. Telch C.F., Stice E. (1998) Psychiatric comorbidity in women with binge eating disorders: prevalence rates from a non-treatment-seeking sample. *J. Consult. Clin. Psychol.*, **66**: 768–776.
56. Wilfley D.E., Cohen L.R. (1997) Psychological treatment of bulimia nervosa and binge eating disorder. *Psychopharmacol. Bull.*, **33**: 437–454.
57. Agras W.S., Telch C.F., Arnow B., Eldredge K., Detzer M.J., Henderson J., Marnell M. (1995) Does interpersonal therapy help patients with binge eating disorder who fail to respond to cognitive-behavioural therapy? *J. Consult. Clin. Psychol.*, **63**: 356–360.
58. Grilo C.M., Masheb R.M., Heninger G., Wilson G.T. (2002) Controlled comparison of cognitive behavioral therapy and fluoxetine for binge eating disorder. Presented at the International Conference of the Academy of Eating Disorders, Boston, 28 April.
59. Hudson J.I., McElroy S.L., Raymond N.C., Crow S., Keck P.E., Carter W.P., Mitchell J.E., Strakowski S.M., Pope H.G., Coleman B.S., *et al.* (1998) Fluvoxamine in the treatment of binge-eating disorder: a multicenter placebo-controlled, double-blind trial. *Am. J. Psychiatry*, **155**: 1756–1762.
60. Devlin M., Goldfein J.A., Raizman P.S., Walsh B.T. (2001) Treatment of binge eating disorder with psychotherapy and medication. Presented at the Eating Disorders Research Society Annual Meeting, Bernalillo, 2 December.
61. Wilfley D.E., Agras W.S., Telch C.F., Rossiter E.M., Schneider J.A., Cole A.G., Sifford L.A., Raeburn S.D. (1993) Group cognitive-behavioral therapy and group interpersonal psychotherapy for the nonpurging bulimic: a controlled comparison. *J. Consult. Clin. Psychol.*, **61**: 296–305.
62. Wilfley D.E., Welch R.R., Stein R.I., Spurrell E.B., Cohen L.R., Saelens B.S., Dounchis J.Z., Frank M.A., Wiseman C.V., Matt G.E. (2002) A randomized comparison of group cognitive-behavioral therapy and group interpersonal psychotherapy for the treatment of binge eating disorder. *Arch. Gen. Psychiatry*, **59**: 713–721.
63. Agras W.S., Telch C.F., Arnow B., Eldredge K., Marnell M. (1997) One-year follow-up of cognitive-behavioural therapy for obese individuals with binge eating disorder. *J. Consult. Clin. Psychol.*, **65**: 343–347.
64. Marcus M.D., Wing R.R., Fairburn C.G. (1995) Cognitive behavioral treatment of binge eating vs. behavioral weight control on the treatment of binge eating disorder. *Ann. Behav. Med.*, **17**: S090.
65. Nauta H., Hospers H., Kok G., Jansen A. (2000) A comparison between a cognitive and a behavioral treatment for obese binge eaters and obese non-binge eaters. *Behav. Ther.*, **31**: 441–462.
66. Beck A.T. (1976) *Cognitive Therapy and the Emotional Disorders*. International Universities Press, New York.
67. Stunkard A.J. (2002) Binge eating disorder and the night eating syndrome. In *Handbook of Obesity Treatment* (Eds T.A. Wadden, A.J. Stunkard), pp. 107–124. Guilford Press, New York.
68. Agras W.S., Telch C.F., Arnow B., Eldredge K., Wilfley D.E., Raeburn S., Henderson S.D., Marnell M. (1994) Weight loss, cognitive-behavioural and desipramine treatments in binge eating disorder: an additive design. *Behav. Ther.*, **25**: 225–238.

69. Gladis M.M., Wadden T.A., Vogt R., Foster G., Kuehnel, R.H., Bartlett S.J. (1998) Behavioral treatment of obese binge eaters: do they need different care? *J. Psychosom. Res.*, **44**: 375–384.

70. Porzelius L.K., Houston C., Smith M., Arfken C., Fisher E., Jr. (1995) Comparison of a standard behavioral weight loss treatment and a binge eating weight loss treatment. *Behav. Ther.*, **26**: 119–134.

71. Gormally J., Black S., Daston S., Rardin D. (1982) The assessment of binge eating severity among obese persons. *Addict. Behav.*, **7**: 47–55.

72. Greeno C.G., Marcus M.D., Wing R.R. (1995) Diagnosis of binge eating disorder: discrepancies between a questionnaire and clinical interview. *Int. J. Eat. Disord.*, **17**: 153–160.

73. Sherwood N.E., Jeffery R.W., Wing R.R. (1999) Binge status as a predictor of weight loss treatment outcome. *Int. J. Obesity*, **23**: 485–593.

74. Garner D.M., Wooley S.C. (1991) Confronting the failure of behavioral and dietary treatments for obesity. *Clin. Psychol. Rev.*, **11**: 729–790.

75. Howard C.E., Porzelius L.K. (1999) The role of dieting in binge eating disorder: etiology and treatment implications. *Clin. Psychol. Rev.*, **19**: 25–44.

76. National Task Force on the Prevention and Treatment of Obesity (2000) Dieting and the development of eating disorders in overweight and obese adults. *Arch. Int. Med.*, **160**: 2581–2589.

77. Raymond N.C., de Zwaan M., Mitchell J.E., Ackard D., Thuras P. (2002) Effect of a very low calorie diet on the diagnostic category of individuals with binge eating disorders. *Int. J. Eat. Disord.*, **31**: 49–56.

78. Carter J.C. Fairburn C.G. (1998) Cognitive-behavioural self-help for binge eating disorder: a controlled effectiveness study. *J. Consult. Clin. Psychol.*, **66**: 616–623.

79. Fairburn C.G. (1995) *Overcoming Binge Eating*. Guilford Press, New York.

80. Loeb K.L., Wilson G.T., Gilbert J.S., Labouvie E. (2000) Guided and unguided self-help for binge eating. *Behav. Res. Ther.*, **38**: 259–272.

81. Wilson G.T., Fairburn C.G. (2000) The treatment of binge eating disorders. *Eur. Eat. Disord. Rev.*, **8**: 351–354.

82. Stunkard A.J. (1997) Eating disorders: the last 25 years. *Appetite*, **29**: 181–190.

83. Vitousek K.B. (2002) Cognitive-behavioral therapy for anorexia nervosa. In *Eating Disorders and Obesity* (Eds C.G. Fairburn, K.D. Brownell), pp. 308–313. Guilford Press, New York.

Commentaries

5.1
As Many Questions As Answers: Evidence-based and Evidence-generating Practice

Glenn Waller[1]

Terence Wilson has provided a timely and comprehensive review of our evidence base for the psychological treatment of eating disorders. Overall, the evidence to date is a real curate's egg—good in some parts and bad in others.

On the positive side, there is strong evidence that we can achieve substantial levels of remission and symptom reduction in bulimia nervosa and binge eating disorder. It may even be that progress is being made in the field of anorexia nervosa (a false dawn that has been heralded often in the past, so we must await further work here). Particularly important moves are being made in understanding the role of motivation [1, 2] and how it needs to be built into our everyday therapeutic stance [3], rather than simply being treated as a "bolt-on" component.

The news is far from all good, as any clinician would agree. Wilson shows how cognitive–behavioural therapy (CBT) is the reference point against which other treatments need to be judged in some eating disorders, probably because CBT is inherently self-testing, attracting clinicians keen to work with testable hypotheses and overt, observable clinical phenomena (rather than hypothetical, unverifiable constructs). However, CBT has a long way to go in demonstrating its superiority with anorexia nervosa (if such a position can be established at all).

Some treatments remain to be tested adequately. My clinical impression is that follow-up studies will not show long-term benefits from pharmacological treatments. Other treatment approaches appear to be inherently resistant to developing an evidence base. It particularly concerns me that the empirical base for the plethora of psychodynamically derived treatments for eating disorders is so poor, given the number of clinicians who still work within such a framework. A valuable first step would be clear operationalization of those approaches, allowing objective testing of

[1] Department of Psychiatry, St. George's Hospital Medical School, University of London, London SW17 0RE, UK

their accuracy and treatment utility. The failure to take that step is a glaring omission. Such research is needed if the potential benefits of psychodynamic approaches are not to be dismissed as the self-serving biased perceptions of practising clinicians. The same criteria should hold for other therapies, however, including some recent developments from cognitive–behavioural models (e.g. dialectical behaviour therapy, cognitive analytical therapy and schema-focused CBT).

CBT has shortcomings of its own, so there is no place for complacency. One of its key problems is that much of the evidence base is founded on a treatment approach whose rationale emerged before the development of a more comprehensive understanding of the psychopathology of eating disorders. Wilson points out how Fairburn's treatment model is predicated on the role of rigid and dysfunctional dieting, but much of the evidence of the past decade suggests that binge eating is driven as much by affective state and social cues as by hunger or food cravings [4]. There is a clear need to consider the roles of affect and of cognitive levels not relating directly to food, shape and weight [5]. Because CBT is predicated on the linkage of cognition, emotion and behaviour, improvements in its capacity to produce behavioural change might depend on modifying the therapy to address those cognitions and emotions.

A further problem, which Wilson touches on, is that many therapies developed in research settings fail to translate to the clinic. In part, this will be a product of the more mixed populations found in such settings, but it is also clear that much of what is labelled "CBT" fails to adhere to the principles or the protocols of this proven therapy. If clinicians do not apply the treatment appropriately, then why would one expect it to be effective?

When faced with the ugly, we often avert our gaze, hoping that it will simply go away. We have many such blind spots in our evidence base. First, our proven successes have been largely with diagnosed disorders that centre on binge eating. There is much to be done in understanding and treating cases where purging behaviours are central to the pathology. This is particularly true in purging anorexia nervosa and in many multi-impulsive cases (the groups where there is generally the highest level of psychopathology). Second, the eating disorders are inconveniently heterogeneous. Fewer than half of the referrals to a specialist eating disorders clinic meet the full DSM-IV [6] criteria for anorexia nervosa or bulimia nervosa [7]. Patients who do not meet full diagnostic criteria have substantial clinical needs, but the existing clinical evidence base barely considers them (except where treatment targets symptoms rather than syndromes). Last but not least, what about obesity?

In conclusion, the evidence base that Wilson has summarized is impressive but has many holes. Those who are seeking a clear picture of where we are up to in our understanding would do well to learn its lessons.

However, the holes in the research demonstrate that we are at a stage where complacency would be dangerous. Evidence-generating practice is as critical as evidence-based practice right now.

REFERENCES

1. Geller J., Cockell S.J., Drab D. (2001) Assessing readiness for change in anorexia nervosa: the psychometric properties of the readiness and motivation for change interview. *Psychol. Assess.*, **13**: 189–198.
2. Serpell L., Treasure J., Teasdale J., Sullivan V. (1999) Anorexia nervosa: friend or foe? *Int. J. Eat. Disord.*, **25**: 177–186.
3. Geller J., Williams K.D., Srikameswaran S. (2001) Clinician stance in the treatment of chronic eating disorders. *Eur. Eat. Disord. Rev.*, **9**: 365–373.
4. Meyer C., Waller G., Waters A. (1998) Emotional states and bulimic psychopathology. In *The Neurobiological Basis of Eating Disorders* (Eds. H. Hoek, M. Katzman, J. Treasure), pp. 271–289. Wiley, Chichester.
5. Hollon S.D., Beck A.T. (1994) Cognitive and cognitive-behavioural therapies. In *Handbook of Psychotherapy and Behavioural Change* (Eds. A.E. Bergin, S.L. Garfield), pp. 428–466. Wiley, Chichester.
6. American Psychiatric Association (1994) *Diagnostic and Statistical Manual of Mental Disorders*, 4th ed. American Psychiatric Association, Washington.
7. Turner H., Bryant-Waugh R. (2001) Eating disorder not otherwise specified (EDNOS): profiles of patients presenting at a community eating disorder service. Presented at the 5th International Conference on Eating Disorders, London, 3 April.

5.2
Mind Over Matter in the Eating Disorders
Regina C. Casper[1]

Affluence in the Western world following World War II has been associated with a rise in the so-called eating disorders, but documents that have traced anorexia nervosa to the Middle Ages and bulimia nervosa to Ancient Greece indicate that cultural influences alone do not account for either disorder. As Bruch [1] noted for anorexia nervosa, eating disorders "are more than dieting out of hand". Biological and psychosocial confluences interacting with a range of personal and psychiatric disturbances ultimately produce the clinical phenomena [2] and studies have shown prognosis and

[1] *Department of Psychiatry, Stanford University School of Medicine, 401 Quarry Road, Stanford, CA 94305-5723, USA*

long-term outcome to be a function of the severity of the comorbid psychopathology [3].

Little is known about the biological mechanisms governing the physiological processes that have gone awry, culminating in an unusual ability to dysregulate body weight to pathologically low levels in anorexia nervosa and leading to a wilfully induced disruption of the rhythms regulating the cyclic pattern of eating and abstinence, of activity and rest and of waking and sleep in bulimia nervosa. Lack of knowledge about the aetiology has not prevented clinicians and researchers from testing virtually every psychotropic medication to treat anorexia nervosa, to little avail. By contrast, drug treatments, in particular with antidepressants, which have a wide spectrum of efficacy, have been used with greater benefit for bulimia nervosa, the disorder more often associated with an affective, anxiety and/or substance abuse disorder [4].

Terence Wilson's comprehensive and learned overview focuses on those psychological interventions, mostly the cognitive–behavioural psychotherapies, that have undergone stringent efficacy testing in controlled studies in bulimia nervosa, in anorexia nervosa and in binge eating disorder. Psychologically, what is shared in anorexia nervosa and bulimia nervosa is the wish for self and weight control to counter personal unhappiness arising from individually determined developmental or family conflicts, not infrequently re-enforced by psychiatric disturbances. The disorders differ in thought content. Whereas in anorexia nervosa hunger sensations signal successful control over body shape to a mind dominated by ideas revolving around means of caloric restriction, the mind in bulimia nervosa proves powerless to maintain control over food intake once prolonged food avoidance, in other words dietary restraint, has disrupted the orderly rhythm of initiating and terminating regular meals. Instead of being able to redirect thoughts to intellectual pursuits or considerations of daily life, an overwhelming urge to eat produced by food abstinence cannot be contained, despite the best intentions, and leads to eating binges. The binges override the satiety signal and the ensuing fears of overweight lead to the decision to regurgitate the food. The conscious mental content in bulimia nervosa resembles that of a food-deprived, ravenously hungry person, constantly assailed by images of food as a result of a disregulated hunger and satiety system. Dietary and cognitive restraint play a minor role in binge eating, the disorder with the least psychopathology; instead, the pleasurable and comforting qualities of food entice to overeating.

The differences in thinking and control might explain why cognitive–behavioural therapies that offer practical guidance for regulating the eating pattern and teach skills for coping with situations that trigger binge eating and hence purging have been so helpful for about 50% of bulimia nervosa patients in overcoming the disorder, leading also to psychological improvements. In experienced hands, interpersonal psychotherapy, which is considered less directive but encourages thought and reflections about current personal relationships, has been found nearly as effective as cognitive–behavioural therapy when re-evaluated 1 year later. Pharmacotherapy, the first treatment to be tested for bulimia nervosa [5], is now considered more of an adjunct and is used mainly for the more psychiatrically disturbed—the high negative affect, high restraint group that responds less well to cognitive–behavioural therapy.

Wilson points out that cognitive structural therapies have had little success in changing the mindset in anorexia nervosa. Whether or not the bulimic subtype [6] responds differently to cognitive psychotherapy than the restricting subtype has not been studied systematically. A quite different approach, emotional re-engagement within the context of family therapy, has allowed young adolescent patients with anorexia nervosa to rediscover values other than a wasted body. If they can have a dialogue with others, alongside the inner monologue with their body, then there is hope. In giving voice to a patient with restricting anorexia nervosa, the attempt to reach out and trust others can be a perilous, painful process: "Alone, I am—in a cage of thorns and dead roses. A few of the needles are poisoned. Is the risk of encountering one going to stop you? It is ok, I will understand; besides I am hungry for nothing—but starving for all."

In binge eating disorder, not cognitive therapies but behavioural weight loss programmes that eliminate the temptation of tasty food (through low caloric, low carbohydrate diets) have successfully curbed overeating and overweight. Intriguingly, in this condition binge eating is mitigated rather than triggered by dietary restraint. Wilson argues that binge eating disorder might not require professional assistance, because self–help strategies have reduced binge eating frequency, weight concerns and general psychopathology.

The cognitive psychotherapies have revealed the healing power of benevolent proactive guidance. A significant proportion of patients with eating disorders—the most chronic, the most psychiatrically disturbed—fail to respond to any treatment. Novel treatments will need to be discovered to help this population, most likely treatments that take their efficacy from new knowledge about the complex aetiology underlying the eating disorders.

REFERENCES

1. Bruch H. (1974) *Eating Disorders: Obesity, Anorexia Nervosa and the Person Within.* Routledge Kegan Paul, London.
2. Casper R.C. (1998) Behavioural activation and lack of concern, core symptoms of anorexia nervosa? *Int. J. Eat. Disord.*, **24**: 381–393.

3. Wentz E., Gillberg C., Gillberg I., Rastam M. (2001) Ten-year follow-up of adolescent onset anorexia nervosa: psychiatric disorders and overall functioning scales. *J. Child Psychol. Psychiatry*, **42**: 613–622.
4. Brewerton T., Lydiard R., Herzog D., Brotman A.W., O'Neil P., Ballenger J. (1995) Co-morbidity of axis I diagnoses in bulimia nervosa. *J. Clin. Psychiatry*, **56**: 77–80.
5. Mitchell J., Groat R. (1984) A placebo-controlled, double-blind trial of amitriptyline in bulimia. *J. Clin. Psychopharmacol.*, **4**: 186–193.
6. Casper R., Eckert E., Halmi K., Goldberg S., Davis J. (1980) Bulimia: its incidence and clinical significance in patients with anorexia nervosa. *Arch. Gen. Psychiatry*, **37**: 1030–1035.

5.3
Broadening the Evidence-based Net
Nicholas A. Troop[1]

Earlier reviews of the effectiveness of psychotherapy came to the general conclusion that *everyone has won and all must have prizes* [1]. It is encouraging, therefore, that Terence Wilson's review leads to clear recommendations as to the treatments of choice, at least as far as bulimia nervosa and binge eating disorder are concerned, if not for anorexia nervosa. A case can also be made that it is a good thing that there are no reliable predictors of change for these disorders. Although we cannot predict who will respond best to a particular treatment, there are no contraindications for using cognitive–behavioural therapy (CBT) in bulimia nervosa and behavioural weight loss (BWL) in BED, so these treatments are probably suitable for all patients.

It is also encouraging that, in moving from considerations of efficacy through effectiveness towards efficiency [2], attention has turned from exclusively determining what is the gold standard to assessing how this treatment can best be delivered within a treatment service. For example, a range of studies have suggested that CBT in a self-help format can help a substantial number of patients when delivered alone [3,4], as the first intervention in a stepped-care approach [5] or guided by a non-specialist [6]. Even when not sufficient to produce remission on its own, a self-directed treatment manual can significantly reduce the amount of subsequent or concurrent therapist contact required, substantially reducing the resources needed [7]. Other studies have begun to investigate whether the effectiveness of CBT can be enhanced by increasing patients' readiness to change [8,9]. These avenues offer the promise of help for a wider range of sufferers, including those in primary care or even those who have never

[1] *Department of Psychology, Calcutta House, London Guildhall University, Old Castle Street, London E1 7NT, UK*

sought and never will seek formal psychiatric treatment, as well as increasing engagement and reducing premature termination in those who do seek treatment.

Although convincing evidence does suggest that particular treatments can be recommended, it does not necessarily lead to their uptake [10]. Indeed, faith in particular treatments can be difficult to shake even in the face of contradictory or questionable evidence—witness, for example, the debate over the use of eye movement desensitization and reprocessing in the treatment of post-traumatic stress disorder [11]. However, caution should be shown before embarking on a crusade to convert the unconverted. There are still some gaps to fill before we reach that position. For example, most of the available evidence has been generated from randomized controlled trials (RCTs) carried out in English-speaking countries such as the USA, UK, Canada, Australia and New Zealand [12]. For reasons that I will come to, one may reasonably ask, therefore, how widely applicable this evidence is to, say, the non-English-speaking parts of Europe (i.e. most of it). Furthermore, the vast majority of this evidence is published in English language journals, which may be an obstacle to getting the message across to most clinicians in primary and secondary care in non-English-speaking countries.

Differences in health beliefs between patients and clinicians can represent a very real challenge for the success of any treatment. CBT for any disorder typically begins by describing the cognitive model of that disorder to the patient in order to provide a rationale for the treatment. However, where a treatment rationale does not match the specific health beliefs of an individual concerning the illness under consideration, then that treatment will be considered implausible, which may lead to problems with engagement and effectiveness. In this case resistance to treatment is not merely a reflection of the lack of motivation or ambivalence about change, but a fundamental mismatch between what the clinician and what the patient expect to be effective. This has not generally been investigated in psychiatry, although it has been investigated in medical settings. Even within the UK there is great variability in the health beliefs of both patients and clinicians and this variability can be even greater if other countries and cultures are considered.

Although multicentre studies are clearly warranted, this is especially so in the case of investigating treatments across Europe. However, RCTs may be difficult to implement, given the diversity of treatment services and experience in Europe (see, for example, the recent series of articles in the *European Eating Disorders Review* from July 2001 to June 2002). Comparing 16 weeks of CBT in a country where outpatient treatment is the preferred option with 16 weeks of CBT in a country where inpatient treatment is generally preferred presents problems, given the systematic difference in delivery. Because of the way in which health services are structured and funded, there are long waiting lists in Britain but these are almost non-existent in other parts of Europe [13]. This is likely to lead to vast differences in retention rates and drop-out, because patients in some countries can leave one treatment and walk straight into another whereas patients in other countries with different healthcare systems cannot [13]. Treatment non-completion therefore may mean very different things in these countries, so calculating the efficacy on the basis of intention to treat is problematic.

It is for these reasons that the COST Action B6 initiative was begun, with a view to investigating the naturalistic treatment outcomes in approximately 100 clinics across nearly 20 European countries involving 5000 patients. The course of recovery (or non-recovery) can be plotted using this large set of pooled data across many treatment modalities and in many different contexts and systems of delivery. There are many questions that this massive comparative "audit" can answer that RCTs cannot, although there are many other questions that can be answered only by RCTs.

It is perhaps unfortunate that so much faith has been put in RCTs to the detriment of other forms of "good" evidence. The RCTs attempt to emulate the best principles of laboratory experimental design applied to clinical settings. Unfortunately, however, there is no such thing as the "perfect" experiment and this is even more true in clinical settings than in psychological laboratories. To give one example, even where the same therapists administer all treatments, given that psychotherapists cannot be blind to the treatment they are providing, any previously published evidence in favour of one treatment over another cannot help but influence their expectations as to which of the treatments they are providing is likely to be the more effective. As we know from the use of placebos, such outcome expectations can lead to self-fulfilling prophecies.

However, I do not wish to overstate this as a problem in RCTs, because there are also problems inherent in naturalistic studies. Nevertheless, and broadening the scope of Lazarus and Folkman's [14] argument, it is unlikely that any single type of evidence can unequivocally determine the best treatment. Rather, the convergence of results from RCTs and well carried out naturalistic studies will be more convincing than one favourable result from even the best RCT.

REFERENCES

1. Luborsky L.I., Singer B., Luborsky L. (1975) Comparative studies of psychotherapies. *Arch. Gen. Psychiatry*, **20**: 84–88.
2. Andrews G. (1999) Efficacy, effectiveness and efficiency in mental health service delivery. *Aust. N. Zeal. J. Psychiatry*, **33**: 316–322.

3. Treasure J.L., Schmidt U.H., Troop N.A., Tiller J., Todd G., Keilen M., Dodge E. (1994) The first step in the management of bulimia nervosa: a controlled trial of a therapeutic manual. *Br. Med. J.*, **308**: 686–689.
4. Carter J.C., Fairburn C.G. (1998) Cognitive-behavioral self-help for binge eating disorder: a controlled effectiveness study. *J. Consult. Clin. Psychol.*, **66**: 616–623.
5. Treasure J.L., Schmidt U.H., Troop N.A., Tiller J., Todd G., Turnbull S. (1996) Sequential treatment for bulimia nervosa incorporating a self-care manual. *Br. J. Psychiatry*, **168**: 94–98.
6. Thiels C., Treasure J.L., Schmidt U.H., Garthe R., Troop N.A. (1998) Guided self-change for bulimia nervosa incorporating a self-care manual. *Am. J. Psychiatry*, **155**: 947–953.
7. Treasure J.L., Troop N.A., Ward A. (1996) An approach to planning services for bulimia nervosa. *Br. J. Psychiatry*, **169**: 551–554.
8. Treasure J.L., Katzman M., Schmidt U.H., Troop N.A., Todd G., de Silva P. (1999) Engagement and outcome in the treatment of bulimia nervosa: first phase of a sequential design comparing motivational enhancement therapy and cognitive behavioural therapy. *Behav. Res. Ther.*, **37**: 405–418.
9. Feld R., Woodside D.B., Kaplan A.S., Olmsted M.P., Carter J.C. (2001) Pretreatment motivational enhancement therapy for eating disorders: a pilot study. *Int. J. Eat. Disord.*, **29**: 393–400.
10. Wilson G.T. (1998) The clinical utility of randomized controlled trials. *Int. J. Eat. Disord*, **24**: 13–29.
11. Joseph S. (2002) Emperor's new clothes? *Psychologist*, **15**: 242–243.
12. Fairburn C.G. (1997) Towards evidence-based and cost-effective treatment for bulimia nervosa. *Eur. Eat. Disord. Rev.*, **5**: 145–148.
13. Treasure J.L. (2001) Case mix leading to treatment match. *Eur. Eat. Disord. Rev.*, **9**: 71–73.
14. Lazarus R.S., Folkman S. (1984) *Stress, Appraisal and Coping.* Springer, New York.

5.4
Seeing the Wood for the Trees
J. Hubert Lacey[1]

Somewhat irreverently, it sometimes seems that bulimia nervosa can respond to any structured therapy—indeed an initial therapeutic assessment interview can lead to marked improvement and some brave clinicians have even boasted a cure! It says something about these disorders that no-one would ever dream of claiming this of anorexia nervosa. For clinical researchers of bulimia, the last two decades have been a therapeutic success. The evidence base of the treatment of adults with anorexia nervosa, however, has changed little: treatment remains empirical and response perplexing to the rational clinician. Little wonder that researchers in this

[1] *Department of Psychiatry, St. George's Hospital Medical School, Tooting, London SW17 0RE, UK*

field have mixed emotions—proud and satisfied of their achievement in treating bulimia, but frustrated that anorexia fails to respond consistently to treatment, including those carefully crafted from successful treatments in bulimia.

Terence Wilson rightly focuses on those treatments that have been evaluated in clinical trials. For bulimia nervosa, her advice is clear and right: manual-based cognitive–behavioural therapy (CBT) or interpersonal therapy, with or without selective serotonin reuptake inhibitor (SSRI) medication, is the treatment approach of choice for the majority. In practice such purity, although desirable, is not essential. In motivated patients, a significant reduction in the frequency of binge eating or purging will follow the use of behavioural techniques, which are often quite simple techniques. It is the maintenance of improvement or remission that is difficult, i.e. it is what is added to behaviour therapy that converts temporary improvement to cure. Cognitive, interpersonal and focal-interpretative therapies [1], and indeed many others, have all been shown to be effective. In the hurly-burly of general clinical practice, these therapies often have more in common than is admitted. What one therapist deems cognitive is judged interpretative by another. This observation, although cynical, leads to another. Patients do best when they and their therapists run with the flow of the illness using cognitive or interpretative techniques as needed, rather than adhering slavishly to a particular therapeutic model, however much evidence supports its use. This means that we should be less concerned than we might otherwise be that CBT is used relatively infrequently by clinical practitioners. What is important is that the patients be treated by professionals trained in a broad range of therapeutic skills in specialist centres. These centres must have a number of clinicians working together to provide peer audit. A number of scandals, on both sides of the Atlantic, have emphasized the importance of this and, indeed, that the treatment centres have sufficient patients on which therapists can maintain their skills.

The real treatment problem is anorexia nervosa. In marked contrast to bulimia nervosa, few control treatment trials exist despite the seriousness of the disorder. Adolescents with early onset and short duration have the best prognosis, and family therapy is the preferred treatment option. Most adult anorexics are wary of family therapy and prefer to deal with family issues in individual or group therapy, or in specialist treatments such as psychodrama, all underpinned with fact-based family information sessions. Joint therapy with a partner has face validity, because weight gain leads to emotional and sexual changes that profoundly affect the relationship.

An issue that bedevils the treatment of anorexia nervosa is the difference between treatment that is life-saving and treatment aimed at getting better. Often the treatment of one merges imperceptibly into the other without review by either patient or clinician. This is probably the single most common reason why patients in the early stages of treatment relapse.

There needs to be a range of practical clinical options: treatment that is life-saving; treatment aimed at remaining ill, but safely; brief treatment to get over a particular hurdle; and treatment that cures. In practice, these are best formulated into programmes. Too often, recovery programmes are seen in simplistic terms: should treatment be given as inpatient or outpatient; should the model be CBT or dynamic, or whatever? Clinical experience suggests that other factors are more important. Is the patient fully informed about the recovery programme? Is there an agreed ethos and philosophy of care? Are the goals, aims and methods agreed by both patient and clinician? Is there an alliance between that part of the patient that wishes to get better (recognizing that there is also a part that does not) and the staff? Is there availability of sustained, quality psychotherapy contact of a skilled kind from the onset? [2].

If treatment is to be successful, patients must change psychotherapeutically within the context of weight gain to normal levels. The final weight must be compatible with full psychological and physiological maturity. Patients find it easier to gain weight within the structure and safety of an inpatient or partial-hospitalization programme. These programmes are lengthy, expensive and raise understandable concern. If they are used, however, only on the basis of the factors mentioned above, then drop-out is avoided and clinical success gratifying. It does mean, however, that fewer patients are likely to enter the recovery programme, hence the need for other treatment programmes with other therapeutic goals.

Treatment is best provided by a multi-disciplinary team, which should include those trained not only in psychotherapies and nursing but also (and perhaps particularly) in practical skills such as social therapy. Again, the therapeutic orientation of the team is probably less relevant than its management. Multi-disciplinary teams do not work effectively if clinical decisions are taken by the responsible psychiatrist alone. Decisions should be made by the clinicians dealing with a particular patient, using a democratic consensus process, the whole being audited by other team members not directly involved in treatment. The psychiatrist therefore has the role of chair of the clinical management meeting and accepts that she/he often can be over-ruled. Once a decision has been made, all agree to be bound by it and not to change policy, unless after discussion at a subsequent meeting. Disagreements or changes will not therefore take place outside the meeting and the patient is able to ally him/herself with a strong, unified and consistent team.

No-one knows which therapies particularly benefit anorexic patients. In all probability, they vary from patient to patient. Individual and group therapy delivering psychodynamic, cognitive and didactic therapies are commonly employed, and in many units they provide an eclectic mix. Multi-impulsive patients [3,4] in whom the anorexia is associated with addictive and self-damaging behaviour, benefit additionally from a more structured behavioural approach and are best treated separately from other anorexic patients.

The research evidence base of anorexia cannot be limited to therapeutic models—programme-mix, structure, ethos, therapeutic goals and the composition of multi-disciplinary teams and their management style are just as relevant.

REFERENCES

1. Lacey J.H. (1983) Bulimia nervosa, binge-eating and psychogenic vomiting: a controlled treatment study and long-term outcome. *Br. Med. J.*, **286**: 1609–1613.
2. Crisp A.H. (2002) Treatment of anorexia nervosa: is "where" or "how" the main issue? *Eur. Eat. Disord. Rev.*, **10**: 233–240.
3. Lacey J.H., Evans C.D.H. (1986) The impulsivist: a multi-impulsive personality disorder. *Br. J. Addict.*, **81**: 641–649.
4. Lacey J.H., Read T.R.C. (1993) Multi-impulsive bulimia: description of an inpatient eclectic treatment programme and a pilot follow-up study of its efficacy. *Eur. Eat. Disord. Rev.*, **1**: 22–31.

5.5

Efficacy, Effectiveness and the Implementation of Evidence

Eric F. van Furth[1]

Randomized controlled trials (RCTs) on the psychotherapy of eating disorders have been conducted only since the last two decades of the previous century. Presently, the body of knowledge on the treatment of these disorders looks somewhat like a Swiss cheese.

In bulimia nervosa, the proponents of cognitive–behavioural therapy (CBT) have produced a wealth of state-of-the-art RCTs showing the short- and long-term efficacy of manualized CBT. The abstinence rate for bingeing and purging following 16 weekly sessions of outpatient CBT is about 50%, while much higher rates of reduction in binge frequency are obtained for most patients. However, depending on one's bias (the cup is either half-full

[1] *Robert-Fleury Stichting, National Center for Eating Disorders, PO Box 422, 2260 AK Leidschendam, The Netherlands*

or half-empty), CBT as conducted in RCTs does not achieve the desired result in about half of the participating patients. More effective methods need to be developed for CBT non-responders.

Almost paradoxically, the advocates of CBT have provided us with an adapted form of interpersonal psychotherapy (IPT) that has proved to be an almost equally effective treatment for bulimia nervosa. Although the modus operandi of IPT may very well be different from CBT, we are not yet able to match patients to specific forms of treatment (let alone therapists) with the aim of optimizing treatment effects.

Now that the efficacy of CBT in clinical trials with patients suffering from bulimia nervosa has been established, there is a dire need to evaluate its clinical utility through effectiveness studies. The complementary role of the latter is needed to assess the generalizability of the results of the CBT RCTs in everyday clinical practice. The effects of patient selection, therapist training, patient motivation and participation, comorbidity and concurrent therapy can then be assessed within the more ecologically valid environment of mental health service provision [1].

Despite its strong empirical underpinning, CBT is rarely used as a treatment of choice. In a recent US-based study, only 6.9% of the 353 individuals with probable bulimia nervosa were reported to have received a full course of CBT in the past [2]. A survey among 60 psychologists whose caseload included at least 5% patients with eating disorders showed endorsement of CBT as the treatment of first choice by 38.8%. However, 65.2% of the psychologists who reported using CBT as their primary theoretical approach did not receive any training in the use of manual-based CBT for working with patients with bulimia nervosa [3]. The implementation of evidence-based treatments in mental health services has many hurdles to take. Careful bottom-up exploration of both the professionals' needs and their resistance to manual-based treatment is needed. On-site training, supervision and intervision may complement the existing conference workshops and teaching days. Professional organizations, such as the Academy for Eating Disorders, face a challenging task.

Evidence-based medicine can be established properly only if there is sufficient high-quality evidence to evaluate. In the case of anorexia nervosa, this is hardly the case [4]. Wilson summarizes the methodological, practical and ethical issues regarding this problem. The best established treatment is outpatient systemic therapy, involving either the whole family or subsystems (i.e. parents), following hospitalization for adolescents with anorexia nervosa. The effectiveness of inpatient treatment for both adolescent and adult patients with severe anorexia nervosa has not been established empirically [5–7].

During the past 5 years, 19 European countries participated in a European Union prospective follow-up study in which 1509 patients with eating disorders were followed for 2.5 years. The follow-up at 1 year after the beginning of treatment showed that only 37% of the patients with an initial diagnosis of anorexia nervosa did not meet any of the DSM-IV [8] criteria (no significant weight loss, no bingeing or compensatory behaviour, no extreme fear of becoming obese and no distorted body image).

The results of the three participating Dutch centres, where patients with anorexia nervosa were treated primarily as inpatients, were slightly better: 49.5% of patients improved to remission at the 1-year follow-up. However, the mean duration of inpatient treatment in the Dutch centres was more than twice that, for example, of German centres (28.2 vs. 11.6 weeks). Also, the intensity of the therapeutic programme was much higher in The Netherlands when compared with Germany (30 vs. 13 h per week) [9]. Obviously, the costs of such an intensive long-term inpatient treatment are high and the pressure to decrease the duration of inpatient treatment is increasing everywhere. This may be understandable from a political point of view, but examples in the USA show that the quality of treatment may suffer [10].

For many clinicians, inpatient treatment for adult patients with severe anorexia nervosa is the first choice. However, an empirical base to substantiate (or refute) this choice is badly needed. The long-term efficacy, cost-effectiveness and the patients' perspective on the quality of treatment all need to be addressed.

Binge eating disorder (BED) is not a formal diagnosis within the DSM-IV, but is mentioned under the category of eating disorders not otherwise specified (EDNOS). Despite the fact that the majority of patients with eating disorders fall within this category, RCTs have excluded patients with EDNOS for various reasons. In contrast, the inclusion of the criteria for BED in the DSM-IV has engendered a lot of research interest. Much remains to be said about the delineation from bulimia nervosa and obesity [11]. Although several empirical-based treatments are now available, many eating disorder centres hesitate to offer their services to this patient group. The reasons for this are unclear. Lack of training in the identification and treatment of these patients and the hesitation to offer the limited resources to patients other than those suffering from anorexia or bulimia nervosa may play a role. Consequently, BED patients may fall between two stools (internal medicine and psychiatry) and not receive adequate treatment.

REFERENCES

1. Black N. (1996) Why we need observational studies to evaluate the effectiveness of health care. *Br. Med. J.*, **312**: 1215–1218.

2. Crow S., Mussell M.P., Peterson C., Knopke A., Mitchell J. (1999) Prior treatment received by patients with bulimia nervosa. *Int. J. Eat. Disord.*, **25**: 39–44.
3. Mussell M.P., Crosby R.D., Knopke A.J., Peterson C.B., Wonderlich S.A., Mitchell J.E. (2000) Utilization of empirically supported psychotherapy treatments for individuals with eating disorders: a survey of psychologists. *Int. J. Eat. Disord.*, **27**: 230–237.
4. Treasure J., Schmidt U. (2001) Anorexia nervosa. *Clin. Evid.*, **5**: 1–12.
5. Meads C., Gold L., Burls A. (2001) How effective is outpatient care compared to inpatient care for the treatment of anorexia nervosa? A systematic review. *Eur. Eat. Disord. Rev.*, **9**: 229–241.
6. Gowers S.G., Weetman J., Shore A., Hossain F., Elvins R. (2000) Impact of hospitalisation on the outcome of adolescent anorexia nervosa. *Br. J. Psychiatry*, **176**: 138–141.
7. Ben-Tovim D.I., Walker K., Gilchrist P., Freeman R., Kalucy R., Esterman A. (2001) Outcome in patients with eating disorders: a 5-year study. *Lancet*, **357**: 1254–1257.
8. American Psychiatric Association (1994) *Diagnostic and Statistical Manual of Mental Disorders*, 4th ed. American Psychiatric Association, Washington.
9. Kächele H. (1999) Eine multizentrische Studie zur Aufwand und Erfolg bei psychodynamischer Therapie von Essstörungen. *Psychother. Psychosom. Med. Psychol.*, **49**: 100–106.
10. Wiseman C.V., Sunday S.R., Klapper F., Harris W.A., Halmi K.A. (2001) Changing patterns of hospitalization in eating disorder patients. *Int. J. Eat. Disord.*, **30**: 69–74.
11. Dingemans A.E., Bruna M.J., Van Furth E.F. (2002) Binge eating disorder: a review. *Int. J. Obesity*, **26**: 299–307.

5.6
Further Perspectives on Psychological Interventions for Eating Disorders

Denise E. Wilfley and Elizabeth Rieger[1]

As thoroughly reviewed by Terence Wilson, psychological treatments have been more well-studied for bulimia nervosa as compared with anorexia nervosa and binge eating disorder (BED). Cognitive–behavioural therapy (CBT) is widely recognized as the first-line treatment for bulimia nervosa because of the scope, rapidity and good long-term maintenance of its effects. In spite of this fact, CBT remains relatively under-utilized by practitioners in the USA, which may be due, in part, to its cognitive and behavioural focus. Consequently, it is critical to cultivate alternative, efficacious treatments that may be embraced more readily by practitioners and widely implemented in routine clinical care. Interpersonal psychotherapy (IPT) is theoretically and procedurally distinct from CBT. The

[1] *Department of Psychiatry, Washington University School of Medicine, 667 South Euclid, St. Louis, MO 63110, USA*

interpersonal focus of IPT may be particularly appealing to practitioners, given that it better mimics the type of treatment that is traditionally administered in community-based practices. Moreover, IPT is the only treatment for bulimia nervosa that has demonstrated long-term outcomes comparable with those of CBT up to 6 years following treatment [1,2]. IPT has been rated also as being more suitable than CBT by patients with bulimia nervosa [2,3].

Despite IPT rivalling the effects of CBT in all long-term outcomes, it is not regarded by scientists as being comparable with CBT, owing to two findings from the recent bulimia nervosa multi-site trial [4]. First, IPT was significantly slower than CBT in achieving its therapeutic effect. Second, the outcomes achieved for IPT (i.e. remission from binge eating and purging) were not as impressive as was found in the earlier Oxford CBT–IPT trial [2,5]. Understandably, these two findings have raised questions about the role of IPT in the overall management of bulimia nervosa. However, because IPT does appear to have specific effects in bulimia nervosa and good long-term maintenance of change [1,2], it seems prudent to evaluate methods for improving its efficiency and effectiveness. For instance, it may be that the slower and less potent effects observed in IPT compared with CBT were due to the manner in which IPT was implemented [3,5]. Specifically, in order to minimize procedural overlap with CBT, the research application of IPT for bulimia nervosa has not included an ongoing focus on making links between symptomatology and interpersonal functioning, which is in stark contrast to how IPT was developed and tested for depression [6]. In future studies, the efficacy and efficiency of IPT may be enhanced by including a specific focus on the core symptoms of bulimia nervosa and their connection with interpersonal issues throughout the course of treatment. Such refinements of the content and delivery of IPT may further strengthen its utility in the treatment of bulimia nervosa.

Anorexia nervosa is a condition associated with substantial morbidity and mortality for which there are few methodologically sound treatment outcome studies, and for which even the most promising treatment approaches can yield limited results (e.g. one study evaluating family therapy for adolescents found that nearly 40% of patients experienced a poor outcome [7]). As such, Wilson's emphasis on the need to prioritize research on "promising psychological treatments" for anorexia nervosa is timely. In addition to the comprehensive review of cognitive–behavioural and family therapies provided by Wilson, one approach that has been the focus of increasing theoretical and empirical attention for the treatment of this condition is motivational enhancement therapy (MET).

The rationale for investigating the effectiveness of MET in the treatment of anorexia nervosa arises from the fact that, as Wilson notes, the disorder is typically experienced by patients as ego-syntonic. The high value that patients accord their symptomatology frequently translates into low levels of readiness to recover (e.g. one study found that approximately 80% of inpatients with anorexia nervosa were not yet ready to work actively on change [8]). Although procedures for enhancing motivation to recover are increasingly becoming a standard feature in treatment recommendations for anorexia nervosa [9], there are, as yet, no published randomized control trials (RCTs) investigating MET for anorexia nervosa. Indeed, only one preliminary RCT has been conducted on the effectiveness of MET for bulimia nervosa [10]. Suggestive of the effectiveness of MET for anorexia nervosa, however, is one study that found that a 4-week group intervention utilizing MET among 19 eating disorder patients (12 of whom were diagnosed with anorexia nervosa) resulted in increased motivation to change [11]. Although it is unclear from this study whether increased motivation leads to improved outcome, other research indicates that higher levels of readiness to change are indeed associated with improved outcome (e.g. one study found that higher levels of readiness to recover at the commencement of inpatient treatment predicted greater weight gain during the subsequent 8 weeks of admission) [12].

In addition to evaluating the effectiveness of treatments such as CBT, family therapy and MET, research is required to investigate the optimal sequencing and combination of alternative approaches for anorexia nervosa. MET, for instance, may prove to be beneficial during the engagement phase of treatment as a preparation for behavioural change, whereas approaches such as CBT may be most helpful for weight-restored patients to reduce the high rates of relapse associated with the weight-maintenance stage of recovery [13].

Currently, there is no definitive answer as to what constitutes the most efficacious treatment for BED and controversy exists about whether to recommend treatment for the overweight first, the eating disorder first or both problems simultaneously. For instance, Wilson concludes that behavioural weight loss (BWL) is the first-line treatment choice for BED, whereas other experts recommend addressing the binge eating and associated psychopathology first, rather than making weight loss the focus. This latter viewpoint is justifiable for the following reasons. Firstly, CBT is the most well-established psychotherapeutic treatment for BED, having been shown to be superior to delayed treatment groups, to have better maintenance of change than two different forms of psychological treatment (i.e. BWL and supportive psychotherapy) [14,15], to be superior to fluoxetine and fluvoxamine [16,17] and to augment the effects of BWL [18]. Secondly, the specialized psychological treatments of CBT and IPT have been shown to have marked and long-lasting effects on binge eating, associated eating disorder psychopathology, general psychiatric impairment and other measures of psychosocial functioning (social adjustment, self-esteem). In contrast to this documented evidence of long-term efficacy for up to 1 year post-treatment [19], the existing long-term data for BWL are limited and incomplete. Long-term evaluation of BWL is needed especially because BWL is characterized by progressive weight regain during the follow-up period, which may exacerbate problems with binge eating and associated psychopathology. Thirdly, specialized psychological treatments have been shown to lead reliably to modest, long-term weight loss in those who cease binge eating, a subset of whom even lose clinically significant amounts of weight [19]. Moreover, individuals who achieve and sustain abstinence from binge eating are significantly more likely than non-abstainers to benefit from weight loss treatment [20,21]. Finally, a subset, albeit a small number, of BED patients presenting for treatment are not overweight. In these cases, guided self-help (GSH) could be considered the first step within a stepped-care framework, followed by a course of specialized psychological treatment if the individual was not responsive to GSH.

BWL is easily defensible as a first-line treatment in those individuals with BED who suffer from the highest levels of obesity and medical morbidity risks. Clearly, further work is needed to clarify the most efficacious overall treatment for BED (singular, combination or sequential) and to identify subgroups for whom specific treatments are indicated.

REFERENCES

1. Fairburn C.G., Norman P.A., Welch S.L., O'Connor M.E., Doll H.A., Peveler R.C. (1995) A prospective study of outcome in bulimia nervosa and the long-term effects of three psychological treatments. *Arch. Gen. Psychiatry*, **52**: 304–312.
2. Fairburn C.G., Jones R., Peveler R.C., Hope R.A., O'Connor M. (1993) Psychotherapy and bulimia nervosa. Longer-term effects of interpersonal psychotherapy, behavior therapy, and cognitive behavior therapy. *Arch. Gen. Psychiatry*, **50**: 419–428.
3. Agras W.S., Walsh B.T., Fairburn C.G., Wilson G.T., Kraemer H.C. (2000) A multicenter comparison of cognitive-behavioral therapy and interpersonal psychotherapy for bulimia nervosa. *Arch. Gen. Psychiatry*, **57**: 459–466.
4. Agras W.S., Crow S.J., Halmi K.A., Mitchell J.E., Wilson G.T., Kraemer H.C. (2000) Outcome predictors for the cognitive-behavioral treatment of bulimia nervosa: data from a multisite study. *Am. J. Psychiatry*, **157**: 1302–1308.
5. Fairburn C.G., Jones R., Peveler R.C., Carr S.J., Solomon R.A., O'Connor M.E., Burton J., Hope R.A. (1991) Three psychological treatments for bulimia nervosa. *Arch. Gen. Psychiatry*, **48**: 463–469.
6. Klerman G.L., Weissman M.M., Rounsaville B.J., Chevron E.S. (1984) *Interpersonal Psychotherapy of Depression*. Basic Books, New York.
7. Eisler I., Dare C., Hodes M., Russell G., Dodge E., le Grange D. (2000) Family therapy for adolescent anorexia nervosa. The results of a controlled comparison of two family interventions. *J. Child Psychol. Psychiatry*, **41**: 727–736.

8. Rieger E., Touyz S.W., Beumont P.J.V. (2002) The Anorexia Nervosa Stages of Change Questionnaire (ANSOCQ). Information regarding its psychometric properties. *Int. J. Eat. Disord.*, **32**: 24–38.
9. Vitousek K.M., Watson S., Wilson G.T. (1998) Enhancing motivation for change in treatment-resistant eating disorders. *Clin. Psychol. Rev.*, **18**: 391–420.
10. Treasure J., Katzman M., Schmidt U., Troop N., Todd G., de Silva P. (1999) Engagement and outcome in the treatment of bulimia nervosa. First phase of a sequential design comparing motivational enhancement therapy and cognitive behavioural therapy. *Behav. Res. Ther.*, **37**: 405–501.
11. Feld R., Woodside D.B., Kaplan A.S., Olmsted M.P., Carter J.C. (2001) Pretreatment motivational enhancement therapy for eating disorders. A pilot study. *Int. J. Eat. Disord.*, **29**: 393–400.
12. Rieger E., Touyz S., Schotte D., Beumont P., Russell J., Clarke S., Kohn M., Griffiths R. (2000) Development of an instrument to assess readiness to recover in anorexia nervosa. *Int. J. Eat. Disord.*, **28**: 387–396.
13. Kaplan A. (2002) Psychological treatments for anorexia nervosa. A review of published studies and promising new directions. *Can. J. Psychiatry*, **47**: 235–242.
14. Nauta H., Hospers H., Kok G., Jansen A. (2000) A comparison between a cognitive and a behavioral treatment for obese binge eaters and obese non-binge eaters. *Behav. Ther.*, **31**: 441–461.
15. Kenardy J., Mensch M., Bowen K., Green B., Walton J. (2002) Group therapy for binge eating in type 2 diabetes: a randomized trial. *Diabet. Med.*, **19**: 234–239.
16. Grilo C.M., Masheb R.M., Heninger G., Wilson G.T. (2002) Controlled comparison of cognitive behavioral therapy and fluoxetine for binge eating disorder. Presented at the International Conference of the Academy of Eating Disorders, Boston, 25–28 April.
17. Ricca V., Mannucci E., Mezzani B., Moretti S., Di Bernardo M., Bertelli M., Rotella C.M., Faravelli C. (2001) Fluoxetine and fluvoxamine combined with individual cognitive-behaviour therapy in binge eating disorder: a one-year follow-up study. *Psychother. Psychosom.*, **70**: 298–306.
18. Devlin M.J. (2002) Psychotherapy and medication for binge eating disorder. Presented at the International Conference of the Academy of Eating Disorders, Boston, 25–28 April.
19. Wilfley D.E., Welch R.R., Stein R.I., Spurrell E.B., Cohen L.R., Saelens B.E., Dounchis J.Z., Frank M.A., Wiseman C.V., Matt G.E. (2003) The psychological treatment of binge eating disorder (BED): a comparison group of cognitive behavioral therapy and interpersonal psychotherapy. *Arch. Gen. Psychiatry* (in press).
20. Agras W.S., Telch C.F., Arnow B., Eldredge K., Marnell M. (1997) One-year follow up of cognitive-behavioral therapy for obese individuals with binge eating disorder. *J. Consult. Clin. Psychol.*, **65**: 343–347.
21. Raymond N.C., de Zwaan M., Mitchell J.E., Ackard D., Thuras P. (2002) Effect of a very low calorie diet on the diagnostic category of individuals with binge eating disorder. *Int. J. Eat. Disord.*, **31**: 49–56.

5.7
Establishing the Evidence Base for Psychological Interventions for Eating Disorders
Adrienne Key[1]

Over the last three decades, we have witnessed an exciting exponential rise in the number of publications in the field of eating disorders. We have started to advance our knowledge in many areas including assessment, epidemiology, aetiology and treatment outcome. Despite this, there are substantial areas that remain relatively unexplored, or areas in which our knowledge is fragmentary. As Terence Wilson highlights, the evidence base for the psychological treatment of all eating disorders remains very limited. The studies with sufficient power and scientific rigour have concentrated mainly on bulimia nervosa, establishing cognitive–behavioural therapy (CBT) as the treatment of choice. The evidence base for the other disorders—anorexia nervosa, binge eating disorder (BED) and eating disorder not otherwise specified (EDNOS)—is sparse. Our task to establish empirically based effective treatment interventions for the future is vital because of the high rates of mortality and morbidity associated with eating disorders [1]. The financial implications for both the individual and healthcare services are also of utmost importance.

What are the obstacles to progress? The low prevalence of the eating disorders, particularly anorexia nervosa, means that studies with adequate power can be achieved only through multi-site trials. This requires coordination, cooperation and continuity of therapeutic model between centres. Services have established either variations on models of care or evolved their own therapeutic stance over decades of clinical experience, making comparisons difficult. Treatment programmes need to be manualized in order to be tested adequately and replicated by other practitioners. Once good quality evidence is confirmed, efforts can be directed towards refining and improving models. CBT has been established as the current treatment of choice for bulimia nervosa [2] but even in successfully delivered trials the success rate is still only about 50%. In clinical practice, patients present with atypical eating disorders and comorbid conditions, making treatment less successful. Clinicians are now moving towards using innovative ideas and exploration of the curative factors of these manualized treatment programmes in order to develop enhanced CBT models. Some authors have adapted related models, e.g. schema-focused CBT, with some success.

[1] Department of Psychiatry, St. George's Hospital Medical School, Tooting, London SW17 0RE, UK

The treatment of anorexia nervosa remains complex, compounded by comorbidity, problems of nutritional deficits and other physical complications. As the author highlights, few controlled treatment trials exist and therefore there cannot be a recommended treatment of choice. Once again, a low prevalence of the disorder and high drop-out rates from treatment intensify the difficulties. The behavioural methods applied in the past did not produce sustained psychological or physical change. CBT has not produced significant results in this patient group and indeed a recent outpatient study comparing interpersonal psychotherapy (IPT), CBT and standard medical care demonstrated the latter to be the most effective [3]. Although a series of studies from the Maudsley Hospital has found family therapy to be effective in the treatment of some adolescents with anorexia, the treatment of adults has not been examined empirically. There is, however, a wealth of clinical expertise on the treatment of anorexia nervosa spanning the last four decades, which enables us to understand more fully the difficulties of establishing the treatment of choice for the disorder. Engagement can be a dominant problem with this ego-syntonic disorder, leading to the high drop-out rates. This means that the therapeutic stance needs to be flexible and a clinically advisable approach is to incorporate motivational techniques [4]. The empirical base for this approach is gathering momentum and will be facilitated by a recently developed instrument: the Readiness and Motivation Interview [5]. These motivational techniques particularly aim to empower patients, encouraging their expression of ambivalence about treatment and weight restoration. This approach is useful to apply at all stages of treatment.

Clinicians familiar with anorexia nervosa recognize both a spectrum of severity of the disorder, requiring different treatment facilities, and also treatment stages requiring different therapeutic interventions. The use of inpatient facilities is expensive, but at the current stage of knowledge it can be the only alternative, particularly if the patient's life is at risk or physical complications are escalating. Matching patient variables to treatment intensity is a guiding clinical principle but it may also indicate fruitful areas for future research [6].

Binge eating disorder is a relative newcomer to the diagnostic categories and so research has been very limited. It frequently presents with additional problems such as comorbid depression and obesity and it is generally accepted that the bingeing behaviours are amenable to CBT. Behavioural weight loss (BWL) is seen as cost effective and an easily disseminated method of treatment by Wilson, but studies have failed to demonstrate that weight loss is maintained. The long-term health consequences of obesity are profound and it is generally regarded as the major public health issue of modern times. The binge eating is amenable to treatment and also may wane naturally over time [7]; the obesity, however, remains. Weight loss therefore needs to be a long-term goal of treatment, and interventions that sequence strategies to stabilize eating behaviours and then address weight reduction are being developed [8].

Psychological interventions are the current mainstay of treatment for all eating disorders, but the empirical evidence defining the most effective model is incomplete. As services rapidly develop, two guiding principles need to be stressed: practitioners need to familiarize themselves with the application of proven treatment models for bulimia nervosa, and planning how we can establish the evidence base for the treatment of other eating disorders is imperative.

REFERENCES

1. Agras W.S. (2001) The consequences and costs of the eating disorders. *Psychiatr. Clin. North Am.*, **24**: 371–379.
2. Agras W.S., Walsh B.T., Fairburn C.G., Wilson F.T., Kraemer H.C. (2000) A multicenter comparison of cognitive-behavioural therapy and interpersonal psychotherapy for bulimia nervosa. *Arch. Gen. Psychiatry*, **57**: 459–466.
3. Joyce P. (2002) A comparison of three psychotherapies for anorexia nervosa. Presented at the International Conference on Eating Disorders, Boston, 25–28 April.
4. Treasure J., Ward A. (1997) A practical guide to the use of motivational interviewing in anorexia nervosa. *Eur. Eat. Disord. Rev.*, **5**: 102–114.
5. Geller J., Cockell S.J., Drab D.L. (2001) Assessing readiness for change in the eating disorders: the psychometric properties of the readiness and motivation interview. *Psychol. Assess.*, **13**: 189–198.
6. Kaplan A.S., Olmsted M.P., Carter J.C., Woodside B. (2001) Matching patient variables to treatment intensity. *Psychiatr. Clin. North Am.*, **24**: 281–292.
7. Fairburn C.G., Cooper Z., Norman P., O'Connor M. (2000) The natural course of bulimia nervosa and binge eating disorder in young women. *Arch. Gen. Psychiatry*, **57**: 659–665.
8. Agras W.S., Telch C.F., Arnow B., Eldredge K., Wilfley D.E., Raeburn S., Henderson S.D., Marnell M. (1994) Weight loss, cognitive-behavioural and desipramine treatments in binge eating disorder: an additive design. *Behav. Ther.*, **25**: 225–238.

5.8
Psychoanalytical Psychotherapy in the Eating Disorders

Marilyn Lawrence[1]

Terence Wilson's comprehensive review of psychological treatments for eating disorders focuses on the treatment modalities of cognitive–behavioural therapy (CBT), interpersonal therapy and family therapy.

In this commentary, I will suggest that psychoanalytical psychotherapy is emerging as an effective treatment for anorexia and bulimia nervosa. I will briefly review the literature and suggest that a psychoanalytical perspective can be a particularly useful tool for practitioners in day and inpatient settings, because it suggests that the behaviours associated with eating disorders are meaningful and can be understood.

One of the difficulties of comparing the effectiveness of psychoanalytical psychotherapy with other forms of psychological intervention in eating disorders is that many of the published reports consist of case studies, either single or serial. The appropriateness of designing randomized controlled trials (RCTs) for psychoanalytical interventions has been discussed thoroughly [1–3]. Margison et al. [4] reviewed developments in measurement relevant to psychotherapy. However, the effectiveness of psychoanalysis and the therapies deriving from it is well established in the mental health field in general [5]. Martindale et al. [6] convincingly argue the benefits of psychoanalytical therapy in the treatment of serious psychotic disorders. Milton [7] discusses and evaluates the paradigms of CBT and psychoanalytical psychotherapy, including research evidence on effectiveness. One of her conclusions is that psychoanalytical psychotherapy is more likely to have a lasting effectiveness in cases where symptoms are linked to underlying personality problems.

Psychoanalysis and psychoanalytical psychotherapy for patients with eating disorders have been reported in the literature for at least 60 years [8,9]. Many of these papers focus on single cases, although Thoma [10] reported on a series of more than 60 cases treated with analytical therapy. In this brief commentary, I will focus on some of the contemporary accounts.

Writers basing their work on a psychoanalytical theory of the drives have noted that the sexual drive and the appetite for food are frequently linked. Freud [11] himself mentions the well-known neurosis that occurs in girls at puberty in which aversion to sexuality expresses itself in anorexia. This line of thinking has been most influential in British psychiatry, where the "regression hypothesis" [12] remains a popular explanation.

[1] Tavistock Clinic, London, UK

A turning point was reached in the development of our thinking about eating disorders when psychoanalysts began to conceive of each patient's inner world as unique and peopled. Symptoms such as anorexia can be understood as expressing a relationship to these internalized "people" or objects.

Eating disorders can be understood as a depiction of relationship disorders, often of a very serious nature. Much has been written about the relationship with the mother in anorexia and bulimia. Brusset [13] describes the sense of two people sharing the same skin. Rey [14] comments on the violence of the struggle of the anorexic patient with her internalized mother. Psychoanalytical psychotherapy, unlike some other forms of psychotherapy, works through the relationship between the therapist and patient. Elements of the relationship difficulties with early figures, most often the parents, are re-experienced and worked through with the therapist in a treatment situation. Birksted-Breen [15] describes analytical work with an anorexic patient in which there is a phantasized fusion or merging of patient and analyst. Williams [16] describes a situation in which the infant who later goes on to become anorexic is reacting to the experience of having the unbearable feelings of the mother projected into her.

Lawrence [17] sees eating disorders as a special version of the manic defence, involving in particular a phantasized murder of the parental couple. She further explores this refusal of the father, of the parents as a couple, in a subsequent paper [18].

One of the strengths of psychoanalytical approaches to the treatment of eating disorders is that they provide not only an effective treatment modality but also a way, or ways, of understanding these perplexing symptoms. Hughes [19] demonstrates how the therapist's use of his/her own countertransference reactions to the patient can be a powerful tool in understanding the underlying mental state of the patient. A psychodynamic approach can be invaluable in understanding the reactions of the patient with an eating disorder to the inpatient or day-patient setting [20].

The literature on the use of psychoanalytical psychotherapy remains sparse. The journal *Psychoanalytic Psychotherapy*, which focuses on work in the National Health Service and public sector settings, plans a special issue on eating disorders in 2003, which reflects the growing interest.

REFERENCES

1. Crits-Christoph P. (1992) The efficacy of brief dynamic psychotherapy: a meta-analysis. *Am. J. Psychiatry*, **149**: 151–158.
2. Wampold B. (1997) Methodological problems in identifying efficacious psychotherapies. *Psychother. Res.*, 7: 21–43.

3. Gunderson J., Gabbard G. (1999) Making the case for psychoanalytic therapies in the current psychiatric environment. *J. Am. Psychoanal. Assoc.*, **47**: 679–703.
4. Margison F., McGrath G., Barkham M., Mellor J., Audin K., Connell J., Evans C. (2000) Measurement and psychotherapy. Evidence-based practice and practice-based evidence. *Br. J. Psychiatry*, **177**: 123–130.
5. Fonagy P. (2000) *An Open-door Review of Outcome Studies in Psychoanalysis.* International Psychoanalytical Association, London.
6. Martindale B., Bateman A., Crowe M., Margison F. (Eds) (2000) *Psychosis. Psychological Approaches and their Effectiveness.* Gaskell, London.
7. Milton J. (2001) Psychoanalysis and cognitive behaviour therapy—rival paradigms or common ground? *Int. J. Psychoanal.*, **82**: 431–447.
8. Waller J., Kaufman M., Deutsch F. (1940) Anorexia nervosa: a psychosomatic entity. *Psychosom. Med.*, **11**: 3–16.
9. Binswanger L. (1944) Der Fall Ellen West. *Schweiz. Arch. Neurol. Psychiatrie*, **53**.
10. Thoma H. (1967) *Anorexia Nervosa.* International Universities Press, New York.
11. Freud S. (1918) *From the History of an Infantile Neurosis.* Hogarth, London.
12. Crisp A.H. (1982) *Let Me Be.* Academic Press, London.
13. Brusset B. (1999) *Psychopathologie de l'Anorexie Mentale.* Dunot, Paris.
14. Rey H. (1994) *Universals of Psychoanalysis in the Treatment of Psychotic and Borderline States.* Free Association Books, London.
15. Birksted-Breen D. (1989) Working with an anorexic patient. *Int. J. Psychoanal.*, **70**: 30–40.
16. Williams G. (1997) Reflections on some dynamics of eating disorders; no entry defences and foreign bodies. *Int. J. Psychoanal.*, **78**: 927–942.
17. Lawrence M. (2001) Loving them to death: the anorexic and her objects. *Int. J. Psychoanal.*, **82**: 43–55.
18. Lawrence M. (2003) Body, mother, mind. Anorexia, femininity and the intrusive object. *Int. J. Psychoanal.* (in press).
19. Hughes P. (1997) The use of the countertransference in the therapy of patients with anorexia nervosa. *Eur. Eat. Disord. Rev.*, **5**: 258–269.
20. Marsden P. (2001) Food and violence: factors in the inpatient treatment of eating disorders. *Psychoanal. Psychother.*, **15**: 225–242.

5.9

To Prove or Not to Prove? Limitations of Evidence-based Choice of Treatment in Eating Disorders

Michel Botbol[1]

Beyond their clinical differences, eating disorders have in common the fact that they challenge significantly any programme designed to treat them. The number and diversity of proposed psychological programmes is proof of this. It is crucial to promote therapeutic evaluations to be able to choose

[1] *Clinic Dupré, BP 101, Sceaux 92333, France*

between these very disparate psychological approaches, especially as eating disorders are rather resistant to pharmacological treatments.

Two general remarks have to be made here: a) although there are quite a number of randomized controlled trials (RCTs) studying cognitive–behavioural therapies (CBT), there are only a few RCTs dealing with other specific psychotherapies; b) in the results of the RCTs, there is a big discrepancy between those dealing with bulimia nervosa, which are rather clear, those dealing with binge eating disorder (BED), which are less obvious, and those dealing with anorexia nervosa, which are quite contradictory.

Terence Wilson's paper is an accurate reflection of this complex picture. In bulimia nervosa, he brings evidence of the superiority of CBT on pharmacological treatments and on behavioural therapy. This superiority does not appear as clearly when CBT is compared with interpersonal therapy (IPT). When differences exist, they are small and disputable, requiring some methodological specifications. First of all, CBT actually implies a relation, even if it does not use it as a therapeutic mean; on the other hand, in a therapeutic context, a non-interpretative and non-directive IPT will generally have to deal with cognitive aspects of bulimia nervosa. In this frame, to compare CBT with IPT is to compare a manual-based CBT with a more impressionistic IPT with cognitive aspects. Obviously this may favour the manual-based technique rather than the less standardized one, this being a bias for such studies. On the other hand, none of the papers quoted by Wilson compare CBT or IPT with specific psychoanalytical approaches or with family therapy, or with the many-sided inpatient treatments that are broadly used in France and characterized by the fact that different psychological approaches are not only possible but even favoured. If evidence is given upon CBT or IPT efficacy, no evidence is thus given that they are the only ones to be efficacious or that they are superior to others that have not been compared with them. In other words, there is no evidence-based data that the above-mentioned alternative treatments are not efficacious in bulimia nervosa, making Wilson's conclusions arguable on evidence-based principles.

The same point can be raised for BED, because the papers quoted by Wilson compare CBT only with educational approaches.

Wilson's conclusions on treatment for anorexia nervosa are less straight-forward, even from his CBT-oriented position. His review reveals that, because of CBT limitations, other specific psychological treatments were taken into account by well-designed RCTs [1]. The conclusions drawn by these last studies were confirmed by recent RCTs comparing behavioural therapy, psychoanalytically oriented treatment and family therapy. These RCTs show that all the specific approaches are equally more effective than a "routine treatment" in producing weight gain, none of them being superior to others [2,3]. Wilson's conclusions on CBT in anorexia nervosa are cautious and may be true, but they are not evidence based.

RCTs are not equally feasible with all types of treatments; from this point of view the greatest handicap is for "many-sided" treatments, i.e. treatments not clearly founded on a specific theoretical point of view or defining their practice on the basis of more than one theory. This is the case of the programme that we propose in the Clinic Dupré in Sceaux. Apart from the many-sided community treatment they receive in this programme, most of our patients with eating disorders benefit also from a psychoanalytically oriented psychotherapy (weekly individual psychotherapy or individual psychoanalytical psychodrama) and/or family therapy (monthly sessions); on the other hand, their inpatient everyday life is marked by many non-specific cognitive–behavioural interventions by the nursing staff. Patients are referred to us by many French specialized departments, most of which work during the acute phase of the disorder on the basis of the weight contract model designed by Jeammet and his team. Our long-term post-acute treatment finds its place in this contract. The whole is globally referred to as psychoanalytically oriented community treatment theory; as we already said, this does not mean that psychoanalysis is the only reference for the different therapeutic aspects of this treatment. This programme is funded by the French national health insurance system and is free of charge for all patients. Immediate outcomes are similar to those found in other intensive programmes [4,5], with 52% of good outcome, 35% intermediate and only 13% of poor outcome [6]. For the moment this programme has not been tested in any RCT, because of methodological and ethical difficulties.

To conclude these brief remarks, I would like to suggest that, because of the scarcity of available data, it might be too early for an evidence-based selection of treatment for eating disorders. At present, clinical tradition, theoretical considerations and case studies may still be of more help for this selection. However, as Wilson points out, RCTs must be promoted, but I think that it will be of much help if future RCTs focus not only on systematized techniques or theoretical points of view but also on questions raised by existing practice with mixed theoretical backgrounds. Moreover, it seems to me that efforts are still needed to avoid the methodological tendency to consider that measurements are the only way to reach accuracy.

REFERENCES

1. Crisp A.H., Norton K., Gowers S., Halek C., Bowyer C., Yeldham D., Levett G., Bhat A. (1991) A controlled study of the effect of therapies aimed at adolescent and family psychopathology in anorexia nervosa. _Br. J. Psychiatry_, **159**: 325–333.

2. Treasure J., Todd G., Brolly M. (1995) A pilot study of a randomized trial of cognitive analytical therapy vs educational behavioural therapy for adult anorexia nervosa. *Behav. Res. Ther.*, **33**: 363–367.
3. Dare C., Russel G., Treasure J., Dodge L. (2001) Psychological therapies for adults with anorexia nervosa. *Br. J. Psychiatry*, **178**: 216–221.
4. Jeammet P., Brechon G., Payan C., Gorge A., Fermanian J. (1991) Le devenir de l'anorexie mentale: une étude prospective de 129 patients évalués au moins quatre ans après leur premiére admission. *Psychiatr. Enfant*, **34**: 381–442.
5. Hsu L.K.G. (1986) The treatment of anorexia nervosa. *Am. J. Psychiatry*, **143**: 573–581.
6. Botbol M. (2000) Rapport d'activité de la clinique Dupré. Unpublished manuscript.

5.10
Different Psychotherapeutic Approaches: For What Reasons?

Philippe Jeammet and Nathalie Godart[1]

Eating disorders, especially anorexia nervosa and bulimia nervosa, are characterized by symptoms that are uniform across populations, although the severity and course of the disease vary significantly, being affected by the degree of malnutrition and the comorbidity with DSM-IV [1] Axis I or II diagnoses. Although the primary target of treatment is the eating disorder, the outcome of comorbid conditions, especially personality disorders, cannot be ignored. The presence of personality disorders is among the predictors of treatment utilization. Moreover, several patients with personality disorders, particularly borderline personality disorder, are highly disturbed, impulsive and emotionally dysregulated individuals, which has implications for the choice of therapy. Can we assume the efficacy of a given type of psychotherapy if only its effects on the symptoms of the eating disorder are evaluated?

As noted by Terence Wilson, the efficacy of cognitive–behavioural therapy (CBT) in bulimia nervosa has been demonstrated thoroughly in the literature, yet it appears that "CBT is used relatively infrequently by clinical practitioners". However, numerous practitioners have treated bulimic patients over the years using various methods (such as psychoanalytical approaches and family therapy) and have had satisfactory results. Undeniably and unfortunately, these classic treatment approaches have hardly or never been evaluated. Evidence of the efficacy of methods such as CBT should not lead to an invalidation of other apparently satisfactory approaches because their efficacy has not yet been demonstrated

[1] *Department of Adolescent and Young Adult Psychiatry, Institut Mutualiste Montsouris, Paris 75014, France*

empirically. As Wilson reports, the effectiveness of interpersonal therapy in bulimia could also be shown. This should encourage us to promote research on the different treatment modalities used today. The profiles of patients with eating disorders are so diverse that clinicians may choose approaches that correspond better to certain profiles or certain moments than others. Moreover, bulimia nervosa can take such an erratic course that different models may need to be tested out before an appropriate and effective treatment strategy is found. When one considers treatment outcome over the long term, the unfortunate conclusion is often that effectiveness is only partial. In a literature review on the outcome of bulimics, Keel and Mitchell [2] tentatively conclude: "Treatment interventions may speed eventual recovery but do not appear to alter outcome more than five years following presentation".

Although research results concerning CBT for anorexia nervosa are not as convincing as in bulimia nervosa, several studies focusing on existing clinical practices are available. Recently, Dare and Eisler [3] showed that, in anorexic adults, a year of focal psychoanalytical therapy and family therapy was significantly superior to a control treatment (low contact "routine treatment"). Terence Wilson cites research on family therapy. Whereas family therapy seems more effective than individual psychotherapy in early-onset anorexia of brief duration [4], it does not follow that individual psychotherapy is not useful or even preferable for patients whose different characteristics would be worth knowing. Why is it that research results are comparable and even in favour of individual psychotherapy for older patients with longer disease histories? Is the difference simply a matter of age? Or is the personality involved?

Longitudinal studies, lasting from 4 to 20 years (with a mean of 11 years), show that, even if eating disorder symptoms due to anorexia disappear, depressive symptoms, social withdrawal and paranoid tendencies remain to a varying degree in nearly 50% of cases [5].

We have, in fact, little information on the long-term effects of psycho-therapeutic treatment of these patients. Under these conditions, it seems wise to pursue longitudinal research evaluating the effect of different treatments also on comorbidity associated with eating disorders. This could be of immense value and allow us to understand better the factors of change that, once identified, could become the subject of a large number of research projects. While waiting for the knowledge that we lack, it seems important not to disqualify certain clinical practices, in particular individual psycho-analytical psychotherapy and methods combining different individual and family therapy methods. Finally, therapists' motivation and personality seem to be important factors for change in patients. Many clinicians recognize that patients are highly sensitive to the therapeutic environment and to the image of themselves that their therapist reflects back to them.

REFERENCES

1. American Psychiatric Association (1994) *Diagnostic and Statistical Manual of Mental Disorders*, 4th ed. American Psychiatric Association, Washington.
2. Keel P.K., Mitchell J.E. (1997) Outcome in bulimia nervosa. *Am. J. Psychiatry*, **154**: 313–320.
3. Dare C., Eisler I. (2001) Psychological therapies for adults with anorexia nervosa. *Br. J. Psychiatry*, **178**: 216–221.
4. Eisler I., Dare C., Russel G.F.M., Szmukler G., le Grange D., Dodge E. (1997) Family and individual therapy in anorexia nervosa. *Arch. Gen. Psychiatry*, **54**: 1025–1030.
5. Jeammet P., Brechon G., Payan C., Gorgé A., Fermamian J. (1991) Le devenir de l'anorexie mentale. Une étude prospective de 129 patients évalués au moins 4 ans après leur première admission. *Psychiatr. Enfant*, **31**: 381–442.

5.11
Eating Disorders—Family Business or Not?

Eia Asen[1]

Terence Wilson's review admirably covers the depth and width of the available treatment methods and research evidence. This commentary focuses on the place of the family in working with eating disordered patients.

The evidence for the effectiveness of family therapy for adolescent anorexia nervosa is clearly compelling, as several reviewers have recently concluded [1,2], and on current evidence this is probably the treatment of choice. It is important to recognize, however, that this may be, at least in part, due to the lack of research on other treatments. Conclusions about the comparisons between different kinds of family interventions have to be cautious. Treatments that encourage the parents to take an active role in tackling their daughter's anorexia nervosa seem the most effective and may have some advantages over involving the parents in a way that is primarily supportive and understanding of their daughter, but encourages them to step back from the eating problem. Not involving the parents in the treatment at all leads to the worst outcome and may considerably delay recovery. Seeing whole families may have disadvantages for those in which there are high levels of hostility or criticism. Such families can be difficult to engage in family treatment [3], because feelings of guilt and blame can be increased as a consequence of criticisms or confrontations occurring during family sessions.

[1] *Marlborough Family Service, 38 Marlborough Place, London NW8 0PJ, UK*

Multiple-family therapy day programmes in Dresden [4] and at the Maudsley Hospital in London [5] are recent developments in the treatment of adolescent anorexia. Here, up to six families attend simultaneously for whole days, initially 4 days in a block and subsequently once monthly for another 9 months. The therapeutic factors of multiple-family work include reducing social isolation, de-stigmatization, enhancing opportunities to create new and multiple perspectives, learning from each other and neutralizing chronic staff–patient relationships [6]. Families are encouraged to explore how the eating disorder and the interactional patterns in the family have become entangled. The sharing of experiences among families and the intensity of the treatment programme make this a very different experience for families than the more conventional outpatient family therapy. It allows many parents to re-stake their claim to parenting and parental authority in a very literal way, by taking very firm charge of their daughter's eating until she is out of physical danger.

Preliminary findings in Dresden and London show that the drop-out rate is very low in both centres. In many teenagers there have been surprisingly fast somatic improvements (increased weight, return of menstruation, stabilization of eating, reduction of bingeing and vomiting, decreased laxative abuse). Family tension and dispute are significantly reduced within the context of a cooperative and supportive working environment.

Proponents of different models of psychotherapy are often prone to make exaggerated claims for their own particular therapeutic approach, leading to a polarization between treatment models. Asay and Lambert [7], in summarizing many years of psychotherapy research in a variety of disorders, have estimated that, when different psychotherapies are compared, as little as 15% of the outcome variance is accounted for by factors that are unique to a specific mode of psychotherapy, with the rest being divided between individual therapist factors (30%), patient and environmental factors (40%) and a general placebo or expectancy effect (15%). This should not be taken to mean that it does not matter what therapeutic approach we adopt. There are many studies that have shown that while more than one treatment may be effective, there are also treatments that are ineffective. For instance, the study by Fairburn et al. [8], which showed a similarity in outcome between cognitive–behavioural therapy and interpersonal therapy, also showed that behaviour therapy was ineffective in the long term, despite initial positive responses to the treatment. Similarly, the Maudsley study of outpatient psychotherapies in adult anorexia nervosa [9] showed little difference between family therapy, focal psychodynamic therapy and cognitive analytical therapy, but high-lighted the greater effectiveness of these specialized treatments in comparison with routine treatment.

REFERENCES

1. Wilson T., Fairburn C. (1998) Eating disorders. In *Treatments that Work*, 2nd ed. (Eds P. Nathan, J. Gorman), pp. 559–592. Oxford University Press, New York.
2. Carr A. (2000) Evidence-based practice in family therapy and systemic consultation. I: Child-based problems. *J. Fam. Ther.*, **22**: 29–60.
3. Szmukler G.I., Eisler I., Russell G.F.M., Dare C. (1985) Parental "expressed emotion", anorexia nervosa and dropping out of treatment. *Br. J. Psychiatry*, **147**: 265–271.
4. Scholz M., Asen E. (2001) Multiple family therapy with eating disordered adolescents: concepts and preliminary results. *Eur. Eat. Disord. Rev.*, **9**: 33–42.
5. Dare C., Eisler I. (2000) A multi-family group day treatment programme for adolescent eating disorder. *Eur. Eat. Disord. Rev.*, **8**: 4–18.
6. Asen E. (2002) Multiple family therapy: an overview. *J. Fam. Ther.*, **24**: 3–16.
7. Asay T.P., Lambert M.J. (1999) The empirical case for the common factors in therapy: quantitative findings. In *The Heart and Soul of Change. What Works in Therapy* (Eds M.A. Hubble, B.L. Duncan, D.M. Scott), pp. 23–55. American Psychiatric Association, Washington.
8. Fairburn C.G., Jones R., Peveler R.C., Carr S.J., Solomon R.A., O'Conner M.E., Burton J., Hope R.A. (1991) Three psychological treatments for bulimia nervosa. *Arch. Gen. Psychiatry*, **48**: 463–469.
9. Dare C., Eisler I., Russell G.F.M., Treasure J., Dodge E. (2001) Psychological therapies for adult patients with anorexia nervosa: a randomised controlled trial of out-patient treatments. *Br. J. Psychiatry*, **178**: 216–221.

5.12

Nothing is as Practical as a Good Theory

Anita Jansen[1]

Terence Wilson exhaustively reviews the state of the art in the psychological treatment of eating disorders, and it is clear that one of the major developments in psychotherapy during the past decades is the systematic and successful application of cognitive–behavioural therapy (CBT) to bulimia nervosa. Many well-controlled large-scale studies convincingly show that manual-based CBT currently is the treatment of choice for bulimia nervosa. However, methodologically sound research on the effectiveness of treatments for the other eating disorders—anorexia nervosa and binge eating disorder (BED)—is scarcely out of the egg. Well-controlled powerful clinical trials designed to evaluate treatments for anorexia nervosa are completely lacking: up to now there is no consistent evidence for the efficacy of any treatment for anorexia nervosa, and preliminary data on

[1] *Universiteit Maastricht, Research Group Experimental Psychopathology, Faculty of Psychology, PO Box 616, 6200 MD Maastricht, The Netherlands*

BED treatment shows that CBT is not superior to alternative psychological treatments, but this might reflect a power problem. Anyhow, there is an urgent need for proper clinical trials that evaluate treatments for anorexia nervosa and BED.

But there is more. Although manual-based CBT definitely is the most effective treatment for bulimia nervosa and the best we can offer, a closer critical look at the long-term CBT effects shows that 6 years following treatment 37% of the patients still meet the diagnostic criteria for an eating disorder [1]. So there is considerable room for improvement, and clinical researchers should ask themselves how the effectiveness of treatment could be expanded. Making treatment more complicated and longer for patients with severe bulimia nervosa, or non-responders in particular, might be a natural human response, but there is no empirical motivation at all for thinking that this is the best strategy.

What is needed now in the field of eating disorders is more strategic experimental research aimed at identifying the mechanisms that maintain an eating disorder. First we should identify what we need to treat and then think up the specific treatment; when we understand why eating disorders continue to exist, then effective interventions will be more or less apparent.

Also CBT is based on several assumptions about the maintenance of the eating disorder, and it consists of several cognitive and behavioural procedures to tackle the alleged maintenance mechanisms, but the empirical evidence for the validity of most of these maintenance mechanisms is limited. For example, CBT for bulimia nervosa is based on the assumption that restrained eating unavoidably leads to binge eating, which is why CBT for bulimia nervosa aims to reduce restraint. A striking fact, however, is that increased restraint in the case of bulimia nervosa is believed to be responsible for increased binge eating, whereas increased restraint in BED is believed to be responsible for decreased binge eating. The idea that restraint leads to increased binge frequency in bulimia nervosa is based largely on retrospective self-reports and correlational experimental designs. The retrospective self-reports have profound methodological limitations and the quasi-experimental laboratory studies show, at the very most, a correlation between restraint and manipulation-induced overeating (and we all know that correlations do not infer anything about causality). Some authors recently argued that it is a tendency towards overeating that triggers restraint, instead of the other way around. They state that restraint is a fight against eating more than is needed, instead of eating less than is needed [2]. If that is true, discouraging restraint in patients with bulimia nervosa might be disastrous for them, because they need their restraint to succeed in maintaining their weight, and possibly binge frequency and body satisfaction, on an acceptable level.

We do not know which of the CBT treatment components are effective, necessary, sufficient, redundant or possibly counter-productive. By definition, CBT assumes that both the cognitive as well as the behavioural interventions are needed for a successful treatment. Data indeed show that reduction of the treatment to the behavioural intervention increases relapse [1], but to my surprise and best knowledge little or no attempts are made to reduce treatment to a pure cognitive intervention. Cognitive restructuring is effective in tackling cognitive processes related to the loathing of one's body, which is supposed to be the heart of the eating disorder. But do we really know these cognitive processes? What is the exact nature of the body dissatisfaction? And how can the dissatisfaction with one's body be reduced? The popular idea is that the feelings of unattractiveness reflect a distorted body image. Is there indeed something wrong in the information processing? We found, as expected, that women with symptomatic eating evaluate their bodies as much less attractive than normal controls, despite a normal body mass index and waist/hip ratio. But what we did not expect was that large naive forums also evaluated the bodies of such subjects as less attractive, without knowing that half of the sample had eating symptoms and the other half did not [3]. Our data suggest that dissatisfaction with one's body may be associated with a body that is objectively less attractive but certainly not too fat. The dissatisfaction with one's body might be transferred mistakenly to weight. It is, after all, easier to do something about body weight than about narrow shoulders or short legs. These data are just to illustrate that we first need to know precisely what kind of cognitive processes lie at the heart of the eating disorders and only then we will be able to manipulate the processes considered responsible for maintenance of the eating disorder. Experimental manipulation of the responsible processes should elicit changes in the behaviour that we aim to explain.

It was argued that models of maintenance mechanisms in eating disorders could still be greatly improved. It was also argued that nothing is as practical as a good theory: research into parsimonious models of relevant mechanisms, as well as experimental tests of the validity of these models, is a very effective way to develop the most effective treatment strategies.

REFERENCES

1. Fairburn C.G., Norman P.A., Welch S.L., O'Connor M.E., Doll H.A., Peveler R.C. (1995) A prospective study of outcome in bulimia nervosa and the long-term effects of three psychological treatments. *Arch. Gen. Psychiatry*, **52**: 304–312.

2. Lowe M.R. (1993) The effects of dieting on eating behavior: a three-factor model. *Psychol. Bull.*, **114**: 100–121.
3. Jansen A. I see what you see: are the negative body images of eating symptomatic subjects cognitive distortions or not? (submitted for publication).

5.13
Great Expectations, Yet Anorexic Results

Táki Athanássios Cordás,
Daniel Boleira Guimaraes and Cristiano Nabuco de Abreu[1]

Eating disorders are probably among the few psychiatric entities for which psychotherapy, instead of pharmacotherapy, is regarded as the first treatment option. However, psychotherapies that are performed in clinical practice are often different from those whose efficacy is proved by research.

There are still very experienced doctors who use non-systematic treatment practices in anorexia nervosa, in which the therapist takes an almost paternalistic stance that swings between discipline and affection. This therapy, based on psychological ascendance over the patient, seems to have changed very little since William Gull and still reminds us of Pinel's moral treatment.

Ryle's statement that the treatment must include "explanation, reassurance, distraction, and firm treatment of starvation", and if necessary a nurse who would sit with the patient until her food was eaten, still holds a very modern appeal, even though it was published more than 60 years ago [1].

Terence Wilson's authoritative and comprehensive review shows the paucity of controlled trials of psychotherapeutic interventions for anorexia nervosa. This is due in part to practical obstacles: low incidence, frequently intensive inpatient treatment, ethical risks of "no treatment" or "waiting list", high comorbidity and refusal of treatment.

Early clinical descriptions and empirical studies revealed clinical and personality differences between restricting and binge/purge types of anorexia nervosa. The relevance of these differences to psychotherapeutic treatment has not been studied systematically.

Another important aspect that can interfere with the adherence to treatment and with its outcome is neuropsychological impairment. In psychiatric patients, the identification of cognitive deficits generally predicts a poor clinical outcome. Neuropsychological and brain abnormalities found in patients with anorexia nervosa are among the most impressive physical consequences of the illness and in particular of

[1] *Department of Psychiatry, Faculty of Medicine, University of São Paulo, Brazil*

starvation. It had been assumed that these brain anormalities reverse with weight restoration. Nevertheless, recent evidence [2] has shown that it is not true in all cases. This is a relevant aspect, because psychotherapeutic treatments are often carried out or begun with undernourished or underweight patients.

Wilson's review points to the fact that family therapy is effective as long as those assisted are adolescents; the benefits of family therapy on adult patients are less clear. Dare *et al.* [3] showed some benefits with focal therapy and family therapy in a group of adult patients, but more than two-thirds remained abnormally underweight at the end of treatment.

Regarding the psychological interventions for bulimia nervosa, cognitive–behavioural therapy (CBT) is found consistently to be effective in controlled clinical trials of manual-based protocols. However, it is well known that the combination of CBT and antidepressant medication shows some advantages compared with psychotherapy alone. A systematic review by Bacaltchuk *et al.* [4], evaluating 12 trials, showed that the remission rate was 42% vs. 23% when combination treatment was compared with antidepressants alone, and 49% vs. 36% when combination treatment was compared with psychological approaches. The real problem is the drop-out rate: 16% for psychological treatments vs. 30% for combination therapy, possibly due to medication side effects or rejection of medication by bulimic patients.

Data collected in our treated population of bulimic patients showed that some non-specific factors predicting drop-out from psychological interventions can be identified. Forty-five patients were followed up for 12 months while receiving either group CBT or psychodynamic group psychotherapy or a psychoeducational intervention. The global drop-out rate was high (77%), but this was a non-selected clinical sample. The group of drop-outs showed a significantly longer duration of illness, a higher comorbidity with depression, a lower educational level and a high frequency of use of appetite moderators (largely consumed in Brazil) [5].

An important problem that exists in developing countries is how to engage these patients in treatment. Cheaper alternative formats of CBT, such as self-help orientation programmes, brief psychoeducational groups and short-term CBT groups, should be first-line choices [6].

Finally, it is important to highlight that there is a very significant difference in how psychotherapeutic work is conceived across the continents. For instance, cognitive therapy is often practised in South America through a significant alteration of the original principles. In Brazil, instructing patients on how to use record diaries of dysfunctional thoughts may be interpreted as a joke. Thus, when we talk about "cognitive interventions", we should not forget to fit them into the given region and the specific cognitive universe (which currently comprises over 25 distinct types of psychotherapy).

Another important factor is how cognitive therapists are trained. In Latin America, cognitive therapy is still in a germinative status, where very few professionals succeed in receiving appropriate technical education, compared with other psychotherapeutic schools such as psychoanalysis.

REFERENCES

1. Ryle J.A. (1936) Anorexia nervosa. *Lancet*, **ii**: 893–899.
2. Hendren R.L., De Backer I., Pandina G.J. (2000) Review of neuroimaging studies of child and adolescent psychiatric disorders from the past 10 years. *J. Am. Acad. Child Adolesc. Psychiatry*, **39**: 815–828.
3. Dare C., Eisler I., Russell G., Treasure J., Dooge L. (2001) Psychological therapies for adults with anorexia nervosa. *Br. J. Psychiatry*, **178**: 216–221.
4. Bacaltchuk J., Trefiglio R.P., Oliveira I.R., Hay P., Lima M.S., Mari J.J. (2000) Combination of antidepressants and psychological treatments for bulimia nervosa: a systematic review. *Acta Psychiatr. Scand.*, **101**: 256–264.
5. Guimaraes D.B.S. (2002) Avaliação dos fatores de abandono no tratamento psicoterápico grupal ambulatorial da bulimia nervosa [Evaluation of dropout factors in outpatient group psychological treatment for bulimia nervosa]. Unpublished thesis, University of São Paulo.
6. Wilson G.T. (1996) Treatment of bulimia nervosa: when CBT fails. *Behav. Res. Ther.*, **34**: 197–212.

5.14

A Recipe for the Psychological Management of Eating Disorders

Stephen William Touyz[1]

Terence Wilson's authoritative and comprehensive review of contemporary treatments for patients with eating disorders illustrates the vexed nature of the task at hand. There is an urgent need to develop more effective and long-lasting treatments for these debilitating and often serious disorders. One is encouraged by the optimistic treatment outcome data for patients with bulimia nervosa. However, we remain somewhat sobered by the daunting prospect that awaits researchers to do likewise for patients with anorexia nervosa and to a lesser extent binge eating disorder (BED). Ground-breaking genetic research may discover biological evidence of a genetic underpinning to anorexia nervosa. It is not beyond the realm of fantasy that such genetic discoveries may have a profound effect on the

[1] *School of Psychology, University of Sydney, New South Wales, Australia*

ways in which we treat our patients with eating disorders in the years to come.

Since manual-based cognitive–behavioural therapy (CBT) for the treatment of bulimia nervosa was pioneered by Chris Fairburn in 1981 [1], numerous studies have been conducted comparing its effectiveness with other psychological treatments, such as interpersonal psychotherapy (IPT) and more psychodynamically focused interventions. Furthermore, studies comparing the relative and combined efficacy of CBT and antidepressant medication have been the subject of extensive investigation. The findings that have emerged have been most encouraging in that we now have evidence-based treatments with proven efficacy. There is no doubt that CBT has the shibboleth, with a more rapid onset of action resulting in a more sustained improvement following the first 2 months of treatment, and that a selective serotonin reuptake inhibitor (SSRI) should be considered only if a severe comorbid depression is evident.

Despite the effectiveness of CBT and IPT, many rural and remote patients are denied evidenced-based treatments because of the lack of appropriately trained clinicians or cost. We should therefore not become complacent but continue to explore more cost-effective and readily assessable treatments, such as nutritional management provided by highly trained dietitians [2], grouped-based CBT [3], guided self-help (GSH) [4] and/or innovative family physician shared-care programmes [5].

There have been excellent descriptions of anorexia nervosa in the published literature dating back to 1689, but surprisingly few controlled treatment trials have been conducted. Wilson cites numerous reasons for this, including the length of treatment required. This is lamentable, especially as anorexia nervosa has the highest mortality rate of any mental disorder. The use of behaviour therapy to refeed patients with anorexia nervosa was initially greeted with much enthusiasm. However, this soon waned when subsequent research revealed that many patients relapsed when they were discharged. Such operant programmes became demonized as being inhumane, because they were perceived to remove all control from that of the patient, i.e. patients were often kept in bed in a single room without access to their family, friends or personal possessions. However, when applied in a more humane and lenient fashion, they have shown promise as an adjunct to inpatient management [6]. Such programmes continue to be used in this fashion and warrant further investigation. Both CBT and nutritional counselling have been impressive clinically, but unfortunately the published studies to date have compared them with one another rather than combining these two treatments. Our group has also developed an innovative exercise counselling programme [7], as well as using videotape feedback to improve eating behaviour [8]. These specific treatments targeting excessive exercise and abnormal eating require further examination.

There is now much interest in the model of family therapy originally developed at the Maudsley Hospital in London [9] and now further refined by James Lock, Daniel le Grange and their colleagues [10]. This treatment assists parents to assume direct responsibility for modifying their daughter's eating and is showing early promise, but requires further investigation.

Arthur Crisp's somewhat unexpected but rather striking finding that patients with anorexia who were treated with brief outpatient therapy gained as much weight as those receiving much longer intensive inpatient treatment has resulted in more attention being given to outpatient and/or day patient treatment [11]. We have proposed recently a "stage of change" day hospital intervention programme that is currently being evaluated [12]. It is likely that almost all patients with anorexia nervosa soon will be treated as ambulatory patients, with only those with serious medical or psychiatric complications (i.e. suicidality) being admitted to inpatient units. It is therefore a matter of some urgency that we develop more cost-effective ambulatory programmes for patients with anorexia nervosa.

Controversy abounds as to what should be considered the treatment of choice in BED. Should it be behavioural weight loss (BWL) programmes that entail both moderate and severe caloric restriction, or CBT and IPT that have been shown to be equally effective in BED? I strongly support Wilson's argument that BWL should be the first choice, especially as such treatment does not require the professional expertise demanded by CBT and IPT and can be administered by many more healthcare professionals. A stepped-care approach makes good sense in BED, in which patients are first exposed to GSH. Should they fail with either GSH or BWL, then CBT or IPT can be chosen with no evidence to separate them.

The development of novel and innovative treatments for patients with eating disorders is gathering momentum. The next decade will be an exciting one as advances in genetic linkage findings combined with new psychological treatments will no doubt result in further advances in alleviating suffering from these debilitating disorders. This is particularly pertinent in anorexia nervosa, with which patients often struggle for many years before finally overcoming their illness.

REFERENCES

1. Fairburn C.G. (1981) A cognitive behavioural approach to the management of bulimia. *Psychol. Med.*, **11**: 707–711.
2. Laessle R.G., Beumont P.J.V., Butow P., Lennerts W., O'Connor M., Pirke KM., Touyz S.W., Waadt S. (1991) A comparison of nutritional management with stress management in the treatment of bulimia nervosa. *Br. J. Psychiatry*, **159**: 250–261.

3. Chen E.Y., Touyz S.W., Beumont P.J.V., Fairburn C.Y., Griffiths R., Butow P., Russell J., Schotte D.E., Gertler R., Basten C. (2000) A comparison of group and individual cognitive-behavioural therapy for patients with bulimia nervosa. Presented at the 9th International Conference on Eating Disorders, New York, 4–7 May.
4. Fairburn C.G. (1995) *Overcoming Binge Eating.* Guilford Press, New York.
5. Beumont P. (2000) Anorexia nervosa as a mental and physical illness: the medical perspective. In *The Encultured Body* (Eds D. Gaskill, F. Sanders), pp. 80–94. Queensland University of Technology, Brisbane.
6. Touyz S.W., Beumont P.J.V., Glaun D., Philips T., Cowie I. (1984) Comparison of a lenient and strict operant conditioning programme in refeeding patients with anorexia nervosa. *Br. J. Psychiatry*, **144**: 512–520.
7. Beumont P.J.V., Arthur B., Russell J.D., Touyz S.W. (1994) Excessive physical activity in dieting disorder patients: proposals for a supervised exercise program. *Int. J. Eat. Disord.*, **15**: 21–36.
8. Touyz S.W., Williams H., Marden K., Kopec-Schrader E., Beumont P.J.V. (1994) Videotape feedback of eating behaviour in patients with anorexia nervosa: does it normalise eating behaviour? *Aust. J. Nutr. Diet.*, **51**: 79–82.
9. Russell G.F.M., Szmukler G.I., Dare C., Eisler I. (1987) An evaluation of family therapy in anorexia nervosa and bulimia nervosa. *Arch. Gen. Psychiatry*, **44**: 1047–1056.
10. Lock J., le Grange D., Agras W.S., Dare C. (2001) *Treatment Manual for Anorexia Nervosa: a Family-based Approach.* Guilford Press, New York.
11. Crisp A.H., Norton K., Gowers S., Halek C., Bowyer C., Yeldham D., Levett G., Bhart A. (1991) A controlled study of the effect of therapies aimed at adolescent and family psychopathology in anorexia nervosa. *Br. J. Psychiatry*, **159**: 325–333.
12. Touyz S.W., Thornton C., Rieger E., George L., Beumont P.J.V. (2003) The incorporation of the stage of change model in the day hospital treatment of patients with anorexia nervosa. *Eur. Child Adolesc. Psychiatry* (in press).

5.15
Psychological Interventions for Eating Disorders: Much Done, Much to be Done

Phillipa J. Hay[1] and Josue Bacaltchuk[2]

There is now a substantive body of knowledge to guide psychological treatments for eating disorders. In anorexia nervosa most major studies are of family therapy, whereas in bulimia nervosa (and binge eating disorder) most are of cognitive–behavioural therapy (CBT). Significant contributions for the former have been from researchers at the Maudsley Hospital in the UK, and for the latter from Fairburn and Agras and their colleagues. However, despite support from trials, evidence for superiority of these

[1] *Department of Psychiatry, University of Adelaide, Australia*
[2] *Department of Psychiatry, Federal University of São Paulo, Brazil*

treatment approaches is not yet compelling, and a number of other therapies, notably interpersonal psychotherapy (IPT) for bulimia nervosa and variants of CBT for anorexia nervosa, have also emerged over the past two decades.

In reading Wilson's comprehensive review we were struck by the differences, but also similarities, in what is known about psychological treatments for each eating disorder. A notable difference is the variance in both the quality and quantity of the "evidence base" for therapies. In anorexia nervosa invariably the trials are small, with a mean size of less than 50 and subjects commonly allocated to groups of between 10 and 20. In bulimia nervosa trials are larger in both absolute number and size. Wilson notes several reasons why gathering evidence is problematic in anorexia nervosa, including its low incidence, the duration of treatment required and the reluctance of many to engage in treatment. In addition, because of high morbidity and mortality, there may be reluctance by clinicians to refer their patients with anorexia nervosa to research trials. However, the result is that the clinical recommendations for anorexia nervosa are limited, in this and similar reviews, to advice based on "clinical experience and preliminary research evidence". This lack of empirical support for psychological treatments in anorexia nervosa is arguably the single greatest challenge facing those who work in the area.

A similarity across the disorders is the paucity of reliable predictors of response to treatment. For bulimia nervosa it has been difficult to find consistent predictors of response, although the presence of personality disorder appears to predict a poorer outcome, and an early response to CBT a better outcome. In anorexia nervosa, family therapy appears more successful in those with earlier onset and shorter duration of illness when compared with individual psychotherapy. In addition, a recent systematic review concluded that an indicator of a good prognosis in anorexia nervosa is a short interval between onset of symptoms and the beginning of treatment [1]. Also, Baran et al. [2] found in 22 women that those discharged while severely underweight had a higher rate of re-hospitalization and were more symptomatic than those who achieved normal weight at discharge from hospital. Taken together, these findings emphasize the importance of early detection and early treatment, namely secondary prevention for people with anorexia nervosa and other eating disorders.

Secondary prevention is, however, difficult to achieve in eating disorders. It is known, for example, that in bulimia nervosa the overwhelming majority of sufferers do not access care, in spite of the good evidence that treatment is effective. Training of primary care practitioners in recognition of this disorder is imperative, and would be helped by having a wider dissemination of treatments. Modifications of manual-based CBT can be delivered successfully by non-specialists (in guided self-help forms) for binge eating disorder, as Wilson describes, but also for bulimia nervosa, as found in a recent study by Paxton et al. [3]. Such approaches provide a way forward to address the under-recognition and under-treatment of eating disorders in the community. Further evaluation of patient-centred factors in accessing appropriate care through community-based studies of the understanding of eating disorders and their treatments is also important.

Wilson addresses the need for enhancement of CBT. In the largest study of CBT versus IPT, only 29% of those treated with CBT and 6% of those treated with IPT had ceased binge eating and purging for a month at the end of treatment. CBT may be enhanced by the addition of other psychotherapies, such as motivational enhancement therapy, and a component of IPT or dynamic therapy. Early studies of enhancement of CBT with exposure response prevention were not positive [4] and enhancement with other therapies requires empirical evaluation.

Wilson emphasizes the contrasting relationship between binge eating disorder and obesity. As she notes, CBT in itself is unlikely to result in weight loss, but the addition of behavioural weight loss strategies does not exacerbate binge eating in the short term, and is associated with weight loss. The largest controlled study to date by Wifley et al. [5] also supports a small but clinically significant reduction in weight with both CBT and IPT, and replicates the finding that patients who cease binge eating lose significantly more weight than those who do not. Wilson hypothesizes that in bulimia nervosa binge eating represents a breakdown in dietary restraint, whereas in binge eating disorder there is little dietary restriction between bingeing episodes. More empirical research is needed, because there is a large body of evidence supporting the relationship between dietary restriction and binge eating; in the short term, the binge eating frequency in binge eating disorder may improve, but longer term studies are needed to show that this is sustained over time.

In conclusion, there is good evidence for psychotherapy in eating disorders, but the review highlights several major challenges for future research. These include the need to redress the paucity of trials in anorexia nervosa, to have a better understanding of outcome by identifying consistent prognostic predictors, to develop and test strategies to enhance the effectiveness of therapy, and to achieve a wider dissemination of treatments.

REFERENCES

1. Treasure J., Schmidt U. (2002) Anorexia nervosa. *Clin. Evid.*, 7: www.evidence.org.
2. Baran S.A., Weltzin T.E., Kaye W.H. (1995) Low discharge weight and outcome in anorexia nervosa. *Am. J. Psychiatry*, 152: 1070–1072.

3. Paxton S., Banasiak S., Hay P.J. (2002) Conducting guided self-help for bulimia nervosa in primary care settings: accessible and effective treatment. Presented at the Academy for Eating Disorders International Meeting, Boston, 25–28 April.
4. Hay P.J., Bacaltchuk J. (2001) Psychotherapy for bulimia nervosa and binging. *Cochrane Database Syst. Rev.*, **3**: CD000562.
5. Wilfley D.E., Welch R.R., Stein R.I., Spurrell E.B., Cohen R.L., Saelens B.S., Dounchis J.Z., Frank M.A., Wiseman C.V., Matt G.E. (2002) A randomized comparison of group cognitive–behavioral therapy and group interpersonal psychotherapy for the treatment of binge eating disorder. *Arch. Gen. Psychiatry*, **59**: 713–721.

6

The Economic and Social Burden of Eating Disorders: A Review

Scott J. Crow and Carol B. Peterson

*Eating Disorders Research Program, Department of Psychiatry,
University of Minnesota, 2450 Riverside Avenue, Minneapolis,
MN 55454-1495, USA*

INTRODUCTION

The eating disorders are unusual among psychiatric disorders in that there is evidence that they have become increasingly prevalent over the latter half of the 20th century. As such, these illnesses represent a relatively new economic and social burden. Perhaps because eating disorders have only received extensive research attention for the past 25–30 years, little is known about most aspects of the burdens of these illnesses. Medical complications and mortality (particularly for anorexia nervosa) in these illnesses are well recognized, but other social, occupational and economic costs have received little attention.

Here, we will review the available information about the various burdens of these illnesses. First, we will provide an overview of what is known about the morbidity and mortality associated with eating disorders. Subsequently, the limited available information about the social, occupational and family burdens will be reviewed. The growing literature on the cost and cost-efficacy of treating these illnesses will be examined. Finally, the ample opportunities for future research in this area will be discussed.

MEDICAL BURDENS OF EATING DISORDERS

Morbidity

Extensive attention has been paid to the medical complications occurring in eating disorders, particularly for anorexia nervosa and bulimia nervosa.

Eating Disorders. Edited by Mario Maj, Katherine Halmi, Juan José López-Ibor and Norman Sartorius.
©2003 John Wiley & Sons Ltd: ISBN 0-470-84865-0

Several recent reviews [1,2] have thoroughly surveyed this area and the many possible complications will not be reviewed in depth here. Nevertheless, it is worth noting that certain complications such as electrolyte imbalance and dehydration are commonly encountered, often require repeated laboratory monitoring and can require oral or even intravenous therapy to correct. Hospitalization for medical stabilization is not uncommon, although the rates with which this occurs are undefined.

In clinical practice, when a diagnosis of anorexia nervosa is first considered, it is common to conduct a medical work-up to rule out other potential causes of weight loss. After such a work-up is negative, the diagnosis of anorexia nervosa is typically made and treatment is begun. By contrast, the diagnosis of bulimia nervosa is often postponed by 5 or more years following the onset of symptoms [3]. In this interim, it appears that some individuals make frequent medical visits for the evaluation and treatment of physical complaints (e.g. gastrointestinal symptoms) that are directly attributable to bulimia nervosa (which is typically not considered, because its existence is unknown to the clinician involved). Of course, these medical costs are incurred at an age when most individuals have little in the way of medical utilization.

In addition to the host of short-term medical complications that appear likely to resolve when eating disorder symptoms are improved, there are at least a few medical complications that may have longer term consequences. One such example is osteoporosis. It is well recognized that osteoporosis occurs frequently in eating disorders [4]. Existing evidence suggests that a return to relatively normal healthy eating behaviours and healthy weight does not necessarily lead to the resolution of osteoporosis, and a number of trials have been conducted or are underway to try to identify effective treatments [5–8]. The impact of developing osteoporosis at a very young age is uncertain but it may increase the risks of osteoporosis later in life.

A second eating disorder complication with potential long-term effects is the gastrointestinal dysfunction seen in association with long-term, high-dose laxative abuse. There is evidence to suggest that laxative abuse can lead to the loss of normal colonic motility, and clinically, when these changes occur, improvements in gastrointestinal function are often slow to occur and incomplete recovery of gastroinstestinal function is often seen [1]. A third long-term complication might, theoretically, be associated with the use of phenolphthalein-containing laxatives. These agents have been removed from the market owing to reports associating them with the later occurrence of colon cancer. Although the literature is conflicting and recently some have concluded that in fact this connection is spurious [9,10], if it is a true risk it seems logical to assume that it might be most likely to occur in those using such laxatives in the remarkably high doses often seen in people with bulimia nervosa.

A final long-term complication to consider is the effect of recurrent vomiting on dentition. The dental enamel erosion seen would not be expected to reverse itself and it does appear that increased dental caries and other dental problems are more likely to occur following this enamel erosion [11], but the frequency of this problem and the costs it brings are not well defined.

Mortality

The fact that anorexia nervosa carries an increased risk for mortality has been recognized since early descriptions of that illness [12]. The studies examining mortality in anorexia nervosa have consistently found relatively high rates. These findings are well summarized in reviews of all-cause mortality and suicidal mortality by Harris and Barraclough [13,14]. These authors concluded that only opiate dependence carried a higher overall mortality risk than eating disorders (considered as a broad group). Furthermore, it is worth noting that, in examining suicide rates, the standardized mortality ratio (the ratio of observed deaths to expected deaths, adjusted for age and ethnicity) was higher for eating disorders than for any other psychiatric condition.

An excellent meta-analysis by Sullivan [15] found an annualized mortality rate for individuals with anorexia nervosa of 0.56%. In reviewing the studies used in that meta-analysis, as well as other literature in this area, it does appear that studies with longer periods of observation, as well as higher ascertainment rates, yield higher observed mortality rates [16,17]. The issue of ascertainment in such studies is a critically important one. In an illness where the long-term mortality rate is often cited to be around 10%, failing to find 10–20% of the individuals in a long-term follow-up study can have tremendous consequences for the accuracy of estimating mortality rate. Standard practice is to assume that individuals who cannot be located are living but, for some reason, unreachable. Although this is undoubtedly often true, the misassignment of vital status as living for a modest fraction of this group could lead to very large underestimates of mortality.

Much less is known about mortality in bulimia nervosa. Fewer long-term studies are available than for anorexia nervosa. In a review of these long-term studies, Keel and Mitchell [18] found a very low mortality rate of around 0.2% (although they also noted that studies with higher ascertainment and longer follow-up were more likely to report mortality within their cohorts). One might have predicted relatively higher mortality rates, at least from suicide, given the high comorbidity between major depression and bulimia nervosa. It may be that methodological limitations have prevented the full appreciation of the rate of mortality in this group. Perhaps some individuals with bulimia nervosa do die of medical complications of the illness in the period between onset of symptoms and initial diagnosis and are thus never identified in such studies. Alternatively, it may be that binge eating and purging behaviour have a regulation role (as has been suggested previously) that serves to diminish the risk of suicide due to mood disorder.

Finally, very little, if anything, is known about the mortality associated with eating disorder not otherwise specified (EDNOS) and binge eating disorder (BED), in spite of the fact that EDNOS appears to be the most commonly encountered eating disorder in many settings. Clearly, the obesity commonly seen in BED would be expected to raise the mortality risk [19].

Impact on Fertility

One area in which eating disorders have a clear medical impact with resulting social and economic burdens is fertility. There is a very clear relationship between anorexia nervosa and fertility, to the extent that amenorrhoea is required in the current DSM-IV nomenclature for a diagnosis of anorexia nervosa in females. However, menstrual irregularity and amenorrhoea are also seen fairly commonly in bulimia nervosa [20,21]. Furthermore, some studies [22–24], but not all [25], suggest that fecundity may be impaired in individuals with eating disorders. Conversely, studies examining eating disorders among women attending infertility clinics suggest that such a group is at high risk for disordered eating [26,27].

ECONOMIC BURDENS OF EATING DISORDERS

The study of the economic costs of eating disorders has begun gradually to receive some focus. As far back as in 1989, Silber *et al.* [28] reported on a series of 20 individuals with anorexia nervosa admitted to a hospital. In that series, all 20 individuals met a fairly rigorous set of medically based admission criteria for hospitalization; in spite of that fact, the third-party payer involved denied hospitalization for 4 out of the 20. Conflicts with third-party payers over appropriate intensity and amount of treatment has led to work examining the effectiveness of current hospitalization practices and the cost efficacy of certain treatments.

Attempts to examine costs in the eating disorders can be split into three broad areas. The first is to measure the indirect costs (e.g. time lost from other activities due to eating disorder symptoms or their treatment). The published literature is devoid of work in this area. The other two areas of potential inquiry are to examine the broader costs of eating disorders within the healthcare system and to examine the cost-efficacy of specific treatments; a limited literature does exist in these areas and it will be reviewed below.

Healthcare Utilization Costs

One study to date has examined healthcare costs within a large database for individuals with eating disorders [29]. In this study, examining 1 year's worth of data for roughly 1.9 million male subjects and 2 million female subjects, healthcare costs for eating disorder treatment were compared with treatment costs for schizophrenia and obsessive–compulsive disorder. In this cohort, 0.14% of all female subjects had received treatment for an eating disorder; this exceeded the rate for men by approximately tenfold, as expected. Hospitalization rates were low, with only 21.5% of females with anorexia nervosa hospitalized during the year; lower rates were seen for bulimia nervosa and EDNOS. In female patients, mean costs in the year for all treatments were as follows: anorexia nervosa, $6045; bulimia nervosa, $2962; EDNOS, $3207; schizophrenia, $4824; obsessive–compulsive disorder, $1930. Thus, the total mean costs for anorexia nervosa and bulimia nervosa were similar in magnitude to those seen in the treatment of schizophrenia. On the other hand, these authors point out that, in a careful analysis of the data, there is evidence for undertreatment in this population. For example, individuals with bulimia nervosa received, on average, 16 (for women) and 9 (for men) outpatient visits, which falls short of published treatment guidelines and most of the treatment literature [30].

It is important to note, in considering the results of this study, that because costs were captured based on diagnostic codes used to bill the services, these costs most likely represent an underestimate of the true costs of these illnesses. For example, if a patient with purging anorexia nervosa is seen for dehydration and hypokalaemia, any outpatient emergency room and hospital charges associated with that problem may well be billed under a diagnostic code for dehydration or hypokalaemia. This is particularly true if the eating disorder diagnosis is not yet clear, but is likely sometimes to be the case even if the eating disorder is known. In either event, such costs are difficult to measure accurately.

Cost Efficacy of Treatment

A slightly larger literature has examined the cost-efficacy of various treatments for eating disorders. Much of this work has actually focused on the relative cost inefficiency of not providing an adequate treatment.

Commerford *et al.* [31] found that individuals who achieved a target weight did better on a wide variety of outcomes than those discharged while still at low weight. Similarly, Baran *et al.* [32] found that partial weight restoration was associated with substantially higher readmission rates. Over the last 15 years treatment practices have changed substantially in the direction of earlier discharge and shorter lengths of stay. Wiseman *et al.* [33] examined this trend. Specifically, they found in their programme that the average length of stay over 15 years went from almost 150 days to 24 days and correspondingly the discharge body mass index dropped from 19.3 to 17.7. In this large sample (1185 subjects) the readmission rate rose from 0% in 1984 to 27% in 1998.

One corollary change has been a move to more aggressive use of partial hospitalization and day hospitalization to try to provide a bridge between inpatient treatment and outpatient, clinic-based treatment. Unfortunately, it has not been shown yet whether this strategy is or is not effective; however, one study [34] cautions that a lower body mass index at discharge is predictive of failure in the process of day hospital transition.

Finally, two studies have attempted to examine directly the cost-effectiveness of specific interventions. Koran *et al.* [35] performed a *post hoc* analysis of the relative cost-efficacy of the various interventions in a five-cell study comparing cognitive–behavioural therapy, medication or both for various lengths of time for patients with bulimia nervosa. Based on the number of patients achieving abstinence, as well as assumptions about the costs of medications and psychotherapy interventions, cost-efficacy indices were calculated. In this study, cost-efficacy analyses were performed after 32 weeks and 1 year. At the 32-week mark, medication given for 16 weeks was the most cost-effective treatment; medication given for 24 weeks was the most cost-effective at 1 year. Combination therapy, consisting of cognitive–behavioural therapy plus medication for 16 weeks, was the least cost-effective intervention. Two caveats are important in interpreting these data. First, this analysis was conducted *post hoc* and the study did not plan initially to conduct a cost-efficacy assessment. Second, although medications given for either 16 or 24 weeks appear to be the most cost-effective intervention (i.e. providing the greatest improvement per unit of spending), this treatment was not the intervention with the greatest overall clinical efficacy (i.e. providing the largest total improvement, independent of cost). This finding represents one of the major challenges in conducting and interpreting such work.

Another cost-effectiveness analysis of treatments for bulimia nervosa compared individual cognitive–behavioural therapy, group cognitive–behavioural therapy and medication using 60 mg/day fluoxetine [36]. This cost modelling study indicated that individual psychotherapy was the most expensive. Group therapy with frequent visits was comparable in price to pharmacotherapy with fluoxetine. Group therapy with weekly visits and an emphasis on abstinence was the least expensive. This finding is notable, because a comparison of the two types of group therapy found comparable results at the end of treatment [37]. However, these group therapies have not been compared directly with individual psychotherapy; whether the outcome would be comparable is unknown.

One additional study has examined the possible role of other treatment settings for individuals with eating disorders [38]. This study reported on a 6-week summer camp designed for adolescents with eating disorders in which the majority (86%) of participants reported the programme to be beneficial. Of pertinence to cost-efficacy, the cost of such a camp was in the neighbourhood of $100 per day, at a time when inpatient hospitalization would typically cost roughly ten times that much.

ACADEMIC, OCCUPATIONAL AND SOCIAL BURDENS OF EATING DISORDERS

An important domain in which eating disorders cause substantial problems is social function, including occupational and educational impairment. These illnesses are most common at an age when people are completing their secondary schooling, going on to college or other advanced schooling and beginning working careers. Many of the prevalence studies for eating disorders have been conducted among college populations [39,40], with a limited number among graduate education populations [41], and it is clear that full and subsyndromal eating disorders are a common problem among these groups. In light of the amount of time spent engaged in eating-disorder-related behaviour or absorbed by eating-disorder-related cognitions, there are undoubtedly major time costs with these illnesses. However, formal attempts to measure these costs have not been reported. On the other hand, social adjustment in individuals with eating disorders has been studied extensively and we will review that information.

Social Adjustment

A large number of studies have examined social adjustment in bulimia nervosa. Multiple cross-sectional studies have documented that problems with social adjustment are more common in women with eating disorders than control groups or, in some cases, individuals with other illnesses. For example, Herzog et al. [41] studied 550 female students of medicine, law or business and found an overall rate of bulimia nervosa of 12%.

Measured using the Social Adjustment Scale, Self-Report Version (SAS-SR) [42], higher social maladjustment was seen in the individuals with bulimia than in those without eating disorders. Of particular note, in this study, even individuals with limited bulimic behaviours falling short of the full diagnostic criteria (e.g. one binge/purge episode per week) showed worse social adjustment than individuals without eating disorder symptoms. In another study, Norman and Herzog [43] assessed 40 women with bulimia nervosa, again using the SAS-SR, and found them to have worse social adjustment than 277 community comparison subjects and 35 women with schizophrenia, but better social adjustment than 155 acutely depressed women. Among individuals with bulimia nervosa, it appears that the domains in which social adjustment is impaired are multiple. For example, Mitchell et al. [3] found interpersonal impairment in 69.5% of individuals, family impairment in 60.7%, financial impairment in 53.3% and work impairment in 49.6%.

Similar findings exist for anorexia nervosa. In a study examining 31 women with anorexia nervosa using the Young Loneliness Inventory Scale, O'Mahony and Hollwey [44] found that the severity of eating behaviours was associated with social maladjustment as measured by this scale. Also, individuals with anorexia nervosa had higher measures of social maladjustment than comparison groups.

A second important aspect of social adjustment in eating disorders involves the longitudinal course of adjustment. Several studies examining individuals with bulimia nervosa have found no change in social adjustment over time as measured by the SAS-SR [45,46]. Others have seen some improvement in overall social adjustment [47]. Similarly, Norman et al. [48] found improvements on marital and parental subscales after a 1-year follow-up. In other studies from that group, improvements have been seen in the work subscale scores of the SAS-SR [46]. In a longer term study, Keel et al. [49] reported modest improvements in social adjustment among women with bulimia nervosa followed up 10–15 years after initial diagnosis. However, in that sample, some impairments were seen in recovered individuals, leaving them a level of social adjustment as measured by the SAS-SR that fell short of published community norms. There was only a limited association between eating disorder outcome and social adjustment outcome in that study. Finally, Rorty et al. [50] compared 39 women with active bulimia nervosa, 40 women who were recovered from bulimia nervosa and 40 control women using the SAS-SR and a measure of social support. The actively ill group had the poorest overall social functioning and reported less social and emotional support. This finding echoes research conducted by Grisset and Norvell [51], who compared social support and a measure of social competence among 21 women with bulimia nervosa and 21 control women; these researchers found that levels of social support and measures of social competence were both lower among bulimic women than the controls.

A limited literature has examined attitudes about dating as they pertain to eating disorders. Two reports [52,53] both found that people without eating disorders believed that it would be more difficult to date someone with an eating disorder and they would be less comfortable becoming engaged or having a long relationship with someone with an eating disorder. It is noteworthy, however, that in the Sobal and Bursztyn study [53] men participating in the study reported that they would be even less comfortable dating someone who was obese than someone with anorexia nervosa or bulimia nervosa.

Thus, in summary, this literature suggests that social impairment is common among individuals with anorexia nervosa and bulimia nervosa and (in a very limited literature) EDNOS. The relationship between social adjustment and causation of eating disorders is unclear. It may be that problems with the social adjustment, social competency and social support networks represent a predisposing factor to the development of eating disorders; it is also plausible that the presence of eating disorder symptoms may have an adverse impact on social adjustment. Although studies do conflict, it appears that the long-term course of such social adjustment problems, at least for bulimia nervosa, involves improvement that perhaps does not reach the prevailing community levels of social adjustment. Finally, it appears that the presence of an eating disorder (once disclosed) may have an adverse impact on dating.

SUMMARY

There are substantial medical, economic and social burdens that accompany eating disorders. An extensive literature exists on medical morbidity and mortality, and on social adjustment. On the other hand, little is known about the economic costs or the educational/occupational burdens, and work to date has largely excluded BED and subthreshold variants of eating disorders.

Consistent Evidence

Consistent evidence in the literature supports the following conclusions:

- A wide variety of types of medical morbidity is observed among individuals with eating disorders.

- Amenorrhoea always occurs (by definition) in anorexia nervosa and is common in bulimia nervosa. Associated with that, infertility appears to be common among individuals with a history of anorexia nervosa.
- Anorexia nervosa clearly has an extraordinarily high mortality rate relative to other psychiatric illnesses.
- Social adjustment is impaired among individuals with eating disorders.
- A separate, but related point is that attitudes of non-eating-disordered individuals towards those with eating disorders suggest that dating is impaired among the latter.

Incomplete Evidence

- The mortality rates for bulimia nervosa remain somewhat unclear. Most studies have found low rates, but the methodologies used have not been optimal and, given the high comorbidity with depression, one would predict higher rates than have been shown so far.
- There is a limited body of evidence on the cost-effectiveness of a wide variety of different treatment settings and treatment modalities, which falls well short of that needed to draw consistent conclusions.
- There is somewhat conflicting evidence at this point relating to the impact of bulimia nervosa on fertility.

Areas Still Open to Research

- The full scope of the costs of medical complications from these illnesses should be described. One important component of this work will be to describe the costs of evaluating and treating medical complications (such as dehydration, electrolyte imbalance) for persons receiving treatment for eating disorders. Perhaps it is more important to examine the cost of potential long-term complications. For example, the implications of having severe osteoporosis by the age of 30 years and the risk for fractures, medical complications and costs at the age of 60 or 70 years or beyond are not known. The magnitude of this problem and its costs can be studied even as attempts are made to develop effective interventions.
- The true mortality associated with eating disorders should be defined further. As discussed, although previous studies have documented startlingly high rates of mortality, methodological issues suggest that these may still be underestimates. Furthermore, the mortality associated with subsyndromal eating disorders (or EDNOS) remains undefined and yet several lines of evidence suggest that it may be substantial. Finally, the long-term medical complications described above, including

osteoporosis, could conceivably yield elevated risks for mortality well beyond the time of successful treatment of the eating disorder; only continued observation of individuals with eating disorders (both in remission and with chronic symptoms) will answer this question.

- Attempts should be made to measure the indirect costs of these illnesses and their treatment, including impacts on academic, occupation and inter-personal function. Such studies could readily involve measures of quality of life, as well as time lost from other activities due to the eating disorder.
- Attempts should be made also to measure the direct costs of these illnesses. Such direct costs would include the provision of effective treatments and relapse prevention strategies, as well as the costs of medical complications described above. The impact of disordered eating on fertility and the costs of infertility treatment also should be examined.
- Future treatment trials for eating disorders should consider the inclusion of a cost-efficacy component. Although the importance of this work cuts across system and national boundaries, it may be particularly pertinent at present in places such as the USA, where third-party payer decisions to limit treatment may be, in the long run, remarkably cost ineffective. Large studies with ample statistical power might ultimately uncover treatment predictors that would permit some degree of treatment matching.
- Published treatment trials to date focus on one or a limited number of treatment components, most typically outpatient-based. This is a significant limitation: most treatment programmes and published treatment guidelines emphasize the importance of integrated treatment approaches with multiple levels of care, the long-term cost of which is unknown. These studies are expensive and complex, but will be highly informative

ACKNOWLEDGEMENTS

This review was supported by research grants from the McKnight Foundation and the National Institute of Mental Health (R01-MH59234) and the National Institute of Diabetes, Digestive and Kidney Diseases (R01-DK61912, R01-DK60432, P30-DK50456).

REFERENCES

1. Pomeroy C. (2001) Medical evaluation and medical management. In *The Outpatient Treatment of Eating Disorders: A Guide for Therapists, Dietitians, and Physicians* (Ed. J.E. Mitchell), pp. 306–338. University of Minnesota Press, Minneapolis.

2. Sharp C.W., Freeman C.P. (1997) Medical complications and management. In *Ballière's Clinical Psychiatry: Eating Disorders* (Eds D. Jimerson, W.H. Kaye), pp. 303–318. Ballière Tindall, London.
3. Mitchell J.E., Hatsukami D., Eckert E.D., Pyle R.L. (1985) Characteristics of 275 patients with bulimia. *Am. J. Psychiatry*, **142**: 482–485.
4. Rigotti N.A., Nussbaum S.R., Herzog D.B., Neer R.M. (1984) Osteoporosis in women with anorexia nervosa. *N. Engl. J. Med.*, **311**: 1601–1606.
5. Iketani T., Kiriike N., Nakanishi S., Nakasuji T. (1995) Effects of weight gain and resumption of menses on reduced bone density in patients with anorexia nervosa. *Biol. Psychiatry*, **37**: 521 527.
6. Rigotti N.A., Neer R.M., Skates S.J., Herzog D.B., Nussbaum S.R. (1991) The clinical course of osteoporosis in anorexia nervosa. *JAMA*, **265**: 1133–1138.
7. Klibanski A., Biller B.M.K., Schoenfeld D.A., Herzog D.B., Saxe V.C. (1995) The effects of estrogen administration on trabecular bone loss in young women with anorexia nervosa. *J. Clin. Endocrinol. Metab.*, **80**: 898–904.
8. Hartman D., Crisp A., Rooney B., Rackow C., Atkinson R., Patel S. (2000) Bone density of women who have recovered from anorexia nervosa. *Int. J. Eat. Disord.*, **28**: 107–112.
9. Longnecker M.P., Sandler D.P., Haile R.W., Sandler R.S. (1997) Phenolphthalein-containing laxative use in relation to adenomatous colorectal polyps in three studies. *Environ. Health Perspect.*, **105**: 1210–1212.
10. Coogan P.F., Rosenberg L., Palmer J.R., Strom B.L., Zauber A.G., Stolley P.D., Shapiro S. (2000) Phenolphthalein laxatives and risk of cancer. *J. Natl. Cancer Inst.*, **92**: 1943–1944.
11. Milosevic A. (1999) Eating disorders and the dentist. *Br. Dent. J.*, **186**: 109–113.
12. Morton R.R. (1689) *Phtisiologia—or a Treatise of Consumption*. Smith, London.
13. Harris E.C., Barraclough B. (1998) Excess mortality of mental disorder. *Br. J. Psychiatry*, **173**: 11–53.
14. Harris E.C., Barraclough B. (1997) Suicide as an outcome for mental disorders: a meta-analysis. *Br. J. Psychiatry*, **170**: 205–228.
15. Sullivan P.F. (1995) Mortality in anorexia nervosa. *Am. J. Psychiatry*, **152**: 1073–1074.
16. Crow S.C., Praus B., Thuras P. (1999) Mortality from eating disorders—a 5- to 10-year record linkage study. *Int. J. Eat. Disord.*, **26**: 97–101.
17. Eckert E.D., Halmi K.A., Marchi P., Grove W., Crosby R. (1995) Ten-year follow-up of anorexia nervosa: clinical course and outcome. *Psychol. Med.*, **25**: 143–156.
18. Keel P.K., Mitchell J.E. (1997) Outcome of bulimia nervosa. *Am. J. Psychiatry*, **154**: 313–321.
19. Calle E.E., Thun M.J., Petrelli J.M., Rodriguez C., Heath C.W., Jr. (1999) Body-mass index and mortality in a prospective cohort of US adults. *N. Engl. J. Med.*, **341**: 1097–1105.
20. Russell G.F.M. (1979) Bulimia nervosa: an ominous variant of anorexia nervosa. *Psychol. Med.*, **9**: 429–448.
21. Copeland P.M., Sacks N.R., Herzog D.B. (1995) Longitudinal follow-up of amenorrhea in eating disorders. *Psychosom. Med.*, **57**: 121–126.
22. Abraham S. (1998) Sexuality and reproduction in bulimia nervosa patients over 10 years. *J. Psychosom. Res.*, **44**: 491–502.
23. Mitchell J.E., Seim H.C., Glotter D., Soll E.A., Pyle R.L. (1991) A retrospective study of pregnancy in bulimia nervosa. *Int. J. Eat. Disord.*, **10**: 209–214.

24. Bulik C.M., Sullivan P.F., Fear J.L., Pickering A., Dawn A., McCullin M. (1999) Fertility and reproduction in women with anorexia nervosa: a controlled study. *J. Clin. Psychiatry*, **60**: 130–135.

25. Crow S.C., Thuras P., Keel P.K., Mitchell J.E. (2002) Long-term menstrual and reproductive function in bulimia nervosa. *Am. J. Psychiatry*, **159**: 1048–1050.

26. Allison S., Kalucy R., Gilchrist P., Jones W. (1988) Weight preoccupation among infertile women. *Int. J. Eat. Disord.*, **7**: 743–748.

27. Bates G.W., Bates S.R., Whitworth N.S. (1982) Reproductive failure in women who practice weight control. *Fertil. Steril.*, **37**: 373–378.

28. Silber T.J., Delaney D., Samuels J. (1989) Anorexia nervosa: hospitalization on adolescent medicine units and third-party payments. *J. Adolesc. Health Care*, **10**: 122–125.

29. Striegel-Moore R.H., Leslie D., Petrill S.A., Garvin V., Rosenheck R.A. (2000) One-year use and cost of inpatient and outpatient services among female and male patients with an eating disorder: evidence from a national database of health insurance claims. *Int. J. Eat. Disord.*, **27**: 381–389.

30. American Psychiatric Association (2000) *Practice Guideline for the Treatment of Patients with Eating Disorders (Revision)*. American Psychiatric Association, Washington.

31. Commerford M.C., Licinio J., Halmi K.A. (1997) Guidelines for discharging eating disorder patients. *Eat. Disord.*, **5**: 69–74.

32. Baran S.A., Weltzin T.E., Kaye W.H. (1995) Low discharge weight and outcome in anorexia nervosa. *Am. J. Psychiatry*, **152**: 1070–1072.

33. Wiseman C.V., Sunday S.R., Klapper F., Harris W.A., Halmi K.A. (2001) Changing patterns of hospitalization in eating disorder patients. *Int. J. Eat. Disord.*, **30**: 69–74.

34. Howard W.T., Evans K.K., Quintero-Howard C.V., Bowers W.A., Andersen A.E. (1999) Predictors of success or failure of transition to day hospital treatment for inpatients with anorexia nervosa. *Am. J. Psychiatry*, **156**: 1697–1702.

35. Koran L.M., Agras W.S., Rossiter E.M., Arnow B., Scheider J.A., Telch C.F., Raeburn S., Bruce B., Perl M., Kraemer H.C. (1995) Comparing the cost effectiveness of psychiatric treatments: bulimia nervosa. *Psychiatry Res.*, **58**: 13–21.

36. Mitchell J.E., Peterson C.B., Agras S. (1999) Cost-effectiveness of psychotherapy for eating disorders. In *Cost-Effectiveness of Psychotherapy: A Guide for Practitioners, Researchers and Policy Makers* (Eds N.E. Miller, R.M. Magruder), pp. 270–278. Oxford University Press, New York.

37. Mitchell J.E., Pyle R.L., Eckert E.D., Pomeroy C., Zollman M., Crosby R., Seim H., Eckert E.D., Zimmerman R. (1993) Cognitive behavioral group psychotherapy of bulimia nervosa: importance of logistical variables. *Int. J. Eat. Disord.*, **14**: 277–287.

38. Tonkin R. (1997) Evaluation of a summer camp for adolescents with eating disorders. *J. Adolesc. Health*, **20**: 412–413.

39. Schotte D.E., Stunkard A.J. (1987) Bulimia vs. bulimic behaviors on a college campus. *JAMA*, **258**: 1213–1215.

40. Drewnowski A., Hopkins S.A., Kessler R.C. (1988) The prevalence of bulimia nervosa in the US college student population. *Am. J. Publ. Health*, **78**: 1322–1325.

41.   Herzog D.B., Norman D.K., Rigotti N.A., Pepose M. (1986) Frequency of bulimic behaviors and associated social maladjustment in female graduate students. *J. Psychiatr. Res.*, **20**: 355–361.
42.   Weissman M.M., Prusoff B.A., Thompson W.D., Harding P.S., Myers J.K. (1978) Social adjustment by self-report in a community sample and in psychiatric outpatients. *J. Nerv. Ment. Dis.*, **166**: 317–380.
43.   Norman E.K., Herzog D.B. (1984) Persistent social maladjustment in bulimia: a 1-year follow-up. *Am. J. Psychiatry*, **141**: 444–446.
44.   O'Mahony J.F., Hollwey S. (1995) Eating problems and interpersonal functioning among several groups of women. *J. Clin. Psychol.*, **51**: 345–351.
45.   Johnson C., Tobin D.L., Dennis A. (1990) Differences in treatment outcome between borderline and non-borderline bulimics at one-year follow-up. *Int. J. Eat. Disord.*, **9**: 617–627.
46.   Norman E.K., Herzog D.B. (1986) A 3-year outcome study of normal-weight bulimia: assessment of psychosocial functioning and eating attitudes. *Psychiatry Res.*, **19**: 199–205.
47.   Fairburn C.G., Kirk J., O'Connor M., Cooper P.J. (1986) A comparison of two psychological treatments for bulimia nervosa. *Behav. Res. Ther.*, **24**: 629–643.
48.   Norman D.K., Herzog D.B., Chauncey S. (1986) A one-year outcome study of bulimia: psychological and eating symptom changes in a treatment and non-treatment group. *Int. J. Eat. Disord.*, **5**: 47–57.
49.   Keel P.K., Mitchell J.E., Miller K.B., Davis T.L., Crow S.J. (2000) Social adjustment over 10 years following diagnosis with bulimia nervosa. *Int. J. Eat. Disord.*, **27**: 21–28.
50.   Rorty M., Yager J., Buckwalter J.G., Rossotto E. (1999) Social support, social adjustment and recovery status in bulimia nervosa. *Int. J. Eat. Disord.*, **26**: 1–12.
51.   Grissett N.I., Norvell N.K. (1992) Perceived social support, social skills, and quality of relationships in bulimic women. *J. Consult. Clin. Psychol.*, **60**: 293–299.
52.   Smith M.C., Pruitt J.A., McLaughlin-Mann L., Thelen M.H. (1986) Attitudes and knowledge regarding bulimia and anorexia nervosa. *Int. J. Eat. Disord.*, **3**: 545–552.
53.   Sobal J., Bursztyn M. (1998) Dating people with anorexia nervosa and bulimia nervosa: attitudes and beliefs of university students. *Women Health*, **27**: 73–89.

Commentaries

6.1
A Spectrum of Costs
Niva Piran[1]

Crow and Peterson indicate in their review both the well-substantiated evidence for the long-term morbidity of eating disorders and the relative paucity of research that has concurrently examined the treatment efficacy and cost-effectiveness of clinical services for eating disorder patients. This commentary will centre on three dimensions relevant to future developments in the field: a) the research continuum—from randomized controlled trials (RCT) to quasi-experimental designs and other practice-based research; b) the epidemiological continuum—from clinical eating disorders to subclinical patterns of disordered eating; c) the intervention continuum— from treatment to indicated or selected prevention.

The most desirable study of cost-effectiveness of treatment involves an RCT where both cost and symptomatic, medical, psychological and social outcomes are assessed in the long term. Such studies allow for the comparison of both cost and treatment efficacy in the same patient group. However, it is of relevance to note that multiple barriers exist to conducting such studies, including ethical and clinical considerations, selective drop-out rates, divergent policies of health insurance companies, or strict inclusion criteria that limit the participation of individuals displaying comorbid conditions and, hence, limit the generalizability of results to clinical practice [1]. Some of these challenges have been raised and debated about in relation to the costly National Institute of Mental Health (NIMH) Treatment of Depression Collaborative Research Program [2]. Considering the multiple barriers in the practice of RCT, it is likely that cost-related data will accrue through practice-based studies, quasi-experimental designs and the use of varied meta-analytical procedures. In addition to questions regarding the cost and treatment efficacy of varied treatment modalities, practitioners in the field of eating disorders need to evaluate the impact of varied intensities of treatment and their sequencing on cost and treatment efficacy [3,4]. These questions have intensified in the USA in relation to

[1] *Department of Adult Education and Counselling Psychology, Faculty of Education, University of Toronto, 252 Bloor St. West, Toronto, Ontario M5S 1V6, Canada*

managed healthcare [5]. Progress in this area of research will require the broadening of approaches to research and inter-centre collaboration.

Another key dimension in the consideration of the medical, psychological and social costs of eating disorders is the continuum of difficulties in disordered eating patterns and body dissatisfaction [6]. According to Gordon [7], the prevalent occurrence and the observed continuum stem from the social causes of eating disorders. The phenomenological continuum of disordered eating and body dissatisfaction produces unique challenges in the assessment of cost of eating disorders. The reported low rates of identification and treatment of clinical forms of eating disorders are even lower in subclinical forms [8]. This is likely to make the medical costs of subclinical conditions even harder to trace. Moreover, the social and psychological costs are likely to be ignored owing to their "prevalent" and even "normative" presentations. It is of relevance here to compare two sets of data. The first is that described in Crow and Peterson's review and collected by Mitchell *et al.* [9] in 275 bulimic patients, of whom 69.5% had difficulties in interpersonal relationships, 60.7% in family functioning, 53.3% in financial circumstances and 49.6% in work adjustment. The other set comes from an eating patterns and substance use survey of 530 female university students (ages 18–25 years), in which Piran *et al.* [10] included a short questionnaire, derived from substance use surveys, about participants' perception of disruption in different domains of their lives due to engagement in varied target behaviours. Of the 310 (58.5%) individuals who had ever dieted, 17.4% reported harmful effects of dieting on their social life, 35.6% on their health, 21.4% on their family relationships, 20.9% on their studies/employment, 9.4% on their finances and 54.4% on their outlook on life. Of the 206 (38.9%) who had ever binged, 27% reported a harmful effect on their social life, 68.8% on their health, 23.5% on family, 25.2% on studies/employment, 17.5% on finances and 73.9% on their outlook on life. Similarly high rates of disruption were reported regarding vomiting and the use of laxatives. In addition, it is worth noting that the reported disruptions tended to exceed disruptions reported from the use of marijuana, tobacco or alcohol. This survey strongly suggests that eating behaviours that can be considered "normative" (such as dieting) or relatively common (such as bingeing) exert a disruptive toll in the life of many individuals who engage in them, even when compared with commonly used substances. The continuum of difficulties in disordered eating patterns and body weight and shape preoccupation introduces unique challenges to the calculation of cost in the area of eating disorders.

In considering the cost of services to individuals with eating disorders, especially the subclinical group, delineating a clear boundary between stepped-down treatment and selective prevention may be challenging. Brief, less-intensive and less-expensive care proposed by professionals such as Treasure *et al* [4] as a first step in the care of individuals with eating disorders may not differ from approaches to secondary prevention with selected individuals, such as the group-based prevention programme for weight-preoccupied women developed by Stice *et al.* [11] or the CD-ROM "Student Bodies" programme developed for weight-preoccupied women by Taylor *et al.* [12]. The costs of intervening and of not intervening with selected individuals who display subclinical levels of body weight and shape preoccupation should be included in the calculation of costs, even though some of this research may emanate from the prevention rather than the treatment domain.

Multiple challenges are present in calculating the costs and burden of eating disorders. Nonetheless, this area of study should be pursued in tandem with therapy efficacy research.

REFERENCES

1. Mitchell J., Maki D., Adson D., Ruskin B., Crow S. (1997) The selectivity of inclusion and exclusion criteria in bulimia nervosa treatment studies. *Int. J. Eat. Disord.*, 22: 243–252.
2. Persons J.B., Siberschatz G. (1998) Are results of randomized controlled trials useful to psychotherapists? *J. Consult. Clin. Psychol.*, 66: 126–135.
3. Commerford M., Licinio J., Halmi K. (1997) Guidelines for discharging eating disorder patients. *Eat. Disord.*, 5: 69–74.
4. Treasure J., Schmidt U., Troop N., Tiller J., Todd G., Turnbull S. (1996) Sequential treatment for bulimia nervosa incorporating a self care manual. *Br. J. Psychiatry*, 168: 94–98.
5. Howard W., Evans K., Quintero-Howard C., Bowers W., Andersen A. (1999) Predictors of success or failure of transition to day hospital treatment for inpatients with anorexia nervosa. *Am. J. Psychiatry*, 156: 1697–1702.
6. Shisslak C.M., Crago M., Estes L.S. (1995) The spectrum of eating disorders. *Int. J. Eat. Disord.*, 18: 209–219.
7. Gordon R.A. (1999) *The Spectrum of Eating Disorders*, 2nd ed. Blackwell, Malden.
8. Fairburn C., Welch S., Norman P., O'Connor M., Doll H. (1996) Bias and bulimia nervosa: how typical are clinic cases? *Am. J. Psychiatry*, 153: 386–391.
9. Mitchell J.E., Hatsukami D., Eckert E.D., Pyle R.L. (1985) Characteristics of 275 patients with bulimia. *Am. J. Psychiatry*, 142: 482–485.
10. Piran N., Thompson S., Affleck D., Downie F. (2000) Preoccupation with body weight and shape among women: explorations of the social context. Presented at the Canadian Psychological Association Annual Convention, Ottawa, 23 May.
11. Stice E., Mazotti L., Weibel D., Agras W.S. (2000) Dissonance prevention program decreases thin-ideal internalization, body dissatisfaction, dieting, negative affect, and bulimic symptoms: a preliminary experiment. *Int. J. Eat. Disord.*, 27: 206–217.

12. Taylor C.B., Winszelberg A.J., Celio A. (2001) The use of interactive media to prevent eating disorders. In *Eating Disorders: Innovative Directions in Research and Practice* (Eds R.H. Striegel-Moore, L. Smolak), pp. 255–269. American Psychological Association, Washington.

6.2
Reducing the Multiple Burdens of Suffering: Accessing Care for Eating Disorders

Ruth H. Striegel-Moore[1] and Debra Franko[2]

Eating disorders are "newcomers" to the psychiatric nomenclature, and the relatively recent history of these disorders means that major gaps remain concerning the personal, social and economic burdens associated with them. Crow and Peterson provide a comprehensive summary of the literature that illustrates the clinical significance of eating disorders. The high rates of medical and psychiatric comorbidity, elevated health services use and impaired social functioning speak for the need to find ways to reduce the burden of suffering that is associated with eating disorders. The economic and social costs of eating disorders may be reduced by decreasing their prevalence (by preventing the onset or reducing the duration of the disorder), lessening or diminishing the rate of secondary complications and developing more cost-effective treatments. As Crow and Peterson illustrate, ample evidence attests to the clinical severity of eating disorders. How costly it is to treat these disorders is less well established; to date, treatment studies have focused primarily on the question of what treatments work rather than the cost of effective treatments. Crow and Peterson offer a compelling list of suggestions for future research. We wish to add to this list one further suggestion: the need to examine the barriers to accessing care for an eating disorder.

Despite the evidence of the profound personal and societal costs associated with experiencing an eating disorder, and despite the availability of proven treatments, only a minority of individuals enter treatment specifically for the eating disorder [1].

Eating disorders are highly stigmatized conditions and stigma may be one barrier to accessing care. In the media, these disorders often are portrayed as problems of celebrities, associating them with affluence and a lifestyle centred on the pursuit of beauty and fame. These reports belie the complexity of the aetiology by reducing eating disorders to the consequence

[1] *Department of Psychology, Wesleyan University, 207 High Street, Middletown, CT 06459, USA*
[2] *Department of Psychology, Northeastern University, Boston, MA, USA*

of vanity "run amok". A national survey conducted in Great Britain found that one-third of respondents thought that individuals with an eating disorder should "pull themselves together" and "have only themselves to blame" for their condition [2]. In clinical practice it is not uncommon to encounter patients who have kept the eating disorder a secret from health professionals for years, due to a profound sense of shame about the disorder. In a community survey, about one-third of women with a current eating disorder reported that fear of being stigmatized (35%) and feeling ashamed about the eating disorder (31%) were reasons why they had not sought treatment [3]. Women from ethnic minorities may feel particularly stigmatized because eating disorders are often seen as occurring only in white women. Research is needed to determine whether efforts to reduce the stigma associated with eating disorders will result in a greater willingness by the sufferers to seek out treatment.

Even when individuals access healthcare, their service provider may not be prepared to diagnose the eating disorder. A study of over 3000 primary care providers found that the provider was aware of the eating disorder in only 10% of all cases; in contrast, identification of mood and anxiety disorders, albeit far from perfect (61% and 43%, respectively), was significantly higher [4]. Relatively low rates of detection and diagnosis also may reflect time pressures on primary care clinicians, which reduce the ability to enquire about eating disorders, as well as clinician discomfort with managing these illnesses [5,6]. In light of the increasingly common practice in the USA of accessing healthcare through a "gate keeper", the role of the primary care provider in detecting mental health problems, eating disorders in particular, is critical. Research is needed to develop cost-effective means for identifying eating disorders in primary care settings as a first step towards appropriate treatment. As Crow and Peterson describe, health service use is elevated in individuals with an eating disorder; if this service use does not effectively treat the disorder, it is likely that the patient will continue to experience the need for further treatment.

The lack of affordable care represents a major barrier to seeking treatment. Even patients with health insurance may find that their policy explicitly excludes coverage for the treatment of an eating disorder. As Crow and Peterson describe, eating disorders may result in several serious and often irreversible or difficult to treat medical complications, including infertility, osteoporosis, obesity and dental decay. In addition, studies have documented high rates of psychiatric comorbidity consistently, both in community samples and patient populations, which add significantly to the economic and social burden of eating disorders. Studies are needed that document the cost offset incurred by early and effective treatment. Finally, Crow and Peterson's review reminds us that not all costs are economic and that the personal and social benefits of good mental health may justify interventions even if they require the allocation of new resources.

ACKNOWLEDGEMENTS

Supported by grants from the National Institute of Mental Health and the National Institute of Diabetes, Digestive and Kidney Diseases (R01-MH-57897 and R01-MH-64022).

REFERENCES

1. Garvin V., Striegel-Moore R.H. (2001) Health services research for eating disorders in the United States. In *Eating Disorders: Innovative Directions in Research and Practice* (Eds R.H. Striegel-Moore, L. Smolak), pp. 135–152. American Psychological Association, Washington.
2. Crisp A.H., Gelder M.G., Rix S., Meltzer H.I., Rowlands O.J. (2000) Stigmatisation of people with mental illness. *Br. J. Psychiatry*, **177**: 4–7.
3. Cachelin F.M., Rebeck R., Veisel C., Striegel-Moore R.H. (2001) Barriers to treatment for eating disorders among ethnically diverse women. *Int. J. Eat. Disord.*, **30**: 269–278.
4. Spitzer R.L., Kroenke K., Williams J.B. (1999) Validation and utility of a self-report version of PRIME-MD. *JAMA*, **282**: 1737–1744.
5. Whitehouse A.M., Cooper P.J., Vize C.V., Hill C., Vogel L. (1992) Prevalence of eating disorders in three Cambridge general practices: hidden and conspicuous morbidity. *Br. J. Gen. Pract.*, **42**: 57–60.
6. Kaplan A.S., Garfinkel P.E. (1999) Difficulties in treating patients with eating disorders: a review of patient and clinical variables. *Can. J. Psychiatry*, **44**: 665–670.

6.3
Where Does the Burden Come From?
W. Stewart Agras[1]

Eating disorders pose significant burdens to health and well-being, as well as incurring high health costs. Society is beginning to recognize these burdens, as demonstrated by the passage of legislation in some states in the USA, listing eating disorders among diagnoses such as schizophrenia, bipolar disorder and obsessive–compulsive disorder, that should be given

[1] *Department of Psychiatry, Stanford University School of Medicine, 401 Quarry Road, Stanford, CA 94305, USA*

parity with severe medical conditions for the coverage of healthcare costs. Crow and Peterson, in their interesting review, pull together the emerging literature on this issue, delineating what is known and exposing gaps in our knowledge that need to be filled.

From a theoretical perspective, it is interesting to speculate as to which of the burdens posed by the eating disorders arise from the disorder itself or from the comorbid psychopathology that accompanies these disorders. Over 50% of those with eating disorders have a lifetime history of major depression, and there are high rates of anxiety and personality disorders, all of which are associated with both social and economic burdens.

- *Medical burdens.* It seems clear that the medical burdens posed by anorexia nervosa and bulimia nervosa are due to the eating disorder itself, because they arise directly from the physiological consequences of disordered eating. In the case of binge eating disorder, however, it appears that the major health consequences, which are many, arise from the comorbid obesity. It is unclear at this point how much the binge eating contributes to the obesity, although it has been shown that maintained cessation of binge eating is associated with modest weight losses and the prevention of continued weight gain [1]. Additionally, disturbed eating patterns, not necessarily those associated with full syndromal status, may affect health. For example, 29% of adolescent diabetics with disturbed eating patterns had significantly higher haemoglobin A_{1c} than those with normal eating patterns. At a 4-year follow-up, those with disturbed eating were more likely to demonstrate retinopathy [2].
- *Mortality.* As Scott and Peterson point out, both overall mortality and suicide rates are high for eating disorders, although the majority of this burden is attributable to anorexia nervosa. About half of the deaths in the latter condition are attributable to the effects of starvation on various organs, whereas the remainder are attributable to suicide. Presumably, the latter deaths are mainly due to comorbid depression, although starvation itself contributes to depressed mood. Because the majority of patients with binge eating disorder are also overweight or obese, these patients should share the higher mortality rate attributable to obesity.
- *Fertility.* The major burden upon fertility appears to be associated with anorexia nervosa. In addition, anorexia nervosa poses an additional burden on the infant, with higher rates of prematurity, perinatal morbidity and mortality. These complications are clearly attributable to the eating disorder. Some studies further suggest that eating disordered mothers have a disturbed relationship with their infant, particularly over feeding but also in other interactions.

- *Economic burdens*. Importantly, Scott and Peterson point out that anorexia nervosa is associated with higher treatment costs than schizophrenia, and that eating disorders as a whole have costs that are similar in magnitude to those associated with schizophrenia. It is unclear what portion of these costs is attributable to comorbid psychiatric or physical conditions (obesity), although one would assume that most of the costs are attributable to the eating disorder, because that was the primary diagnosis under which the costs were incurred.
- *Social burdens*. It appears that social adjustment is impaired in all the eating disorders, with limited data for eating disorders not meeting the full syndromal criteria. Moreover, adjustment is impaired in the family, in personal finances and in work status. At this point no work has appeared that attempts to separate out the effects of the eating disorder and the effects of comorbid psychopathology.

Overall, many of the costs of eating disorders appear to be contributed to by both the eating disorder and the comorbid physical and psychopathological conditions, although it is possible hypothetically to separate out "cause" in some circumstances, and it should be possible to delineate the separate effects in future studies. It is possible that within each of the diagnostic entities there are individuals at higher and lower risk of incurring excessive costs.

Certainly the literature suggests that eating disorders compare in health and social costs to the most serious of the mental disorders, including schizophrenia and obsessive–compulsive disorder. Although enough is known about the social and economic costs of eating disorders to spur further investigation, it is clear from Scott and Peterson's review that much remains to be done. The opportunities for research delineated in the review will hopefully spur further action in this interesting area, which has important implications for health policy.

REFERENCES

1. Agras W.S., Telch C.F., Arnow B., Eldredge K., Marnell M. (1997) One-year follow-up of cognitive-behavioral therapy for obese individuals with binge eating disorder. *J. Consult. Clin. Psychol.*, **65**: 343–347.
2. Rydall A.C., Rodin G.M., Olmsted M.P. (1997) Disordered eating behavior and microvascular complications in young women with insulin-dependent diabetes mellitus. *N. Engl. J. Med.*, **336**: 1849–1853.

6.4
Economic Burden and the Eating Disorders
Paul Garfinkel[1]

Although anorexia nervosa was described in the medical literature almost 400 years ago, and symptoms of bulimia date back to the Babylonian Talmud, eating disorders have received increasing attention in recent years as knowledge of their frequency, mortality and morbidity has accumulated. At the same time, Crow and Peterson are correct in emphasizing how little is known about the economic and social burden of these disorders. This is especially true when one factors in the partial syndromes (what DSM-IV describes as eating disorders not otherwise specified, EDNOS) and the burdens of some of the frequent complications or sequelae.

Core features of the eating disorders centre around the extreme drive for thinness and morbid fear of fat in the case of anorexia nervosa, in spite of emaciation, and in bulimia nervosa with extreme efforts to compensate for binge eating. Clinically significant differences between bulimia and anorexia nervosa have been delineated in the past 20 years; and, more recently, subtypes of anorexia and bulimia have shown important implications for course and costs. Although Crow and Peterson have noted the increased frequency of these disorders, the increase in recent years has been in bulimia nervosa. This has occurred with a reduced age of onset [1] and in all countries that become more westernized.

The symptoms of eating disorders vary greatly, and some of the core features may be ego-syntonic (e.g. the desire for thinness). People with anorexia nervosa also display a denial of illness and those with bulimia great shame and secrecy. It is not surprising then that many people do not come forward for treatment, delay treatment or go unrecognized by the clinician. Treatment frequently may be provided for the complications—osteoporosis, erosion of dental enamel, depression, etc.—rather than the underlying illness.

The high frequency of the partial syndromes and their relationship to full syndromes limit our knowledge of the burdens to these states. Earlier work has shown partial syndrome anorexia nervosa to be about three times as common as the full syndrome (1.4% vs. 0.6% in young women) and corresponding figures exist for bulimia nervosa (2.3% vs. 1.1%) [2,3]. People with partial syndromes display significant comorbidity for depression, alcohol-related problems and anxiety disorders, which would have to be accounted for in any evaluation of the costs to these disorders.

[1] Centre for Addiction and Mental Health, 1001 Queen Street West, Toronto, Ontario M6J 1H4, Canada

Probably the greatest area for underreporting of the burden of eating disorders relates to their frequent complications and after-effects. Crow and Peterson correctly comment on the physiological effects of chronic starvation and dieting. The psychosocial sequelae are of even greater importance here.

There is considerable overlap between eating and affective disorders. This is true in terms of the shared familial predisposition and co-occurrence, but also in the course after recovery for the eating disorder. Over half of the people with an eating disorder experience at least one depressive episode. Even after recovery, Toner *et al.* [4] reported that 60% of anorexic patients later experienced depression. The burdens of depression have been studied in greater detail than for eating disorders, and have been shown to be more marked than for many chronic medical conditions. Similarly, about 30% of bulimics and 5–7% of anorexics develop alcohol misuse, which again is associated with significant morbidity and cost. Anxiety disorders are also frequent in people with eating disorders and, whether it is agoraphobia, obsessive–compulsive disorder or generalized anxiety disorder, there would have to be significant effects in terms of social withdrawal and lost productivity. Crow and Peterson have appropriately identified obesity, which is common in binge eating disorder and in bulimia nervosa, as having its own set of problems from increased mortality and many causes for additional burdens.

One important but often overlooked comorbidity with eating disorders relates to the personality disorders, especially those with poor impulse control. This is particularly true for those with the bulimic forms of these disorders, of whom about 25% display some form of borderline-narcissistic spectrum disorder. These people are liable to disrupted work and personal relationships, affective lability and episodes of other impulsive acts such as suicide attempts, drug use and self-mutilation.

Given the above, it is not surprising that so little is known about the social and economic burden of eating disorders. The healthcare utilization costs described by Crow and Peterson would have to be tempered with the knowledge that most people with an eating disorder receive no treatment or receive treatment for another condition, grossly undervaluing the burden of eating disorders.

The limited work on cost-efficacy is interesting and points to areas where there has been some improved understanding. There is now a consensus that weight restoration is critical for treatment, and psychotherapy while the individual is still starving is quite limited. The trend for shorter lengths of stay may lead to an unfortunate tendency to discharge patients before they are ready, increasing the likelihood of relapse. Partial and day hospitalizations are proving to be valuable for weight restoration and nutritional stability at a fraction of the cost of in-hospital treatments.

Effective treatments for eating disorders have resulted from the clinical research of the past two decades. We know that specific forms of psychotherapy and antidepressant medications, and their combinations are useful [5,6]. The work quoted by Crow and Peterson demonstrates that the treatments with the greatest cost-effectiveness may not necessarily be the best for clinical efficacy. An antidepressant drug may be the most economical for producing the highest number of abstinent bulimics per dollar spent, but this would not be recommended in terms of treatment of people in a clinic. Treatment should begin with cognitive–behavioural, interpersonal or family therapy, and medication should be added only when symptoms do not seem to improve or when depression is significant.

REFERENCES

1. Garfinkel P.E., Lin B., Goering P., Spegg C., Goldbloom D., Kennedy S., Kaplan A., Woodside B. (1995) Bulimia nervosa in a Canadian community sample: prevalence and comparison of subgroups. Am. J. Psychiatry, 152: 1052–1058.
2. Dancyger I.F., Garfinkel P.E. (1995) The relationship of partial syndrome eating disorders to anorexia nervosa and bulimia nervosa. Psychol. Med., 25: 1019–1026.
3. Garfinkel P.E., Lin B., Goering P., Spegg C., Goldbloom D., Kennedy S., Kaplan A., Woodside D.B. (1996) Should amenorrhea be necessary for the diagnosis of anorexia nervosa? Evidence from a Canadian community sample. Br. J. Psychiatry, 168: 500–506.
4. Toner B.B., Garfinkel P.E., Garner D.M. (1986) Long-term follow-up of anorexia nervosa. Psychosom. Med., 48: 520–529.
5. Kaplan A. (2002) Psychological treatments for anorexia nervosa: a review of published studies and promising new directions. Can. J. Psychiatry, 47: 235–242.
6. Zhu J., Walsh T. (2002) Pharmacologic treatment of eating disorders. Can. J. Psychiatry, 47: 227–234.

6.5
Eating Disorders: Time to Count the Cost
Arthur Crisp[1]

Crow and Peterson convey the ubiquity and seriousness of the eating disorders and the great personal, social and economic burdens that accompany them. The term "eating disorder" itself colludes with the public's defensive need to deny or trivialize these conditions in the face of their apparent ego-syntonicity and associated disempowerment of others. The term bears a similar relationship to the underlying and psychologically

[1] Department of Psychiatry, St. George's Hospital Medical School, London SW17 0RE, UK

destructive dyslipophobic psychopathology and related body weight concerns, as does the symptom of a "cough" to its basis in, say, lung cancer. Treating the cough alone is a serious error! To illustrate the point, recently we reported on an anorexic patient in the UK who occupied a hospital bed for 3 of the 4 years that she languished *in extremis* and undiagnosed [1].

Crow and Peterson focus on the report of a domestic study [2], examining health insurance claims of nearly 4 million individuals. Claims in connection with those with anorexia nervosa were greater than for those with other major psychiatric disorders; there were lesser claims in respect of bulimia nervosa. These authors remind us that claims may be made also for the cost of assessing and treating many of the severe physical complications of the eating disorders, where the underlying psychopathology is not recognized or reported. In an effort to estimate some of these costs within the UK National Health Service (NHS), in 1991 we conducted a study of 20 successive patients with anorexia nervosa referred to our service. It was retrospective, carefully recording and checking on all previous contacts with the health services, i.e. both primary and secondary care systems. The considerable problems of estimating costs were examined. Calculated costs to the NHS ranged up to more than £56 000 ($82 000). Cost per year of illness ranged up to £11 479 ($17 000). The details of this study are contained in a university thesis [3]. In the UK we would need to identify separately the costs to social services in respect of anorexia nervosa, which are probably at least as great as those to the medical care system.

The full extent of morbidity and mortality costs can only be speculative. For instance, because anorexia nervosa is a seriously egosyntonic disorder and the other eating disorders are also often strenuously concealed and denied, much of the immediate related physical morbidity is never revealed in its true diagnostic colours. Running a psychiatric liaison service 40 years ago, I identified 26 cases of anorexia nervosa in a female medical ward run by two very progressive and clinically and academically alert physicians who had nevertheless not always detected the disorder within the welter of physical symptomatologies and signs that were presenting [4]. As Crow and Peterson also point out, eating disorders are well represented although often concealed within clinics dealing with infertility. Unwise artificial facilitations of conception/child-bearing in women still afflicted with eating disorders and likely to have a post-natal intensification of the disorder can bring in their wake a plethora of developmental problems for the offspring, with related further (and probably long-term) costs to the healthcare system.

Death from an eating disorder might, from a national cost perspective, be thought to bring down the curtain on the tragedy, but this is not necessarily so, especially if there are offspring by that time. The impact of loss on parents in mid-life can also prompt its own morbidity.

Crow and Peterson remind us that studies reveal widespread subclinical eating disorder pathology in teenage females in particular. The academic, social and economic impacts of this are probably profound and deserve investigation. For instance, it is clear that among teenage females cigarette smoking is often an immovable defence rooted in weight gain concerns and the awareness that smoking reduces food intake [5]. The knock-on effects of increased cigarette smoking in the female population in the UK are now beginning to be felt in terms of serious mid-life respiratory disorders.

There is a significant but tiny positive side to the matter of morbidity and mortality costs. Many years ago we noted that people with anorexia nervosa seemed much less likely to suffer from colds and influenza than the remainder of their family. Possible explanations in this respect seemed to be their social isolation and perhaps some diet-related phenomenon such as hypoglycaemia. In fact we found that they had a more robust antibody response to influenza vaccine [6]. In an overall study of the mortality of our patient population, accumulated between 1960 and 1995 and with year of onset between 1935 and 1995, we found an almost significant tendency for there to be less deaths from cancer of both the breast and uterus. Such a finding is clinically plausible.

Meanwhile, there are few disorders so personally and socially crippling as the main eating disorders themselves. Loss to productivity [7] is a major concern for individuals with anorexia nervosa. Personal and family economic burdens accrue. Twenty-five years ago I found myself talking with a crowded hall of parents in New Jersey, USA, some of whom had spent all their life savings and mortgaged their properties to the hilt in futile efforts to help their anorexic children. The barrenness of existence that confronts so many sufferers is a quality-of-life factor that is painful and probably impossible to quantify.

Reluctance of health insurance companies to pay for lengthy hospital admission for individuals with anorexia nervosa probably impairs the efficacy of treatments aimed at prompt weight restoration. In the UK, Meads *et al.* [8] recently reported their systematic survey of the literature on the relative efficacy of inpatient and outpatient treatments for anorexia nervosa. They drew upon our randomized controlled trial of treatments, including psychotherapy (addressing the maturational problems of patients with anorexia nervosa) [9]. This trial revealed the superior effectiveness of the treatment irrespective of setting [10]. The costs of the outpatient options were one-tenth those of the inpatient package. In an earlier cohort of patients treated in similar ways, we demonstrated a 20-year outcome where overall mortality is just 4%, with 1% suicide instead of the usual 5–7%. This population, treated and with 70% fully recovered, has demonstrated its potential healthy fecundity, having produced 115 live offspring and just one death. Treatment can work and the illness "costs" shrivel.

REFERENCES

1. Howlett M., McClelland L., Crisp A.H. (1995) The cost of the illness that defies. *Postgrad. Med. J.*, **71**: 705–706.
2. Striegel-Moore R.H., Leslie D., Petrill S.A., Garvin V., Rosenheck R.A. (2000) One-year use and cost of inpatient and outpatient services among female and male patients with an eating disorder: evidence from a national database of health insurance claims. *Int. J. Eat. Disord.*, **27**: 381–389.
3. Taylor R. (1993) Anorexia nervosa: patterns of service utilisation. Unpublished thesis, University of London.
4. Crisp A.H. (1968) The role of the psychiatrist in the general hospital. *Postgrad. Med. J.*, **44**: 267–276.
5. Crisp A., Sedgwick P., Halek C., Joughin N., Humphrey H. (1999) Why may teenage girls persist in smoking? *J. Adolesc.*, **22**: 657–672.
6. Armstrong-Esther C.A., Lacey J.H., Crisp A.H., Bryant T.N. (1978) An investigation of the immune response of patients suffering from anorexia nervosa. *Postgrad. Med. J.*, **54**: 395–399.
7. Croft-Jefferies C., Wilkinson G. (1989) Estimated costs of neurotic disorder in UK general practice 1985. *Psychol. Med.*, **19**: 549–558.
8. Meads C., Gold L., Burls A. (2001) How effective is outpatient care compared to inpatient care in the treatment of anorexia nervosa? A systematic review. *Eur. Eat. Disord. Rev.*, **9**: 229–241.
9. Crisp A.H. (1997) Anorexia nervosa as flight from growth: assessment and treatment based on the model. In *Handbook of Treatment for Eating Disorders* (Eds D.M. Garner, P.E. Garfinkel), pp. 248–277. Guilford, New York.
10. Crisp A. (2003) Treatment of anorexia nervosa: is 'where' or 'how' the main issue? *Eur. Eat. Disord. Rev.* (in press).

6.6
The Hidden Burdens of Eating Disorders
Robert L. Palmer[1]

The clinical eating disorders have an image problem. They tend to be thought of either as devastating but rare conditions or as commonplace but trivial. In truth, they are neither. They are ordinary psychiatric disorders and they constitute a significant public health problem. The review of their associated burdens by Crow and Peterson is timely.

Some of these burdens are clear, but some are less so. Some are easy to ascertain for the individual but even these may be difficult to quantify for a population. Thus, the excess mortality of sufferers is evident even if its size is uncertain. Likewise, clinical osteoporosis diagnosed in a young person

[1] *University Department of Psychiatry, Brandon Unit, Leicester General Hospital, Leicester LE5 4PW, UK*

with anorexia nervosa may, in the extreme case, be manifest as pathological fractures. But are there cohorts of former sufferers who will have evident problems only in later life, perhaps long after their eating disorder has resolved?

Some burdens and costs may be difficult to quantify even in principle. For instance, what about the restriction and derailment of people's lives that the disorders involve? Any disorder that afflicts young people as they enter adult life is likely to be disruptive in ways that are difficult to measure. What would have happened if the disorder had not occurred? Such questions are difficult to answer and yet they are the stuff of concern for sufferers and their families. Of course, an eating disorder does not arrive out of the blue. Many people who succumb to them have troubled lives and some observers speculate that an eating disorder arises as a way of coping that has gone wrong. If another way of managing the trouble had been adopted, what then? But this line of thinking moves quickly into the unanswerable and imponderable. It is more straight-forward to think of the direct associations of having an eating disorder. However, even then, the data that might answer the questions are not always available.

The majority of those afflicted by eating disorders are not in contact with appropriate clinical services even when these are potentially available. This may be especially true for bulimia nervosa, which is an easier condition to hide. Sufferers have mixed feelings about their condition and these may include shame, embarrassment and fear of change, making the seeking of help feel risky. Studying patients (i.e. those who do present to services), therefore, might give a misleading impression of what is typical. It certainly underestimates potential treatment costs. Crow and Peterson suggest that there is evidence for the undertreatment of people who do present, perhaps because third-party funders baulk at the cost. However, there is greater potential demand from those who do not present. There is likely to be a complex relationship between the provision of service and the willingness of sufferers to seek out treatment despite their mixed feelings about doing so. Good services encourage demand, and so they should. But good services cost money. There is a dilemma here for clinicians and funders. Should they encourage the provision of services even in the face of low apparent demand, or should they act upon the likelihood of there being many people out there who could benefit from help but who are not currently demanding it? It seems ethical for good services to be made easily available when people are suffering and effective help could be provided. But the temptation when resources are limited would be to let sleeping dogs lie and not to be too active in offering expensive help to those who are not actively demanding it. The ambivalence of the sufferers may promote a parallel ambivalence in those who could help them.

Another kind of third party may be involved with people suffering from eating disorders, i.e. their family and friends. They too may experience real difficulty. One study suggests that the load upon the relatives of someone with an eating disorder was no less than that upon the relatives of those with psychosis [1].

The eating disorders are a significant public health problem. However, they have a complex relationship with another greater problem, i.e. obesity. Eating restraint (slimming) seems to play a key part in the risk of developing eating disorders. However, slimming, in some sense, is part of a rational response to rising weight in an individual and in a population. Public health messages are best kept simple but on this issue the reality is complex. For the population as a whole the health benefits of slenderness need to be promoted in the face of tempting excess, but the necessary messages may all too easily become entangled with the distorting self-doubt of the potential eating disorder sufferer. How often do our patients—even those who are evidently ill—claim to be eating "healthily"? Are they, in any sense, casualties of the public health battle against obesity?

There is much that remains uncertain about the details of the burdens that eating disorders place upon individuals and populations. Nevertheless, it is clear that they are substantial. Those of us working in the field need to be willing to issue repeated reminders of this to our colleagues and to those who fund our work, so that eating disorders may receive the attention and resources that they deserve. We should not have to do this, but, because eating disorders have an image problem, we do.

REFERENCE

1. Treasure J., Murphy T., Szmuckler G., Todd G., Gavan K., Joyce J. (2001) The experience of caregiving for severe mental illness: a comparison between anorexia nervosa and psychosis. *Soc. Psychiatry Psychiatr. Epidemiol.*, **36**: 343–347.

6.7
Differential Treatments for Eating Disorders Might Reduce Social and Economic Burden

Maria Råstam[1] and Christopher Gillberg[1,2]

As reviewed by Crow and Peterson, there is evidence for undertreatment in eating disorders. In a Swedish community screened sample, including a total birth cohort, 1.1% of all girls developed anorexia nervosa before their 18th birthday. However, 24% (12 out of 51 individuals) never sought any psychiatric or other medical services for their illness [1]. Only 55% received treatment (defined as psychiatric/psychological treatment given on eight sessions or more) and only a fraction of this proportion could be considered "comprehensive". In bulimia nervosa, according to a community screening in The Netherlands, only 6% received mental healthcare [2]. It is clear that, in spite of the medical risks, many individuals with eating disorders go untreated. Even so, the economic costs according to Crow and Peterson are substantial. Treatment is shown to be very expensive, at the same level as treatment in schizophrenia. Furthermore, although the frequency of anorexia nervosa seems to have levelled out, broader spectrum eating disorders, including bulimia nervosa, appear to be increasingly more common [2]. A future increased demand on psychiatry from persons with eating disorders is therefore to be expected.

The well-known, sometimes life-threatening, consequences of eating disorders make early detection and treatment mandatory. However, long-term outcome after treatment is not clearly distinguished from the natural course of the disorder [3]. Recent studies of adolescent anorexia nervosa followed prospectively for a minimum of 10 years, with all cases accounted for, found zero mortality, suggesting that anorexia nervosa with classical teenage onset may have a better prognosis [4–6].

Comparing quality-of-life measurements in eating disorders, angina and transplant candidates [7], impairment in social life seemed to be the worst aspect of anorexia and bulimia nervosa. Eating disordered patients were only slightly better off than men under the age of 60 years awaiting coronary surgery for angina, and worse than candidates for heart/lung transplantation. Reporting on the impact of eating disorders on the families with a sick family member, one study found that in anorexia nervosa (but not in bulimia nervosa) the psychosocial situation was impaired at a level similar to that reported by families with a grown-up child with schizophrenia [8].

[1] Department of Child and Adolescent Psychiatry, Göteborg University, Göteborg, Sweden
[2] Department of Psychiatry, St. George's Hospital Medical School, London, UK

Positive changes in eating behaviour correlate with higher quality of life, including social life, but in most anorexia nervosa studies the psychosocial problems tend to persist in some individuals. This might be due in part to impairment related to starvation-induced brain abnormalities [9], or the social isolation, which is one of the first symptoms of the illness. Furthermore, the young individuals are affected at a time of life that is very important for their socialization. In some cases with eating disorders, however, there is evidence of childhood obsessive traits and weak social skills [10,11]. In the anorexia nervosa study mentioned above [6], poor overall outcome was found in cases with persisting eating disorder and in recovered individuals with lifelong problems with social interaction and obsessive–compulsive behaviour, in some cases fulfilling the criteria for an autism spectrum disorder. At the age of 25 years, 4/51 individuals had disability pension because of eating disorder, autism spectrum disorder or both. Outcome was not related to treatment. It is pertinent that in anorexia nervosa associated with autistic traits, according to our clinical experience, common treatment methods have little effect. Instead, a more psychoeducational approach is warranted.

In the case of autism spectrum disorders, a lifelong dependence on psychiatric services can be expected. There are many other secondary/ comorbid/overlapping conditions associated with eating disorders, e.g. obsessive–compulsive disorder, affective disorders, personality disorders and substance abuse, each with psychosocial, physical and economic consequences. Considering the costs and scarce availability of treatment, it would seem important to optimize the treatment given. The very limited effect of even well-established treatments in eating disorders [12] points to the heterogeneity of the disorders. Studies show that different background factors account for different outcomes in eating disorders, e.g. childhood feeding problems, early personality traits and life events may colour "the end result" just as much as, and sometimes more than, the eating disorder *per se* [13]. Early assessment of such factors in the individual case— matching treatment to patient—could improve the results.

REFERENCES

1. Gillberg C., Råstam M., Gillberg I.C. (1994) Anorexia nervosa: who sees the patients and who do the patients see? *Acta Paediatr.*, **83**: 967–971.
2. van Hoeken D., Lucas A.R., Hoek H.W. (1998) Epidemiology. In *Neurobiology in the Treatment of Eating Disorders* (Eds H.W. Hoek, J.L. Treasure, M.A. Katzman), pp. 97–126. Wiley, Chichester.
3. Ben-Tovim D.I., Walker K., Gilchrist P., Freeman R., Kalucy R., Esterman A. (2001) Outcome in patients with eating disorders: a 5-year study. *Lancet*, **357**: 1254–1257.

4. Strober M., Freeman R., Morrell W. (1997) The long-term course of severe anorexia nervosa in adolescents: survival analysis of recovery, relapse, and outcome predictors over 10–15 years in a prospective study. *Int. J. Eat. Disord.*, **22**: 339–360.
5. Herpertz-Dahlmann B., Muller B., Herpertz S., Heussen N., Hebebrand J., Remschmidt H. (2001) Prospective 10-year follow-up in adolescent anorexia nervosa—course, outcome, psychiatric comorbidity, and psychosocial adaptation. *J. Child Psychol. Psychiatry*, **42**: 603–612.
6. Wentz E., Gillberg C., Gillberg I.C., Råstam M. (2001) Ten-year follow-up of adolescent-onset anorexia nervosa: psychiatric disorders and overall functioning scales. *J. Child Psychol. Psychiatry*, **42**: 613–622.
7. Keilen M., Treasure T., Schmidt U., Treasure J. (1994) Quality of life measurements in eating disorders, angina, and transplant candidates: are they comparable? *J. Roy. Soc. Med.*, **87**: 441–444.
8. Santonastaso P., Saccon D., Favaro A. (1997) Burden and psychiatric symptoms on key relatives of patients with eating disorders: a preliminary study. *Eat. Weight Disord.*, **2**: 44–48.
9. Hendren R.L., De Backer I., Pandina G.J. (2000) Review of neuroimaging studies of child and adolescent psychiatric disorders from the past 10 years. *J. Am. Acad. Child Adolesc. Psychiatry*, **39**: 815–828.
10. Sharp C.W., Clark S.A., Dunan J.R., Blackwood D.H., Shapiro C.M. (1994) Clinical presentation of anorexia nervosa in males: 24 new cases. *Int. J. Eat. Disord.*, **15**: 125–134.
11. Thornton C., Russell J. (1997) Obsessive compulsive comorbidity in the dieting disorders. *Int. J. Eat. Disord.*, **21**: 83–87.
12. Wilson G.T. (1999) Cognitive behavior therapy for eating disorders: progress and problems. *Behav. Res. Ther.*, **37** (Suppl. 1): S79–S95.
13. Råstam M., Gillberg C. (1992) Background factors in anorexia nervosa. A controlled study of 51 teenage cases including a population sample. *Eur. Child Adolesc. Psychiatry*, **1**: 54–65.

6.8
The Burdens of Eating Disorders are Rarely Recognized

Pauline S. Powers and Yvonne Bannon[1]

Among the major mental illnesses, only substance use disorders, affective disorders and anxiety disorders are more common than eating disorders [1]. Eating disorders affect at least 5 million people in the USA and are more common than Alzheimer's disease (which affects 4 million people), schizophrenia (which affects 2.2 million people) and obsessive–compulsive disorder (which affects 3.3 million people). Within the general categories of affective and anxiety disorders, frequently recognized specific disorders are

[1] *Department of Psychiatry, College of Medicine, University of South Florida, Tampa, FL 33613, USA*

less common than eating disorders. For example, bipolar disorder affects 2.3 million adults and panic disorder affects approximately 2.4 million adults. However, despite the high prevalence of eating disorders, very little work has been done regarding their medical, social and economic burdens.

The reasons for this omission are many. Only in the last three to four decades have eating disorders been recognized as relatively common and, perhaps, increasing in incidence. Furthermore, information regarding eating disorders often has focused on anorexia nervosa (which is the least common eating disorder), many studies of incidence and prevalence have been carried out on college campuses and most reports of treatment outcome have come from tertiary care centres. In addition, most reports of eating disorders focus on females, even though a large minority of patients are males. For example, it is not widely appreciated that in the USA there are more males with bulimia nervosa than females with anorexia nervosa [2]. Many treatment centres exclude male patients, and the only drug approved for any eating disorder (fluoxetine) was studied in trials that excluded male patients [3–5]. Male patients may be less likely to seek treatment or may be unable to access treatment [6].

Only in the last few years has an attempt been made to determine systematically the demographic and clinical characteristics of eating disordered patients seen in a wide variety of treatment centres. The International Eating Disorder Database located in Fargo, North Dakota, is now collecting information, and the first report of findings from the USA was presented recently [7]. A key finding was that the most common eating disorder was eating disorder not otherwise specified (EDNOS), which included 53% of the 526 patients enrolled in the Database. Of the 53% who had EDNOS, 11.4% had binge eating disorder; the majority of the other patients in the EDNOS category had atypical or subsyndromal bulimia nervosa or anorexia nervosa. This large category of patients with EDNOS has made it difficult to estimate the social and economic burdens of eating disorders and also has made it difficult to plan for appropriate interventions, because most treatment outcome studies have focused on full syndromal anorexia or bulimia nervosa.

However, there is evidence, as noted by Crow and Peterson, that the physiological complications of EDNOS are likely to be as serious as with the syndromal conditions. This observation is strengthened by the research of Garfinkel et al. [8]. The current diagnostic criteria are useful for certain types of specific research (such as the genetic contribution to eating disorders) but are very limited in promoting our understanding of the extent and burden of eating disorders.

Until recently, most research funded by the US National Institute of Mental Health (NIMH) was for cognitive–behavioural therapy for bulimia nervosa and certain studies of neurotransmitters, particularly in anorexia nervosa. The actual NIMH research funding for eating disorders (excluding obesity) for the year 2000 was $14 673 000 [8]. By contrast, the funding for Alzheimer's disease was $59 721 000, even though this disease is less common than eating disorders and affects individuals at the end of their life rather than during adolescence. The cost differential is even more marked for the comparison between eating disorders and schizophrenia: $234 799 000 was expended on research for schizophrenia in the year 2000. The average expenditure on research for patients with eating disorders averaged less than $3 per affected individual, compared with $107 per individual affected by schizophrenia.

Pharmaceutical companies generally have not funded research into eating disorders. The fluoxetine studies for female patients with bulimia nervosa are the major exception. Given the enormous direct medical costs of treating eating disorders in the USA ($5–6 billion per year) compared with the yearly global cost of antipsychotic medication ($7 billion per year) [9], perhaps this will change.

REFERENCES

1. National Institute of Mental Health (2002) *The Numbers Count*. http://www.nimh.nih.gov.
2. Powers P.S., Spratt E. (1994) Males compared to females with eating disorders: 15 years of clinical experience. *Eat. Disord. J. Treat. Prev.*, **2**: 197–214.
3. Fluoxetine Bulimia Nervosa Collaborative Study Group (1992) Fluoxetine in the treatment of bulimia nervosa: a multicenter, placebo-controlled, double-blind trial. *Arch. Gen. Psychiatry*, **409**: 139–147.
4. Goldstein D.J., Wilson M.G., Thompson V.L., Potvin J.H., Rampey A.II., Fluoxetine Bulimia Nervosa Research Group (1995) Long-term fluoxetine treatment of bulimia nervosa. *Br. J. Psychiatry*, **166**: 660–666.
5. Romano S.J., Halmi K.A., Sarkar N.P., Koke S.C., Lee J.S. (2002) A placebo-controlled study of fluoxetine in continued treatment of bulimia nervosa after successful acute fluoxetine treatment. *Am. J. Psychiatry*, **159**: 96–102.
6. Andersen A.E. (1999) Gender-related aspects of eating disorders: a guide to practice. *J. Gend. Specif. Med.*, **2**: 47–54.
7. Powers P.S., Mitchell J.E., Garner D.M., Munson N. (2002). International eating disorders database: preliminary findings. Presented at the International Eating Disorders Conference, Boston, 27 April.
8. National Institute of Mental Health (2000) *Budget Actuals for Fiscal Year 2000*. National Institute of Mental Health, Bethesda.
9. Striegel-Moore R.H., Leslie D., Petrill S.A., Garvin V., Rosenheck R.A. (2000) One year use and cost of inpatient and outpatient services among female and male patients with an eating disorder: evidence from a national database of health insurance claims. *Int. J. Eat. Disord.*, **27**: 381–389.

6.9
Counting the Cost of Counting the Calories
Lois J. Surgenor[1]

Even seasoned clinicians in the area of eating disorders remain sensitive to and are staggered by the burden of these conditions, not only on those affected but also on the health, economic and social systems in which these are embedded. Indeed, few psychiatric disorders are so comprehensively disabling and distorting of self. In the face of a possibly increasing prevalence of eating disorders, a focus on the burden of these conditions is timely.

Researchers typically have appraised the economic burdens in terms of healthcare utilization, especially that of hospital resources [1]. Something is known of the direct costs of inpatient programmes, as illustrated by Crow and Peterson's description of the large database study led by Striegel-Moore *et al.* [2]. In this respect, hospital admissions appear to be very expensive options for health providers—not to say sometimes also distressing for the patient. Although there is increasing criticism of the international trend towards brief admissions [3,4], Crow and Peterson remind us that the jury is still out regarding the clinical efficacy of inpatient treatment over cheaper options [5,6]. Obtaining better quality information regarding the very pressing issues of treatment cost-effectiveness and clinical efficacy remains a frequently stated call in the field of eating disorders, but the mechanics of this are not easy [7]. In the absence of sufficient evidence, it is important that those meeting the current economic burden do not read this as justification to suspend such options. As has happened previously in the history of eating disorders [8], economic incentives, misinformation and other clinical pressures have led to wildly oscillating treatment fashions, and not all of these have been helpful.

The costs of associated psychopathology, such as significant mood and anxiety disorders, also must form part of this appraisal. Such comorbidity can be crippling and sometimes devastating. Counting the cost of eating disorders in isolation from this is likely to underestimate significantly every facet of this burden. It is a disturbing trend that comorbidity seems to be increasingly common in clinical practice and, as such, it is probable that the overall burden of eating disorders may be increasing.

Crow and Peterson argue that people with eating disorders also experience significant social, interpersonal and career disabilities. Much less is known about these domains. Clearly, many of these costs occur at the

[1] *Department of Psychological Medicine, Christchurch School of Medicine and Health Sciences, University of Otago, PO Box 4345, Christchurch, New Zealand*

time of illness, whereas other costs incubate or indeed may continue to occur well after the illness has resolved. This hints at the complexities that must be grappled with when appraising the wider burden. Ideally, such appraisals need to delineate between the direct effects of the eating disorders versus the effect of having lived with any disabling condition, whether this is medical or psychiatric. Likewise, future appraisals of the cost from the patient perspective may help to elaborate existing models of burden. People with eating disorders know their condition well [9], and their priorities regarding the respective burdens, how these are experienced and what is effective in ameliorating such burdens may be different from those espoused by clinicians or "known" by researchers. Finally, eating disorders have an effect on family and care-givers as well. These issues must figure in future attempts to understand the true cost of eating disorders.

REFERENCES

1. Agras W.S. (2001) The consequences and costs of the eating disorders. *Psychiatr. Clin. North Am.*, **24**: 371–379.
2. Striegel-Moore R.H., Leslie D., Petrill S.A., Garvin V., Rosenheck R.A. (2000) One-year use and cost of inpatient and outpatient services among female and male patients with an eating disorder: evidence from a national database of health insurance claims. *Int. J. Eat. Disord.*, **27**: 381–389.
3. Baran S.A., Weltzin T.E., Kaye W.H. (1995) Low discharge weight and outcome in anorexia nervosa. *Am. J. Psychiatry*, **152**: 1070–1072.
4. Pike K.M. (1998) Long-term course of anorexia nervosa: response, relapse, remission, and recovery. *Clin. Psychol. Rev.*, **18**: 447–475.
5. Meads C., Gold L., Burls A. (2001) How effective is outpatient care compared to inpatient care for the treatment of anorexia nervosa? A systematic review. *Eur. Eat. Disord. Rev.*, **9**: 229–241.
6. Zipfel S., Reas D.L., Thornton C., Olmsted M.P., Williamson D.A., Gerlinghoff M., Herzog W., Beumont P.J. (2002) Day hospitalization programs for eating disorders: a systematic review of the literature. *Int. J. Eat. Disord.*, **31**: 105–117.
7. Shaw B.F., Garfinkel P.E. (1990) Research problems in the eating disorders. *Int. J. Eat. Disord.*, **9**: 545–555.
8. Garner D.M., Needleman L.D. (1997) Sequencing and integration of treatments. In *Handbook of Treatment for Eating Disorders*, 2nd ed. (Eds D.M. Garner, P.E. Garfinkel), pp. 50–63. Guilford Press, New York.
9. Jarman M., Walsh S. (1999) Evaluating recovery from anorexia nervosa and bulimia nervosa: integrating lessons learned from research and clinical practice. *Clin. Psychol. Rev.*, **19**: 773–788.

6.10
What About The Family Burden of Eating Disorders?

Angela Favaro[1]

The family burden of eating disorders is undoubtly a neglected topic. Most of the literature on the family has been aetiological, emphasizing the negative role of parents in the development of the illness. A few studies have been performed to evaluate the role of the family in the maintenance of eating disorders or in the response to treatment. However, we should learn from the lessons of schizophrenia and consider the assessment and treatment of the family burden in eating disorders as a powerful tool for successful treatment in a cost-effective perspective. The literature on schizophrenia suggests that family interventions aiming to improve the way relatives deal with the burdens have a positive impact on the course of the illness. In addition, these interventions have direct beneficial effects on the relatives' own mental health [1].

Clearly, the characteristics of patients with eating disorders imply that the family burden is considerable: anorexia nervosa is an illness with a high risk of mortality and chronicity; patients with bulimia nervosa are often characterized by impulsivity and self-aggressiveness; in both disorders patients usually show a great resistance to seeking treatment and low motivation when referred to clinics. The most common age of onset of both disorders is adolescence, further stressing how important it is to consider the consequences of such disorders on the family members.

After a preliminary study on a smaller sample [2], we investigated 74 key relatives of 42 patients with eating disorders. The sample included 31 relatives of patients with the restricting type of anorexia nervosa, 14 relatives of patients with the binge eating/purging type of anorexia nervosa and 29 relatives of patients with bulimia nervosa. To assess the objective and subjective family burden among key relatives, we used the self-administered Family Problems Questionnaire [3]. The distinction between objective and subjective burden was introduced by Hoenig and Hamilton [4]: the former concerns objective problems related to the patient's illness, whereas the latter is the burden perceived subjectively by the key relatives.

The burden reported by the key relatives is remarkable. The area of objective burden is less problematic, especially with regard to items such as financial difficulties, the need to stop working or change jobs and other work difficulties and absenteeism. However, a large number of relatives report problems with social relationships and limitations on leisure activities: 68% complain of poor social relationships, 53% about neglect of

[1] *Department of Neurology and Psychiatry, University of Padova, Italy*

hobbies, 38% report difficulties in inviting friends or relatives and 36% in taking holidays. The subjective burden appears to be greater: 70% of relatives feel depressed, 70% of them report worries that the patient might hurt herself, 68% feel unable to cope and 66% express the need for a rest period. The binge eating/purging type of anorexia nervosa is the most burdensome subgroup: the subjective burden reported by the relatives of this subgroup is not significantly different from that reported by 34 relatives of 21 very severe cases of schizophrenia, which we used as a control group. In another study performed on patients with anorexia nervosa who had experienced an episode of inpatient care, the effects on general health and problems in care-giving were significantly greater for relatives of patients with anorexia nervosa than for relatives of a group of psychotic patients [5]. Furthermore, the general health of relatives and the problems of care-giving were significantly linked.

In our sample, we found a significant correlation between relatives' psychiatric symptoms (measured by the Hopkins Symptom Checklist) and subjective burden, but no correlation with objective burden. Moreover, we explored the correlations between family burden and the characteristics of the patients with eating disorders. In bulimia nervosa no significant correlations emerged, whereas in anorexia nervosa both objective and subjective burdens were significantly associated with negative body attitudes, perfectionism and hostility in the patients. A heavier objective burden also was significantly associated with more severe depression, whereas body mass index, duration of illness and number of failed treatments did not correlate with the burden reported by relatives.

In conclusion, clinical practice and research appear to show that relatives of patients with eating disorders suffer a considerable burden. Psychoeducational or other types of treatment for the family are used in many eating disorder units, but their effectiveness in reducing the family burden is not known. Further research is needed to study in greater detail the factors that influence the severity of the burden for relatives and the effectiveness of specific treatment for the health of the family and the patient's outcome.

REFERENCES

1. Fadden G., Bebbington P., Kuipers L. (1987) The burden of care: the impact of functional psychiatric illness on the patient's family. *Br. J. Psychiatry*, **150**: 285–292.
2. Santonastaso P., Saccon D., Favaro A. (1997) Burden and psychiatric symptoms on key relatives of patients with eating disorders: a preliminary study. *Eat. Weight Disord.*, **2**: 44–48.

3. Morosini P., Roncone R., Veltro F., Palomba U., Casacchia M. (1991) Routine assessment tools in psychiatry: a case of questionnaire of attitudes and burden. *Ital. J. Psychiatry Behav. Sci.*, **1**: 95–101.
4. Hoenig J., Hamilton W. (1966) The schizophrenic patient in the community and his effect on the household. *Int. J. Soc. Psychiatry*, **12**: 165–176.
5. Treasure J., Murphy T., Szmukler G., Todd G., Gavan K., Joyce J. (2001) The experience of caregiving for severe mental illness: a comparison between anorexia nervosa and psychosis. *Soc. Psychiatry Psychiatr. Epidemiol.*, **36**: 343–347.

6.11
A Field with Important Issues Awaiting Investigation
Aris Liakos[1]

As most clinicians working with eating disorders know, denial and secretive behaviour associated with these disorders, as well as their long course, present the investigator with a formidable task. The variety of medical complications of the disorders are often disguised and confused with other medical and endocrine conditions, producing additional difficulties in estimating their cost and often requiring multidisciplinary teams of investigators.

Although mortality rates from eating disorders other than anorexia nervosa are uncertain, it is worth noticing that mortality rates from anorexia are found to be consistently high and amount to 10% in the long run. Suicide rates are higher than in any mental disorder. These findings are clinically important, in spite of depression comorbidity in anorexia nervosa.

Economic burden is a complex matter with extensive social consequences and quite a few methodological, measurement and definition problems. The area has received little research attention. However, healthcare system costs have been studied extensively in spite of difficulties in measurements. As Crow and Peterson state, the findings are specifically important in the USA, where third-party payments are involved, but also carry weight for planning and organizing psychiatric services in European and other countries, where psychiatric reform is taking place. It is worth noting that the costs of treating anorexia or bulimia nervosa are similar in magnitude to the costs of treating schizophrenia.

Social maladjustment is also severe in anorexia and bulimia nervosa, extending to a broad range of social functioning areas such as interpersonal and family relationships, economic self-sufficiency, work performance and dating. These findings are in concordance with clinical experience, and the

[1] *Department of Psychiatry, University of Ioannina, Greece*

severity and extent of maladjustment carry implications for the management and rehabilitation of these disorders.

I think that the data related to cost-efficacy of treatment are also important and have considerable implications for planning effective treatment of the disorders. Findings show that medication treatments are better in cost-effectiveness, but a combination of drugs and psychotherapy treatments is more effective therapeutically. Setting seems also to have relevance to the effectiveness of treatment, a fact that should be taken into consideration in planning treatment services.

Eating disorders start in early adolescence—often at secondary school age—and considerable education impairment is to be expected, as observed by clinicians. No research is available in this area.

The family of the anorexic patient is often involved in an ambivalent relationship with the patient that usually includes the patient's eating behaviour. The strain to the family members is considerable, and this is more evident in Southern European countries, where the extended family tradition still holds and dependence of offspring to the family is more prolonged. Under these circumstances severe psychological burden is to be expected for all members of the family. This kind of burden is well documented and researched in other serious psychiatric disorders such as schizophrenia and depression [1]. Suitable instruments for measurement have been developed [2] and research in eating disorders in this area should prove to be fruitful.

REFERENCES

1. Jenkins J.H., Schumacher J.G. (1999) Family burden of schizophrenia and depressive illness. Specifying the effects of ethnicity, gender and social ecology. Br. J. Psychiatry, 174: 31–38.
2. Chene A., Tessler R., Gamahe G. (1994) Instruments measuring family and care giver burden in severe mental illness. Soc. Psychiatry Psychiatr. Epidemiol., 29: 228–240.

Index

Eating Disorders. Edited by Mario Maj, Katherine Halmi, Juan José López-Ibor and Norman Sartorius.
©2003 John Wiley & Sons Ltd: ISBN 0-470-84865-0